EXCESS AND RESTRAINT

EXCESS
AND
RESTRAINT

SOCIAL
CONTROL
AMONG A
NEW GUINEA
MOUNTAIN
PEOPLE

RONALD M. BERNDT

THE UNIVERSITY
OF CHICAGO
PRESS

Library of Congress Catalog Card Number: 62-10996

THE UNIVERSITY OF CHICAGO PRESS, CHICAGO & LONDON
The University of Toronto Press, Toronto 5, Canada

© 1962 by The University of Chicago. All rights reserved
Published 1962. Printed by THE UNIVERSITY
OF CHICAGO PRESS, Chicago, Illinois, U.S.A.

Preface

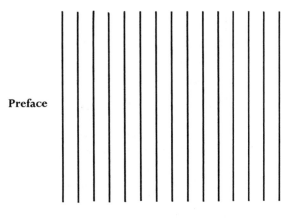

The theme of this volume is social control and social order among people belonging to four language units located in the eastern Highlands of New Guinea. It deals, that is, with a specific topic: the dual concept of conflict and co-operation, order and disorder, conformity and non-conformity. All the major ingredients may not be included here, but an effort has been made to show something of an ongoing society and culture in the process of change.

One of the basic tenets in the study of anthropology is that, ideally, every society or culture should be seen as a functioning unit in all its interrelated complexity. With some notable exceptions this has rarely been carried through. The tendency today is in the direction of seg-mentary studies, emphasizing particular features rather than the broad scope I have suggested here. Both approaches, of course, have their short-comings. The second may provide a series of books on a range of topics or problems relating to one region or society, each perhaps "complete" in itself but, all together, hardly ever providing that unity or "wholeness" we might expect to find. The first, however, limiting depth of discussion in terms of detail, actually answers a different range of questions: it is multifaceted in approach. And the intention is to get the full impact of one society and culture. Although this broad overview is primary in the present study, since we are exploring the nature of social order in New Guinea, a number of subsidiary issues, directly relevant, make their appearance. The problems arising here are seen in perspective.

Any discussion of social order must inevitably take up the problem of conflict. It is within such a context that I offer this work as a contribution to the sociology of conflict, in both its positive and negative forms.

Relatively full studies of New Guinea and Papuan societies are rare. Even rarer are recent studies of New Guinea peoples still primarily oriented along traditional lines and having a minimum of contact with others. A number of such studies have been and are currently being made; but conditions are changing so rapidly that, for instance, some of what I write in the present tense (the present of 1951–53) relates, today, only to the past. The trend is clear throughout this volume, intensified by growing pressures from the outside world. Change is seen in terms of (for example) variation in behavior, a widening or narrowing range of choices, alterations in role, and differing means employed to achieve what are in one sense the same ends as before: the struggle and jockeying for power and prestige, with the translation of "traditional" values to cope with current demands.

The essentially unsophisticated people with whom my wife and I carried out field work are bound to have changed greatly in the last eight years. Where once we climbed laboriously up and down native tracks, jeep roads have been put through, making distant districts accessible in a matter of an hour or so. When we first knew them, many men and most women had never visited Kainantu patrol base, and numbers of them had not seen Europeans before. Now, however, apart from intensified missionary and administrative activity, the Kuru Medical Research Clinic has been established at Busarasa (see R. Berndt, 1958, pp. 14–15), which during our time was on the fringe of the "uncontrolled" region. Cannibalism and warfare and the more dramatic aspects of sorcery may now have been completely suppressed or rechannelized. But it is permissible to look back, somewhat nostalgically perhaps, in order to underline the theme of rapid change.

We look back, however, not necessarily to regret the passing of "traditional" life in the sense in which it is seen in this book. The very word "traditional" is itself ambiguous and certainly relative. Nor are we thinking in terms of the "good old days." If we permit evaluation to enter here and measure them against what we know to be actuality in many societies, these "good old days" seem to have been quite bad.

But in their contemporary perspective (dealt with in the present volume), I am sure they were never considered "bad," and any such evaluation as did take place was in personal terms only.

According to the standards of our own kind of society, these eastern Highlanders do not make a very good showing, and much of what I write about does not make particularly pleasant reading. But are they worse than the majority of human beings elsewhere? I don't propose to answer this question, since this is not intended to be an apologia for the eastern Highlanders. In any case, the standards against which we measure "the right ways of behaving" are by no means universal.

I have said that these people at the time of our work were unsophisticated. This is misleading because, quite obviously, they were and are sophisticated in terms of their own culture. I mean, however, that they responded quite frankly to both inquiries and observation; and it is this frankness that I have endeavored to convey. They had not, at that time, realized that there were people who behaved and thought so very differently from themselves, although in some respects they were beginning to do so.

Looking back over our period in this region, experiences crowd together, distorted perhaps to some extent by the passing of time. On the whole, our two main bases, Kogu and Busarasa, were not easy places in which to live and work. At times we did not like these people, but just as frequently we did; and this fluctuation is mirrored to some extent in their own response to life—aggressive and violent excitement contrasted with extreme and sometimes tearful sentimentality as expressed, for example, in the love songs. Inevitably, we made enemies as well as friends; but we like to think the latter were more numerous.

Because the area at the time we visited it had experienced so little alien contact, something must be said here about our initial reception, our gradual adjustment, and the people who helped us to understand what social living meant in their terms.

To begin with, we spent a week of orientation at Raipinka Lutheran Mission station, getting together our stores and finding carriers for the trek south. Dr. Reo Fortune was also at Raipinka at this time, having come in from his camp near Finintegu, to the northwest.

As we left there on our first trip south, an irregular line of carriers stretched before us; but we could not converse with them directly. All our instructions, our questions and responses, had to be given through the medium of pidgin English to two interpreters. This long line of muscular brown men talked, sang, and grumbled as they walked.

Interpreters aside, there was no way in which we could tell, except by guessing from their facial expressions and their actions, what they were talking and thinking about. At each village we passed, a scattering of children and adults came running out to look at us. When we arrived at Jababi for the first night, dozens of people rushed noisily to embrace us, flinging themselves upon us, caressing and feeling our bodies. A European woman had not visited their district before, and many of them had never seen one; and no "white man" unaccompanied by native police or evangelists had come their way. On the second day an excited mob accompanied us and our carriers, grabbing at us and pulling us back, making sucking and hissing sounds, shouting and calling to us, greeting us with their welcoming words "I eat you!" Little clusters of district dignitaries met and addressed us at each village; but only the gist of their speeches was translated to us. A crowd of men, plumed and decorated, danced and sang before us, twanging their bowstrings, rushing backward and forward, shouting, stamping, and singing in unison. And when we eventually arrived at Maira, in Kogu, a newly built house awaited us, garden produce was heaped before us, pigs were killed, and dancing and singing went on until well after dark. (The significance of these preparations and welcome has been discussed in R. Berndt, 1952–53, *Oceania*, XXIII, No. 2, pp. 150–51.)

In marked contrast was our second walk through the same districts, when we had some command of the local languages, could understand what was being said, could joke with people and engage in repartee. There was much less excitement this time. Apart from several scenes when my wife was set upon by crowds of shrieking women, we encountered in most places chiefly the greeting of friendship, the discussion of events that had taken place since our departure, the almost silent embracing and crying as we entered our old "home" in Kogu. The bizarre, the exotic, the unknown quality, the air of having entered an alien world—that is to say, feelings arising from ignorance of the situation and the people—had, within such a short period (a year), almost completely evaporated. In its place had come some knowledge of the society and culture, some comprehension of the significance of events, some understanding of the meaning of what we saw and heard. And the only way this state of affairs could have been brought about was through learning the local languages and not relying solely on interpreters.

In the first week of our arrival in Kogu a large round working house was built. It was regarded as an extra men's house and, like our sleeping quarters, was located within the village limits. In it I spent most of my earlier days, with a selected group of men from Maira and from adjacent villages and districts. They were chosen on the basis of such diverse considerations as their willingness, friendliness, desire to impart knowledge and teach, their age, social status, and so on; but the initial selection rested heavily on my interpreter. Virtually no pidgin English was known throughout the region, and there was little knowledge of Europeans. We were viewed as returning spirits of the dead who had forgotten the tongue of our fathers and wanted to relearn it. I was able to begin immediately with the recording of phonetic texts on a variety of subjects—food collection, gardening, domestic life, and myths. As I recorded, I was learning the language, and each new subject introduced new themes, new ideas and words used in a combination of different contexts, suggesting questions and points for amplification. I was learning the language in the quickest and most desirable way and at the same time building up a store of empirical data which was gradually to provide me with a key to social and cultural behavior. But learning did not end with formal recording in this way. It was a process that continued from the moment we awoke until the moment we went to bed. Even then, lying awake, we could hear the almost incessant talking from the surrounding houses—incomprehensible at first but later transformed into valuable data. I concentrated on Jate and, during the second research period, to some extent, on Fore; my wife, on Kamano, Usurufa, and, later, Fore.

But all this did not run as smoothly as I have suggested. The people's overwhelming exuberance and enthusiasm were tempered with wariness and timidity. We were spirits and aliens, on the one hand identified with themselves, on the other viewed as strangers there for their convenience. We were assumed to be capricious and undependable, possessed of "power" such as ghosts and malignant spirits have, to do them harm if we felt so disposed—beings who had to be propitiated by lengthy recordings and descriptions and explanations. This led to a certain strain in interpersonal relations and served as a basis for some misunderstandings. Stories were current that we had ulterior motives in learning their languages; that we should be distributing goods freely instead of expecting some return for them; that we were trying to trick them into revealing what they really thought and how they really behaved, so that we could report to the Government; that we were going to round them all up and take them to jail, first cutting off their hands and even their heads! This kind of thing could be overcome to some extent in the course of everyday interaction with them and through discussions held at odd times, when something of Australian life, and of our intentions in carrying out such work, could be explained. Still, some rumors persisted; and the Kogu people, especially, became possessive toward us. On one occasion, for instance, virtually all the Kogu men stood guard over us, with drawn bows, to prevent one of the southern districts from kidnapping us and our stores.

Day after day hundreds of men, women, and children from adjacent and distant villages came to trade and sell vegetables. We were overwhelmed with numbers and could not buy all that was offered. Linguistic difficulties at first did not improve matters. Even when we could cope more readily with the situation and made selections from different villages on the basis of the help they gave us in our general research, when we could make ourselves and our intentions understood, as we thought, fairly clearly, difficulties still arose—sullenness and anger, quarrels between villages or individual persons submitting their produce. But this did not prevent hundreds of people from assembling for the festivals and ceremonies, when one district would compete with another in providing dance emblems and decorations (see C. H. Berndt, 1959). Great quantities of food were cooked and distributed among all taking part; and such periods provided ideal occasions to use our knowledge of a local language, to meet new people and build up our information on a wide variety of topics. Conventionally, such ceremonies continued through the night until sunrise, when from continual dancing and the monotonous reiteration of their singing the participants would emerge dazed and exhausted, reluctant to engage in any conversation and ready only to fall down anywhere to sleep.

But even when we knew a language well enough to communicate through it, however much we engaged in participant-observation, there were always some of both sexes who remained unwilling to act as informants. This was probably inevitable in such a situation. There were women, especially at first, who were afraid of my wife, or through some pretext or other (having to mind the pigs, or attend to a garden, a sick husband, or a child) managed to evade any prolonged close association. They did not mind transient contacts; but apart from these, in their view, Europeans were dangerous and best avoided. Similarly, though not necessarily for the same reasons, there were always men willing enough to sit and listen to others but unwilling to express their own opinions or offer anything much to a discussion. But where dancing, singing, acting, or food-selling were concerned, no one showed any hesitation.

Any amount of talking in the local language will, of course, not convince a man if he does not wish to be convinced—if he has, in his own view, good reasons for resisting. Again and again, accusations and counteraccusations of sorcery between people and villages would cut across the smooth course of field-work procedure. During our second period, before we left Kogu for Busarasa, dissension and ill-feeling became apparent. The Kogu people could not understand why we wanted to leave, why we were taking some of our stores (which they viewed as their own) to an alien district, a potential enemy. We were their property, just as much as, for instance, their fertile gardens were; and there was no real comprehension of why we should "desert" friends for people they regarded as vastly inferior. During this period there were nightly disturbances caused, we were told, by sorcerers now attacking their territory as we prepared to withdraw our "power" and patronage; running feet, and clattering bows and arrows, as men raced in pursuit of these sorcerers; a stretch of bush going up in flames one midnight as men and women hunted for intruders; armed guards over ourselves and our house at night, to prevent, they said, attacks by stranger groups. . . . At last we withdrew to Busarasa; and the Kogu people's fears materialized when later an official patrol passed through, pulled down some of their huts, allocated part of Maira to a traditional enemy, Asafina, snubbed and ill-treated the village headman, and declined their gifts of food; when our old house was defiled by a local police official; when in defending it they received the worst of a fight; and when several deaths occurred, which were attributed to sorcery.

At Busarasa we noticed a different atmosphere. The physical environment itself was different. Kogu was partly closed in by trees, hills, and jungles; Busarasa and Moke, in open kunai grass country, were sparsely wooded and much colder (about 7,000 feet above sea level). The main center at Moke was relatively deserted; people preferred to live away from it, in their own small settlements. In fact, the official Moke is really Pintagori hamlet in the Busarasa district. Fear of sorcery and of interdistrict fighting led most of the occupants to leave Pintagori in 1952 for their lineage strongholds.

There was much more talk of sorcery in this area. Interdistrict distrust was always apparent; men frequently went armed, as they had done during our first visit to Kogu. Although the same non-sacred ceremonies were held, not so many took part. And, as our Kogu friends had warned us, the people were timid and afraid of us at first; there were no local demonstrations of enthusiasm and embracing. That was to come later, when they got to know us. We had to spend much time in persuading men and women to help us in formal recording. We needed to spend time on this, for now we were in a different language area. Our knowledge of adjacent languages, although Jate was understood to some extent, could not serve wholly to gain their confidence. But presently they grew used to us. Men and, less frequently, women came in from distant villages to look at us; they could not stay, they apologized, because their districts were too busy fighting. Although these people were more reticent in their approach to us, when they began to understand what we wanted they were just as frank and helpful as our best informants at Kogu. Nevertheless, fights and quarrels and accusations of sorcery were constantly taking place, even within my own working camp where I had representatives from antagonistic districts.

In the area of which I am speaking, actions in a wide range of social behavior were observed. These had best be noted here, because in so many anthropological monographs there is no clue as to what was actually witnessed by the inquirer and what is simply hearsay evidence. I am not disparaging material obtained from informants and unsubstantiated through observation; there are many aspects which, partly because of limitations in time, cannot be personally observed, and here it is necessary to rely on the indirect approach. Just as I have discussed our entry into this situation, because so often in anthropological studies we are introduced to the field of study without any indication of how the inquirer got into the area or contacted the people, I shall mention here some of the features I myself observed. In much of this region while I was there, apart from the modifications I have noted, everyday life was continuing almost as if there were no such thing as alien control. It was only during our second stay, when the Administration intensified its drive to push through roads and bring the southern areas under its authority, that this picture began to change. My wife and I, together or singly, were able to observe the majority of features discussed in this volume, some of them not once or twice but many times, in Kogu and various adjacent districts, as well as in the Busarasa-Moke area: birth, initiation rituals, the rites of the cult of the ancestors and the sacred flutes, the pig festival, the sweat house, cane-swallowing, ritual operations, secular ceremonies and dramatic enactments; courtship, betrothal, and marriage; quarreling, interdistrict fighting, sorcery scares; some aspects of cannibalism, and attempted suicide; the holding of informal courts and the punishments meted out; and so on. In fact, the range of direct observation was comparatively wide, for after leaving Raipinka we spent all the time of both our research periods, apart from walking from one place to another, in native villages. That is to say, we were able to witness a great deal of ordinary everyday activity. There was, however, as there must always be, much that we could not see: for example, violence during cannibal feasts, sharp fighting and confusion when a village was raided, certain extra-marital ventures, and so on. Although by all accounts these were still taking place south of Wanevinti, it would have been unwise and dangerous to attempt research there at that time. (This region was officially "restricted." During our second period, when we were assumed to have some knowledge of the local languages and of local conditions, we were given verbal permission by the Assistant District Officer at Kainantu to venture as far south as we thought could be done with safety. Our information on the state of affairs then existing convinced us that it would be foolhardy to attempt to go beyond Wanevinti, or even to visit some of the hamlets on its slopes, without a strong patrol.)

Every informant is a member of his society, with a limited range of action within it, and a limited range of insight into its arrangement and working. The reliability, the validity and scope of his information, will vary with his age, sex, and social status. I have mentioned already that in this particular area I found it necessary to select a number of adult men (a nucleus varying between twenty and thirty) for purposes of formal recording. These and others who worked with me over a period (i.e., excluding casual informants) and who were consistently helpful received a return for their services. This followed their own conventional practice: even between close kin, every minor service must be reciprocated.[1]

This kind of recording, in both Kogu and Busarasa, was carried out almost entirely in the special men's house built for the purpose. Women and children were excluded from it. Every day and night it was crowded with men who spent much of their time there, eating, talking, and sleeping. Visitors and local men came and went in the course of their affairs—their gardening, hunting, quarreling, attending to religious rites or secular ceremonies; and quite often I went with them. But even when we stayed in one place, from my vantage point in the village I could observe as well as listen and talk, ready to follow up any new and

[1] Minor "payments" in the shape of matches, shells, salt, and so on were made every weekend; each man's and woman's regular work was assessed on the basis of its importance in widening our knowledge of certain problems or extending their range. At the end of our periods of field-work, twice at Kogu and once at Busarasa, gifts were distributed on the same basis. Occasional contributions were made to festivals, ceremonies, and so on, comparable to those normally expected from participants. There were also other ways through which people could obtain gifts from us: for instance, through the sale of food or of certain ethnological specimens.

interesting line of activity. The material which I recorded formally is all in the Jate language, in the shape of narrative accounts and songs. When it related to the past, as it did in many cases, I tried to insure that all the main protagonists, if they were living, were represented. And because these accounts and discussions took place in a "public interview" situation in which men from all the surrounding areas were free to listen and comment, with undertones and overtones of antagonism and cross-cutting interests, between persons and between social units, I supple-mented them with more private conversations which were not subject to the same limitations. In formal recording sessions, all the main warrior leaders, the "strong men," and all the local native officials considered that they had a right to participate. They were in the forefront of action in other spheres and took this new involvement very much for granted. To keep a balance, I insisted that the nucleus should include not only Kogu leaders (or, for that matter, Usurufa leaders, who at first tried to keep this potential source of power and of wealth to themselves) but also men from outside that range, both spatially and in the matter of status. Statements made by "strong men" were checked against other statements, both public and private, from men of lesser status, from women (talking to my wife), and from the speakers themselves at different times and in different contexts. During our two periods of field work, my wife and I visited the majority of the districts mentioned in this volume, as far south as the valley below Mount Wanevinti. On leaving the area after the second period, we walked through Jate territory, staying briefly at Taramu, skirting Mount Michael, and so through Kami to Goroka.

This volume takes up some of the problems with which I was con-cerned in the course of research in the area. It does not attempt to provide a complete account of all facets of local life nor a complete record of my own participation in that life. Nor does it consider some of the issues of methodology and techniques directly relevant to this kind of situation, where firsthand observation must be supplemented by reference to the past, mediated through people's accounts of it as recorded in the present, with no documentary evidence to provide an extra dimension of inquiry. The material presented here will, I hope, be supplemented by further reports (some at present in course of prepara-tion, several virtually completed) amplifying various points which in the present study can only be touched on in passing.

This study, then, is based on field work carried out in the Trust Territory of New Guinea in two periods, during 1951–52 and 1952–53.

At that time I was a member of the staff of the Department of Anthropology at the University of Sydney. My wife, Catherine Berndt, who was also attached to that department, was with me during both visits. An original draft of this work was prepared while I was a postgraduate student at the Department of Anthropology, London School of Economics and Political Science, University of London, and was written as a thesis for the degree of Ph.D. The writing-up of this material was made possible initially by a Nuffield Dominion Travelling Fellowship (1953–54), and later (1954–55) by the help of a Leverhulme Award from the London School of Economics. Between October, 1955, and March, 1956, under a fellowship (to myself) from the Carnegie Corporation of New York, my wife and I were able to visit various anthropological and sociological departments and institutes in the United States of America and Canada. Apart from various other reasons for visiting these countries, it served as an excellent opportunity to discuss with a number of anthropologists some of the problems dealt with in this volume.

During 1956–59, in between responsibilities of instituting courses and developing teaching and research in Social Anthropology (Comparative Sociology) at the University of Western Australia, I was able to reassemble the original thesis and substantially rewrite the whole work. The typing of this was made possible by a grant from the research committee of that university.

I would like to take the opportunity of acknowledging first the encouragement, supervision, and help of Professors Raymond Firth and I. Schapera, of the London School of Economics, as well as Professor Max Gluckman, of the University of Manchester, and Dr. Phyllis Kaberry, of University College, University of London. In addition, a number of other colleagues have helped indirectly in the basic orientation of this study. My acknowledgments must include Emeritus Professor A. P. Elkin, for his encouragement over the years (particularly when he was an incumbent of the Sydney Chair of Anthropology) in relation to my Australian Aboriginal as well as New Guinea research.

On the field, it is difficult to single out specifically all those who have directly and indirectly helped me. Various members of the New Guinea and Papuan Administration and the Lutheran Mission, among others, stand out most notably. Particularly, I should like to mention here my debt to the many Kamano, Usurufa, Jate, and Fore people (whose names appear from time to time in this volume) who through their friendship (through manifestations of both co-operation and conflict) have made available a relatively frank statement of their social and cultural life.

But this to my mind should not be just a one-way affair, important both theoretically and empirically to the social anthropologist. It is unlikely that many of them will read this volume for some time, perhaps not for a couple of generations; and when they do, as likely as not they will be upset or shocked by some of the things they will read. If and when this occurs, they will do well to remember that this study is intended to be relatively objective and does not evade the empirical situations any more than their implications. This, to the best of my knowledge, is how life was lived in this region up to 1953. And changes which are taking place now or will take place in the future must be both directly and indirectly influenced by what is happening today. On the other hand, there is sufficient in this volume of practical significance for the administrators of this region—not just in terms of the traditional society and culture and the changes that are taking place, but in the indication of specific trends which are entirely relevant here. How the Administration will react to them is another matter.

As far as acknowledgments are concerned, the most important is the debt one owes to a co-worker with whom one is in constant contact, able to discuss both practical and theoretical questions as they arise; this cannot be estimated, or adequately acknowledged, and such assessment is even more difficult when the co-worker is one's wife. Apart from these considerations, she has helped quite considerably in the re-orientation of the original manuscript.

Finally, I have anglicized native words wherever possible to facilitate reading, while conforming broadly with the system of spelling suggested by Capell (e.g., 1948–49). The symbol ^{c} indicates the glottal stop. For a preliminary consideration of the Kamano, Usurufa, Jate, and Fore languages see C. Berndt (1954, pp. 289–317). All vowels should be given their full weighting; and "j," as used here, is equivalent to the English "y." Also, I have deliberately kept diagrams to a minimum; village and house plans, garden ownership, and so on need separate treatment and could not be included here without distracting attention from the main theme.

Personal names used in this volume have been altered to avoid the possibility of identification.

Many of the incidents described here, particularly those relating to violence, cannibalism, and sexual aggression, no longer represent current behavior. The Administration has suppressed both interdistrict warfare and cannibalism, and the predominantly traditional situation in which I carried out field work in 1951–53 has now undergone quite radical changes.

RONALD M. BERNDT

Contents

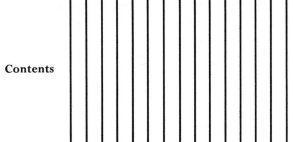

Contents

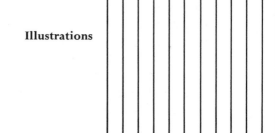

Illustrations

Part 1   Introductory

Chapter 1   Introduction to the Problem

New Guinea is still a country of romance. There is still a flavor of the exotic, of opportunities for widening and deepening our knowledge of alien ways of living. Such a feeling on an anthropologist's part is entirely legitimate and highly desirable: it is, surely, the essence of all scientific inquiry. But as we proceed with our research, our ignorance gives way to growing acquaintance with the situation. The zest of discovery, of charting an uncharted sea, so to speak, is always present; but we begin to see our subject matter in perspective. The glamor and the romantic elements recede, and in their place remain, or should remain, understanding and explanation—for it is on these factors that Social Anthropology rests: it is a science "only to the extent to which it can explain." [1]

[1] S. F. Nadel (1951, p. 20 *et seq.*).

The Central Highlands

It is now a quarter of a century since the central Highlands of the Mandated Territory of New Guinea were discovered,[2] and in the ensuing period much of the native population has come to know something about Europeans. In some areas contact was intensified during the recent war, while in others a depleted official patrol staff obliged the natives to fall back on their own resources. There were concentrations of military personnel at Mount Hagen, Goroka, and Bena Bena, the bombing of Administration posts and Mission stations at Mount Hagen, Ogelbeng, Chimbu, Goroka, and Kainantu, and active land fighting near Kainantu with Japanese coming up from the Markham Valley. Indentured laborers were recruited from Bena Bena, Goroka, Chimbu, and Mount Hagen; dysentery was introduced, and malaria became endemic.[3]

After the initial explorations of Leahy, Dwyer, and Taylor in 1930, more prospectors came, followed closely by the establishment of Government posts and Mission stations.[4] Toward the end of 1934 or the beginning of 1935, the Highlands were closed to further European penetration, although some missionaries and miners were allowed to remain. This restriction was maintained up to the time of the Japanese invasion. During the war, and after, conditions changed. The central Highlands were no longer closed; a number of administrative posts have been opened within recent years; and there was a drive to bring most of the region under full control by 1955, a tentative date, later (in 1956) put forward to 1959. Nevertheless, the years immediately following the war were spent largely in consolidating Government control and in patrolling regions surrounding the main settlements. Many of these patrols have since been pushing rapidly further afield, among people who have, or had, little or no knowledge of Europeans: at Mende, southwest of Mount Hagen, in Papua; at Churunki, west of Wabaga; Jimmi, north of Mount Hagen and

[2] See M. Leahy and M. Crain (1937); E. W. P. Chinnery (1934, pp. 113–21); L. P. Mair (1948, pp. 29, 35, 37); J. Nilles (XIV, No. 2, 1943, p. 105). It is possible that Hermann Detzner visited some of the Highland districts from 1914 until after the armistice, during the four years after his escape from Singaua. He did not, however, reach the Sepik River, nor did he penetrate beyond the Mount Hagen district. From his map (see Lloyd Rhys, 1942, pp. 40–41, or H. Detzner, 1920) it would appear that he visited the eastern Highlands, but I have not been able to verify this.

[3] L. P. Mair (1948, pp. 197–98). Natives were not at that time recruited from the Kainantu district. See W. E. H. Stanner (1953, pp. 45–56, 131–44); R. H. Black (1956, pp. 136–42).

[4] L. P. Mair (1948, p. 37); K. E. Read (1952a, pp. 229–38); C. H. Berndt (1953, pp. 112–38), specifically in relation to the Kainantu district. Also R. M. Berndt (1952–53, e.g., pp. 40–41).

Ogelbeng; Sua, northwest of Mount Michael, and Lufa on its northern fringe; Taramu, southeast of Mount Michael; and so on (see map A). There still remain territories through which patrols have only passed, areas and villages unvisited by Europeans, where the main stream of native life is virtually untouched. Such territories are called "restricted" or "uncontrolled." In contrast are those peoples who have officially appointed leaders like the *luluai*, *tultul*, and "boss-boy" or "mouth-boy," outwardly, at least, welcome the Christian missionaries and their native evangelists and the Administration and its native police, and no longer engage in interdistrict fighting.

The Eastern Highlands

Across the Highlands from west to east lie the main administrative settlements of Wabaga, Baiyer River, Ogelbeng, Mount Hagen, Nondugl, Kerowagi, Chimbu, Kainantu, and Goroka. Only a handful of Europeans is settled at each of these, although their numbers are increasing; Goroka had a nonindigenous population of about 120 in 1953. These focal points with subsidiary outstations represent a thin thread of European penetration. Throughout the region is a large native population, which so far has not been systematically assessed [5] but exceeds half a million.

The part dealt with here embraces sections of two administrative subdistricts, Kainantu and Bena. The principal administrative post for the first is at Kainantu, and for the second at Goroka, the control base for the eastern Highlands and originally the administrative center for all the central Highlands. The area to be considered in this volume is indicated in the accompanying map (see map B).

All the villages surrounding Kainantu, excepting those on the south, began to come under Australian control from 1930–31 onward, and by the time World War II began the process was apparently completed. The position changed as civil authorities and missionaries withdrew and patrols became even less regular than before. Fighting flared up again,[6] and there was a period of convulsion. Then control was gradually re-established, and patrols began to penetrate into the "uncontrolled" areas. The end of the war saw the return of the Civil Administration, of European missionaries, Lutherans and Seventh Day Adventists, and of solitary gold prospectors. People from the surrounding areas and even further afield came drifting in, on voluntary or forced visits—looking for work, selling vegetables,

[5] Anthropological research on this eastern side has not been intensive or extensive, except for two or three areas; a list of published work appears in the bibliography.

[6] See C. Berndt (1953, p. 113).

bringing grievances to the official "courts," or spending periods in hospital or jail. Men from southern districts two and three days' journey away or more, whose knowledge of Europeans was based almost entirely on hearsay, came into Kainantu to see the place for themselves. But the actual "controlling" of this region was a slow process, even though superficially it appears to have been rapid.

In the area where we carried out anthropological field work, the first official patrol was made toward the end of 1947, when fighting was still in progress. The patrol met with a mixed reception. Some villages gave it an exuberant welcome, others were wary or hostile. All were ordered to stop fighting and throw down their fortifications, and by the end of 1950 or beginning of 1951 the whole region as far south as Moke was declared "controlled." Mission native evangelists, pushing gradually into the region, had contacted many districts before official patrols arrived; but this did not begin in earnest until the missions were re-established after the war. In 1951 a Lutheran Mission outstation was finally set up at Taramu, half a day's walk southwest of Kogu, in the Bena subdistrict. The country southeast, south, and southwest was still restricted or "uncontrolled" at the time of our second visit, and a number of villages had not been visited by Europeans.

Before any Europeans entered the region, so we were told, the local people received their initial shock with the advent of the first airplane in the 1930s. Their response to this strange new "thing" is described as one of awe and fear; but as passing planes became more common, and as rumors began to reach the southern districts from the newly established Kainantu base, they began to adjust their minds to these strange events and seek explanations for them. During this period, too, small items of European manufacture were handed down from village to village as rare and exotic goods. But as a result of further rumors, now of a different type, they became afraid and tried to take preventive action against the dangers which threatened. This developed into a series of reaction movements which have continued, in varying manifestations, up to the present day.[7]

One of the most important points revealed in the official patrol reports is that all through this region alien impact has been largely of an indirect kind. That is to say, apart from the drive against fighting and cannibalism, the changes which have occurred are not a result of direct force or threat. On the other hand, the patrol reports are inevitably superficial, so that

[7] See R. Berndt (1952–53; 1954a).

important local trends have been overlooked or simply ignored. Here, of course, we are faced directly with introduced forms of social control.

The Fieldwork Area

The people we are considering belong to four major language units: Kamano on the north, Fore on the south, with Usurufa in between, and Jate adjoining all three of these on the west (see chap. 3 and map C). These units are made up of a number of named divisions, or districts, each with its localized settlements, villages, or hamlets, with a more or less sedentary population.

This is a region of subsistence horticulture, based on shifting cultivation, with some elementary rotation of crops (see A. J. Schindler, 1952). A few gardens lie close to the houses, others at varying distances from them—on hillside slopes, roughly terraced and fenced against pigs, or on the more level ground between them. The period of most intensive cultivation is the wet season, from approximately November to April. Staple foods are sweet potatoes in the north, yams and taros further south, supplemented by a wide range of garden produce, both indigenous (or described as such) and introduced—such as maize; sugar cane; various legumes; edible gourds, marrows, cucumbers; edible leaves; and many varieties of bananas. There is the small-leafed native tobacco, smoked in bamboo pipes; and crotons and *dracaenae* are grown in the gardens as well as outside them. Other plants, wild and cultivated, provide fiber of different kinds for twine and for such things as skirts and belts; vegetable dyes for netted bags and ceremonial emblems; bark, which is pounded to make emblems and sometimes small capes; and bamboo for making arrows, water containers, and sacred flutes. For protein, the local people rely mainly on pigs, a few fowl and dogs, and occasionally keep wild cassowaries for fattening in pens; but the dry season, when gardening is slack, is the time when they make use of the resources the bush and jungles have to offer: small animals, birds, and reptiles; wild fruits and fungus; and leaves and bark for chewing in the sweat house (see chap. 5).

The routine work of gardening falls most heavily on the women; the palms of their hands are rough and ingrained with dirt from constant use of digging sticks and from weeding, planting, and tending the growing crops. Men are responsible for the rougher tasks—felling trees, making fences, and clearing away the undergrowth to make new gardens. Conventionally, in every village or hamlet a group of men, claiming agnatic kinship, shares a common house for eating and sleeping, owns local garden land, and collaborates in joint enterprises like warfare and religious ritual. Their wives, coming from other villages, live in separate houses, together with their children—boys until the first initiation, girls until marriage at or about puberty.

Near Kainantu and Raipinka the villages have been moving down to fairly level ground, a process which has been taking place apparently since about 1947. Around a central clearing, a ceremonial or communal meeting ground, are houses roughly rectangular in shape (under European influence), with a church standing a little apart, and an official rest house. Before one has walked half a day southward, however, hillside villages appear, made up of typical round houses of varying size, with kunai grass roofs, protruding center poles, and eaves sweeping gracefully to within two or three feet of the ground. Another day's walk, and they become smaller, a men's house dominating a number of women's houses, while the only rectangular house may be the rest house or village church. Such a village was Maira, in the Usurufa district of Kogu, in which our first period of research took place (November, 1951, to April, 1952). This village was strategically placed for our purpose, within easy walking distance of other Kogu villages and about three-quarters of a mile from Moiife, another Usurufa district, and with Jate and Fore districts adjoining it on the west and south.

Three days' walk southwest of Kainantu are other villages where contact with Europeans has been minimal. Their houses are not so neat, their women's houses much smaller, some only four to four and a half feet across. Pig houses are within the village allotment, and so are small fowl coops, raised above the ground. There are gaping round water-filled holes in the village cleared-place, and piles of blackened stones, the earth-ovens; gardens adjoin houses, with the large men's house usually on slightly higher ground. Some villages have still kept their wooden palisades or part of them, built in much the same way as Assistant District Officer Skinner observed in his 1947 patrol. Such were the Busarasa, Moke, and Ora districts in which we carried out our second period of work (November, 1952, to March, 1953). Immediately opposite us to the south rose Wanevinti; beyond, to the northwest, cloud-covered Mount Michael, with the new Lutheran Mission outstation at Taramu clearly visible to one side. Between us and Wanevinti lay a long narrow valley containing a fringe of villages and districts where occasional raids took place. Beyond Wanevinti, toward the Papua–New Guinea border, only three Administration patrols had ventured. East of Moke precipitous mountains separated this region from the Lamari River, although the smokes of Kawaina could be seen.

There are certain contrasts between these two areas in which we worked. Kogu, for instance, was declared "controlled" at the end of 1949, the Busarasa–Moke districts at the end of 1950, while a native police official was stationed there in January, 1951. Kogu is a series of scattered hilltop hamlets, with virtually no remaining stockades, and with a tendency to centralize beside the patrol road. During our first period it was accepted, collectively, into the Lutheran church without understanding much about what it meant but conforming because it was the sophisticated thing to do.

Busarasa, Moke, and Ora, away from the official rest house and native police official,[8] consist of small hamlets, a few surrounded by tall wooden stockades and guarded doors. In the gardens where the women work, men stand guard with bows and arrows. These weapons are almost invariably carried in this region; further north, at Kogu, they are now kept hidden away until they are needed. In the Busarasa-Moke-Ora constellation interdistrict feuding is still a thing of the present. On the third day after our arrival at Busarasa a man working on a house for one of our native assistants was killed, while a fortnight before we left the area several hundred people took part in an interdistrict fight, using arrows, axes, knives, and planks of wood, and there were attempts to fire some hamlets before the fight was brought under control. Fighting, feud, sorcery, cannibalism, stockades, in fact virtually all concomitants of life before alien impact, are present but in modified form. It is because of this modification that the area is classified as "controlled," as far as the Divide on which most of the Ora-Busarasa-Moke hamlets are situated. Just beyond, in the valley and along the slopes of Wanevinti, the country is "restricted"; and further south, in the "uncontrolled" region, such features are subject to virtually no external restraint.

In 1948, if we may rely on verbal information from local sources and on patrol reports, the region to be discussed in this work showed some uniformity as far as these elements were concerned. But when we were there, in 1951–53, conditions were changing. Very broadly speaking, we had before us a panoramic view of three areas that merge into one another, depending on the extent of administrative influence. We may well suppose that, for instance, Moke a year or so hence would be much like

[8] The native police official was absent during most of our period in the field. We received the utmost co-operation from the administrative staff in Port Moresby, Kainantu, and Goroka, and were given a completely free hand in this region. During our first period we had no visit from a patrol officer. During our second period we had one short visit at Kogu from the A.D.O., Kainantu, one from the same A.D.O. on patrol through Busarasa, and one from a Goroka patrol officer from Taramu.

Kogu, while beyond Wanevinti conditions in two or three years' time would be much like those we found in Moke. This would depend on the regularity of patrolling and on the assumption that contact with the main patrol base at Kainantu continued to be maintained. Because we are dealing with the whole region (from certain points within it), these variations in change, these local differences, present some methodological difficulties. But before we consider them, the situation calls for further comment.

Busarasa, Moke, and Ora are only half a day's walk from Kogu. Nevertheless, they belong to a different linguistic unit. In the first three the Fore language predominates, with some Jate. In the fourth, Usurufa is the main language, but Jate or Kamano may be used as a lingua franca (see chap. 3). Allowing for these linguistic differences, and apart from the question of European influence, cultural and social variations between the two regions are, broadly speaking, slight; but there are numerous details which may appear to be of greater or less significance according to the context in which they are being discussed.

Problems of Description

At this juncture each of the four linguistic groups can be taken as a society, in that each is the widest social unit which is territorially defined and linguistically fairly uniform, with a recognized commonalty of culture. In discussing them I allow for their separateness in these terms, but over and above this I consider them in linked totality. Broadly speaking, then, and acknowledging the dissimilarities and limitations already indicated, we can, on the basis of empirical material, make tentative assumptions for the whole area under consideration. In talking about this area I talk about these four societies, their common culture with local variations, and the interrelationship and co-activity of the people concerned. No one linguistic unit could have been isolated for the purpose of this study at the expense of those adjacent to it. We are obliged to view them as a constellation in order to reach a greater understanding of what happens within them, although this is more than just a matter of expediency for purposes of description. Further, the modifications traceable to external pressure, we may tentatively assume, have taken place only within the last ten years or so. To understand social conditions at the time of actual field research, we cannot ignore events and incidents which occurred within that period, for they have a direct bearing on contemporary action.

Thus the material we consider falls within a time range and consists of data concerning events which took place some time before our two visits, in between them, or while we were there. This covers a period of approximately a decade and a half, with most cases falling between 1944–45 and 1953; but occasionally it extends as far back as a person's memory could go.

Excluding for the time being legend and mythology, the oral literature of these people, the material to be used here is broadly of three orders. First, we have that which relates to events which occurred in the past but were not witnessed or participated in by the people who reported them; in other words, experiences and incidents about which they have only secondhand knowledge and for which no verification is available. A criterion of its usefulness may be found in the extent to which people believe in it and insist that it is true. Second, we have that relating to events which occurred before the period of research but which were personally witnessed and participated in by those we talked to, their veracity substantiated as far as possible by other informants. Third, we have that which relates to events occurring during both periods of research.

For our purpose, the "ethnographic present" takes into account the period just prior to the first official patrol through the region in 1947 and extends to the time of writing, 1953. This covers what we may broadly term contemporary life, including all the necessary conditions for our examination. Fighting, for instance, was taking place at Kogu in 1946–47 as it was in 1953 near Busarasa-Moke; Kogu was "uncontrolled" then, as the country south of Busarasa was restricted in 1953. We thus have a regional range in space and time as a basis for understanding the various modifications brought about by alien influence.

When I discuss a particular situation, with a view to indicating norms, dominant themes, generalizations, and so on, I am considering the ethnographic present, as defined above. I allow for variations, noting them when necessary, but the picture I attempt to give is an over-all one. And finally, when I discuss specific events or cases in comparative detail, or refer to a particular incident, I endeavor to indicate their relevance in a time sequence.

There is general agreement on the whole concerning the range of factors which enter into any control system,[1] although most social anthropologists have preferred to concentrate on one or two of them: law, political organization, warfare, and so on. Possibly because of this emphasis, there has been a tendency to consider social control as involving, above all, coercive force. What is more, features coming under this heading are more clear-cut and much easier to handle. Nevertheless, social scientists have been increasingly concerned with those which are more informal and subtle.

Another difference, as between various writers on this subject, lies in the extent to which they have focused on the issue of change due to external pressures in any given society.

Within this broad framework of social control a number of topics will serve as focal points for our study, and before turning to the discussion of the empirical situation a few words should be said about them.

Processes of Socialization

Under this heading comes the regulation of conduct, consciously or otherwise, in both formal and informal ways: that is, by means of child training and other educational and enculturative mechanisms which continue throughout life. These include initiation, ceremony and ritual, myth and religion—possibly the most important features here, because they embody and reinforce the basic values which permeate all aspects of social life (see chap. 4). This is both indoctrination and habituation, relating on the one hand to the maintenance of order, on the other, more specifically, to the socialization of individual persons.

Coercion and the Social Order

Here attention is focused on the deliberate regulation of conduct.[2] At one extreme are various forms of disciplinary action on an interpersonal

[1] See bibliography for background references on the subject.
[2] These two divisions should not be regarded as entirely separate but merely as a broad

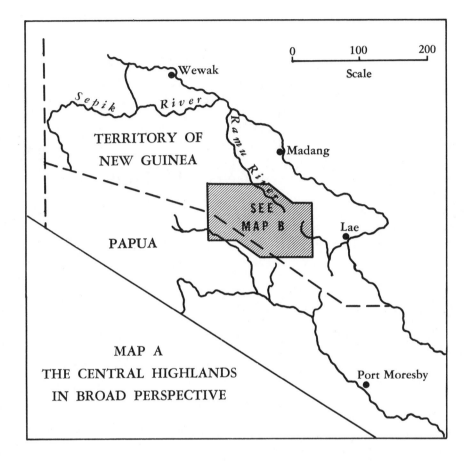

MAP A
THE CENTRAL HIGHLANDS
IN BROAD PERSPECTIVE

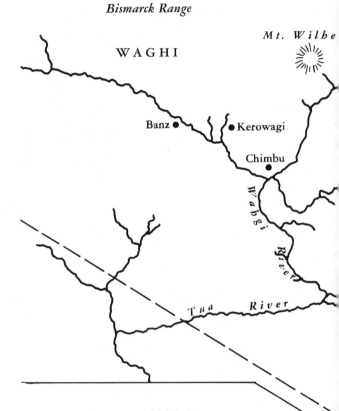

MAP B

SKETCH MAP OF A SECTION OF
THE CENTRAL HIGHLANDS

Shaded inclosure shows main area of
field work in relation to the rest of
the Highlands. (See enlargement, Map C.)

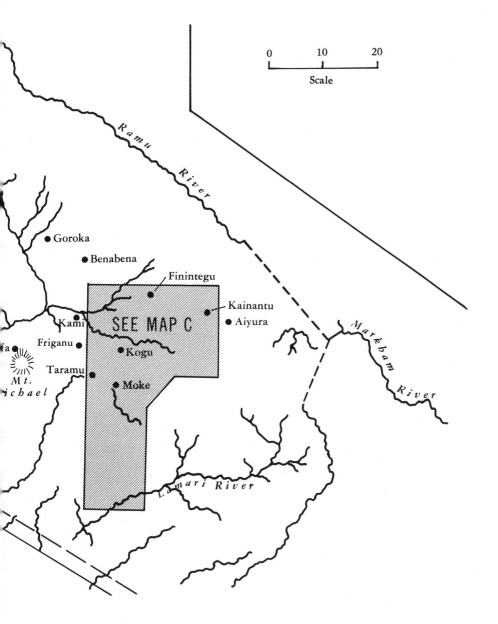

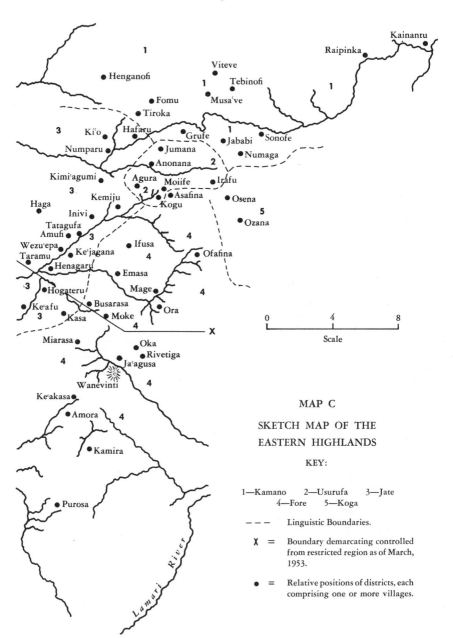

● Finintegu

1

● Henganofi

Viteve
● Tebinofi

1

Raipinka

Kainantu

1

Fomu ●
● Tiroka

Musa've ●

3

Ki'o ●
Hafaru ●
● Grufe

Numparu ●
● Jababi
● Sonofe

1

● Jumana
● Numaga

● Anonana

2

Kimi'agumi ●

Agura ●
Moiife ●
● Irafu

3

Kemiju ●

2

● Asafina
Kogu

● Osena

Haga ●

Inivi ●

5

● Ozana

Tatagufa
Amufi ●

3

● Ifusa

4

Wezu'epa ●
Taramu
● Ke'jagana

4

● Ofafina

Henagaru ●

● Emasa

3

● Hogateru

Mage ●

4

Ke'afu ●

3

Busarasa ●

● Ora

Kasa
● Moke

4

Miarasa ●

Oka ●

4

● Rivetiga
Ja'agusa ●

X

Wanevinti

4

Ke'akasa ●

● Amora

4

● Kamira

● Purosa

Lamari River

| 0 | 4 | 8 |

Scale

MAP C

SKETCH MAP OF THE
EASTERN HIGHLANDS

KEY:

1—Kamano   2—Usurufa   3—Jate
4—Fore   5—Koga

- - -   Linguistic Boundaries.

X = Boundary demarcating controlled from restricted region as of March, 1953.

● = Relative positions of districts, each comprising one or more villages.

basis—between husband and wife, or parent and child. At the other are institutionalized fighting, warfare, and organized judicial mechanisms, either simple or elaborate. A central theme in all this is conformity, which can be brought about up to a point by making transgression difficult or impossible. In other words, the methods devised to achieve it do not rely entirely on socialization, although it may be seen as, ideally, the end result of that process. Physical prevention is an important factor when combined with socialized habits. Coercion, or the threat of coercion, seems to be a necessary feature of social living, indispensable to the maintenance of any given social order.

In both divisions a certain "range of conformity" is acknowledged, a normal range of variability. Within it, ideally, socialization takes place. Outside it falls behavior considered to be either dangerous or undesirable, judged by both individual and social standards, or actually deviant. The former is subject to corrective measures of varying intensity and severity; the latter is rather different, although it may be subject to the same sanctions. The deviant may have a definite and accepted place in community life, or he may be an outcast or misfit.[3]

Broadly speaking, all societies have means by which the behavior of their members can be channelized, either more or less successfully. Social control thus covers all the processes and procedures which regulate behavior, in that they exert pressure on persons and groups to conform to the norms. They fall into various categories, some of them guarded by provisions or sanctions of either a positive or negative kind,[4] designed to counteract tendencies toward divergency or disobedience. All this has to do, ultimately, with the selection and definition of goals and the range of behavior conducive to the realization of these. It concerns, too, the fixing of rewards and punishments (positive and negative sanctions), how these are to be enforced, by whom, and in reference to whom. We may say that the regulators of behavior, and therefore the instruments of social control, are in turn linked with a system of values.

---

operational classification for handling the relevant material. Force enters into many aspects of socialization, and conformity rests also on a number of features which belong under that heading, such as public opinion, example, gossip, incentives relating to status and prestige, guilt feelings, and so on. See R. K. Merton (1949/57, chap. IV, pp. 131–60); Talcott Parsons (1952, p. 258).

3 This question will not be explored here. See, e.g., Nadel (1951, pp. 95, 389); Parsons and Shils (1952, pp. 156–58). Deviance should be conceptually distinguished from variation, although the one may merge into the other.

4 Cf. Malinowski, in Hogbin (1934, pp. xxxvi, lxx); Radcliffe-Brown (1952, p. 205).

Values

To speak of social controls implies some concern with the social standards or values on which they depend. Why do people do this as against
that? What influences their choice of one line of conduct as against
another, when both are socially acceptable? There are ways or modes of
action to which most people in a given community broadly conform; and
there are those which seem to show a much wider range of variation.
Briefly, we can speak tentatively of a core of values which are basic and,
at a secondary level, of values which may be actually in conflict. The first
comprises values taken very much for granted. The second are "considered values," involving a weighing of conditions, summing up a situation and choosing accordingly, nearly always on the basis of perceived
self-interest in either its long-range or short-range aspects.

The question of whether social anthropologists should use the term
"values" is a mildly controversial one. Its opponents claim that it has a
mystical quality, encouraging overreliance on intuition, or the substitution of "feel" for "fact"; that it represents a residual category in which
the "unexplainable" can be neatly pigeonholed; or that it leads to the
illusion of achieving either "deeper" or "super" explanations of social
phenomena. While recognizing the dangers here, nevertheless I consider
that the concept of "values" can offer one sort of perspective, and a
useful one, in a study such as this. Other anthropologists have taken the
same broad stand. To Firth,[5] for instance, the term value involves "judge-
ment on a preference scale, a grading. It implies primarily positive
qualities, ideas of desirability or worth. . . ." Nadel[6] agrees, seeing it as
"an idea of worthwhileness governing a class of actions and imparting to
each the index 'good' or 'bad,' or 'desirable' and undesirable,' as the
case may be." Kluckhohn,[7] too, has explored this concept.

It is often useful to distinguish between the "near ideal," sometimes
called the norm, and the "distant ideal," which may be regarded as unattainable, not drawn on directly as a guide to actual behavior. In much
the same way, we can identify two categories of values: value-acceptives,
as I would call them, or values-*desiderata*; and values-*desideranda*, where
the normative aspect predominates. The first category is more straightforward, whatever the choices involved, whereas in the second the
"ought" quality is much more obtrusive. To frame it crudely, this is the

---

[5] R. Firth (1951, pp. 42–43; 1953, No. 231, pp. 146–53).

[6] S. F. Nadel (1951, pp. 264–65).

[7] C. Kluckhohn, in Parsons and Shils (1952, pp. 388–433); see also F. Kluckhohn, in
Grinker, ed. (1957, pp. 83–93); E. Vogt (1955, pp. 3–13).

contrast between what one wants and what one *ought* (or feels one ought) to want. The interplay between "ought" (of various kinds) and "is," the one influencing the other as a series of compromises and adjustments, represents one of the most interesting problem areas in the field of social order and social control.

Law and Legal Procedure

Controversy on the use of the term "law" centers in the main on the distinction between law and custom,[8] between codified law and customary law, and, oddly enough in view of the common derivation of the two words, between law and other "legal" phenomena. On the one hand there is the view that "law" presupposes a formal written code and a formal judicial procedure operating within the context of a nation-state.[9] This was the position of, for example, Radcliffe-Brown and Seagle.[10] On the other hand there is Malinowski's[11] broad approach, which in demarcating law from custom stretches the term legal to include a wide range of customary or traditional rules of behavior. In between come such definitions as that put forward by Schapera, who does not restrict the term law to nation-states but does use the criterion of judicial enforcement to distinguish it from custom. Gluckman, on the other hand, following Malinowski in the view that "law must be allowed to cover some methods of social control in societies without courts," uses the term accordingly, reserving "legal" for rules sanctioned by judicial procedure.[12]

Where there are no courts but coercive sanctions are invoked in regard to certain areas of behavior, it is useful to have a special term for this intermediate category of control mechanisms, within the general field of culture, or "custom." Because the term law has been so consistently associated with courts, there is a lot to be said for not trying to extend it further.[13] In contrast, the word legal seems to be less provocative, yet it

[8] The term "custom," often used in this context even by anthropologists, perhaps because of its association with "customary law," seems to be identical with "culture" in the anthropological sense; cf. I. Schapera (1938/55, pp. 35–38); M. Gluckman (1955, pp. 236–37, 261, 359, 362).

[9] E. A. Hoebel (1940, p. 45). For a different approach to this issue of "law," see Bohannan (1957, pp. 4–6, 208–14).

[10] A. R. Radcliffe-Brown (1952, pp. 205, 212); also in Fortes and Evans-Pritchard, eds. (1950, pp. xi–xxii); W. Seagle (1937, pp. 275–90).

[11] E.g., B. Malinowski (1949, p. 59). See also Hoebel (1954, pp. 177–210) and Gluckman (1955, p. 230). For a brief but comprehensive summary of Malinowski's position see Schapera, in Firth, ed. (1957, pp. 139–55).

[12] M. Gluckman (1955, pp. 164, 229–31, 345, 366); see also his use of the term "alegal."

[13] But see S. F. Nadel (1947, pp. 499–500; 1951, pp. 133–35).

is so close in meaning as to make the distinction seem almost arbitrary. Hoebel, taking it in its broader sense as I am doing here, suggests that legal phenomena need not be associated with courts, provided they involve the use of socially sponsored coercive force or threat of force. In other words, "the legal has teeth," which in principle differentiate it from other "rules of custom." [14] The distinction is not clear-cut. Insofar as we can make it, however, it rests not so much on the relative severity of sanctions, as Nadel [15] seems to suggest, as on the procedure adopted in enforcing them.

The relationship between custom and law has sometimes been seen as an evolutionary one, with contemporary non-literate peoples serving as a medium for speculations on the "origin" of law. But it is more rewarding to consider in such a society the processes by which certain aspects of culture, what I have been calling legal aspects, may become crystallized into "law." [16]

In judicial procedure we have to do with the general problem of the allocation of authority, but here specifically in relation to internal mechanisms of order and control. It rests on retaliation, on power to inflict or threaten punishment; and on power to enforce a settlement judged appropriate to the offense. This presupposes a body of arbitrators having a socially defined role; but, as Radcliffe-Brown has pointed out, there may be considerable diversity here, in that they may or may not be in a position to use physical coercion or to insist on a settlement.

But coercive sanctions, whether or not associated with courts, represent only one type of pressure toward conformity. For this reason there is a growing preference for the inclusive term "social control." The broadness of its coverage has certain disadvantages, not least as regards choice of a particular line of approach within it. Nevertheless, it does indicate clearly enough the main problem with which all studies of this sort, whatever their content and range, are primarily concerned.

The procedure adopted in the present volume is first to outline the main social features in this particular region, then to discuss something of their cultural content, the basic assumptions and values as expressed in mythology and ritual. Drawing on both these perspectives, we go on to

14 Hoebel (1940, pp. 46, 47; 1954, pp. 21, 23, 28, 274); Llewellyn and Hoebel (1941, pp. 283–84); Radcliffe-Brown (1952, pp. 212–13).

15 Nadel (1947, p. 501). But see his discussion of the "social range of offences" (ibid., pp. 501–2).

16 W. Seagle (1937, pp. 283–84); but his framework here rests on an evolutionary sequence.

consider the process of socialization, learning with its counterpart of teaching, the local prescriptions for achieving social adulthood, and the ways in which these are put into practice. Next we turn to coercive controls, discussing under this heading suicide, sorcery, and warfare as well as, finally, the judicial mechanisms which are emerging as a consequence of outside pressures.

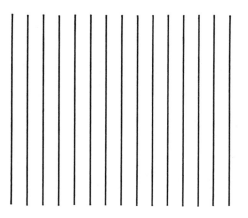

Part 2   The Social and Cultural Setting

Chapter 3   Social Structure and Organization

The Linguistic Units and Their Environs

Kamano (Kafe), Usurufa (Uturupa), Jate, and Fore are language names as well as general names for the people who speak them. The Kamano number about 12,000. They occupy a region of perhaps 320 square miles, stretching west and northwest (into the Bena subdistrict), south and southwest of Kainantu. On their west are the various Goroka–Kami–Henganofi–Bena Bena groups such as the Hofagi around Bena Bena and the Gafuk^c (Gahuku) near Goroka. The Kamano, Jate, Usurufa, and Fore speak of these groups as Ketori, and say that the Ketori call them, collectively, Jagarijavi. On the north and northeast the Kamano adjoin the Agarabe (Agarve), and on the east the Taiora (Taiarora) and Gadsup (Gazup); the Gadsup occupy at least three localities, separated by Taiora and Koga. On the south the Kamano meet the Usurufa, Fore, and Jate, and on the southwest also the Jate.

There are only about 900 Usurufa, in an area of no more than twelve square miles. On their north are Kamano, on their west and southwest Jate, on the south and southeast Fore, and on the east Fore, Gadsup, and Koga. The Kamano, Jate, and Usurufa confuse Gadsup with Koga, although they do trade, fight, and have other contacts with them. The Koga are said to have outposts about a day's walking distance east of the Usurufa but are mainly located east and southeast of the Fore, west and east of the Lamari River, in steep, mountainous grassland country with timbered ridges and gullies. They are called Hoga by the Fore.

The Fore, approximately 10,000 at the very most, occupy possibly about 240 square miles of country; but this general name seems to cover a number of subgroups in the "uncontrolled" region beyond Wanevinti. On the north of the Fore are Usurufa, Kamano, and Jate, on their east Koga and Gadsup, on the west Jate, and on the south Hatia, or Ati^c, Pamusa, Irasa, Purosa, and Jau^c (Jau^cgi or Jau^cgomana), Agirabu, Sumi-sumi, and Tavo^c. Nothing is yet known of these last groups, and they may not even be linguistic names.

The Jate extend west and south over a fairly large area, with a population which may exceed 20,000. They are divided roughly into a number of local units, representing dialectal variations.[1] The most important for our purpose here are the Ke^cjagana, Kemiju, and Friganu Jate. The latter is spoken and understood as far as Kami, about fourteen miles by direct track from Goroka, although the territorial boundary of this subgroup lies a little to the south of Kami. The Jate are bordered by the Kami and Goroka groups on the northwest; on the west by the Lufa and Mount Michael groups (Agugunehi^ce) as well as by the so-called Fogamiga; on the southwest by another Ke^cjagana group, apparently not Jate but possibly having Jate affinities; and, further southwest, by the Solwajani. On the east and southeast they meet the Fore, with whom they have the same southeastern perspective.

The assessment of population throughout the eastern Highland region

---

[1] Not all members of the subgroups I am calling Jate would agree. This applies particularly to the Friganu, some of whom never refer to themselves or their language in this way. Classifying them under the heading of "Jate" is to some extent an artificial device, a matter of ethnographic convenience. Nevertheless, other Jate-speaking subgroups regard the Friganu as linguistically and culturally akin to themselves, and Friganu as merely a regional name: and this is the opinion also of some of the Friganu. The issue here appears to be the over-all language name to be employed and not the acknowledgment of linguistic and other cultural affinities.

is tentative; more than half of it is still restricted or uncontrolled. Fairly accurate census figures are available for the Kamano but not for the Jate, Usurufa, and Fore.

The boundaries for each linguistic unit are well defined (see map C). The same is the case with the main Jate subdivisions. Even in border villages, where people usually have some knowledge of the neighboring language, they are quite definite about their own linguistic identification. Nevertheless, these four units can be said to represent, very broadly, a cultural bloc within which dissimilarities are acknowledged but over-all conformity to a common way of life is taken for granted. They fight and make peace with one another, intermarry, and know what to expect from one another. Generally speaking, and with some qualifications, although they claim separate linguistic identity, members of these units do not view one another as "strangers" to the same extent as they do others outside this range.[2] On the whole, their mythology affirms this view, emphasizing their common origin. In spite of this, they do not see themselves as a single social or political entity, nor as being in any sense genealogically related on this scale. There is not, or was not, free movement through the entire region covered by the four units any more than within each unit itself. But each district (see below) has a sphere of influence which normally covers all adjacent districts, and even those some little distance away, and transcends linguistic differences. Although we may regard the linguistic unit as the widest social grouping, its members do not consider themselves as united or as possessing common interests; and they, or their representatives, never meet collectively in the name of that unit.

The District, the Village, and the Patrilineage

Each linguistic unit contains a number of local subdivisions, "big names," a term here translated as "districts." It is the district name which these people generally use in talking of their home territory. Map B gives a partial distribution of such districts with their linguistic affiliations. The Kamano have approximately 67, the Usurufa only 6; the Kemiju-Jate subgroup has 33, the Keᶜjagana-Jate subgroup 41, and the

---

[2] I am speaking here mainly of the southern Kamano, Usurufa, Fore, and Jate; the northern Kamano have a slightly wider perspective. Within the last few years all of them have begun to realize that besides the Europeans at Kainantu, Goroka, and Henganofi there are many peoples living in all directions beyond their former social horizon. They are still rather vague about all this. However, such information is spreading rapidly, through contact with Government and Missions, native police and evangelists from other areas, and anthropologists. For a brief discussion of this subject see C. H. Berndt (1957).

Friganu-Jate at least 12 and possibly twice that number. According to Kamano, Jate, and Usurufa reckoning, there are 45 districts in the Fore unit, but according to Fore assessments there are 36. According to Usurufa and Jate estimation, there are approximately 14 Koga districts, but the Fore count reaches 27; this, of course, covers only those definitely known to them.

The population of each district varies considerably (ranging from about 50 to 480) and so does the area each district covers. At least half is usually unoccupied or uncultivated, with shifting cultivation the rule. Land is fairly plentiful in this part of the Highlands, although not all is equally fertile. There is not the same pressure of population here as around Kainantu or Goroka, a pressure intensified by European contact and settlement. The question of land use and occupation is seen principally in terms of fighting prowess. A refugee group may be allocated land, but not on a permanent basis. Land, the actual ground itself as contrasted with what it produces, is traditionally inalienable. Now (1953), however, claims to the land they occupy have been made by refugees who no longer look on themselves as such. A stronger and more clearly articulated conception of "land ownership through use" is in the course of development.

Within each district are several "small names," or place names. At some of them there are gardens, at others villages or hamlets, usually situated on high ground and fortified with wooden palisades. In the northern part of the region a village or hamlet-cluster, known by the "small name" of the site on which it stands, is occupied by a local clan containing one or more patrilineages.[3] The following list shows how a few districts are subdivided.[4] Most district, village, and patrilineage names have special meanings and linked with them is a great deal of pseudo-historical and mythological material which falls outside our present range of interest.

Linguistic Unit: Usurufa.

District	Village or Place Name	Patrilineage
Kogu	1. Maira	*a* kogu
		b kogu

---

[3] See A. R. Radcliffe-Brown, in Radcliffe-Brown and Daryll Forde, eds. (1950, p. 40); M. Fortes (1945, pp. 30ff.); (1949, pp. 4ff.); (1953, pp. 17–41); R. Berndt (1954*b*); K. E. Read (1951; 1954); M. Reay (1959, esp. p. 35); P. Brown (1960, pp. 25, 32).

[4] For convenience all names except those of patrilineages are given in Ke⟨jagana-Jate, mostly without the locative endings often used in ordinary speech. Fairly complete lists are available, but it would take up too much space to include them here. For convenience, too, most vernacular terms throughout this chapter are also in Ke⟨jagana Jate.

District	*Village or Place Name*	*Patrilineage*
Kogu	2. Juwe	*a* kogu
		b ke^canoza
	3. Alilo	*a* wagimuaipa
		b wagimuaipa
		c wagimuaipa
		d wagimuaipa
	4. Kiave	*a.* wagimuaipa (breakaway from 3*a*)
	5. Fufusa	*a* kogu, or fufusaga
Anonana	1. Kuneja	*a* jumana
	2. Juveri^cme	*a* anonana
Agura	1. Amura	*a* agura
	2. Karete	*a* kinu
	3. Uwasa	*a* uwasa
Moiife	1. Anamu	*a* irafu
		b kiki
	2. Kugu	*a* irafu
		b kiki
	3. Waninu	*a* irafu
		b irafu
Irafu	1. Wanisu	*a* wagami
		b koga
		c koga
Jumana	1. Gume	*a* ke^canoza
	2. Amuba	*a* krevea

Linguistic Unit: Kemiju-Jate.

Numparu	1. Ihamugu	*a* irafu
		b kiki
	2. Kadju	*a* kiki
	3. Sifo^co	*a* ki^co
Kemiju	1. Nise^cja	*a* ja^cagusa
		b gaguna
		c tigana
	2. Avige^cme	*a* henagagu
		b tiaguta
	3. Kagaguawate, or Tofe	*a* agatu
		b una
	4. Sosofe	*a* agatu
		b agatu
		c nupaguni

Linguistic Unit: Ke^c^jagana-Jate.

District	*Village or Place Name*	*Patrilineage*
Ke^c^jagana	1. Asonita	*a* hai
		b omisaro
	2. Kotutu	*a* hogateru
		b hogateru
	3. O^c^nu	*a* kasa
	4. Kinanovi(ga)	*a* hogateru
		b hogateru
	5. No^c^hire	*a* kasa (split from 3*a*)
		b kasa (split from 3*a*)
	6. To^c^jafore	*a* hai (split from 1*a*)
		b omisaro (split from 1*b*)
	7. Iita	*a* hai (split from 1*a*)
		b hai (split from 1*a*)

Linguistic Unit: Kamano.

Grufe	1. Fomu^c^o	*a* imusa
		b imusa
	2. Esimpi	*a* krevea
		b krevea
Tebio (Tebi^c^o, or Teve^c^o)	1. Tafure	*a* tebinofi
		b tebinofi
	2. Imusa^c^o	*a* karokaro
		b karokaro
	3. Tiane (Tihane)	*a* onu
		b onu

Linguistic Unit: Fore.

Busarasa	1. Jajumi	*a* anumpa
	2. Kaboma	*a* inivi
	3. Agagu	*a* inivi
	4. Kabi	*a* inivi
	5. Ibarera	*a* kiki
	6. Kaboma No. 2	*a* inivi
	7. Inaisa	*a* kasa
	8. Tosang^c^gamu	*a* kasa
	9. Punaningga	*a* kasa
	10. Kaiawani	*a* kasa
	11. Puna	*a* kasa
	12. Inominggajampuri	*a* inivi
Moke	1. Aibijugantisa	*a* obabisa
		b moke
		c ke^c^afu
	2. Egunitisa	*a* moke
		b obabisa
		c ke^c^afu

District	Village or Place Name	Patrilineage
Moke	3. Masamipintisa	a kasoru
		b pamia
		c keᶜanoza
	4. Kevia	a keᶜanoza
		b kasoru
	5. Wasapi	a kasoru
	6. Sawananta	a moke
Ora	1. Igoginogari	a anumpa
	2. Wenta(gori)	a anumpa
	3. Isa(gori)	a anumpa
	4. Akitaamu	a anumpa
	5. Aburu	a anumpa
	6. Katuri	a anumpa
	7. Jagai	a anumpa
	8. Nagu	a anumpa
	9. Tukasina	a kasaru
		b tategu
	10. Amuja	a kasaru
		b waniababi
	11. Amorantagu	a kotuni
	12. Igivi	a kasaru
	13. Arojagu	a kasaru
	14. Toruvi	a kasaru
	15. Ivija	a kotuni

The patrilineage or "line" (*agunagani, nagana; nofi* in Kamano; *nogani* in Usurufa; *runi* in Fore) consists of men and women tracing genealogical descent through males to a common remembered male ancestor. Genealogical knowledge is not extensive. As with the *dzuha* of the Gahuku-Gama,[5] it normally covers a span of no more than four generations, so that the "ancestor" in question may be a father's father or his father. Male members of a lineage, with their families, and unmarried, divorced, or widowed female members usually live together in a village or hamlet. They share certain gardening land, co-operate in various activities such as house-building, and jointly own sacred flutes and associated tunes.

Among the Kamano, Usurufa, and Jate a clan consists of one or more patrilineages occupying the same village. Whether or not they share the same name, they claim common descent, without being able to trace this relationship genealogically. This is the case, for instance, with the two

[5] K. E. Read (1951, p. 155). See also M. Reay (1959, p. 34).

lineages of one name, *kogunogani*, at Maira in Kogu. But the lineage of the same name at Juwe, also in Kogu, claims no relationship, except in a classificatory sense, with those at Maira. It is aligned with the *ke^c anozano-gani*, and with it forms a clan in the sense in which I am using the term here. The name alone, then, is no clue to clan membership. Throughout the whole region all these names are very much alike, but similarity alone is said to be no indication of relationship. For instance, the Fore *ke^c afuruni* claims to have taken its name from the Jate district of Ke^c afu; the Fore *obabisaruni* from Obabi (Ofafina), a Fore district; the *iniviruni* of Busarasa (Fore) from Inivi, a Jate district; Numparu, a Kemiju-Jate district, contains a lineage named *irafunagani*, but Irafu is an Usurufa district. And so on.

Among the Fore the villages are usually much smaller than they are farther north; it might be better to speak of them as hamlets or isolated house-clusters. Here lineages of the same name occupying different villages within one district consider themselves interrelated, whether or not they can work this out genealogically. This relationship cuts across village membership, where the emphasis is on coresidence. For instance, the *kasaruni* in Busarasa are five patrilineages, occupying separate sites but regarding themselves as "one": in my terms, a clan, which can be seen here as a political subunit. The Busarasa *anumparuni*, however, stands alone in that district as the only one of this name. Coresidence is not entirely ignored: for certain purposes, and in certain situations, when two or three patrilineages occupy the same village they acknowledge some degree of common interest and common action; but these local bonds are viewed as much weaker than those between linked lineages of the same name.

All through the region, adult males in a village or hamlet traditionally share a communal house; women and children occupy a series of smaller houses, one to each wife in the case of polygynous unions. Among the Fore, where changes in the settlement pattern have not been so striking, house-clusters continue to be small and dispersed. Among the Kamano, Jate, and Usurufa, however, the lineages now spread out over the district may have been more closely knit prior to 1947. Examination of the remaining Usurufa stockades seems to indicate this. If so, it would mean that the clans were rather larger than they are today. Now that they feel fairly safe from organized attacks by other districts, these people have shown a tendency to scatter. At the same time they have been under pressure from the Administration to concentrate in larger villages where they are more accessible and more easily supervised. Many of the Kamano near Kainantu and Raipinka have moved down from the ridges to valley sites, and this trend is spreading southward.

The patrilineage, like the clan, has no totemic affiliations, for we cannot take their names alone to signify this. But the ground on which a village is built or "grows" has traditions associated with it and spirit beings who belong to it and whose activities are described in local mythology. If a village is occupied by two or more lineages, the land is divided between them. In the final count it belongs to the district and if threatened from outside may be defended on that basis. Ordinarily, however, it is seen as patrilineage "trust" property, allocated among its members. A man is expected to share his part of the lineage lands among his sons when they marry, keeping enough for his own use during his lifetime. This distribution covers not only cultivated gardens but land lying fallow, or unworked ground near his home village. The division is not fixed but always subject to revision, especially after the death of one of the "owners." A woman leaving her village in marriage retains some right to her own patrilineage land and if she returns to it will expect to work in one of her brothers' gardens. Very rarely, she may take up a section of that land and work it herself. In principle, then, she does not relinquish her claim to her father's land.

Routine gardening work is largely women's responsibility. The produce is individually owned by a man, his wife, or wives and children who have shared in its cultivation; his father and brothers have no claim on it. In the gardens patrilineage dead and their adherents are buried or eaten, or both; and this and the rites associated with it are held to increase the fertility of the earth.

The Patrilineage and its Composition

The basic structure of the lineage may be diagramed as on p. 26. The diagram shows an ideal patrilineage, a paradigm, as Fortes puts it. The shortness of genealogical memory is encouraged by a relatively high death rate, so that a man's paternal grandfather's brothers might have died before he was born and their male descendants be genealogically lost to him. Most middle-aged men remember the names of both grandfathers and at least one great-grandfather, but few can give any information about the brothers of these and their offspring, who automatically formed "new" lineages. Female members of the patrilineage are not shown in the diagram because, although they still belong to the patrilineage after marriage, they do not serve to perpetuate it. (I am not dealing here with the matter of adoption, including the exchange of children between

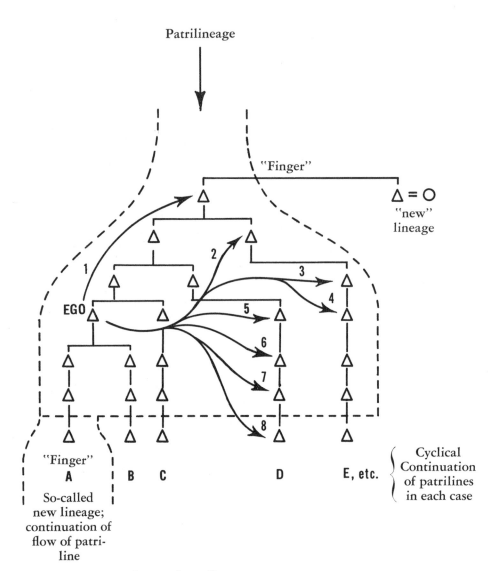

Patrilineage

"Finger"

$\triangle = \bigcirc$
"new"
lineage

EGO

"Finger"
A

B C

D

E, etc.

So-called
new lineage;
continuation of
flow of patri-
line

⎱
⎰ Cyclical
Continuation
of patrilines
in each case

Arrows from Ego:
 1. "Finger" (see text).
 2. Classificatory father's father.
 3. Classificatory father.
 4. Classificatory brother.
 5. Parallel cousins; "siblings."
 6. Classificatory parent-child.
 7. Classificatory grandparent-grandchild.
 8. "Finger."

brother and sister.) It extends lineally in a cyclical fashion, but its lateral spread is restricted by the continual breaking away of various sections to form similar units. One of its most important attributes is its fluidity, expressed through changing personnel. The only stable feature is the male descent line from father to son, conceptualized as a continuous process in time and symbolized by a growing creeper, or "rope," linking generation with generation.

A man calls both his father's father's father and his son's son's son "my finger" or "fingernail" (naginagumu^{c}e). The assumption here is that he can expect to see his great-grandchild only as an infant; when he extends his finger, the child grasps it and plays with it.[6] He uses the same term for all those of the fifth descending kinship grade, conventionally signifying the juncture at which the cycle repeats itself. It thus limits patrilineage perspective, encouraging segmentation, without affecting the concept of linear continuity.

On the one hand, then, is this formal system in which segmentation appears as an automatic process, a matter of genealogical distance. On the other hand are the named units found in the actual situation, varying in size and in genealogical composition, but all called by the same term and viewed, structurally, as equivalent.

Kinship

For most children in most human societies the first few years of life are spent in a setting where the major interpersonal relations are organized in terms of kinship. It is in this setting, the family in its various forms, that the process of socialization begins. Whether or not we agree that the pattern established in this way is strong enough to shape the perception of all subsequent relationships, it is clear that its influence must be considerable.[7]

The second diagram is a schematic and condensed representation of the kinship system(s) as ideally conceived by the Kamano, Jate, Usurufa, and Fore.[8] This particular construct is not derived from quantitative analysis

[6] The Jate term may also be translated as toe, or toenail, with the same implication. Cf. A. R. Radcliffe-Brown, in Radcliffe-Brown and Daryll Forde, eds. (1950, p. 29).

[7] M. Fortes (1949, pp. 344, 346).

[8] See R. Berndt (1954b), where tables presenting terms used by the four linguistic units are given in rather more detail.

During the first period of our field research the genealogical material took into account some 1,770 persons of both sexes. In the second period, some 1,652 persons were considered in some detail in Kogu and adjacent districts, and some 606 in the Moke-Busarasa-Ora districts. These genealogies cover southern Kamano, eastern Jate, Usurufa (completely), and northern Fore.

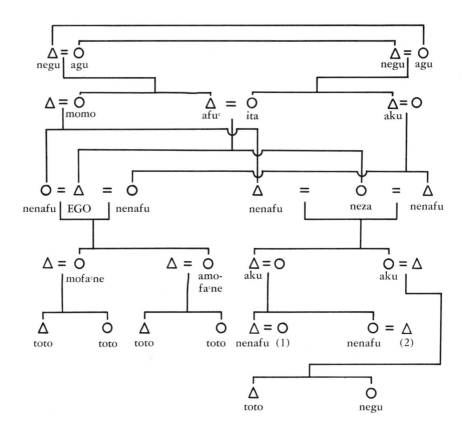

(1) partial identification with Ego's sister.
(2) partial identification with Ego.

of genealogical material, which would require a series of diagrams and much more discussion; but it does offer one kind of basis from which to approach the actual behavior involved in social relations. There is more or less complete over-all agreement on it between members of these four units, although the Fore diverge on a number of points. For convenience I am using only Ke^cjagana-Jate kinship terms: terminological differences do not affect the content of the relationships, insofar as this concerns us here.

The basis of this formal system is the ideal type-marriage(s) made by a man with females he calls *nenafu*, which can be translated broadly as cross-cousin. He may marry either his mother's brother's daughter or father's sister's daughter, or both. Another eligible *nenafu* is his (not full) sister's son's daughter, who in this ideal scheme is also the daughter of his mother's brother's son. His sister, too, may marry either or both cross-cousins, although not simultaneously, or her classificatory son's son. Among the Fore, marriage may take place within the clan, the linked lineages of one name, and also within the village or hamlet-cluster if this contains more than one patrilineage. The immediate patriline itself is, here, the only truly exogamous unit; that is, a man may marry his "sister" (Fore, *namanani*) or "daughter" (Fore, *araganeni*). On marriage, however, throughout the region the term changes in relation not only to the woman concerned but also to her close kin. The change indicates a new range of duties and rights, superseding or supplementing those formerly expected.

A man calls his actual father's sister *momo*, although the mother of a marriageable *nenafu* should be *neimo* or *aku*. He may call his father's sister's husband "father" (*afu^c*). Alternatively, he may call him *noka*, a term inherited, so to speak, from his father, who called that particular man his wife's brother or his sister's husband. A mother's brother is an *aku*; his wife, if not otherwise related to him, *nogago(^ce)*; and in conventional terms his daughter is the most desirable wife. In Kamano a mother's brother's wife is called by the same term as father's sister, *momo*; in Usurufa she is called "mother." A man calls his sister's children *aku*, the same term that they use for him. Although his sister's son's children are *nenafu* to him, his sister's daughter's children are *toto* and *negu*, grandchildren. The terms for actual parents-in-law depend to some extent on how they were viewed before that marriage took place. But the conventional term for wife's father and mother, as such, is *neimo*, extended to wife's father's sister and mother's brother.

There is no need to discuss here all the categories of relationship which make up the kinship system, the alternative choices permitted within it, and the associated behavior to which each term provides a key. Only a few of the more important will be indicated briefly, to provide a framework for our later discussion.

Siblings

Close male siblings normally remain together in the paternal village, not moving out of it on marriage as their sisters and fathers' sisters do. Especially before they are both adults, an elder brother is assumed to dominate a younger. He has some say in a younger brother's initiation and in arranging his marriage. Full brothers are supposed to be bosom companions in fighting, to stand as one with members of their lineage or clan in the event of a raid, to speak with one voice in village discussions, and so on. Nevertheless, there is also the expectation of some antagonism between them. One source of rivalry or resentment is the father's allocation of gardens: a man frequently favors his eldest son in this. Another is competition for wives. The eldest conventionally has first choice, regardless of any attachments formed by the others. Once betrothal arrangements are in hand, the girl and her sisters are cut off sexually (as *ato*) from the younger brothers. They may be compensated for this eventually through the junior levirate, but that again may lead to trouble between them should a younger son blatantly anticipate the elder's death.

When a man dies, his wife or wives may (in certain circumstances) pass to his younger brother. It is sometimes said that, ideally, a man's full younger brother is not eligible to marry his widow, that only half- or lineage- or more distant younger brothers may claim her. In practice, however, this limitation is certainly not strictly observed. If a man is already married to a sister of his elder brother's widow, the widow may not come to him. The avoidance relationship with *noka*, wife's sister, unlike the *ato* relationship, does not lapse on an elder brother's death. Should the elder die while the younger is still a boy, in this case, too, the widow may not go to him as wife. Instead, she may take up the role of "mother" and call him "son."

During her husband's lifetime a woman calls his elder brother by the same term as he does. Among the Kamano and Usurufa she does not address his younger brothers, close or otherwise, by any kinship term at all. If she finds it necessary to refer to one of them, she uses a term which could be broadly translated as "newly initiated youth." She refers in the same way to her husband's *nenafu* and *nefaru* (age mates). All three categories share the common feature of eligibility to marry her in the event of her husband's death.

The relationship between female siblings, as contrasted with males, receives much less emphasis. This may be because it is not seen as a competitive one. For instance, two sisters rarely marry the same man. Nor is it structurally important in the same sense as the male sibling tie or the tie between siblings of opposite sex. Rights and obligations between sisters are not clearly or precisely formulated. If they have married into the same village or even the same district, the bond of affection already assumed to exist between them is likely to be intensified through mutual interdependence. But the same term is often used both for people related through genealogical kinship and for those whose husbands are so related, that is, women who have married into the same lineage or clan. In both cases co-operation and mutual assistance are expected. However, where the kinship tie is unsupported by common residence or common enterprise, in other words where the ascribed relationship is not reinforced in the course of social living, it is taken to be no more effective than the tie which links women in the first place through their husbands and in the second place through their sons.

As against this, the bond between close brother and sister is one of central importance, not just in personal terms but in its direct bearing on other social relationships; for instance, in the ideal that these two should exchange children in marriage, the cross-cousin union which is said to be the most desirable of all. The bond between them is highlighted on such occasions as her betrothal and subsequent marriage with the arrangement and payment of her bridewealth; and on her death he will be one of the main recipients at the mortuary distribution. Although marriage payments are conventionally made to her father's youngest brother, her own brothers expect to receive a share. In fact, she may actually view this man as a "brother" if he has been adopted by one of his older brothers, perhaps by her own father.

A brother and sister are expected to avoid looking directly at each other, talking frivolously, or discussing erotic matters; it is sometimes said that there should be very little conversation of any sort between them. However, there is no name taboo between them; and while she is still living in her home village a girl may cook her brother's food, if he is still unmarried, and take it to him in the men's house. After marriage she looks to him to protect her rights, especially as against her husband and his kin. Women speaking of their own villages and lineages usually refer first of all to their brothers, much less frequently to their fathers. Conversely, a man can normally count on a close sister's help in times of trouble and fighting. Under cover of this affectionate bond some double-dealing seems to take place at times. A man learning that members of his district plan to attack the village in which his sister lives might slip away to warn her on the pretext of visiting his gardens. For this he would accept payment from her husband. Later he might warn his own kin that the village into which his sister had married was preparing for war and for this information receive further presents.

A woman's husband may also help her, if her mother is dead, in arranging and preparing gifts for the betrothal of her younger brother. Conventionally he would call this man *noka*, brother-in-law. Acting in this way, however, would be accompanied by a change in terms. She would now be a "mother," not a sister, to the boy; her husband would now be a "father" to him, and if he belonged to the same district would assist in the boy's initiation. The woman whose marriage they had arranged would now be a son's wife, *nanoferu*, to them, although normally a woman calls her brother's wife *so^ciju*.

Cross-Cousins (nenafu)

Even when male *nenafu* belong to different villages or districts, and despite the name taboo between them, this relationship is said to typify comradeship and freedom of association; it is like a "brother" bond, but without its latent rivalry and jealousy. Two close male *nenafu* may walk together with arms about each other's shoulders, talk freely, and participate in erotic adventures together. One will mourn deeply the death of the other: he may slash his nose vertically so that blood flows freely down his chest, or cut his nasal septum; he may spend several nights in vigil over the grave, perhaps violently repulsing local efforts to eat the corpse. In extreme cases he may even try to commit suicide in his grief. Mythology, like contemporary life, is rich in examples of friendship between two male *nenafu*. This is most enduring when it is not interrupted by the marriage of one of them to the sister of the other. In that case, when the two are not affinally related, when a man's wife has no kin tie with his male *nenafu*, a situation rather like the levirate may develop. The assumption is that she becomes a special kind of *nenafu* to this man whom he himself calls *nenafu*, who may have sexual access to her during the husband's lifetime and is eligible to marry her on his death.

Ordinarily, however, should one *nenafu* marry a woman whom the other calls sister, or both exchange sisters, the term changes to indicate a new affinal relationship: *noka*, brother-in-law, with all the economic obligations which this involves, accompanied by restrictions on speech between them.

The *nenafu* relationship, then, is of two kinds. A man has his own close and classificatory female *nenafu*, but there are others whom he calls by that term in virtue of their marriage to his male *nenafu*. These last he may have sexual access to and later marry; but should he marry one of the former her actual sisters become *noka*, or should his brother marry one she becomes his *ato*. A wife's sisters do not become *nenafu* again until she dies or leaves him, while he may take his brother's widow only if he is a younger brother and not married to her sister.

The relations between male and female cross-cousins are thus affected by their respective marriages, as those between female *nenafu* are not. If they remain affinally unrelated, friendship and intimacy may continue between them, with implied sexual freedom. But they do not become so deeply or demonstrably attached to each other as do male *nenafu*. The strength of the tie between them is influenced by genealogical closeness, with a man's "true" *nenafu* his full cross-cousin. With the proviso already noted, he may always have sexual access to her. When she quarrels with her husband, she may accuse him of being only a classificatory *nenafu*, not her proper husband; and there are cases in which a woman has left her husband for this actual *nenafu*. The choice might seem to offer some difficulties when several brothers are involved, but often the eldest is given priority. Even so, a woman may rationalize the matter to suit her own preference.

A man calls his wife's sister's husband *honi^c*; and, except within the same lineage or clan, this means name-avoidance and speech restrictions. The idea is, as one man put it: "I already have a *nenafu* from that particular family. Some other men must have my wife's sisters." However, when the son of a man's *honi^c* is old enough to be initiated, the boy's mother's sister's husband may perform the nose-bleeding operation upon him. On the death of a man's *honi^c*, the widow, his wife's sister, may come to him as wife. This seems to be the only approved instance where sisters may be co-wives. The children of two *honi^c* call one another "brothers" and "sisters" until they become adult, and then *nanogai*. Should one male *nanogai* die, his widow may go to the other. The *nanogai* bond is seen as a close and affectionate one, comparable to that between *nefaru* or *nenafu*; it is also a "neutral" one in warfare.

Name-Avoidance

The taboo on uttering personal names extends over a range of kin, both consanguineal and affinal. One of the most intimate relationships, that between two male *nenafu*, or a male and a female *nenafu*, involves this. So do those of a man with his *neimo* (parents-in-law), *nanoferu* (son's wife), father's sister, mother's brother and his wife, sister's son, sister's husband, wife's sister and her husband, wife's brother and his wife, and elder brother's wife.

The only name-avoidance within the patrilineage is that between a man and his father's sister, for with his own sister there is merely a relationship of restraint. Both these women move out of the patri-village on marriage but retain their emotional links with it, conventionally typified in the brother-sister bond. The relationship between a man and his father's sister is an extension of this, perpetuating in a different form the close association which existed between her and his father. He cannot expect the same help from his father's sister as his own father could. Nevertheless, he can expect special treatment from her, and it is this expectation which is expressed in the relationship of restraint between them. She gives him food and, if living in the same village, looks after him just as an unmarried sister does. If not, he can visit her when circumstances permit and receive food and attention. They may even joke together. "You are my *aku*'s wife," he may say. "Why may I not open your bark skirt and look at your vulva?" (To part the hanging bark threads of a woman's skirt is tantamount, symbolically, to having sexual intercourse.) This relaxation and channelizing in erotic jokes of the formal restraint between them is something which could not occur between siblings of the opposite sex or between a man and his mother or her sisters. With no other agnate, in fact, can he behave in this familiar way; but the degree of familiarity is predetermined and restricted. Underlying it is the significant fact that this father's sister may become his mother-in-law, for her daughters are his *nenafu*.

Agnates and Cognates

Social relations within the patrilineage are based upon common agnatic descent. Cognatic ties, however, spread beyond the patrilineage, embracing not only the district but also members of adjacent districts in the same or other linguistic units. All the members of a patrilineage have more or less identical lineage ties, defining their common status as against the members of other such units; but only siblings of the same parents have exactly the same cognatic kin.[9] The kinship terminology reflects these two spheres, which are seen as being to some extent in contrast, if not in opposition. The first is basically the co-operative sphere, at a more than individual level. It is extended by the adoption of males who may help to perpetuate the units of which they become members, and by the perception of certain common interests and aims within the linked lineages, the clan. The second sphere involves mutual ties of sentiment, reciprocal duties, and help in particular circumstances, but not on a group basis.

Extradistrict relations are seen as a personal matter. Members of the same district call one another by kinship terms, whether or not they can explain their relationship in detail. District membership itself carries with it this assumption of common kinship, as against the assumption of non-kinship outside it except in interpersonal terms. Only agnatic kin within a certain range consistently and ideally live together, so that local and kinship bonds mutually reinforce and define each other. But other categories of kin ordinarily occupy different villages if not different districts and, therefore, except among the Fore, are not necessarily bound by common interests in war. Kin living outside the district are in potentially hostile territory and conventionally should be viewed with caution, although certain relationships, especially those between *nenafu* cross-cousins, or between close brother and sister, remain, ideally, free from antagonism or suspicion.

For own kin who become affines, the change in terminology has more than nominal significance. Active co-operation, especially in regard to the passing of certain goods or the performance of certain services, is still expected of them; but this now takes rather different forms and, what is more, is set in a different emotional context. The strong bond between male cross-cousins turns into a *noka* relationship should one marry the other's sister. Other cognatic kin who become affines may or may not become actively antagonistic. Affines between whom there were previously no acknowledged kinship ties, however, are seen as potential or actual enemies.

When a wife leaves or is forced to leave her husband, in the event of a divorce or estrangement, he normally keeps their male children while she takes the females. (If the children are separated at an early age this may weaken the bond between them.) Or a woman living in her husband's village, finding herself suddenly a widow, may flee to her paternal village,

9 Cf. M. Fortes (1949, pp. 13–14).

taking her children of both sexes with her—although usually, it is said, the males are claimed by her husband's younger brothers. Apart from adoption in the ordinary way, there are also some cases where children have been stolen and brought up among strangers in other districts, so that in later years they do not know or will not acknowledge their real parents.

Although the claims of maternal kin are acknowledged to be strong, this kind of relationship is treated as if it were almost entirely personal. Rights and obligations in respect of them, or at least the more significant of them in local perspective (especially mother's brother, mother's brother's children, mother's father and mother), are fairly clearly defined; but there is no suggestion that the mother's patrilineal descent group as such is of an importance equal to that of the father's. From another angle the situation is exactly the same where a man's father's sister's husband and her children are concerned. From the viewpoint of his patrilineage or clan, they are members of potentially hostile units, with different and conflicting loyalties. It is patrilineal kinship which counts in this connection.

One particular relationship which overrides genealogical kin links actually underlines the importance of the group of male kin who share a common territory and join together in certain major activities, even though in practice the people who acknowledge such a relationship do not always belong to the same district. Children born of different mothers within a district at the same time and place, or initiated together, call one another age-mates, *nefaru*. This itself is said to be stronger than the ordinary sibling tie; but when both are combined, as in the case of two close brothers, the relationship is an exceptionally intimate and binding one.

Conventionally, a man views with respect as well as affection all close kin of his grandparents' generation, male and female; but this is more marked in the case of his father's father. He is the virtual head of the patrilineage, in the process of becoming an "ancestor." If both a man's parents are dead, his father's father will lead him to his initiation and draw blood from his nose. (If his mother is dead, his mother's brother may not do this.) The paternal grandfather will also take a leading part in arranging his marriage.

A man accumulates wealth through patrilineage and clan distribution. For example, a lineage- or clan-sister may marry. A sister, actual or classificatory, or an elder brother's daughter, is a direct source of income. Wealth may be obtained also through gifts made by a *noka* or a male *nenafu*, or through the death of a father or brother. Gifts between *noka*, *nenafu*, or male and female siblings are, however, reciprocal in essence. A man cannot accumulate goods in any marked degree through these channels, as he can through others.

In arranging a marriage, a man's father and male members of his patrilineage, and to a lesser degree his own mother, select a particular girl, haggle with her parents, brothers, and father's brothers, and finally, when an agreement is reached, hand over the bridewealth. When festivities for the consummation of the marriage are in progress, the reciprocated bridewealth is paid by the girl's parents and patrilineage. Rarely does any of it come to the bridegroom. Occasionally a man's second or subsequent marriage is financed not by himself or by members of his patrilineage but by his first wife or wives and his own sons. The material wealth essential for arranging a marriage is not acquired by a man's own personal effort; this is the duty of his parents and his patrilineage. Nor does he gain wealth through his marriage, for this increases his obligations. Throughout his life he must make gifts to his wife's brother, which may or may not be reciprocated.[10] Marriage is a responsibility, a call on his wealth. This becomes more marked when his sons marry; and although he is an indirect receiver on his daughter's marriage, he must subscribe toward her reciprocated bridewealth.

Changes in terminology and in associated behavior take place almost entirely within the framework of the formal system, as part of that system. The outstanding example of this is marriage, involving as it does the formation of a new set of affinal relationships, some of which were formerly phrased in terms of consanguineal kinship. But there are other changes which (up to a point) may also be seen within that framework, to the extent that it includes a range of acceptable alternatives. However, choice of such alternatives, as of those which are regarded as less acceptable, in itself helps to widen this range and in so doing to make a more obvious distinction between social and biological kinship. Adoption is one case in point. Another is marriage in which choice of partners rests less on kinship eligibility than on other factors, such as the amount of bridewealth which can be obtained.

From one point of view we can say that asymmetrical relationships are those between, for instance, parent and child, elder and younger brother,

---

[10] That is, if the wife's brother does not marry his sister. If two *nenafu* have exchanged sisters, the gift exchange between *noka* is fairly equally balanced. If a man's sister goes to a classificatory wife's brother, he will still share in some of the gift exchange, for any husband of a sister is a *noka* and is bound to continue payments to him as wife's brother.

a man and his wife's brother or wife's parents; but where duties are more or less equivalent, as between grandparent and grandchild, brother and sister, *nenafu*, *nefaru* age-mates, *honi^c*, *nanogai*, and so on, we can speak of a symmetrical relationship. It may be argued that no relationship is really symmetrical, that there is only an approximation of reciprocity in terms of tangible and intangible mutual benefits. Basically, however, from the viewpoint of any given person, there are those with whom he is on equal terms; those with whom he must be diffident, respectful, and obedient; and those over whom he stands in authority. Many subtle differences exist between these three types of status relationship. All are alterable, in terms of personnel, through time: of ascending kinship status through age, marriage, parenthood, and so on. Or a symmetrical relationship may be transposed into an asymmetrical one, for example male *nenafu* becoming *noka*, and vice versa, through the junior levirate or through divorce. But every adult man and woman stands in relationship to defined kin in one of these three ways.

Here we are concerned primarily with some basic assumptions which are contained in, and find expression through, a body of popular knowledge. This knowledge is verbalized in the shape of ordinary tales, stories, and general information as well as mythology. It is part of the nonempirical background of social action. We are concerned also with ritual action, or at least with certain elements of it.

For the purpose of discussion, verbal knowledge in this area can be classified under three main headings. The first presents a broad picture of the natural and social environment. The second concerns myths which, among other things, substantiate certain rituals. The third, not treated here, comprises a large body of "non-sacred" mythology which can be differentiated in some respects from the other two. It is within this problem area that conflicting values are most clearly expressed, whereas in the body of knowledge with which we shall be dealing values operate largely in terms of basic assumptions, or "givens." In the "non-sacred" mythology, patterns of conformity and nonconformity, conflict and consistency, are developed as it were alongside one another, providing not only a set of moral standards but also a charter for misconduct.

The first division comprises a motley of assumptions[1] relating to the nature of the universe and man's place in it. The problem of cosmology as nonempirical belief in relation to religion has been mentioned by Talcott Parsons,[2] who holds, as Durkheim did, that all such beliefs which reflect "man's moral attitudes and value-orientation patterns" are of a religious nature. This all-inclusive view is taken by a number of anthropologists writing today—Herskovits, Firth, and Nadel,[3] for instance. Others have suggested that it would be better to abandon the term religion in favor of a more neutral one such as Honigmann's "ideational culture."[4]

---

[1] In this context reference should be made to the volume edited by Daryll Forde (1954).

[2] See Talcott Parsons (1952, pp. 359–60, 368).

[3] M. Herskovits (1949, chaps. 21–22); R. Firth (1951, p. 221); S. F. Nadel (1954, pp. 2–3, 7–8).

[4] J. Honigmann, cited by C. Kluckhohn in A. L. Kroeber, ed. (1953, p. 509).

In the present instance I am using the term rather loosely, in much the same manner as Firth and Nadel. Cosmological ideas in the eastern Highland region are not regarded by the people themselves as specifically "religious." They comprise rather a body of knowledge linked only indirectly with sacred ritual, providing accounts of natural phenomena in mythological terms or in nonempirical statements.

The second category of myth, which might be called an "origin" myth or cycle, concerns the adventures of two Creative Beings, Jugumishanta and Morufonu, who are said to be responsible for peopling the whole country occupied by the Kamano, Usurufa, Jate, and Fore. They did not make the entire world that these Highland people know, but they made human beings (although there are contrary beliefs), planted gardens, trees, and so on, and instituted various behavior patterns and ceremonies. They are responsible for the social and cultural world, are cited as the originators of almost everything except most natural phenomena, and are associated with most sacred ritual. There is a further series of myths which account nonempirically for certain aspects of ritual action but do not show how ritual should be carried out.

That part of myth which relates to ritual need not offer a description of it, although it may attempt to account for it.[5] Ritual does not refer only to social action occurring in sacred situations (allowing for the fact that here I am not defining the term sacred),[6] and myth in current usage does not have this limited connotation. But ritual usually, although not invariably, has some mythological substantiation. Mythology, on the other hand, while serving to account for certain kinds of ritual, presents a much wider field of belief content.

It is in this sphere, the creation of human beings and the establishment of social life as it is known today, that we find sentiments which can most conveniently be described as religious. We find also a number of obvious inconsistencies overlooked by the narrators. There are many versions, although a fair amount of agreement on essential details. Most versions are fragmentary, told without regard to sequence. There is no attempt to present a co-ordinated and full account, with all the various incidents arranged to form one myth. In a sense we may say that there are not one but many myths about them.

[5] The myths are not enacted, but the ritual actions which do take place serve to symbolize certain features. This refers to sacred ritual and not to the dramatization of some myths in the third category of non-sacred mythology.

[6] I would agree with Leach (1954, p. 12) and others that we cannot draw a strict dichotomy between sacred and profane as Durkheim tried to do.

The outline of the material to be discussed here was gathered at various times throughout both periods of field work. It consists largely of fragments told to novices going through the age-grading rituals, not by way of formal instruction, but in stories when the novices are gathered in the men's house; or when men, secluded in the sweat house, sing and tell tales. It is usually the older men, considered to possess more knowledge in virtue of their experience, who relate these stories; but it is not their sole prerogative. Women also know the broad outline of these myths, although some features are conventionally kept secret from them. It is not this secrecy which marks it off as sacred. The whole range of mythology in this category can be viewed as sacred.

The Creative Beings

Both Jugumishanta and Morufonu are intimately connected with the cosmos. They are said to have emerged from the sacred ground at Rivetiga (Arigi), near Oka, about half a day's walk southeast of Busarasa-Moke. Rivetiga is a swamp, and the name itself is derived from *rigina*, a species of cane used for swallowing. Some versions claim that they emerged from the swamp covered with slime and foliage, others that they were simply living there. This seems to contradict the original statement that they made the world. The explanation here is that Jugumishanta herself is the earth, and as a spirit, in one of her manifestations, she emerged from it; she is viewed as emerging from herself. Jugumishanta, indeed, is stressed much more than Morufonu. Like him, she has many names which represent her different manifestations. Thus she is Rivetiga, the swampy site, Kabito, a type of red croton, or Jagami or Jugu, a special variety of "salt."[7] She is called also Jugu^cjugufanta, meaning a species of grass used in nose-piercing, and Guriguri, the stone barrier of a waterfall. On the Jate side she is more often known as Fami^c, a type of bean.[8] Morufuno or Magafono is derived from *tafo*, the hornbill. He is also called Jagojugu, meaning taro, among the Jate, or *gerigeri*, the sound of a

---

[7] These are her three principal names. Red croton leaves are immersed for some time in the swamp water at Rivetiga, then dried in the sun. This yields a thin layer of "salt," which is a particularly important commodity in the region. Collected in this way it is chewed and expectorated over food for seasoning or it used in propitiation to avoid sickness, sorcery, and so on. Net bags, too, are left in this water and on being dried are stiff with "salt."

[8] She is likened to a bean pod which "gives birth" to many seeds. Among the Fore she is sometimes called Anggarosa. In some versions Anggarosa is said to be the ghost of Jugumishanta, in others her sister, and in yet others the original place from which these Beings emerged.

waterfall; and in one popular manifestation he is *wojafa* or *wajafa*, a red parakeet.

At Rivetiga they lived under a black hardwood tree which grew from an arrow they carried. They planted bamboo, crotons, and other trees and grasses. At this time they did not resemble human beings. Jugumishanta made herself: she put on skin and fashioned arms and legs and cut a vulva for herself. She then turned to her husband, who had no mouth, no eyes, no skin, and at the top of his head a large hole from which issued flames; his penis was within his belly. First she got water and poured it into the hole at the top of his head, quenching the flames. With the sap from the *fukina* tree, she covered up the hole. She placed a taro leaf first on the upper part of his face, cutting two eyes, then lower down, cutting a nose, and finally a mouth. Then she placed the taro leaf at the base of his abdomen, cut, and pulled out his penis. She went on pulling it out until it was long; then she put it into her vagina, and they copulated. In this way she became pregnant.

In the garden of Figagiat at Rivetiga [according to another version] are two stones, a "male stone" upon which Morufonu "sharpened" his penis, and a "female stone" upon which Jugumishanta "sharpened" her vagina. They sat separately, one at each side of the garden; Morufonu looked at his wife's vagina, and his penis grew long and stretched out across the garden. Jugumishanta "sharpened" her vagina on the stone, making it large; Morufonu "sharpened" his penis, making a pointed apex to facilitate entry. They were both working at opposite sides of the garden. He now extended his penis so that it went across the garden and entered her; but after he had ejaculated, Jugumishanta turned around. "What is this that enters my vagina? Ah, it is his penis!" She caught hold of it and cut it. Morufonu drew it back and began to "sharpen" it to a point again, and Jugumishanta also "sharpened" her vagina. The same thing happened again. She turned, exclaimed, grabbed hold of his penis, and cut it. This continued until his penis was the normal size, and the two could enjoy intercourse in the usual manner. Jugumishanta then became pregnant.

The significant point here is that copulation is occurring in the garden; Morufono is fertilizing the earth, symbolized by Jugumishanta.

Jugumishanta gave birth at Rivetiga first to a female and then to a male child; but they had no flesh, they were only skin and bone. She put them down, wondering what to do. From Tabajaka,[9] the place of the wind, in the far southeast, from a cave near a waterfall, *jasia*, the wind, came blowing. All the nearby country was bare. *Jasia* came on, catching the banana leaves, the leaves of many trees and of yams. Pushing them before him, he came to where Jugumishanta and Morufonu lived and showing them all these leaves said, "You have put these yams, these trees, these bananas, and they have grown well." He swirled around,

9 In some versions it is said that the Creative Beings came from Tabajaka, leaving behind them Anggarosa (identified with Jugumishanta). Tabajaka means in this context, so it is said, the branching limb of a tree; the place is also called Koripika, referring to the burning of the grass when they prepared gardens to plant yams, sugar cane, and other food.

catching up the leaves, blowing hard on the newly born pair until his spirit entered their bodies, swelling out their skin, making them like human beings.

It is said, too, that *jasia* caught up the spirit of man and placed it within each of these two children of Jugumishanta, telling her, "You have put men now, and they have grown well." In this way men came to have each a spirit (*hangkaru*), making them come alive, making them breathe (*tabamuna*, derived from Tabajaka): it is the spirit which breathes, which keeps them alive. Then the sun shone on these two children, their skin became even better, and they grew into adults.

Although we are led to believe that no people existed at this period, except the spirits of the cosmos, the Creative Beings themselves, and their new creation, man, we are told that Kaiteniwaja^c^mogi (Jate: "story men") were there and shot at Jugumishanta and Morufonu. Morufonu drew his bow and shot back at them, but his aim was inaccurate. Then Jugumishanta took his bow and changed around the toughened bamboo slat (used in place of a string) so that the arrow butt rested upon the slippery surface. She handed it back to Morufuno, who shot them. The two pulled the dead bodies down the face of a hillside, one by one, making furrows in the ground. This occurred at Koripika, an alternative name of Tabajaka.

Most of the versions at this stage tell how men were placed in various districts, and how the Creative Beings planted trees, bushes, and so on. A few abbreviated examples can be given.

At Rivetiga, Jugumishanta and Morufonu planted crotons and put people who spoke Fore. Then they set off on their travels, planting bamboos and crotons as they went. They put the Koga people, the Ati^c^, the Jate, Kamano, Usurufa, and so on, naming each district, and decreeing what language was to be spoken there.

At Agwinatogu, below Kimi^c^agumu in Jate territory, they rested under a *nupa* tree. They prepared a large oven for bean roots, but had no water for pouring into it to make the steam rise. "Where shall we find water?" they asked each other. And as if in reply they heard the croak of a frog from the base of the *nupa* tree. From the hardwood *nekamana* tree they cut and sharpened a pole. "What is this that cries?" they asked. They plunged the pole into the ground at the base of the tree and water came gushing out, running into the hole at the top of the oven. [Today water from the Numparu River runs down into this large hole in the rocky gully.] When the bean roots were cooked they took them out and put them in their net bags. Then they played the sacred flutes for the first time: first the flute named *sowopa* [a wad of tobacco used in the bowl of a pipe]; then the *kenami* [bamboo of Agwinatoga]; then *fagamo* [the bean flute]; the *kamairu^c^* [red bark of the *bara* tree]; the *hupevi* [*evi*, sugar cane]; and the *tegepa* [fire from the head of Morufonu—see above]. They carried these in their net bags to distribute among the people. They came to Oaguni [near Kimiᶜagumu] and put people . . . [lists of place names in Jate territory are given].

Another version accounts for the scarcity of shells used in exchange and in decoration.

At Rivetiga, Jugumishanta and Morufonu put shells into the swamp. But as they were doing so they were observed by a small bird named *jawojawo* or *jagojago* [from *joa*, or *zago* shells], who called out *"Kanagesiosio!"* ["I see you!"]. Removing the shells, they went on to Nesaka [near Kasa] and put them into the water there. Again the bird observed them. [This is repeated across the whole countryside until they eventually reach Osagajatega, near Tiroka, in Kamano territory, where they put the shells in a small cave in the stone cliffs.]

Leaving Tabajaka, the two came with all their belongings to Gobuguriga [pine tree place], where they made a large men's house and planted bamboo and crotons; there they put the Tavoᶜ people. They came on to Rivetiga [mentioned above as the place of emergence]; there they built a large house, planted bamboo, crotons, beans, the *kagavefa* tree [and other trees listed], cane [used in cane-swallowing], the *koeᶜ* tree,[10] wild "garoka" pandanus palms, the bow tree, the hardwood arrow top tree, wild betel-nut trees, gum trees [the bark of which is beaten, specially treated, and made into twine, or into shoulder cloaks], the *megufa* [leaves eaten with pig meat], sugar cane, and yams, to name a few of the more important items. They put also various snakes, frogs, wild pigs, cassowaries, small animals, rats, and so on, giving instructions to each as to how it was to behave and where it was to live—e.g., in the ground, in the jungle, in a tree, in the kunai grass. They put a man and a woman at each named place, showing them how to build houses and stockades, to make bows and arrows, to cultivate gardens, and so on. They instructed them in all the normal activities of daily living, telling them to "look after the ground." They also told them how to make the sacred flutes, how to play them at the pig festival, at the killing of the pigs; and they spoke to them about the age-grading ceremonies. Eventually, after passing through all the Fore, Usurufa, Jate, and Kamano territories, they arrived at Josaᶜjagura, near Kainantu in Taiora country. Here, they said, ended the people who were culturally the same; they were now going to pass into alien territory. They warned the people that they must not pass out of that country— if they did so, they would be killed and eaten; if those beyond came into their country they would be killed and eaten. And they sang:[11]

> *mirenireni marenireni warona*
> *tafokeo koke koke* . . . .

"Kill them! Kill them! Kill and eat, as we dance moving our bows. . . ." Then they passed on to the Markham River, coming to Tuaᶜguwuga in the mountains [Taiora country]. Here they put more people. By this time, both were growing old. They went further and finally put "white" people, Europeans.

---

[10] This is a red flowering tree, usually the feeding place of flocks of birds—which, however, are never killed while on it, since it is connected with a menstruation myth.

[11] Language unidentified; translation general, not literal.

Before passing to the final phase of their adventures, which concerns the Land of the Dead, I shall give a general rendering of a typical myth as told in the men's house. It concerns points already covered in the abbreviated versions given above.

At Agwinatoga, Jugumishanta and Morufonu put salt and also a man and a woman. Thus they talked to them: "Break off some of your skirt, or some of your net bag, and place it in the water. Put it in your house to dry. Then eat the salt that is on it." And they planted bamboos. Thus they put these two. They went down to Ketoriga near Taramu among the stones [a name referring to the *kopefa* leaf from a species of orchid]. There they put a man and a woman. Thus they talked to them: "You look after this ground, these trees, these bamboo, these crotons." They put the *kopefa* among the stones and spoke to the man and woman: "You two break these leaves, chew them and spit on sweet potatoes giving them to your pigs—plenty will then come up." They came to Taramu, where there is big bush. They looked and saw a wild fig tree which had fallen down. Gathering its dry leaves, they made a fire and burnt off the grass. Then they planted pitpit, edible leaves, sugar cane, bananas, and other varieties of food. That night they slept at the base of a large tree and in the morning looked at their garden and saw that all the plants had grown well. With stone axes they began to clear away more bushes, to enlarge their garden. Many of the plants flowered and attracted birds. The blue bird of paradise, *feta*[c] [Duke of Saxony], came first and fed off the flowers and the edible leaves. Then came the *pisiwa* [bird of paradise, the sun], the *tufimo* [species of hornbill], the *wojafa* or *wajafa* [a red parakeet], the *kainanifa*, the *susuke*, the *uwena*, the *kogonina* [another bird of paradise], and all the many varieties of birds. There they were feeding from the flowers. Jugumishanta and Morufonu broke a limb from a tree and removing its leaves used it to kill some of these birds, obtaining the feathers and giving them to the man and woman who occupied this place. They talked to them thus: "You two can shoot such birds in the bush; you can shoot small animals for eating. Use the birds' feathers for decoration in ceremonies. Clear away the bush so that the kunai grass grows, and like this grass many people will come up." They made a swamp at Futigi, so that many pigs would come there. They instructed them in methods of fighting: "You two will stay here, and others will shoot you." They went to Anipagetaga, near Taramu, and planted the bow tree, and there they put men and women. They talked to them: "Men will shoot you." At this place they told the mosquito to shoot men. . . . They came to Nunawatanoga, near Tatagufa, where they put many stones. They made a large house, put many gardens, made a large oven in which they cooked yams, taro, banana, bean roots, and so on. When the food was cooked, they opened the oven and removed it, putting it in their bags. Some they left growing for men. And they put there a man and a woman. . . . They came to Tegifamega, near Kimi[c]agumu. There they put a man and a woman, planted gardens, and built a house, and they said: "You two look after this ground, hold pig festivals, and initiate young boys. When you have a child, 'shoot his nose.' Catch all the young boys and push rough leaves up their nostrils until blood flows; then give them cane to swallow."

Jugumishanta and Morufonu showed them how to swallow the cane properly so they would not die. . . .

The myth continues from place to place. Gardens are planted, people are put to look after the ground and instructed in the arts of living and in the ceremonies and rituals they must perform. The pig festivals and the age-grading ceremonies are performed, so Jugumishanta and Morufonu tell these people, in order that the crops may grow, the pigs propagate and increase, and that they themselves may eat and continue to live, in the way the spirits have planned.

When Jugumishanta and Morufonu passed over the boundary demarcating the Kamano, Usurufa, Jate, and Fore from the peoples to the northeast, they passed through Agarabe country to the Kampi of the Markham. There, in the vicinity of Markham Falls, they entered Anabaga, the Land of the Dead, where in their spirit form they are sometimes said to have remained. According to one version, all the spirits of men after death come to this place, where they live in conditions similar to those they knew in life. It is possible, too, for them to visit their old haunts. Sometimes, it is said, they are helpful. At other times, especially to strangers, they may do harm. Ghosts always have light-colored skin, so that Europeans coming into this region for the first time were hailed as spirits of dead kinsfolk. Thus most versions of the myth conclude with their disappearance into Anabaga and mention their responsibility for the creation of Europeans. There are two main views. Either the Creative Beings directly gave birth to Europeans, placing them in various territories outside the physical and social range of the Kamano, Usurufa, Jate, and Fore; or the Europeans are the local people themselves, returning after death. This attitude was important during initial contact, although it has since lost ground, especially among the more sophisticated who have been influenced by native police and Mission evangelists.

There is no final agreement as to just where the Land of the Dead is located. Some versions place it below the earth, others in the sky. Wherever it is, Jugumishanta and her husband preside over it; and since they can be in any number of places at the same time, and can transform themselves at will, there is no suggestion that different versions must be reconciled. One account has it that when these two reached the Markham Falls they passed through a doorway, going down into the earth, to Anabaga. Spirits of the dead take the same path. They come to a flowering tree; after they have eaten some of its blossoms the doorway is revealed to them, and they pass through. In other versions the spirit then follows a special road and eventually meets Jugumishanta and Morufonu, who stand blocking his pathway and ask, "Why have you come? You had better go back." The spirit replies, "You called out to me, and I have come." Then Jugumishanta pulls aside her skirt, revealing her genitalia, and the spirit comes to her and sucks them. Morufonu pulls aside his bark fringe and offers his penis to the spirit, who does the same to it. They then allow him to pass. In performing this act, the spirit symbolically acknowledges that he is of the same flesh and spirit as themselves: he is their son, having been born as it were from their genitalia.

Significance of these Beliefs

Here the primary concern is the peopling of the region, with the establishment of gardens and the introduction of various creatures and plants which are of direct use to man. Accounts of this usually give long lists of "big" or "small" names, allocating to each a man and a woman, with various foods, bamboos, and crotons. There is no explicit reference to lineage formation, or the establishment of the nuclear family. In each case the two original ancestors, being children of Jugumishanta and Morufonu, are full brother and sister, although most versions do not draw attention to this. Nor do they name any of them or the lineages they are to establish.

All human beings, it is said, must be descended from these two Creative Beings. Nevertheless, the social world of these people embraces only the four linguistic units, together with borderline cases, sometimes included and sometimes not, like the Agarabe, Taiora, and Koga. As a basis for this social perspective, they sometimes cite Jugumishanta's pronouncement as she passed into Taiora and Agarabe territory. It does not restrain them from fighting one another. For instance, it is not used as an argument against interdistrict warfare or intradistrict dissension. Yet it was significant during initial European contact and partly explains why patrols into the region first met with little resistance. It was only later, when they realized that the newcomers were after all the same as themselves (children of Jugumishanta), but not close kin returning to take up their old ties, that the local people began to distrust them, crediting them with the same motives they themselves would have when entering alien territory.

The various versions of these myths, then, often fragmentary and uncoordinated,[12] offer no detailed account of social institutions, specific relationships, or behavior patterns. They do not put forward an ideal code

[12] This is much as we would expect, in view of the social configuration here. Each district stresses the places within its own boundaries associated with Jugumishanta and Morufonu, with only a secondary interest in others. Moreover, versions from any one district tend to include only incidents relating to its immediate zone of interaction,

or a set of moral values to which men must adhere. Nor do they bring in
supernatural sanctions to enforce conformity with divinely articulated
rules or "laws." There is no detailed description of how ritual and ceremony should be performed, what songs should be sung, what actions
should take place. They do not enshrine a specific doctrine. Nor do they
demonstrate and explain sacred ritual, although they are viewed as the
source and substantiation of that ritual.

This being so, what is the relevance of these myths to the local situation?
In the first place they concern the basic needs of man in this region.
Second, they serve as the medium through which a body of symbolic
references is expressed. Third, they substantiate the social order as the
accepted way of life. For the present we are concerned only with these
three points, which are relevant to our basic theme.

Jugumishanta is viewed as a fertility mother, identified with the earth
itself, who must have sexual intercourse and become pregnant before
giving birth to the first human beings. The scene of this is a garden, and
the analogy here is the breaking of the soil with digging sticks in order to
plant crops and insure growth. By breaking garden-ground, impregnation
of the mother is suggested. We have seen that one of the focal points of
these people's interest is the gardens, which are also the burial place of
local dead. A body which is not eaten is "given to the earth"; the eating
of human flesh often takes place in gardens, and the bones are buried or
reburied there. Blood, either pig or human, is poured over the ground,
offered as a libation to the earth, as if to give renewed life to it. Predominantly, this part of the mythology has to do with the fertility of the
earth. The Creative Beings instruct the people they leave behind to look
after the ground, to attend to the gardens, and to perform special rituals.
Only through this can man continue to live. We are to assume that the
first two requirements, plus garden-burial, blood-libations, and so on,[13]

covering districts which may or may not be regarded as enemies at the time and may or
may not be adjacent. The myth, then, broadly indicates or "reflects" this kind of
linkage. The beginning and ending may be conventional; but the Creative Beings, emerging from Rivetiga, come directly into the sphere of influence of the district concerned,
passing out of it to the northeastern boundaries and thence to the Land of the Dead.
Nearer Rivetiga, much more detail is given concerning the initial emergence and the
birth of the first human beings; but here again, the origin place may or may not be
pushed further back to Tabajaka. Rivetiga itself, however, is acknowledged by members
of the four linguistic units as the most important and most sacred site in the whole region.
Although I observed its surrounding jungle through binoculars from Busarasa and Moke,
I could not visit it because of the hostility between adjacent groups in the restricted area.
[13] There are also certain forms of garden magic associated with archaeological stones:
see R. Berndt (1954c).

are not enough but must be supplemented by specially designed ritual. Yet this aspect is not elaborated. Jugumishanta and her husband indicate what should be done, and why, but not the exact procedure. The inference is that this is already known. On the other hand, although the main reason for the rituals is given there is room for the inclusion of secondary themes; and these are important for understanding the relationship between ritual and everyday activity.

One sort of symbolism apparent in this mythology relates to what are regarded as basic needs of man, food and sex. Further, we have already noticed the significance of a few of Jugumishanta's names. The special red croton, symbolizing blood, is used extensively in the rituals and age-grading ceremonies. It is planted over garden-graves and in other parts of the gardens, and also in a village, to signify an unavenged death. Salt, or mineral ash, is one of the most valuable commodities in this region, used not only for seasoning food but for what may be called ritual purposes. It is especially significant at times of human crisis, when people are most vulnerable: at childbirth, marriage, menstruation, and during sickness. Salt, as the body or essence of Jugumishanta, protects the partaker. It is not just the salt itself which is said to have this power; the eating of it is in a sense an offering to Jugumishanta, whose strength and help are required. To take another of her names, the cane grass for nose-piercing indicates that this rite causes blood to flow as a libation to Jugumishanta and her husband and to various spirits. But it has the further significance of providing strength to those who perform it.

It is evident that the Jugumishanta and Morufonu mythology provides a framework for the explanation of much social activity, without being concerned with its actual content. Although it does not mirror this content, it points to the dominant pressures perceived by these people, outlining the broad setting of social and cultural life itself. It emphasizes man's dependence on nature (for Jugumishanta and Morufonu, in combination, are equivalent to nature), and his reliance on ritual to supplement his routine activities; and it suggests the inevitability of warfare. For instance, the first people are instructed in fighting methods and warned that others are bound to fight them. Jugumishanta and Morufonu themselves fought an unspecified number of "story people." What we are dealing with in this mythology is a body of knowledge deriving from basic assumptions, similar to those found in other cosmological beliefs. The myth does not dwell on any inherent conflicts in social relations; it simply offers a series of statements about a particular way of life.

The Mythology of Ritual

We have discussed something of the mythology of ritual action. In this section we find more than nominal substantiation. Part of it can be described as an extension of the Jugumishanta and Morufonu mythology, although it is not always viewed in this way by the people concerned. It is seen rather as an extra "explanation," should this become necessary at any time, of the use of certain ritual objects and the performance of certain ritual actions. Primarily, it accounts for men's possession of the sacred flutes and the practice of cane-swallowing. Only a section of this mythology will be given, to illustrate basic social values and conflicting elements within it.

Jugumishanta and Morufonu were living at Koripika. Jugumishanta built a small segregation-hut where she slept by herself, her husband having built a large house for himself. At her place Jugumishanta planted wild ginger. She cut a length of bamboo and bored a hole in its surface, making a flute, and this she hid in the ginger foliage. Later she took it out and hiding it in her skirt left the camp. Reaching a secluded place, she began to play the flute; and from his own hut her husband heard its cry. "What is this that cries?" he said. "I would like to see it, but perhaps it would kill and eat me." So he thought to himself, and was afraid. Day after day Jugumishanta played her flute, and her husband became increasingly curious. Returning one night, she plucked out some pubic hair and placed it in the barrel of the flute; this would enable it to cry out if handled by someone other than herself; she then hid it in the ginger foliage. Later, when she went out to work in her garden, Morufonu made sure she was out of sight. Then he went down to her house and following her footprints eventually found the ginger bush and the flute. He dug up the ginger and took it back to his own house, where he planted it and began to play the flute; but the flute was playing by itself, warning Jugumishanta. As he lifted it to his mouth, the pubic hair within the flute touched him, and he immediately began to grow facial and body hair. [This explains why men are now much hairier than women.] When Jugumishanta heard her flute, she ran back to her house and finding it and her ginger gone came over to Morufonu and asked him, "Who stole my flute?" Morufonu replied, "I heard something playing outside your hut, and I grew angry. I came down and found it. You couldn't play it properly, but I do it well. You must not look at it now, it is something belonging to me." He then placed the flute [14] in the ginger foliage; it "turned" [became transformed] and grew into a large clump of bamboos with ginger growing at its base, seen today at Koripika.

The myth offers no further account of Jugumishanta's reaction to the new situation, which symbolizes the ritual subjugation of woman. But one version concludes with the following statement:

[14] *Usugopa* is the name of the bamboo, and the special name of the flute was *gumevinopa*, from the *gume* tree.

Now men cut bamboo and make flutes, playing them in the bush at night during the pig festival so that pigs will increase. During the night, too, they enter the village, decorated with branches of foliage, playing their flutes, while women, children, and young boys fasten their doors and stay in their houses. Moon after moon the flutes are played, increasing the pigs and making them grow larger, improving and advancing the crops, until finally pigs are killed and a festival is held. If a woman looks at a flute, she is killed; if a young boy is caught looking at the players, his nose is bled.

A further fragment concerns the origin of the bullroarer (*pubunani*, meaning a type of fungus; the connection could not be explained):

Morufonu thought about the flute: Jugumishanta had made it. What would he make now, something about which she would know nothing? He set to work and shaped a bullroarer and swung it, listening to the noise it made. Jugumishanta heard it too and was afraid; she stayed in her house, fastening the door.

Or again:

Morufonu in his own house prepared cane for swallowing. Each day Jugumishanta brought food to his doorway. He would eat this, then take his cane and go out into the bush where he swallowed it,[15] vomiting the food. When he returned, Jugumishanta asked him, "I gave you food. Where did you go? Did you go out to defecate?" But he would not tell her. Each day he went out and vomited. Her curiosity aroused, Jugumishanta went out to her husband's feces-pit and saw that it was empty. She waited until next he went out into the bush, followed, and watched. Then she came back to her house to wait, and when he came she spoke to him: "Why do you always finish all the food?" "I am a man," he replied. "I do not defecate!" Then he planted his vomiting cane, which grew into a large bush.

The following statement indicates when the vomiting cane should be used:

Man, if a woman gives you food, take this cane and swallow it, and vomit. Should a menstruating woman give you food, take this cane and swallow, and vomit. Should a pregnant woman give you food, take this cane, swallow, and vomit. Should a man commit adultery with your wife and she give you food, take this cane . . . and vomit. If you do not do this, your body will become no good, you will become like an old man, and you will die. This is something good, hold firmly to it. This that has been put is good and will make your body strong. If you

[15] The cane is looped, one end held in each hand; the loop is put down the throat until only two short ends protrude from the mouth. It is then slowly drawn up, causing vomiting. This was first reported by E. W. P. Chinnery (1934, pp. 113–21, figs. 5–6). Chinnery says that Taylor (one of the early administrative officials associated with the opening of this region) was told women would die if they saw this rite; it was mentioned to him that this practice prevents sickness and is sometimes used to induce vomiting after heavy feasts (*ibid.*, p. 118). Fig. 6 in Chinnery's report is evidently posed. The cane itself is not unlike a thin pencil in size, varying in length from two to three feet.

eat food from the hand of a menstruating woman, it will turn to blood in your belly. If you take food from the hand of a pregnant woman, your belly will become large. Take food only from the hand of a "good" woman. Thus spoke the ancestors.

Before we consider the implications of these injunctions and the suggestive points raised in the myth itself, let me offer two additional examples. The first exists in many versions, some more detailed than others. This particular account comes from Moiife.

A number of young girls were living at Aifo, close to Moiife, where they had built a large house. There they played the flutes named *tuevinofa*, *inaruefa*, *juwagahu*c*nia*, and *inavego*c. One man, however, was living at Jabota and could hear their sound. "My skin, what is this that cries?" he asked himself. So he obtained a woman's skirt and wound it around himself, and placed on his head a net bag covering his hair and falling down his back; he rubbed earth over his face [signifying his association with digging in the gardens]. He then left his hill and went in search of the cry of the flutes. By the time he arrived there, all except one small girl had gone to the gardens. He came into the house and sat with her, pretending to be a woman. But he sat carelessly, his skirt not properly adjusted, so that she saw his penis. Making excuses, she left him in the house and went out to the gardens, where she told the other young girls that it was not their grandmother who had visited them but a man. Some of the others did not believe her; they beat her, telling her that it was indeed her grandmother. The man apparently remained with them for several days without being discovered. One day when they had all gone to the gardens leaving him with the small girl, he went to a clump of crotons and there found a flute. Taking it up he began to play it, running away from the house to his mountain. All the young girls heard its sound. They ran to their house, where the little girl reproached them for not listening to her. She ran after the man, who had thrown away first his skirt and then his headgear. But she stopped in fear at the cry of the *feta*c [Duke of Saxony] bird of paradise, one manifestation of Morufonu. The thief went to a place called Wulwul near Moiife. There he put his flute, which transformed itself into a large clump of bamboos; and today, when the wind blows through these bamboos, the sound it makes resembles that made by men when they play their flutes.

In another version:

Two young girls were in possession of the sacred *inegure* flute and lived on top of a mountain. The track leading up to their house was greased with pig fat. After a great deal of difficulty two young men reached the top of the mountain and persuaded the girls to let them blow the flute. Finally one man grabbed it and ran down the slope. The two girls followed close behind, but the men ran faster and escaped. As they ran they blew the flute, and it cried, "Oh mother, oh mother!" [referring to the two girls]. Then the cry of the flute turned to "Oh father, oh father!" [referring to its new owners].

In this way the flute was "given" to men. Because the flutes were stolen from women, women today may not look at them or at the men playing them, under pain of death.

The following cane-swallowing myth, in two of many versions, again shows the influence of women:

A man, after working in his garden with his wife, went down to the creek with a number of other men. She followed to find out what they were doing and saw them squatting in the water swallowing their lengths of cane. They did not leave the two ends protruding from the mouth, but swallowed it completely, drawing it out through their navels. She pulled them out of the water and began to sew up their navels, telling them only to swallow the cane and draw it up through the mouth. [A number of injunctions are then given.] "You must hide this thing from women. You must not eat from the hand of a menstruating woman, nor may she touch anything associated with cooking your food; if you eat of this and neglect to vomit, the result will be [similar to that mentioned above]. If you do this your body will be good, you will grow strong. All the women will look at you and like you. They will ask you to show them what you do, but you must not tell them. Should women see you doing this, you will all be transformed into red parakeets, and the women will remain by themselves without men."

A woman gave birth to a male child who eventually grew to a young man. He began cane-swallowing in the following way. He obtained a length of cane, looped it, and tied a croton leaf at the loop end. This he swallowed, pushing it down into his belly until it came out of his anus, cleansing him internally. He then inserted it into his anus, pushed it upward, and drew it out, and he grew to be strong. All the young girls liked him; they came in great numbers, desiring to be his wives. But his mother grew worried and asked him, "Why do all these young girls come to you? How is it that you attract so many?" The young man replied that he swallowed the cane, and it was because of this that they came. But his mother pointed out that many of the women were married already—trouble would be sure to follow, if this continued. She then instructed him not to draw it through his anus, nor through his navel (which she sewed up), but only to put it down his throat and then withdraw it the same way. She plucked some of her pubic hair and placed it on his upper lip, saying, "You are now a man. If you copulate with other men's wives a big fight will come up. Men did not get 'hot belly' before when you had no hair; now they will fight. They will shoot arrows; they will fight with axes, with sticks. They will fight men who copulate with their wives."

Implications

This mythology is sacred; but it does not mean that women are excluded from hearing or transmitting it, as they do among themselves in certain situations. They know that women possessed the flutes in the first place. They talk about flutes, although conventionally they are not supposed to do so; yet they do not normally discuss the conditions under which men play them, and they rarely mention cane-swallowing. The myths given here, with their accompanying injunctions, are told at times when young men or novices are shown these objects and their use. There is a direct relation between them and ritual action. In the first place, like the myths specifically associated with the adventures of the Creative Beings, they provide justification for ritual. But they do more than this. They state specifically why men carry out such rites and women do not. Flute-playing and cane-swallowing are two features which mark off men from women. There are other ritual practices, like making blood flow from the nose; but this is not treated specifically in the mythology of this category because it is also performed by women.

In all versions relating to the sacred flutes, women are said to have had them first and to have lost them only through the duplicity (in a few cases, physical violence) of men. Men give this as the main reason for segregating themselves from women while performing such rites: "They must not see us, because we are doing something associated with them." Moru-fonu, for example, although he had stolen the flute, had really nothing of his own. To assert himself he made a bullroarer and used this to "frighten" women, just as he himself had been afraid when he first heard the flute-playing of Jugumishanta. This section of the myth throws a certain light on the relations between men and women in this society. Moreover, it is an aspect on which some comparative material is available.[16] It may indicate co-operation between the sexes, an identification of common interests with the recognition of social and ritual spheres of independence, a defined division of labor; or it may indicate a fundamental cleavage, based on dissension, antagonism, and distrust. It depends, of course, on how these features are interpreted; but interpretation must hinge on what we know of the local situation, a consideration of these factors in relation to others.

Because this part of the mythology makes so much of man's reliance on woman, we might well expect that the ritual associated with it will be oriented in the direction of purely female activities. This is not to say that men, having nothing comparable in everyday life, must look for compensation in this sphere. Enough has been said to show that the sexes are seen as essentially interdependent.[17] The acknowledgment of physiological paternity, for example, finds expression throughout the mythology. Also, although there are male and female flutes, one representing

[16] See M. Mead (1950, pp. 102–3); R. Berndt (1952, pp. 56–58 et seq.); and for the Gahuku-Gama, K. E. Read (1954, p. 25, n. 35).

[17] The converse of this situation of what I call male-female interdependence is postulated by K. Read (1954, pp. 24–25) for the Gahuku-Gama of Goroka.

Morufonu and another Jugumishanta, these are usually phallic objects symbolizing male dominance. In another context, ritual bloodletting is said to symbolize the menstrual flow. Although the aspect of fertility is fundamental both to the core of basic knowledge and to ritual life, it is overlaid with certain other features which either have grown out of it or have been superimposed through symbolic inference.

Nevertheless, what is explicitly brought out in the injunctions appended to the myth, and implied in the myth itself, is the subjugation of women. Jugumishanta has no redress when her flute is stolen. Nor have the women living at Aifo, nor those who greased the pathway up to their home. No indemnity is paid to them. In the accompanying injunctions the position becomes even more apparent: women are killed if they see the playing of flutes, or the flute itself, or the rite of cane-swallowing. Yet who know more, intuitively, so it is said, than the women themselves, to whom this esoteric knowledge and practice are denied? Most revealing is the concluding warning attached to one myth: "Should women see you do this [that is, cane-swallowing], you [men] will all be transformed into red parakeets"; but the women will not suffer, nor be transformed. The red parakeet is one representation of Morufonu. It is acknowledged that the male is the dominant sex, "the holder of the arrow" (penis). Yet this is strength gained, by inference, from women: it is female pubic hair which turns the male from an effeminate creature into a man with warlike qualities, his maleness assured by possession of ritual prerogative. And this is maintained by his subjugation of the female: his right to enforce his opinion and retain his dominant status through physical coercion, with resistance punishable in certain cases by death.

This is not the complete picture. Women can be aggressive and forceful too, although mainly in relation to their own sex. Nor are they invariably subordinated to their menfolk. But formally and conventionally this pattern holds good, as we shall see in looking at relevant case material.

The flutes, as ritual objects, symbolize the dominance of men. Their use in ritual reinforces this constellation of ideas but expresses also the wider implications relating to fertility—apparent in the injunctions appended to the myth but not in the myth itself. Given local assumptions about the origin and maintenance of life, the myth, as a symbolic representation, is sufficient without further elaboration. The flute-playing rites are primarily a matter for the community as a whole, with only passing reference to individual participants, and are always associated with certain important ceremonies. In contrast to this, cane-swallowing, although carried out during some ceremonies, can usually be practiced privately without the presence of others and is relevant mainly to the performer himself. Although both cane-swallowing and flute-playing have much the same ends in view, there are differences in means, in the processes by which men seek to achieve those ends. Flute symbolism has both social and individual implications; but cane-swallowing refers obliquely to a symbolic framework which is not apparent until it is transformed into action.

In the myth, the reasons for cane-swallowing are to provide a substitute for defecation or a method of internal cleansing. The injunctions underline these, linking them with the belief that internal cleanliness leads to physical perfection. The practice marks men off from women, and to an extent even greater than the ritual of the flutes, for however much the aspect of maleness is stressed in flute-playing it infers a division of labor in the pursuit of common goals. Cane-swallowing is designed primarily to protect man from the weakening influence of woman. A secondary point which receives some attention is that overeating impairs one's health and undermines one's vigor; thus a man may resort to his cane if he feels uncomfortable after a feast. There are some features in the cane-swallowing myths which I shall not attempt to interpret, such as the statement that originally the cane was drawn through the navel or through the anus. No adequate explanation is offered for these acts, nor is it necessary that it should be at this juncture and at this level. One suggestion is that such purging made a man so perfect physically that women were irresistibly drawn to him, as in the example given above. The mother helped him to avoid the inevitable and disastrous results of such a procedure by showing him how cane-swallowing should take place to accentuate his masculine appearance. This may imply that it is associated with peculiarly female characteristics, an argument which gains weight when one considers the main reason put forward for it.[18]

There is, then, a current idea that women are potentially dangerous to men, apart from any consideration of interpersonal relations and lineage affiliations. This danger is intensified during certain periods: at menstruation, at pregnancy and childbirth and for a defined period afterward, and on the occasion of a wife's adultery. It is not that woman is at such times ritually unclean,[19] although we might view it in this way; there is no

[18] Men when asked whether women carried out cane-swallowing responded first with a shocked silence, then with the reply that the Moon did this for them naturally (i.e., through menstruation) without artificial manipulation.

[19] That is to say, it is not classified under a concept of filth, as is the case among the Nyakyusa. See M. Wilson (1954, p. 235).

word used in this context which can be so translated. What is suggested is, rather, a state of danger.[20] It is not the menstrual blood itself which is dangerous but the condition associated with it. All those who might have been in close proximity to a menstruating woman immediately before her segregation put salt on their food. A man and his wife or wives are in a specially critical condition when a girl betrothed or married to him menstruates for the first time. They must be warned at once so that they will not eat anything before it has been rendered "safe" by the addition of salt. The real danger lies in the harmful influence which may be transmitted through food, and this is intense where the husband is concerned, although in varying degrees it may concern any man in relation to any woman. Even when a husband has no reason to suspect that his wife has handled his food when in such a condition, he may use his cane for vomiting as a precautionary measure. Or should he eat food which he finds has been so handled, he resorts to his cane. The danger lies in his neglecting to do so or in unknowingly eating food which has been contaminated in this way. One of the most provoking insults is to tell a person to drink the menstrual blood of his wife. If his physical strength becomes impaired, he may blame his wife for her lack of care or accuse her of adultery. In this belief lies one reason for the severe treatment of adulterous wives. It is not so much the act of adultery which is punished as the woman's carelessness in exposing her husband to this danger. There are a number of contradictions here. For instance, it is specifically stated that the blood associated with menstruation and childbirth will weaken a man. Yet men themselves imitate the menstrual flow during certain ceremonies. Similarly, it is not the act of birth as such which is dangerous: this theme is, ritually, of considerable importance.

Cane-swallowing always takes place in running water so that the vomit is dissolved and washed away, to guard against sorcery. Every adult male possesses and carries about with him lengths of rolled cane[21] as a necessary part of his equipment. Personal cleanliness means physical fitness, and the injunctions insist that this practice will insure a strong body attractive to the opposite sex. There is no symbolic reference or implication here. The injunctions state why the rite should be carried out; the

[20] E.g., Max Gluckman (1954, p. 7) comments, ". . . during their menstrual periods [Zulu] women were a constant threat of danger." They could rob a warrior of his strength.

[21] In the northern part of the region cane-swallowing is less frequently practiced and in some districts no longer carried out. This is partly through Government pressure, but also a direct result of Mission influence. In the area I am discussing, however, its use was still general at the time of my field research.

myth tells how and offers a precedent. And here there is complete agreement with contemporary practice. At the same time, the rite refers
symbolically to male dominance through strength and physical aggression.
The achievement of such strength is, we are told, the aim of all men.
Cane-swallowing is designed to this end, just as this is one of the aims of
the festival of the flutes.

This category of mythology, then, embodies a fairly wide range of basic
assumptions, a series of more or less symbolic statements about fundamental values. We cannot provide answers to the question of how these
came about, but we can examine how they take form and in what aspects
of social and cultural living they are manifested. The values expressed
through the body of belief represented by the two categories of mythology
dealt with here are those which appear to be the most strongly held, being
in the nature of value-acceptives (see chap 2). Moreover, they serve as a
basis of all control mechanisms and can themselves be described in one
sense as aspects of control.[22] They influence opinion, attitudes, judgment,
and action of all kinds; and choices in specific situations are made against
this framework.

[22] See M. C. Albrecht (1954, pp. 425–36): "Literature is interpreted as reflecting
norms and values, as revealing the ethos of culture." It maintains and stabilizes the social
order, "which may be called the 'social-control' theory" (ibid., p. 425). For reference
to the "social-control" function of literature see Albrecht (ibid., pp. 431, 432).

Chapter 5   Ritual Action

In the course of this discussion we have indicated the relation of myth to ritual action, representing this as a system of belief translated into social action, of which ritual is one aspect. Values expressed in ritual action are still in symbolic form; this may or may not be the case where other forms of activity are concerned. Further, the nexus between symbolic representations in ritual and those in mythology may not always be recognized. The basic values in ritual may be overlaid by other features, just as symbolic representations in ritual may be extended. There is no one-to-one relationship between mythology and ritual; the former may contain broadly the same symbolism and values but offers a far wider framework for their expression and patterning.

Ritual, to follow Firth, is "a kind of patterned activity oriented toward control of human affairs, primarily symbolic in character with a non-empirical referent, and as a rule socially sanctioned."[1] That is to say, it need not be classified as sacred or religious;[2] it is distinct from technique by its use of symbolic statement.[3] It can be identified, in this context at least, by its nonempirical relationship between means and ends and by what it says symbolically. Nevertheless, we shall be considering here only those apsects of ritual which may be called religious, and this is in accordance with the kind of distinction made by the eastern Highlanders.[4]

We are concerned with symbols which can be comprehended by the people themselves: as Nadel observes, "their social effectiveness lies in their capacity to indicate."[5] The context in which a symbol is used or

[1] R. Firth (1951, p. 222).

[2] To M. Wilson (1954, p. 240), ritual is primarily religious action, differentiated from ceremony. In the present discussion, too, they are not regarded as identical. While much ritual is accompanied by ceremony, ceremony can take place without ritual.

[3] See Leach (1954, pp. 10–13).

[4] Nadel (1954, p. 114) speaks of ritual form becoming part of the machinery which maintains the efficient working of a society of a given social structure. Moreover, with him we may say that ritual accumulates further aims and ideas, or, if we like, further values are enunciated, through symbolic expression or otherwise.

[5] Leach (1954, pp. 15, 86); Nadel (1954, pp. 108, 262); A. R. Radcliffe-Brown (1922, p. 264; 1952, p. 157); A. Richards (1956, passim); M. Wilson (1954, pp. 236–37).

expressed defines its meaning and representation. It is a social symbol precisely because it is "agreed upon" by a group of people. If such a symbol (that is, excluding "private" symbols derived from personal experiences) means several things to one person, it means the same things to others within that particular group. The meanings and significance granted it are dependent upon a number of factors—social alignment (group and cult membership), sex, age, status, and role in various situations. Symbols are identifiable in their cultural context and in the social alignment of individuals who use them.[6]

Ritual, then, is a form of symbolic expression: it can contain a whole series of acts which cover a range of symbolic representations. As Leach points out, in its cultural context it is a pattern of symbols;[7] but these symbols do not directly indicate structural elements. Rather, they serve to enunciate the cultural content of social relations and alignment. Further, they embody values of a basic nature. I call these "value-acceptives." Others have referred to them as expressions or sentiments on which the constitution of a society depends, or suggest that rituals reveal values at the "deepest" level.

Again, ritual is significant as a medium of control. Stated in the simplest possible terms, this can be looked at in two ways. Ritual is defined by its specific ends, which are to be achieved nonempirically: it is marked by the symbolic content of the action or actions designed to bring these about. It is designed in a way ceremony is not and relates to a sphere in which ordinary techniques are of no avail, or thought to be of only incidental value, in controlling the affairs of human beings. For instance, the ritual acts relevant to the pig festival, the playing of the sacred flutes, and so on, are generally considered to increase the supply of pigs and garden produce; and the practice of cane-swallowing, which appears at first glance to be a straightforward technique, insures individual purification.

---

[6] Leach (1954, p. 262) says that two individuals or groups of individuals may accept the validity of a set of ritual actions without agreeing at all as to what is expressed in those actions. Agreement on symbolic expression, however, depends largely on social alignment. If not, then we are not dealing with symbolism of social significance but with symbolism of a different order. Traditional poetry (through medium of song) in ritual deals with images which are of symbolic social significance. Poetry composed by individuals without being traditionally based, although being in the cultural idiom and using accepted forms of expression, has not this common medium. It is dependent on social alignment but relies much more heavily on individual personal experience. The use of symbols in this respect is determined predominantly by individual interpretation within the cultural context. In the region under discussion we find individually "composed" poetry, as song, communicated during ritual, or in the context of ceremony (see below).

[7] Leach (1954, p. 15).

This aspect of control or attempted control is perhaps its most obvious role. The symbolic representations apparent in a ritual act are expressions of certain values. They permeate the whole of social life and serve to control behavior by influencing choices and decisions.[8]

For the purpose of discussion we shall focus our attention on two ceremonies in which ritual occurs. Ritual takes place in a variety of social contexts, as at birth, marriage, and death (to name the three most obvious life crises), in a whole range of age-grading ceremonies, in the training of warriors, in sorcery practices, and so on. We shall be considering the ritual content of some of these in succeeding chapters. The ritual with which we are concerned at the moment has the dual aim of controlling the affairs of human beings on the "natural" as well as on the social plane. On the one hand, it has to do with the maintenance of garden crops and the increase of pigs. On the other, it reinforces group attitudes, demarcating the roles of men and women, helping to maintain the status quo. The very performance of such ritual may have the almost mechanical effects for which it is designed, but it also serves as a vehicle for the formal training and instruction of the young. It is not, however, only for the young. Rather, it is a process which for male adults continues throughout life—a process, moreover, of continual strengthening and reinforcing (enculturative, in Herskovits' term). Rituals of this nature, having this social significance, are what I would call religious.

The two rituals to be discussed should be viewed as part of a series of initiation ceremonies. Because both are performed at times without the presence of youths for instruction, we may temporarily isolate them from their sequence. Yet we view them as instruments of training. The first are ceremonies and rituals involving the sacred flutes, substantiated by the mythology already discussed; we already know something of their signfiicance. The second concerns the *avagli*, the sweat house ceremonies, which are not substantiated by the mythology reviewed but owe their inspiration to a pseudohistorical incident. Discussion of these two will be necessarily brief and in summary, with the minimum of attention to the interrelationship of the persons concerned.

The Pig Festival

Months before the actual festival, men go out into the surrounding bush at night to play their flutes. At times they enter the village after dark, playing flutes. No woman or young boy may see them, under the threat of death by arrow. Inside their houses, the women sit about their fires,

[8] See Radcliffe-Brown (1952, p. 157).

gossiping or sleeping, occasionally listening. The men insist that they are trembling with fear; and should any woman later ask what the sound was, the conventional reply will be that it was the cry of a malignant spirit. Women, however, are less ignorant of this ceremony than they appear to be. Men say that secrecy is maintained to frighten them, since in the beginning they owned the flutes and had their own communal house, like the men's house. At that time, men add, they themselves were afraid; but now the situation is reversed, and it is the women's turn to be frightened. As the time draws near for the main festival, the flute-playing is intensified; men enter the village playing them and swinging bullroarers. Women hand out pig meat to feed the spirit, allegedly to avoid being killed and eaten themselves; and the men take it to their house to eat. Or they may capture young boys, taking them out into the bush and thrusting wild cane up their nostrils to make blood flow before showing them the flutes.

These preparations continue until the gardens are ready and the main crops fully developed.[9] Thus the playing of the flutes brings about the requisite conditions for the festival itself. But in conjunction are the episodes in which the flutes are revealed to novices.

At Maira, in Kogu, there was a series of preliminary ceremonies:

After inviting several surrounding districts to attend for singing and dancing, men collected large quantities of food from their lineage gardens. They themselves prepared ovens and cooked the vegetables, the women being warned not to go to the gardens. At night the invited groups arrived, one after another entering Maira carrying emblems and dancing and singing. This continued until early morning, when bundles of food were distributed and the visitors returned to their respective villages and districts. In the following weeks men and women from Kogu decorated themselves and made emblems, visiting and receiving food from each of the groups which had visited them. The visits completed, the playing of flutes was continued in their own villages. Preparing an initiation site near a creek, the men again collected food from the gardens and cooked it themselves, taking it to their communal house. Then, fully decorated, carrying their bows and arrows, they entered their village to "catch" the young boys. [They are sometimes taken forcibly from their mothers and sisters, who mourn for them.] Down in the river their noses were bled and the flutes shown to them. Brothers and fathers, actual and classificatory, bled their own noses, too, and swallowed cane, in addition to other operations to be mentioned later. The novices were

---

[9] Read (1954) mentions that, among the Gahuku-Gama, pig festivals take place each year or at longer intervals, depending on how many pigs are available. As here, they are connected with initiation; but those we are discussing do not directly concern the betrothal of warriors. They are, Read notes (ibid., p. 18), essentially competitive and connected with prestige; but in our example they serve only indirectly to confirm political ties. M. Reay (1959, pp. 20–22) writes of the "pig complex" among the Kuma of the middle Wahgi Valley.

warned not to talk to women about what they saw; above all, they must guard the secret of the flutes. A whole series of admonitions followed. Then they retired to the men's house and feasted. Men from other villages in the district received their share of the food and returned home. Late on the next afternoon they played their flutes in the surrounding bush, and that evening after dark re-entered the village. The women closed their doors, while the men paraded about playing the flutes; some planted rows of red croton leaves around the village clearing. Before daybreak they ceased playing and retired to the men's house to rest. Women emerged from their huts and saw the crotons, crying that a malignant spirit had visited them during the night. In the meantime, some of the men out in the bush began to play the flutes again. Others called out to the women, telling them that their female pigs were now bearing young, the litters were increasing, soon the pig festival would be held.

These preparations extended intermittently over approximately six months and had begun many months before. The description stops at the stage when pigs are to be produced for the ceremony. When these pigs grew big, they would be used for the festival, which would take place in approximately a year's time. In the intervening months the flutes would have to be played at intervals to insure the growth of the pigs.

In a culminating festival witnessed at Sosofe, in Kemiju, the preliminaries had continued for five "gardens," i.e., approximately five years, the festival being held on the maturing of the sixth "garden." Huge quantities of food, collected and prepared by men, were placed in a specially built house near the men's house. Firewood was cut, ovens cleaned out and arranged, water collected in lengths of bamboo, and bundles of banana leaves piled up, along with edible leaves.

One morning pigs, trussed up on poles, were brought in from the various villages in the district and arranged in rows. They were then killed one by one by a blow on the snout, so that blood flowed from the nostrils to the ground— like men having their noses bled, the blood falling to the ground being a libation to the earth, a manifestation of Jugumishanta. Then, picking up bamboo knives, the men to whom the pigs belonged first cut the foot, singing,

biribirio mira zapazapa biribiro . . .

"Cut thus, at [this] ground. . . ." ["I do not cut this ground belonging to me, I cut a pig."] The blood spurts out; the man offers the blood to the ground.[10]

The men then cut up the meat, which had been placed on banana leaves, spitting over it chewed bark and salt for seasoning. At this juncture there was some dancing by men and women, and singing. Ovens were built up, the belly meat and liver being cooked and eaten that evening by the local people. The rest of the meat was arranged in a line near the men's house. Early next morning ovens were

[10] The meanings of these songs and all others considered in this work were given by the people themselves; there is no free interpretation on my part.

started up and vegetables cooked. In the distance could be heard approaching groups, representatives of various villages and districts with which arrangements had been previously made. Six districts were represented. Decorated with shells, feathers, and colored leaves, carrying bows and arrows, the people came dancing and singing [there is a wide range of songs which need not be discussed here] into the village. The men came first, followed by heavily laden women with net bags full of produce, some carrying pig meat, most smeared with pigs' blood, with skin and entrails stretched over their heads. In the meantime the local people had arranged their rows of food and meat, whole pigs complete with heads being stretched out on poles. When all the visitors had arrived, they arranged themselves in lineage groups at one end of the village clearing. On the opposite side the local people prepared for the distribution. Lineage headmen, forming a group, called the name of the first district and lineage to receive food. As the name was called, the headman or warrior leader danced forward to receive his share; pig meat stretched out on poles was put on his back and with it he danced back to his own group; it was then removed from his shoulders by his younger brothers. Again and again names were called and meat placed on the shoulders of dancing men who returned to their groups. The distribution completed, all the visitors left almost immediately for their own villages.

The visitors to whom the pig meat is given are those belonging to what I call here the sphere of political influence. Peace between some of the units within this range has been established, for the time being at least. The group which arranges a pig festival is the district, which is the co-operative unit for ceremonial occasions, and the culminating ceremony of distribution may be held in any village of that district. But ruptures may occur at any time, so that the final distribution may be delayed. Rarely, it seems, were more than six or so districts involved. And the end of the festival was a sign that hostilities could be resumed: "We put away our flutes and take up our bows and arrows for fighting."

In the northern part of this region the pig festival is no longer held. In the area of which I write, however, the traditional pattern continues. The shifting alliances are reflected in the units taking part in any festival. When one has completed its own series, it becomes a recipient in a further constellation, which may or may not include all those groups who visited it; but eventually it expects to receive from all those to which it has given.

The following account outlines the preliminaries before final distribution, when pig meat is offered to the spirits.

During our second period at Kogu, when the pigs had grown sufficiently large, thirteen male pigs were brought to the village clearing at Maira, trussed up on poles. In the surrounding bush flutes were played. During the late afternoon one pig was killed and cut up while flutes were played from the men's house, and men and women danced. In the meantime, lengths of bamboo had been cut and within the men's house flutes were being made. Blood, brought on croton leaves from the slaughtered pig, was smeared over all the flutes, old as well as new. Two men then emerged from the back of the men's house and blew their flutes in broad daylight. They were not seen by the women, who were all either dancing or assembled around the oven. A number of croton leaves were smeared with pigs' blood and the pig meat placed in the oven for cooking. All the old men of the Kogu district sat around the oven and, taking up the bloodstained croton leaves one by one, began to split them, waving them in the air and calling the ancestral spirits or ghosts [hangkaru]. "Negivigo^{c}moka; juwego^{c}moka; kiavego^{c}moka; miago^{c}moka. . . ." "Negivi ground, you; Juwe ground, you; Kiave ground, you; Mia ground, you. . . ." The names of various places were called, each associated with ancestral spirits. In this way the spiritual essence from the blood itself and the oven was given to them. In addition a request was made: "Do not hold our mouths, do not restrain us from playing these flutes well." [The ancestors were said to be present at the feast.] The flute-playing was continued; then out came all the men blowing the non-sacred flutes or whistles, and dancing and singing continued into the night. Next day food was collected from the gardens and the remaining pigs killed; visitors came from nearby villages and districts.[11]

The pig festival, as indicated, must be seen in the perspective of the initiation ceremonies. The following account concerns such a ceremony held in conjunction with a section of the age-grading cycle in Busarasa (Fore).

Once it was decided to hold this ceremony, the men told the women to prepare gifts for the novices. The men constructed a shelter in which the pigs would later be killed. This took about a week, during which time firewood and oven stones were collected. Flutes were played each day in the bush, and during the night men entered the village while the women remained behind closed doors. At last the women told the men that they had completed their task of making net bags and arm bands of orchid cane, and messages were sent to nearby villages and districts with invitations to the feast. [Most of the main visitors were nenafu and mothers' brothers to the novices, with a sprinkling of their fathers' sisters' husbands' lineage kin, various matrikin, and some related to them only indirectly through their nenafu and mothers' brothers.] By late afternoon of the following day most had assembled, entering Busarasa with singing and dancing. The ovens were started up. During the night men collected bark from the specially cultivated trees in their gardens and brought it back to the men's house. Mothers, sisters, and brothers' wives, as well as nogago [mothers' brothers' wives, resident outside the village], then brought their partially finished orchid fiber waist bands, bags, and armbands to the men's house, handing them in from outside. There the men set to work to finish the plaiting, adding the bark they had collected. Others dried bamboo leaves over the fire and when they were

---

[11] During the festivals pig fat is rubbed over women's bodies, over their skirts and hair; men rub fat only over their short bark fringe skirts and hair, not over their bodies, because of the avagli (see below, p. 73).

brittle broke them into a wooden dish, mixing them with grease. When this was ready they awaited the arrival of the novices, who were driven toward the men's house by their fathers, brothers, mothers' brothers, and *nenafu*, singing as they beat them with branches:

> *Noparanu noperiperi sanggu pirio i,*
> *no[m]periperi sanggu pirio i. . . .*

"Inside the house, inside the house you go. . . ." [The song refers to the novices' being forced to enter the men's house.]

The men then took hold of them and rubbed the mixture on their bodies. They put the fringed waistbands on the boys, cutting and fastening them, hung the net bags from their shoulders, and put on the armbands, slipping *waku* leaves under them for decoration. They decorated bows and arrows, tying *kavi^c* at the center of their shafts. A long series of songs was then sung:

> *kena^cnimo jokeru tiriso kenai kena^cnimo. . . .*

"My skirt, sit quietly [as we] cut. . . ." Sung as the skirt is put around the novice, this refers to its cutting and fastening. The novice is advised that this is a mark of adulthood; he must not play about any more but "sit quietly."

> *Ibonani . . . tentenbo najampini tentenbo . . .*

"My boy, thus I made [it], my arm . . ." The novice's father, brother, or mother's brother sings of the armbands he is putting on him.

> *Soribubu namio namio sori:i . . .*

"Hitting with branches . . . we trick you . . ." They hit the novices with the branches again, but this time they say it is only to "trick" them; it is not meant in earnest. "You are no longer small, you may eat pig meat."

> *Anumamuja:i warara mamuja:i kofi^cnanto*
> *oji kasi mamuja:i warara i: . . .*

"Cassowary plumes: red bands of feathers [We] put round [your] head . . ." Bands of cassowary and red parakeet feathers are placed around their foreheads.

> *anumaja koko mijijuwe majujuwi . . .*

"Hold the central pole. Thus you grow . . ." The novices now hold the central post [from the *wa^ciga*, man tree] of the men's house, moving around in a circle: "You must be strong like this central pole—so you will become big men."

> *ja:ni a'kisako ja:ni ja:ni tapomi . . .*

"Strong trees [you will] break . . ." ["As we break this stick easily, so you will cut down large trees, because you will be strong."]

> *jagumija:u tarugie fongge fongge*
> *jagamataja:o . . . jarasuja:u tarugie waguja:u tarugie . . .*

"The large *gumi* tree. [Thus you] will become. The *gamatai* tree . . . the *tasu* tree; the *wagu* tree." "These trees are large and strong, as you also will be."

> *esa:esa:wi wabamuntiga esa:esa:wi . . .*

"Bark of the *jonin* tree, sap of the *jonin* tree . . ." Bark from this tree is obtained, chewed, and expectorated on leaves, and the novices' fringed waistbands rubbed with it to produce a red coloring. Sap from this tree is also collected and rubbed on the waistband.

Next morning the pigs were killed and ovens made. The meat was cooked with great quantities of vegetables. When this was ready, the ovens were opened and the food placed in wooden platters arranged in a long line; it was then sprayed by mouth with salt and chewed ginger. Men of the novices' patrilineages, particularly their fathers and brothers, and their mothers, distributed the food among the boys' mothers' brothers, *nenafu*, maternal grandparents, and classificatory fathers, mothers, and brothers among the visitors. The mothers' brothers and *nenafu* reciprocated with strings of shells and beads to be hung around the boys' necks. Fathers and mothers of the boys then filled their net bags with meat and cooked vegetables and passed it through the door of the men's house. The evening and night were spent in feasting, and flutes were played. In the morning all the *nogago*, who stood as mothers' brothers' wives to the novices, arranged themselves around the entrance to the men's house and called to them: "Take up your bows and arrows and come outside." The boys left the house and holding their decorated arrows pointed downward presented them to their *nogago*. The women returned them point upward, saying, "You shoot wild pig at Iboti [near Rivetiga, the place of Jugumishanta and Morufonu]. You are strong now, you must shoot a man." Holding their arrows upright, the novices returned to the men's house. The pig festival was finished, but the initiation of the youths continued.

The pig festivals are directly concerned with fertility. In emphasizing this aspect, they are underlining the basic concepts apparent in the Jugumishanta and Morufonu mythology. The desired conditions can be brought about only through the use of flutes, played in a special way, together with certain other ritual actions. The part played by women is of a secondary nature: they may sing and dance and eat at the feast, but they have no hand in the main rituals and ceremony. Sex demarcation is strictly observed.[12] The ritual and ceremonies associated with the flutes, as symbols of male dominance, accentuate it. Men apparently feel that they must exert this pressure, continually reassuring themselves that they are superior to women. Whenever the question of women's seeing the flutes is raised in discussion in the men's house, there is an immediate outburst that the women will be killed should they look, quickly followed by the explanation that women once possessed these flutes but lost them through the craftiness and strength of men. One has an impression almost of guilt, marked by a desire to justify possession by emphasizing that men are the

---

[12] Compare with Mundugumor ceremonies of the flutes discussed by M. Mead (1935, p. 181 *et seq*.). But see also in reference to the Orokaiva: E. W. P. Chinnery and W. N. Beaver (1915), F. E. Williams (1930, plate xxiv, pp. 88, 99, 180); here there are male and female flutes (*ibid*., p. 185) as among the eastern Highlanders, but among the Orokaiva no sacred character is attributed to them (*ibid*., p. 197).

real owners. So strong is male opinion against women seeing the flutes that there are only a few cases available for discussion of what happens when this occurs.[13]

In one incident, said to have taken place just before Kogu was declared controlled [in 1949], a young woman had the misfortune to observe two men playing flutes out in the bush. They did nothing immediately but discussed the matter with her father and brother. All decided that she must die. Her father and brother caught hold of her and dragged her into the bush; protesting vehemently that she had not seen the flutes, she composed a song [in Kamano]:[14]

> *nagara ongke^cnowe owa aie jo:o*
> *intevi intevifana ongke^cnowe owa eo . . .*

"I, I did not see the flute [playing] I did not see . . ." Men gathered around her and, drawing their bows, shot her dead as she sang. Her father and brother carried her back to their village, killed a pig, held a feast, and buried her in their lineage garden. Men declare that the women were very much afraid after this.

Two mechanisms of control are in operation here: public opinion, backed by male action if necessary, and fear, the taken-for-granted sexual demarcation expressive of the value-acceptive element. Yet since the northern area has been under control, and there is less likelihood of killing without an inquiry and public court, some women have allegedly tried to bribe men (offering to copulate) to describe and even show them the flutes. But men have argued that they can get sexual satisfaction without going to these lengths. They declare that "all women" are interested in the flutes; and novices, in the course of initiation, are warned not to reveal the nature of the flutes to women.

A woman, it is said, hears the sound of the flutes: she is curious and hides near a bush track, waiting for some young man to come along. When she sees one coming, she holds him and asks, "What is that sound? Show me, and you may copulate with me." The young man replies, "Yes, I will show you." They copulate. Afterward he tells her, "It is just like a woman, with the same skin as you, wearing a skirt; but it has a hole under each armpit, no eyes, although it has a mouth. The cry comes from the armpit holes; it holds its hand over one armpit and cries from the other; then it does the same with the other side." She asks again, "You will show this to me?" They copulate again. She presses her request, but he refuses to add any more. "I have told you about it, I cannot show you. It

---

[13] See chap. 11. *Ja^co* sorcery was used to punish two women who played a flute and danced.

[14] It is the custom at times of stress to "compose" songs. People feel apparently that they can express themselves better this way than in ordinary speech. Further, the song will possibly be remembered as their other words may not.

is something which belongs to all the men; if you look, they will kill us. They will shoot us, and only the kunai grass will remain. I have told you about it, that is enough." In this way he evades the issue, but it is fairly certain [see below] that she is not deluded.

The rituals rest on the assumption that the flutes must not be seen by women. In the northern districts, when women have seen the flutes, all the associated rituals and ceremonies immediately collapse. The flutes are the focal point. It is the fact of observing them, not of knowing about them, which is deemed important.

Yet women in most of the region we are discussing may desire to maintain the status quo: they want their menfolk to be strong, as they themselves must be strong. There is no apparent feeling of injustice because the flute is a peculiarly male possession. Women have their role, men theirs. To illustrate this attitude, here is a contemporary song from Busarasa:

> winewul bakabaka mamiounti gora igurari ireiinara . . .
> nantunantu usaro asaro jababara nantunantu umburere kinanu . . .
> gupena jawuljawul mameguwantu^{c}o avitirino^{c}u . . .

"[Oh] mother! [What is that?]" "Don't speak [the mother replies]. You have no penis. Rain [falls].
"Flutes sound. Flutes sound from Nantunantu, from the bush. Men [are there]!
"[But you have] blood. Don't cry, you [are a] woman. You don't hear [understand]!"

[A mother tells her daughter: "Do not speak about them, you have no penis. The rain is falling and the flutes cry from the mountains, from the bush: there men are playing. But blood stops within your body. Do not cry. You sit down and blood will fall upon the ground, you are a woman." As if to say: "If I had borne a man instead of a woman you would have looked at this; but you are a girl instead of a boy, blood will flow from you like water. This is the same as the playing of the flutes."]

The point noted before is important. Women may know something about the flutes, but they may not see them. The extent of their knowledge is suggested in a series of oni^c [15] songs heard in the Busarasa district and said to come from women living in districts adjacent to Rivetiga. The songs give relatively accurate accounts of flute-playing and of the nature of the flutes. They are not known farther north in, for instance, the Kogu and Kemiju districts, yet women there are not as ignorant as men assume them to be.

---

[15] Songs composed on the basis of visits from spirit familiars, during trances induced by chewing a special bark.

Here is an example of a similar song:

> *Umburebawu pibirasajamu*
> *tatarantuwanu . . .*
> *jabakinana miritonoibu . . .*
> *si^cabawu keberu^cabawu*

"[The] flute sounds at Pibirasajamu, defecating [as it goes] . . . Near the tree [the flute-woman] sits, crying . . . at Si^cabawu, at Keberu^cabawu."

The incident, although having possibly occurred in Fore territory [perhaps Busarasa, where the song was sung], is placed in the Mania region to the southwest so that the singer can be treated as anonymous. A Keimu woman is working in her garden; she hears the sound of a flute playing from Pibirasa Mountain. Later she goes to this place, curious to find out who plays it. She finds feces. She takes up a stick and poking them lifts them to her nostrils, smelling. First, so we are told, she thinks that the flute-woman has left them; but after smelling she knows it is "a village man" [that is, an ordinary human being]. The song is sung by Miarasa women shut up in their huts at night, when men come playing flutes and hoping for pig meat.

The sound of flute-playing is said to be irresistibly attractive to women, as in this song (attributed to a woman of Kigupa, on the slopes of Gurupina near Taramu, in Jate territory):

> *. . . asaru asoru*
> *agonetenu*
> *vigio namatiagabia agonetenu*

"[The] flute sounds. Copulate with me. He goes [playing]: [the flute sounds like the] *tiaga* bird . . ."

Women sing in their houses as the men play the flutes: "The cry of your flute is like the blue *tiaga* bird—copulate with me!" The same theme of eroticism appears, as we have seen, in the cane-swallowing ritual and is apparent, too, in the *avagli*.

Interesting, in the light of this relationship between men and women, is the fact that women may call the flute co-wife (e.g., *nagomepa* in Jate, or *nabaimu* or *namaramu* in Fore, where it is more usual). That women should call the flute *iberu*, "female flute," seems contradictory after what has been said of it as a symbol of maleness. Yet this is not so incongruous if one considers its mythological background. Men gain their strength from and through women and much of their ritual is associated with physiological features primarily relevant to women, while flutes used by men are called by terms denoting male and female (and referring to the two Creative Beings). For example, the following song, sung by a Miarasa woman, refers to her co-wife, the "female flute," who cries and cries and eventually enters the men's house to sleep.

> *Namaramuo umburereji tubebedji . . .*
> *karisigontagovinti saginapaja kanantanai:je*
> *urerebo terebo . . .*
> *mempangk gajuguvintirigaji . . .*

"Co-wife, flutes sound, flutes sound. From the base of the *karisi* tree, this woman comes. Flutes sound; flutes sound [as] she enters the men's house."

Use of the term "co-wife" implies sharing a husband, common duties, and, ideally, co-operation. As the song suggests, this ritual "wife" goes to sleep in the men's house, a place forbidden in most circumstances to her human counterpart. But I shall not press this parallel too far, although it is significant for our understanding of the ritual relationship between men and women.

On the conclusion of the pig festival men usually spend some time in their communal house, playing the flutes and eating meat. When the meat is finished, and after dark, they enter the village, playing their flutes and going from door to door. The women may put meat on the end of an arrow and pass it out through the door. The men remove the meat and substitute cassowary feathers on the tip of the arrow or smear saliva on it. The woman who has passed out the arrow sees that the meat is gone and thinks, so it is said, that her co-wife has taken it: there is her saliva, there her hair! Many women, if not all, realize that it is the men who take the meat; but the pretense is maintained that they are feeding their co-wives. Some women, however, do not co-operate, just as is the case among human co-wives.

Anugabujema, an *anumpa* lineage man of Busarasa, sings of such a woman (Arugisa, also an *anumpa* of Busarasa: he calls her *ato*, sister-in-law):

> *Anumparu wenta kabiba agori*
> *arimpagagawul namaramuwe kampinta*
> *araganamaii meapinti'meuntatu*
> *iberusemigunu nanamantibara*
> *wakinagaivi kaisinarugapinti maremiu*
> *kabu kabaikinakaima*
> *migagarawu usasaginagaima*
> *tumpunabumajuwul notataiinasunobagajawu*

"*Anumpa* woman, open the door [of your house]. I look, [it's] not [my] co-wife. . . . [I am a woman yet] she puts nothing into my hand! The *iberu* flute-woman goes crying into the bush. She goes down to Kaisinarugapinti, angry like a snake. Stay there! [But] I am a man [who] plays [it]. I become ashamed, sorry, because of this—this flute."

A general rendering of this song is as follows: "Woman of Busarasa, is your door open?" [The flute-woman speaks to her]: "I look for my co-wife, but she is not there. I am a woman, but she puts no meat into my hand." The flute-woman goes crying into the bush, into the creek bed at Kaisinarugapinti, there to stop, angry like a snake. "I am a man of this ground," [16] says Anugabujema. "I played the flute. Now I am sorry and ashamed because of this happening."

A flute is said to be co-wife to any woman, irrespective of the relationship existing between the player and the woman who is asked for meat. In the above example, the woman who refuses is the man's *ato*, an "avoidance" relationship. He is ashamed, not just for himself but because her action is a slight to the sacred flute. Yet he takes no action against her, merely protesting in song; and the situation is summed up in terms of customary behavior between co-wives: "Some women perform the duties which are part of this relationship; others do not."

This relationship between men and women in the ritual and ceremonial sphere is central to our main theme. We speak of men's dominant ritual status—their desire to hide certain knowledge from women, their power (even though, as above, they may not always exercise it) to enforce their opinion and retain their position through force and fear. Yet in one sense this is a matter of formal appearance. The influence wielded by women is less obvious; it serves both to support and accentuate the ideology of male supremacy and to increase men's dependence on them.

The flutes are potent; they are instrumental in bringing about fertility because they have been anointed with pigs' blood. Blood is a vital life-giving and life-symbolizing essence. Pigs' blood, flesh and skin, entrails, and so on, are smeared over and worn by men and women as they dance in the pig festival. Blood splashed on the earth gives life to it and makes the crops grow. There is further symbolism here: the blood-smeared flute is like a penis stained with blood after coitus with a menstruating woman.

We saw that during the feast places associated with ancestral spirits are invoked and the spiritual substance of the food offered to them. It is suggested by some that the spirits have come from Anabaga, the Land of the Dead. There is, too, a direct connection between them and the flutes. Each man possesses at least one flute, which is specially named. It is part of himself, containing part of his spirit, and this part is his physical strength. Should a woman see it, his strength fails; should he play it, his strength is enhanced. He and his male lineage kin play one tune; should it be played by another lineage not entitled to it,[17] this is grounds for

[16] This is of the same order as statements such as "I am a man, not a woman!" "I am a man, not an animal!" "Man gave birth to me!" "I am a man of a village, not a man of the bush or a spirit of no domicile," insisting on superior status in the human and nonhuman world. "I am a man, how can people treat me so!"

[17] A number of lineages in one district may play the same tune, thus inferring their common relationship, although, as we have seen, this may not be otherwise acknowledged.

warfare. On his death a man's flute is broken and buried with him or his bones: his physical strength has disappeared.[18]

Finally, there is the association of these ceremonies with initiation. The ritual we have been considering here stresses the development of the novice's strength. He must grow strong like the central pole of the men's house; he must be able to cut down strong trees; he must grow as strong as some of the largest trees. When the youths are called from the men's house by their *nogago*, to whom they offer arrows, they are instructed to shoot well, not only wild pig but also men. The significance of the rite, apart from emphasizing this aspect of male aggression specifically sanctioned by the women, lies in its symbolism. The youths are called out by their *nogago*, who are potential mothers-in-law—that is, wives of mothers' brothers who are not fathers' sisters, implying marriage with a matri-cross-cousin. The *nogago* acknowledge the youths as potential sons-in-law, now eligible. The down-pointed arrows signify detumescent penes before their mothers-in-law; the women hand back the arrows with the points upright, implying that a virile man has an erect penis. They instruct the youths, however, that they must kill pigs in order to make gifts of food to their prospective parents-in-law; and they must kill a man before they can marry. These rituals are associated with training for aggression—not diffuse or generalized, but oriented along specific lines. A network of obligations is set up, involving not only members of the lineage and linked lineages but also matrikin, actual and classificatory *nenafu*, and certain other kin, if only in a classificatory sense. The pig festival itself creates obligations which devolve on the novice as a member of a specific lineage and district. The driving of the youths into the men's house by their fathers, brothers, mothers' brothers, and *nenafu* symbolizes their subordinate status in kin terms, and in regard to relative strength. The fastening of their ritual skirts confers on them the status of manhood; but the repeated beating with branches by the same group of kin, while described as a mere gesture (for the youths are now socially adults and the taboo on the eating of pig meat is lifted), appears to stress status differentiation.

Avagli

Our second example of ritual and ceremony concerns the sweat house. Before discussing it even briefly, as we must do here, we shall consider two accounts of its origin.

The first of these is pseudohistorical and not mythological in the

[18] A man must refrain from blowing his flute for a certain period after an older brother's death.

conventional sense of the term. It tells of an unnamed Inivi (Jate) woman who went out to dig rats at Ifajutoga:

She went on digging a hole till nightfall, when she blocked it up and returned to her village. During the night, the rat to which the hole belonged came to her in a dream and spoke: "I lie in water." She replied, "I too lie in water." In the morning she got up and saw she was covered with *avagli*—her face, breasts, buttocks, hands, skirt. It was running down from her "like water." She showed herself to the men, who asked her what she had been eating to cause this. She told them how she had gone to Ifajutoga and of her dream. All the people admired her.

The second (Fore) account tells of two brothers, one older than the other, both orphaned and in the story unnamed:

They made an oven, cooked food, and ate. Afterward, the younger brother rubbed the elder's body with ashes from the oven and the elder did the same for the younger. As they were doing this, a *wore^cworefa*, a potentially malignant spirit, came along. His body was dripping with *avagli*. As he walked, it fell upon the leaves of bushes he broke down and upon the ground; it was like pig grease. He came up to where they were sitting and spoke: "Your skin is like ashes; why do you do that?" But they became angry and chased him with axes. He ran off, splashing the grass, bushes, and trees with *avagli*. As they came close to him, he transformed himself into a tree. On reaching it, they asked it, "Why have you turned into a tree?" But it was growing dark, and at last they returned to their house. In the morning they again made an oven and rubbed their bodies with ashes; and again the *wore^cworefa* appeared and taunted them, "Your skin is no good, it is only ashes." Again they chased the spirit, who changed into a tree. They asked it, "Why do you do that, tricking us?" The elder brother told the younger to go home; and he waited there. Presently the spirit turned into red-stemmed sugar cane which grew alongside the tree, reaching to its head. "What can this be?" asked the elder brother. He began to cut it down, and as he did so out spurted the *avagli* all over his body, covering him completely.[19] He cut the cane and stacked it in a bundle and took it home, but gave none to his younger brother. Instead, he planted it in a garden. The younger brother seeing him with *avagli* asked, "Elder brother, what have you been eating that this thing has come up? Show me." "No, it came up by itself." Relenting afterward, however, the elder brother showed him where he had planted the sugar cane, telling him to cut only the older sticks and not to touch the new shoots. Later, the younger brother went to the garden and, discarding the old cane, cut a new shoot. Immediately *avagli* spurted out all over his body. The elder brother, suspicious, came to the garden and saw what had happened. "How did you get this?" he asked. "What have you eaten?" When there was no reply, he grew angry: "You have cut the new shoots. Who told you to do that? I told you to cut old sugar."

[19] In other versions the juice of the sugar cane, into which the spirit has transformed himself, is his blood. On drinking this the elder brother loses his coating of ashes and is covered with *avagli*.

Maira village, in Kogu. The road at left
leads to Moiife district.

Juwe village, in Kogu. An
earth-oven is being dug
out.

Women at Pintagori (Busarasa) bundling scraped sweet potatoes in
pandanus leaves ready for the oven. Note nose ornament of flying fox
bone worn by woman in right foreground.

Women at Maira (Kogu) with contributions for a feast.

Removing vegetables and meat from a steaming oven at Pintagori.

On the road from Ke^cjagana (Jate), near Kemiju (Jate). Visitors to pig festival.

Picking up his ax, he struck his brother, killing him, and then buried him in the sugar garden.[20]

From these two stories we learn very little about the significance of this rite or the nature of *avagli* itself, other than its association with physical attractiveness. Its origin is ascribed on the one hand to a woman, on the other to a spirit. Nevertheless, they serve to substantiate the ritual in much the same way as the Jugumishanta myths do for the flute-playing and cane-swallowing.

The ceremony associated with the *avagli* is called *noneflegi*. Special leaves are collected, and all adult males, except perhaps a few of the old men, enter their communal house. There the leaves are cut up finely with ginger and with *megufa* leaves, mixed with scraped bark of a certain tree, placed on a banana leaf, and sprayed with salt. The men bleed their noses by thrusting cane or pitpit leaves up the nostrils and scrape their tongues with coarse leaves until blood flows. Then the mixture is passed around, and each eats a little. All the men remain for approximately five days in the house, where a large fire is kept blazing. Sweat then begins to run over their faces, chests, and backs, forming designs on their bodies. This is the *avagli*. During the period of the sweat house there must be complete abstinence from sexual intercourse; otherwise, the *avagli* will not appear. Each day, wives, daughters, and mothers resident in the village cook edible leaves and bring them with lengths of sugar cane and bamboo containers full of water to the entrance of the men's house, where they pass them in to their menfolk. They also make orchid fiber armbands and net bags and the fringed bark skirts worn by men. When the fifth day is over, they bring wood and oven stones to the village clearing. Then they collect food from the gardens—sugar cane, bananas, taro, yams, sweet potatoes, pitpit, edible leaves, marrows, and so on, which they cook in a large oven. In the meantime the men decorate themselves with shells. The women hand the new bags and skirts through the doorway, and the men put them on. They fasten on headbands of feathers and of animal fur and put lengths of white quartzite through the nasal septum. When the oven is ready, the food is removed and arranged in a line, and the women and old men call out. The men take up their bows and arrows and emerge singing from their house (this is the *matataglifia*). They dance up and down the clearing, singing, being admired by their womenfolk, and finally sit down to the feast.

At Maira, in Kogu, a large house was built for this purpose and firewood cut and placed inside. Middle-aged men collected the special leaves and bark and

---

[20] This story resembles closely in form and content a version found in the category of non-sacred mythology. Note its theme of male sibling antagonism.

prepared the mixture, spraying it with salt. Then the inside of the house was decorated. All the men entered, a fire was built up, and they arranged themselves around it. They bled their noses and scraped their tongues so that blood flowed, cleansing their faces. Then they ate some of the leaf mixture and waited for the appearance of the *avagli*, while young boys almost ready for the initial age-grading ceremonies were brought in to watch. Songs were sung all night long during the whole period, the days being spent mostly in sleeping. Each day, women brought food.

The *avagli* does not "come up" as readily on some men as it does on others. To induce it, men cane-swallow to purify themselves so that the *avagli* will be unhampered or chew the red *zomana* flower mixed with *tipajana* leaves in case the first mixture has not been potent enough. It appears first around the forehead and eyes, running down at each side of the nose and from the ears, then down the mustache and chin. From there it drips to the chest, running to the navel, and is then "guided" into designs by the use of a sharpened cassowary bone. This is as far as the substance runs on the average man, on whom it is said that "one leg (or line) of *avagli* runs down." The "big men," the really strong warriors, can make it flow down their backs or sides from under the armpits: for them, the "fighting-shield of *avagli* runs down," a shield insuring magical protection. On the most outstanding it is said to reach the penis.

On the fifth night the women came to the house with burning flares of dry grass and bark and looked through the doorway at the men, admiring them. Then all emerged from the house. The younger men who had attended their first sweat house were met by their mothers and fathers, who told them, "You are big and strong now. You must not copulate with women while you have this *avagli* upon you, or it will dry up and you will lose your strength; you may only rub jaws with young women [i.e., in the conventional courtship manner]."

The *avagli* is primarily a means of attaining power and strength. The more apparent and prolific the *avagli*, it is said, the greater the warrior. The youths who have emerged from their first sweat house have become strong because they have the *avagli* on their chests and bodies, and now their parents warn them: "The designs caused by the *avagli* are attractive to women. Beware that this does not weaken your strength; abstain from intercourse, be content merely with courting." But older men do not abstain from coitus; and there seems little reason to suppose that it detracts, in their opinion, from the strength they have gained.

Let us pause to consider several songs in order to underline this significance, for it is in the songs (of which a large series was obtained) that this aspect is best demonstrated. They are not of a strictly traditional nature, although in form and content their range is somewhat restricted. They are contemporary, "composed" by individual men and women, and sung during the sweat house period.

Women bring firewood to the men's sweat house. They dance toward the door and through it, singing:

> Wojafa i: i: marimarita pinti mamata pinti
> maisuwe wojafa i: i: . . .

"Red parakeets: [shall we] put [it] here or there? [We come] red parakeets . . ."
[In Fore: "Where shall we put the wood, here or there? You are like red parakeets (wojafa, or wajafa)!" The women refer to their husbands and sons, and other men.]

Inside the house, the men sing about the youths who are undergoing the avagli for the first time:

> Mantitabawewe tonavikintati kaso^c^kaso
> tonanajatari kaso^c^kaso waja^c^wewi . . .

"At Mantitabawewe [Miarasa] the avagli runs; down the chest it flows; flowing further, it comes: red parakeets!" ["There at Miarasa the avagli flows down the body, making you like a red parakeet, making the body strong."]

The women come dancing into the sweat house with lengths of bamboo containing water and decorated with red flowers and crotons, singing (in Fore):

> Kopugarampi kiroso kiroso kama^c^a kikirampi
> kiroso kama^c^a
> kanu kamisio kamanampanabi kamuwe
> kama^c^a kamisio . . .

"At Kopugarampi, we bring leaves of red flowering creepers . . . Not your mothers give you [this]. Your sisters give you [this]. We bring, we give . . ."
[Here at the places mentioned, we women bring leaves of the kiroso for you. Your mothers are dead, your fathers are dead, but we your sisters and your wives give to you.]

The men sing (in Jate) that those within the house are of one "line" (lineage):

> Nagai^c^namawaja dzu^c^nanu zezuzawarie
> mai^c^negejanagio ko^c^ni jananajamerugai
> zozavarie . . .
> mai^c^negejanagio nagai^c^namawaja dzu^c^ni^c^amo
> nagai^c^ zezuzawarie

"My birds, red parakeets, my lineage, at Zezuzawa [Kogu]. It remains [thus], my ground at Janana [Kogu]. Zozavarie [confirms this]. It remains [my ground], my birds, red parakeets, my lineage, at Zezuzawa."
Reference is made to two places associated with the lineage participating, members of which are likened to red parakeets. A woman is named, wife of the district headman; it was she who drew this comparison. She identifies herself here with her husband's lineage, not her own.

A mother sings (in Jate) of her son in the sweat house:

> Mojazanani wajuwaju wajuhumologio
> mojazanani wajuwaju humologio maigewe^cjameroga
> hajo hajau maigewe^cjameroga
> moreta^cfezani haraua haraua moreta^cfezani . . .
>   morenupijamurega
> hajo hajau morenupijamurega moreta^cfezani . . .

"My orchid fiber, pull, pull, pulled. My orchid fiber, pull, pull, pulled [out] at Maigewe^cjameroga [near Inivi]. It comes, it comes [out] at Maigewe^cjameroga. My orchid fiber, pull, pull, pulled [out]; my orchid fiber [at Wunepinka]. It comes . . ." The literal meaning is that the wild orchid fiber is pulled and comes out at the places mentioned in the song. Symbolically, it refers to the umbilical cord of her son. She sees her son emerge from the house with *avagli*; his skin is good, his body strong.

Men sing (in Jate) of a particular incident relating to a fight. Kemiju men prepare an ambush at Mipotoga, on the track between Kemiju and Tatagufa. A war party comes, consisting of men from Inivi, Taramu, Amufi, and Kimi^cagumu districts. The party is surprised by the Kemiju men and, collecting their dead, its members return home.

> Nama haniganagana auu:ti^camuanu
> avikerelga hu^cnegajanigio wokagatagata epa
>   agujagimagunowa
> hai^cna^cni agegigamonageo ao^cnio io^cnio
> amuatagujagimaganowa hai^cna^cni
> agegigamonageo nama haniganagana . . .
> papati^camu^co mai^cnikaizamenigio

"Like birds, they shot us, our brother(s)! I mourn there. I go there, to Woka-gatagata [near Inivi], our lineage place. I go [there] and we look at each other. [I leave you.] To Amuata [Inivi], the men's place, I go . . . We look at each other. They have shot the birds. [Only] our fathers remain . . ." ["They shot us like birds, killed our brother(s). I go and stay there, mourning him (them), at Woka-gata, the place of his lineage. I look at you; you look at me; now they have killed you. I go to Amuata; I look at the birds (men) they have shot. Only our fathers remain."] Note the pidgin English word papa, used here in place of the ordinary Jate word for father.

The women sing (in Fore) when they are requested to bring bamboos of water, dancing around the sweat house before bringing them in:

> Mempangk waiaguvintima
> kanavilotu waribue ewaii e . . .

"[In the] sweat house, in the men's house, they are angry with us, [coming with] leaves . . ." Holding the lengths of bamboo, decorated with leaves, the women tell the men that they are angry with them: "You are always calling out for water—you are angry at us!" Note that the word for "sweat house" is often one of the ordinary words for men's house.

The men reply as the women enter the sweat house:

> *Mirumpiru agagajemingganipi*
> *kenasie kerunasie o*
> *miru agagaiwanipi*
> *kenasie o*
> *patasa:aratagajau merunaio*
> *irunaio kenasie o*

"*Miru* birds, in the water: [like the] sound of water falling. Who will drink? . . . *Miru* birds; sound of water falling. Who will drink? Stay in your village. [But] we can get it. Who will [then] drink? ["We are like *miru* birds in the water. You make a sound like a waterfall as you urinate into the bamboo lengths, filling them with your urine. Who will drink it? You stay in the village without getting us water; we ourselves can get our own water."] The men reprimand the women for their slowness in filling the bamboo containers.

Men warn the youths undergoing the *avagli* not to eat from the hand of a menstruating woman or their *avagli* will dry and they will lose their strength. The following song, in Kamano (with a "Jate accent"), is from Kogu.

> *. . . egu amofo kajanegi^cna*
> *o^cnegowe kajana bugibugi*

"[From the menstrual hut] you come, your woman's hand, cooking; I do not look at your hand. . . ." The song refers to a woman who has offered a youth food. He refuses this because of her association with the menstrual hut.

Or a parallel is drawn between the flowing *avagli* and menstruation:

> *Aga^cno jawuljawul marijotozie . . .*

"Fine grass, [from which] it flows down the body . . ." This song, in Fore, refers to a fine grass used as a menstrual pad; the blood seeps through this and flows to the ground; similarly, the *avagli* runs down the body of the men and drips to the ground.

The ritual of *avagli* is a specifically male activity, but there is no secrecy associated with it. Women pass fairly freely in and out of the sweat house when they bring water and food, although they do not linger there. They desire to see their menfolk with *avagli* upon their bodies and liken them to the red *wojafa* (or *wajafa*) parakeet[21] with its beautiful plumage, or to red flowers; they desire to have the imprint of the *avagli* upon their own bodies, as may happen during coitus. There is an allusion to this in the following Fore song:

> *Arumata katatetuwe*
> *igoki igokikama. . . .*

[21] The red parakeet, it will be remembered, is one manifestation of Morufonu. Usually the comparison is drawn only in reference to men, although there are cases, as in songs, when it refers to particularly attractive women.

"Yesterday I left you, [like] a dry tree trunk. . . ." ["Yesterday I (we) left you
women and came to this sweat house. You are now dry like a tree trunk."] The implication is that later, after copulation, the women too will have the *avagli* on them.

Or the song sung in Fore by women:

> *Arumata natatitani i:*
> *mempangk waiaguvinti*
> *galwaᶜa gama . . .*

"Yesterday you left me, [in the] sweat house, in the men's house. The *galwa*
penis-nuts!" ["Yesterday you left me (us) and entered the sweat house. The
nuts [22] of the *gama* tree are like your penes!" That is, "when you emerge from
the house you will imprint the *avagli* upon us."]

The following song is in Jate:

> *uhajari kajana ario*
> *uhajari kajana ario*
> *vemogi korikofani eae kajana*
>   *ario vemogi . . .*
> *matawu hajari kajana ario matawu hajari*
>   *ario waiamogi* [or, *vemogi*] *. . .*

"In your hand, hold the leaf . . . For men [it is like] wild ginger . . . [like a]
water reed, a leaf. In your hand, hold [it] . . ." [A man holds the vulva (leaf) of
a woman who sings, "Hold it as if holding on to a tree." She wants something
which the men have (i.e., the *avagli*). She says her vulva is "sweet" like ginger;
men eat it as they eat ginger to induce the *avagli*. "The base of the water reed
is like a vulva; you hold it as you hold the leaf of this plant."] [23]

The final example refers to a woman's desire for coitus with an *avagli* man:

> *O nenafuᶜnimokagio a'feregi a'feregetigi*
>   *ozuo mafitotajano*
> *erigete negowe erigete negowe*
>   *mafitotajanowe . . . o nenafu—*
>   *nimokagio a'feregi*
> *erinabebonimamau hanaglaglie*
>   *hanaglagligetea manegaipiana*
> *eritenegowe a'glitenegowe manegaipiana . . .*

"Oh, my *nenafu*, don't look back on the way to Mafitota [near Inivi]. Holding
you, I look on the way to Mafitota. Oh, my *nenafu*. My man, take [this] . . . look
back—[as you go to] Manegaipi. I hold you looking. . . . [From] Manegaipi [I
hold you] . . ." [A woman sings, "My *nenafu*, go along that track to Mafitota
without looking back: I cannot leave you. You come back; I keep this vulva for
you. You look back as you go to Manegaipi, but I hold you, I look (at you, I have
your *avagli* upon me).")]

[22] The *galwani* nuts are made into tops which are spun by hand around the men's house
during the season when taro and sweet potatoes are shooting; the top is a penis fertilizing
the earth. Jugumishanta told people how to do this.

[23] This song refers to Egopagiᶜja, wife of Agojagia at Tatagufa, and her *nenafu* Aninetipa,
also of Tatagufa. She sings it as the men emerge from the sweat house.

Conclusion

While the *avagli* concerns members of the patri-village, the pig festivals usually involve the combined efforts of the district as the main unit of ritual action. There are, however, further contrasting features. The pig festivals tend to cement unity within the district, giving shape, as it were, to the political unit. It is only the intermittent concerted efforts of this group, the combined effort of flute-playing over a period, which can bring the festival to a successful culmination. But this is not just the concern of the district alone. Other districts, too, are brought within its influence. It is convenient, almost a necessity, that barriers of hostility should be thrown down, at least nominally, for the time being; and in addition there is the attraction of pig meat. But the distribution itself, the attendance of an alien village or district at the festival, the participation in the common ceremony (if not the ritual), the acceptance of obligations between receiver and giver, do not in themselves constitute a binding tie of peace. There is no guarantee that the groups which come for the distribution will not prove actively hostile on arrival; a great deal depends on the quantities given. Formal statements indicate that weapons were temporarily laid aside, to be taken up immediately after the festival. In practice, however, this does not seem to have been so. Members of a host district may be reasonably sure of those they invite. (Ties of kin offer no certainty of good will; yet there must be a certain degree of confidence if the festival is to proceed.) But they are not certain of those whom they have not invited. A district may be at peace with many others, yet there are others with which it may be considered to be on hostile terms. But if we assume one function of this festival to be the maintenance of peace, another (the training for strength) is directly concerned with warfare or with potential warfare.

The *avagli*, in contrast, except among the Fore, affects only the one or more lineages within a village, but occasionally members of breakaway lineages are included. Among the Fore, the tendency seems to be for lineages of the same name within a district to come together in the hamlet or village occupied by one or more of them. In this way, in both cases, it reinforces the solidarity of the clan as the subpolitical unit. At such times, conflicts within the lineage or linked lineages are discouraged even more strongly than usual. Nevertheless, a ritual like the *avagli*, which concerns itself with physical strength and sexual attractiveness, offers further grounds for dissension between brothers: the *avagli* of one may extend further down his body, for instance, or his patterns be better, or he may be stronger or physically more attractive than his brother.

In considering together these two rituals and ceremonies, then, we can observe certain differences. The flute ceremonies are centered upon specific aspects of fertility, the growing of crops and pigs, libation to the Creative Beings, and the propitiation of the ancestral spirits. They find validation and precedent largely (though not entirely) in the mythology of Jugumishanta and Morufonu, and there is much secrecy where the flutes themselves are concerned. There is concern with both the natural and the social environment, a desire to bring about through ritual performance a state of affairs recognized as the "right" way of life. In the *avagli* ritual there is overwhelming preoccupation with physical strength and attractiveness, no supplication to spirit beings, and much less use of myth as a source of justification. Yet we may view the *avagli* as religious. It attempts to control the affairs of human beings through a specific ritual which, like cane-swallowing, might almost be declared a straightforward technique; but we cannot so dismiss it, because *avagli* itself provides a magically protective power through achieved strength. The instigation of the *avagli* is technical in a sense, for we must regard the mixture itself, the use of specific leaves, roots, and flowers, and the heat of the fire in the sweat house as factors which in themselves bring about the required physical condition. But once induced, once the body patterning is formed, the *avagli* has a particular magical significance; and the means by which this is achieved is ritual. This significance, too, concerns not just the individual but the village as a whole. It is seen as a necessary factor in village defense and offense. The *avagli* is associated with age-grading and with the ritual acts of cane-swallowing, nose-bleeding, and tongue-scraping. It involves not only the men undergoing it but also their womenfolk; for the ceremonial actions of the women, even if primarily oriented around mundane duties like providing daily food and water and finally a feast, are essential to the efficacy of the ritual.

Different as these rituals are, they have common elements which link them in expressing similar aims and motives and in giving direction to specific action. Both show preoccupation with acquiring strength, with becoming physically attractive, and both emphasize male dominance. There is association of ritual with women: the first *avagli* story quoted above attributes its inspiration to a woman's dream, reflecting the tendency noted in the mythology connected with the flutes and with cane-swallowing. It is to these aspects—male dominance, strength, physical attractiveness, aggression, and the interrelationship of the sexes—that much of our attention must be directed in this analysis.

In the mythology we are concerned with here, there is no formula for the carrying-out of ritual and no specific directions which must be adhered to in order to achieve the desired results. But the values which permeate it, the sentiments and the intentions, are indicated either directly or in symbolic terms. Although there is a stylized ritual procedure which may be classified as traditional, there is no mythological validation of that stylization. It is enough that it depends on the symbolic representations, on the basic values, and on the specific use of ritual objects. Apart from this, the detailed procedure to be followed is not stipulated; it is dependent on conservative opinion. Opinion, conditioned by the mythology, gives scope for individual interpretation; but this is interpretation within the confined range of personal, firsthand experience.

While certain features of ritual remain relatively constant, then, the over-all procedure varies from one performance to another. No two are exactly the same, nor is it essential that they should be. In other words, there is in this context no formalized "ideal" which may serve as a pattern in actual life; but there is a common acceptance of basic values in relation to it and awareness of appropriate sentiments, together with acknowledgment of the intention and the aim. Thus variation is present in the examples discussed, but it is most evident in the songs which are sung. Songs, although appropriate to the occasion, are attributed to contemporary individual "composers," the only exception being those sung during the instruction of novices in the course of the pig festival or those which form a part of the non-sacred mythology. While the songs make use of familiar concepts and ideas, they introduce an element of conscious variation with attitudes which, while conforming broadly to conventional standards, express at times what appear to be contrary points of view. We have seen some examples of these, revealing for instance a woman's curiosity about the nature of the flutes, women's knowledge of the flutes and their appropriate ritual, and the element of the erotic in the pig festival and the flute-playing as well as in the *avagli*. Yet there are precedents for such approaches, not least in the mythology. Women first owned the flutes, were associated with both cane-swallowing and the *avagli*; it was from them that men obtained much of the ritual. Further, some of the symbolism relates to peculiarly female characteristics. The aspect of eroticism is one outcome of the primary emphasis on strength and maleness.

The songs provide images of symbolic social significance—put forward by individual "composers," taken up on ceremonial occasions, and later reappearing in different combinations as new songs. They reflect opinions and attitudes which may or may not be generally held. They express individual points of view, but they also represent miniature "constructs" of specific situations. In this sense they perhaps mirror fairly convincingly the agreed-upon reality of such situations in such a way that there is little or no clash with ritual assumptions. But within their range they are pliable, and this pliability is in turn reflected in the ceremonial aspect of ritual action. It is this aspect which is most subject to change and, indeed, like the songs, is continually changing. There is through time a constant reshuffling of elements and of patterns, centered about the hard core of ritual expression. This is not simply a question of "ideal" in contrast with "actual." It is primarily a question of symbolic representations maintaining their dominant quality through time in the face of structural reorientation and cultural variability. This assumption needs further consideration.

Basic values, in their direct or symbolic expression, reinforce and maintain "the hard core of ritual expression." They are controlling factors in conformity, providing form and structural continuity through time. They relate to that element of consistency which insures social order. Yet are we right in regarding them as such factors of control? How do they respond to the forces of alien contact and deliberate external interference? Although at this juncture we cannot answer such questions, it is necessary that we should both ask and, eventually, answer them. For example, the focal point of the pig festival is the flutes—and the fact that they may not be seen by women. Should women see them, so it is said, men will lose their strength and the ritual and ceremonial associations become meaningless. Much the same would result should a woman observe a man in the process of cane-swallowing. Yet in the northern part of this region (among, for example, the northern Kamano) alien pressures have forced the public showing of the flutes to women, and cane-swallowing has been ridiculed and forbidden. All the rituals and ceremonies associated with these objects have consequently been abandoned, together with associated age-grading rituals and ceremonies. With the banning of fighting and warfare came the curtailment of the *avagli* ritual almost to the fringe of the area we are discussing. In such circumstances we cannot legitimately regard ritual action as possessing "hardness," when it will possibly be the first to feel the strain of alien pressure. The point is rather that dominant values, such as those we have been discussing here, are not reflected solely in the ritual; they do not disappear should the ritual disappear: they are apparent in all aspects of culture and of social life, a part of the belief system itself.

Part 3   Socialization and Enculturation

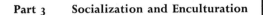

Chapter 6   The Road to Adulthood

We turn now to the regulation of conduct as part of the process of preparation for adulthood. Here we have informal and unreflecting, as well as conscious and deliberate, means of control operating during the processes of socialization and enculturation. Although socialization may be differentiated from the use of coercion in maintaining the social order, I do so simply as a matter of convenience for purposes of discussion. At the empirical level the two are not separable. A distinction can be drawn, however, between coercion which occurs within the range of conformity (that is, coercion, disciplinary action, injunction, and admonition, restraining variation in behavior and action within loosely defined limits) and coercion aimed at forcing back within these limits behavior and action considered dangerous or undesirable. We are concerned, at the moment, with the former.

Menstruation

In beginning our section with this topic, I stray from the conventional introduction to a discussion on socialization. Admittedly, of course, menstruation has little or no influence on the social life of the child in relation to its mother. My object is to focus attention on what is regarded as one of the most marked physiological differences between men and women. This difference is to some extent a symbol of the female's weakness, her subordination to the male, in the terms of the societies under review; but more subtly it symbolizes her strength. We have seen that this physiological function has a direct bearing on men's ritual life. Although it is possible to correlate certain male rites with menstruation, it would be oversimplifying the matter to offer this as a complete explanation.[1] Other factors are present, other concepts or values involved. Nevertheless, this is one interpretation put forward by men themselves when discussing certain aspects of initiation. It is mainly for these reasons that I begin with this point. Further, menstruation has to men[2] a dual significance. As a diffuse, generalized concept, it is ritually and symbolically expressive of life, energy, power, and strength; but in actual situations in relation to specific women, menstruation is potentially dangerous to man.

Most fathers, we are told, warn their sons by telling them the following story:

A man and his wife lived in a certain village. One day she went to the menstrual hut used by women married to men of her husband's lineage. Her husband was curious. Turning into a *wojafa* [red parakeet], he flew up to a tall flowering tree near the menstrual hut and perched there, eating the flowers. His wife came out of the hut and spoke to him, "Oh, my man, there you are eating *igatu* flowers. Where is my man?" As she looked at him, the bird fell to the ground and lay dead at her feet in the shape of a man.

[1] K. Read (1954, p. 26), speaking of the Gahuku-Gama, says: "Men recognize that in physiological endowment men are inferior to women, and, characteristically, they have recourse to elaborate artificial means to redress this contradiction and to demonstrate its opposite." I would not say this was consciously recognized by men in the region we are discussing: it might very well be a projection of our own feeling about this feature. Read adds (*ibid.*, p. 27) that "initiation rites in consequence serve the same purpose for the male as menstruation for women. The one is explained in terms of the other, and the same idea, the cyclical expulsion of blood, lies behind the men's ritual of nose-bleeding." "Men must thus practice nose-bleeding at regular intervals to ensure that they achieve physical maturity and superiority." See also M. Reay (1959, pp. 156, 162, 175–84).

[2] I am considering here primarily the beliefs and attitudes of men. All the information discussed here and in other sections was obtained from men, unless otherwise noted. There is thus a male bias. In interpretation this has been balanced to some extent by checking against material obtained by Catherine Berndt from women.

The warning continues:

If your wife goes to the menstrual hut, you must not seek her out and look at her face. It is not good that women should look at men at such times. She will stay there for five days and on the sixth will come to her own house; but five more days must pass before she may handle a man's food, and then only after washing her hands and rubbing them with aromatic leaves.[3]

During her seclusion a woman is said to "hide" from men, who are "afraid" of her. In practice, however, it seems to be only her husband who is "afraid." When she returns to her house and he asks her for food, she is said to protest, "I cannot give it to you; you must go to your own garden and obtain it for yourself." She may tell him, "You are a good [i.e. strong, attractive] man. If I give you food now, you will die. It will make you no good, weakening you; you will become like an old man, and then what? I would have to marry another man; and he might beat me, not look after me well. He might scold me. Let us stay together." A wife might speak in this way to a husband of whom she was fond, warning him of her dangerous condition. But there are women, so we are told, who do not like their husbands and do not warn them, giving them food from their hands. Then the man's belly fills with blood. He does not move outside his house, but sleeps. His body becomes weak, and he dies.

It is generally believed that intercourse brings on menstruation, although it is also said that at such times the moon "kills" or wounds a woman. A wife may advise her husband of her impending condition by telling him, "Your mother bore you; you have fingers and toes. I am about to go to the seclusion hut." A hint is enough for him, and he abstains from contact with her and eats no food from her hand for the customary period.

During a girl's first menstruation the procedure is more formal. She is taken out to a small house accompanied by her mother and sisters, while her father and brothers collect firewood and make her a fire. Much depends on whether she is already married. If so, she may be accompanied only by such of her close kin as are present in the village or district or by women married into her husband's lineage or clan. Although betrothed, a girl is often not married until she reaches puberty. Before this she may have been having sexual relations with her betrothed and with others; and, now, feeling at last the premenstrual pains, she tells her mother, "Such

---

[3] This does not conform with the results of personal observation. In no case noted did an adult woman remain in the menstrual hut for longer than four days at a time, sometimes three; and within a day or so after her return she would frequently be seen in the gardens obtaining food.

and such a young man [her betrothed] has copulated with me. I carry
blood.'' The mother or some other relative then takes steps to arrange
with the youth's parents for betrothal payments. In any case, whether the
man be married to her or merely betrothed, he must undergo a cleansing
rite. His father, mother, and brothers take him to one side of the village.
There they build a fire and heat stones, wrap them in special leaves and
grass, and pour water on them so that an aromatic steam rises. This is
blown over his body, removing the smell of menstruation which is said to
adhere to him and making him pleasantly scented. It also removes the
hagari and *fen* menstrual water-snakes, which take away with them on
their old skins all the undesirable substances. As they cast the old skins,
revealing new ones, so his own body and skin appear clean and fresh. He
squats over heated stones while his parents and brothers place another at
his feet. They prepare yams, taros, sweet potatoes, and bananas, spit salt
over them (as a protective measure), and give them to him.

The rite which the husband or betrothed husband undergoes has much
in common with the menstrual rite itself. Through it his body is being
cleansed, just as the girl's is being cleansed by the emission of blood.
Because he is linked with her in actual or potential marriage, this is for
him a period of danger; his strength must be preserved, and no harm must
come to his body. This performance need not be repeated for her subsequent periods. It is conventional, however, for a wife to make quite clear
her reason for going to the seclusion hut, in the way already indicated. It
might seem that this repetition is unnecessary, that it should be enough
for her simply to tell him where she is going. In the course of their age-
grading rites, men have learned the dangers of taking food from a menstruating woman. But the reiteration is explicable in the light of the
formal pattern of distrust between husband and wife, which may exist
alongside apparent affection. In thus warning her husband a wife is guard-
ing against the likelihood of blame should he become ill or be killed in
fighting. At the same time, we may perhaps read into her words a veiled
threat: ''I do not give you food from my hand at such a time, because I do
not want you to die; I do not want to marry another man who may beat
me and be cross without reason. But you are always good to me, you do
not ill-treat me, you look after me well. If someone copulates with me
against my will, I come to tell you immediately and you fight him. We
stay good together.'' Her attitude thus depends on his treatment of her;
it is in his own interest to treat her well. But this is not enough in itself,
and in any case men do not always restrain themselves in their dealings
with their wives.

As already noted, it is not external contact with menstrual blood which is dangerous but the fact that it may be taken internally. This is especially relevant to a husband, because except for his young sons he is normally the only man who consistently eats the food his wife cooks. The power a woman has over men during this period is dependent on the range of those to whom she customarily gives food. The men most vulnerable to her are those to whom she stands as wife, mother, sister, or brother's wife; but this potential danger receives less attention in the case of a mother or sister. Another point which receives little attention in discussion, both of actual cases and of the situation in general, is the belief that a husband who does eat food which has been handled by a menstruating wife or other woman may have to resort to cane-swallowing. The trouble is that he may eat contaminated food unknowingly, and for this or some other reason the cane-swallowing may take place too late to save him. No examples are available of a husband who has actually been in this predicament; but the assumption is that it might happen and that cane-swallowing will serve to prevent it.

Conventionally, a woman should abstain from sexual relations while she is in the seclusion hut and for perhaps six days afterward, until she is properly cleansed. Men say that no husband would think of having such a close association with his wife during that time; yet apparently this does not debar other men from doing so should she be willing. Conventionally, the seclusion hut, like the men's communal house, is forbidden to persons of the opposite sex; and women may retire to it when they want privacy or do not want their actions to be observed by the general community. Nevertheless, this arrangement is not always adhered to. For instance, women sometimes receive lovers there, even during menstrual periods; but it is impossible to estimate how often this takes place.

We can recognize in the actions and beliefs surrounding menstruation certain mechanisms of control which operate in a fairly obvious fashion to consolidate existing marital ties and to ameliorate interpersonal relations between husband and wife. As against these, however, a woman is believed to be capable of manipulating her "natural" powers to the detriment of her husband's lineage; and this assumption points to marital distrust and antagonism.

Birth and Growing Up

Among these people, the physiological facts of conception are relatively well known, at least in outline. The significance of coitus is acknowledged; and it is said that the accumulation of semen and menstrual blood combines to form the fetus. There are said to be no restrictions on sexual intercourse until the pregnant woman actually leaves for the seclusion hut; it may recommence approximately six months after childbirth, depending on personal inclination. An expectant father (though not an expectant mother) must observe a number of small taboos, mostly relating to gardening, the eating of certain vegetables, and so on. These taboos are intended chiefly to safeguard the child and facilitate its birth. For instance, the father must not drive a fence post into the ground, in case the mother's vagina be obstructed and the child be prevented from emerging; he must not loop or knot twine or creepers, in case the child should be strangled by the umbilical cord. But at least one prohibition is designed to safeguard the father's own well-being. For some time before and after the child's birth he should not eat edible leaves—because these, when cooked in the usual way, are said to resemble the feces of a young baby. By eating them, therefore, the father is in danger of losing his strength and becoming as weak as a baby.

I shall not dwell here on the topics of pregnancy and birth, beyond a few remarks to put this section in perspective. Nor shall I consider toilet training (which rarely begins until a child can walk), the details of a child's growth, the way in which he is fed and looked after by his parents, and the way in which he learns to distinguish various categories of persons (including categories of kin, or the contrast between kin and non-kin). Such a discussion would be entirely relevant to the present study but at the same time would add considerably to its length.

Briefly, then: when the unborn child's bones become strong it is said to ask itself, "Which road shall I take? The doorway is there below!" Then, in a normal birth, it emerges head first from its mother, finally being pulled out by the body and hands by another woman (the mother's sister, mother-in-law, co-wife, or even, conditions permitting, her own mother): the afterbirth is covered up in a nearby hole in the hut. On the day following the birth the child is rubbed with cassowary or pig fat, and intermediaries tell the father whether the baby is a male or a female. If it is a boy, the father may prepare a paste of animal fur and scraped bark and send it to the hut to be rubbed into the child's chin and upper lip to retard the undesirable growth of facial hair. On the third day the child drinks milk for the first time. On the fifth day his skin and face are said to look "good," and on the following day mother and child return home. There the father particularly may make a great deal of fuss over the child, rubbing his body with cassowary fat to make him strong so that he will grow quickly. Much the same attention is paid to a girl, but with less emphasis on the development of strength.

Socialization begins when the child is brought into the village from the seclusion hut, and this is acknowledged, too, when children are rubbed and massaged with special paste and fat containing bark which is said to have magical properties. (The same process takes place in regard to pigs.) It is the commencement of a practice which will be repeated intermittently until the boy is between about five and nine years old and begins the age-grading rites. For a girl, the procedure is more casual and more informal.

During their first few years most children, both boys and girls, are petted and made much of and rarely punished except in anger. They are decorated with shells and with armbands and necklets of pig or human genitalia to encourage growth. With all the indulgence lavished on them there seems to be some impatience where the matter of physical growth is concerned. They are regarded in a sense as small adults, pushed into situations that are adult or reflect adult activity; and one has the impression that they are expected to become full social adults in the shortest possible time. Small boys before their initiation, and young unmarried girls, sleep with their mothers in the women's houses. There is no restraint in speech or action before them. As babies and small children their genitalia are fondled. In the women's houses, as in the bush and in the gardens, they observe sexual intercourse and erotic play. They may be taken with their mothers to the gardens, and little girls are encouraged to help while they are still too young to take any serious part in garden activity. Small children dance with their elders during the ceremonies held in the village clearing; they watch erotic farces with evident enjoyment; they stand listening during fights between co-wives, between their parents, or others. They are excellent as informers and are encouraged to "tell tales." They hear the evidence given at informal courts and are present during the punishments that may follow. They are subject to relatively few food taboos until their initiation. The only obvious restrictions relate to keeping away from the women's seclusion house and from the ritual activities of the men; during fighting, their place is with the women. In other words, children are expected to be present, as interested spectators if not participants, during most forms of adult activity. Their play frequently centers on their own interpretation of such activity. Boys who have gone through the first age-grading rites often play various fighting games; but often, too, they play in mixed groups, when "wives" are allocated from among the small girls available and domestic life is acted out, with food-collecting, adultery, fighting, ritual, and ceremony. Boys may be reprimanded for choosing "wives" from among their sisters, but this is not taken seriously; there is a good deal of erotic play, and coitus is simulated as a matter of course.

Indulgence, in these circumstances, means the accentuation of desirable traits. I am ignoring here the frustrations that may arise through such indulgence and stimulation, as well as the differences in personality, birth order, and so on, between children, and speaking in general or "construct" terms. Indulgence, then, encourages the development of the ideal personality type in the growing boy or girl. The child most liked and admired by adults, particularly by his (or her) close male kin, is the one who commands attention by tantrums, by a dominating approach to his fellows, by bullying and swaggering, by carrying tales to his elders. These actions epitomize the characteristics so desirable in the "strong" man and woman—one who by forceful persistence can hold his own in all situations in which he or she may be involved. They are the mark, too, of the fighter and warrior. By such means responsibility is forced on the child, the small girl assuming in miniature the role of the adult woman, the small boy that of the adult man.

It would be grossly oversimplifying the situation to say that children are taught, informally, to want and to like what their elders consider they should want and like; but, very broadly speaking, this is the case. Small children seem to be on the whole secure in their parents' affection, whatever they do. The main exception lies in sudden outbursts of rage on the part of the parents, when a child may be violently punished for some trivial offense which at other times provokes little or no response, or perhaps even a favorable one. This apparent inconsistency on their part is possibly not interpreted as such by the child. On the contrary, violent physical action in the context of what may be loosely labeled "rage" or "excitement" (especially sexual excitement) is itself consistent and distinguishable from the relative mildness of action in other contexts. That is not to say that violent action is always associated with obviously emotional states. But children do seem to associate violent action with excitement, with "hot belly." This appears in their play and is intensified for the boys during their formal training for warfare.

Adults and older children pay the greatest attention to the active, self-assertive child who dominates his peers, encouraging him to develop these traits at the expense of others. The rewards are largely of an intangible sort. Material rewards, in a situation where durable goods are comparatively scarce but food normally plentiful, are of secondary importance.

The process is not so much one of deprivation of goods or affection but a more positive singling out of certain kinds of behavior for special praise. The child is afforded the gratification of being the center of attention, sought after to some extent by adults, dominating as best he can his peers and especially his juniors, and encouraged to identify himself with those who through these very traits dominate the adult scene. The pressure for power and prestige in interpersonal relation is thus overtly encouraged and, one might say, manipulated by adults, not only with both the training of children and the wider social issues in view, but also because they enjoy these situations for their own sake. From among all the varied behavior that a child observes, he is shown more or less consistently that certain attitudes and actions lead to rewards, intangible and otherwise, and moreover offer the only secure defense against similar attitudes and actions on the part of others. His selection of models for imitation, in varying degrees, follows broadly along these lines.

These attitudes are most consistently and intensively crystallized, in regard to specific persons, between young male children living in the same village and district and typically calling each other siblings. The same situation of mixed co-operation-competition persists into and through adulthood, reinforced by stronger social pressures, and on a more serious basis, frequently and conventionally within the same group of male kin.

The whole period of childhood, interrupted for the boy at initiation but for the girl continued until puberty or some little time before, dependent on betrothal, is one of learning through imitation, informal training, and spasmodic guidance. By the time a boy is ready for his initiation he is, in a manner of speaking, a replica of an adult, corresponding in some measure to the ideal personality type: what he will be, as an adult, is said to be already reflected in him. Although there has been no systematic training for aggressive action associated with male dominance, the pressures have been such that most children are already oriented in this direction when more deliberate and organized training begins at initiation.

Becoming a Social Adult

Formal instruction through the male initiation grades which follow this period, then, has already a substantial basis on which to work. The whole process ostensibly revolves around the teaching of novices, but this is not its sole concern. Men do not participate in its ritual and ceremony merely for the purpose of initiating boys or making them into men. From another point of view, initiation involves the coming together of people other than those of a single village or hamlet-cluster. Although it concerns primarily members and adherents of the lineages to which the novices belong, matri-kin and others from within and outside the district are also expected to attend. This presupposes that peaceful relations have been established, at least for the time being, between the districts participating. For just this reason, and because in many cases it is difficult to make peace, it is said that initiations are often carried out only in part, or protracted over a long period, or in some cases begin without the presence of certain matri-kin, and so on. Notwithstanding these difficulties, every boy has to undergo his age-grading rituals before being recognized as socially adult. Further, much preparation is entailed on the part of women, as well as expenditure in terms of pigs, vegetable foods, and small animals for feasting, shells, feathers, arrows, bush beads, and so on, as gifts. A boy's parents and lineage kin are concerned in this; and those who sponsor him are involved in a network of prestations.

Our first example is a brief construct of the various stages undergone by a novice; it refers more particularly to the southern Kamano, Usurufa, and Jate. The second example is a similar construct from the Fore. Both are summaries based on actual observation. We are not following the same novices throughout but considering rather the various sequences which took place while we were in the area, relating to different novices at different stages.

The Nose-Bleeding

A father massages his son at intervals to help him grow. When the boy is considered old enough, preparations are made for his initiation. Messages are sent to those kin regarded as personally involved. The boy's father has set aside pigs for a ritual feast and has made the boy orchid fiber armlets. The mother has made a special net bag for her son.

Several days before the first initiation the boy goes to sleep in the men's house. When the day comes, there is much preparation. Parents of the novices, all of whom should belong to one clan, are helped by members of the lineage or lineages and most of the adult women in the village. In addition there is an influx of visitors from other villages in the district and of members of adjacent districts who have kin ties with the novices and their parents. Firewood and stones are collected and the ovens prepared; food is brought in from the gardens, and pigs lined up and slaughtered. The majority of the men [except actual fathers], all fully armed in customary fashion, go down to a nearby river, choosing a shallow section where the banks are relatively close together. Here croton leaves and various bushes are arranged to fringe the banks. *Nenafu* of the novices bleed their own noses by forcing wild pitpit leaves up the nostrils, and the blood is dropped along the decorated fringe. A small bough shelter is made, and from it the sacred flutes are blown throughout the ceremony by two men who are lineage kin to the novices. Sugar cane is broken[4] and placed upright along the ground leading to this shelter, with lines of crotons. In front of it stands an elder of one of the lineages concerned, his face disguised by a mask of bush beads and shells; he is naked and holding a drawn bow; the point of another arrow pierces his foreskin, to which a horizontal length of sugar cane has been attached. (There are several variants of this.) He is there as guardian of the flutes and to strike fear into the hearts of the novices.

When the scene is set, men return to the village to catch the novices and bring them to the site. As they draw near, men standing in the water begin to bleed their nostrils; others cane-swallow and vomit; others, standing with drawn bows and arrows, enclose the whole site. The novices are brought up and shown the blood on the leaves; their guardians tell them, "You novice, your toe is no good! Take up that blood and eat it. Look, your toe is no good!" [That is, the novice is accused of menstruating and dropping the blood on the leaves.]

The novices are then taken toward the bush shelter in which the flutes are playing and behind which a bullroarer is swung. They are shown the guardian with impaled penis and told that he is a malignant spirit.[5] They tremble, urinating and defecating in fear.[6] Then they are seized from behind, their arms and heads held, and their noses bled. They cry out in surprise and pain, but the operation takes only a few minutes. By this time it is evening, and they are taken back to the men's house.

The ovens are opened and wooden platters arranged in rows. Pig meat, sweet potatoes, yams, taros, bananas, and sugar cane are heaped on them or arranged in mounds nearby. Meat is sprayed with chewed ginger and salt. Food is sent up to the novices, and all the men who participated in the initiation are given a share of the food—for example, those who held a novice and bled his nose receive a share, as do all others present, according to their lineage membership. During

[4] Sugar cane is broken ritually on many occasions, particularly during marriage and peace ceremonies. It is significant, too, as we have seen, in the *avagli*.

[5] Before the novices are taken out to the ground, their fathers tell them that the sound made by the swinging bullroarer is the voice of the spirit called *guᶜnagu gosunamu* (bullroarer old man). He is described as having no belly but a large mouth. He is blue in coloring and lives in the water, from which he emerges to catch and swallow small boys. The fathers then collect ripe bananas and taking them down to the water throw them in; this persuades the spirit to vomit the boys and accept the bananas instead. The spirit who lives in the water is, actually, the initiators who catch the boys and "release" them in return for their parents' gifts.

[6] Defecating and urinating during situations of emotional stress appear to be quite common—even, in some circumstances, during the sexual act.

M. Mead (1935, pp. 41–42) correlates low sphincter-control among Arapesh adults during highly charged situations with infant experience: "When an infant urinates or defecates, the person holding it will jerk it quickly to one side to prevent soiling his or her own person. The jerk interrupts the normal course of excretion and angers the child." This is not the case in the region we are discussing, where mothers allow babies to urinate and defecate over them with no apparent discomfort and ordinarily without bothering to remove them. Yet we find low sphincter-control in adulthood during disturbing situations —that is, in relation to extreme pleasure, fear, physical pain, or public humiliation.

the night the boys' parents come to the men's house, bringing armlets, net bags, shells, feathers, bush beads, and so on, with which they decorate their sons.

In the morning more pigs are killed by the parents—not only their own but others belonging to members of the novices' lineages. Ovens are built up and the meat cooked. Several net bags filled with meat are given to the novices to last for a few days. Vegetables have been cooked and placed in rows with the meat. The parents then call out to the boys' mothers' brothers who have helped in the initiation and make them gifts of food.

All the men now assemble with the novices either in the ordinary men's house or in one specially constructed. Women of the village, with others who are visiting, cook more pig meat. Men call out asking the women whether the meat has been prepared, and the women reply that it has. This verbal exchange is repeated again and again, until eventually they come up carrying the meat completely encased in bamboo wrappings. They speak to the men and novices: "We come with a little something. We women have carefully tended these pigs, we have looked after them all the time. Now we have prepared and cooked them. You eat." The men take the bamboo container and break it open, arrange the meat on platters and spray it with salt and ginger, then share it among all the men and women present.

While the feast is in progress, the men harangue the novices: "You must not steal food from another man. You must not abduct the wife of another man. You must not steal another person's pig, nor his fire. You must not do these things. But you may shoot men; you may use your bow and arrow. If a man uses sorcery against another, you may shoot him. You must be strong, you must be ready to fight. You must grow strong, you must be big so that you can do these things. You must look after your gardens. You must build fences about it; you must clear ground for gardening and dig furrows; you must plant crops. Thus you will grow to be a big man. . . . You must not eat from the hand of just any woman. If a woman offers you food, refuse it; if you eat from the hand of women [unspecified] you will lose your strength, you will become thin. You have hands, you have hair, you have good eyes, you are a young man. Cook your own food now and you will become big and strong, you will be like your fathers. You must not eat from the hands of young girls, only from those of an old woman or man . . . [repetition about taking food from the hand of a young girl]. You must not eat from the hands of young men, for they have been copulating with their wives; if you do, it will make your body just skin and bones." [Then follows, usually, much repetition relating to the above, pointing out the various circumstances in which it is excusable to kill men: these relate to wrongs against the lineage and clan, against the individual and his property, against his wife, his children, his pigs, and his gardens.]

The novices remain in the men's house and do not return to the women's houses to sleep. Here they are at the older men's beck and call; and they are responsible for keeping the men's house supplied with water and firewood. They eat food cooked by themselves or given them by the old men, by their mothers, or by older women. They are more consciously aware of their maleness. They continue to play much as before, except that usually they try to keep away from children of the opposite sex. This sexual division in play and ordinary association does not seem to be rigidly enforced, and the main point they must observe is in regard to the eating of food from young women and girls. But as they grow older they are more in the company of adult men; they spend more time about the men's house and join men in their normal activities. They are learning by example and direct training what is required of a man.

The Charcoal Period

Until he is adolescent, and facial hair appears, the novice attends the nose-bleeding rites of younger boys as well as of adults; he is present during part of the *avagli* ritual. At adolescence he is taken out into the nearby bush by the men and rubbed all over with charcoal.[7] This is the beginning of a series of tests designed to keep him strong through his active fighting career. Anklets and arm bands of plaited orchid cane, decorated with bunches of leaves, are placed on him, and a pig bone is put into his net bag. He remains for some weeks near the men's house, where he sleeps at night. Finally he is taken down to the water and washed, his old net bag is thrown away, and his anklets and arm bands are broken. Then follow a number of operations extending over a period of several months.

Although there is no hard and fast sequence, these rites usually begin with the piercing of the nasal septum: this is done with a salt-smeared bamboo sliver, which is then twirled around in the hole. Next comes the tongue-cutting. The boy is held from behind and his tongue kept in position by two twigs, one below and one above. It is then pierced at the right side and cut horizontally at its base to make blood flow. It is also rubbed with a rough-surfaced leaf; this causes the novice's body to tingle, and he shivers. (The same measure is employed in healing, to revive and strengthen the patient.) Later, the index fingers, as well as others, are pierced under the nail in order to draw blood, and the apex of the penis is rubbed with a rough-surfaced leaf or cut to allow blood to flow. This last is done in a series of actions when warriors dance before the youth, posturing with bows and arrows, and then shooting one arrow after another. They are both demonstrating the use of this weapon and encouraging the novices to ignore the pain. The novices must strengthen themselves, and this can be done only by submitting themselves to the rites through which they are now passing. The primary and avowed aim of the rites is to insure strength—which, in this view, can be achieved only through enduring pain and causing blood to flow. These rites do not end

---

[7] The charcoaling is also a prelude to the *avagli* rites; see above. The charcoal is prepared from charred *kunai* grass and bamboo leaves mixed with pig fat.

with initiation but must continue throughout every adult male's lifetime, especially during his active fighting period. It may seem then that most if not all of this ritual is oriented toward practical ends—not surprising in the light of the main stresses already discussed. It has, however, a further esoteric significance. The blood is a libation to the Creative Beings and to the ancestral spirits of the lineage. It is an offering to insure their spiritual patronage so that they will sustain the "giver." The periodic shedding of blood is also directly equated with female menstruation.

Toward the end of the "charcoaling period" the novices again have their noses bled, this time by the adult method: several leaves of wild pitpit cane are tightly packed together, tied, and sprayed with salt. The novice, standing upright, is held while the two packs are forced simultaneously up his nostrils. They are twirled, then withdrawn, and blood flows profusely. During the operation he may struggle and cry, calling out for his parents to help him.

At this time, too, boys are taught to use the cane for vomiting. At the end of each section of the long series of rites, some of which are repeated, admonitions similar to those mentioned for the nose-bleeding are reiterated.[8] Finally the youths are pronounced adults, ready to engage in interdistrict fighting. They have received training in the arts and magic of warfare. The management of weapons is, of course, something which they have been learning since early childhood and in which they have been constantly encouraged over the years. And they are told that they must copulate with no woman, nor may they marry (that is, consummate the union which normally, by this time, has already been arranged) until they have killed more than one man. A number of food taboos are associated with the various stages of initiation, and finally lifted with ritual eating of the forbidden food.

Penis-Bleeding

The youths have already been shown the sacred flutes; but it is not until he is a social adult, until he is ready for fighting, that a man may possess one himself and play it in the festivals. Even then possession of a sacred flute may be delayed until his prowess is proved and he succeeds in killing someone. It is at this time, too, that the youths join the older men in the sweat house, increasing their strength and physical attractiveness through *avagli*.

[8] During the "charcoal period" there are subsidiary feasts. The boy's parents, helped by his father's lineage kin, give presents to those who perform the operations; and on his emergence as a social adult, further gifts are made to all the men who have taken part.

They have reached the age of perhaps eighteen to twenty years. They are now ready to undergo an operation which, like other rites, will be repeated periodically over the years:

To the accompaniment of flute-playing, the novices are taken to the nearby river. Each leans backward across the lap of a brother [his own or another] and is grasped firmly around the neck; another holds his arms while his legs are opened, flexed, and held securely. An elder then inserts into the penis duct a length of "spear" grass which has first been treated with ashes.[9] It is pushed in as far as possible, and the novice cries out that it feels as if it is reaching the anus. It is then withdrawn and replaced by a special twig together with a length of wild orchid fiber, which is twirled around until the youth, crying in pain, urinates. It is then removed, sprayed with salt, and reinserted until he defecates, crying in great pain;[10] but there are no cases reported of fainting. This procedure is said to cause an emission of seminal fluid which, with the discharge of blood, is caught in bamboo and used to anoint arrows to insure that they always find their mark.[11] After this operation the youth is carried to the men's house, where he sleeps for about six days, eating little food. When urinating he must hold his penis because of the pain.

After an interval, usually of a few weeks, he is taken out to undergo this operation for a second time. Special leaves are bunched together, tied to the size of a pencil, and forced up the urethra. This time, although it is painful and the man cries, he can also speak. He may say, for instance: "Oh! I eat your wife's vulva. Let me go! Let my penis alone—it pains! I eat your wife's menstrual blood. Let me go! You are copulating with my penis [that is, pushing the leaves up and down in the penis duct, which is likened to a vagina]. Let me go! Mother, come and hold me! Father, come and hold me!" He continues crying in this way. Then the leaves are removed and blood flows, with seminal fluid. He is carried back to the men's house.

This is followed by a further, similar operation. The apex of the penis is cut with a bamboo knife. The thin sharpened bone from a pig's leg is first inserted into the duct, then replaced by bundles of leaves, the size of a pencil, which are forced up the urethra and twirled around by hand. Seminal fluid and blood flow and are collected. Again the youth cries out to the operator in much the same was as before, adding, "When you copulate with your wife, I eat the seminal and vaginal fluids which drop from her! Let me go!" Again he is carried to the men's house to recover. His tongue is then scraped with a rough leaf until blood flows,

[9] The spear grass may afterward be worn, placed in the hair or headband above the forehead so that it protrudes outward.

[10] Men may involuntarily defecate under duress—during the penis insertion or during, for example, the cutting of the tongue. The feces are collected and used in smearing arrows to insure accuracy of aim; but it is said also that the feces may be removed surreptitiously and used in sorcery against the warriors.

[11] Arrows are dipped in this substance and then placed on platforms above the central fireplace of the men's house; the constant heat is said to accentuate their potency. During serious fighting they are shared out among members of the lineage and when shot "always" find their mark.

and he uses the cane for vomiting. When he has completely recovered and his penis is healed, men of his lineage prepare a banana cake which is cooked in lengths of bamboo and given him to eat, to strengthen his body.

This marks the completion of his initiation, and he is looked upon as a man.[12] One is to assume that at some time during this period the youth has killed a man, for having eaten the banana cake he may receive his promised wife and copulate with her. The avowed object of these rites is to make the novice strong, so that he may be able to withstand pain, and to make him a proficient warrior. The insertion of objects into the penis duct is said to make the penis itself strong; for if this is strong, so will be the arrows he shoots, directly aided by the substance with which they are anointed. The banana cake itself is a symbol of maleness, as the bananas used are likened to penes. After this, the periodic operations must be performed by himself voluntarily, without show of weakness.

The Fore Initiation

Before discussing some of the points raised here, let us consider briefly a Fore initiation sequence. This example is from a series which took place in the Busarasa district. The procedure is not uniform throughout the region, but the broad pattern is all that concerns us here.

When the pig festival draws near, it is agreed that the first initiation ceremonies can begin. The boys are taken to the men's house. Women married into the novices' lineages are asked to make net bags, orchid fiber arm bands, and so on. When this is done, the men build a special house with a central pole of strong wood, which symbolizes the strength of the lineage, and a stockade is also constructed around it. Special leaves and crotons, and a special variety of sugar cane, are collected and fastened to the central house pole; these give sustenance to the pole, strength to the lineage. Firewood is cut and stacked, together with oven stones. People are then summoned from the nearby districts, particularly matrikin (such as mothers' brothers) and various nenafu of the novices. When all have arrived, the first night is spent in talking and sleeping. In the morning pigs are killed[13] and cooking commences.

The banks of a shallow creek have been decorated with an edging of special leaves. The mothers' brothers "catch" the novices and leave them with their

---

12 The completion should also be marked by a feast, when pigs are killed by the youth's parents and the meat distributed among those who have helped him during his initiation. Some is formally given to the youth himself, his father telling him: "You are now a big man: you must kill men. We have given you food to eat, we have looked after you. Now you must look after us. All this we have done for you, and looked after you. When we grow old, you must attend to our fire and water and give us food . . . ."

13 During the pig festival, the feet are cut first, to the accompaniment of singing, and the blood falls to the earth as a libation. The intention here is to increase the supply of pigs.

elder brothers [actual and classificatory] while they themselves go to the ritual ground and bleed their noses over the leaves. Then they bring the boys down. The scene is very much the same as that already described. The boys are shown the blood and told "Women's toes are always no good [that is, they are always menstruating: this is a form of circumlocution]. This is the blood of women: you may eat it. You are not to get angry. You are not to say the name of this blood." Then the novices are held and cane is inserted up their nostrils so that blood flows. Following this, each novice is handed a length of cane and told to swallow it in the approved fashion, to cleanse himself because he has eaten menstrual blood.[14]

Some take the cane boldly, saying, "I can eat it. I am no woman." Others show some hesitation and are held by their brothers while the cane is forced down their throats by a mother's brother. Occasionally a novice shows real fear. In such a case the men desist and symbolically hold the cane against his chest, "marking him," observing that later on when he is a big fellow he will do it properly—he may now see how it is done; and they hang the cane about his neck.[15] The reason for the vomiting is then explained to the novices, and they are told how dangerous it is to eat from the hand of a woman. They are also warned not to eat food given to them by their mothers: "The moon strikes her, and she goes to the seclusion hut. Do not eat food from her hand, or it will turn to blood in your belly. Vomit it out by using the cane. When you nose-bleed, this is menstruation, too. Always cane-swallow afterward. . . ."

In the main village the novices' parents have been preparing the oven. When everything is cooked, they spread out large leaves on which they place sweet potatoes, yams, sugar cane, taro, and pig meat, and spray salt over them. Then they decorate themselves with shells and feathers. Women [who are mothers, sisters, nenafu, nogago, actual and classificatory, to the boys] decorate themselves with crotons, shells, and feathers, take up bows and arrows, and hold the long wooden shields. Then, leaving the village, they go toward the track leading to the ritual ground and when about halfway there hide in the surrounding kunai grass like warriors waiting to ambush an enemy.

The men bring the novices along the track, singing [in Fore] and dancing as they come:

> Warebuna runtu . . . runtu wai tunturuntu o . . .
> wajau . . . iwu . . . aiaju . . .

"Red warebu leaves we bring!" ["We bring the novices back: their skin is red like the warebu leaf—it is good!"]

As they reach the place where the women are hidden they pause. The women jump out of the kunai grass, "frightening" them. They shoot dummy arrows at them and act out a typical ambush scene, driving the men back and being driven

---

[14] In the examples I have seen in the northern part of this region, around Kogu and Kemiju, this rite was not undergone by novices until their charcoal period. It does, however, vary. The contention is that they had better know how to cane-swallow as early as possible.

[15] They do not force the novice to swallow the cane unless they are sure he will not clench his teeth on it, biting through the cane so that it remains in the stomach.

back themselves. They call out to the men, "We gave birth to those boys; but now you have caught them. You have spoilt their nostrils; you have beaten our children. And now you take them to the men's house. They do not come back to us to sleep in our houses—you stop them from doing that! When they were small they stayed with us. Now they go to the men's house." The women work themselves into a conventional fury, and both sexes appear to derive a great deal of enjoyment from this mock fight. Finally the men dance forward, with the women behind them, and enter the village. They take the novices to the men's house.

The food is then arranged and distributed. Large portions are given to the novices' mothers' brothers and to all those who helped in the initiation or in the preparation of the ground: to the boys' brothers, sisters, *nogago*, *nenafu*, and so on, male and female. Pig meat is also given formally to the novices themselves. That evening the boys' parents fill net bags with pig meat and with shells, arm bands, feathers, and so on, enter the men's house; there they hang the bags around the walls, and decorate their children to the accompaniment of songs.

> *Mamuwe nora mamuwe warara isugo . . .*
> *asogowa uwe . . . uje aje . . .*

"Parakeet and hornbill feathers. [We are] fastening . . ."
[Strings of parakeet feathers are fastened on the novices as headbands.]

> *. . . kabari migarinari oawo . . .*
> *susuke o migarinari . . .*

"Red bird feathers . . . [We] put around you . . ." ["As we put these red feathers around you, so will you stay here like these bird feathers; your skin is like these feathers."]

The parents leave, and a series of scenes is now enacted. A fully decorated man carrying bow and arrows comes stealthily through the doorway of the men's house. Reaching the central pole, he breaks off some of the sugar cane attached to it and, peering about to make sure he is not observed, disappears through the door again. The men turn to the novices and say, "You must not break another man's sugar." Another man enters the house and coming up to the central pole looks at the remaining sugar cane. "Who has cut my sugar?" he demands and, angrily seizing his weapons, runs from the house.

Various edible leaves and pitpit are "planted" in the ground around the central fireplace, including sweet potatoes with their spreading leaves above the surface of the ground. "Look at this" the men tell the novices. A man enters the house. He comes over to the "garden," digs out the vegetables, puts them hastily into his net bag, and goes away. Another man enters to find his vegetables stolen. In a rage, he marks with bamboo sticks the places from which they have been dug; he will not withdraw these until he is compensated or has his revenge. The warrior leader of the lineage now talks to his novices, threatening them with a firebrand. "You must not steal from another man's garden. You must not take another man's wife. If you do you will be killed. When you were a small boy you stole; now it is different. We have made your nose bleed, and quickly you have grown big. You are now like a man. You must think of gardening; you must hold well this pitpit, these sweet potatoes, these edible leaves and sugar cane; hold well in your hand bananas and pigs. Plant your gardens so that food comes up and you will always eat. [That is, you must possess good gardens and pigs and not neglect them.] If this food does not come up, it is your own neglect and you will think of stealing. If you think of stealing from other men's gardens, you will steal their pigs and their wives. Listen to our words. If you do these things you will not live a long time, you will die soon. What we tell you is good; hold it in your bellies, and you will stay good. This talk is finished.

"Now hear this other talk. Do not eat from the hand of your mother, nor from that of your father [the food may be tainted through his copulation with his wife]. Take up your own net bag and go to your parents' garden and there collect vegetable food and cook it yourself. If a young woman offers you food and you eat it, your skin will become no good. You must not eat from such a woman; her hand is taboo. If an old woman offers you food you may eat it. There is only one word: you may eat from the hand of an old woman [16] or from an old man. If you do this your skin will be good, your body strong. Quickly you will become a big man. You will kill men, and we will stay by your feet; we will stay by your hands. This talk you must not lose; hear this with your ear. Some boys hear this and hold it; others do not hear it. . . . This talk is finished.

"Now hear this other talk." A man dressed as a young girl enters the men's house, followed by a man who makes advances to "her." He pulls aside her grass skirt and pushes her to the ground: with erect penis he mounts her and pretends to copulate. From the doorway of the house the "girl's husband" watches: he draws his bow. The young man sees him and jumps up, grabbing his weapons: the girl tries to escape, and the two men fight. They leave the house. The warrior leader continues to admonish the novices. "If the wife of another man comes to you, resist her. Do not hold women when you are in the garden. If you meet a young woman, do not look at her face; if you look at her and she looks at you, then you will copulate. If you do this, something will come up all over your skin, your body will be spoilt. Hear what we say.

"Now another talk comes up. When you go to the bush to hunt, kill small animals and birds and bring them back to give to the elders, to the old women, or to the young men or to small children. Do not eat them yourselves. If you do this everyone will be friendly toward you.

"Help your father in making fences around the gardens and in cutting sticks for the support of sugar cane. Help your lineage in making the stockade around the village. . . . Some boys hear what we say, others do not."

The warrior leader turns to the older boys who are also in the men's house: "We talk to you young boys, too, not only to these small boys. Listen to what we say. If you meet a woman as you walk along a bush track, stand to one side keeping your weapons well away, let her pass without looking at or talking to her. If you touch her inadvertently, she will quickly tell her husband and he will shoot you. If a woman likes you and holds your hand, ask her, "Why do you hold my hand?" Go quickly and tell her husband, so that he may ask her why she does this and beat her. Hold well what we tell you, and your body will not pain. If

[16] Some say, however, that the novices should not eat from the hand of any women. While they reject food from young and middle-aged women, they may pretend to take it from old women, feeling "sorry" for them, but must secretly throw it away.

you do not listen to us, you will not live long. He who listens to us will live long, and will die an old man. . . .''

For the next six or seven days the novices remain in the men's house. Their brothers prepare food from their parents' gardens and cook it in an oven nearby and give it to them. During this period, too, the evenings are spent in singing, which increases the strength of the novices.

After the seventh day all the pig meat is assumed to have been eaten, and the novices' parents come to the men's house and speak to them: "Up to now you have eaten food cooked only in an oven. If you had eaten vegetables cooked in the ashes of a fire your skin would be like ashes." The novices are then taken into the bush, where a platform is built and vegetables placed on it. Sweet potatoes are cooked in an open fire and given formally to the novices with pig fat. The taboo on food cooked in the ashes is broken.

This section of the initiation is now completed, and the novices' parents may resume sexual relations. They have abstained during the initiation period, to avoid contaminating the pig meat they give the boys.

From this point, the sequence of initiatory rites is similar to that already outlined. There is the "charcoal period," which includes further nose-bleeding, the scraping of the tongue with a rough-surfaced leaf, and the piercing of fingers beneath the nail. This is followed by the introduction to the sacred flutes, when the novices are beaten until blood flows from cuts. They are told:

"Blood flows from your body, but you must not get angry. Your mother, your sister, your little brother will look at this and ask you how it happened. You are to answer that a branch has fallen on you and caused these scratches, or that you fell from a tree when cutting wood. You are not to tell them that you have been beaten. If you do, we shall shoot you. You are not to tell them about the flutes; these do not belong to us alone, but to all the men. . . .''

(But it is not until their final initiation that they may play the flutes.) Among the Fore there is no penis-bleeding or cutting of the penis. During this period they concentrate on nose-bleeding and cane-swallowing, on strengthening the novice's body, and on purifying it from time to time; and there are a number of food taboos. At this time, too, novices attend their first *avagli* rituals.

When another pig festival is held, the initiation continues in the way discussed in Chapter 5. The novices are now past adolescence, and after decorated arrows have passed between them and their *nogago* (mothers' brothers' wives) they are considered old enough to shoot men. The presentation of arrows is a formal acknowledgment of this new status. About five days' later the novices are taken down to the river, where the warrior leader and older lineage members prepare a large banana cake, approximately five by two feet in size. This is cooked in an oven, cut into sections, and sprayed with chewed bark. The novices are washed and clad in new skirts. They nose-bleed by inserting the special pads of leaves smeared with salt. Their net bags are filled with banana cake, the eating of which is said to have a strengthening effect, and they return to the village as men. A further series of rites is held periodically, mostly a repetition of the above, but involving a greater degree of participation on the part of the youths. They are not full participants, however, until they have proved their prowess in warfare and are finally married.

Puberty Rites of Females

The ceremonies and rituals carried out by women focus attention primarily on distinctive physiological characteristics. Broadly speaking, the rituals consist of certain actions clustered around menstruation and childbirth, features regarded as parallel and in some measure complementary to the male initiation rites. Their center of interest is the seclusion hut, from which men are normally excluded, as are women from the men's house. We can draw a fairly clear demarcation between the two realms, especially when we consider the local view of the weakening effect of woman on man. This may appear artificial when their interdependence in all social activity is seen in total perspective; nevertheless, without extending the argument at this juncture, we can say that the two spheres, the male and the female, are seen as opposed, not because they represent direct opposites but primarily because of their similarities. Men use the physiological facts of menstruation and childbirth, translated into symbolic forms, to achieve strength; women use these same features in a direct and natural way to achieve strength for themselves. There is a conflict here between the natural or "real" and the derived or symbolic. For example, women may be "dangerous" to novices during certain physiological crises; yet, in symbolic terms, it is exactly from these crises that the novices derive their strength. Menstruation is dangerous to the young man, yet his well-being is attained through its acknowledged equivalent. Extending this, we can see a more obvious antagonism developing when the strength achieved by either sex is used (or thought to be used) for different purposes: the male's strength used in defense of his lineage, his village, and his district, the female's in support of her own patri-kin. While this distinction is not so sharply defined in actual situations, and is modified by other factors, it receives, nevertheless, considerable attention.

The female counterparts of male initiation and religious ritual are, then, mainly the physiological events of menstruation and childbirth. The actions relevant to such events are themselves considered to be ritual insofar as they are classified with other actions which can be so described, although they do not represent ritual in our terms. Songs and some dancing are associated with them.

When a girl's first menstruation is thought to be imminent, other women resident in the village [that is, her own relatives or her husband's] take her to the seclusion hut. Here she is decorated, and some dancing takes place: women dress as men and posture with bows, arrows, and shields. Leaves of various kinds have been collected. The girl lies on her back, held by another women, while her sister [actual or classificatory] inserts into her vagina a tightly wrapped wad of leaves, twirling it around and working it up and down. Each of a number of leaf wads is inserted in the same way, until finally a certain rough-surfaced leaf draws blood; it is followed by the leaf of a variety of red croton. Blood is now flowing profusely.[17] This is to induce the menstrual flow; it is also said to be like coitus, which brings on menstruation. Afterward, the girl's nose is bled in the same way as in the case of male novices. A few food taboos are associated with these rites. The shedding of blood has the same significance for the female as for the male. It not only induces the menstrual flow, which is secondary and would in any case be accomplished naturally; it is primarily to make her strong, to improve her bodily attraction: her skin glows "blood red." In order to maintain this strength and physical well-being, both vaginal- and nose-bleeding are carried out periodically. This usually takes place after menstruation and childbirth, for strength and purification, but also before marriage, or when a woman is angry and wishes to fight or intimidate people.

Although we may observe some basic similarities between male and female initiation, the former has a far wider range. The reason for this lies primarily in the different emphasis on training. In the case of females, training is largely informal and unorganized. The only exception takes place shortly before her marriage and may or may not coincide with her puberty ceremony. She is subjected then to a series of admonitions, but these are briefer and rather more casual than in the case of males, and the whole ritual is shorter and less dramatic. The control mechanisms operative in informal training involve both girls and boys, but in the case of boys are channelized and crystallized through initiation. This difference is linked with differences in the ascribed roles of the sexes in adult life.

Implications

Nearly all the ceremonies and rites which have to do with age-grading may be viewed, both explicitly and implicitly, as they are by the people

[17] If a man sees or hears of this, it is said, he will be killed by the women through sorcery. Nevertheless, it is from men that the above information was obtained, conforming with that observed and collected from women by Catherine Berndt. Cf. M. Mead (1935, p. 93).

Distribution of pig meat at festival in Sosofe village (Kemiju), mentioned in Chapter 5. In the background is large "rest house" for visiting patrols.

A young novice at Pintagori. From his headband protrudes a sharpened stick for nose-bleeding (see Chapter 6) or for *sangguma* sorcery (see Chapter 11).

Initiation sequence in Busarasa. Armed men line pathway decorated with crotons and salvia, leading to place where cane-swallowing and nose-bleeding take place (see Chapter 6).

Entrance to sacred initiation ground in Kogu. Armed guardian holds shield on left and another shield is used as barrier on right. Other guards line decorated path leading to scene of the ritual.

Men playing the sacred flutes move down pathway between rows of armed guardians (Busarasa). They crouch as they play, hiding their faces with foliage.

Flute playing during initiation sequence in Kogu, in shaded creek. The flutes are thinner than those used at Busarasa.

themselves, in three ways: first, in terms of man's relationship to woman; second, as an esoteric exercise leading to the achievement of strength; third, as a force in maintaining the social and cultural status quo. Each receives different stress and each is a corollary of the other. The third is the framework within which the series is constructed; the first, the fabric from which it is constructed; the second, its dominant and derived feature, is its central theme.

Man's relationship to woman has been dealt with sufficiently for our purpose; we need only underline some of the empirical points. All forms of ritual bleeding are equated with menstruation. We have seen that during the ritual the novice is told to eat the symbolic menstrual blood; in the Fore ritual, this is followed immediately by cane-swallowing and vomiting for purification. In the more advanced phases of penis-bleeding, the verbal exchanges between novice and operator have an obvious sexual connotation. It is not simply a matter of using obscenities during emotional and physical stress: the words and phrases are conventional and do not cover the whole or even part of the range which could be classified as obscene. A sexual association is inferred between operator and novice, connoting the kind of situation in which such remarks are appropriate. The insertion of the leaf pad rod into the novice's penis, and the actions of the operator during this process, are viewed as coitus, the novice being the "female"; the novice then threatens to assert his manhood. At the same time, the pain is so great that the novice offers to humiliate himself, if released, in what must be considered an extreme degree. Symbolically equivalent as man's initiation is to woman's natural physiological crises, the antagonistic elements are obvious. Outside the ritual ground this is formally apparent only when the women dressed as warriors meet the men on their return and wage a mock fight, calling out their reasons for doing so. They are angry because the novice has been removed from their sphere of influence; but this is a conventional anger which is designed primarily for a release of tensions, an opportunity for the women to assert their point of view and to impress on the men their indebtedness to females. (This is a feature which appears, for example, during the first nose-bleeding ritual and the subsequent feasting when the women bring the men pig meat wrapped in a bamboo container.) But in most other contexts associated with age-grading there is an interdependence between the sexes. Women reinforce the customary male attitude. Certain female relatives co-operate with the men as an essential part of the ceremonial content of male age-grading. Male-female antagonism or apparent conflict is not incompatible with mutual co-operation and common interests and aims.

The second element, the attainment of strength, is the most obvious feature. It is, one might say, carried almost to the point of obsession. There are reasons for this. The object of most of the age-grading ritual and ceremony is to provide or develop strength, fighting prowess, and physical perfection in all participants, although the novices are the chief concern. In this respect, it is expressive of those basic values already noted, and here made more or less explicit. The blood drawn from various parts of the body is, as we have seen, a libation to the Creative Beings and to local and lineage spirits, to enlist their help and to counteract antagonistic influences. In this sense the rites are hortatory and propitiatory. But they have the direct practical aim of toughening participants and novices, and it is this which receives most emphasis. It illustrates, one may say, the achievement of strength through pain and physical suffering. This is not my interpolation of an alien viewpoint; explicit statements are made by the people themselves, particularly during age-grading. Over the years the physical pain endured is intensified, culminating in the rite of penis-bleeding. Repetition of such operations develops, not immunity to pain, but what appears to be (with some exceptions) acceptance, accompanied by a show of indifference. From first nose-bleeding to first penis-bleeding covers possibly ten to twelve years, during which more or less formal training takes place. The novices' bodies are being constantly strengthened; they are becoming warriors, the purpose for which they are being trained. This is particularly noticeable in the final penis-bleeding rites, when not only the penis is said to be strengthened by such an operation but also a man's arrows and his shooting ability. The man with a strong penis is a strong warrior.

The third aspect of age-grading is its relationship to the status quo, its concern with conformity within a certain range, its maintenance of established custom, and its embodiment of a consciously expressed ethos. Some of these elements have already been considered. We must underline the obvious point that initiation has wider implications than its expressed aim of developing strength. The rituals are associated with the increase of crops and pigs, with the maintenance of the physical world in its accustomed form. In this respect its expresses the rhythm of nature linked with the periodic occurrence of ritual, like the menstrual rhythm of the female. But it also concerns the maintenance and continuance of the social order. The values articulated (directly or symbolically) in ritual and ceremonial procedure are those which these people find important. They are not confined to this sphere alone but are apparent throughout social life. But it is in the matter of organized training to insure adherence to what is considered to be the established way (conformity, in other words) that this aspect is clearest. We have already seen that this is achieved by age-grading, by subjecting novices to certain ritual actions and operations, by drawing them into ceremonial activities, by concurrently training them in fighting methods and inculcating attitudes and sentiments which stem from basic values. All this is instruction and guidance, formally conceived and reinforced by coercive measures. In addition, there is the use of injunctions and admonitions, of particular interest here; but before they are discussed one further point must be mentioned.

All males undergo initiation; there are no exceptions. No cases of evasion were mentioned to us, and reference in mythological or pseudo-historical tales are extremely rare. There are, however, allusions to the severity of earlier initiation rites and their subsequent modification. There is, too, recognition that not all boys or youths can participate fully (that is, some are not physically able or so inclined) in certain of the rites, and not all will be fitted for active fighting. For example, in the case of cane-swallowing, novices who express great fear are merely marked symbolically with the cane on chest and belly. In certain cases the severity of nose-bleeding, tongue-cutting, and penis-bleeding is also relaxed, depending on the attitude of the novice. This is not just a result of indirect alien contact, for it is apparent too in the Busarasa-Moke districts where indigenous features of initiation have been virtually unaffected.

During the "charcoal period," older men decide which youths will be the fighters and warriors, the ones who will defend them in times of need. Those with effeminate faces, or those who have not stood up to the ritual operations, are not expected to be of much help here. The fact that this variation is recognized, that there is no enforcement in these matters, is of paramount significance, particularly in a society oriented toward ideals of male aggressiveness and dominance. It means that even in so conventional an institution as age-grading, choice is allowed: choice within the range of maleness on the one hand and outside that range on the other. This would seem to suggest that the processes of socialization have failed in their object of establishing conformity within a certain range; and it raises the question of whether the effeminate youth, or the novice who will not or cannot stand up to the necessary tests of manhood, is considered a deviant. In local terms, he is not. He is, rather, a person who has chosen a certain course. He is not ostracized. There is no effort to make him conform or to punish him because he chooses a different way. He is not actually classed with the women. In certain circumstances, he may still fight; he still joins in the activities of men and also marries; but he is by nature mild and non-aggressive. Such men, however, are few, in any one district not usually more than two or three. They are men for the most part inconspicuous in village and district affairs, rarely making their presence felt.

There is another type, the "no-good" man. He again cannot be classed as a deviant, although he may be physically undersized, have bad skin, be untidy in his appearance, wear old skirts, not be accomplished as a warrior, and so on. There seem to be always at least a couple of such men in each district. Sometimes they remain like this all their lives, the butt of others; but just as often they may vindicate themselves and pass into the category of the ordinary man.

An intrinsic part of these initiation processes is the formal verbal instructions or admonitions, repeated over and again. They are similar in form to certain African instructions or speeches,[18] being phrased in an emphatic and categoric style: the values inherent in them are laid down for the hearers to accept. In Firth's terms these would be "moral rules" relating to what kinds of conduct are right and what are wrong.[19] Through their formalized expression they are necessarily stereotyped and are, indeed, meant to be no more than this. They are admonitions exhorting novices to do certain things and avoid others: they give advice and they warn, stating what will happen if the admonition is neglected. Remarks in this style are usually couched in terms of "Do not do this, but do that," or "Do this but not that," "If you do that, this will be the result of your action," and so on. Thus all have both positive and negative facets. Notwithstanding, we can distinguish two broad categories, one associated with positive sanctions, the other with negative sanctions.[20]

The positive admonitions are couched in such terms as: be strong, be ready to fight, kill men, listen to what we say, help your father and his lineage, attend to your gardens and stockades, and give food to others. These are the broad principles on which men are exhorted to base their actions. Novices are not told whom to kill and why, whom or when to fight. The implication is, anyone outside the district, anyone outside a certain range of kin; and the reasons for and circumstances of fighting and killing are assumed to be understood. The first three are associated with the dominant trend. Being strong, attaining warriorhood, is itself its own

---

[18] Cf. G. Herzog in S. Sargent and M. W. Smith (1949, p. 101). M. Reay (1959, p. 172) also mentions the lecturing of Kuma novices.

[19] R. Firth (1951, p. 183).

[20] A. R. Radcliffe-Brown (1952, p. 205).

reward. It is, for men, the most desirable of all conditions, and it has the approval of the majority. But failure to achieve this status, to carry out this injunction, involves no direct negative sanction. All men are committed to this course of action because they are within this particular social order, but all do not necessarily fulfil these requirements. For the few who do not, there is no sanction except public opinion, and this operates only in oblique fashion. Such an achievement appears to be so highly valued that there is no need for enforcement or punishment in case of nonconformity. Again, with the remaining positive admonitions, there is the idea that these are good in themselves, they are what all men will automatically do—in their own interest, and in that of their lineage and district. But evasions do occur, and failure in this respect brings no corrective measures, no real sanction.

The negative admonitions can be divided into two groups: those relating to undesirable results from action against a person, and those relating to undesirable results from the transmission of food, under certain circumstances. The first concerns stealing, association with another man's wife, and relations with young women and/or all women. These features are impressed upon novices not only by emphatic verbal warnings but by the acting out of scenes which show the repercussions likely to result. Implicit in such action and verbal statement is the understanding that the admonition relates to behavior within the political unit, not outside it. Failure to observe such injunctions arouses punitive counteraction where stealing and interference with another man's wife are concerned: the sanction involves both disapproval and action against the offender. Association with young girls and women is seen in terms of a weakening effect on the novice. Fear may prove a sufficient deterrent, requiring no further reinforcement; but attraction between the sexes, and the encouragement of impulsive behavior from early childhood, may render this particular admonition ineffective as long as the second category is not involved.

The second set of admonitions seems to be the most important because it is concerned primarily with the development and preservation of strength, of all manly qualities, of ability and prowess in warfare, status and prestige, attractiveness to the opposite sex, and so on. Such admonitions concern the eating of food from the hand of any woman, unless she is elderly (past menopause), irrespective of whether or not she is menstruating. Here is not just fear that some power antithetical to strength may be transmitted through food taken from the hand of (or cooked by) a menstruating woman, but the suggestion that in taking food from any woman some weakening effect may be suffered by the eater. This concerns, too, a novice's mother (and his father, who copulates with her); nor may the boy take food from young men who are married, because they engage in regular sexual relations. Failure to heed such admonitions involves an automatic sanction implying a loss of physical strength and even death by "supernatural" or "non-human" means. It would seem that this harm can be counteracted by self-purging with the cane; yet in the case of novices this remedy is never mentioned. There are, however, no cases known to us of a novice's failure to conform in this respect. On the other hand, we are faced with the question of the kind of sanction operating here. It is not what we might, for convenience, call a religious sanction;[21] and to call it "supernatural" or "non-human," as I have done, is to ignore the local interpretation. It is not pollution, uncleanness, or sinfulness which, in Radcliffe-Brown's terms, can be removed or neutralized by lustration, sacrifice, penance, confession, or repentance. Failure on the part of the novice to conform involves physical harm, transmitted to him in a straightforward way through food containing a germ of weakness or as a counteracting influence from a female whose "oppositeness" to the male is particularly apparent during her physiological crises and during sexual intercourse. It is the germ of femaleness which can be harmful to man under certain conditions, and this belief is apparent throughout other areas of culture and social relations.

In the second group of admonitions, also, are those relating to the eating of certain foods during various stages of initiation and for most of a man's active lifetime. We may call these generally food taboos, which are relevant in a variety of contexts: they have ritual value and status, insofar as ritual is not confined to a "religious" sphere. Again, no examples are available of a man's violation of such a taboo, nor is there any clear idea of what would happen in such a case. The food itself would cause harm to the eater; but in some cases this refers to harm which another person, a child for instance, might suffer should a father eat taboo food prior to and after the child's birth; or eating taboo food would interfere with the course and efficacy of a magical rite. These are rules with specifically defined sanctions, but in the general context of initiation they refer more directly to the effects on a novice's strength. The over-all sanction in all admonitions is the flat statement or warning, not truly a threat: "Some boys hear what we say, others do not." "If you do these things you will

[21] Cf. Radcliffe-Brown (1952, pp. 206–7).

not live a long time; you will die soon.'' The novices are shown the way to behave. If they do not heed this advice, such action will bring its own punishment. It rests primarily with the individual person; social life itself resolves such departures from conformity. It is precisely because these categories refer to strength and its impairment that they are important. If these admonitions represent what we term the ideal, then the actual is more or less an approximation. We have no available cases of failure to comply, no instance where the relevant sanction has been invoked. Men do not knowingly eat from the hand of a menstruating woman; novices do not eat from the hands of women. If such does occur we have no direct or indirect knowledge of it: and it is the same with food taboos. Yet a relatively elaborate mechanism to control the behavior of novices in this respect has been constructed, simply because of the premium placed on physical strength and ability, on its importance to the individual and to the social unit.

With the other negative admonitions, however, the sanction is not primarily in terms of endangering one's physical welfare. The responsibility rests on the individual in a different way. The warning is in a sense noncommittal, and the statement that early death may result in the event of violation embodies a likely and not particularly fearful expectation. The nature of social life itself lived according to idealized precepts in terms of strength, fighting, and aggression offers, actually, no markedly different alternative. If a man or a novice is restrained from going contrary to admonitions in this group, it is not because he fears an early death but rather because such action may jeopardize his position in the lineage, village, and district. He is restrained because of his position in the network of relations involving interpersonal sets of obligations; outside this range no sanction does or could apply. But it is in this particular area that conflict between ideal and actual is more noticeable. The sanctions which do operate here are weak, and the ideal (as expressed through the admonitions) bears little resemblance to the actual; nor is it intended to do more than this. Yet sanctions in themselves provide a guide to approved and disapproved action and are regulative. They serve as factors in maintaining social control.

Chapter 7   Adulthood Means Marriage

Before the young warrior goes out to kill for the first time, he acquires power to withstand enemy markmanship, although not sorcery, by eating food sprayed with a specially prepared substance. *Fijozita* leaves and a sprig of *aipieta* briar-rose, together with dry *hufahaita* fern, *hopahaita* pitpit fiber, and *azageja* tapioca root, are obtained by his father and other lineage members. These are crushed and cooked over a fire and sprinkled with small pieces of *atijafana* (bow stone—possibly petrified tree bark, which is broken up), and the mixture sprayed by mouth over his food. Small fragments of the same stone are chipped and placed beneath his thumbnails, and his mustache, armpits, and anus are rubbed with a *faigeti* rough-surfaced leaf by a brother or by his mother's brother if he happens to be present. Then he is handed a bow and a bundle of arrows and told to use them for killing a man. But equally important are the attitudes necessary for the kind of activity that is expected of him.

Throughout his early life a child is not shielded from the "reality" of a situation: he is subject to the hardships of warfare like everyone else of either sex or any age. He has apparently learned to appreciate fighting and warfare, to enjoy the excitement and action it provides, and to take pride and pleasure in his strength and physical prowess. This is not just a matter of preparation for defense, for survival, as something considered necessary. On the contrary, warfare is viewed as an integral part of living, as something good in itself. This is illustrated in the many songs associated with fighting, which are sung at night in the men's house, for instance after returning from a successful fight. Although the rhythms are traditional, the words (or rather, combinations of words) are not; composed on appropriate occasions by warriors, they may be taken up by other members of the lineage. A few examples will show their general nature.[1]

aiwi aiwi . . . wiju aiwi gora^cnuni kisinu . . .

"Cry, [from] sleep. [As] blood flows: pulled by the hair . . ." ["As the enemy

---

[1] These are in Fore and Jate. There are many such songs, each usually associated with a particular event. In addition, there are many war songs recording dreams in which certain events were allegedly foretold.

sleep, we shoot them; they cry as their blood flows. Pulling their hair, we return." The enemy are dragged by the hair back to the village, where they will be eaten.]

> kanani mopanuta . . .
>   ʃagiᶜmo kanani i: i: a:au . . .

"Red croton at Mopanuta [Keᶜjagana] . . . Eaglehawk [swooping] . . ." ["As the eaglehawk swoops to a marsupial or pig, I will shoot you." The red croton signifies that the singer's threat is associated with retaliation.]

> jua:o we o jua:o ea . . .
>   sinajumpini sepo eva eva sinajumpini . . .

"In the taro garden, at the base of the gabiba bush he [lies] . . ." ["I killed an enemy in the taro garden. There he lies by the base of the gabiba bush."]

> waja kopintontanaja arami arami
>   o o waja vije vije o o . . .

"Burning [your] houses [we] scatter [you] strong as the faja leaf. . . ." ["We burn your houses, scattering you: we are strong like the faja nettle."][2]

> ejuwe eja aruguma . . .
>   oke ake . . . eja eja . . .

"[With] erect penis [we] hide [for ambush] . . ." ["Our penes are erect like our arrows: we go to hide in ambush."]

> kabi tumbanabureinabure putambeka
> kanatuwe igamunterampi gobeja gobeja
> uwamamiewu egunitambi gobeja gobeja
> takija kimaruwe kabi kimaruwe . . .

"[They] open our door to steal. [We] come to Igamunterampi [Mt. Awanti, Kasa]. Shells [they stole]. [From] Egunitambi [Moke]. Shells [they stole]. [We] fasten our doors strongly . . ." ["The Awanti Kasa people came to our doorways, opening, entering them to steal shells; thus they left us. Now we come while you are inside your houses; we fasten the door, set fire to the houses, shoot you."]

> wanumenu kasarinani . . .
>   wo wo e je wanumenu . . .

"[Like a] small dead animal he [lies] stinking. . . ." ["We shoot a man, leaving his body in the bush to stink like a wanume animal."]

As we have seen, a young warrior has to kill at least one man, but usually from perhaps two to five, before he is permitted to marry. Men who have married since 1947 in the northern area (that is, around the Kogu-Kemiju-Keᶜjagana region, or since 1950 in the area immediately surrounding Moke-Ora-Busarasa, have not necessarily fulfilled this obligation, although apparently many have done so. (As a substitute, killing a

---

[2] The faja (waja in the song) is used to restore those who are exhausted or sick.

man by sorcery is just as creditable.) This point may be illustrated in the following case, reported from Busarasa.

Jona᷉o's father Ta᷉nepa [of the *anumpa* lineage] arranged for his son to marry Agaja [*inivi* lineage, in the same district] and gave substantiating gifts.[3] The day came when the bride was brought to *inivi* lineage ground. The conventional sugar cane stick was set in the ground, together with the bridewealth; this included four trussed-up pigs. Jona᷉o, as custom ordained, was sitting in the newly built house awaiting his bride. Men and women of both lineages, together with many others, were awaiting the distribution when an old man, Hetase [half brother to the girl], intervened: "You are not to buy this girl: you must wait. Jona᷉o must shoot a man first, then you may buy him a wife. It is not good that he look at a girl's vulva before shooting a man. . . ." As he strode through the group, shouting angrily, Jona᷉o rushed from his house and snatching up a bamboo knife cut the ropes which tied the pigs, letting them run away. Ta᷉nepa hastily seized his bow and arrows and called out to Jona᷉o asking why he had done this. Jona᷉o picked up his bow and arrows and began to shoot. Ta᷉nepa shot back at his son, but neither hit the other. Ta᷉nepa repeated his question. Jona᷉o answered that Hetase was angry with him and because of that neither he nor his father would continue with the marriage arrangements. But the fight subsided, and the pigs were caught. The girl's brothers accepted their bridewealth payments and handed over the reciprocating payments; and the girl came to live with Jona᷉o. Jona᷉o, however, was still smarting under Hetase's accusations, which were tantamount to calling him a weakling who was unable to vindicate his maleness. He copulated with Agaja twice and then spoke to her: "All the men talk against me. They are angry. They call me a young boy, saying that I am not old enough yet to marry. So I cannot marry you. You must return home." While the girl got ready to leave, Jona᷉o collected together several of his friends, Owapa, a half elder brother, Kamuga, a half father, and Jarigu, a *nenafu* cross-cousin. They waited until the girl was returning along the track leading to her village; then they sprang out from behind some bushes and threw her to the ground, copulating with her in turn. Jona᷉o then told her to go for good.[4] Jona᷉o's father on hearing of this was extremely annoyed, saying, "Your father stayed alive and bought you a wife for you to copulate with; but you turned your penis upon yourself and copulated with your anus. . . ." Jona᷉o replied that his father was angry because he had not shot a man; he was treating him as a child. Later Jona᷉o went with a party of Tatagufa men and shot a man at Karite. On his return he spoke to his father: "Now I would like a wife. You can arrange matters for me." Ta᷉nepa arranged a marriage with a girl named Arajaga from Emasa, who came to live with him. [Before his marriage Jona᷉o called her half sister.]

___

[3] It will be recalled that among the Fore marriage may take place between a man and his half sister, as well as with other close classificatory relatives. Jona᷉o called Agaja half sister.

[4] Agaja returned to her village of Kabumanti. Nothing further was done in the matter, and no action taken by members of her lineage; the bridewealth was not returned. Marriage negotiations were eventually opened with another man, Ija of Ke᷉akasa, to whom she was sent.

Some interesting points are revealed in this case. Jona^co's hurt pride had to be vindicated. The girl was in no way in the wrong, but her half brother had slighted her husband and she had to suffer. Public opinion, expressing disapproval of a marriage where the man had not fulfilled the obligations of manhood, forced Jona^co to break up his marriage against the wishes of his father and to seek someone to kill. Only in this way could his marriage be at all satisfactory.

Before a young man fulfilled the requirements proving manhood, his betrothal usually would have been arranged; and after his final initiation ceremony, although it is ideally desirable for him to keep away from young girls, he is drawn toward them and may engage surreptitiously in premarital relations. In the northern part of this region, too, there is the formal "courtship," or period of conventional love-making. There is also a considerable body of love magic lore, mainly in the possession of and used by older men who are already married.

Courtship and Betrothal

Formal courtship or love-making seems to be broadly of two varieties: one arranged by older men, who invite young girls to visit their village for this purpose, the other involving parties of young girls who go from village to village to engage in love-making. This practice, however, is not common and depends on the existence of peaceful relations between the villages immediately involved. One purpose of the specific invitation is to provide young people with an opportunity of meeting and to point out approved and marriageable *nenafu* so that attachments can be formed and betrothals arranged. When betrothals already have been arranged, this enables the pair to get to know each other. It seems to be considered a socially, or, rather, publicly, accepted practice whereby members of both sexes can achieve a certain amount of sexual satisfaction at a period when this is particularly desired. Virtually all the girls who take part are unmarried and either pre- or postadolescent. The youths have passed their final initiation and have begun their *avagli*. Some are in the process of becoming proven warriors. Others, having achieved their killings, are awaiting their parents' and lineage kin's negotiations for their wives. Where no such formal meetings are available, the youths may manage to make arrangements with female *nenafu* through intermediaries—or simply meet young girls in the bush. Should they become attached to each other, either or both may approach their respective parents so that marriage negotiations can be initiated.

Behind the holding of these public courtship parties, and the apparent freedom to choose a spouse in a relatively private way (that is, through meeting a girl surreptitiously, as is also socially approved), lie some of the important factors already noted in discussion of the earlier phases of socialization and of initiation. Youths, for instance, are trained to be aware of the advantages and necessity of strength, which is to be channelized primarily into aggressive action through warfare and fighting, in maintaining the dominance and prestige of their particular lineage and district. This is development along lines of maleness in contrast to femaleness. Outlets must be found in activities other than fighting, and erotic activity with members of the opposite sex is one of them. This does not become obvious until the relations existing between married adults are examined, for marital and extramarital association is viewed as aggressive action heavily weighted in favor of the male. This brings up certain points which have already been touched on. Free as choice of a marriage partner appears to be, both parties are primarily dependent on their separate families and upon their lineage. "Payments," for example, are required by the bride's group and reciprocated "payments" by the bridegroom's group. These are accumulated and made only by the respective groups involved; otherwise, the marriage does not take place. Circumstances are different, however, as regards the operation of the levirate or, in the case of an elopement, a seduction by force, and so on.

A courtship party may take place in the following way:[5]

Let us suppose that men of Kemiju district have completed their *avagli*. Many of the young men are decorated with body designs, said to be attractive to the opposite sex. The older men arrange for a party of young Tatagufa girls, with their brothers, to visit Kemiju for the *ajafahawaise* [chin-rubbing]. On arrival, the visitors arrange themselves on the elevated ground near the men's house or in a specially constructed shelter. The Kemiju youths form one line and the young Tatagufa girls another immediately opposite, each facing a *nenafu* [actual or classificatory]. They begin to rub chins. The young men's parents meanwhile prepare an oven, sharing out the food when it is cooked. The participants are given lengths of sweet potato runner with which they hit one another, amid much joking and laughter. The girls' brothers supervise the proceedings. Should a girl not be pleased with her partner as they rub chins, she rests her hands on the ground; should she like him, she rests them on his shoulders. This continues for perhaps two days, the evenings being spent in feasting and the daytime in chin-rubbing. On the third day the Kemiju youths present plaited rope, arrows, shells, salt, and so on, to the girls, who then depart for home.

Some little time afterward the Kemiju young men go down to Tatagufa with their sisters; the latter line up opposite young Tatagufa men, and the same chin-rubbing performance begins. Ovens are prepared, and there is much feasting.

[5] Compare with the *Katuyausi* of the Trobriands: see Malinowski (1952, pp. 227–31).

The chin-rubbing continues well into the night; some couples remain in the house, others may retire into the darkness outside for copulation.[6] Next morning the girls receive gifts from the Tatagufa men, hand them on to their brothers, and return to Kemiju. Exchange visits are then made to a number of other districts and villages. For example, the young Kemiju girls may be taken by their brothers to Tofenaga to rub chins with Haga youths, who in turn bring their sisters to Kemiju. The Haga men may then take their sisters to Numparu; the latter in turn visit Haga, then Kiᶜo; Kiᶜo men may bring their sisters to Numparu, then to Hafaru, which returns the visit; and so on, a whole network of exchange visits being made within the particular sphere of influence of any one district.

In other examples, the pattern is much the same, with slight variations. When the participants belong to the same district, the young men may visit the unmarried girls who occupy a special house. Usually, however, it is an interdistrict affair.

At Kogu the young men, brothers of a selected group of young girls considered ready for chin-rubbing, prepare *zefajana* love magic, making a small mound of earth [an *agoja*, a hill or penis], with an aperture in which they put salt and chewed leaves. They then build a bench upon which they place cooked sweet potatoes, spraying them with the *zefajana* leaves. Collecting their sisters, they bring them to this place and perform nose-bleeding, forcing up their nostrils sticks smeared with *zefajana*; this is said to break down their shyness and make the girls desire to join in these activities. The blood falls into the *agoja* hole in the mound as they bend over it and is later covered up. The girls' brothers then give them the food which has been prepared, and they all prepare to visit Kemiju. That night when all the youths are asleep, or pretend to be asleep, the Kogu party enters Kemiju and surrounds their house, shrieking and pulling off the kunai grass roof. Some girls enter the house, where the young men are huddled together not offering resistance, and remove their possessions—shells, arrows, drums, salt, and so on. They take off, too, the youths' decorations and waistbands, leaving them naked. They give these things to their brothers. The young Kemiju men then emerge from their house, singing:

> morio zakaikai . . .
> inanopi mazezuwe . . .
> vovo voa o . . . haia haia . . .

"Chin-rubbing . . . In which house am I to sleep . . ." ["In which house shall we chin-rub."]

The brothers of the girls also begin to dance, singing in reply:

> kamorena emenamia afeteve tangguwe
> emenamio wajoaje
> hanoreve tangguwe wajoaje
> mogwondawe hanoreve tangguwe jowaveo . . .

[6] While sitting opposite each other rubbing chins, they may play with each other's genitalia and copulate, the man drawing the girl on to his thighs.

"I give [my sister] to you for chin-rubbing. . . . Come give me, or I'll burn your penis . . . I'll burn your penis . . ." [That is, some men bring their sisters for chin-rubbing; others do not send theirs in return.]

The term *hanoreve* for "penis" means semen; the inference is that the men have brought their sisters so that they can collect this for sorcery; i.e., heating a victim's semen over a fire in order to weaken and if possible kill him.

They lead their sisters by the hand to the Kemiju house, where young men sit down opposite their *nenafu* partners and begin chin-rubbing. In the morning they go to the higher ground near the men's house and forming into two lines, singing, repeat the process. Partners are changed until each is more or less satisfied with the choice made, the girl signifying this by placing her hands on the shoulders or thighs of her partner, or touching his penis. Throughout the day the girls' brothers dance down the long lines of lovers, pushing their buttocks into their faces, singing:

> *mofakana hogove wana*
> *lukevokovo kabojuva . . . juaowajua o . . .*

"I show you the girls' road! Look at my anus—this road!" ["I show you the girl's road, the vagina. Look at my anus—come, eat it!"]

The lovers try to push them aside. Old men also walk down the lines poking them with sticks, joking erotically. They may continue in this way for most of the day. Ovens are made, food cooked and distributed, and all eat. They go down to the creek, wash, and return for more chin-rubbing. Finally the girls' brothers intimate that they must return to Kogu. The Kemiju men bring out their gifts, supplemented by pig meat, and present them to the girls, who hand them on to their brothers. They all return to their home villages.

During the period of chin-rubbing, genuine attachments may be formed. A young man may tell his parents, who approach the girl's brothers with extra gifts; if these are accepted, they are counted as part of the bride-wealth payment. The girl and her brothers also speak to her parents. His parents may prepare food and salt and bring them to hers to see the response and to decide how much they should offer. But there is much variation in the arrangements leading to formal betrothal.

Once a young man is betrothed, others may tease him, telling him he has chosen a girl whose genitalia are covered with sores, one who is physically undesirable. He may worry about this, however often he has heard it said to other young men in a similar position—especially since during this period he is not supposed to visit her (and so find out for himself). His lineage brothers may insist that they have seen the sores with their own eyes and laugh at his angry protests. This is a stock joke, the theme of a farce which is performed during ordinary ceremonies. Several versions of it are found in the non-sacred mythology. In the following version, the young man sets off to reassure himself:

Briefly, he magically enters a certain tree through a small hole, casting his skin and turning into a small boy. In this guise he comes to his betrothed wife's village and sits down outside crying. The women of the village come out and carry him inside, where his betrothed lifts him up in her arms, asking him why he cries. But he does not stop. They take him to the garden; he looks at her skirt and cries. She offers him some sweet potato, but he pushes it aside; she offers him sugar cane, with the same result. He keeps on looking at her skirt, and when she sits down comes crawling over to her, trying to get under it, but she pulls him away. She parts her skirt fibers to look for lice, and in doing so partially reveals her vulva; he laughs. She stands up to continue her gardening, and the disappointed child cries. She sits down and opens her skirt to look for lice, and he laughs. But she soon gets up to begin working, and he cries again. Realizing why he cries, the girl sits down, opens her skirt, and shows her vulva to the child, who laughs and fondles it. He cries no more and accepts the food offered to him and goes back to the tree, where he turns into a man again. Returning to the men's house he takes up his *tofugona* [jew's-harp] and plays a tune which the girl hears.[7] She realizes what has happened and is "ashamed," and sits down crying. Her parents see her and think she is crying for her betrothed; they are sorry for her and hasten the marriage proceedings. [In several versions she commits suicide, but to the best of my knowledge this is never shown in the farce. There the parts of the girl and the child are acted out by two men, to the great enjoyment of all the spectators.]

Marriage

Usually, whether or not a young man or woman has indicated a preference, it is a father's obligation to seek out a wife for his son (although, as we have seen, certain other persons may do so). Here is one example to illustrate the general procedure:

A Tatagufa father visited several districts with which his own was on relatively peaceful terms. Eventually, in Kemiju, he found a young girl who would possibly be suitable. He indicated his intentions to her parents, who were noncommital, and "marked" the girl [that is, indicated a claim on her] by giving her some sugar cane. Returning to Tatagufa, he told his brothers, who discussed the matter with other lineage members. The youth's father pointed out that the chosen girl had a half father who was his son's mother's brother; the girl was his son's matricross-cousin, a desirable spouse. The father described her and asked his brothers whether they would contribute bridewealth. After deliberation they agreed, and some little time afterward the father's younger brother went down to Kemiju, where he spoke to the girl's brothers [or to the girl's father's youngest brother]: "We would like to buy your sister; we will give you gifts." "You may not buy her," they replied and, in assumed anger, left him sitting there; but a little later they returned and indicated their willingness to negotiate. The youth's father's younger brother went back to Tatagufa and reported his success. When the

---

[7] There is a series of tunes played on the jew's-harp, each with a different meaning, and used as sign language between lovers.

bridewealth had been collected, the father himself went to Kemiju to tell the girl's brothers and lineage members that the bridewealth was ready. He then returned to his village. Next day the Kemiju party came down to Tatagufa, where they slept the night in the men's house. In the morning racks were put up in the village clearing and the bridewealth placed on them, arrows resting on the horizontal poles, with lengths of various kinds of threaded shell, bush beads, waistbands, salt, and six trussed-up pigs. When these had been arranged, the Kemiju party were called to look and to signify acceptance. The girl's brothers, her father's younger brothers, their wives, and others crowded around to discuss the quantity and quality of the gifts. "No," they said at length, "this is not enough. It is no good. Come, put more!" Tatagufa men brought forward another pig and then another before they were satisfied. "Enough, now we shall take it." The goods were then shared out; the girl's brothers stored away the shells and other goods into bags and tied up the arrows into bundles, the pigs were distributed between the father's brothers, and so on. So laden, they left Tatagufa and came along the road leading to Kemiju. The betrothed girl, who had been hiding, saw them coming in the distance and called out to her age-mates and friends, young girls and youths [lineage brothers]. The girls armed themselves with sticks, the youths with bows and arrows, and all hid at one side of the road just outside the village. As the returning party approached, they jumped out, surprising it, beating its members with sticks, threatening to shoot, breaking arrows over them, demanding their share, threatening to take it by force. But presently the excitement died down. They entered the village and stored away the goods, after showing them to the other villagers. Then they went to the gardens and collected yams, taros, and sweet potatoes, cooked them in the ashes, scraped them, and arranged them on dishes; sprayed with salt, they were given to the betrothed girl. This was her betrothal-confirming feast, shared by herself and the young girls of the village.

At Tatagufa the youth's parents also went to the gardens and collected yams, taros, and sweet potatoes, cooked them in the ashes, scraped them, sprayed them with salt, and gave them to him. This was his betrothal-confirming feast, which he shared with his age-mates and lineage brothers.

Next morning at Kemiju preparations continued. The girl's mother, sisters, brothers' wives, and others prepared her skirt, adding strands of shredded bark to cover her bare thighs, cutting them to a suitable length. A number of skirt lengths were also completed and put away. This continued on the following day, more lengths being added to the skirt. On the third morning they went to the gardens and collected more vegetable food and cut firewood, bringing it back to the village. In the afternoon the girl's sisters took her down to the creek, where they bled her nose, then brought her back to lie down in her mother's house. During the evening her mother, father, brothers, sisters, and all the other young girls and women gathered around this house and proceeded to offer advice. This is the conventional lecturing [monoke] or discussion, usually referring to meetings in the men's house. It runs much as follows: "You are now a wife; you must stay with your husband. If he calls out to you, if he tells you to do something, listen to what he says. Do not ignore it. If another man looks at you and pulls your arm, tell your husband. If you hide this, he will beat you. . . ."

Next morning all the vegetables were heaped up in the middle of the cleared place: sweet potatoes, yams, taros, pitpit, bananas, and so on. One or two pigs were killed and placed in ovens to cook. In the meantime, messages had been sent to Tatagufa, and the youth with his parents, lineage members, and others came to Kemiju. He was shy and remained very much in the background. The betrothed girl was led out from her mother's hut by all the young girls, who placed her on top of the heap of food and, surrounding her, began to rub her body and theirs with warm pig fat. Her father called out in pride, "She is a man's child, and I am losing her. She is no dog's child, no spirit. Treat her well, she is a daughter of this lineage. She sits there on all this food." [The reference here is to her potential fertility.] The pig meat, removed from the ovens, was cut into portions and put into the girl's net bags and into those of the young man's parents. The girl stood in the center of all the vegetables, shining with pig fat, surrounded by the young girls. An elder sister handed her a full length of sugar cane, complete with leaves, which she held upright between her legs with both hands [as an emblem of fertility, a symbol of the male element in her subsequent impregnation]. Her sisters then proceeded to put skirts on her, one after the other, until they reached to her navel and above. [This ritual "rounding" of the skirts is one of the most important features of the whole range of ceremonies; it signifies a girl's assumption of marital status.] From her head they hung a net bag of pig meat, the cord passing across her forehead.

The youth's mother now came forward and took the girl's hand; the girl's brothers called out for the husband, but he, being shy, had already started off for Tatagufa. His parents, with their new daughter-in-law, also set out for Tatagufa. The bride carried an arrow in her hand and was helped in carrying her possessions; these constituted her dowry, over which she had personal jurisdiction; the bags of pig meat given to the husband's parents were part of the reciprocated bridewealth. The mound of food at Kemiju was divided among the girl's brothers, half fathers, mother's brothers, nogago, nenafu, and grandparents, and was either carried away or cooked in ovens and eaten then and there.

During the afternoon, the girl's parents collected quantities of food and pig meat and came along the Tatagufa road, crying and wailing, to give them to the youth's parents; and this was the reciprocated bridewealth. This meat was then cut up into portions and given to all those who had helped in supplying the initial bridewealth. Then the Tatagufa people collected from their gardens quantities of yams, taros, and sweet potatoes, while men of the lineage took the new husband down to the creek and bled his nose. This food, cooked in the ashes and sprayed with chewed bark of various kinds mixed with salt, was then given to him. [The nose-bleeding and spraying of the food counteracts the female influences which may harm his strength and manhood.] The arrow which the girl had carried was then presented to her husband, symbolizing her willingness to aid him in fighting —an attempt to avoid the conflict of loyalties which might normally be expected.

It is this meal which the bridal pair are supposed to eat together, but this is not always so. Both the bride and bridegroom are often shy of each other [goriᶜ, "fear," is the word used]; and this resistance must be broken down. The youth's parents may cut two large pieces of pig meat and put a bone skewer in each, giving one to him and one to his wife; he cuts off a piece, sticks the skewer in, and offers it to his wife, who eats it; she then does the same for him. The exchange of food is said to ease any strain between them. Sometimes this is less easily achieved, especially if the girl is very young. The two may avoid each other for a period, until her breasts are larger and he enters her flesh [that is, has coitus].

There are, however, numerous variations in which there is much less formality; and there may be no negotiations leading up to the central ceremony. In such cases, the issue of sexuality is of dominant importance.

Contrary to the admonitions which accompany the initiation rituals, a newly made warrior may spend much of his time (when not actively engaged in training and in fighting—which, after all, is not a daily occurrence) with members of the opposite sex. These entanglements in some cases lead to marriage, but more often they are simply brief premarital liaisons. This position is aggravated sexually to a point where it becomes a game, a trial of strength, which has its counterpart in the ideal aims of the initiation training. His sexual activity is looked upon as "fighting," both having that element of excitement through which satisfaction is attained. This aspect will receive some attention in the following chapter. In the meantime, let us consider a few of the associations which may lead to marriage.

A youth attracted to a girl in a neighboring village may wait in hiding by the stream when she comes with her bamboo container for water. If he is well-received, he will have sexual relations with her. She returns to her house, which she may be sharing with other girls, and during the night he may join her there. A period then follows when they contrive to meet, either by day in the gardens where she is working or in the bush collecting firewood or in her house at night. Eventually, the girl goes to the menstrual hut. Should her mother ask why this has taken place so early, she may tell about the young man, giving his name. Her parents then go to his asking for "pay" [bridewealth]. Since it is the girl's parents who have "pushed" the matter, the payment will be much less than in the case of formal negotiations. Finally, her parents prepare vegetable foods, hold a feast, put skirts on her without the central ceremony, and send her to her husband.

Or a young man, seeing a girl who catches his fancy, may ask his sister to act as an intermediary. Since she may depend on him for the same purpose, she will let the girl know that her brother wants to meet her surreptitiously in the bush for chin-rubbing. If the girl is willing, this is arranged. Afterward he will send her, through his sister, gifts of meat; and she may also arrange for her own brother to meet his sister.

After a certain amount of chin-rubbing, they are stimulated to such an extent that this is no longer satisfying. When he comes to her house by night, to share food and to chin-rub, she may catch up a firestick and burn him; he may do the same to her. They begin to fight, hitting each other with sticks, and during the struggle he pulls off her skirt and they copulate. This is repeated several times during the night, until shortly before dawn he returns to his own village men's house. There now ensues a period when they take every opportunity to meet. During the night he visits her, and the time is spent almost entirely in erotic play. During the day they sleep or meet in the gardens. If they become attached to each other, the girl may press him to approach his parents. "I like your penis. You copulate, and it is sweet," she may say. "Go talk to your mother and father, and ask them to buy me for you." In such a case there is little delay. It is a mere formality to put on her skirts denoting marital status and send her to her husband.

In another example we see how elastic marriage arrangements are. We are, it will be remembered, considering only young girls and youths who have not previously been married and have no other commitments.

A young man with his mind on a particular girl may go into the bush and shoot a bird or a small animal, and then go to hide behind some bushes in the garden where she is working. When the other women are occupied elsewhere in the garden, he attracts her attention by breaking a piece of wood; she looks toward him, and he offers her his catch. Leaving her digging stick, she comes into the bushes and takes it, asking, "Why do you give me this?" "You may like us to copulate." If she does not reply or run away, he throws her to the ground. To avoid comment she goes back to work but returns to him at intervals during the afternoon. They decide that they like each other and take every opportunity to meet. During the night he comes to her house, or they arrange to meet nearby; he gives her food, and they eat together. He watches for her departure in the mornings for the gardens, or for the bush to collect firewood, and seizes the opportunity when she is apart from her companions. But as time goes on they find that these meetings do not give them enough time together to satisfy them. The girl may say angrily, "I shall go and get my mother's skirt and fasten it around me, and then I will come to you!" The youth returns to his lineage group and awaits developments. The girl returns to her own village and puts on some of her mother's skirts; she then comes to his village and sits with him. An uproar follows, and the girl's parents, brothers, and other lineage members hasten to his village to demand bridewealth. This is usually handed over almost immediately by the youth's parents, who will kill about three pigs. If these are accepted, the bride's family then go home to collect vegetables and kill a pig, and returning offer it to his parents, who distribute it. A marriage has taken place.

On other occasions, the proceedings can be even more informal:

Omaju of Moiife, going down to the local stream to get water found his *nenafu*, Aisau^cru [also from Moiife], cutting a bunch of bananas. He threw aside his bamboo water container and copulated with her while standing. Then they lay down and continued to play, rolling into the shallow water. As they were so engaged the girl's parents, Wojavi^cmi and Awaja, came down for water and saw them. Omaju told them crossly to go away. Later in the same day, the parents fastened on her skirts and without any formality sent her to him as wife. Certain gifts were afterward given to Aisau^cru's brothers [i.e., as the usual gifts to brothers-in-law].

Many such examples could be given, each revealing a different aspect of this subject and showing the element of individual choice within a certain range. There are cases where girls taken in interdistrict warfare later marry their captors without any ceremony, feasting, formal fastening of skirts, or exchange of bridewealth. On the other hand, such girls may be properly "bought" so that the marriage is validated. Warriors who capture girls in fighting are as a rule already married. For instance, take the case of Marepe^cna, of Kemiju:

In a fight with Inivi, Marepe^cna captured a young girl named Jejemiso^c. He brought her back to Kemiju, where she was looked after by his two wives, Kohajaho and Arata. After a while Marepe^cna decided that she was old enough for intercourse. He went down to one wife's house, where the girl was, and told her that she was to marry no man other than himself. He spread out a pandanus mat and placed her on it; then kneeling before her with erect penis he sang,

Jejemiso a'gujumo a^cnehunu
somajapa a'gojuno ionehunu . . .

"Jejemiso^c's vulva cries; Somajapa's penis cries . . ." [That is, "Jejemiso^c's vulva cries for coitus; Marepe^cna's penis cries for coitus." He calls his future child's name, Somajapa; the inference here is that he will make Jejemiso^c pregnant and she will bear his child.]
He copulated with her. His first two wives then decided to collect the bridewealth for her. When they had done so, they took it to Inivi and gave it to her half father, Oifa; he in turn came up to Kemiju with pig meat and food, and the marriage was ratified.

In considering marriage in this region, we have a range of conventional proceedings which lead up through negotiations to the point when the girl is the center of a ritual which highlights her feminine characteristics, as the essence of fertility. But these proceedings may be so perfunctory that the only consideration is the fastening of a skirt and the exchange of gifts, and even these steps may be omitted in certain circumstances. This is not a matter of an ideal, contrasted with actual behavior. Within the accepted range the procedure is determined by a variety of circumstances such as conditions of war and peace or the inclinations of the couple involved. War may temporarily confine a youth's attentions to girls within his own district; or if a marriage is contracted with a former enemy group, the negotiations and proceedings may be drawn out and formal. Even in hostile districts, however, youths will have their *nenafu* whom they may meet freely and with whom they can engage in erotic adventures which may lead to marriage. There are no controlling mechanisms which insure the following of specific marriage procedures or restrict premarital relations or choice of partners (except in the case of certain close relatives).

A lineage group supporting a marriage, its various members subscribing toward the bridewealth which is paid over by the youth's parents to the girl's lineage, expects in return a woman who is fertile, who will carry out her prescribed work, and who will bear children for the good of the lineage. Her own lineage, while losing an active member, hopes to gain not only bridewealth but later a girl for one of its male members. The latter is the long view, the more immediate one being the marriage settlement and the distribution of goods. A marriage between the two lineages, however, is not viewed as a form of alliance. The relationships growing out of any marriage between two districts develop areas of aid and amiability which are meaningful only to specific individuals, not necessarily to their lineage or village group as a whole.

In marriage, people seek primarily a means of engaging in regular sexual activity. Partners are chosen and discarded largely according to the degree of sexual satisfaction attained, although other factors such as economic co-operation may be involved. There seems to be no doubt that this is the most important factor in marriage, especially for those who are relatively young, and the desire for children is viewed as a necessary accompaniment. Generally speaking, women show little reluctance to bear children, and when their period of seclusion and abstinence is over normal sexual activity is continued. There is a desire on the part of girls as well as boys to develop their sexual powers to the maximum [8] through the stimulation of the conventional courtship meetings or in the permitted freedom during the premarital stage. But although this is to some extent channelized in marriage, the development of sexuality, along with other factors, apparently can find satisfaction only in extramarital liaisons of a spasmodic or permanent nature. There is a tendency to sexual excess, which in local terms is not excess (except from the viewpoint of a husband who becomes aware of his wife's infidelities) but an entirely natural activity. It is within this sphere, however, that dissension occurs. What we call a "double standard" is operative here. While men conventionally regard any woman outside the prohibited range, married or not, as a potential sexual partner,

[8] See A. W. Hoernlé in I. Schapera, ed. (1937, p. 159); I. Schapera (1940, p. 259); L. P. Mair in A. Phillips, ed. (1953, p. 11).

their own wives, they consider, should remain faithful to them. They themselves do not expect to be in any way restricted in the matter of extramarital activity, although their wives may censure them for it. A woman does not proceed against her husband in such a case, although she may show her jealousy in other ways. A man does run a risk of being embroiled in a fight, however, if his sweetheart's husband becomes aware of what is occurring.

In the advice a woman receives on marriage, three major points are made. She must stay with her husband, thus insuring marital stability; she must take notice of all he tells her; and she must avoid having sexual relations with other men. These admonitions obviously concern ideal rather than actual behavior. They are, moreover, offered by her own lineage kin and the wives of lineage kin. No explicit attention is paid to such aspects as marital distrust, the pull of each partner's own lineage, the strong siblings-of-opposite-sex relationship, and so on. They do not need to be verbalized at such a time because they are taken for granted. When a father calls out to the assembled groups, as his daughter sits on the heap of vegetables, that he is losing her; when both her parents come wailing to the village into which she is married; this does not mean that they relinquish all claim to her. It is true that they have lost her as a worker or as a person of whom they can dispose; they have ceded to her husband their control of her sexual and reproductive functions; but they and her brothers will continue to expect her aid and sympathy. Although she leaves her lineage, she does not lose her allegiance to it.

Much in the way of actual behavior, then, runs contrary to the admonitions offered during initiation. Even after initiation, until a man's prowess is proven and his marriage is arranged, he should, he is told, keep well away from all young girls and women. But while proving themselves as warriors, young men may participate in the formal courtship meetings; and this is also a period of sexual preoccupation. There is no restriction on their activity. Older men do not usually reprove them or condemn this behavior. They have already offered advice, and it now rests with the youths themselves: "Some hear what we say, others do not." But the apparent contradiction is explained by the belief that real harm or risk to a young man comes only if he eats from the hand of a woman. This is the point of the bridal meal, sprayed with a special prophylactic substance; of the exchange between the pair of pig meat impaled on skewers, to break down shyness. The sharing of food by the newly married couple signifies their dependence on each other, and the husband's trust in his wife's willingness to guard against his being harmed through any fault of hers.[9] In premarital liaisons, it is the eating of food together which will most surely lead to marriage.

The training of a young man encourages an ambivalent attitude toward females. They are looked upon as "dangerous" and in a sense forbidden. He must always be on his guard with them. Those on whom he will look with sexual interest are not of his lineage and, apart from the conflict of loyalties, can do him physical harm. Nevertheless, he is attracted by them physically. The sexual urge is stimulated in the initiation rituals by the tremendous stress placed on strength, physical attractiveness, and aggressive maleness. Through sexual activity a man justifies his status as a male; and the more he engages in this activity, the more highly are his strength and prowess assessed. His sexual relations with women are viewed as a kind of armed combat. It is conventional to force a woman, however willing, to the ground; in erotic play the pair burn or beat each other; in coitus a man uses his penis like an arrow, and the ejaculation is "shooting"; sexual intercourse is frequently referred to as fighting, and the couple bite each other's chins as an expression of enjoyment. Such behavior is common enough, and it would be unwise to overstress it in relation to the sexual act. Nevertheless, it is significant.[10] We could perhaps see in this relationship the attraction-antagonism aspect made so much of elsewhere, the interplay of contrasting male-female elements. Yet this would be to underestimate the situation. Both male and female are aggressive, and men do not always take the initiative in love-making. A young girl, for example, may persuade her lover to approach his parents to set marriage arrangements in train; she may take the initiative in courtship meetings; she has normally some choice as to whom she marries; and she can send packing unwanted suitors.

For both men and women, marriage is an inevitable feature of adult life. Whatever a person's associations with eligible members of the opposite sex, this relationship is of central importance. The bond between husband and wife is, conventionally, supplemented by new ties between them and the children they are expected to bear; marriage is inseparable, here, from the notion of "family of procreation," just as it is inseparable from the broader network of lineage and kin relations.

The question is not, then, whether or not a person should marry,

9 Cf. also, for instance, M. Mead (1935, p. 95), in reference to the Arapesh, where a girl at marriage eats a meal prepared by her husband, and a piece of yam is kept aside for potential sorcery to insure her loyalty to him.

10 Compare with the Mundugumor: M. Mead (1935, p. 215 et seq.); and in reference to Truk, T. Gladwin, and S. B. Sarason (1953, p. 111). Also, generally, C. S. Ford and F. A. Beach (1951).

because the answer is taken for granted. The point at issue is choice of partners within that framework. For a man, the range of choice is wider. He is not only in a better position to engage in extramarital affairs but also is not restricted to one spouse at a time. A woman's personal wishes are more easily overridden. In any serious clash of interests with a man, she is at a disadvantage. She may have sweethearts, if she can overcome the risks involved, but cannot legitimately live with more than one husband simultaneously. But in either case, once a person becomes an adult and is in a position to make such a choice, this is, potentially, a focus of dissension.

Chapter 8   Foci of Dissension

Two important areas of dissension in the arranging of a marriage concern the jilting of suitors and the payment and distribution of bridewealth.

Jilting of Suitors

Although rivalry between "brothers" for the hand of a marriageable *nenafu* is the source of much bickering and quarreling, it does not usually have serious repercussions. A suitor from outside the district who is jilted may occasionally bear a grudge and await an opportunity to "hit back." There is always an element of danger in declining a specific request for a girl, and this is avoided whenever possible. Yet it is not wise for a girl's parents to go contrary to her desires. If she is attached to some young man, he is a potential suitor, and to override her choice might arouse his hostility. Her commitments must be considered, and her paternal kin must weigh the merits of the case in terms of alliances and pressures.

Ozaze^cna, originally of Ke^cjagana, was staying with his father and brother at Tatagufa in company with his mother's brother. They had been driven away from Ke^cjagana during interdistrict fighting. He formed an attachment to his mother's brother's daughter and found his liking reciprocated; but no formal arrangements had been made. About this time a Kemiju man came down and approached her brothers, wishing to negotiate a marriage. The girl, hearing of this, told her brothers that if they were to contract with Kemiju, and she were sent there in marriage, she would immediately return to Tatagufa. The Kemiju man's offer was therefore refused, and he returned home disgruntled. Some time afterward a Fore man came to Tatagufa with the same intention, attempting to claim the girl [in order to begin negotiations] by giving taro to her brothers. They immediately approached her in the matter; but she replied that they must not eat the proffered food, for she had no intention of marrying into the Fore. So the Fore man took back his taro and went away. Ozazen^ca then thought that he would approach his lineage kin to institute proceedings. He left Tatagufa for Henagaru to see his father's brother's sons. [His father's younger brother had also left Ke^cjagana during the fighting, and gone to live temporarily at Henagaru among matri-kin.] Here he broached the subject of his marriage. His "brothers" offered to find him another woman as wife and to accumulate the bridewealth; they anticipated trouble from a woman who had already jilted two suitors. Their lineage was dispersed, like their district, and they could not hope to carry out prolonged fighting. Ozaze^cna, however, insisted on his choice, and eventually an elder brother accompanied him back to Tatagufa to start negotiations with the girl's brothers. The suit was accepted, and they were invited to come down to Henagaru to collect the bridewealth on the following day. Next day they came, with others, and collected the pigs, arrows, shells, waistbands, salt, and so on from Ozaze^cna's half brothers, members of parallel lineages, as well as from his own father and brother who had come down for that purpose. The Tatagufa people set off for their home village, but on the way a group of young girls and boys swooped down on them, attacking them with sticks and arrows in the conventional manner. Ozaze^cna's father and brother returned to Tatagufa, went to the gardens they were using, and brought back vegetables, which they cooked and sprayed with salt in the approved way. These were given to Ozaze^cna, who passed them on to the young men of Tatagufa with whom he was living, but did not eat himself. Next morning his mother's brother came to him and said, "We have received the bridewealth now. This girl says that we tried to send her to another place, but she always came back to you; she threw aside her bridal skirts and returned to you unmarried."

On the following morning pigs were brought in and killed, ovens made, and people went out to collect vegetables. They were ready to take the girl down to the water when word came that a fighting party was approaching. Warriors from Kemiju, Henagaru, Amufi, Kogu, Emasa, Moke, Ke^canoza, Etazena, and Ifusa had temporarily combined to oust Tatagufa and the remaining Ke^cjagana people. Some of the Henagaru people had accepted bribes from Kemiju and Moke, as representing the two jilted groups; there were other reasons behind this, but the jilting brought it to a head. The girl's skirt was fastened hastily and without the usual ceremony. Ozaze^cna's brother took her down to Henagaru, and with them went others carrying the pig meat and other possessions. Once there they bribed all those who had helped them in accumulating the bridewealth by distributing the reciprocated bridewealth in addition to other goods. Ozaze^cna remained at Tatagufa. There was some skirmishing around the stockades, and a few men were wounded, but eventually the attackers dispersed to their separate districts. Some little time afterward Ozaze^cna's mother died at Tatagufa, and a message was sent to his brothers at Henagaru. They came up with Ozaze^cna's wife and wailed over the body, killed a pig, poured the blood over her, and buried the body next day; the pig meat was cooked, cut, and distributed. Ozaze^cna's brother returned to Henagaru, leaving Ozaze^cna with his wife. But soon afterward more warriors from Kemiju, from certain Fore districts, and from Henagaru again surrounded the Tatagufa villages. This time they succeeded in sacking them, but not before Ozaze^cna, his wife, and father had escaped with their belongings to Kimi^cagumu and then to Numparu. After a time the trouble died down. Altogether this covered a period of two to three months.

Distribution of Bridewealth

Examples here are plentiful and varied, but I shall mention only a few:

Igalwa of Ja^cagusa approached Esoiba of Moke with a request that he be allowed to open negotiations for Tomuga. He wanted her to marry his son Kagonaria, whom she called classificatory *nenafu*. Tomuga was the daughter of Esoiba's elder brother. Esoiba, however, refused the request. Some time afterward Igalwa came again to Moke and asked for Tomuga. Esoiba replied that he had already refused, but since Igalwa seemed so anxious he would send a deputation to Ja^cagusa to view the bridewealth and decide. The following then went down to Ja^cagusa: Igoefa [Esoiba's wife], Apa [Tomuga's elder sister], Tobaru [Apa's husband, and Tomuga's *noka*], Igimimi [Tomuga's brother], and Ontari [a young man, Apa's son]. The bridewealth, already laid out, was accepted by the party, who collected it and started for home. They were met on the road at Paboi, in Ja^cagusa territory, by Esoiba, who examined the "pay" and decided that it was insufficient. He told them to go back and get another pig. They did so, a brother of Kagonaria, Branaga [also an *ato* of Tomuga], supplying a large one. This was taken to Moke, where it was accepted; the bridewealth was distributed, and the marriage proceedings continued.

It is usually assumed that a certain amount of haggling will accompany the bridewealth negotiations; but carried too far, this may lead to fighting:

In the case of Toni^c, a younger brother of Kama of Kogu, bridewealth was paid to Asafina for a young girl named Jaraja. After receiving the goods and pig meat, her brothers and lineage kin said they did not want it. Kama went to Asafina with more gifts, which they refused. He returned to Kogu with these, but he could not recover what had originally been given. Asafina is relatively close to Kogu, and so next morning Kama went down to the gardens to look for Jaraja. He found her and took her forcibly to Kogu, where he gave her to his brother as wife. The Asafina men, on hearing of this, caught up their bows and arrows and shields and met Kogu in a pitched fight. A Kogu man was killed, but finally Asafina was driven back and Kogu demanded a pig in compensation. Asafina gave a pig, and the fighting stopped. The dead man was carried into his village, the pig killed, and both man and pig were placed in ovens and eaten. Women present in the village put a bridal skirt around Jaraja,and she was declared married to Toni^c. No further gifts were given or received in relation to this marriage.

The fact that a young girl can be "marked," or claimed, by more than one negotiating party shows the unsureness of such initial contracts. They are not in any real sense binding. The brothers of a girl are anxious to obtain as much bridewealth as they can, and this is a major consideration. When personal affection between the couple is not a factor in the betrothal arrangements, the aspect of economic advantage is dominant. The same element enters into the establishment of political alliance in warfare by bribery. But it may arouse or intensify ill-feeling, the seriousness of the situation depending on just how far the negotiations have gone and on amounts already paid. If the arrangements fall through, a common practice is to retaliate by abducting the girl (as in the case above), fighting, or working sorcery, or, today, to take action through the informal courts.

Dissension over the distribution of the reciprocated bridewealth within the lineage or clan can lead to serious rifts between, for example, brothers, despite efforts to control them:

Jasona of Kogu was betrothed to a young Ke^cjagana girl named Ativio. His father in collecting together the bridewealth took a pig belonging to his son, Jasona's younger brother, Konu, without asking his permission. The bridewealth was eventually paid and the girl arrived in Kogu. By this time Konu had found that his pig was gone. Angrily he went to Ativio, who was previously his *nenafu*, and copulated with her. Jasona heard about this and threatened Konu with his bow and arrows, asking him why he had done it. Konu replied that because his pig was used in the bridewealth, without his consent, he was entitled to claim compensation—and this was a legitimate way of doing so. Jasona, to avoid further trouble in the lineage, acknowledged this claim. The blame was cast on Ativio, who was beaten by both her husband and her lineage brothers and warned to stay with her husband without causing trouble. Ativio, resenting this, ran away to Inivi but was brought back to her husband by Ke^cjagana men and remained with him.

Interesting here is the shifting of blame to the girl. It occurred, too, it will be recalled, in the case of Jona^co, who was accused of marrying before proving his manhood by killing. Or take the following case, the marriage of Tuse^co of Numparu to his *nenafu*, a Moiife girl named Jaga^ce:

The bridewealth was paid to the girl's father's younger brother, Seseo, and to her full brother, Kesosa. Preparations were made for the marriage ceremonies. Seseo approached Kesosa, asking him to bring a pig for killing and promising to do the same. Kesosa agreed, but said he would kill his at his own hamlet, and Seseo could do the same with his. Then they would fill the girl's bags so that she could go to Numparu. The girl's nose was bled and her skirts fastened; Seseo's pig had been killed, cooked, cut, and distributed to the bridegroom's parents. Jaga^ce's bags were ready and were then filled by Kesosa, but instead of placing good meat in them he put only bones. Seseo noticed this but did nothing at the time. When the excitement of the marriage had died down and Jaga^ce had left for Numparu, Seseo found Kesosa and his wife, O^cmata, his *nanoferu*, eating meat which should have gone to Jaga^ce as part of the reciprocated bridewealth. In a rage, he took hold of O^cmata and began to strike her, then turned to Kesosa and struck him with a stick. Kesosa spat out what he was eating and ran away. Seseo, taking up his weapons, ran after him, but after some threatening words and actions the trouble died down.

The events leading up to and surrounding marriage offer many opportunities for disagreement, especially since it is likely to bring together two potentially hostile groups. But even in cases of marriage within the district, similar conflicts may arise:

Oga^cu of Kogu, the young daughter of Arojabu, was "bought" [i.e., initial gifts were handed over for her] by a woman called A^cna, also of Kogu, who wanted the girl for her brother's son Hagani^cmo. [Arojabu was A^cna's clan brother, and

Oga^{c}u her *nogago*.] However, Mania of Kogu objected to this; he was Arojabu's younger brother and called the girl "daughter." [A^{c}na was Mania's clan sister.] He wanted the girl to marry outside the district. Soon after this a Kemiju man named Ma^{c}avi came to Kogu to negotiate a marriage for his son. He acknowledged no kin relationship, even in a classificatory sense, to Mania, but called A^{c}na *nanoferu*. His suit was rejected. Arojabu then went to Moiife and contacted an old Kogu man named Pusa^{c}i, asking him to intimate to his son, Wanoi^{c}na, that if he approached Mania the latter would be willing to negotiate with him so that Oga^{c}u could go as bride to Wanoi^{c}na's son, Amepi, whom she called *nenafu*. [Pusa^{c}i was a classificatory father to Mania and Arojabu, as well as to A^{c}na, and called Oga^{c}u *toto*.] Wanoi^{c}na came to Kogu and asked Mania if he would be willing to accept the bridewealth from him. Mania accepted the proposal, and on the following day he and his lineage brothers and others went to Moiife to collect it. They brought back to Kogu six pigs, shells, and other objects. These were distributed between Mania himself, Tu^{c}avu, and Asa^{c}ja [younger half and full brothers respectively of Mania], and Ano^{c}igi [Mania's father's brother's son], as the chief recipients, and various actual and classificatory brothers of Oga^{c}u [of the same or linked lineages, as well as those scattered throughout the Kogu district]. This was mainly a distribution of pig meat. The girl, with due ceremony, and with her bags full of pig meat, was sent to Moiife as wife to Amepi. Some time afterward a man named Agaja, a classificatory brother of Oga^{c}u, came to Mania and accused him of neglecting to give him a share of the bridewealth received from Moiife. An argument followed when Agaja threatened Mania with bow and arrows. To avoid further trouble, Mania took one of his own pigs and gave it to him in compensation.

This is a favorite trick of a classificatory brother who has been ignored in such a distribution. By not pressing his claim during the feast, or by being absent, he has more chance of obtaining a larger share. A brother, however far removed he may be, always has a claim on his sister's bridewealth payments. His insistence on this right depends on how far he may be regarded as a "strong man"—on how far he can reinforce his claim with actual force or threat. The above example, besides showing those who are primarily involved in a marriage arrangement, demonstrates certain aspects of social alignment in terms of relationships. (For instance, there is the importance of a girl's father's younger brother, who has the final say in declaring to whom she may go as wife. It illustrates, too, the desirability of marriage with a cross-cousin. Certainly Hagani^{c}mo and Amepi were both *nenafu* to Oga^{c}u, but the second was more distant.) The primary consideration here is individual decision within an accepted framework.

Resistance to a Marriage

One other focus of dissension should be mentioned in this context, since it may have serious repercussions. A girl's wishes may be overridden in the matter of her marriage. She may object to a certain man but finally be sent to him after pressure from her father, father's brothers, and even her own brothers. She may finally become reconciled to the marriage; or, making the best of a bad bargain, she may engage in extramarital affairs and so obtain satisfaction while perhaps awaiting an opportunity to elope. Alternatively, she may run away—returning to her own village, eloping with a lover, or simply seeking the protection of a "brother" or *nenafu* in another village. But she may oppose the match so strongly as to persuade her patri-kin that to continue with the arrangements would lead only to trouble. Again her position is determined by the relative "strength" of the persons involved. Refusal on her part, no matter how expressed, is likely to cause dissension. On the other hand, a bridegroom, seeing his potential bride, may become opposed to the match; he may find her physically unattractive or for some other reason not want to marry her. There are several cases where a bride, after going through the marriage ceremonies, has arrived at her husband's village only to be told to return home merely because she did not appeal to him. But these are rarer than cases in which a girl opposes her projected marriage or dislikes the man to whom she is sent:

Kepo^cgo, an Inivi man, was betrothed to a young girl named Fenakizu, whom he called *nenafu*, living in the same district. Okiona, the girl's brother, was the major recipient in the bridewealth. The marriage ceremonies were concluded, and the bride sent to Kepo^cgo. She stayed some time with him but did not like him, being attracted to a Ke^cjagana man [her *nenafu*] named Joa^c who was visiting Inivi. Subsequently, she left Inivi and went to live with him. Her father Aisakea went down to Maneviga village in Henagaru where the pair had gone and called out to his daughter, asking her to return to avoid trouble. She went back with him to Inivi, but insisted that she would not remain with Kepo^cgo and would return to Joa^c. But two men, Ka^ceavu of Kogu [of no relationship to Fenakizu; a refugee in Inivi] and Fami^c of Ke'jagana [who called her mother's brother's wife, being a nephew of Kepo^cgo] ordered her to remain in Inivi. She replied that she would go to Ke^cjagana. The two men grabbed her arms and pulled her along the track to Maneviga. Once there they threw her to the ground and beat her on the pubes until she howled with pain and left her lying in the village clearing. Some Henagaru women were sorry for her and heating pig grease and water tended her wounds. They carried her to Inivi, where she remained with her father until she was well. Afterward she rejoined Joa^c, who paid bridewealth to her father. None, however, was paid to her first husband, nor was the original bridewealth returned. The girl had been punished, and Joa^c's lineage and village were powerful. No action was taken against Joa^c, and the girl was considered to be entirely to blame.

In another case, a Miarasa girl named Toruta was sent in marriage to a Busarasa man, Sivina:

Frightened of Sivina, she refused to copulate with him and ran back to her parents. Jona^co, a younger lineage brother of Sivina, went down to Miarasa and brought the girl, whom he called *ato*, back to Busarasa. On the way he had intercourse with her, and again on arrival at Busarasa when he took her into a nearby garden. From there he called out to Gopai, his classificatory father [*nenafu* to Sivina, and *ato* to Toruta], who came and also had coitus with her. Then Jona^co took her to another garden and copulated. Afterward he sent her to Sivina, but she again ran away. Sivina and Jona^co then went down to Miarasa together, and brought the girl along the road to Busarasa. At Pojeti, Sivina asked Jona^co to have coitus with her while he kept watch so they would not be observed. Then Sivina did the same. Jona^co told him he would not have coitus with her again but that she was to remain married to Sivina.

Toruna of Busarasa was married first to Waribu of Emasa, her classificatory brother, who died during a dysentery epidemic. She then passed to Oni, his younger lineage brother; but she did not like him and wanted to return to Busarasa and marry there:

Her brother Tabie, hearing of this, came to Emasa, where Toruna cried, "I am married to a no-good man. I must return home. Help me carry my belongings, and we will go." Tabie then told Oni that he could not remain married to Toruna because he had previously had as wife Tabie's mother's brother's wife. [Oni therefore called Tabie half son. This would have provided no obstacle to his marrying Toruna but was merely brought forward to justify her leaving him.] Tabie then took his sister and returned to Busarasa, where she was eventually given to Jogi as wife. Now this marriage caused some complications, for Jogi's father was Asea^co, a brother to Asonaga, who was married to Gumina, the sister of both Toruna and Tabie. Jogi called Toruna mother. [This is a typical Fore marriage. She was not married to Asonaga, although a potential spouse to him, because he already had her sister as wife. Jogi now began to call Toruna "sister."] On hearing of her marriage, the lineage brothers of Oni came in an armed body from Emasa and approached Tabie. "You came to Emasa and took away your sister. Where have you hidden her?" "Ask Jogi," replied Tabie. They went to Jogi and demanded Toruna, seizing her by the arm. Asonaga then made an appearance and showered abuse on her. "Why are you living as wife with Jogi? You are married to your own son," and he hit her with a stick. Just as Tabie had used the excuse of Oni's having been married to his mother's brother's wife, so Asonaga, having already condoned the union, tried to cast blame on Toruna in order to avert the hostility of the Emasa men. Then the Emasa men began to drag Toruna away. Tabie, supported by a number of age-mates and lineage brothers, stepped forward to defend her, pointing out to the Emasa men that she was a good woman who looked after her gardens at Busarasa and gave food to her brothers. He took her, forcibly, and returned her to Jogi. The Emasa men, temporarily outnumbered, returned home. They collected a number of warriors and came down in a large group to Busarasa, ranging themselves ready for fighting. Then they called out to Jogi. "You want to marry this woman. Now pay us or return her to us. Otherwise we will fight." Jogi replied that he was willing to pay them. Gifts were then brought out and given to the Emasa men, who left satisfied.

In such examples we can see the areas of dissension to which reference has been made. From one point of view, analysis can proceed along the lines of the relationships involved: rivalry between brothers, the type of marriage, the strength of the brother-sister bond, the importance of lineage and village solidarity, the implications of bridewealth distribution according to claims of particular kin. But at the same time, running to some extent contrary yet within a defined framework, we have the pull toward individual choice—personal wishes and interests dictating the course of events.

What exactly is nonconformity here? If forceful action or public opinion is required to make a young girl return to her husband; if only threats can force payment of compensation; are these controlling mechanisms functioning to maintain conformity? Alternately, do these foci of dissension themselves represent acceptable, conforming behavior? And if such be the case, what is the function of controlling mechanisms? "Focus of dissension" means here that certain combinations of factors, as found in various situations, give rise to social upset, leading to a greater freedom of personal choice among possible alternatives. The choice of alternatives is not necessarily in terms of conformity-nonconformity but simply in terms of conformity within a range. A marriage, for instance, may be carried out in one of a number of conventional ways (that is, empirically, not ideally speaking), the selection being influenced by personal choice and interests. It is necessary for any member of a society to be able to predict what others will do in given circumstances, but such prediction must always take personality factors into account.

Next we shall consider briefly the relations existing between wife and husband and between co-wives.

Relations Between Husband and Wife

No extra status is accorded a man just because he has more than one wife; nevertheless, many men seem anxious to have more than one. The reasons given are usually sexual, although sometimes phrased in terms of economic advantage or of a wish for more children. Having several wives does not restrict a man's extramarital liaisons. Most men have had during their lifetime more than one wife, not necessarily simultaneously, and partly as a result of the inheritance of widows. But tentative examination of genealogies shows that, generally speaking, a woman is likely to have had more husbands, though not simultaneously, than her husband has had wives. Nevertheless, there appears to be often real affection between spouses, and many marriages appear to be relatively successful.

A husband and wife were happily married at Henagaru. She had gone to him as a young girl, and they grew so fond of each other that they made a vow: on the death of one, the other would sever the genitalia from the corpse and dance with them. Shortly after this, Amwe men from south of Taramu are said to have bribed with shells Henagaru men of the husband's clan to perform sorcery on the wife. In any event, she died, and the body was cut up. The husband in grief told his lineage kin [with their womenfolk] to eat the flesh, with the exception of the vulva which he wanted for himself. This he tied to his hair so that it hung at one side of his forehead. The rest of the corpse was in the ovens cooking, with a pig which had been killed for the purpose, and Amwe men entered Henagaru singing to join in the feast. As they moved across the village clearing, singing and dancing, the widower got up and began dancing too, singing and twanging his bow-string; the vulva flapped against his face, and the blood ran down his chest. The ovens were opened and the meat removed. He was offered pig meat but refused it; he continued dancing until exhausted. The Amwe men were given pig meat and returned to their district; the others went on with their feasting.

The same affectionate themes appear in the songs, not only between husband and wife, but between lovers, between *nenafu*, and so on. In fact, one may say that these people are extravagantly sentimental, perhaps as a counterbalance to their aggressive displays, or representing a different facet of them. In both, they show a tendency toward lack of restraint. We shall speak of certain sexual excesses in the next section, mostly in relation to extramarital behavior; yet many husbands and wives, particularly the wives, are said to remain sexually faithful. On the other hand, sexual constancy is not particularly highly valued.

A husband may dispose of his wife to another man, as he may do also in the case of widows whom he inherits. But other men, too, may claim such widows.

There is the case of Asiwa of Ora, whose parallel lineage [*anumpa*] elder brother, Sena^cau, died from *krana* sorcery and was eaten. The three widows, an Ifusa woman named Janu, an Ora woman [*kasaru* lineage], Eginu, and Pia, an Emasa woman, all of whom Asiwa called *ato*, came under his protection but did not yet become his wives. They remained in Asiwa's women's house; while they were there, Wamaisu [*anumpa*, "elder brother" to Asiwa] opened the door; he lay down beside Eginu and copulated with her, then ran away. Eginu immediately told Asiwa of this, but she did not know who the man was. The next night Asiwa hid in the hut under a mat. Wamaisu came to the door and indicated that he wanted Eginu, who told the other women she was going outside to urinate. As she went through the doorway the man grabbed her and began to copulate. Asiwa threw aside his mat and held their arms. "Why do you do this?" he asked Wamaisu. "Her husband has only just died. His spirit still remains with us, in the branches of a tree, at its base, or in the bamboo clump. It is watching us. When his spirit has gone to Gapisesera [Anabaga], you may copulate with her." Wamaisu then went away. Asiwa continued to look after the three women. Some time afterward Eginu asked Asiwa, "Asiwa, have you no penis? You look after us, but you do not have intercourse with us. Instead, all the other men come and copulate with us!" Asiwa then took Eginu into the bush near his garden where Janu was working. There he met Akiru [also *anumpa*], who told him that on the following day they would hold a feast [ending the mourning period], and the three women would be allocated to their new husbands. Asiwa was angry at hearing this, as he wanted to copulate with them first. However, Eginu set to work digging a hole, while Asiwa watched; when she lay down to burrow, he opened her skirt and mounted her from behind. Rising, he saw that Janu had been watching and, on being seen, had turned back to the village. Asiwa was worried about this.

Next morning all the men of the *anumpa* lineages prepared an oven and feasted to end the mourning period of the widows. When they were finished, they called Asiwa to join them, so they could allocate the women. But Asiwa, who had looked on the women as his property, refused to come out and told them to go ahead. They then called Eginu's name: "Eginu, you dig the garden of Akiru." "Pia, you dig the garden of Isana." "Janu, you dig the garden of Isana." [Isana was Asiwa's "brother," of the *anumpa* lineages.] Hearing this, Asiwa grew angry ["hot belly"], and shouted to the assembled men, "Why don't you give one to me? I looked after them!" He gathered together his belongings and his weapons, and went to a place called Joboi [in the bush, in what was originally Asafina territory, before members of that district had been driven away by Ora]. Eginu ran away to join him there, and they copulated. Akiru, however, caught up his weapons and followed them. He spoke to Asiwa: "You are not to marry this woman." Asiwa replied, "I like her, and I will pay you." "No," said the other. "I want to marry her." Asiwa warned him, "This woman won't stay with you. She will go to one place and then another and another." But Akiru took Eginu back to Ora. Asiwa followed in a rage. On reaching Ora he called out to the three women, reallocating them: "Pia, you go to Oka [district]. Janu, you go to Mage [district]. Eginu, you go to Ifusa [district]." The women replied, "You, Asiwa, have made good talk. You looked after us, but they did not give one of us to you. If they had done so, we would have remained here, but now we won't." Next day the three women ran away. Pia went to Oka, where she married Jaboroda [classificatory younger brother to Asiwa]. Janu went to Mage, where she married Jemi [also a classificatory younger brother to Asiwa, but a "half brother" to Janu]. Eginu went to an Ifusa man whose name was unknown by the Ora men. The *anumpa* men said to one another: "Leave them, let them go; they do not like us"; but Isana and Akiru grabbed their weapons and threatened to fight Asiwa. Asiwa, however, was "strong." He replied, "I can shoot you; but it's no good fighting. The women have gone." And the other two returned to the men's house and dropped the matter.

Conventionally, widows should refrain from intercourse until the end of their mourning period, when their widows' weeds (old skirt, torn net bag, covering of charcoal, mud, and feces) are thrown aside. Actually, complete abstinence seems to be rare. The interesting point is that a "strong man" (in this case Asiwa) can override the decision of lineage and clan kin (in this case the *anumpa* lineages of Ora). Further, the case indicates the status of widows, who may be disposed of without reference to themselves or to their own lineage.

Tabu^cno, an *anumpa* Busarasa man, was married to Nigibi [also *anumpa*, of the same clan, but not lineage: he called her "sister"]. Tabu^cno was killed in a fight at Obonemi, in Henagaru. He was carried back to Busarasa and buried, and subsequently disinterred and eaten. After the mourning interval his widow passed to Jona^co, younger brother of Tabu^cno, without further payments to her parents. But she always cried when Jona^co tried to have intercourse with her. "Why are you afraid?" he asked. "Have you not a hole like all the other women? My body is good; there are no sores on it. I am a good man. Why then are you afraid?" One day he came to her house and sat down by her fire to cook pitpit. When he had finished eating, he pushed her over, but again she began to cry. Later, when she was asleep, he parted her skirt and taking a piece of bark from the fire put it into her vagina. She awakened with a start. Jona^co then pulled out the bark and copulated with her. After this, she pulled off her skirts and cried, so that the whole village was attracted. Some of the men were angry with him and asked why he had burnt her. He replied that he wanted to have coitus with her, but she did not care for him. "So I burned her vagina. Leave it, there is no need to fight. If she dies, you may cook and eat her." The others then turned on Nigibi and scolded her: "Have you no hole? Why are you afraid of Jona^co? You are not a little girl!" Jona^co did not go near her again. When she had recovered, another Busarasa *anumpa* man named Awakabara [an age-mate, *nefaru*, of Jona^co, who called Nigibi "sister"] asked him for her. Jona^co arranged that Awakabara should "pay" him [one pig, beads, salt, arrows, and waistband], and on receipt of this he sent Nigibi to him as wife.

A widow who is unattached, not under the protection of a prospective husband, and moreover outside the control of her own or her deceased husband's lineage, can expect little consideration. She may resist her new husband, as Nigibi did Jona^co; but here public opinion is against her, particularly in regard to her refusing intercourse. Refusal gives the aggrieved husband grounds for aggressive action. But a widow who has not been reallocated or remarried is liable to be "snapped up" by any man with an inclination in that direction:

There is the case of Taja of Emasa, married to Kaju, also of Emasa. Because Ifusa allegedly performed *sangguma* sorcery on Kaju, he died. His widow went to stay with her younger sister, Jasaru, who was married to a Busarasa man named Ubuta. Taja was working in her brother-in-law's garden at Paenggamuti when Tabie passed by. [Tabie, of Busarasa, called Taja *ato*, being brother to Ubuta, *inivi* lineage.] He asked Jasaru, "Why has this woman come?" She replied that Taja was only visiting them. Tabie went into his own garden, dug some sweet potatoes, and while cooking and eating them thought that he would like to have this woman as wife. He hid near the track leading from the garden and when the two women came along sprang out and grabbed Taja's arm. "Why do you do this?" asked Jasaru. Tabie replied that he wanted to marry Taja. He took her and put her into his house, where he copulated with her and considered her to be his wife. However, an age-mate of his, Riema, who also called Taja *ato*, took a liking to her. He came to the house, thinking she was alone; but Tabie was there. Hearing Riema coming, Taja spoke loudly to warn him [and so avoid a fight between the two], telling Tabie to make up the fire. But Tabie was suspicious. He went up to the men's house, where he asked the others who had come to his house. [There are always men in and around the men's house, keeping watch.] They replied that it was Riema. Tabie then went to Riema, and asked him, "Why did you look in my house?" Riema denied the inference that he had special interest there, saying he had merely heard someone talking and had looked in out of curiosity. But Tabie was not convinced. He said he would give up Taja and Riema could marry her. Riema answered that he did not want her. Tabie then went to his house and got Taja, and both went to his garden. There Tabie told her that he had been thinking about what had happened, how she had warned Riema in order to avoid a fight [whereas a dutiful wife, approached by another man, should immediately tell her husband], and that possibly afterward Riema had visited her. "You did wrong," he told her, "I can't remain married to you." He then tore off her skirt. Taja asked if he wanted intercourse or was only "tricking" her. Tabie assured her that he was not tricking her. Taja therefore lay down; but Tabie seized her skirt and threw it into a feces pit. [This was to guard against sorcery being performed on him, since her skirt had some of his semen adhering to it.] He then left Taja, who went to live with his mother. [Taja did not remarry but was later killed, allegedly by *sangguma* sorcery performed by Awanti men. Her corpse was taken back to Emasa by her brother, Guruba; a feast was held there, a pig killed, and her body cooked and eaten.]

When the above cases occurred, the informal court was not operating in these districts. Even if it had been, it is doubtful, since widows were involved, whether the men concerned would have approached the matter differently. In acting as he did, in running contrary to the dictates of the lineage, Asiwa revealed a fundamental conflict between self-help[1] on an individual basis and the demands of the social unit. He too had rights on his side, and the group did not proceed against him because he was expressing the fundamental principle of "strength." It might be argued that the actions of the group as well as that of Asiwa fall within the range of conformity. But when Jona°o forced his attentions on Nigibi, and subsequently injured her, he was performing a coercive act which had what I would call a legal quality. Local opinion, in so far as this was expressed, shifted from censuring Jona°o to censuring Nigibi on hearing why she had been punished. Tabie, in first claiming Taja and then discarding her, was behaving neither legally nor illegally but within the range of conformity. He was in one sense "punishing" her by discarding her; but he was not

[1] See C. K. Allen (1951, pp. 55–56), M. Gluckman (1955, pp. 225, 262–63), S. F. Nadel (1947, pp. 500–507); E. A. Hoebel (1954, pp. 27–28, 259) speaks of private law.

regulating her conduct, and his action was primarily a matter of self-interest.

Co-Wives

The maintaining of amicable relations between co-wives depends largely upon their respective temperaments. It is clear that in many cases co-wives live together with the minimum of friction. Some women have negotiated and gathered bridewealth to supply their husbands with additional wives. In other instances there is real dissension between them, leading to brawls and fighting. A co-wife may use magic to make the new wife leave voluntarily or elope, or she may persuade or pay her female friends to attack the intruder. It may be necessary for the husband actively to intervene or to placate them. The first wife may drive away the new wife, or vice versa, and in some instances the quarrel comes before the informal court. Ordinarily, the regulation of affairs within the marital unit, when there is no introduction of a third party, concerns only those within it; that is, the husband and his wife or wives. But in certain circumstances others are involved—when a co-wife calls on her brothers or lineage kin for help, or when others take sides in a fight. We shall consider briefly several cases:

Tewapi, a Kemiju man, broke some sugar cane from the garden of his second wife Aᶜumu and brought it back to his house. Aᶜumu asked him for some; but he turned to his first wife, Avusuza, and gave it to her. Aᶜumu went angrily to her mother Grofeteja, who was living in the same district, and told her about this unfair treatment. The mother, sorry for her daughter, went to Avusuza and belabored her with a stick. She was soon joined by a younger sister, Oᶜnio, as well as by Aᶜumu herself, and the three set to work to beat Avusuza thoroughly. Avusuza picked up a stick and brought it down on Aᶜumu's head, drawing blood. By this time Tewapi had grabbed his cane and in turn attacked the women, dispersing them. He then spoke to Aᶜumu: "You must not fight Avusuza. This is all on account of the sugar cane I broke. Now you may grow vegetables in your garden, but I will not accept them. They are your own business, you eat them yourself. If you want to marry another man, you can go." [Tewapi did not intend to force Aᶜumu to leave him; he was "hot belly," but not as angry as that.] To placate the other women, including Avusuza, he gave them money and paper [nonindigenous trade items].

Such behavior on the part of co-wives is, up to a point, taken for granted by the husband. He expects to have to keep order to some extent. It satisfies his conception of himself as a dominant male sought after by females. But it can take a more serious turn. For instance, each co-wife may send up to the men's house a wooden platter piled with vegetable food for her husband. He may have a preference for one and eat only her food, neglecting the rest. This may continue for some weeks or even longer, during which period he does not visit the other's house at night. The withholding of sexual favors, the considered neglect of a wife by a husband, capped by the direct insult of refusing to eat the food she prepares (thus inferring that she is habitually unclean and desires to do him harm), do not justify her leaving him or blatantly engaging in extramarital liaisons. She may consider herself justified, but her husband does not; and he will proceed against her either by force or through the informal court if this is operative.

Another example is the case of Mare^c^e, originally of Kogu, who was married first to an Asafina man, Agiasa, but was abducted while working in a garden at Goritaopinti [Asafina, near Ora]. Two Ora men, Takasu and his age-mate Berebi [both of the *anumpa* clan] saw her. Takasu declared, "I want this woman." [Takasu called Agiasa *nenafu*, but this did not stop him.] They took hold of her and brought her back to Igivinti in Ora, where Takasu already had as wife Wabaso [an *anumpa* of Ora]. Wabaso resented her coming and fought with her. "I alone am here. Why do you come to my man?" Takasu tried to make peace between them: "I can marry her. Why do you two fight?" And Berebi added his opinion [as dominant warrior leader]: "Why do you fight? Takasu wants to marry her, he abducted her for that purpose." Mare^c^e pretended to be menstruating and went to the seclusion house. Rain was falling and the villagers remained indoors; Mare^c^e ran away. Onaba [*anumpa*, who called Berebi and Takasu "father"], from the men's house at Masagari, saw her running away. He went after her, caught her, and copulated with her. In the meantime the other two men, suspecting that she might go, looked in the seclusion hut and found it empty. They picked up their weapons and went after her. Berebi came first and saw Onaba copulating with her. "Why do you do that?" he asked. "She is married to another man." Onaba replied that he had seen her running away and consequently caught her. Berebi then improved on the situation and told Onaba to copulate again while he held him at the back. This he did; and Onaba, enjoying it, remarked, "I am copulating properly now. My penis reaches to her anus. . . . I will look after your garden and give you plenty of taro." Takasu, however, came up then and seeing them so engaged was angry. He threw Onaba to the ground and beat him with a stick, asking, "Why do you copulate with her? She is married to me." But when Onaba managed to explain, Takasu, sorry for what he had done, said, "She is no wife of mine. I abducted her." They then each copulated with her. When they had finished, Berebi told her to lie down and taking up his bow shot her in the thigh. By this time others, including Takasu's first wife, had come upon the scene. Wabaso and her husband carried her back to their house, the latter first removing the arrow. He tended her and brought her food each day until the wound was healed. Some time afterward Mare^c^e made the same excuse and went to the seclusion hut; from there she ran away to her first husband, Agiasa. Finding her gone, Takasu and Berebi, fully armed, followed her to Asafina, where they met Agiasa. Agiasa spoke to them: "You like this woman, and you have copulated with her. She is my woman, and

I want her back. I will pay you both.'' Berebi and Takasu accepted the offer and received a bundle of arrows, salt, beads, shells, and so on. Agiasa said, as he handed it over, ''You two are strong. You take this woman, and now I give you pay. In future you are not to abduct her.''

Berebi and Takasu were not in the wrong when they abducted Mareᶜe. Only force or what is in effect bribery could restrain them; and as they were acknowledged to be stronger than Agiasa, he paid them to leave his wife alone. There is no legal influence to restrain this behavior, which is simply what is expected between hostile groups; the controlling factor is the relative strength of opposing units. With the development of the informal court, however, settlement could be effected legally, although the same principles come into play. Mareᶜe, as a woman, has little influence on the course of events which so directly concern her. She is abducted against her will but has no redress. Her escape from this predicament is considered unjustified, and consequently she is punished.

A co-wife, then, often feels herself injured by the entry of another woman into her circle because of the attention her husband will undoubtedly pay to the new wife. But what are the reasons for this jealousy?

Kokiema of Keᶜjagana was sent as wife to Nanggito of Awanti Kasa. When he was shot by Miarasa men, Kokiema was taken to Eraki in Busarasa and later a feast was held there to end her period of mourning. Jonaᶜo, who was at Pojeti in Emasa, came down to Eraki and saw the widow, whom he called *nenafu* [he had called her husband classificatory younger brother]. He arranged that she should elope with him, and they went to Pojeti together. There they were received angrily by Jonaᶜo's first wife, Arajaga, who caught up a stick and began to hit them both. Jonaᶜo, attempting to ingratiate himself, pulled aside his skirt and showing his penis pointed out that he had not yet copulated with Kokiema: why was she angry? He declared that Arajaga should be sorry for the other woman, particularly after having beaten her. Arajaga then appeared to forgive her, and both women worked together in their husband's gardens. Kokiema then persuaded Arajaga that it would be a good idea if they both ran away to Keᶜjagana and married other men; but at the same time she warned Jonaᶜo that his first wife planned to leave him. The two women collected their belongings [Kokiema doing so in order to allay any suspicion on the part of Arajaga] and started off. Jonaᶜo was waiting hidden beside the track they were to take, and as they came along he jumped out and shot Arajaga in the leg: turning, he then shot Kokiema. After this he gave Kokiema to his age-mate, Uwakabara, saying, ''When she is well again, you can marry her.'' Uwakabara gave him gifts.

In most cases, jealousy between co-wives is described as being primarily of sexual origin; but, as we have seen, other sources of potential conflict such as unequal treatment by the husband may also be present in this relationship. On hearing for the first time that her husband is bringing home a new wife, especially a younger one, a woman may anticipate this and react violently, because she believes that through a show of strength the relationship may be stabilized or weighted in her favor. She pits her strength not only against her new co-wife but also (less directly) against her husband. Further, the situation is one in which a woman can, with relative freedom and with advantage to herself, resort to physical aggression. It is in just such a situation (the suggestion of insecurity in her personal position; fear of being thrown into a worse predicament by being cast off by her husband; fear of punishment for what she considers unjust treatment) that she is likely to resort to open aggression. Primarily, then, she is not jealous of another woman solely for sexual reasons, although this element is undoubtedly present, any more than a man resents, as a matter of sexual or personal affection, the adultery of his wife. What he does fear is the effect that adultery may have on him and his strength; and what she fears is that her security may be jeopardized.

Aggressiveness is manifested in a number of culturally defined ways, and one setting in which it finds considerable scope is the field of sexual relations. This is obvious perhaps, yet there is here a certain lack of restraint, a tendency toward what might be regarded as excess, which illustrates the theme particularly well. It will appear again in the context of the informal courts.

Both men and women seek extramarital affairs as a form of relaxation or diversion. As long as these are not discovered, they need not have social repercussions, yet a great deal of dissension is directly due to them. A man confronted with the fact or assumption of his wife's adultery may feel it necessary to fight, to demand compensation, or to shoot her or her lover or both. The quarrel may involve other members of his lineage as well as of theirs. Adultery within the lineage or village is often condoned, or at least does not have serious repercussions. Adultery outside the village but within the district can lead to fighting, while outside the district it is likely to be a matter of warfare, of retaliation by the social unit acting nominally as a whole. Within this field too must be considered interdistrict elopements and abductions.

The attitudes of these people toward sex in general and the sexual act specifically are not easy to clarify. There is no prudishness; and they are frank in discussion, as in all aspects of social life where this subject is concerned. Women frequently sleep naked at night; men's pubic fringes, casually worn, do not hide the genitalia; young children often run naked. The sexual act itself is largely a private affair between the couple concerned. Nevertheless, it is often observed; and in many cases it is knowingly performed in front of others—such as a co-wife, or daughters of the house, or, in erotic adventures, in the company of other men and women. The sexual act is considered to be a natural phenomenon, like eating, and the urge for it is satisfied without undue concern for others. Children grow up in this atmosphere, and their initial curiosity is not restrained. A small girl fingering her father's penis may be told that "it belongs to mother." Small children of both sexes are excellent informers, perhaps running to tell other adults that mother (or father, as the case may be) is having coitus. Adults joke with children; a woman may call a small boy her lover, remarking on the size of his penis, and a man may talk in a similar way to a small girl. Yet, with all this frankness there is the desire to intensify eroticism, to treat it as a topic for the expression of humor.

Farces

On ceremonial occasions, men, never women, dramatize incidents from the secondary myths or from everyday life. Those on erotic topics have by far the greatest appeal. As the actors move from one part of the ground to another, crowds of children and adults follow them to watch the same scene being repeated again and again. Four examples show something of their content and presentation:

Two Irafu men take part. One represents a woman, complete with skirts and bag, the other her classificatory son. He picks up his bow and arrows, preparing to go out to fight: but she persuades him not to go, telling him that she has seen his death in a dream. [This is merely a ruse on her part.] He is convinced; and the two prepare an oven. As he breaks the firewood, she opens her skirt and shows him her vulva. [Laughter.] "I can copulate with you," he says; "I am sorry for you." [Laughter.] He erects his large bark penis [about eighteen inches in length] and holds it up in front of her. [Laughter.] She speaks: "Come, try it. Put your penis here; I have a mouth here. Come, give me food so I can swallow it." [Laughter.] "Come mark me with it, with the creeper rope of the *gabiag*! ¹ Draw back the prepuce and shoot me!" [Laughter.] The young man replies: "Thus you speak, I will try your mouth." [Laughter.] He throws aside his ax and pushes away the wood he has been chopping; the woman lies down with her legs apart. [Laughter.] As he is about to mount, the woman cries out, "Leave it! First I must defecate; first I must urinate! Then you can ejaculate. . . ." [Laughter. Defecation and urination have here an erotic connotation.] She gets up and runs off, and he runs after her. He searches for her among the crowd of onlookers, rushing up to various women and young girls, and also to men, with his bark penis, speaking to them and making motions of coition. [As he comes up to them there are shrieks of laughter.] At last he finds her, and the scene begins again.

A Kemiju man dressed to represent a young girl newly married is followed by another representing her husband. He comes up to her as she rests in her house [i.e., lying down on a mat in the village clearing, completely surrounded by spectators]. He simulates coitus; but she says his penis is too short, it does not fill her vagina as it should. [Laughter.] She leaves him. Another man appears; she comes up to him and pulls his arm [laughter], then lifts up his skirt fringe to look at his penis. [Laughter.] "Ah," she says, "Here's a long penis!" [Laughter.] She

¹ Reference is made to the creeper of the *gabiag* tree, which when broken peels back like the foreskin of an erect penis; the foreskin drawn back with penis erect is like a bow drawn taut for shooting.

tells the man, "My husband does not copulate with me properly. His penis is too short. But you have a long one, I have seen it. You copulate with me." [Laughter.] The man then "copulates." [Laughter.] "Ah, it goes inside my belly; you copulate well!" she says. [Laughter.] The two then move around the village clearing followed by a crowd of spectators. Choosing a spot, they plant a fragment of pitpit in the ground. [This symbolizes their hiding place in the tall wild pitpit cane beside the road.] Then each puts beside it a forked headrest. [This signifies that they are to sleep there.] They lie down together. [Laughter.] Other men walk past and see them "copulating." [Laughter.] Then ensues a conversation between the couple. The man has cut his hand on the razorlike edge of the wild pitpit cane, and it is bleeding. He asks her, "Will you eat this blood?" She replies, "I can eat it," and makes a noise of lapping it up. [Laughter.] Then she asks him: "This blood of woman [menstruation], would you like to eat it?" He replies, "I can eat it," and makes a noise of lapping it up. [Laughter.] He now asks her, "This blood of man [i.e., blood shed at the penis- and nose-bleeding rituals], would you like to eat it?" She replies, "Yes, I can eat it," making a noise of lapping it up. [Laughter.] She asks, "This blood from afterbirth, would you like to eat it?" And he replies, "I can eat it," making a noise of lapping it up. [Laughter. These are subjects about which men and women do not ordinarily talk together, except in "swearing" during quarreling or during the erotic talk of lovers.] Then she asks him, "My husband doesn't copulate with me properly. Will you marry me?" He answers, "Yes." [Laughter.] They get up and repeat the performance in another part of the dancing ground.

The third example was performed by three visitors from another district called Kogu (in the Jate area, near Mount Michael):

Two are dressed as middle-aged women, the third as an old man. [The background of the farce concerns a disagreement between the man and his two wives over the negotiations for the betrothal of his son.] He says to them, "Why didn't you come and tell me all about it?" Then, turning to one, "I will shoot you!" [Laughter.] He erects his large bark penis [laughter] and "copulates" with her. [Laughter.] The other wife begins to beat him. [Laughter.] He withdraws his penis and threatens to shoot her. [Laughter.] He then "copulates" with her and is beaten by the other in her turn. [Laughter.] This is repeated again and again, the interest of the audience apparently never flagging.

The last example was performed by Kogu men (Usurufa):

A mother goes to the gardens leaving her daughter in the village. [The daughter sits before a circle of onlookers; she is supposed to be a small child.] A man comes up to her and asks, "Has your mother gone away?" [Laughter.] "Yes," the girl replies, "she has gone to Belimaka [garden name]." [Laughter.] The man erects his bark penis. [Laughter.] "I'd like to copulate with you," he says. [Laughter.] He copulates with her hair [laughter]; he copulates with her eyes [laughter]; he copulates with her nose [laughter]; she is too small for ordinary intercourse. Then he goes away, and the mother returns. This happens each time the mother goes to the garden. At last the small girl tells her. The woman is angry. "Why does he come here tricking us?" she asks and hides herself in a nearby house. The man comes up and asks his usual questions, and on hearing that the mother has gone to the gardens begins to copulate with the child's hair. The mother emerges from the house and throws hot ashes and coals at him [laughter], and he runs away into the bush. [Laughter.]

These farces are exceedingly popular, particularly during night ceremonies when large blazing fires light up the scene. No matter how often they are repeated, there is the same apparent excitement, the same uproarious laughter. People say that their purpose is to entertain, to create a diversion during the singing and dancing. It may be suggested that they serve to release tensions, to bring into the open aspects of the forbidden which must ordinarily be repressed. Up to a degree, this may well be so. Against it, there is the point that the behavior portrayed represents not only an area of absorbing interest but also an accepted part of everyday life. In a sense it is, given the focus of interest, the ordinariness of the event, what has happened on one occasion and may happen again, which provides the humorous twist. The mother entices her son, but when he is ready for intercourse she makes excuses; this simply underlines the lasciviousness of women, even of elderly, classificatory mothers. It is commonly said that a long penis is most attractive to women, and the second farce thus points out that a woman must find sexual satisfaction. The old man who fights his two wives offers a lesson in tactful handling of such a situation, as well as an expression of co-wife rivalry. The final case is humorous because it deals with a man who is unable to control his sexual impulse. But there is more in these farces than a desire to present a humorous situation and to entertain onlookers; they provide circumstances in which erotic conversation can occur between the actors, with appropriate actions, and by this means they serve also to stimulate the spectators.

Extramarital Relations

In this social environment, young men and women grow up to regard sexual relations as a normal part of the process of living, a satisfaction which need not be confined to marriage. Men have been taught that physical strength is of paramount importance, and this strength is maintained and enhanced by fighting and by erotic adventure. Both men and women desire sexual satisfaction. Their appetite is whetted by the farces which accentuate the erotic.

Kokote of Kogu came on a young girl at Fugufinaga [near Numparu], and on looking at her immediately felt sexual desire.[2] "Ah, my sister," he greeted her,

---

[2] "To look a woman in the eyes is to desire her." A rope running through the body, it is said, connects the eyes with the penis: as one looks the rope grows taut, making the penis erect. See B. Malinowski (1952, p. 141) for comparison.

using this as a term of endearment. He made arrangements to meet her in the garden and on doing so said again, "Ah, my sister! Lie down!" He took hold of her and threw her to the ground and copulated with her. While this was taking place, the girl defecated. He ejaculated and withdrew, then copulated with her again. The girl was very young and his penis too large. She defecated in surprise and initial fear and bled as a result of being deflowered. Then she told him to hold her head as he copulated; they fought together, he pulling her hair. Afterward he got up and removed the feces, using leaves which he threw into the water [to guard against sorcery].

The point of this example is that the man (in his own words) enjoyed the act, particularly in causing the girl initial pain, in making her defecate and bleed. These two facts combined to provide him with a tale to tell his age-mates and his *nenafu* and others, and added considerably to his prestige in matters of sex.[3] The next case is somewhat similar:

Asinaga of Ofafina came upon a young Tatagufa girl named A^cuve. He ran after her and eventually caught her, then threw her to the ground and copulated. As he did so she cried and sang:

> *kapi^cnaowe kapi^cnaowe jugukana*
> *nago^ckekani afukana nago^ckekani*
> *hafruwe . . .*

"Kapi^cnaowe [Asinaga's alternative personal name] . . . the shell road.[4] On one road, the pig road . . .[5] Oh, I die!"[6]
She drew in her breath and fainted. Two other men, her "brothers," found her and revived her by applying warm leaves to her breasts and pubes. She then went to Asinaga as wife, her bridewealth being paid without any negotiations. Asinaga was a well-known warrior, and his lineage and hers were at that time on friendly terms.

The circumstances of various liaisons reveal certain patterns of behavior which illustrate and illuminate the themes we are discussing. Take, for instance, this example:

Nagaba, a young girl of Moke, formed an attachment for her *nenafu*, Esoiba, also of Moke, and told him, "If another man marries me, I will return to you." Eventually she was sent in marriage to Barenu of Kasa, who called Esoiba classificatory younger brother. However, she took an opportunity to return to Moke

---

[3] This is not just a matter of idle boasting, as nearly all such examples are vouched for by others as well, such as a male companion or a sexual partner. It is probable, however, that an element of exaggeration appears here. This is almost impossible to control, in this context, and is in itself an interesting indication of current attitudes toward the subject.
[4] "Road along which shells come," i.e., her vagina.
[5] "Road along which pigs come," i.e., her vagina.
[6] His penis is so large that she faints.

to see her parents; on the road at Pomavinti she met Esoiba, and pulled his arm, saying, "I spoke to you before. Do you remember?" Esoiba replied that he remembered; and they went into the grass and copulated. She asked him, "Would you like to take me [i.e., elope], and we will go back to Moke together?" But Esoiba answered, "No, your husband would shoot me. You like me, and I copulate with you, that is all." So the girl returned to Kasa. Some little time afterward she came to Moke again and saw Esoiba at Jabakamuti. He spoke to her: "I told you to stay with your husband, but you are 'strong.' You can sleep with my mother, and tomorrow you must return." He took her to his mother's house, where they copulated, and he remained with her for most of the night. Next day Barenu came to Moke to look for his wife but did not find her. First Esoiba hid her in a house, then he took her into the bush at Eguninti, hiding her by a *karu* tree, where they copulated. Leaving her there, he went down to a nearby stream. While he was away, two young Moke men, Obu and Ibanggi, age-mates of Esoiba, who had been cooking sweet potatoes for him, went in search of him and came on Nagaba asleep. They placed the sweet potatoes by the tree and first one and then the other copulated with her, holding her down and stopping her from crying. Then they ran away. Returning, Esoiba asked why she cried, and she told him what had happened. He replied that he would look into the matter later on but would now take her to the road leading to Kasa so that she could return to Barenu. They ate the sweet potatoes, and he took her to the road. She asked him why he was leaving her and added that she would return to him. He told her, "I don't want this any more. I have finished copulating with you. I won't marry you." Nagaba then returned to her husband. He asked her where she had been, saying that he had gone in search of her, but she said that she had been with her mother and father and had come back to Kasa by a different road. A little later she returned to Moke again and went to her mother's house. An old man named Kaguwanita, who called Esoiba half father and Nagaba half daughter, gave Esoiba some bean roots; he gave these to Nagaba. Everyone but Kaguwanita had gone to the gardens. Esoiba looked out of the doorway, saw no one about, so returned to Nagaba and copulated. She told him that she didn't like her husband because his copulation was not sweet and that she would stay with Esoiba. Kaguwanita, however, suspected something and coming up to the house asked Esoiba what he was doing there. Esoiba replied, "A woman came to live with me, and I have put her here." "Whose woman?" asked the other. "Barenu's," answered Esoiba. "She is another man's woman. You are not to marry her. This Barenu is your half brother. Leave her, let her go back." "Oh, father," replied Esoiba, "I cannot throw aside your words. I haven't abducted this woman, she simply came to me. She came herself, because she liked me. I will leave her." Esoiba then took her along the Kasa road, and she returned to her husband. Next day Esoiba went to Kasa and spoke to Barenu: "Your wife comes to me all the time. I am angry with her. Speak to her; look after her well." Barenu gave her a thrashing and kept a closer watch on her.

This could be viewed, in one light, as a more or less genuine attachment between *nenafu*, broken by an enforced betrothal and continued as an extramarital liaison. *Nenafu*, as we have seen, are appropriate sexual partners; but the sanction of the woman's husband is more or less obligatory. Without it (especially since Barenu was Esoiba's classificatory elder brother, and his wife therefore, ideally, sexually taboo to Esoiba) difficulties can arise. Esoiba realized this, and when the affair threatened to become public he protected himself by warning Nagaba's husband. No questions were asked about the young men who copulated with Nagaba, since inquiry would only have caused dissension within the district.

Tunggabaso, an Ora woman, was married to Agagantuma of Moke, who went on a trading trip for shells to Grufe, in Kamano territory. While he was away she came to a Moke garden at Karapinti, which was adjacent to a roadway. There she hid in the wild pitpit cane and waited in the grass. Obebu of Moke, who called her *ato* and her husband *nenafu*, came along the road, and as he passed the woman scratched him with a length of pitpit. "What scratched me?" he asked. He parted the cane and found Tunggabaso, who laughingly threw aside her skirt and lay down, asking him to copulate with her. Obebu, reluctant, protested that he could not do so; he was going out to cut creeper rope to be used to lash the planks of the stockade. She replied, "Cut it, but copulate first." She was "strong," and so Obebu copulated with her. Then she said to him: "My husband has two wives; he copulates with the other woman first and only afterward with me, and I don't like that. But you copulate with me well. It is sweet. . . . I scratch the skin of your buttocks." "I must go and cut rope," said Obebu. But Tunggabaso held him: "Go and cut it, but copulate again first. I hold you." Again Obebu did so and then got up. "I will go and dig sweet potatoes. I'll wait till you cut your rope and meet you on the road," she told him. Returning, he found her waiting and copulated with her again. She gave him some sweet potatoes, and after making a further assignation Obebu returned to Ora. During the night he came to her house and copulated. This went on for some considerable time, even after the return of her husband. They managed to meet on the occasion of ceremonies, in the gardens or in her house. Tunggabaso became so blatant that she came down to where Obebu was engaged in attending to his stockade. He replied that he feared her husband would see them and shoot him. But she was "strong," and they copulated. Later Tunggabaso went to Ifusa, where Obebu met her in a garden at Warigasiga; she pulled his arm. Obebu said, "I walk through the bush and my skin is cold; I come through the kunai grass and my skin burns. Why do you pull me?" Tunggabaso, however, was "strong," and they copulated. She then returned to Moke and was living at Egujaganti when her husband was shot by Kabara, a mother's brother to Obebu. After the period of mourning was over, she came to Obebu and told him that she could now be his wife. Obebu accepted her offer; but afterward, as he was fighting the Hatia, she died of sorcery.

This example shows a man's relations with his *nenafu*'s wife, an *ato*, who gave the excuse that she was not sexually satisfied and allegedly took the initiative. The implication is that through her adulterous activities she

weakened her husband, making him vulnerable so that eventually he was
shot and died.

During the sacking of Kogu by Moiife and Kemiju, a man named Kaᶜi made his
escape to Ifusa carrying his small son, Tera. Here two sisters, Uraᶜo the elder and
Tagaru the younger, came walking along with net bags full of pandanus nuts which
they had been cooking. They saw Kaᶜi with his crying child and being sorry for
him gave Kaᶜi some of the nuts; they took small Tera along with them to the
sugar garden. After some little time they called out to Kaᶜi to come and fetch his
child. At first Kaᶜi was frightened, thinking it might be a ruse to get him away
from the village and perform *sangguma* sorcery on him. However, he went to the
garden in order to get his son. "Come!" the two women called to him. "Give
me my child," said Kaᶜi, "and I will go." "You can't get this child," said one.
Turning to her sister, she told her to keep watch while she copulated with Kaᶜi,
promising that afterward she could do the same. Tagaru then kept watch nearby,
while Uraᶜo lay down and placing the child on her chest, spread out her legs, and
invited Kaᶜi to come to her. Kaᶜi was frightened: "Ifusa men will shoot me, I
can't copulate with you." After a while Tegaru returned and asked, "What's the
matter with you two?" Her sister replied that nothing had happened. She then
went to keep watch while Tagaru lay down and invited Kaᶜi to approach. Again
he refused, giving as the reason his fear of the Ifusa men. Then he took the child
and returned to the village. Later he saw Uraᶜo and gave the child into her care.
During the night he came to her house and copulated with her, unknown to her
husband Waᶜema, then returned to the men's house where he slept. This went
on for some weeks while he lived at Ifusa, meeting her in the gardens, along the
roads, or at night, until she became pregnant, when the liaison ended.

The husband, Waᶜema, was under the impression that the child was his
own. After the child, named Akerojema, was born, Waᶜema died,
allegedly as the result of *krana* sorcery administered by Etazena. Uraᶜo
then went to Etazena and married Jaberoti, the *luluai* of that district.

Here again the initiative is said to have been taken by women. Kaᶜi was
restrained by the thought of the Ifusa men, his hosts. He was a refugee
living under their protection. If he were caught committing adultery with
one of their womenfolk, a fight would ensue in which he would be hope-
lessly outnumbered.

In another instance Arojabu of Kogu went to Ontenu, near Numaga. Here he
met a woman named Jasano, whose husband Taiku had gone to Forenofi [close to
Osena]. Arojabu asked her to get water for him. This she did, and in return he cut
firewood and arranged stones for an oven. When the oven was finished they ate,
together with others; then Arojabu went away to sleep, as it was beginning to
rain. As he lay on his back asleep, Jasano entered the house and lifting up his
fringe fingered his penis until it was erect. Then she squatted over him and put it
into her vulva and began to copulate. Arojabu woke up. "What are you doing?"
he asked. "Your husband will kill me." But Jasano replied, "My husband has

gone to another place, and I hold you. I am an Ontenu woman, I can hold you; my husband cannot see you.'' He copulated with her then. For the next few days, whenever they were alone, they did the same. Finally, Arojabu decided to return to Kogu for fear her husband might come back and surprise them. At Kogu he received a gift of pig meat from his ''brother,'' Kama [in settlement of a quarrel between them, when Kama had shot arrows at Arojabu in a dispute over garden land]. Accompanied by Tajoganina, also a ''brother,'' he returned to Ontenu and gave the meat to Jasano. She asked Tajoganina to go into the bush for some leaves, but he returned almost immediately, and she sent him again. While he was away, and since most of the people were in their gardens or otherwise engaged, Arojabu copulated with her. When Tajoganina came back, they returned to Kogu. Arojabu made several visits surreptitiously until, hearing she was pregnant, he became afraid and did not return. [The child, Tana^{c}u, was claimed by the woman's husband as his own, as he was unaware of her liaison.]

Such examples show that a woman may take the initiative in sexual matters just as in the courtship meetings. Even when the man himself resists, through fear of the consequences, she may override his opinion. She inverts the usual sexual position and ''fights'' the man. But usually it is a man who takes the initiative.

The theme of the lascivious woman makes its appearance again and again, in the face of male dominance. We may view it as a complementary manifestation. Through sexuality, a woman can engage in aggressive action. She is looking for sexual satisfaction, and any excuse will serve. At the same time, she is being ''strong,'' forcing the man as he forces her to conform to his demands. By seeking variety in sexual affairs, and taking the initiative in them, a woman is conforming to the ideal personality type—one of aggressive self-interest. She is obtaining pleasure, too, not just through the sexual act but through the risk involved. All adulterous affairs involve risk and are desirable just for this reason, providing enhanced stimulation beyond the immediate physical act; this is an important consideration. And in order to achieve her purpose, or to pursue it, a woman may threaten her lover with exposure:

A pig belonging to Asiwa's mother's brother, Ape of Ora, died. He called together some youths of his lineage and gave it to them and to his wife, Mara^{c}muga [originally from Haga; Asiwa called her not mother's brother's wife, but son's wife]. They took it to Fenavinti [at Ora], some little distance from the main villages, and there built a house and prepared an oven. [It was thought that, under the circumstances, it would be well to eat it away from the village in case the feces, since the pig had died from sickness, should later be eaten by other pigs, and they too should die. This would, however, not affect human beings.] When the meat was cooked, they called out for Asiwa: ''Would you like to eat?'' Asiwa replied that he would come and look and perhaps eat. He came up to where they were cutting the pig and was offered some. ''I have pigs of my own,

I can't eat this,'' he said. But they pressed him and he ate. He remained in the house with them until the meat was finished. Ape returned to his village, leaving his wife with the others. During the night they ate and at last arranged themselves for sleep, the youths around the wall of the house and Asiwa and Maraᶜmuga in the middle, with small boys between them. During the night Maraᶜmuga looked at Asiwa and saw that his penis was erect. She moved aside the small boys and squatted over Asiwa, inserting his penis in her vagina, at the same time awakening him and whispering, "Do you like this or not?" Asiwa was afraid and complied, copulating with her. Then they slept. In the morning Asiwa sent the young boys to the gardens for sweet potatoes to eat with the meat. Maraᶜmuga stayed behind, copulating with him until the boys returned. Then he went down to a nearby stream for a drink, and Maraᶜmuga followed him to fill her bamboo container. Here she again showed him her vulva. "Do you like it?" she asked. Asiwa replied that he feared her husband, who would shoot him if he found out. Maraᶜmuga answered, "He is not here; he remains in the village." They copulated again, then she returned to the house and Asiwa followed later. This kind of thing continued during the day when the boys were absent and at night when they were asleep. Asiwa became so exhausted that he built a rough shelter some little distance away; but Maraᶜmuga still visited him. He built another shelter further away, but still she came to him. He told her he was afraid of repercussions and, although some meat still remained, would return to his village. He did not escape her attentions, for she visited him there and asked for intercourse. Asiwa replied, "You copulate with me all the time, but your husband is another man; you are not my woman." She threatened him with exposure, but Asiwa had had enough. In anger Maraᶜmuga went to her husband and told him [as a dutiful wife should] that Asiwa had made advances to her. Ape caught up his bow and arrows and ax and called out for Asiwa, who armed himself. Ape made to fell him with his ax, but Asiwa said, "I did not seduce your wife, she made advances to me. She copulated first with me, she liked my penis—you ask her." With the end of his ax Ape hit Maraᶜmuga, then turned and struck Asiwa. A fight followed. Again Ape asked, "Why did you copulate with her?" Again Asiwa told what had happened: "She came to me. She lay upon me. She liked my penis. If a woman does this, a man has to copulate." Ape then beat his wife. Others interfered, saying, "Stop! If Asiwa had made the advances you could shoot him, but the woman did and he is not to blame." Then they went back to their separate villages. Next morning they began to fight again, exchanging arrow shots. Asiwa said, "I did not approach the woman, but I copulated with her. Are you going to shoot me, or is this now finished?" Ape replied, "You speak the truth. The woman approached you, and you copulated a great deal. My belly was hot, but it is now finished."

This case adequately illustrates the initiative taken by the woman (although standing in a sexually taboo relationship), the element of risk, the pressure on the male, excess, and the threat and subsequent fighting between him and her husband, including the thrashing of the wife. It was not as serious as it could have been because both men belonged to the *anumpa* lineages.

One other example shows a slightly different aspect:

Kama of Kogu was in his sugar garden when a young woman, Tavava^ce, came along, entered the garden, and broke some sugar cane. "Who told you you could break that?" Kama asked. She did not reply but merely began to chew the cane. Kama went over to her, threw her to the ground, and copulated. Tavava^ce then told him, "I did not come for sugar cane, I came for copulation. You copulate well, it tastes sweet." Next morning Kama met her down by the stream as she was getting water; he held her, and they copulated. That evening she apparently became ill. Her husband, Kiki^co, also of Kogu, a classificatory brother to Kama, came to him because of his reputation as a healer. "Someone has made poison against her and she will die. I will kill the man who did it." He asked Kama to help her, to give her "power" to make her better. Kama then went down to her, while Kiki^co remained in the men's house. Entering her house, Kama found her sleeping naked by the fire with her legs apart. He told her to get up, and show him where the pain was; but she continued to lie there, and asked him to blow smoke on her.[7] Kama began to do this, but then his penis became erect and he copulated with her. They continued doing this for some time, biting each other's chins and playing together. . . . When Kama could continue no longer, he blew tobacco smoke over her and returned to the men's house. There he told Kiki^co that he had cured her and demanded pay for his trouble. Next morning Tavava^ce was quite well, and Kama received his pay.

In most of the examples available to us, little fear of women is shown. Although youths are warned that women have a weakening effect on them and must be avoided, this is counterbalanced by other pressures. With full adulthood comes an intensification of this activity, until for some it becomes almost an obsession. Generally speaking, and with partial reservations in regard to certain kin ties, men do not trust women or women men. Moreover, in marriage self-interest is a primary consideration. Complete sexual satisfaction is rarely to be obtained from one legitimate partner. The pleasure a man receives from his wives soon becomes monotonous and devoid of excitement. The opportunity to "show off," to gain prestige through sexual prowess and through risk, is lacking.

Men usually sleep in their common house and eat separately, except at gatherings and feasts, and visit their womenfolk primarily for sexual intercourse and erotic play. The position of their sleeping quarters and the conventional dichotomy between the sexes provide ample opportunities for either to indulge in activities unbeknown to the other. Men

---

[7] That is, on the painful parts of the body. Pipe smoking, it is said, was originally the prerogative of older men; but this had apparently been changing before indirect European contact, until now most people smoke. They also use newspaper, when they can get it, in rolling "cigarettes" of native tobacco.

cannot constantly keep watch over their womenfolk down in the women's houses, although they know from their own experience what happens there. Women are not interested exclusively in their husbands, whatever affection they have for them. The men are providers of meat, guardians, defenders; they give a measure of security through the strength of their fighting arms; but the relationship is predominantly a sexual one. This being so, some of them at least come to regard their spouses in terms of how well they can satisfy them, an attitude which leads eventually to extramarital activities. The unofficial advice to newly married men is to copulate with their wives as frequently as is physically possible, this being the only sure means of restricting their adulterous activities. This, men say, is the primary interest of females, and women's actual behavior to some extent corroborates this point of view. The situation is intensified through the high value placed by both sexes on strength and aggressiveness.

Even menstruation is no bar when sexual intercourse is desired. In practice, too, men readily accept food from women, even from those of alien districts. The assumption here is that they can avert any potentially harmful effects by cane-swallowing if they suspect that the food is contaminated. Yet there are restraining influences. A man may hold back from intercourse because he fears the likely consequence of his action. He fears armed conflict, although he himself is ready for it; or rather it is not just this that he fears but the justified anger of an aggrieved husband backed by majority approval. Yet in a way he desires this risk because he has been taught to desire it, to expect it. The woman is in the same position. She seeks out risk, which may involve her directly in a fight. She presses the man, forcing him to comply. She is "strong," she speaks forcefully, she insists on copulation and takes the initiative. The most telling taunt she may utter clinches the matter: "Are you a woman that you fear risk, that you fear to fight? Have you no penis? Can't you fight my husband?" The man's pride in his strength and in himself is questioned; he can only try to show that he is really a better man than her husband. Yet in some measure he is restrained by fear of the consequences, including the possibility of sorcery. Ka‘i, for example, was afraid that the two women who tried to seduce him were acting as decoys for sangguma sorcerers. In other cases, men fear that the semen collected by women during spasmodic unions will be used by them or given by them to their enemies for purposes of sorcery. A man cannot trust such women not to do this. The whole question of adultery is tied up with beliefs relating to semen. Although an adulterous wife impairs the strength of her husband, it is not her relations with other men as such that he disapproves and fears but the fact that the alien seminal fluid in his wife's vagina can harm him. It is this which makes a man severe in his treatment of the sexual lapses of women yet lax in regard to his own actions which cause similar trouble to other men. Weakened by his wife's adultery, he may be wounded or killed in a fight; and this is what she may desire if she really dislikes him or wants to marry someone else.

In many cases men seem to have sexual relations with women casually met, or at least with those not normally accessible, without much thought of the consequences—or at least of the use to which their semen may be put. Other examples, however, demonstrate this fear and show the preventative measures taken:

A young woman named Gufemoga of Asafina, married to Obuja of Ora, had a reputation for indulging in adulterous affairs. She was working in her garden at Tuwenti [Ora] when Takasu [also of Ora] came and pulled her into some tall wild pitpit cane and copulated with her. [Takasu called her classificatory mother and Obuja "father."] Berebi [an age-mate of Takasu, who called Obuja "father," all three belonging to the *anumpa* clan], coming through the garden, followed their tracks and saw them. "Why are you copulating with another man's woman?" he asked. Takasu replied, "Come, let us both copulate with her." [Complicity in the act might prevent Berebi from revealing Takasu's adultery.] The two men spent the afternoon copulating with her. Afterward Gufemoga returned to the garden and dug some sweet potatoes, which she gave them, saying, "You have copulated with me well, it tasted sweet." Next morning she was working in her garden when again Takasu came along, pulled her into the grass, and copulated with her. On the following morning he went to the garden with a companion, Ko^cmari, of Ora [his "elder brother," also *anumpa*], and found her there; they pulled her into the pitpit and copulated. Then the two men spoke together: "This woman will take our semen and give it to some enemy, who will shoot us with *imusa* poison." So they performed *sangguma* sorcery on her. Berebi, on his way to copulate with her, saw them doing this. By that time she was almost dead, and Berebi returned to his village without saying anything. She was afterward found by an old man, Tona^ce, an *anumpa* of Ora, her classificatory father, who brought her to her house where she died.

Violence in Adultery, Elopement, and Abduction

The majority of quarrels and fights within the village, and a fair proportion of the others, are directly provoked by cases of adultery, elopement, and abduction. The same is true of the cases which come before the informal courts.

Manafia was married to Wa^cju of Ke^cjagana, but while she was staying at Haguglifinaga [near Ke^cjagana] her husband's younger brother Mugisa pulled her into the undergrowth and copulated with her. He was observed by Wa^cju's *nefaru* age-mate, who went at once to Wa^cju and told him about it. Wa^cju angrily caught up his bow and arrows and went in search of Mugisa; but Mugisa, frightened, ran off to a place called Aiwa^ckifaga [in Ke^cjagana]. Wa^cju waited in ambush and shot him in the thigh, then returned to his village, leaving him there. Konu,[8] and Wanizara, both from Kogu [then living in Ke^cjagana], found Mugisa and carried him to the nearby village; they placed him in a house, removing the arrow. In the meantime Wa^cju was shouting at his wife, asking why she had not come to him immediately and accusing her of hiding the affair; he then struck her on the body and head with his ax. Other women carried her away and put her in a house. Wa^cju made another attempt to shoot Mugisa, but Konu prevented him; and finally his anger subsided. Some days later, when the wounds of both Mugisa and Manafia were partially healed, Wa^cju made an oven and called out to his brother. They ate food together and embraced, signifying that their quarrel was now ended.

This is a common enough occurrence: an incipient fight which could have serious consequences yet because it is an affair between brothers, members of one lineage, is settled amicably. Konu as Mugisa's *noka* protected him, but not to the extent of drawing his bow. Primarily it was an affair to be settled between the brothers, a legitimate procedure, as was also the punishment of the adulterous wife.

In another case, a Kogu woman, Ketu^cna, was married to a Moiife man, Wari^co. One evening, returning from the gardens after dark, she bent down to open the small door of her house. As she did so Manigu, Wari^co's *nenafu*, also of Moiife, came up from behind, held her head, bent her further down, and began to copulate with her. She cried out and twisting around broke off a piece of his shredded bark waist-fringe. Manigu ran off into the darkness. Ketu^cna went directly to her husband with the bark fragment and told him what had happened. During the night Manigu obtained a new skirt fringe, kept his weapons beside him, and awaited events. Wari^co also collected his weapons and early next morning walked around Moiife showing the piece of bark to all the women and men, trying to identify it. They all laughed as he told how it was obtained. At last he came to Kerimi, his *nenafu* as well as Manigu's, and showed him the bark. He recognized it at once and spoke to Wari^co: "You have shown it to all the women! I am ashamed. I look at this piece of bark, and I am ashamed!" He seized his weapons and led Wari^co to Manigu's house, calling for him, and as he appeared shot him [not fatally] with an arrow. Magori, *nenafu* to Manigu and Wari^co, was Kerimi's full elder brother; he ran up and shot Kerimi, wounding him. Some Kogu men who were present, brothers of Ketu^cna, also went to the help of Manigu. Some Moiife men stood with Wari^co and shot at Manigu and his supporters; others shot back, wounding Wari^co. The fight was then called to a halt, and Manigu ordered one of his pigs to be brought. He killed it and gave it to those who had helped him. Wari^co did the same, giving a pig to Kerimi. An oven

[8] Konu was Mugisa's *noka*, since Mugisa was married to Asera, Konu's father's brother's daughter; Wanizara called Konu "brother," and Mugisa *noka*; both called Wa^cju elder brother (classificatory).

was then made and the two pigs cooked and shared among all those who had participated.

Here we have an interesting case arising from adultery within the district, leading to a fight in which armed men take sides. It is halted because it is primarily an internal fight within the district and because serious repercussions are likely on account of the presence of men from another unit, Kogu. It illustrates one important point, among others—reliance cannot be placed upon ties of relationship. Manigu might have argued that his attempted seduction of his *nenafu*'s wife was, after all, nothing to quarrel about; yet even before being identified he expected trouble. Wariᶜo was inclined to treat it as a joke, as did those to whom he showed the piece of bark. Yet Wariᶜo's other *nenafu* identified the bark and stood by him in preference to his *nenafu*, Manigu, whom he wounded. Magori took his *nenafu*'s side and wounded his younger brother. Here we have *nenafu* taking sides against *nenafu*, and also combining against *nenafu* and younger brother. In addition the Kogu "brothers" of Ketuᶜna took the side not of their sister and her husband but of Manigu.

A Teveᶜo woman, Jegonaso, was married to an Asafina man named Kaᶜjebu. One day she was sheltering from the rain in a small hut in her husband's garden, close to Kogu, where a Kogu man, Goᶜari, was out hunting birds. He too went to the hut for shelter and seeing Jegonaso there took hold of her and copulated. [He called her husband classificatory elder brother and called her by the taboo term for "elder brother's wife."] Kaᶜjebu happened to be nearby and saw them. He ran back to his house and seized his weapons, but by the time he returned Goᶜari had run away. Kaᶜjebu searched for him, but meeting with no success hid in the undergrowth by a pathway leading into Kogu. At last Goᶜari came along, and Kaᶜjebu shot an arrow at him; Goᶜari returned the shot. A number of arrows were exchanged, without either being wounded. Goᶜari then went to Moiife and slept there. [Moiife and Kogu were on friendly terms at that time.] Next morning both Goᶜari and Kaᶜjebu armed themselves with shields and with their respective supporters began to shoot at each other. Asafina, led by Kaᶜjebu, tried to kill Goᶜari, who was joined by both Moiife and Kogu men. Some of the Moiife men changed sides and went to the help of Kaᶜjebu, shooting Kogu men. A number were wounded, but none killed. Finally a halt was called, when the Asafina men were forced to return home.

Cases such as this suggest that the seduction of a married woman in another district is likely to lead to violence when both parties have the wholehearted support of their respective units. In the above example a third unit, Moiife, is embroiled. The reason was not so much that they supported Goᶜari himself, although he had matri-kin in Moiife and also a betrothed wife there at that time, but the fact that Asafina, an intruding refugee (Fore) group from near Ora, was encroaching on both Moiife and Kogu gardening land.

Other examples illustrate different facets of extramarital behavior.

Aufiagegoja was married to her *nenafu*, Tewapi [then "mouth-boy," now *luluai* of Kemiju]. She ran away to Kogu, to Go^cari, asking him to marry her. Go^cari refused; then, thinking better of it, tried to pull her into the bush for coitus. Aufiagegoja resisted, saying she had come to Kogu for another man, and beat him on the head with a stick. Go^cari let her go, and she went to Hafoza, also of Kogu, who called her classificatory sister. Hafoza, anticipating trouble, called out for Noka, the *luluai* of Kogu. When Noka came, Aufiagegoja told him [her *nenafu*] that she had really come for him. "Come, take me, and let us elope," she said. Noka then took her to Anonana, where he slept with her, and from there they went to Agura. Here an Agura man, Nakaka [Noka's classificatory father; Noka came originally from Agura, although he was *luluai* of Kogu], and his wife Jotefoi expressed their pleasure that Noka had married Aufiagegoja; they gave pandanus nuts to both of them, and they ate together [signifying their married state]. Noka left her with Nakaka and his wife and returned to Kogu. There he met Ka^ceavu [mother's brother to Noka, *noka* to Tewapi, and classificatory brother of Aufiagegoja], who said, "You are not to marry that woman; Tewapi will shoot you. Go and bring her back." Noka, angry, went back to Agura. Here an Agura man, Kisega [who called Noka *noka*] told him that he had been copulating with Aufiagegoja. Noka replied, "I am a man. I took this girl and put her here. I won't give her to you." Taking her, he returned to Kogu and put her in the house of a woman, Tane^cme [wife of Ka^ceavu], who was lying there sick. During the night Noka came to this house and played with Aufiagegoja; as he was beginning to copulate, Tane^cme called out from the other side of the fire: "If you two copulate and then give me food it will make me really sick, and I will die." Noka, who was fully occupied, called back, "Don't you understand about coitus? Aren't you a woman who is copulated with?" But Tane^cme continued to grumble and Noka grew angry and went to sleep. Next morning, Ma^cavi, *nenafu* to Aufiagegoja and elder brother [father's brother's son] to Tewapi, came from Kemiju to get the girl; but Aufiagegoja slipped away to a pig hut at Toto^cjapa. Ma^cavi called out for her, but she did not reply. Noka, who by this time had decided to return her to Kemiju to avoid fighting, sent two young Kogu men, Ava^co and Sinotaba [both *nenafu* to him] to find her. They went down to Toto^cjapa and called her, but she would not come out of the house. She was afraid: "Another man calls out for me; I won't come." They returned to Noka and told him. Noka then spoke to Ava^co, Sinotaba, and Wa^cjava [also his *nenafu*], telling them to wait in the bush while he went to get the girl, and after he had copulated with her they could do likewise. The three young men were a bit dubious, thinking that Noka would run away with her to Agura. Their surmise was almost correct; he got Aufiagegoja and took her to Ijananapa [in Kogu], then went away. The three youths had followed them. Waiting until Noka had gone, they surrounded the girl and held her for coitus. Ava^co took hold of her, but she grabbed a stick and felled him. Sinotaba then held her and tried to throw her on the ground, but he too received a blow on the head. By this time Noka had returned, and Aufiagegoja hit

him too, saying, "I came to marry you, but instead you sent these men to me."
She continued to attack the four men. Hafoza then came up and taking a stick
defended Aufiagegoja, hitting the others as they ran away. Hafoza took her to his
house. By this time Ma^cavi had returned to Kemiju to report. Another Kogu man,
Kekia [Hafoza's age-mate and Noka's younger "brother"], then approached her,
asking to marry her. She replied that she would not live with him and, catching
up a firebrand as he made advances, hit him with it. Tewapi then arrived, supported by armed men, including Waja^cipi, the *luluai* of Numparu, and took her
back. Once they had left Kogu and were on the road leading to Kemiju they
pulled off her skirts, threw her to the ground, and pulled her legs apart and
fastened them to two posts which had been driven into the ground. They showed
the other men her vulva—pointing out that here was a vulva of a lascivious woman.
Tewapi then copulated with her, followed by Waja^cipi. Then they loosened the
cords which bound her legs and dragged her naked along the road, hitting her.
Tewapi, her husband, called out, "You think I am a no-good man, and you leave
me for someone else!"

Here are several interesting developments. This is not just an elopement; this is a woman in search of sexual adventure, taking what
opportunities offer, with men availing themselves of these and accepting
whatever risks may be involved. In the process, the sexual violence already
mentioned makes its appearance, particularly in relation to punishment or
debauchment. Noka, for instance, in telling his *nenafu* to debauch Aufiagegoja, was implying that she should be punished. At the same time he
was trying to create a cover for his own activities. The three youths, in
attempting to copulate with her, were simply looking for entertainment.
Tewapi, her husband, by assaulting his wife publicly (relatively speaking)
with his companion, Waja^cipi, by stripping her naked and tying her to two
posts and beating her, was punishing her for the offense of adultery and
elopement.[9] He was endeavoring to shame her, to hurt her because his
pride was shaken; his masculinity and sexual prowess had been called in
question by her preferring someone else to him. He was reasserting himself aggressively. Male sexual violence in this respect is a controlling
influence on a woman's behavior, limiting her adulterous activities or at
least insuring that they are carried out with a certain degree of secrecy.
No informal court was held, and the matter was settled between the
parties involved. Such incidents are relatively common throughout
the whole region, but they are becoming increasingly the concern of the
informal court.

Sexual violence or collective copulation may be employed deliberately
as a punishment or may appear simply as enjoyable acts of aggression (for
aggression, here, has this pleasurable quality).

[9] Cf. M. Mead (1935, p. 232), in reference to the Mundugumor.

A young Jababi girl, Wanapa, was sent as wife to a Fomu man, Agijavi. Obebu of the ke^{c}afu lineage, Moke, was the husband's age-mate and consequently called Wanapa ato. Going to Watokerifi in Fomu [close to Grufe] he saw her there. Later she ran away from Fomu to Karapinti [in Moke] and went to the house of Obebu's mother, Ria. Obebu, passing this house, heard voices. "What woman talks within?" he asked. Hearing her name, he entered and seized her arm, taking her to the gardens of Morabuvinti [close to Karapinti], where he had built a pig house. He took her inside; after they had made a fire they had intercourse. Then she said, "You came up to Fomu and I looked at you and you 'pulled' me. Now I come to you; I will stay with your mother. You are not to leave me!" Obebu replied, "Other men are not to come to you." However, a number of men, Wakiri [of pamia lineage; Obebu's nenafu], Jaberu, Tunggono and Utegia [all of the ke^{c}afu lineages, Obebu's age-mates], and Kiaga and Igimo [of a linked ke^{c}afu lineage; classificatory younger brothers of Obebu], came looking for Obebu. First they spoke to Ria, then followed the tracks to the pig house. "Why have you come? This woman came for me, and we are now married," said Obebu. "Let us have intercourse with her first," they said, "then you can marry her." "All right," replied Obebu, "take her. I will not marry her, I will leave her." Utegia threw her to the ground. The other men became excited. Kiaga, kneeling down ready to begin when Utegia finished, began pulling her leg. Utegia moved away, but before Kiaga could take up his position the girl sprang up and semen poured from her over his face. He told her to wipe his face. As she did so, she said, "I came to Obebu, not for you men. Now you come and do this! My belly is hot, and so I poured that over you. But no matter, you can all copulate with me." She lay down again. Kiaga then took his turn, followed by Jaberu, Wakiri, and Igimo, and then by Tunggono. While the latter was thus occupied, Kiaga took hold of her hand and placed his penis into it, and Obebu squatted over her head and put his penis into her mouth. "Don't bite off my penis," called Obebu and continued until he had ejaculated into her mouth. Jaberu knelt down, pushing his penis into her ear. Kenabaju [a nenafu of Obebu] then came up and asked, "Now you have all had intercourse with her. Give her to me, and I will marry her." But Wanapa replied, "I won't marry you. I am going to Obebu." Obebu interrupted her, "I won't marry you; you came to me, but I have finished with you. Kenabaju can marry you." But she refused to go to Kenabaju and returned to her husband at Fomu. He shot her in the leg for running away from him; nevertheless, she remained with him.

In this case there was no punitive intent (except on the part of her husband, when she returned to him). Wanapa was unattached, and Obebu's associates did not take his reference to marriage seriously; nor could he resist their combined pressure. Their main purpose was to enjoy the situation with the minimum of risk, and the orgy which followed was apparently not unusual under such circumstances when restraints were relaxed. For example, the "abnormal" features have a parallel in the farce already noted when a man attempts to copulate with a small girl's hair, eyes, and nose. There is the element of force: Obebu's opinion, with that of Wanapa, was overridden. Obebu even joined in the orgy, while Wanapa acquiesced without much protest. The element of sexual abnormality is difficult to explain when it appears in conjunction with normal sex relations. All that may be said is that sexual excess may be associated with violence; the situation is such that inhibitions are relaxed, and this is one possible consequence.

Much the same is seen in the following example:

Igatiema and her husband Tutujema came to Ora as refugees from Hogateru. While they were working in a garden which had been allotted to them, Berebi came past and was attracted to the young woman [whom he called *ato*, although he had no relationship with her husband]. He went over to her and dragged her away. Her husband went to her defense, and he and Berebi fought with their fists. Berebi managed to get away from him and tore off the woman's skirts; again her husband attacked him, and again he was beaten off. But Berebi was strong, and the husband gave up. Berebi copulated with her, then tied a cord around her waist and cut some croton leaves to cover her pubes and back. He took her to Amujati [in Ora] and put her in a house there; then he gathered together his weapons and waited. In the meantime Tutujema had returned to Hogateru and in late afternoon arrived back in Ora with members of his lineage fully armed. They approached Berebi and demanded the woman, but Berebi refused. "I won't give her to you. You go!" he said, striking Tutujema. Berebi was supported by a large number of Ora men; the others retired. Berebi's *ato*, Talwaria, then fastened new skirts on to Igatiema, whom she called *nenafu*, and she went to live with Berebi. However, Tutujema bribed with shells an Ora woman named Oberesa [*ato* to Berebi and *nogago* to Igatiema] to take her to a nearby road so that he could get her. This Oberesa did. Berebi took no further action in the matter, beyond remarking, "Here I am, married to this woman, and she has run away. I wanted to pay for her; but no matter, leave it."

Here again is the principle of "might is right." An unprotected stranger, even though a refugee, can expect no immunity, and the man's wife is abducted before his eyes simply at a whim.

Ubojema [*luluai* of Busarasa], Abonaga^c a [his classificatory elder brother], and Fusa^c i and Goria [his age-mates] were collecting wild pandanus nuts at Tabise [Busarasa] when coming along the road they saw Kabuntu of Miarasa and his wife, Pana^c ina. "Ah," they said, "here is a no-good Miarasa man with a good young girl; let us chase them." At Magiti stream Abonaga^c a attacked Pana^c ina, who fell partially into the water. As he opened her legs, Kabuntu came forward with drawn arrow; Abonaga^c a ran away. The couple then hurried off as fast as they could, but the four men ran after them. At Kegeti, husband and wife became separated; Abonaga^c a took hold of the woman and threw her down and began to copulate with her in the middle of the road. Kabuntu turned back and fired an arrow at Abonaga^c a, wounding him; the latter jumped up, and the husband grabbed the woman and pulled her along. At Etavinti, Goria seized the woman and copulated while Ubojema and Abonaga^c a fought her husband; arrow shots were exchanged. By this time Goria had finished and, grabbing his weapons, began to shoot. The woman ran after her husband, and they got as far as Hagasiga [in Emasa], where the four men managed to wound Kabuntu. Fusaᶜi took hold of the woman and copulated with her. The husband continued to shoot and drove off the men, regaining his wife and escaping with her into the thick kunai grass. The others returned to Busarasa.

This was apparently nothing unusual. Miarasa was not on friendly terms with Busarasa, and the incident provided entertainment for the Busarasa men. The Miarasa husband and wife had no means of redress, apart from returning home and stirring up their district to fight Busarasa. This would depend on Kabuntu's status as a "strong man," and also on the relative strength of Busarasa. Small groups passing through hostile areas would expect such treatment and would do all they could to avoid meeting armed strangers. Even with such restrictions and risks, numbers of people apparently move about without being molested; yet the principle stands that an unaccompanied woman, even within the district, will prove an almost irresistible attraction:

Gumio, a young girl married to Tunujema of Busarasa, ran away to Anggira, also of Busarasa, her husband's age-mate but her "brother." [Tunujema, *kasaru* lineage, was also Gumio's "brother"; Anggira was of *anumpa* lineage.] Tunujema came after her and shot her in both legs, but as the wounds were not serious she pulled out the arrows and escaped into the bush. Ubojema and Noᶜe, the girl's mother, went in search of her, each taking one side of the bush. [Ubojema, *kiki* lineage, was Noᶜe's *ato*, "younger brother" of her husband Jagagu of Busarasa, *kiki* lineage. Noᶜe, *wanefa* lineage, came from Jababi. Ubojema had no relationship with either Tunujema or Anggira.] Noᶜe found the girl, but just then another Busarasa man, Tunetune ["elder brother" to Ubojema, *ato* to Noᶜe] came up. He took hold of Noᶜe and copulated with her. Ubojema had retraced his tracks and climbed a tree. From this vantage point he saw them and called out, "She is not your wife," and shot one arrow into Tunetune's leg and another into his back, wounding him. Ubojema then returned and told Jagagu what had happened. Jagagu replied that since Ubojema had shot Tunetune for him, the matter could rest there. He killed a pig and gave it to Ubojema; he also refused to have Noᶜe back. Gumio returned to her husband but on recovering from the arrow wounds ran away again to Anggira, who in settlement gave Tunujema two pigs, shells, arrows, and salt.

Tunetune was simply taking the opportunity which offered. He may possibly, however, have been the lover of Noᶜe, since her husband refused to have her back, although this is no certain indication. No action was taken against Ubojema for shooting him, because they were of the same clan, as was also the aggrieved husband. Rather, Ubojema was rewarded for what he had done.

Two women from Ke᷈afu were going to Ora unaccompanied, in search of husbands. They were met on the roadway not far from Moke by Obebu, who asked, "Where are you going?" "We are going to *anumpa* Ora. We want to marry there." "You are not to go there," Obebu replied. "There are plenty of men in Moke. They will marry you." He took hold of them and brought them to Aganamategori [in Moke], where he told them he would marry them both. They replied that they would not stop with him but would go to Ora. They spoke "strongly." Obebu left them while he went to a nearby house. When he returned they had gone. He took up his bow and arrows and went after them, overtaking them at Tikanamanti [Moke]. The elder woman, frightened now, said she would stop with Obebu provided he let the younger return to Ke᷈afu. But Obebu took hold of the young girl and put her on his shoulders; in fear, she urinated over him. He dropped her on the ground, and she immediately started to run away. Obebu drew his bow and killed her. He was angry. He called out, "I wanted to marry you two, but you were afraid of me. I have no sores!" He drew his bow again and shot the other woman dead. Then he dragged the bodies to a nearby stream and threw them into the water. Returning to Moke he told the women married into his lineage to get the bodies and bury them. This they did, at Aganamategori. Afterward a Ke᷈afu man who was living at Ora, Wari᷈namu [classificatory father of Obebu, and father of the elder woman], dug up the corpse of his daughter, leaving the other, and carried her to Fajampinti in Ora, where he buried her. There was some fighting after this between Moke, Ora, and Ke᷈afu.

The point is clear, and will become more so in subsequent examples: sexual activity leading to excess as a feature of tolerated behavior, a merging of *desideranda* and *desiderata*; the elaboration of those factors which have gone to mold these actions and attitudes, in weighting sexual accentuation and according it a definite social value. Sexual excess, as we have seen, produces an asymmetrical relationship between the parties involved; this in itself embodies elements of conflict. The conflict is not inconsistent, nor is it in any sense connected with basic organizational traits of "unbalance." In the sphere of interpersonal relations, however, in the positioning of individuals concerned, nonconformity to the norms of stylized relationship ties is apparent.

Plural Copulation

We have already noted two facets of plural copulation—collective aggressive action by males, two or more of whom have intercourse with a female, occasionally with, but usually without, her consent. The purpose may be merely pleasure (for example, the case of Aufiagegoja and the young men of Kogu; or Wanapa and the Ora men; or Pana᷈ina and her Busarasa attackers), or it may be accompanied by violence as a form of punishment (for example, the case of Aufiagegoja, her husband, and his companion).

Tapama of Inivi and his classificatory father Seseo, of Moiife, were collecting firewood at Kamugokati, near Henagaru, when a young woman named Mesofaᶜja [whom Tapama called *nenafu* and Seseo classificatory sister], the wife of Kokoᶜnapi [*nenafu* to Tapama, *noka* to Seseo], of Wezuᶜepa, Keᶜjagana, came and watched them. When Tapama moved away from Seseo, she came up to the latter and pulling his arm suggested that they should run away together to Tatagufa. Seseo replied that he would not do this, for the Wezuᶜepa men would shoot him. Later she made advances to Tapama, asking him to take her to Tatagufa. Tapama appeared ready to do so, but Seseo pointed out to him that the Wezuᶜepa men would surely shoot them. "Copulate with her and let her go," he advised. Tapama then arranged to meet her in the bush that evening, but he invited other young Inivi men as well. They went down into the bush with torches and all had intercourse with her. Seseo came down also to look for them. Recovering the girl after they had finished, he brought her back, filled up her net bags with food, and took her down to Wezuᶜepa. No mention was made of the affair to her husband.

The restraining influence was the revenge which might be undertaken by the Wezuᶜepa men should the woman elope. But Tapema could not resist copulating with her, and plural intercourse involves all those taking part as associates in complicity. Repercussions resulting from it, if any, are likely to involve all the men concerned. This was debauchment of the girl for pleasure: "If she has come for this, give her what she wants." But there is, too, an element of punishment. The girl is called *gumaja*, a promiscuous female; and her promiscuity must be punished. The term *gumaja* is used so generally as to be almost meaningless, but it is significant that the epithet refers only to women.

In another case an Amufi man, Fanamu, who with his daughter had been staying at Oka, was returning to his home district. On the way he was shot dead at Busarasa by Tabari because Fanamu had killed his father, Panagabara. This happened while the daughter was collecting pandanus nuts in the bush nearby. Jonaᶜo, Tabari's age-mate, immediately went after her and coming up behind her copulated with her as she held on to the limb of a tree; the limb broke and both fell, but Jonaᶜo did not stop. He then took her to Tautauᶜpinta bush [in Busarasa] and copulated again. While he was so engaged, a number of men came on them. Jonaᶜo, dragging the girl, ran down to Jojuminti garden and started again. Then his classificatory elder brother, Nagojavi, came up. Jonaᶜo asked him not to tell the others but invited him to join in; Nagojavi had intercourse with her too. Then they played with her. Nagojavi tied thread from a wild pitpit plant around his penis and copulated; on withdrawing, he found that the thread had remained behind. "What kind of a woman are you?" Nagojavi asked. "I have lost my thread inside your vagina!" [This was considered a particularly witty remark.] The girl replied, "No matter, it will come out. Let us continue." They went on in this way for the rest of the day. [The various things they did together will not be outlined here.] In the meantime, Busarasa men had taken Fanamu's body to

Amufi and now came in search of the girl. At the sight of them Jonaᶜo and Nagojavi ran away, leaving the girl. The others took her into the bush and all copulated with her, then took her to Emasa; from there she made her way to Amufi.

Here we have the men of Busarasa taking advantage of an unprotected girl, but in the case of Jonaᶜo and Nagojavi, at least, she did not actively resist. They did this for pleasure. However, where all the men engaged in copulation there was possibly an element of revenge, an extension of the situation in which her father was killed.

Punishment is more clearly defined in the following case:

Some *kasaru* lineage people from Wasapinti [Moke] came to Kabumanti [Busarasa], among them a woman originally from the *anumpa* lineages of Ora, Tumanggi, married to a *kasaru* Moke man, Tagusi. This woman collected her belongings and ran away. She was seen by Ubojema [see above: he called her "daughter of a classificatory elder brother"; however, he called her husband classificatory younger brother.] He told her husband, who said, "Let her go, I cannot follow her. The *anumpa* [Ora] will shoot me." [He blamed his wife for having instigated a fight between Ora and his lineage, or for carrying tales to her brothers; fearing the repercussions of such an accusation, she ran away.] Ubojema, with other Busarasa men, Magibu [*inivi* lineage; no relationship], Janaga [*anumpa*; no relationship], and Isaᶜangganda [*inivi*; classificatory mother's brother] ran after Tumanggi and caught her at Paintani [near Moke]. Ubojema took hold of her, and they started back to Busarasa, but Magibu spoke to him: "Give me this woman, and I will copulate with her first." So Ubojema handed her over, and Magibu did so. When they arrived at Pintagori [Busarasa, but called the official Moke base], Magibu again copulated with her. Ubojema said he could not do so because she was his classificatory daughter. The four men went down into the kunai grass where all except Ubojema copulated with her. Magibu then told Ubojema, "Give her to me. I will take her to my pig house." But Ubojema insisted that they return her to her husband. Ubojema then took her to his garden at Kabigori and had intercourse with her; he was joined by Isaᶜangganda, and by Jogoᶜna [*tultul* of Busarasa], who did likewise. A large crowd of Busarasa men and women assembled to watch them. The men drew their bowstrings and the women got sticks, calling to the three men, "We will fight this woman first, and later you can have intercourse with her." But Jogoᶜna replied that they were not to beat her, and Ubojema said that they had already copulated with her and the matter was finished. He then took her to a house at Kabumanti, where he left her. Afterward the other men came to her and copulated again. Next day her husband came and thrashed her, then collecting his belongings went with her to Ikoti [Wanitavi]. Afterward they returned to Moke.

This is a typical example in which men combine pleasure with punishment. The woman was accused of having been implicated in the Ora-Moke fighting, of having carried tales to her lineage brothers, and so being responsible for arrow attacks upon her husband. She therefore had to be punished. If not shot by arrow in these circumstances, a woman is beaten and copulated with. Her husband fully sanctioned this, as apparently did the majority of the people, both men and women, who assembled to attack her.

Two final examples will suffice:

A young Ifusa woman named Hagarisoja was negotiated for by Ka°eavu, father's brother to Tegenopi of Kogu to whom she eventually went as wife. Kovi°na°muna of Ifusa, the girl's brother, prepared the reciprocal bridewealth. On the girl's arrival at Kogu, Tegenopi awaited her with drawn bow, standing on one leg with the knee of the other flexed and resting on it. [This is a variation of the ceremony when the bride offers her new husband an arrow; here the situation is reversed, and the bridegroom is expressing his complete jurisdiction over his new wife.] Hagarisoja was put into her own hut. That night Tegenopi came down from the men's house to visit her, but she was afraid and refused his attentions. This occurred several times, the girl finally saying that he was a "no-good" man and was not to copulate with her. Tegenopi then grew angry. He went to Ka°i, his elder brother [father's brother's son], and told him that the girl was afraid of him; they could take her into the bush and copulate with her and then return her to him. Ka°i got together a number of men: Eti and Gusi [younger "brothers" of the husband]; Arojabu and Gumevi [no specific relationship to the husband]; Nogo°o [from Grufe, a visitor]; Tagi°, Kareriku°, Moguga°e and Asonavi [elder "brothers" of the husband], who went into the bush. Ka°i took hold of the girl and carrying her on his back brought her to the others, who copulated with her one after the other. Then they told Gumevi, a young man, to take up his position in front of the girl with penis erect. Ka°i then stood above him with a stick of sugar cane [of a special variety named *ujena*]. Resting it on Gumevi's shoulders, he called out invocations to the ancestors, of different places in Kogu and Anonana: "Aliloka . . . Waninuka . . . Watapika . . . Mairaka . . . Kovawanitaka . . . Negifika . . . Juweka . . .". On calling the last name Ka°i broke the sugar cane over Gumevi's shoulders, and he plunged his penis into her, while all the other men called out "*ei! ei! ei!*" and crowded behind him, pushed, released, and pushed, with regular movements, until he had ejaculated. [This act symbolized the arrow of Tegenopi, ready in his taut drawn bow as he waited to receive his wife on her arrival from Ifusa, and is said to make the girl enjoy intercourse.] Ka°i then heated his penis over a warm fire to make it very hard and pushed it into the girl "like an arrow" so that she cried out and defecated in fear. "Thus my brother Tegenopi can copulate with you," said Ka°i. Then he took Hagarisoja back to Tegenopi.

This was partially punishment for a wife who consistently refused the attentions of her husband. She was young and afraid, not so much of intercourse but because she was in an alien district. The treatment was designed to give her a liking for intercourse, to break down any resistance on her part, and to make her feel at home. The special form this takes differs from that in the previous examples. It is more in the form of a rite,

"Guardian of the Flutes" in posture designed to strike fear in the hearts of novices (see Chapter 6). He holds a magical leaf in his mouth, and bow and arrow are poised in readiness. An arrow pierces his foreskin and a length of sugar cane held beneath.

Two novices in Busa-rasa perform cane-vomiting and nose-bleeding. Note length of cane used by man on left and two nose-bleeding bundles protruding from nostrils of the man on right. The banana leaf at their feet is to catch blood and vomit, which must be destroyed to protect them against sorcery.

Bleeding the nose of an adult (Konu) during initiation sequence in Kogu. Tewapi stands in central background, Kokote stands at right, on log.

Eiumata cane-swallowing during initiation sequence in small creek in Kogu.

Men returning from initiation ground in Busarasa are ambushed by women dressed as warriors and carrying bows, arrows, and shields (see Chapter 6).

A simple marriage ceremony in Busarasa. The bride and her father, surrounded by kin, adjust net bags containing pig meat before she leaves for the bridegroom's village. The pile of sugar cane at her feet is a symbol of fertility.

symbolic of a husband's right of access to his wife. The sugar cane is likened to a penis which, like it, should "taste sweet." The ancestors of various lineage and other grounds in the Kogu district and also in Anonana are invoked to witness this act in the interest of the unit as a whole. Here is a woman from another district who must be assimilated, and this is done through intercourse. Men and women can be adjusted to one another only through intercourse, for this is the basis of their relationship. This important truism is echoed throughout the period of socialization; there is fundamental antagonism between the sexes, and this can be overcome only through sexual relations, as crystallizing the dependence of one sex on the other.

In contrast to this is the more "orgiastic" aspect of such behavior:

Several men and two young women from Jababi came to Kivi, where Hogateru men were killing pigs [i.e. during a pig festival]. They were given pig meat and departed for home. On the way Ijoga, a Kogu man, met them and asked for some meat but was refused. He followed them for some time, repeating his request, but they continued to refuse. Then he ran back to a party of Kogu, Irafu, and Moiife men who were hiding in the bush [having embarked on a fighting expedition] and with them took another track through Fufusa to Numaga. Here they came up with the Jababi party and wounded two or three men and one young woman. On being attacked they threw aside their meat and ran away, but the other woman was caught by the Kogu, Irafu, and Moiife men. They threw her to the ground and copulated with her, one after the other. While one Moiife man, Nooiᶜna, was so engaged, an Irafu man, Awaᶜi, was anxiously awaiting his turn. He called out to Nooiᶜna to hurry, but he would not; Awaᶜi jumped on his back and, putting his penis into Nooiᶜna's anus, began to copulate. Nooiᶜna pulled himself away and pushing Awaᶜi to the ground, placed his penis in his mouth and simulated coitus. Then he pushed it into his nose and ear, and finally, catching hold of Awaᶜi's face, rubbed it up and down in the woman's vulva so that it was smeared with semen. [These two men were nenafu.] This gave rise to a general brawl. While the men were so engaged, a Kogu man, Tuᶜavo [classificatory brother to Nooiᶜna and nenafu to Awaᶜi], caught up the girl; he carried her into a nearby tree with spreading branches and had intercourse with her there. The others soon found them, and he brought her down again. They continued copulating with her. Then they collected the pig meat and took her again, in turn, until they came to Moiife. Next day a band of Jababi men came and demanded the woman: "You have eaten our meat and you have copulated with this woman. Now return her." Moiife handed her over, and the Jababi men departed; they did not question the strength of Moiife, Kogu, and Irafu on their home ground, and the latter paid no compensation.

Here no punishment was involved but simply aggressive action, part of the pattern of warfare. Awaᶜi's act of sodomy was apparently motivated by sexual excitement and a desire to anger Nooiᶜna, while Nooiᶜna's behavior was calculated to humiliate his *nenafu*. Sexual "abnormality" is here an accompaniment of excess, as it was in the case of Wanapa. It may or may not arouse feelings of resentment. It will usually provoke anger when performed on someone of the same sex; but when a woman is the victim this is apparently not the case—or at least she cannot do much about it. In either case it is not regarded as really "abnormal." It may be laughable, as in the farces, or it may be a manifestation of relaxed restraint and excessive stimulation. It is not punishable—except by the men actually involved, as in the last example. In one case, when a youth was caught by an elder brother committing sodomy on a younger boy he was asked whether he knew what a penis was for.

Now, plural copulation may be a consequence of an extramarital affair; the lover, on being discovered, allows or requests others to participate. This means that the others become partners in adultery, signifying their willingness to support the original lover should he be accused by the woman's husband. Her silence is ordinarily assured by threatening her with death or sorcery should she reveal what has taken place. Here we are faced with a problem. However much extramarital relations are sought after, and however common they may be, adultery within the district is punishable if discovered, and if the husband (or his lineage kin) is willing or strong enough to proceed. His ability to do so depends on the circumstances of the case, on the relationships involved, and on the personal inclinations of those concerned. Plural copulation, by implicating a number of persons, represents an endeavor to establish or a move toward a "legalization" of the act of adultery. The more persons involved, the less likelihood that the aggrieved husband will proceed against any or all of them. There is less likelihood, too, that the matter will be made public. This expresses the overriding importance of strength on such occasions, for that alone, in the last assessment, is the main criterion of legality—the threat of force or coercion. But the point must not be overemphasized, as we have seen; adultery is (ideally) viewed as an offense, and in the majority of cases the husband or his lineage can proceed against both the woman and her lover, administer punishment, and in certain circumstances demand the payment of compensation. Their right to do this, however, has now largely been taken over by the informal courts.

In the case of a woman who has been abducted from another district, or has eloped, or has been captured in the course of fighting, this is merely aggressive action against a person not belonging to the political unit, one whose husband, guardians, or lineage kin are classified as "outsiders." It can therefore be described as "legal" procedure, from the point of view of those performing it, on much the same basis as interdistrict warfare. While it does not have articulate majority backing, neither does it receive majority condemnation. The woman's husband, her guardians, or lineage kin may retaliate by war if they choose, demand her return, or pay for her recovery. Occasionally, she may be released and told to return home. (There she may be beaten, sexually assaulted, or wounded for having been abducted or for having eloped.)

Plural copulation carried out within the district, sometimes involving persons from outside it, to punish a woman for promiscuous behavior, for attempting to run away (back to her village, or in elopement), for failing to comply with the wishes or demands of her husband, and so on, the punishment having the sanction and approval, and sometimes active participation, of the husband, can also be identified as legal procedure. It is this right of punishment, in this way, which has been taken over and elaborated by the informal courts.

The Concept of Strength and Achieved Status

In speaking of "strength" we can view it in terms of a strain toward the ideal personality type, particularly as evidenced by men; that is, including those aspects of male dominance, aggression, and fighting prowess already discussed. All men conform to this in varying degrees. But in our examples, and there are a great number (most of them not to be discussed here), there are no clear cases of what I would call deviation. The effeminate youth, the "no-good" man, are not deviants in the normally accepted sense of the term, any more than is the hermaphrodite who must assume the role of the sex he has found, or been taught to find, most congenial. If a man, he must wield his bow, see that a brother keeps his wives sexually satisfied, and "talk strongly" on certain occasions. There are also occasional cases of "masculine" females, who while conforming with other demands of their sexual role are also good arrow shooters and may take part in warfare. But this is not the same as nonconformity to the relevant sexual role, nor does it involve ostracism. On the contrary, as far as we can tell such behavior provokes admiration and envy, although the moral injunctions insist that this should not be taken as a precedent. Women can use the bow, as they do in the initiation rituals; and men can do so-called women's work, when need be. No loss of prestige is apparently involved by thus acting out of character.

On the other hand, the ideal personality type, so rarely if ever completely achieved in real life, embraces what we might regard as an excess of aggressive and violent action. Actually, except in certain defined situations, there are no limits: the concept allows for the relaxing of restraints in relation to sexual assault, cannibalism, and warfare. It serves as a permissive influence in all forms of aggressive action directed outside the political unit. The only major controlling force is the counteracting influence of the same principle, which modifies or restrains the expression of physical violence even while it supports and upholds the dominant criterion of "strength."

Manifestations of "strength" within the political unit are limited by a number of factors. Ties of kinship, the importance of the political unit as the war-making group, and emphasis on the ideal solidarity of the village, lineage, or clan are all important here. Through internal pressure such manifestations are, to some extent, deflected outside the group—but only to some extent, for, as we have seen, "strength" is a determining factor in nearly all situations. In the final count, there is no procedure which can resist its influence. When other men become implicated in an extramarital affair, through plural copulation, a position of strength is established which allows a husband's legitimate grievance to be overridden and majority opinion dissipated in conflicting loyalties. Similarly, a man accused of adultery may avoid punishment or a fight through forceful action and threat of action. By taking a stand the transgressor is simply reiterating the basic concept and in this sense is not behaving "wrongly."

There is no formal system of social stratification here, but through alien influence new categories with loosely defined rights are in the process of being established.

Prestige, outside the zone dependent on kinship (e.g., as between senior and junior brothers) can be obtained in two ways: through wealth and through strength. The first has to do with the holding of feasts at marriages, initiations, deaths, pig festivals, peace ceremonies, and so on, and the distribution of goods, pig meat, and vegetables. The second calls for a dominant, aggressive personality, ability to override others in argument, quickness to take and to give offense, and proficiency and courage in warfare.[10] Traditionally, the leader of a lineage or village is not so much its hereditary head man as the strongest of its strong men. His elders may be

---

[10] A broad comparison can be drawn with material on the Plains Indians presented by B. Mishkin (1940, p. 3), although the situation there is much more highly formalized: "The exaggerated interest of warriors in the performance of war deeds in order to acquire rank and the standardized character of these deeds have led some interpreters of Plains culture to see warfare as a game in which the players maneuver for social recognition." See R. Lowie (1927, p. 356); W. M. Smith (1938); also R. Fortune (1932, p. 135): "In Dobu the race is conceived as going to the strong."

well equipped to train youths at initiation, or to perform magic and sorcery, their kinship status may be "higher" than this, in terms of seniority, but the warrior leader is, physically and temperamentally, better able to cope with affairs calling for enterprise and initiative. Achieved status of this type is bound to fluctuate, depending on a man's ability to maintain his position in the face of competition; and further, prestige attained from the distribution of wealth will diminish unless this process is continued. There is a slight tendency toward hereditary succession, on the assumption that the sons of outstanding warriors will take after them, but the larger the lineage or village the less noticeable this seems to be. Each village, then, possesses at least one war leader,[11] and all these have more or less equal status throughout the district: but usually among them is one outstanding man who tends to dominate the others.

In the northern part of this region the warrior leaders have given place to more or less officially appointed *luluai*s and *tultul*s, and in some cases to "boss-boys" or "mouth-boys." There are, however, certain differences between the traditionally based position of the *kabatie*, and the superimposed *luluai-tultul*–mouth-boy constellation (see chap. 15). Once warfare has been banned, the war leaders can no longer gain the recognition so necessary to them. On the other hand, when the Administration's choice falls on the *kabatie* of the district, all that this man stands for is reinforced and sanctioned officially.

Conclusion

Socialization may be taken to concern primarily the development of a child's personality, encouraging him to conform through formal and informal training and guidance—a process which commences almost immediately after birth and concludes only when social adulthood has been achieved; in this case, by killing enemies before a marriage may be consummated. Yet after this point is reached other avenues of activity are open to a person. His experience is being widened as his life continues, and participation automatically involves learning—automatically because in this respect he has, essentially, no alternative. He has choices; there are degrees of participation dependent on a number of factors, on roles and statuses, on the concept of strength, for instance, or personal inclination at a given time; but participation there must be.

From earliest childhood there is training for "strength" and aggression, for forceful action and forceful talk. These are part of the system of

---

[11] *Kabatie* (Jate); *kavahai^ctie* (Kamano); *kezigawai* (Usurufa); *kiarezeni* (Fore) or *kaba-wajatai^ce* (Kemiju-Jate): "our men." Other terms also are used.

assumptions and values with which a child is indoctrinated, with which
he continues to be inculcated, and which he in turn inculcates. Before
his initiation he appears superficially to be free from coercive pressure.
He is allowed a relatively free hand. There is little restraint in speech or
in action. He is petted and indulged; the nipple is rarely, if ever, withheld from him; his parents' nakedness and sexual habits are there for him
to observe and take for granted. Children are barred from little except
the initiation of elder boys, the secret rites of men, and the menstrual hut.
The training that does take place is informal and subtle and consists mainly
of example. Yet adults are impatient to see children take their place in
social life: they are encouraged to imitate adults and to co-operate with
them. This in itself is coercion. The child is forced to assume increasing
responsibility; he is not shielded from the realities of life and is subjected
to the same social and cultural influences as are adults. There is, or was,
no life for him other than that he observes; and the formative years entail
a grappling with what we might say are adult problems, first immaturely,
and then, as growth continues, with increasing assurance.

Discipline is more obvious, however, in the boy's initiatory period,
when tendencies which have been developed informally are now emphasized explicitly, and a certain measure of enforcement (with some
notable exceptions) takes place. Coercion and force are not only being
exerted upon him; he is also encouraged, and in fact urged, to develop
and use these himself. The admonitions accompanying this period of
instruction offer an illuminating insight into local aims and desires. Parts
of the ritual may be relaxed and carried out symbolically on the novice,
but this does not apply to the requirement that he express himself in the
traditionally formulated way, trying to achieve the ideal personality (even
if actuality in his case falls far short of that ideal). Further, there is the continuing emphasis on "strength," on aggressive action in sex relations, on
indulging in risk, on attempting, through forceful action, to rise above the
rights of those offended, to override the legitimate procedure which may
be adopted as a result of his action.

I have followed Whiting and Child (1953) some distance in discussing
aggression, as manifested here; yet there are points of difference. For
instance, aggressiveness is not specifically a result of severity in socialization and initiation, a natural outcome of severity, or a response to frustration. Taking the initiatory rituals alone, with their stress on physical
operations, bloodletting, and so on, a case could be made perhaps for the
claim that aggressiveness is due to severity in training. This, however,
would imply that aggressiveness is not socially desirable and that it is

simply the physical mechanisms of initiation, or the physical effects of disciplining during the formative period, which have brought it about. We have seen that, on the contrary, it is encouraged and sponsored in the processes of socialization. It is not necessarily a consequence of a severe initiation, although that severity may be designed, as here, to reinforce what is desired.[12] We find here specific "training for aggression"; and this is apparent from early childhood. If we hold the view that aggression is upheld by and developed through the socialization processes, it is difficult to see how it may result from frustration without using the term frustration very broadly and taking it to be inseparable from the period of socialization as such.

In this kind of situation, too, we cannot view aggressiveness as an aspect of deviant behavior, as does Talcott Parsons (1952). The possible isolation of certain forms of aggressiveness as deviant behavior is based on no absolute criteria and must be seen in terms of the sufferer of the aggressive action. Yet if at this juncture we cannot determine the limits of aggressive action, we can indicate the controlling influences which are brought to bear upon it in certain circumstances—that is, the extent of such action within the political unit or outside it, and the nature of the retaliation. A relevant question here is one raised by Nadel (1951) and by Hallowell (1950) regarding compensatory factors in relation to aggression; it may be manifested in one situation and not in another. There are numerous situations in which virtually no aggression appears—the pig festivals, the performance of secular ceremonies, peace rituals, storytelling and song-making. The content of many songs, with their mildness, sentimentality, and poetic imagery, offers a relevant example.

I have assumed here a connection between insecurity and aggression, pointing out that, according to local belief, security can be achieved only through force and suggesting that fear lies behind aggressiveness.[13] The relationship to anxiety is more elusive and at this stage not particularly obvious. We still have other forms of direct, as well as indirect, aggression to review. But the nexus has been established. Moreover, it is

[12] For instance, initiation may be just as severe (in some circumstances, even more so) in certain parts of Aboriginal Australia (e.g., R. and C. Berndt, 1942–45, among the Pidjandjara groups) as in the eastern Central Highlands; and yet aggressiveness is not a dominant or noticeably apparent feature among most Australian groups. Among the Goroka people (Read, 1954), stress on aggressiveness is similar to that discussed for this area; but they are not, apparently, subjected to a similarly severe initiation. Nor are the Kwoma (J. W. M. Whiting, 1941/51, e.g., p. 106). (In reference to Kwoma training-for-aggression, see also J. J. Honigmann, 1954, pp. 284–85.)

[13] Cf. Murray, in Parsons and Shils (1952); Parsons and Shils (1952); W. B. Cameron and T. C. McCormick (1954, pp. 556–61).

possible to suggest that fear and anxiety stem from the socialization period, during which aggression is inculcated. Aggression is learned behavior deliberately taught, both formally and informally, and for this to be effective it is necessary that fear should be established—fear of the "strong" man, fear of losing one's strength, fear of sorcery in certain erotic contexts, fear of eating food contaminated with menstrual blood, and so on. Situations involving dissension, arising from marriage, extra-marital liaisons, and sexual violence, are especially rewarding from this point of view.

Part 4   Coercive Controls

Chapter 10   Suicide

Controls, coercive or otherwise, are concerned with maintaining or insuring conformity to cultural rules and regulations and with making transgression difficult or impossible. At first glance this seems to be a clear and straightforward statement. But is it always so easy to identify these controls? Let us explore this question in three interrelated fields of behavior —suicide, sorcery, and warfare.

The concept of strength includes the ideal of fearlessness, or rather of refusing to show or acknowledge fear. For instance, in the heat of a fight or in quarrels a man or woman should not take death seriously into account or appear disturbed at the prospect of it. Certainly men take great pains to safeguard themselves physically, trying to make themselves invulnerable. Yet in many ways, especially when under the stress of some

179

strong emotion, they are careless of the prospect of death. Behind this attitude is a belief in an afterlife, in possible reunion with the original Creative Beings, and eternal residence in a spirit world; or alternatively, because the belief is not well-defined except in regard to the period immediately after death, in rebirth. But belief in the reunion of kin and especially of spouses is an important aspect in cases of suicide.

Suicide occurs occasionally in the non-sacred mythology, for a variety of reasons. It has, we are assured, "always" taken place. The customary method is hanging—a slipknot around the neck, with the other end tied to a tree, a bench, or a rafter in the house.[1] A more spectacular method, which does not seem to take place in real life but is popular in discussion, appears in certain myths:[2]

Two brothers, under the impression that they are killing their mother's lover, shoot their own father. In revenge the mother summons many warriors; they break through a series of stockades and succeed in wounding one brother, who dies. The remaining brother, grief-stricken, places the body on one side of the fire and, taking his bow (taut, with a shortened bamboo "string"), lies down on the opposite side. He inserts the point of one end into his nostril, arranges the bow so that smoldering ashes will gradually burn through the bamboo, and goes to sleep. Slowly the "string" is burnt through and the bow springs upward, forcing its point up his nostril and killing him.

This incident is the subject of a ceremonial drama, but in the examples witnessed the "bow" method is supplanted by hanging, convincingly enacted, to the delight of the audience. At the same time the bow, with an arrow, is held in a special way as in some real suicides.

During both periods of our field work, this subject was not of primary concern but was examined incidentally. Only forty cases were recorded:

[1] See also C. G. Seligmann (1910, pp. 571–72), for the southern Massim. He speaks of different methods being adopted by men and women, quoting from *New Guinea Annual Report* by A. M. Campbell (1902–03, p. 26). Malinowski (1952, pp. 95, 100, 101, 102, 268, 393, 399, 424, 432, 457, 461, 475–76) also gives for the Trobriands both varieties and reasons. He mentions jumping from a tree for the purpose of suicide, as did Seligmann; but this does not seem to occur in the eastern Highlands. F. E. Williams (1930, p. 213) mentions suicide among the Orokaiva as a result of the death of a spouse or near relative. M. Mead (1935, p. 172) notes a case of "suicide" for the Mundugumor which is not really a suicide in my terms (i.e., death at one's own hand). It is similar to "suicide" mentioned by K. Read (1954, p. 23)—i.e., by voluntary surrender to enemies as a means of achieving redress. In the region we are discussing, a person's voluntary surrender to enemies (except in certain mythological cases) would be taken to mean that he or she was under the influence of sorcery.

[2] For a variant of the myth in which one brother accidentally shoots the other and then commits suicide see C. H. Berndt (n.d., chap. 4).

these comprised twenty-six "successful" suicides (twenty-one women and five men) and fourteen attempted suicides (five women and nine men). In such a large area, with a relatively dense population, this represents an extremely small percentage. Such being the case, why attach so much importance to them? It should be emphasized that the forty cases do not represent a fair sample. They cannot be taken as indicating the actual number of real or attempted suicides between, say, 1945 and 1953. Had we concentrated on recording such cases, it would have taken up a disproportionate amount of our time in the field.[3] Nevertheless, suicide is of interest to us here because in certain circumstances it is regarded as the "right" course of action, although it comes in conflict with a parallel value-acceptive, an ideal against which reality is measured. And these forty cases, inadequate as they are from a quantitative point of view, tell us something about the conditions in which suicide is said to take place.

Another question is how far we can rely on imputed motives for any completed suicide. Where attempted suicide is concerned, we are on safer ground, especially when it is possible to talk with the person involved. But in a successful suicide, the reasons for the final decision may not have been communicated to others. Granted these limitations, the available evidence is more convincing when a person is said to have made a pronouncement beforehand or when the circumstances of the case made suicide a likely outcome. It is inevitable that rationalization should take place after the event. The inference is that in such and such a situation, which itself provided the necessary and sufficient "reasons," suicide was only to be expected. Most recorded cases of suicide, then, have already been interpreted for us by the people who relate them; we see them through their eyes. It is enough that in any given case the available witnesses should be in substantial agreement.

The cases we are considering fall broadly into seven categories. They concern suicide, actual or attempted, as a result of (1) bereavement, (2) marital dissension, (3) illness (both men and women), (3) sorcery (men and women), (5) "shame" at remaining unmarried (women), (6) "shame" at a false accusation, severe criticism by villagers, or a quarrel resulting therefrom (men and women), and (7) fear of attending a court (women). The fifth and sixth categories can possibly be considered under the general heading of suicide resulting from "shame."

---

[3] I have not included a number of cases recorded by Catherine Berndt which in pattern and type conform to the examples discussed here. In genealogies others too are noted; but these genealogies do not cover the whole region, nor are full particulars given on each suicide.

Suicide Following a Death

A widow on the death of her husband is faced with certain choices. Except in some Fore districts, one ideal holds that if she were attached to him, and whether or not she had made a vow, she should commit suicide. It is sometimes said that a widow who commits suicide demonstrates not only her affection for her husband but also her lack of responsibility for his death. A wife is always potentially dangerous to a husband. A strongly affectionate bond between them may reduce this danger; yet if the cause of a man's death is not clear-cut, or if sorcery is suggested, his widow may be the first to be regarded with suspicion. This is most likely at times when her husband's district is at odds with her own. If he has been killed by members of her own clan or district, she may expect his male kin to retaliate by killing her. In such a case she is faced with a choice between being killed or committing suicide to "prove" her innocence, appease them, or conform to the "ideal." (However, she may not have sufficient time to make a choice.) Examples of this appear in genealogies but refer mainly to events said to have taken place a generation or so ago. Recent examples (from, say, 1945 to the beginning of 1953) are few and far between, and no material is yet available for the area south of Busarasa. Of two thousand odd cases of warfare, fighting, raiding, and quarreling which I recorded, in only two instances is a woman deliberately killed by her dead husband's close kin. On the other hand, women were quite often killed in warfare, and it is not always easy to determine whether in each case they had been singled out or merely killed in the course of hostilities. A good percentage, however, does seem to have been shot in the course of retaliation.

Kogu men allied themselves with Ofafina in order to fight their neighbor, Moiife. During the period of their alliance, an Ofafina man named Kutariana was seen to receive pig meat from an Ozana man. In discussion, Ofafina and Kogu men decided that Kutariana was being bribed by Ozana to work sorcery on them, or to reveal their war plans. Ozana, they agreed, must in turn have been bribed by Moiife to do this. "This man will kill us," they said. "He had better die." Some Kogu men then gave *krana* "poison" [sorcery] to Kutariana, thus making him vulnerable to Moiife arrows. [There is some doubt, however, as to who actually administered the *krana*; some say it was really Ofafina.] Although his death was contemplated by his clan and even by his lineage kin, a device was employed to "save their faces." If Kutariana were killed, and they were certain he would be [for *krana* is deadly], his wife [a Moiife woman] would be held and killed also. Consequently, when the Ofafina and Kogu men left to fight Moiife, some old Ofafina men seized her and waited for news. Presently Ofafina men returned from the fight carrying the dead Kutariana and calling out to the old men to kill her. They drew their bows and shot her. Subsequently the two bodies were cut up and cooked in an oven by Ofafina and Kogu. The remaining bones were anointed with blood and buried in the dead man's garden.

The case illustrates two points relevant to our main theme. First, even Kutariana's own kin group apparently agreed on his guilt and hostile intentions, without waiting for further evidence. Then, through a process of rationalization, his wife was held solely responsible for his death— or made to appear so. Since she was a Moiife woman, her death was viewed as avenging his and also assuaged the anger of his lineage at losing a warrior and a kinsman.

Haga men attacking Amuege^c [near Taramu] abducted a woman, and one of them took her as a second wife. Shortly afterward Amuege^c attacked Haga and succeeded in killing her new husband but not in releasing her. In the mortuary feast which subsequently took place at Haga, a pig was killed and cooked whole. The dead man's first wife made a public statement to the effect that the Amuege^c woman had seduced her husband, and that this was why he had been killed. Then, taking up a large knife, she cut off the pig's head, came up dancing and singing, and gave it to the Amuege^c woman, who placed it beside her. Again she danced up singing with the ribs, then with other portions until the whole pig had been given. The Amuege^c woman did not eat but passed it over to her classificatory brothers. Then the other, dancing and singing, came up to her still brandishing the knife and cut off her head. Leaving her body before the assembled crowd, the first wife took a length of rope, climbed a nearby tree, and jumped, hanging herself. All the men, it is said, "felt good" after this incident. They waited till she was dead, cut her down, and buried the two in separate holes before continuing the mortuary feast.

The severing of the pig's head was viewed as a subtle piece of symbolism foreshadowing the first wife's subsequent action. She was avenging her husband's death and simultaneously demonstrating her affection. At the same time, the deceased's clan-fellows felt a glow of pleasure and well-being because the killing had been avenged and the widow had behaved in accordance with the "ideal."

In a fight between Kogu and Ofafina Ima^{c}o, a Kogu man, was killed. He was carried back to his village and received by his widow, Jega^{c}izu [originally from Numparu]. That evening they all cried, and next morning a mortuary feast was held and the dead man buried. This woman, we are told, thought about her husband and how kind he had been to her and came to the decision that she too should die. She dressed herself in a new skirt, rubbed her body with grease, and called out to the people: "You must not loosen the rope around my neck until I am dead. We two will go along the same road. Come and watch me!" In front of a large crowd, she hung herself from a nearby tree. Finally she was buried near her husband, but was subsequently disinterred and eaten.

There was no effort to restrain Jega^{c}izu. It was, as we have seen, the "right thing to do," and moreover (an important consideration) she had made up her mind to die. But an underlying reason is inferred, although not explicitly stated. She came from an alien district and therefore might have been held indirectly responsible for his death; her action, then, obviated the need for revenge. A croton signifying that his killing had been reciprocated was planted over the man's grave.

A Moke man named Mananitoja, reputed to be a powerful sorcerer with a number of *sangguma* killings to his credit, died during a dysentery epidemic, together with his son. His wife, Nemioja, with her small daughter, remained dressed as a widow at the home village. After a time she was approached by another Moke man, Fujarema [her *nenafu* and a father's brother's son of the dead man], who asked her to marry him. She replied that she must wait for a time. "I remember my dead husband. When he copulated with me, his *avagli* dripped from his chin and chest on to my body. It dripped like rain from a kunai grass roof; it flowed like water. I whispered a vow in his ear as he lay dead. I shall stay here for a while, then come to you." Shortly afterward she took her child and went to Fujarema as his wife. A few months later some Busarasa men performed *sangguma* sorcery on her, and under the influence of this she spoke to her husband and friends at Moke: "I have heard! I am about to die, to fulfil my vow. Who will carry and bury me?" That night she put on new skirts, decorated herself with ropes of bush seeds, strings of shells, and a white quartzite nosebone. Carrying two bows she went into the bush and came to Kase^cega, to her dead husband's garden, where a *tegeona* tree [yielding bark for net bags] stood alongside his grave. Here she prepared a length of rope, making a slipknot around her neck, and placed a bow upright in the ground at each side of the tree. Then she spoke to his ghost. "You died. You were a good man to me, and I stayed here. But now something has come upon my skin. Thus I come to your grave. Now I want to come to you." [That is, she is under the influence of *sangguma* and her skin is moist from fever. She is about to fulfil the vow she had made to him. She whispered in his ear, "Like the *avagli* that dripped on me, should something come upon my skin, then I shall commit suicide and come to you." The *sangguma* sorcery caused the fever; and this was the sign for which she had waited.] Taking up a stick she beat the grave, disturbing the spirit to make sure that it was aware of her presence. Then she climbed the tree, fastened one end of the rope to an overhanging limb, and jumped so that her legs rested firmly against the upright bows. Her spirit then came to her brother, Avia, and said, "A woman has committed suicide. Go, look." Avia, thinking someone had spoken to him, asked who it was but received no reply. With his wife he therefore set out to look and eventually found Nemioja hanging dead. Crying, they loosened the rope and carried her and the two bows back to the village. A mortuary feast was held and a pig killed, and woman and pig were cooked and eaten, the bones finally being rubbed with blood and buried. In order to avenge this death, Moke men fought Busarasa and succeeded in killing one man. They returned and planted a croton over her grave. This killing was reciprocated by Busarasa, which later raided Moke, shot a man, and returned to plant a croton over the other's grave.

This case offers an interesting insight into the supposed reasons for a widow's suicide. It could be included under our fourth category, suicide while under the influence of sorcery (in effect, "when of temporarily unsound mind"). Her death was actually attributed to sorcery and therefore avenged in the conventional way. At the same time it is said that the act of sorcery, with its effect on her body, was the sign she had anticipated; and her subsequent actions conformed to the ideal pattern. She was, then simply fulfilling a vow she had made to her first husband. We are faced here, however, with an "explanation" after the event. She had apparently told no one just what vow she had made, although there was a clue in her remarks to Fujarema and the inference could easily be extended. Her speech at her dead husband's graveside was heard by no one and must remain a matter of assumption only. Yet this speech was later reported and discussed with no sign of incredulity by a number of men. When asked how they knew about it, they replied, "This is what was said when the woman's body was brought back to the village."

In another case, a Kasa man named Kogia was shot while allegedly under the influence of sorcery. [The circumstances leading up to this, and the consequences of Kogia's death, involving fighting in which Kasa, Ke^{c}jagana, Wezu^{c}epa joined against Ke^{c}afu, are omitted here.] During the mortuary feast the dead man's brother, Tajoba, requested the widow, Koiu, to kill a pig. Koiu replied that if he did so, she would do the same. Tajoba in anger picked up a knife and slashed the back of her neck. Immediately her brother, Au^{c}ja, sprang to her aid, shooting Tajoba in the chest [a superficial wound]. This began a general fight which died down when Tajoba suggested killing his pig. Ovens were prepared and the feast proceeded without further disturbance. Kogia's body was cut up in his lineage garden, A^{c}neku^{c}zeka, and more ovens prepared. Koiu, however, washed herself and greased her body, put on new skirts, inserted a noseshell, and hung ropes of shell around her neck. Taking a length of rope, she called out to some people, "Tajoba cut my neck. You did this to me first. Now I shall do it properly! Now I shall hang myself!" Going to a bean garden, she hanged herself from a kafifego tree. In the morning people went to get her, and two of her dead husband's brothers, Tajoba and Juvenaga, killed a pig and gave it to her brother for her mortuary feast.

This is what we may term a marginal case. Apparently the widow did not commit suicide because of her husband's death but because she had been "shamed." On the surface it was a quarrel over the killing of the pig, but underlying this was the anger that Tajoba felt at his brother's death. The pig offered an excuse to release this anger and to blame the widow indirectly for having caused it. She belonged to an opposing subpolitical group in Kasa which was closely allied to Ke^{c}jagana; this point is brought out in the circumstances leading up to Kogia's death, not treated here. Tajoba's attack on her, with the cutting of her neck, was designed to suggest that she should hang herself by the neck. She alluded to this (signifying that she had understood it) in announcing her intention. The case is an interesting example of indirect compulsion exercised against a widow.

It is much rarer for a man to attempt suicide on the death of his wife. Widowers apparently prefer to demonstrate their affection through some extravagant gesture such as defending the dead woman's body from those intent on cutting up and eating it, dancing with it or with parts of it, composing a mourning song, or through temporary loss of self-control. In the event of a wife's death, the husband is not faced with the same range of choices, if any. He is in the bosom of his lineage and village, he is not the conventional suspect, and, even if he has been allegedly instrumental in bringing about his wife's death, no sanctions are operative against him. He may be subjected to accusations from outside, but this is no more than he normally expects whether his wife is alive or dead; and he can usually count on the support of his own group.

Ampa, a Kasogana man, married a Busarasa woman named Agampu. While Agampu was working in the garden with her co-wife, Kantu [from Kamira], an Oka man, Bararu, killed her. She was eventually eaten. Her husband declared that he had been married to a woman from a distant district and that she had been a good woman. Taking a length of rope, he proceeded to hang himself from a tree; but as he hung he cried out and was heard by a number of men who ran to release him. A fire was made and warm leaves applied to his body, and he soon revived. When he could speak, he said, "If you had not come I would have died. My spirit came to a door in the sky; I had placed one hand upon the rail of the door and one foot on the step leading into it. I was ready to go inside, but you cut me down and warmed me!"

This does not appear to have been a genuine attempt at suicide, especially since Ampa drew attention to it by crying out. It is possible, of course, that he changed his mind. In any case, the attempt served to translate into violent physical action his frustration and sorrow at the death of a loved spouse.

But at times genuine grief (insofar as we can gauge this) does crystallize in a decision to commit suicide.

Panajabu, an Ifusa man, for example, had a daughter named Fogo°i whose death was ascribed to *sangguma* from Asafina. While her body was lying decorated with shells, her father tried to hang himself from a tall pole in his garden. He was cut down in time and revived by an application of warmed leaves. Next day he made another attempt, this time from a tree, but was again cut down and revived.

In another example an Ofafina woman died, allegedly as a result of *sangguma*. Her son, a young man, decorated himself with shells, put on his mother's skirt, and hanged himself in his garden. He was found later and cut down, and his body was placed alongside that of his mother; a pig was killed, and the bodies carried to his garden where they were cooked and eaten.

Occasionally, too, a man may attempt suicide on the death of a close relative. This is not regarded as a deviation from the norm. On the contrary, judgment, if any, sanctions the act. There is no endeavor to restrain, although there is some readiness to rescue the person if (as in the case of Panajabu) he provides the opportunity by not performing the action properly, or if (as in the case of Ampa) he cries out, inferring a desire for help. Circumstances, too, in any given situation, influence the actions of observers or would-be rescuers.

The ideal is weaker in regard to suicide on the death of a son or daughter, or parent, and even more so where certain other categories of kin are concerned. Yet self-mutilation (the severing of a finger joint, the lobe or a piece of the ear, slashing of the nose or of different parts of the body, according to the type of relative in question) may perhaps be viewed as a sacrificial gesture, with some elements of propitiation, on the principle of a part for the whole. This is evident not only in the case of a surviving spouse, parent, or child, but also in regard to certain other emotionally charged relationships such as nenafu, nefaru, and honi^c, and particularly siblings of either sex. In the mythology and in local constructs, it is these categories of kin which show a tendency to commit suicide (especially a dead man's brother or nenafu); yet in everyday life such examples are rare. This is not really surprising when ideal behavior between brothers is contrasted with the rivalry, suspicion, and distrust so often found in actual situations. But it is more difficult to explain in the case of nenafu, and siblings of opposite sex. One explanation may be that there is more latent dissension in both these relationships than I have indicated, in spite of their apparent closeness.

Self-mutilation may be a substitute for suicide in such circumstances; but structural considerations are relevant here. Females commit suicide more often than males, possibly because there is stronger pressure on them to do so, although this is most noticeable in the marital sphere. Siblings of opposite sex normally live in different villages or districts, and in any case there are no examples of one being blamed for the death of the other. Parents as a rule do live in the same village as their young children and adult sons (with some exceptions because of divorce, abduction, adoption, and a variety of other reasons) but are virtually never blamed for causing the death of one of their own children—although this is a theme which appears in non-sacred mythology. Generally speaking, too, one *nenafu* is never held responsible for another's death; conventionally, no doubt is cast on the integrity of the relationship. In marital suicides, apart from compulsion exerted by the deceased husband's group on the widow, she may be said to be under the influence of sorcery. This may serve as one sort of explanation. On the other hand, she may commit suicide partly in order to propitiate her dead husband. Many mythological or pseudohistorical stories concern a spirit or ghost which returns for the living spouse, enforcing conformity with the ideal (or *desiderandum*) that a wife should travel by the same road as her dead husband. This is much less obvious in relation to a living husband and a dead wife. Certainly propitiation of the spirit of the deceased is one reason for self-mutilation.

Suicide Resulting from Marital Dissension

There is not the same sort of precedent here, in terms of a defined and verbally expressed value. Yet cases falling within this broad category are, perhaps, the most numerous.

Several concern quarreling between husband and wife as a result of his forcing his attentions on her against her will, or more rarely her complaint that she is subjected to too much sexual intercourse. Locally speaking, a man is fully justified in beating his wife for noncompliance in this respect. The sexual aspect of marriage is stressed particularly, as we have seen, and failure to fulfil this obligation is a serious matter unless the wife has good reasons for refusing. If he is repulsed in this way, a man's pride is injured, and he may protest, "Am I a malignant spirit? Have I sores, that she should refuse me? I am a man. No dog, no pig, gave birth to me!" His approach, with public opinion behind him, is direct: physical action is required, and if this fails after a number of attempts the union must be severed. A woman, on the other hand, may not normally proceed so directly if her marital rights are denied her, although some such cases are recorded. Resistance on her part may indicate a fixed dislike of her husband. If she can see no way out of the situation (by taking refuge with her kin, or by eloping), suicide may serve as a last resort; but this cause is not revealed in the available examples. There is also the question of humiliation before her husband's kin and their wives, or before an even wider audience, for these beatings occur publicly and the alleged reasons for them are a matter of common knowledge. She may be "shamed." Alternately, a wife or husband may make a show of attempting suicide, hoping to bring about a reconciliation.

Mai^cmai^c, a Wanitave man, quarreled with his wife Kawege^cja [originally from Ke^cjagana] because she refused to have coitus. Later in the same day she decorated herself with shells, strings of bush beads, a nose-shell, and a new skirt and net bag and, having rubbed herself with grease, went out into the night with a length of rope and hanged herself. She was later found and brought back to the village, where a pig was killed and a mortuary feast held, goods being distributed [payment in compensation] to her brothers. Her body was then eaten.

Owajaga of Ke͗jagana, in another example, had the same trouble with his wife, Ema [originally of Kemiju; many Kemiju people were refugees in Ke͗jagana at the time]. In a rage, he burnt her genitalia with a piece of flaming bark. She responded with abuse and ended her tirade by saying, "I am no malignant spirit: a human being bore me. [That is, I should not be treated like this.] You burnt me, and my belly is hot." That night she decorated herself in the usual way and, taking a length of rope, went to her husband's garden at Jagazaga [near Ke͗jagana] where she hanged herself from a tree. She was found later by her father's sister's son, Kokogi, who was out trapping rats. He returned and told her brother, Mato͗o, who with a number of people went to get her. Mato͗o angrily tried to shoot Owajaga. He was protected by his kin, but Mato͗o succeeded in wounding him and in burning down his house. Ajakiwa [Owajaga's father] then gave compensatory gifts to the dead woman's brothers, who took no further action. The woman's body was carried to a garden, Agojaka [Ke͗jagana], where women cooked and ate her body, afterward burying the bones.

Owajaga's action was evidently resented by the dead woman's brothers, but this was only part of the situation. It was not so much that he had gone too far and was consequently blamed for her suicide; but Kemiju men, her own kin, were present as refugees in Ke͗jagana. Similar resentment on the part of a woman's lineage kin or her own family would possibly always be present in some degree, but the action they took would depend on a variety of factors; for instance, they might be living some distance away. The husband's kin obviously did not condemn him, for they surrounded him in defense. Payment of compensation to her brothers did not mean that the husband's group acknowledged responsibility; such mortuary payments are always, or nearly always, made to brothers and other kin unless a state of open hostility exists between the units concerned. Disposal of the corpse, however, is not so clearly defined.

More difficult to understand, in the light of our previous remarks concerning sexual excess, is suicide resulting (or so it is said) from a husband's excessive demands:

A man named Opie from Jofu, near Taramu, came to Busarasa as a refugee with his wife, Puri. His wife accused him of copulating so much that her body ached. He consequently thrashed her. In anger, then, she decorated herself and, going out into the night, hanged herself from an *isi* laurel tree growing at Mano͗kajate [a Busarasa garden]. Her husband, finding her gone, immediately slashed his ear; then he went to find her and brought the body back to the village, where he killed two pigs for a mortuary feast. Busarasa women took the body to Nokajate garden where they cooked and ate it.

But such cases are not confined solely to sexual incompatibility, if we can call it that, although it may be present as a subsidiary reason:

An Agura man, Afano, had two wives, Javiza [or Ja^{c}ija], of Kogu, and Ona^{c}ena, of Asafina. He preferred Ona^{c}ena, accepting her food and favoring her sexually. As a result the two women quarreled bitterly [bad feeling between Kogu and Asafina was a contributory factor]; and their husband interfered, reprimanding Javiza. Javiza, feeling herself unjustly treated and unwanted by her husband, went out at night to a bean garden at Goritega [near Numparu] and hanged herself from a *kafifogoti* [wild "apple" tree]. She was discovered by Noka, the Kogu *luluai*, and her brother, who with the aid of his half brother, Aipafi, carried the body to Uwazaga [in Agura]. Her husband summoned her actual and classificatory brothers, killed two pigs, and gave these with other gifts as part of the mortuary distribution.

Trouble may ensue should a husband falsely accuse his wife of adultery. A woman may not resent such an accusation if it has some basis in fact. Usually, if we are to gauge from many examples, she will submit to "punishment," be caught up in the machinery of the informal court, or elope. In the case of Ejaku, married to Ika^{c}o, a Ke^{c}jagana man, we see one woman's reaction to a false accusation:

Ejaku consistently gave food to her *ato* [husband's "brother"], Nusa^{c}e. [Nusa^{c}e was a half brother of Ika^{c}o, of the same lineage, and although the *ato* relationship is a sexually taboo one, it may involve the exchange of gifts. The implication here is that the *ato* was a *nenafu* before her marriage, and as Nusa^{c}e was younger than Ika^{c}o he could legitimately expect her to come to him as wife on her husband's death.] She was in her house one day, working on a net bag, when her husband asked for whom she was making it. "For Nusa^{c}e," she told him. At this, Ika^{c}o angrily accused her of copulating with Nusa^{c}e. "You deceive me," he said. "You work the bag for him as a lover's gift." Seizing the bag, he chopped it into small pieces, then thrashed her. Finally he left her lying on the ground. She was helped by other women, who applied warmed pads of leaves. During the night she approached Nusa^{c}e and told him what had happened. [He had, of course, already heard.] Then she obtained a length of rope and went to her father, Woga^{c}mi [*aku* to Nusa^{c}e], who was also in the village, and said, "If I am not in this village, look for me in the gardens." She told her mother the same. Later that night she went to Gujave^{c}gugagifafaga, where her husband had a garden, and hanged herself from a *tiona* tree. Her father, suspecting her intention, had informed several men, who set out to look for her. These men, Anagaze^{c}me, Hifatu, and I^{c}ia [lineage brothers, who called both the woman and her husband *nenafu*], found her, quickly loosened the rope around her throat, and placed her on the ground. At once they began to copulate with her, taking turns. Other men joined them. They continued with this until the warmth of the semen and the action of coition revived her completely. When morning came she returned, quite well, to her house. Her husband asked where she had been that night. She replied that she had slept elsewhere owing to their quarrel but had now returned. A reconciliation followed. She did not reveal that she had attempted suicide, nor did she tell him how she had been revived. Nusaᶜe afterward assured Ikaᶜo that he had not copulated with his wife, but because he was his brother she had given him food and net bags. To prove his point he told him of her attempt at suicide.

Another factor too may enter into the situation. A husband wanting to be rid of his wife may try to achieve this by maltreatment. This method quite often succeeds, the wife eventually either eloping or returning to her own village. It may, however, result in suicide. Such a motive was attributed to a Hajafaga (near Viteve) man:

"If I kill this woman," he is alleged to have said, "I can marry another." He therefore took every opportunity to beat his wife, Evema, even when he was copulating with her. Finally she grew tired of this behaviour and turned on him in a rage: "At first you were all right, but now you hit me. Neither a pig nor a dog bore me! I have always looked after your food; I have never neglected you. But now our marriage is finished." She collected all her personal belongings in her bag and threw them into a nearby stream. In the night she hanged herself from a tree near her house. Next morning her husband found her and cried. He summoned her brothers, killed a pig, and gave them the meat.

What we might term trivial causes may have similar results. They may, however, represent the culmination of a long series of marital troubles. It is often impossible to follow the sequence of events in this respect or to trace all the circumstances leading up to such a decisive act.

Jawagliᶜa, an old Hogateru man, had some choice bananas growing in his garden. To protect them for ripening and also to declare his prior interest in them he put a taboo mark on them [i.e., as far as his family was concerned. Normally a wife has a right to all produce grown in her husband's garden, not only in virtue of her marriage but also because she has expended energy there. This right does not hold in the case of produce which has been declared taboo]. His wife, Jojoso [from Tingkafiᶜo, Kamano], ignored this, cut the bunch of bananas, brought them back to her house, and cooked and ate them. Jawagliᶜa later went to his garden to cut them and found them gone. Angrily, he asked his wife what had happened to them. She replied that she and his children had eaten them a long time ago. Jawagliᶜa then thrashed her about the head until blood flowed and she lay unconscious. Next morning, recovering a little, she went out and hanged herself from a tree. But her half son, Konu, happened to be nearby. He came running, climbed the tree, and cut her down in time. He then called out to her husband, who was sorry for what he had done. He cut much sugar cane and many bunches of bananas, and made a feast.

But it is not always the woman who reacts in this way:

Natuga, wife of Mavi, a Kogu man, accused her husband of laziness, specifically in reference to the erection of a garden fence [which is usually men's work].

Mavi was so deeply offended that he strode out into the bush to commit suicide. Finding a suitable tree, he knotted a loop around his neck, tied the other end to a jutting limb, and, holding his bow poised complete with arrow as if to shoot, jumped. His wife, fearing this would happen, had warned a number of men, who came on him just as he jumped. They saw him hanging there with bow poised and said to each other, "He may shoot us." They came up from behind, loosened the rope, released him, and revived him with warmed leaves.

This is the approved way for a man to commit suicide, holding his weapons in such a way as to warn off would-be rescuers. It has its counterpart in the woman's attention to her toilet, her pains to decorate herself in all her finery before taking such drastic action. Further, it expresses the idea that one should be fairly well equipped to undertake the journey to the other world. It is probably with this intention that, in some cases, the deceased person lies in state, bedecked with shells and surrounded by all his worldly goods.

On the occasion of the opening of the first "church" at Jababi, about 1948, pigs were killed and a feast held. One of these pigs had been supplied by a Kogu man, Keri^co; but it was his wife's and had been taken without her consent. When he returned to Kogu, his wife, Uwa^cai, angrily abused him. With "hot belly," he took the rope with which he had tied up the pig and hanged himself from the top bench in his house. He was later found by Noka, now *luluai* of Kogu. A mourning feast was held and a distribution made. Keri^co's younger brother, Wa^cjava, afterward went to the grave, cut off a piece of his ear, and attempted to hang himself; but he was rescued in time.

Dissension in the marital situation is perhaps more than might reasonably be expected from differences in personality and temperament, and conflict due to expectation of different loyalties has much to do with it. It is not surprising, therefore, that perhaps the majority of suicides can be traced to such beginnings (we could include here suicides resulting from the death of a spouse). On the whole, marital dissension is dissipated in spasmodic quarreling and is more often brought to a head by an elopement or an informal court case. Suicide to escape from what can be taken as unpleasantness is not at all frequent, yet we can say that it represents an alternative course of action which is locally accepted and in some circumstances frankly commended. In such circumstances there is no direct pressure by the social unit desiring to cast blame and obtain a scapegoat. The pressure exerted by a man against his wife is of a personal nature, and her decision is viewed in relation to his attitude and treatment. Condemnation from the victim's kin may follow the suicide; but this can be dissipated by merging the personal responsibility of the man or woman who served to crystallize the suicide decision into that of his (or her) lineage and village, by interdistrict fighting, sorcery, and so on. There is never internal social condemnation either of the victim or of the person believed to be responsible.

Suicide as a Result of Illness

Suicide during illness is usually associated with a morbid condition, with the attitude that life is no longer worth living, or with the desire to avoid further pain. It is said to have been especially common during the dysentery epidemics which spread through this region (the most recent in 1947).

Katawa of Hogateru had severe dysentery and while being carried from Keᶜjagana to his home village by his classificatory brother, Wanizara, continually remarked that he wanted to die. As soon as he found himself unwatched he got up and hanged himself from a tree. Wanizara went in search of him, climbed the tree, and cut the rope with his teeth. He carried him back but was unable to revive him.

The same happened in the case of Taᶜu, wife of Enaᶜo of Kogu, who also had dysentery. After expressing a wish to die, she hanged herself from a rafter in her house. [However, in a version of this case recorded by C. H. Berndt from Taᶜu's brother's wife, the alleged reason was that other women scolded Taᶜu for being ill and causing them extra work in looking after her.]

More recently a Keᶜjagana woman, Vegoᶜe, married to a Hogateru man, was ill with an unspecified sickness [possibly some sort of skin disease]. Becoming depressed when no cure was effected, she hanged herself from a tree. Her son Gozigoja and her classificatory son, Konu [of Kogu], found her soon afterward and cut her down, but she died on removal to her house.

In another example Mogaᶜau, wife of Nomaja of Agura, became ill. Her husband, a native doctor, and several close kin treated her with warmed leaves, massage, special herbs, pig blood, and meat, but she showed no improvement. Her husband left her in a very depressed state in the care of his mother's brother, Auᶜna, while he went to get sugar cane. Returning, he found his wife missing and asked where she was. Auᶜna replied that she had said she was going outside the house to defecate but had not yet returned. They both set out to find her and managed to cut her down in time. After applications of warmed leaves she revived and afterward recovered from her illness.

Such cases are fairly straightforward and need no detailed discussion. There is the assumption that it is necessary to watch over such patients, since any decision to commit suicide will be dictated not by free choice, as it were, but by their abnormal condition.

Suicide under the Influence of Sorcery

Sickness from natural causes is distinguished from sickness as a result of sorcery. In the case of certain kinds of sorcery, it is said that the victim has no hope of survival; usually he waits for the sorcery to run its course and does not hasten death by his own act. But there are other types of sorcery, such as *sangguma* (in pidgin English; *tunakafia* in Jate). During the operation performed on him by the sorcerers (see chap. 11), the victim may be told what to do in order to bring about his own death. Commoner still, however, is that kind of *sangguma* or *krana* ''poison'' which is said to make a man vulnerable to the arrows of his adversaries (as in the case of Kutariana of Ofafina above, p. 182). The victim, under the compulsion of magic, may run out in full view of the enemy, without protection, while arrows are attracted to him; he makes no effort to protect himself, nor is he able to do so.

Four Ofafina men met Ke^conu on the outskirts of Moiife. They showed him ropes of shells, offering to give him these if he would kill a certain man for them; but first, they told him, it would be necessary for him to come into the bush so that they could discuss matters. Ke^conu, attracted by this proposition, went with them; but as soon as they were under cover at Kariga [near Moiife] they turned on him and carried out *sangguma*. During the operation, while their victim was unconscious, they spoke to him, telling him to commit suicide, describing all the actions he was to go through. They then revived him, and he returned to Moiife and slept. Next morning, with his bow and arrows and a spare ''bowstring'' as well as all his decorations, he went to a bean garden at Sanofinaga where an *ogona* tree was growing. Here he dressed in all his finery, knotted the bowstring around his neck, and climbed the tree. Several young boys found him hanging and told the rest of the village; he was cut down, a mortuary feast was held, and he was buried.

In such a case sorcery offers a convenient means of accounting for a death. Indeed (and here we are faced with a problem similar to the one raised before concerning statements made when no one is present), there is no evidence to support the reason given for Ke^conu's suicide. No one knew that sorcery had been worked on him. For that matter, he himself would not have been in a position to tell, for he was allegedly acting under compulsion and not consciously aware of his actions. In certain circumstances, a *sangguma* victim can inform others of his state, but Ke^conu did not do so. The Ofafina men would presumably have been ready to claim responsibility for the suicide in order to enhance their prestige; and news of this claim inevitably would have reached Moiife.

In another case marked by complications leading up to the performance of *sangguma* by two Busarasa men, Ivo^ce and Iasava, on Kajokajopi, a Ke^cjagana man who was decoyed for the purpose, the circumstances are much the same except that some time elapsed before the act was carried out. On being revived, Kajokajopi went back to Ke^{c}jagana and after an interval of several days collapsed in the presence of his *noka*, Nusa^{c}e [Kajokajopi was married to Nusa^{c}e's sister], and his mother-in-law, Fenakizu. These two killed a pig and collected the blood in a bamboo container. They then bled Kajokajopi's nostrils until blood flowed freely, and when it had eased a little poured in the pig blood to give him strength and revive him. This was of little help, so pig meat was cooked, cut, sprayed with a special bark, and given to him. Next morning he announced that he was going to die. Nusa^{c}e, Fenakizu, and others, including his son, Hagina, decided that he was under the influence of sorcery. Kajokajopi instructed them to kill a pig and hold his mortuary feast immediately. This was done, the chief participants being Fenakizu, Nusa^{c}e, Fenakizu's brother's son Meneke, whom she had adopted, and the sick man's wife, I^{c}iota. That night they all slept in the house with Kajokajopi. During the night he tried to hang himself from a rafter but was seen in time by Fenakizu, who awakened Nusa^{c}e and I^{c}iota. They loosened the rope and made him lie down. He told them then that sorcery had been worked on him and that he was compelled to die in this way. Later, when they were all asleep, he got up and pried loose two planks of an upper storage bench, then putting his head between them he let them fall back into position, so breaking his neck. The noise awakened Fenakizu, who called the others; but it was too late. During the mortuary feast which followed, word reached Ke^{c}jagana that *sangguma* had been performed on Kajokajopi by the two men already mentioned.

Here some effort was made by the victim's kin and affines to restrain him from killing himself; but when they realized that sorcery was responsible, they saw that intervention was futile.

Suicide from Shame

The term "shame" (*agaze*) is used in a variety of circumstances.[4] Broadly, however, it seems to have two main meanings. It is used frequently in relation to real or assumed shyness. The farce mentioned in Chapter 7 is a case in point: when the girl found that what she had thought was a small child was really her betrothed husband who had changed his

4 See Malinowski (1952, pp. 393, 424), who mentions suicide from "shame": but his interpretation is slightly different. Fortune (1932, pp. 3, 49, 91–92) speaks of suicide or attempted suicide on the part of offended husbands. He notes that the old feature of Dobuan suicide, in this context, "forcing one's kin to avenge one on one's cruel wife's kindred, is difficult now, owing to the white man's laws against murder being fairly well enforced." Fortune notes, too (p. 79), suicide on the occasion of obscenity being used against a husband by his wife's kin, or between spouses, the injured party attempting to take his or her life. The term *agaze* is used also when declaring an object or item of food taboo to others or in the rite concluding a "story" (a secondary myth) when a moral pronouncement is made. I would agree with Honigmann (1954, p. 294) that the identification of guilt or shame remains too much a matter of intuition: "cultures" cannot be satisfactorily classified on this basis (see, e.g., G. Piers and M. B. Singer, 1953, p. 45).

shape to see whether her genitalia were healthy, she is said to have been
"ashamed." In one version, however, this was equivalent to shyness,
which was overcome upon her marriage. Similarly, on some occasions
the "shame" or shyness of a newly married couple must be overcome by
the performance of a rite. A man is "ashamed" (or shy) when his full
sister's name is mentioned in his hearing and responds with giggling
embarrassment. But shyness shades into what we would refer to as real
shame when, as is sometimes the case, trickery is involved. In one myth,
young men in the shape of birds approached some young women, changed
into men to copulate with them, then changed back into birds; a number
of the women, ashamed, committed suicide. The same word is used for
that "shame" which leads to anger. The shamed person has a sense of
injury and injustice, and there is an upsurge of "heat" from his belly
which forces him to hit out or look for an opportunity of revenge. This is
the case in another version of the farce, already cited. There is ample
evidence to suggest that people may be (or are said to be) ashamed in this
way but do nothing about it. Nevertheless, certain accusations, slights,
injuries, or insults are likely to cause shame, followed by a desire to
reciprocate verbally or by physical action—and suicide is one response.

A young Asafina woman, Ramu, repeatedly asked her parents to send her in
marriage, but after many delays, and haggling with representatives of several
eligible men, nothing was done. At first she was ashamed: "Why don't they send
me? Why do they injure me in this way?" Then she grew angry and cutting some
leaves from a pandanus forced them into her vagina so that blood flowed. She
called out to her parents, "Why do you not send me to a man so he can copulate
with me? That is what I want. Why do you keep me here?" That night she took her
mother's spare skirt and tied it around herself, greased her body thoroughly and
decorated it with shells, and hanged herself from the top bench in her house. She
was found later by her brother, Amori, who loosened the rope and took her
down. He called out to others, and a mortuary feast and distribution took place.
Afterward her body was eaten in a garden at Popoga, near Kogu.

The case is a straightforward one. She had reached the age when it is
usual for a girl to be betrothed and sent to her husband, and she was
ashamed of the delay, yet we can hardly suppose that the thwarting of the
sexual urge was the real reason for her decision, since, as we have seen,
some sexual latitude is permitted unmarried girls. Even had she been
betrothed and not yet sent to her husband, this would not have stopped
her had she wanted coitus. It is more likely that marital status was
involved: all the young girls of her age were married, and she felt strongly
the supposed slight or neglect. This was apparent when she made blood

flow from her vagina, re-enacting a part of the puberty ceremony, signifying her maturity and readiness for marriage. In addition, the act had the same significance as nose-bleeding during the marriage rites. And before committing suicide she dressed herself as a bride. She greased her body and replaced her own skirt, which left the thighs bare, with the skirt of a married woman. Shame had symbolically been removed, and she had achieved marital status; but she still felt deeply injured and angry. In committing suicide she retained the status she had assumed and punished her parents and lineage kin. They had lost a daughter who could have brought them bridewealth; and distributions of meat and goods to her mother's brothers and *nenafu* in another district would have to be made at the mortuary feast.

A somewhat different note is struck in the case of a young woman from Viteve who had as lover a young Ke°jagana man, Hafoza. Hafoza, living in Viteve at the time, had formed this attachment without the sanction of her parents; she was his classificatory *aku* [daughter of a distant cross-cousin]. Their liaison continued more or less in secret until she became obviously pregnant. A number of Viteve men then made it their business to ask her the name of her lover. "Hafoza made me pregnant," she replied. She was "ashamed." That evening she dressed herself in a new full skirt and shells and hung herself inside her house. She was found by her brothers, who loosened the rope. A mortuary feast was prepared, and she was eventually buried. Her father and brothers wanted to take revenge on Hafoza and but for the influence of the Administration in this region would have shot him there and then. Instead of calling an informal court, they captured Hafoza and took him to the patrol base of Kainantu, where he was, presumably, charged and put in jail for a period.

This case has some interesting points. In the first place, there was nothing unusual in the girl's indulging in premarital sexual relations; had the matter been kept relatively secret, probably no action would have been taken by her parents and kin. Premarital sexual relations are often a prelude to marriage, and here there is no virtue in virginity. Nor are association and marriage with a classificatory *aku* frowned upon, although they may provoke discussion and perhaps disparaging remarks. The point at issue was the girl's pregnancy. It is usual for a girl to be married either before or immediately after puberty. If not, this means that her parents are holding out for more bridewealth, that she herself for various reasons is unwilling to marry, or that she is so physically unattractive that no man will initiate or agree to marriage negotiations. Ordinarily, should an unmarried girl become pregnant the marriage proceedings are hastened so that the birth can take place with the full co-operation of the child's father and his lineage. It is important that a child should have a social father, and as far as we can judge there are virtually no cases of socially recognized illegitimacy. This is not to say that physical paternity is not recognized by those immediately concerned—that is, by the woman and her lover, and often (but not necessarily so) by her husband. Extramarital relations which culminate in pregnancy are normally curtailed, the woman so arranging matters that her husband does not suspect the child is not his own.

Here, the Viteve men, by asking the name of the man who had made her pregnant, were suggesting that, since she was past puberty and therefore physically mature, something was wrong with her; otherwise she would be married. "Why," they inferred, "are you evading your responsibilities?" This suggestion made her ashamed, and that was why she committed suicide. There may be other reasons behind this. For example, her parents may have opposed the match on the grounds of the relationship involved, or perhaps had already betrothed her (or intended to do so) to someone else. There is no information on this point, but there is reason to suspect some such crucial underlying factor in the situation. Her parents, for instance, could not have failed to notice her condition; it was their duty then to make arrangements for the marriage. The girl had apparently not approached them in the matter. In committing suicide she obviously intended to punish them. She was not, then, because of a socially disapproved pregnancy, forced into a situation where humiliation and shame could be balanced only through suicide. The anger of the girl's lineage kin was directed against the man she had named. He was blamed for her death; but, for fear of Government reprisal, they were unable to avenge her death by killing or wounding him, and so the case was brought before the European court. (The shift from indigenous to alien control will be discussed later.)

A different aspect of the problem of "shame" in relation to suicide is apparent in the case of Tewapi, who made a name for himself as a warrior, a strong man, and a great talker. He became first a "mouth-boy" (boss-boy) and later a *luluai* of Kemiju. In the example which follows he was a relatively young man.

Tewapi went alone to one of the Amufi villages [near Inivi] and set fire to the large men's house there. Returning to Kemiju, he boasted of his deed to the people of his own village as well as to Tatagufa visitors. The men of his lineage and clan angrily reprimanded him, for there was no current quarrel with Amufi, and in any case he had acted without their authority; they feared reprisals. They took no action against him, but their words were enough to make him feel "ashamed." His sense of injustice turned to anger; he was "hot belly." He gathered together his weapons and strode out into the bush until he found a *karu* tree.

He then tried to hang himself, but the bough broke and he fell to the base of the tree. He was found by some men and carried back to the men's house, where they revived him by pouring pig blood into his nostrils.

The same sense of "shame" and injustice was felt by a Kogu man, Matojaba. He was left in charge of a small boy named Oiituma who was being reared by one of his mother's brothers, Mania, elder brother to Matojaba. While Matojaba was so occupied, his own own son, Arijaᶜo, fought with Oiituma, his *nenafu*. Matojaba, finding his son crying, struck Oiituma, who ran away into the bush. Next day Mania returned and finding him missing asked his sister Woiveku, the child's mother, what had become of him. She said that he had run away because his mother's brother had hit him. Mania, angry, seized a stick and attacked Matojaba. Matojaba did not return the blows. He was "shamed." Later in the evening he grew angry and going out to his garden attempted to hang himself from a tall pole supporting sugar cane. He was discovered by an age-mate, who released him and brought him back to the village where he was revived by applications of warmed leaves. Next morning Mania killed a pig and heaped up vegetables and sugar cane for a feast of reconciliation. Oiituma had returned after spending a night in the bush.

Matojaba resented Mania's action because he himself was just as much a mother's brother to the child as Mania was. A relatively strong bond, an extension of the brother-sister relationship, exists between a man and his sister's child. Whether he was justified in hitting the child is beside the point; there is the question of a parent's rights in this respect, and the normative attitude that only they may punish their children. But Mania was the child's guardian, as the actual father was dead, and in addition he exerted his authority as an elder brother. The shame and anger Matojaba felt were directed against the questioning of his affection for his sister's son as well as the elder brother's authority. His intention was to punish Mania; and Mania's acknowledgment of this was evident in the feast he held after the suicide attempt.

Another case could perhaps be included under the heading of "marital dissension" but belongs more properly to the broader concept of "shame."

Jofangki, of Kogu, a "schoolboy" at Raipinka Lutheran Mission station, came with us on our first visit to Kogu to serve as an interpreter. Although he spoke Usurufa, Jate, Kamano, some pidgin English, and a little Fore, it soon became obvious that he was a hindrance rather than a help. He was inclined to show off, to bully his own kin as well as other local people, to engage in fights and quarrels on his own account while proclaiming that he had the authority of the Administration to do so; and when in any difficulty he cast the responsibility on us. There were numerous complaints from men and women of Kogu and neighboring districts; but serious discussions with Jofangki seemed to make no difference at all.

Finally we told him he must return to Raipinka. This decision was a humiliating one for him, although it had been foreshadowed quite early in our acquaintance. Just at that time Jofangki's wife, Uwa^cai, was about to give birth to another child. Since she also belonged to Kogu, and her own parents were living in Maira village, it was arranged that she would stay there for the time being while he returned alone. However, he tried persistently to remain.

One day of very heavy rain, Jofangki came back to the village in the late afternoon tired, cold, and soaking wet, and asked his wife to give him a small piece of newspaper to roll a cigarette of local tobacco. Annoyed with him on account of the trouble he had been causing, she refused to do so. This led to a quarrel. Shortly afterward the cry went up that Jofangki had hanged himself with his leather belt, and everyone in the village rushed to the spot. However, he had apparently waited until he was sure of being observed and had fastened the belt loosely so that it slipped open again. He was soon revived with wild ginger and salt and a dash of cold water.

Discussion in the village after this focused on the topic of Uwa^cai's sharp tongue. Her first husband, Keri^co, had hanged himself after a quarrel with her, and it was pointed out that the second might well be expected to do the same. The issue of Jofangki's projected return to Raipinka received less attention; but undoubtedly it was of major significance, and the trouble with his wife merely a "last straw." It seems clear, however, that he did not intend his suicide attempt to succeed.

Suicide Resulting from Fear

There are very few cases in this category, and all have some connection with the impact of alien influence. I shall describe only two.

A young woman named Inasa, wife of Mena, a Kasa man, was forcibly taken from him by Bagau (or Baga^cu), a native police official who was stationed for a while at Moke. She accompanied him on several journeys as his mistress and when he grew tired of her returned her to her husband. Shortly afterward one of her *nenafu*, Numugo^c, a lineage brother of Mena, eloped with her to Ofafina. Mena, hoping to bring them before an informal court, came to Bagau and told him what had happened. Bagau went to Ofafina with the intention of "taking in charge" both the woman and her lover. Numugo^c, hearing of this, told Inasa: "This police boy has come for you. You had better go down to talk to him." Inasa refused to go: "I like you, and so I will stay with you. But you are not strong enough to fight this court. I am afraid of what will happen to us. I won't stay here." She began to cry. That night she decorated herself and hanged herself from a *pagaua* cane tree. Numugo^c, thinking over what she had said, decided that they should both run away, but he found Inasa hanging. He cut her down and brought her body back. In the morning her brother, Wanufuto, was sent for, a pig was killed, and a mortuary feast was held. The girl was buried, and Bagau returned to Moke without further interference.[5]

[5] This occurred in about August, 1952. No compensatory payments were made to Mena by Bagau or by Numugo^c. There were apparently no repercussions from these events.

In pointing out that they would have no chance against the courts, Inasa was evidently concerned with the prospect of punishment, of separation from Numugoᶜ, and perhaps of being taken by Bagau. Her hopes of escape must have faded before the threat of direct interference by the Administration in the shape of its agent, Bagau. Numugoᶜ had first suggested that she appeal to Bagau in order to clear the way for their marriage. When she refused, he planned to escape with her to some place beyond Bagau's control, on the local principle that a woman who runs away with her lover becomes his wife if the first husband does not take immediate action. At the worst he would be obliged to pay compensation to the first husband or to fight it out with him.

A somewhat similar event occurred in February, 1952.

A woman married at Haga ran away to live with an Ofafina man. Her husband and his lineage brothers approached a native police official, Tamuka, who was in the region, asking that a court be held. Tamuka came to Ofafina with the aggrieved husband and told the woman they were going to make court against her. "Stay here," he said. "We are going to Kainantu to take the case to the white man. When we return we shall catch you and take you back to Haga." They then set off for the patrol base, where they asked the administrative officer to remand the woman and her lover and to hold a court. In the meantime, she mentioned to several people at Ofafina that she did not like this court business, particularly in relation to a white official, and was afraid of it. Finally she hanged herself. Hearing the news, her lover rushed to her body and embraced it. He too attempted to commit suicide but was rescued in time and revived. The court case was dropped.

The woman feared not only separation from her lover but the punishment which she took to be the inevitable result of such a court. There was the additional possibility that she might be taken to the Kainantu jail.

It is most unusual, as far as we can tell, for suicide to be attempted as a direct result of fear of any specific situation, person, or thing. A widow who expects to be blamed for her husband's death may take this course, but otherwise death is rarely seen as the only possible means of escape. When alien control comes into the picture, it may seem to overshadow any conceivable alternative other than suicide to anyone in such a dilemma. Nevertheless, the great majority of people still refrain from taking this final step.

One other point distinguishes suicide in this category: the absence of any apparent desire to cause injury to others.

Implications

Suicide in this region is an entirely normal (non-deviant) phenomenon. It is part of the cultural heritage, traditionally based, an accepted form of action in certain circumstances. Therefore, notwithstanding the discrepancy between the "ideal" and the "actual," and the smallness of our sample, we can with justification call it institutionalized. The fact that emotional instability might be inferred in some instances, despite the absence of supporting data, is no argument to the contrary. I am excluding, in this particular context, cases in which the subject is under the influence of sorcery, or under extreme stress and pain, as in illness. Although local opinion has it that in such cases personal choice and ordinary reasoning ability are entirely absent, this is possibly not so. Such examples are few.

Two broad, contradictory propositions are relevant here. We have Durkheim's statement[6] that suicide is an index of a society's social cohesion. But it is Nadel's contention[7] that social rigidity is a key to the incidence of suicide. Briefly, that is, to paraphrase Durkheim, the more "stable" (or rigid) the society, the less suicide; to paraphrase Nadel, the more "stable" (or rigid) the society, the more suicide. I have no intention of equating social rigidity with social stability, but it seems to me that in Durkheim's terms social cohesion might be taken as conterminous with stability. And in Nadel's terms social rigidity would mean, in effect, that control mechanisms were strong in relation to conformity; less latitude would be permitted, and the range of conformity would be correspondingly narrower, with the consequence that one could speak of relative solidarity existing within the group. The next step would be to consider stability in relation to aspects of social structure and organization.

How far, then, can such propositions be tested against our empirical material? A number of problems immediately present themselves. I shall mention only a few. Initially, of course, there is the question of what we mean by cohesion; if we substitute stability, there is the same query. If we are to speak of stability at all, our frame of reference must take into account the time dimension and be phrased in some such terms as a fluctuating equilibrium which allows for inconsistencies and conflicts. We cannot, in this context at least, speak of the occurrence of suicide as indicating social cohesion or solidarity, or the reverse. There is a multiplicity of factors operating here. Certainly it is possible to tackle the question of social rigidity in relation to strong mechanisms of social control and severe socialization, so long as we keep in mind its dynamic

---

[6] Durkheim (1930); also, e.g., Talcott Parsons (1949*b*, pp. 324–38, 708 ff.); MacIver and Page (1950, pp. 108–9).

[7] S. F. Nadel (1947, pp. 478–80; 1951, pp. 117–18).

Scenes during an informal court in Kogu. Cases are discussed in Chapter 16.

An informal court (see discussion of Case 17 in Chapter 16).

A mock fight in which a "dead" warrior is brought back to Kogu in the course of the ceremony. The two "human" figures made of beaten bark and attached to sticks at right are ceremonial emblems.

Armed warriors approaching to attack near the gardens at Maira (Kogu).

Breaching a stockade at Maira.

Armed fight at Pintagori, outside the "rest house."

aspect. In the light of examples at hand, we can say that here the process of socialization is relatively severe, if measured against an ideal western European standard (broadly speaking) and if certain physical operations are taken as index. If we consider socialization in its wider perspective, as I have done, certain of these severe features appear to be counter-balanced by others. Assessing the severity of socialization then becomes more difficult.

Furthermore, strong control mechanisms are noticeably lacking in some areas of social action. There are what we may term "hard" and "soft" controls. There is a tendency today for certain control mechanisms to harden with the development of informal courts, due indirectly to alien pressure. In social process we see a fluctuation of the relative "hardness" or "softness" of these controls. But because the range of conformity is relatively wide, because it is flexible enough to allow apparent inconsistencies, and because conflicting elements are of vital importance in any social system, we cannot speak of social rigidity. If "rigidity" means that certain forces are at work to make people conform to common traditional practice, and that the corollary of this is a greater tendency to suicide, then we can answer that here, where there is a some-what contrasting situation, there is also a demonstrable tendency to suicide. The problem of suicide must be considered in relation to both situation and person. In one sense it is dependent on factors of personality, embracing individual experience expressed in terms of personal decision. But personal decision is shaped by cultural facts (traditional procedures) and by the social values which are inherent in these.

There is no social disapproval of the person who commits suicide or attempts to do so, and no hint of differential treatment for such a person in the spirit world. Rather, positive approval is expressed, particularly when a widow or widower takes this step (category 1). (There is a suggestion that a male should perhaps be saved from himself, but this is neither consistent nor explicit.) The consequences in such cases may be regarded as good on the whole by members of the lineage or village, or of the district. We might say that they offer an emotional release for the group which has been disturbed and upset by the first death and can in certain circumstances be interpreted as indicating that that death has now been avenged, if only because members of two different units (districts, or at least villages) have been involved; and this is regarded as implying some sort of balance. This type of suicide underlines as well as exemplifies interdistrict suspicion. Even when it is clearly established that husband and wife were on closely affectionate terms and had exchanged vows, over and above this the interaction between their respective units comes into play. The inference of conflict between spouses, as representing the wider and more articulate hostility of their respective lineages, villages, and districts, appears in all cases where one attempts to commit suicide in consequence of some action on the part of the other.

A fundamental consideration is the principle of reciprocity. A death occurs, another must follow to compensate. An injury is given; an injury must be returned. Gifts are made; they must be reciprocated. No service, however small, is given without expectation of return. In suicide as a result of dissension (as in category 2), the significant point is the balancing of an imagined or real injury. The same mechanism is at work when a son attempts suicide in grief at losing his mother. But it is not apparent in suicide arising from sickness or from sorcery, although such an act will more likely than not set in motion the machinery of revenge.

A problem which cannot be explored in detail concerns values influencing the final decision in cases of suicide which are not directly due to outside pressures. Where humiliation and shame are involved (categories 5 and 6), we have seen that there is said to be a reaction of anger, or "hot belly." This reaction, for both men and women, hinges on the concept of strength and self-assertion, embodying fundamental value-acceptives. These strongly entrenched values appear to re-establish themselves after initial feelings of shame and humiliation and provide a favorable setting for inflicting harm and injury on the supposed offender— even if this takes the extreme form of an act of aggression against the self.[8]

Malinowski's significant contribution[9] is his recognition of suicide as a means of control. Where his contentions differ from mine is in his treatment of suicide as deviant behavior, a point which Talcott Parsons has elaborated as a general proposition.

All controls, by their very nature, involve action or movement designed to establish conformity, to maintain the status quo, or to right what is

---

[8] An example of this sort is mentioned by Hu Hsien-Chin in D. G. Haring, ed. (1944, p. 411); and W. D. Wallis (1947, pp. 28, 36–37) refers to suicide committed in rage to punish an offender. M. D. Jeffreys (1952) speaks of "revengeful suicide." A. Adler (1945, e.g., pp. 7, 238–39, 239–40, 254) draws attention to the aggressive aspect of suicide, with particular reference to melancholia. See also J. M. A. Weiss (1957, pp. 17–18), citing P. Schilder (1951) as suggesting, among other possibilities, "that suicide can serve . . . as a form of punishment for a person who may have earlier denied love to the subject." (Weiss also distinguishes, e.g., pp. 24–25, between successful and "unsuccessful" suicides, the latter involving "an aspect of hidden or overt appeal to society, a call for help.")

[9] B. Malinowski (1949, pp. 94–98).

considered to be a wrong. This is done in a variety of ways. It is not that a person is forced to commit suicide because he or she has deviated from what is taken to be conformity. Certainly pressure is occasionally exerted on a widow and strongly influences her choice among possible courses of action. Disapproval expressed against her may be translated into coercive action, for reasons already mentioned, and she may be killed. She is thus being punished for alleged injury to a person for whom (or on behalf of whom) the group acts through certain of its members. This in itself, of course, is a mechanism of control, like the pressure of public opinion exerted against her; and this pressure has a legal quality. To make this clearer, a widow is never directly told (except in myth) that she must commit suicide. The pressure is always exercised in such a way that she comes to a decision herself, although this may be a consequence of that pressure. If the deceased's group feels strongly enough on the matter, its members resort instead to direct physical violence.

In certain circumstances, then, suicide is seen as balancing a real or imagined wrong. The mechanisms of control set in motion by an actual or attempted suicide have to do with what is viewed as the common good of the social unit affected (the lineage, village, or district). Insofar as it is assumed to have a duty to proceed against the person held responsible for that wrong, or a substitute for that person, forced suicide is one medium through which this can be accomplished. The suicide of a widow, or a person in some equivalent category, "avenges" the death of the husband. She is held responsible for his death, and her suicide serves as compensation. The unit in question thus need not take organized action against an external aggressor since she herself is viewed in this light. This is so even if husband and wife had previously exchanged vows; there is still the concept of her death as "paying," at least partially, for his.

Control mechanisms of a less direct kind may also come into play. Here the focal point is a perceived wrong against which, generally speaking, there is no formal procedure that can be said to have the wholehearted support of the group. Although alternatives in terms of self-help are available, these may not be chosen. There are, broadly, two basic situations which appear in categories 2, 5, and 6 (see pp. 188–93, 195–200). Where marital dissension is concerned, a wife has no legal rights in the village into which she is married (except among the southern Fore). Apart from seeking external help, the only choices open to her are to continue the quarrel with her husband, to leave him, to attempt a reconciliation, or to do her best to injure him. The circumstances may be such as to suggest suicide. Taking this step involves a specific attempt to injure the offending person; the primary intent, however, is to right a wrong. A man who attempts suicide (for example, because of some action on the part of his wife) is proceeding along the same lines and with the same purpose. He is not relying on his male lineage kin, for they may consider the matter too trivial, yet to him it is of extreme importance. Where men of the same lineage are involved in a dispute, there may be no other avenue by which the wrong may be righted except an open breach and continual quarreling. An open breach would lead to a split within the lineage or village. Suicide, or an apparent attempt at suicide, is in that case one means of achieving the desired end. It is, consequently, a device by which undesirable behavior may be regulated, or at least an effort made to regulate it. (Nevertheless, suicide is not always a satisfactory means of achieving this, and has obvious disadvantages.)

We are left with two categories of suicide, (3) as a result of illness and (4) sorcery. Whether or not this is rationalization after the event, the performance of sorcery is an aggressive act designed to bring about a victim's death. To the persons purportedly responsible, the victim is an enemy, and their action is designed to compensate their own social unit for a death said to have been caused by him. Whether or not he was personally responsible or is the most suitable substitute does not matter. The factor of compensation is all that concerns them. This aggression is directed outside the group and in a general sense may be regarded as a mechanism of control relevant to group solidarity (collective pressure in the case of threat). Further, from this point of view it is a legal procedure and as such is a form of social control. The suicide, while ratifying this view, does not itself present such a mechanism; and from the standpoint of the injured group it represents an offense. Sorcery, whether or not it is associated with suicide, is always a form of aggression; and suicide as a result of sorcery may accentuate this point. In any case it is likely to provoke a reaction of reprisal and revenge.

With sickness from natural causes the situation is in most cases entirely different, and should suicide result it cannot be considered as an act directed against another. Nor can suicide as a result of fear (category 7) have that connotation. Both are related to the breakdown of personal controls, and suicide ascribed to sorcery may also be viewed in this light.

Suicide as an approved form of action in certain conditions means that it is a sanctioned form of behavior and, being so, when viewed in relation to social order, is a form of social control in the terms previously discussed. One other point must be emphasized. Whether or not a suicide is contemplated, and the resulting decision acted upon, depends in all instances (even when pressure is brought to bear) on personal decision. Except when sorcery is in question, there are no contemporary cases in which we might say that, from the evidence, suicide is the only possible way out of a given situation. There is always a range of possible alternatives from which choice may be made of a more congenial or more apparently rewarding course of action.

Chapter 11   Sorcery

The threat or performance of sorcery may be used either in pursuit of personal ends, without the approval of other members of the community, or in an attempt to discourage or avenge behavior which those members regard as wrong. In general terms, then, it may be viewed as a crime, an offense against the established social order, or as a means of maintaining that order—or as both. Malinowski [1] (particularly for the Trobriands) and Hoebel [2] (for the Comanche), among others, have considered the problem of the legal implications of sorcery. For Malinowski, [3] "When used in support of the established social order it is a mechanism by which law is enforced"; but for Seagle, [4] with a narrower definition of law, it is a "legal influence" only when treated as a punishable offense. The arguments on both sides rest on the social recognition or condemnation of sorcery in any given context.

Belief in sorcery is common to the whole region under review. To the best of my knowledge, there is no adult, even among Mission converts, who does not share it. It is not always equally obvious, however, but it is accentuated at different times in different places. For instance, between Kogu and Asafina there was a fairly long-standing land dispute which had involved some desultory fighting; because they are no longer able to engage in open warfare, sorcery has become especially important as a medium of hostility between them. There seem to have been no really effective indigenous measures to cope with such a problem, except by direct action; and this was to some extent curtailed by our presence and fear of the intervention of the Administration.

[1] B. Malinowski (1949, pp. 85–94).
[2] E. A. Hoebel (1940, pp. 77 ff., 85–86); also H. I. Hogbin (1934, pp. 216–22); E. E. Evans-Pritchard (1931, pp. 22–51), and in a different context, A. I. Hallowell, in Kluckhohn and Murray (1950, p. 209). But see Hoebel's discussion (1954, pp. 272–74) of the relation of sorcery to law. He considers B. Whiting's (1950, p. 87) contention that sorcery is less prevalent in highly organized societies and more apparent in those limited in politico-legal perspective; and here he speaks of law as a natural enemy of sorcery (ibid., p. 274).
[3] B. Malinowski, in Hogbin (1934, pp. lvii–lx).
[4] W. Seagle (1937, pp. 275–90).

What is important for us here is the suggestion that sorcery, producing a high state of excitement and emotional stress for all concerned, as it evidently does, allows for only one safety valve—physical aggression. The use or threat of sorcery provokes fear, and an accepted local response is aggressive action. This is obvious in cases when a whole group is threatened.

In the Moke-Busarasa area late in 1952, people from several districts were conscripted for road construction. Three or four deaths occurred among them and precipitated a crisis. Typically, in their anxiety people did not turn on the native police or express open hostility to the Administration. At this practical level, they treated it within the existing framework of interdistrict relations. A new village which had been constructed in Busarasa was abandoned, and the inhabitants returned to their separate hamlets to exchange threats of sorcery. One result of this was a series of minor fights, and a larger outbreak in which several hundred people took part.

Sorcery, like warfare, can throw into relief all those conflicts which are an accompaniment of interdistrict relations. Nevertheless, there are no grounds for saying that these people are obsessed with constant fear of sorcery.[5] It is not a new or unusual phenomenon. Almost every adult knows how to perform sorcery; few will admit this knowledge in company, but in private, or in the security of the lineage men's house, the men are not so reticent.[6] It is regarded as part of the natural-social environment of man, something which must be coped with in the ordinary course of human existence. It is acknowledged to be harmful but inevitable. In their view it cannot be eradicated, even if there were any desire to do so; but in some cases its effects may be combated.

It is popularly taken for granted that Melanesians or Papuans believe all

[5] Malinowski (1952, p. 137) mentions the Trobrianders' extreme fear of sorcery, their ever-vigilant suspicion and lack of trust of those around them. Fortune (1932, p. xix) speaks of the Mailu people's dread of sorcery: they are "paralyzed with fear at night"; see also among the Dobuans (Fortune, 1932, p. 137). F. E. Williams (1940, p. 107) notes the varying intensity of fear of sorcery among different Papuan societies. He makes an important point in relation to fear of sorcery (1930, pp. 328–29): ". . . sorcery exercises an important influence on conduct. The threats of it, and the dread of it which is ever-present, together make one of the most powerful deterrents against wrongdoing." See also Malinowski (1949, pp. 86, 93). This conclusion would be difficult to support in eastern Highland societies. Even where the sorcery of punishment is concerned, it is not usually thought of, nor does it serve as, a deterrent, against, e.g., stealing.

[6] Comparison should be made here with R. F. Fortune's Manus material (1935, pp. 95–104).

deaths are due to sorcery, that there is no such thing as "natural" death.[7]
The people of this particular area, however, ordinarily consider cause on
two levels. One is what we would call the real or observable cause (which
they would consider superficial or secondary), the other the magical cause
(which they would consider real). In most cases these two seem to be
differentiated. Nevertheless, in some circumstances only one is acknowledged, and here their views and ours converge: certain deaths are regarded as a "natural" consequence of sickness, old age, childbirth, pre-
birth injuries, accident, and fighting. But just as often such deaths are
attributed to sorcery, or rather to the "natural" or apparent cause plus
sorcery (as in some cases of suicide). It is not easy to see why one death,
say from shooting during interdistrict fighting, is attributed to that cause
alone, and another apparently similar death to the influence of sorcery.[8]

In many cases it is possible to see why the issue of sorcery is raised. In
the first place, there are various signs: the victim acts according to a conventional pattern, and all concerned are quite ready to suspect sorcery.
Certain complaints in particular, including some that we might term
psychosomatic, are attributed to this; and there may also occasionally be
physical signs of sorcery. But a great deal of sorcery involves suggestion.
If a person is ill from a trivial complaint, it may not be long before gossip
accounts for this and allocates responsibility, so that the sufferer may
become convinced that he is a victim.[9] Evidence may accumulate in retro-
spect. The circumstances of the death may call for some discussion;
people may want to know why one person and not another was wounded
or killed, and sorcery offers an "explanation." If further proof is needed,
there is always divination, which not only helps to crystallize opinion but
also is expected to reveal the culprit. But one possible motive for declaring a death to be due to sorcery is a desire to justify retaliation at an interdistrict level. There are always scores to be balanced, real or imagined

7 K. Read (1954, e.g., p. 27). See also M. Mead's discussion (1935, pp. 158–59) in
reference to the Arapesh, where sores are excluded from suspicion of sorcery. Malinowski (1952, pp. 137, 387) says that the Trobrianders regard every death without exception
as due to sorcery, unless it is caused by suicide or by a visible accident, such as poisoning
or a spear thrust. Fortune (1932, p. 150) notes for the Dobuans that "there is no concept
of accident," and F. E. Williams (1940, p. 108) says the same for the Orokolo Bay
people.

8 For example, among the Arapesh (Fortune, 1939, p. 31), "no man is slain in war
except his personal leavings are first in the hands of sorcerers in the pay of the enemy."

9 Honigmann (1954, p. 382) mentions thanatomania as illness or death resulting from
belief in the efficacy of magic; it is said to illustrate well how group membership conditions sensorimotor dysfunctions. Cannon (1942, pp. 170–71) believes that the emotion
of fear together with the profound physiological disturbances associated with intense fear
can, if they endure, kill the organism.

slights to be wiped out, and deaths to be avenged; in the clash of personal and group interests, sorcery is both an outcome and a medium of conflict.

It is entirely legitimate to perform sorcery against members of another district, and this range obviously includes a man's own wife and the wives of his lineage kin, unless they belong to the same district. Use of sorcery within the district, between its members, is strongly condemned, although some cases are known. Dissension between them is said to be better settled by quarreling or fighting, which is easier to control. As for women who have married into it from other districts, the position is not always straightforward. In their case, direct physical aggression seems to be preferred to sorcery. The reason is not clear. Men sometimes use sorcery (or are said to use it) against women living in the same district, but generally they appear to regard it as a supra-military weapon to be used literally outside the district boundaries. (I am not considering certain aspects of destructive magic, or magic to get rid of a co-wife or son's wife without actually harming her.) On the other hand, there is the fear that a woman may be used as an intermediary in sorcery: [10] she is dangerous to a man because she is in close contact with him and because of her loyalty to her own district. Thus in the matter of sorcery there is an imbalance in this relationship. A husband has more occasion to fear his wife (or wives) and the women with whom he has intimate association than they him; direct physical aggression is easier to cope with than the more drastic forms of sorcery. A man should be constantly on his guard to retain his strength, his physical ascendancy, his dominant position as a male. Conventionally, he should be careful even during intercourse with his wife, except when she is a member of his own district. Intercourse with all other women involves this hazard, apart from the possibility of more direct repercussions. But in actual practice such considerations do not seem to restrict extramarital activity.

A word should be added about "leavings" which are said to be used in sorcery. Anything which has been in direct contact with a person (fragments of a bark skirt or net bag, a woman's netted hair snood, an arm band, anklet, or belt) and anything which has been part of his person (hair, nail parings, bodily excretions), is in a sense an extension of himself. Through such material, an essential ingredient in most types of sorcery, he is vulnerable to anyone who wants to do him harm. Nevertheless, many villages of my acquaintance were littered with discarded pieces of

[10] Cf. Read (1954, p. 27) for the Goroka groups. See also Malinowski (1952, p. 137), who mentions the Trobriander's distrust of his wife in matters of sorcery.

food—bones, vegetable peelings, and sugar cane fiber as well as other rubbish. It would be easy for a sorcerer to obtain a large collection if he felt so inclined. When questioned about this, the local people would usually say casually that leavings must be "new" (although much of the rubbish is always fresh), or that it would be difficult to associate any piece of rubbish with a specific person unless he were seen discarding it. On the other hand, men as well as women quite often destroy discarded fragments of food—not just throwing them into the fire, but making sure that they are completely burned. At other times, when passing through villages in strange districts, they are careful to throw unwanted scraps of food into running water and to defecate in a stream. And eating food supplied by an alien group may lead to anxiety about its possible effects (for example, as occurred among the Jate, Usurufa, and Kamano men and women who accompanied us to Busarasa. While traveling, and for the first several weeks at Busarasa, they incinerated scraps left over from our food as well as theirs, for the same reason). People are careful, then, in situations where they perceive some direct or specific threat, but most of the time they tend to be lax in such matters; this seems to be the case too, for men, as far as semen is concerned. They are more careful in disposal of feces. It was fairly common before alien contact (and still is in many areas) for men and women to have separate pits [11] which were carefully hidden by a covering of bushes. Nevertheless, in some villages exposed feces were noted, and there are cases where people have defecated in fear, and no attempt was made to safeguard the feces; some widows smear themselves with their own feces; and sexual intercourse while a woman defecates is said to be especially exciting. But great care is taken in disposing of food vomited during cane-swallowing and of blood during the rites of nose-bleeding, penis-insertion, and so on.

Sorcery is not a specialized craft in this region, [12] although certain men do achieve a reputation as sorcerers. But, generally speaking, the sorcerer is most often the warrior leader.

When a man is asked where he received his knowledge of a particular

[11] In the northern region where the Government has encouraged the people to come down from their hilltop villages to the valleys, an additional problem has been created: instead of the new communal latrines, people defecate in the streams from which they obtain their drinking water. In some villages separate latrines are dug for each house, and while we were at Kogu there was talk of sorcerers coming at night and taking away feces. For instance, several rats were shot by arrow in our deep latrine there; the suggestion was that sorcerers were sending the rats to obtain feces.

[12] There is no formal initiation or undergoing of a mystical experience when various methods of sorcery are revealed, as among certain Australian Aboriginal tribes.

form of sorcery, the usual reply is "from my father." Here is a construct of *naglisa* sorcery:

After a youth has undergone his initiation, his father may decide that it is time his son learned how to use *naglisa*. They go into the bush together and he demonstrates the procedure. "If you want to kill a person, do thus; but you must also observe certain food taboos. During that period you must not drink water or eat sugar cane and edible leaves; you must abstain from coitus. Only by doing this can the sorcery be effective." The youth takes notice of what he is told; but at first he may be doubtful, he must test it for himself. He takes some *naglisa* leaves and asks his father, "Are you tricking me? Is what you tell me true?" "It is true." "All right, I shall try it for myself." He performs the required actions and observes the taboos. Eventually, it is said, his chosen victim dies. He breaks his fast and exclaims, "My father has shown me a good thing. I like this!"

Less specifically, it seems to be the business of the lineage or clan to hand on such information during initiation rituals. As mentioned, it is during this period that a boy is told how to use various forms of fighting magic and (more generally) the various kinds of sorcery. In addition, and this is important since much of this is common knowledge, he learns about it in the ordinary course of conversation. On the whole, it is the prerogative of men to use sorcery, but women occasionally do so. Apart from serving as agents through whom a male sorcerer works, they know its various methods, procedures, and effects, and sorcery is performed against them just as frequently as it is against men.

Sorcery in this region can be classified under two headings. The first covers a range of types according to native categories and shows considerable overlap. For instance, different names may be applied to varieties which have much the same procedure and are distinguishable only as far as intent or effect is concerned. The common feature in all of these is that there is no suggestion of direct physical violence in a face to face situation. In contrast, the second heading covers a number of types said to be characterized by direct aggression. These are conveniently treated together under the (pidgin English) term *sangguma*.

A group which has suffered a loss through death is likely to consider sorcery as the cause of it. There are, of course, exceptions, but usually sorcery is believed to be at least a contributing factor. It is necessary, then, to find out who is responsible. This is the business not only of the dead person's agnatic male kin but also of the adult males of his village, and often of the district. It is necessary to be explicit about the sorcerer's affiliations, if not his personal identity, because of the implications. Blame must be placed on a unit or person who is recognized as an enemy not only of the deceased (since this cannot always be established in cases of sorcery) but of his whole group, because it is only in this way that majority support can be assured; that is to say, usually good reasons are already present before any particular decision is reached. This gives the necessary stimulus for retaliation, involving the unit as such in the repercussions that follow. The choosing of a sorcerer then, either before or after a death, is not a haphazard business. It is influenced by a variety of factors hinging on general relations and current attitudes between the respective units.

Conventionally speaking, the dead man's spirit is not satisfied until a croton indicating that "backing" has been effected is placed over his grave. The lineage has this direct responsibility to a deceased member, particularly in the case of an adult male. Yet in practice, and here appears the customary discrepancy between ideal and actuality, not all deaths are reciprocated. There are cases in which, although the "cause" of death has been established and the responsible party named, no further action is taken. Those immediately concerned may not have felt strongly in the matter, or may have decided that the best policy was to let things slide rather than commence hostilities. They may have been weak at the time; the deceased may have had no strong lineage kin to press the case; or it may have been thought better to leave revenge in the hands of the next generation, for example, until the dead man's sons were grown. Or this death may be regarded as balancing a previous one and the matter allowed to rest there. Ideally, however, most deaths require "backing," and this expectation has contributed to the state of intermittent dissension and warfare in this region.

Imusa

Imusa is associated primarily with the use of a victim's semen, and occasionally of exuviae. A woman's male lineage kin may persuade her to obtain this from her husband; or she may approach any man with that intention. Association of men with women is understood to involve this risk. However, she may not act deliberately in the matter.

There is the case of a Moiife woman who, after intercourse with her husband, went to her garden to work. There she dropped a little semen. This was seen by a Kogu man who was hiding nearby. When she had returned to her village, he collected it on a leaf and put it in a bamboo container, which he hid in the men's house. It so happened that presently a Kogu man died, and Moiife was blamed. The semen could now be used to avenge his death. The conventional way of doing so is as follows:

Two male lineage kin of the dead man build a small house in the bush, complete with feces-pit and a supply of firewood. Here they must stay in seclusion for over five moons, abstaining from drinking water and from eating sugar cane, edible leaves, and certain varieties of pitpit. They may eat and cook over their own fire only sweet potatoes brought to them from time. to time by lineage kin. [When the period is completed and the sorcery effected, they are emaciated.][13] The semen is taken from the container and placed on leaves, the *kokuhita*, the *kagufofaida* [wild taro], the *mazahai*[c] [sweet potato], and *kamufaiaida*. Then a hole is made in a wild taro root, and the semen is put into it. All these leaves are placed around it, with the yellow *naglisa* leaf, and tied into a bundle which is heated over a fire and beaten with a stick. The victim now feels his first pains and as this beating and heating continue he becomes increasingly ill. Toward the fifth moon the victim's spirit visits the two sorcerers and catches up a firebrand from their fire. They know by this sign that the end is near. They take up their magic bundle and going to swampy ground make an oven in which they place it, covering it with earth. The victim begins to bleed from the nose and mouth. The two sorcerers return to their house to perform the last rites. On the sixth moon they kill a rat, saying as they do so, "Thus will this man die. . . ." and throw it into the fire to burn. They then break sugar cane, throw it into the fire, and sing:

> guzino guzi guzino . . .
> anawa guzino guzi . . .
> ojo oii. . . .

"Blowflies [from his body] . . . To Anabaga [the Land of the Dead he is going]. . . ."

The victim, no matter how far away he is, hears this song and dies. The sorcerers emerge from their house, wash and decorate themselves, and going to the grave of their lineage brother plant a croton over it, indicating that the death has been avenged. After death the victim's body swells, particularly his face, tongue, and genitalia. It is said that the body becomes so large it is difficult to get it through the doorway of the house and it takes five men to carry it. It may be cooked and eaten.

A variation relates to the cooking of the bundle on swampy ground. The oven is made, the bundle placed in it and completely covered with earth. The oven smoke cannot escape, and it is this which enters the victim's body and forces his nose and mouth to bleed. The blood runs "like water"; at the same time, due to the smoke, his arms, legs, penis, and testes swell. The same trouble is experienced in removing the bloated body, and if it is not eaten a very large hole must be dug for the burial.

In some cases *imusa* is used without the aid of women. A man visiting a village outside his own district, and sleeping in the local men's house, may have certain exuviae taken by a potential sorcerer. An old grudge connected with his district may be remembered. The sorcerer may see him asleep. "This is a good man," he may say. "I would like to kill him." Some grease or dirt, taken from his body, is

[13] Several very thin old to middle-aged men were pointed out to me as having habitually carried out *imusa*. They themselves admitted this in private discussion, and a few boasted of it. The period of seclusion, however, would vary, as would the degree of abstinence from food.

put in a bamboo container which is filled up with leaves. This is heated in a fire, causing the victim to feel sick and cry out in pain. To hasten the deed, a rat is caught, killed, and put in the container. This is beaten with a stick to which are tied certain red croton leaves [signifying that the act is being carried out in revenge for a death]. As the sorcerer does this, he cries out: "You [name of victim], I break your backbone! You, I break your ribs! You, I break your head!" The victim writhes in pain. The sorcerer then throws the container in the fire and breaks the stick. As these burn, the victim dies.

There is no set pattern for much of this sorcery, and both the procedure involved and the length of time taken to carry it out vary considerably.

Naglisa

Naglisa, involving stabbing with a magical dart, is one of the commonest forms of sorcery. It need not be fatal. It is said that when a sorcerer wants his victim to suffer without dying he will not go through the full series of actions.

Inivi and Kimiᶜagumu were on bad terms. When an Inivi man died, suspicion fell on Kimiᶜagumu. An Inivi man prepared a *naglisa* stick of two prongs bound at the base with the poisonous *naglisa* and orchid cane, decorated with white feathers. He set out for Kimiᶜagumu and stealthily hid beside a garden, waiting for someone to come along. At last he saw a Kimiᶜagumu man. Rising from the bushes he held him with his eyes, raised the stick, and bent back one prong until it broke, calling at the same time, "I break this!" The *naglisa*, shot like a dart, entered the victim. Then the sorcerer returned to his village exhausted and went to sleep pretending to be sick;[14] but the Inivi men knew differently. The Kimiᶜagumu victim too went back to his village and slept; but he continued to do so, awakening only for short intervals. He became very thin and finally died. In the village men's house, after some discussion, it was decided that perhaps this balanced the Inivi death they had previously caused [or for which they had acknowledged responsibility]; it might be better to do nothing for the present but to bide their time. But the victim's parents were not satisfied; they wanted revenge. They gathered together bush beads, various shells, and pig meat and, filling a net bag, the father left his village by night and went to Tatagufa. There he approached a certain man, offering this bribe on condition that he killed an Inivi man. The other agreed, and the Kimiᶜagumu man returned home secretly. Some time afterward the Tatagufa man prepared *naglisa* and going to Inivi selected a man and "shot" him. He too returned to his village exhausted, feigned sickness, and abstained from drinking water and eating certain foods.[15] He simply lay in the men's house sleeping. Eventually, the victim died. When news

---

[14] Compare with Fortune (1932, p. 168), where the sorcerer feigns sickness and abstains from eating so that his body remains hot.

[15] Refraining from drinking water and eating these foods is not apparently obligatory (see above, in reference to training); but in many cases it is explicitly stated that failure to comply will render the sorcery ineffective.

of this reached Tatagufa, the sorcerer broke his fast. That night he secretly left his village and breaking off a length of red croton went to Kimi^cagumu; he offered this to the man who had bribed him, signifying that his part of the bargain had been fulfilled. The other accepted the croton in public and later planted it over his son's grave. Overjoyed, he pressed the visitor to stay. Heaps of vegetables and sugar cane were brought, ovens made, and a pig killed. The Tatagufa man's bags were filled, and he returned to his village. All the dead man's kin were pleased; his death had been avenged.

An interesting point here is that individual demand for revenge can override group decision. No action was taken by Kimi^cagumu as a unit, although it was agreed that Inivi was responsible. Whatever other reasons were involved, it is likely that one was the weakness of the dead man's father or brothers. The relative strength of a victim's immediate agnatic kin is usually a critical factor, influencing the trend of a discussion and swaying the decision. We may assume that in this case the victim's father was not sufficiently strong to enforce his opinion; but apparently he and his wife were anxious for revenge. This brings up another point: the victim's lineage kin may be subject to some external pressure to avenge his death; a *nenafu, nefaru, honi^c*, or even an *aku* (mother's brother) may be at the bottom of this. The inference here is that there was pressure from his mother (a member of another unit) and her male kin. The father, however, took the initiative himself, and when the revenge had been achieved he is said to have received the full support of his group.

Okaza

Okaza is very much like *naglisa*, but it is of special interest here because some examples reveal an exception to the general rule that lineal members of a district normally are not suspected of performing sorcery against one another. This brings up a question which appears in Malinowski's treatment of Trobriand sorcery: what is the position of a person who works sorcery against a member of his own political unit? It would be too much to expect a one-to-one correlation between the general rule and actual behavior, but in spite of examples to the contrary, the assumption is that most sorcery is, and should be, directed outside the district. Two contributing factors enter here: first, possible rifts within the village or district—the formation, for example, of more or less independent sub-political units; and second, the ever-present issue of bribery. Both have a bearing also on interdistrict fighting.

The problem which always confronts us is that of independent action on the part of the "strong man," dictated largely by personal interests and cutting across other expected forms of behavior in an attempt to exploit any given situation. This is not simply a matter of individual personality factors or of "deviant" behavior; in part, it has to do with the pull of certain relationship ties. However much lineage and village solidarity is viewed as an essential *desiderandum*, however much survival is said to depend on it, the relationship bonds that extend outside have an indirect tendency to undermine it. But, even more than this, the emphasis on strength casts ultimate responsibility on the individual. It is for him to achieve this strength through his own efforts, and he alone must guard against its loss. He has been taught to feel morally bound primarily to himself, and only secondarily, and in his own interest, to his group. The way is thus paved for regarding as "good" a self-interested action which may be harmful in the long run to his own group; and it is in this context that the problem of bribery occurs.

In some instances, however, the person who accepts a bribe may have no intention of doing anything further in the matter. Once the payment has been made, the giver has no "legal" power to insure that the agreement is kept, although eventually his group may consider the use or threat of sorcery. In some cases it is possible that a man may take what is offered in the belief that sooner or later a death will occur in his group, and he might as well take advantage of the opportunity; by assuming responsibility under such conditions, honoring the arrangement, finally handing over a special croton to members of the other group, and receiving extra gifts, he is labeling himself as the sorcerer, in their eyes at least. Even in dealing with *nenafu*, risks are involved. He has no assurance that they will not turn on him, or reveal his identity to his own unit.

Guzigli[c] (kuru)

Guzigli[c] (kuru) is said to be carried out in several different ways and with varying results. Most of the victims are women or girls. It is called in pidgin English *guria*, meaning "shaking" or "shivering"; but this term is misleading. It is quite unlike the shivering which accompanies spirit possession.[16] In cases observed (none in the final stages) there was partial paralysis and loss of muscular control. The attacks are described as becoming more frequent and more intense, with death as an inevitable climax. Despite physical difficulty in uttering words, the victims do not appear to be mentally affected, although cases inferring this have been recorded.

[16] See R. Berndt (1952–53, 1954a, 1958).

For the purpose of retaliation, but also in a sense as a punishment [17] [making her pay for the misdeeds of her husband or one of his lineage kin], a sorcerer obtained a small piece of sweet potato thrown away by a woman. He collected bark of various trees, a twig from the *kigi*, leaves from *mofahaida*, some coarse grass [*kanokanomo*^c], some fine grass [*jugu*^c*jugufa*], wild taro leaves [*kagafufa*], hardwood "bara" [*menihai*^c], and gum [*hai*^c*teni*] leaves, as well as green croton and sweet potato leaves, and prepared a special bundle into which he placed the sweet potato. This he bound up tightly, with the *kigi* twig protruding, and buried in swampy ground with the twig showing. The sorcery was now set in motion, and initial mild attacks began. As the weeks went by, he visited his submerged bundle and beat it with a stick. This is said to have been continued day after day, the attacks of *guzigli*^c becoming more frequent and intense. Eventually came a time when the victim was seriously under its influence: she spent her time lying about in her house or attempting to hobble around with sticks. People took her affliction as a matter of course; they would nod in her direction, commenting [in her hearing], "Someone has worked *guzigli*^c on her!"

About this time she began to behave erratically. Stumbling across the village clearing, falling as she did so, she would call out for coitus. Coming on a young man [kinship ties are neglected], she would urge him, "Come and have intercourse with me! Here is my vulva!" But he would reject her. Her death was a foregone conclusion. She now had violent attacks of dysentery and loss of bladder control, with severe pains under the arms; a stench rose from her whole body as she lay in her house; maggots appeared; and finally she died.

Much the same sequence is allegedly followed in the case of a male victim. A fragment of masticated sugar cane is obtained by the sorcerer, who places it in a taro root and makes it into a bundle with certain leaves. This he takes into the bush and puts into a feces pit. The victim has his first attacks of *guzigli*^c. Men continue to use the pit, and the victim's illness intensifies. As time goes on, he becomes worse; his head becomes heavy and aches, and he has increasingly severe attacks of dysentery. He stumbles about the village, falling down; twitching, lack of muscular control, and the usual manifestations of *guzigli*^c become so severe that at last he remains in his house. When the bundle in the pit completely disintegrates, the victim's own body [which has been rotting internally] begins to stink, maggots appear on his body, and finally he dies.

Tugezajana

Tugezajana sorcery is said to be used by both men and women; except for *kenagaglisa*, it is the only variety commonly attributed to women. The following construct shows a typical example:

[17] The term retaliation refers to the "backing" or reciprocating of a real or imagined injury, insult, or wrong experienced by a person or his social unit (here normally the district). Punishment, however, has a moral connotation and implies also the exercise of legitimate authority. It involves the inflicting of some penalty on an offender for committing an action or series of actions considered to be "wrong" (e.g., theft).

F. E. Williams (1930, pp. 327–29) mentions retaliatory sorcery; I would classify some of his examples as sorcery designed to punish.

A woman sees a small boy [who may or may not belong to her husband's lineage and district] stealing sweet potatoes from her garden; she is very angry but says nothing at the time. Taking a little of the sweet potato runner the thief has discarded, she prepares her magic in the privacy of the menstrual hut. The fragment of runner is divided and each piece placed on pitpit leaves; over this are scraped *azatetina*, *tefani*, and *krelkukupagetina* barks. It is then wrapped in two bundles with *haita* and *kakamo* leaves and twigs and each tied with coarse *kaka-kopiᶜna* twine. One bundle is put in the ashes of her fire, the other near her sleeping place. The former, as it is heated, causes the victim's eyes to glaze over as if covered with ashes, and his body takes on the same appearance. The other bundle is placed under her as she menstruates, causing the victim to become emaciated.

About this time the victim is questioned by either his father or a lineage kins-man. "Why have you become like this? Someone has worked sorcery against you. Have you stolen something?" He may reply [as in this case], "I went to the garden of ――― and there I dug sweet potatoes." The other reprimands him, "You are not to steal from gardens," and pulls out some of his hair. He then approaches the sorceress: "You are not to kill this child. It is not good. You must release him." Finally he induces her to confess. At first she justifies herself: "This is my own garden! I planted it myself. I am a human being! Why am I injured in this way? I found him stealing from it and eating. My belly was hot, and I used *tugeza* against him to kill him." But at last she agrees to release him. She takes the bundles from the menstrual hut, unties the twine, and throws them away. She also gives the boy some *megufa* leaves, and after chewing them he becomes quite well; he puts on weight and loses his ashen coloring, and his eyes clear. No compensation is paid to him, nor is any given to the woman; the appeal is made to her as a woman, and there is no other way in which her hand can be forced. Threatening to kill her or to work sorcery in return would only increase her anger without freeing the victim.

The woman is acknowledged to be within her rights in administering a punishment[18] which she alone is in a position to carry out. This is clear when the victim's father or a lineage kinsman questions the boy about the cause of his sickness and reprimands him—reminiscent of the injunctions during initiation, when youths are told not to steal, especially within the boundaries of their own district. (Stealing is, although not always, a feature of interdistrict hostilities. Within the district there are no adequate sanctions to prevent it; but the informal courts are gradually

---

[18] F. E. Williams (1930, pp. 328–29) holds that sorcery serves as a deterrent to wrong-doing. R. F. Fortune (1935, p. 352) states that both Dobuans and Manus use supernatural sanctions to enforce correct and lawful behavior toward neighbors. That is to say, sorcery is in its legal aspect a mechanism of control of primary importance. In the region we are discussing, however, the process involved is not the same. Sorcery or threat of sorcery is not normally used as a deterrent to deviant behavior. It is not used between district members to rectify a wrong, although it may serve as an example to others of what not to do. (This point is not explicitly stated.)

coming to concern themselves with the problem.) The administering of punishment for stealing garden produce and pigs, and more rarely some other commodities, is not primarily the concern of the political unit or even of the village. It is, rather, a matter of personal self-help. This may involve desultory quarreling and fighting, with people taking sides. In other words, theft may lead to intralineage and intravillage conflict. Except where the informal court comes into the picture, the offended person can choose the most appropriate type of punishment. This may or may not be sorcery. When it is, the inference is that the expected penalty for theft, for adult or child, is death.

Theft is an infringement of the ideally conceived rights of human beings, a focusing on personal interests at the expense of others. It is this point which the sorceress used to vindicate herself, and which alone justified her action. The boy on whom she performed sorcery may have been a member of the group with which she was living; the land she used for gardening belonged to her husband and his lineage, but in a sense it belonged to the whole district and thus to the boy as well. What was hers, and what she was obliged to share with her husband, was the vegetables it produced. She herself had worked the ground and tended the crops.

When interdistrict stealing occurs, the customary reaction is to view the theft as an aggressive act against the political unit, to be met by retaliation. In some cases, however, the offended party is left to handle it at a personal level.

A Kogu man stole a pig from Asafina. No action was considered by this district, because interdistrict warfare had been suppressed. Further, there was already sufficient dissension between these two units, and it was decided not to hold an informal court because there was no common meeting ground between them. The offended man was thus left to act for himself. He hunted in the bush and at last found the rope with which the pig had been tied and footprints leading toward Kogu. He learned that a certain man at Kogu had held a pig oven. Returning home with the rope, he set to work to perform sorcery. He scraped various kinds of bark over the rope and placed with it a tree grub. Then he made a special framework of two sharpened sticks and added various leaves, mainly wild taro, to make a bundle, binding it with twine. This he fastened to a tree with the sharpened sticks upright. The victim began to have severe body pains and became very thin. The sorcerer then removed his bundle and placed it in swampy ground. As it gradually rotted, so did the victim; finally he died.

Other versions relate that a victim of *tugezajana* is made vulnerable during interdistrict fighting. When he is shot and his body is cut open, maggots are found; then people know that sorcery has been used against him.

Although the injunctions against stealing are felt to have a more or less universal application, the feeling is correspondingly weakened in relation to outside groups. In situations where there is already strong antagonism or hostility, the moral injunction may be almost entirely lacking. In such cases, the issue may be one of veiled retaliation and nothing more. Yet what we assume when using the term punishment in connection with interdistrict theft is the existence of the ephemeral zone of social inter-action (see chap. 12). Should theft occur between groups which are, for the time being, on more or less friendly terms, open warfare or reprisals may follow. Or it may result in a localized quarrel involving a few people, when the dominant desire on the part of one is to punish the offender. This remains on a personal basis, and the means used to effect punishment may be physical aggression or sorcery. This does not mean that such per-sonal action is carried out quite independently of the respective units. Each may help with the pressure of opinion but restrain itself as far as concerted action is concerned. The very presence of this background opinion is a potent element in achieving rupture. The attempted "punish-ment" may change to retaliation and counter-reprisal, with the severing of peaceful relations, and moral indignation will be submerged in the desire to obtain compensation.

Accounts of sorcery in this region dwell in some detail on the agony felt by the victim. There is a stress on bodily decay; in many cases the internal organs are said to rot away, causing a stench, and the body is infested with maggots. This is all, clearly, part of the sorcerer's intention. It is not solely death which is desired but a slow, painful process which satisfies the avenger and gives him adequate and full compensation. He normally expresses no sympathy for the sufferer. On the other hand, there is the erratic sexual behavior associated with $guzigli^c$ in females (and present also in $neginofi$ "image" sorcery). It is rarely associated with male victims. For instance, a woman under $neginofi$ (or $guzigli^c$ during its final stages) is said to become $(a)negi(ne)$, "foolish" or "silly." The removal of conventional restraints under a spell reveals the female desire for sexual gratification. It is man's prerogative to express his strength through violent sexual activity. But this need is no less true of females. One conse-quence is that men attribute an abnormal sexual appetite to the woman who becomes $(a)negi(ne)$.

Kukubari

$Kukubari$, sometimes called ja^co, is of interest here because it is used against women who have violated one of the men's most important rules:

they must not see or, conventionally, know about, the sacred flutes. If they do acquire this knowledge, not only the individual security of each lineage member but the productivity and welfare of the whole village and district are threatened. Relatively few cases of such infringement seem to have occurred; but in one notable example, said to have taken place in Kogu in about 1943, the punishment was effected by *kukubari* sorcery:

Flutes were heard being played in the nearby bush. Men asked themselves: "Who is that? A young boy?" One went out to investigate and, guided by the sound, came to where two women were secluded, one playing the flute while the other danced up and down with leaves under her arms. After identifying them he returned to the men's house, where the matter was discussed at length: the decision was made to perform *kukubari* on them. Later, after the women came back to their houses, small fragments of discarded food were obtained. A length of bamboo was cut [like a sacred flute] and a hole made on its convex surface. It was then filled with the food scraps and black coarse outer leaves from a pitpit cane and placed on the fire to cook in much the same way as are edible leaves. As it boiled, *teborio* and *naglisa* leaves were put into it; the two women immediately began to feel ill. For several days the same process was repeated, and the victims became worse: sores began to appear on their faces and gradually extended, eating away the flesh of the nose, mouth, and eyes. Finally they died. (*Teborio* is the name of a variety of leaf, and also of a type of sorcery centering on a fragment of the victim's skirt.)

Although the sorcery was carried out by one man, the cooking of the bamboo container allegedly took place in the men's house and received the full sanction of all the men, including the women's husbands. It was viewed as a legitimate punishment. The decision to use sorcery instead of killing the women at once was based on the belief that in this way the maximum suffering, and hence punishment, would result and serve as an additional warning to other women.

Sangguma

Sangguma (or "shoot nail") is the pidgin English term for one of the most feared forms of sorcery.[19] It is accompanied by physical violence and used almost invariably as a means of retaliation; it is, therefore, an important feature of interdistrict hostility. Unlike most other forms of sorcery it is carried out not alone but in the company of at least one other person.

[19] It is called *tunakafia* in Jate, *afa* in Kamano, *ila* in Usurufa, and *tugabu* in Fore. Widely distributed throughout New Guinea and Papua, it has many parallels in Aboriginal Australia. F. E. Williams (1940, p. 106) mentions one type for the Orokolo, the *hara*; Seligmann (1910, pp. 170–71, 187–88) for the Motu-Koita, the *vada*; B. Malinowski (1915, p. 649, 1922, p. 42); R. F. Fortune (1932, pp. 284–87); P. Lawrence (1952, p. 340) mentions *ämale* or *sagarami* (*saguma*; i.e., *sangguma*), but this appears to be of a different sub-variety. There seems to be a basic similarity between all varieties of *sangguma* or *vada*.

In performing *sangguma* the sorcerers have two main intentions in mind. They have received an injury which demands retaliatory action. This action is probably sanctioned by their group, but they want to avoid open warfare. *Sangguma*, they believe, provides a satisfactory answer: it is carried out surreptitiously, and the identity of the sorcerers and their group may not be immediately discovered. Here they delude themselves, for gossip travels quickly; and the fact that when the victim dies crotons are planted over a fresh grave in the sorcerers' village establishes their responsibility. Blame may now be localized, as to unit at least. The other intention is to cast suspicion on someone else. With this in mind, they suggest to the victim a scapegoat who is, or will be, reported to be responsible for his death; this is designed primarily as a cover for their own activity.

The same problem arises here as in our discussion of other forms of sorcery, as well as suicide. How do people know what has taken place? Is most of what we discuss in relation to the *sangguma* operation itself, as well as to the conversation between the sorcerers and the victim, simply reconstruction after the event? What has been said before is relevant here. If people believe that these things occur, that is sufficient reason to consider them. We are not, as anthropologists, concerned primarily with the empirical "reality" of the situation, with whether or not it actually takes place; local belief in it gives that degree of reality which is required for our purpose. Nevertheless, *sangguma* sorcery represents a borderline example, where the observer's scepticism may weaken as he gathers examples and scraps of observed material. I am not saying that *sangguma* occurs as reported, but my impression is that some features of it may do so. We are not dealing solely with magic but with a physical operation under the *guise* of magic.[20] In the majority of cases, the *sangguma* "nails" are projected into the victim only symbolically, but there is some evidence to suggest that more than this may be attempted. A victim may be violently beaten and then released exhausted; because of the widespread belief in *sangguma*, he is convinced that the operation has been performed on him, and this has a detrimental effect on his health.

[20] To account for this type of sorcery, I am postulating a form of hypnosis or suggestion used in conjunction with aggressive physical action. Seligmann (1910) doubted that *vada* was due to a human or a spiritual agent. Fortune (1932, p. 284) speaks of *vada* as hypnotic cutting open of the body of the victim. He holds that "It is emphatically a human procedure," and I would indorse his statement. Malinowski (1915 and 1922) was partially of this opinion. Fortune (1932, p. 294) notes that "The gulf between *vada* and the rest of sorcery is a gulf that should be recognized."

See also B. Malinowski (1952, pp. 305–6, n. 1).

Only sorcerers and victim are party to the actual events. Whatever the empirical reality may be, there is a conventional pattern to which any conjecture will broadly conform, and many men are prepared to boast of their proficiency in *sangguma*. A "victim" returning home under its influence displays certain characteristics. Extreme lassitude, avoidance of normal pursuits, and erratic behavior are taken as clear indications, especially if these are followed by a rapid decline and almost immediate death. Any conversation which takes place between sorcerers and victim is known only to them and would not be revealed by the victim; but its substance is inferred from subsequent events. This is in the nature of sheer speculation, providing evidence to support any accusations which may be made later. But it is based on the events surrounding the death: the victim behaves erratically, and therefore it is assumed that he has been instructed by the sorcerers to do this. A victim is shot without apparent reason; therefore he has been made vulnerable and told that he will die in that way at the hands of these particular people. The victim does not reveal the identity of the sorcerers or of their group. The manner of his death may be designed to conceal this but not the fact that *sangguma* has been carried out; in popular belief, the signs are plainly visible on the corpse.

Many people insist that they have caught or seen *sangguma* men lurking in the bush surrounding their villages. In a number of cases they are said to have been surprised in the act.

A Kemiju man, Opieso, went some little distance from his village to cut wood near the main Kemiju-Amufi road. While so engaged he was surprised by two Amufi *sangguma* men, who threw him to the ground and proceeded to perform the usual operation. But it so happened that coming down the same road was Warema, one of his lineage brothers, taking sweet potatoes to his pigs. He heard a noise in the bush and saw what was happening. Throwing aside his potatoes, he drew his bow and rushed forward. The two *sangguma* men jumped up and turned to run away, but not before Warema had brought one down. The other disappeared into the heavily wooded bush surrounding some Kemiju gardens. Turning to the man he had shot, Warema found that he was wounded. He called out to the nearest Kemiju villages that he had shot a *sangguma* man. Men rushed out with their bows and arrows, followed by women with digging sticks. Surrounding the injured sorcerer, they shot arrow after arrow into his body, while the women beat him until he died. The women then squatted over him one by one, urinating into his mouth, upon his face and over his body, hurling invectives and pushing one another aside in their excitement, some rubbing their genitalia on his face, others pulling and manipulating his penis and testes. Then they carried Opieso back to the village and revived him with heated leaves; except for some bruises, he was unhurt.

In the meantime the other *sangguma* man was hiding close to the garden of a woman named To‑mezia, originally from Amufi but married to Fegono of Kemiju. She had not heard the disturbance, or pretended she had not, because Amufi was involved; she continued with her weeding. As the whole area was being thoroughly scoured by armed men, the Amufi man was forced to seek help from To‑mezia. He approached her and held her arm, crying, "Oh my vulva!" She struggled for a moment, threatening to call out, but he continued, "This is my vulva; how good it tastes!" and brushing aside her skirt he sucked her genitalia. Now in a thoroughly good humor, she remarked modestly, "You eat something of mine, I shall help you." And she made him lie down in the thick undergrowth of the garden, covering him with sugar cane leaves. There he remained until nightfall, while the others searched around him; then he slipped from his hiding place and escaped to Amufi. [This section of the story is said to have been told later by the Amufi man, while the woman concerned related the incident to other women resident in Kemiju. She was not reprimanded for doing this; her own kin and district were recognized as having a greater claim on her loyalty than her husband's group. This does not mean, however, that retaliatory action is never taken in such cases.]

Next morning two Amufi women, To‑mezia and Zaru [wife of Agaja‑gia] were detailed by Iranu‑izu [Agaja‑gia's father and an important "strong" man] to take the dead sorcerer to Amufi. The two women carried him and at Amufi gave the body to their kin. No further action was taken by either side.

In this example we see what might be described as typical treatment of a *sangguma* sorcerer caught in the act. He is an enemy and must be killed; but, further, public disapproval is expressed by the treatment of his dead body. Not only are the victim's lineage kin implicated; the whole co-resident group shows its common dislike and condemnation more or less collectively.

Abuse of a corpse is a particularly interesting feature, and more will be said of it later. It represents one outcome of the emphasis on aggressive and violent action. Controls, as we have seen, restrain this in varying degrees during the more humdrum periods of everyday life. But punctuating these are occasions when excitement reaches such a pitch that only through this kind of behavior, itself conventionalized, can release be achieved. In the above example, the capture of the sorcerer may be viewed as a relief from the expectation of *sangguma* aggression, a reaction to fear; the people now have something tangible on which to vent their feelings. Men shoot arrows feverishly into the corpse, women abuse it as their menfolk stand by approvingly. This is gratifying, this is exciting; and it is undoubtedly, by all accounts, pleasurable.

In the same case, the surviving *sangguma* man is protected and hidden and helped to escape by a kinswoman (a classificatory sister). At first she intends to warn her husband's group; she is afraid of the *sangguma* man;

but because he is a member of her own district, and in consequence of his particular approach, she becomes entirely sympathetic. There is a mythological precedent here: when a ghost or spirit comes along the road leading to Anabaga, he is met by Jugumishanta and Morufonu and must greet them by sucking their genitals. By this means he can enter the security of the Land of the Dead. Further, the touching and fondling of the genitals is a conventional way of expressing greetings and good will. It is designed to indicate, sincerely or otherwise, extreme trust and friendship. The *sangguma* man is thus claiming first her sympathy and then her help; because of the existing bond between them, she cannot refuse after such overtures have been made.

The sexual element appears in *sangguma*, as in certain other forms of sorcery, when the victim is a woman—as in the following example:

Four Asafina *sangguma* sorcerers are said to have set out with the intention of obtaining an Ofafina victim. Reaching the outer gardens of Ofafina, they found a young woman working there alone. They seized her and pulled her into the tall grass, then each in turn copulated with her while the others kept watch. They continued in this way until almost sunset, when they let her return to her village and themselves went back to Asafina. The woman, not suspecting that they were *sangguma* sorcerers but believing them to be only young men out for pleasure, returned to her garden early next day. She had not long to wait before they reappeared and again pulled her into the tall grass; there they spent the day dallying and copulating with her as before until it was almost dark, then left her and returned to their village. On the two following days they did the same; but on the fifth they became bored and worked *sangguma* on her. They did not, however, "shoot" her with *sangguma* "nails" but used oven stones to pound her body until it was thoroughly bruised, leaving her unconscious. On reviving, the young woman staggered home; warmed leaves were applied to her body, and after a few days she recovered. It was after this that she told what had happened, concluding that the reason why she suffered no ill effects was that she had so readily submitted to their sexual demands.

But compliance on the part of the woman will not necessarily save her. A similar case, but with a different ending, concerned five *sangguma* men from Ifusa:

It is said that, setting out for Kemiju, they reached the fringe of the gardens at Tomiᶜfinaga and found a young woman named Jogulgakiza at work. They dragged her into the long grass, threw her upon the ground, and tore off her skirts ready for *sangguma*. But as they looked at her they changed their minds and instead copulated with her in turn. Then they told her to return the following day for the same purpose but not to tell anyone else or they would work *sangguma* on her. Next day she again came alone to the garden and was soon joined by the five Ifusa men, who proceeded to behave as before. This continued for several days until one of the men became impatient. "We are *sangguma* men," he told the others.

"Do we not shoot with *tunakafiagai^c jona* [nails]? Or do we use only our penes for this sorcery? We must kill people! All you do is to copulate with this woman. But I shall kill her, alone." On the following morning he left without his companions and found her waiting. He took her into the grass, choked her into unconsciousness, and proceeded to carry out *sangguma*. The victim walked back to her house; as she was dying she described what had happened but without revealing the men's identity. This was discovered only afterward, together with the *sangguma* men's conversation, relayed by *nenafu*.

Sorcery and Social Control

In regarding sorcery as a mechanism of control, we are faced immediately with the question of how it operates in this respect; and if it is such a mechanism, has it "legal" backing—that is, has it majority backing, either direct or indirect? If so, are there any cases in which it could be viewed as an "illegal" force? Some of these questions are already answered in this chapter, but let me reiterate briefly: Sorcery serves as a legal mechanism, as a means of retaliation, as a factor in maintaining in-group solidarity, or as punishment to achieve order within the political unit. It is a mechanism of control in its own right but may in turn be subjected to other controls. Ignoring the latter point for the moment, we have (*a*) retaliation, (*b*) punishment, and (*c*) sorcery within one's own group in exchange for a bribe, thus assisting interdistrict retaliation.

The first two are straightforward. Sorcery is brought to bear on a member of an alien group, whether or not such a person is resident in one's own district, in order to avenge a perceived injury or wrong. The sorcerer normally has or can expect to have majority backing; he and his group are interested mainly in bringing about the death of a member of another unit in order to plant a croton, to balance the crime against themselves. The process has legal validity and is comparable to the direct physical action of warfare. Sorcery is thus a form of social intercourse as well as a medium of control. A wide variety of sorcery types is available for this, including most forms of the *sangguma* which I have classified as sorcery combined with physical aggression. There are, too, the borderline cases of sorcery used for retaliation and/or punishment; but here I am drawing an artificial barrier between the two categories in order to discuss them in general terms. The control mechanisms operating for retaliation are of one kind, but they also involve repercussions and certain other issues, depending on whether the victim and the sorcerer are co-resident. With punishment, the control mechanism not only has legal validity but is a legal procedure, being designed to punish an offender (real or imagined) in order to right a wrong; the only compensation involved is the victim's suffering. It does not so much regulate as remove the perpetrator of it. Neglect to punish would imply the condoning of unacceptable or "wrong" behavior.

Retaliatory sorcery directed against a victim resident outside the political unit can be seen as enhancing the social solidarity of that unit. The sorcerer acts with its sanction, and even if he does not have this immediately it is ordinarily not long in coming. If such sorcery is directed against a victim living in the sorcerer's own village or district, especially a woman from another district, the sorcerer must normally have majority support to insure his own protection. If he is a "strong" man he may override public criticism, if this is expressed, or he may carry out his sorcery surreptitiously. If hostile feeling is running high against a woman's lineage and village, she may serve as a scapegoat or substitute; the sorcerer's action is legally valid but may serve as a focus of dissension. It embodies retaliation against the out-group which the victim represents; but it may give rise to conflict within the district or village, depending on the relative strength of the persons concerned.

Sorcery as punishment within the co-resident unit may be directed against a woman because of some wrong allegedly suffered by the sorcerer. She may not be the real culprit but a convenient substitute. The sorcerer is thus, in some cases, exerting pressure indirectly upon his own lineage; he is using an entirely legal procedure as a means of evading lineage conflict, although in so doing he may aggravate the situation. In straightforward cases, where punishment of a female culprit is concerned, the control aspect is clearly defined. The woman's offense is most commonly stealing (and occasionally adultery, or the playing of the sacred flutes). There is a strong moral overtone which seems to presage violence when the rule against stealing within the district is broken; but not all cases of in-group stealing are treated in this way. In some the response is sorcery, in others physical violence, in others argument, and in yet others only a few admonishing words. There is no hard and fast rule, and the offended person's response depends on a variety of factors with which we will not concern ourselves.[21]

[21] I have not explored here the relationship between distrust and sorcery. Honigmann (1954, pp. 152–54) discusses sorcery in relation to hypothesis verification. He mentions that Hallowell (1946, p. 222) correlates the anxiety of Northeastern Indians with their atomistic social organization. Honigmann, carrying Hallowell's analysis further, assumes "that the relationship between sorcery and atomistic social structure is probably mutual." "That is, the absence of cohesive behaviour patterns, like chieftainship and a sense of group allegiance, leaves the community without the means for controlling, arresting, or obviating sorcery behaviour." In other words a "tight" social organization presupposes

The third point concerns bribery in relation to sorcery. A man approaches a member of another district, either in person or through an intermediary, and offers him goods to perform a hostile act against a member of his own unit. We might assume that his acceptance, if the transaction were made public, would bring condemnation on his head and embroil him in quarrels with his own lineage, village, and district, that he would be viewed as a dangerous person interested in undermining political unity or at least lineage solidarity; but it is not altogether certain that he would be regarded in this way, although his actions might be acknowledged to have this connotation. Certainly there are cases where members of a unit have taken immediate steps against one of their number who is believed to have accepted payment for such a purpose. And there is the suggestion that he himself considers his action to be "wrong," or at least open to criticism. For instance, he may hide his gifts from other members of his village, trying to conceal the material evidence which might inculpate him. The only party to this may be his wife, herself owing no real loyalty to his group. In any case, by his acceptance he puts himself into the hands of men from another district or districts, who may use their knowledge to injure him. He must weigh the material advantages against the possible risks, and this may mean a measuring of his strength against that of others in his unit. This points to the problem of conflicting values, already indicated. Sorcery performed through an intermediary serves the same function as that used directly for retaliation, but it gives rise to a number of additional features which concern mainly the intermediary himself. We can say that the sorcery performed by him is illegal, and is punishable if his own kin are concerned, but not if it is directed against an "alien" living among them. Further, bribery, although commonly practiced, is an unsatisfactory means of attempting redress for a wrong.

The term bribery is used in this context partly because of the moral implications and partly because no direct sanctions can be brought to bear to insure that the contract is honored except threat of sorcery or of physical action against that person or his group; and even this is designed not to redeem the pledge but to retaliate for the original act of aggression which served as the reason for it. Certainly the same absence of sanctions

---

trust on the one hand and suppression of sorcery on the other, and vice versa. This discussion is highly relevant to conditions in the societies we are discussing.

On the other hand, Clyde Kluckhohn (1944) suggests that in certain communities which try to eliminate interpersonal hostility there is considerable guilt or anxiety in members who are unable to avoid hate impulses; but they are able to direct these impulses into oblique channels, minimizing social disruption.

is evident when, for instance, bridewealth transactions are interrupted by hostilities between the districts concerned; but in this case there is the clear expectation that the contract should be carried through or dissolved in such a way that both parties are satisfied. There is an acknowledgment of a legitimate claim which it is "wrong" to evade, and this is not true where bribery is involved. Bribery can have official sanction when a unit as a whole is implicated. A lineage, village, or district may accept payment and in so doing promise to join forces with the giver or to perform some stipulated action. Here again there is no guarantee that acceptance will necessarily insure fulfilment, and no sanction to enforce it.

Sorcery closely resembles interdistrict warfare, and indeed the same mechanisms of control are operative in the matter of retaliation. Both represent legitimate avenues for the release of aggressive tendencies, and both have the same consequences. That is to say, here we have fear and anxiety, with revenge and counter-revenge, the release and building up of tensions in a repetitive fashion, halted from time to time only to recommence within the same or another constellation. It differs from warfare however, not only in its nonempirical content but in the fact that sorcery may be used on occasion as a means of punishment distinct from retaliation so that action taken against a victim can end there, its purpose achieved. In this respect, the fact that it may have subsequent repercussions does not alter its function.

Chapter 12   Warfare

According to one point of view, warfare can take place only between highly organized nation states: the small-scale skirmishes of non-literate peoples should not be dignified by that term.[1] Against this is the contention that the issue does not hinge on the size and political complexity of the units concerned, or the techniques employed; that warfare is planned violence carried out by members of one social unit, in the name of that unit, against another; and that this is a matter of principle, independent of fluctuations in scale. The distinction between war and feud,[2] not always easy to make, can be framed in these terms.

Like suicide (see chap. 10) and sorcery (chap. 11), warfare may be socially approved and regarded as not only the right but the only conceivable course of action in certain circumstances. Apart from any consideration of ends or aims, it may be held to be good in itself, associated with the highest occupational status a given society has to offer. There are many examples of this, not least in New Guinea itself, which indicate that warfare can be described (even in Nadel's sense)[3] as an accepted social institution. Also, there is the fairly well-established contention that warfare, like sorcery, strengthens the ties within such units by contrasting them with the hostile "out-group." It represents one type of conflict relationship, as against the type of relationship which focuses on cooperation.

Because there is an interdependence between law and political institutions, because when we are dealing with political systems we must, as Radcliffe-Brown has pointed out, consider both law and war, and because,

---

[1] H. H. Turney-High (1942, pp. 21–22); (1949, p. 30); also M. Herskovits (1949, p. 344).

[2] Radcliffe-Brown, in Fortes and Evans-Pritchard, eds. (1950, p. xx), holds that in feuds (as contrasted with war) the aim is merely to compensate for a specific injury, and to achieve neither more nor less than this; but see his position in regard to warfare in 1933 (1952, p. 215). See also Nadel (1947, pp. 151–55, 259, 301–3, 346–48). Hoebel, in R. F. Barton (1949, p. 3), says that if revenge stops at a counter-killing, and does not lead to a feud, this may be called legal-law.

[3] Nadel (1951, pp. 117–18).

as Nadel and others have shown, warfare is primarily a function of the political unit, which by this means attempts to maintain its integrity, we may assume that warfare is a mechanism of social control. It is such because the political unit which sponsors and approves it, through the support of the majority of its members, in so doing directs and determines the use of force for its own ends and for its own preservation, which is the preservation and integrity of its component segments.

Warfare is (or was) the main form of intercourse between the districts in this region, as political units.[4] Broadly speaking, it is justified coercive action on the part of one unit to exact compensation or revenge from another for a real or imagined injury. If this death is attributed to sorcery, the explicit aim may be merely to kill the person, or some member of the unit, held to be responsible, so that a croton may be planted over the grave of the first victim. The actual result could be several deaths or the wounding of participants on either side, the devastation of gardening lands, the destruction and burning of a village and its stockades, the abduction of women, and the looting of pigs, corpses, garden produce, and other commodities. However, wholesale destruction is the exception rather than the rule, and there are relatively few deaths in any one skirmish. Every now and then, members of a district may be forced to leave their home territory and seek refuge elsewhere; but most interdistrict fighting is on the level of "hit and run" raiding. There is a repetitive quality about this, interspersed with peace ceremonies and other interdistrict gatherings, so that there is a constant fluctuation of friendly and hostile relations. All districts other than one's own are potential enemies, as well as friends; but there is no question of fighting people simply because they happen to be enemies or because one has always fought them. Political alliances are mostly transitory, with shifting alignments designed

---

4 Warfare between districts and fighting between segments of a district are not clearly distinguished by special terms, as is the case among the Gahuku-Gama of the Goroka region; see Read (1954, pp. 39–42). But an enemy from another district is a *kamiwajana* ("fight man" in Jate, *havahe* in Kamano), a term never used for an adversary in intradistrict fighting. *Kami* is used only for fighting between districts; it can be translated as "warfare," as contrasted with ordinary intradistrict fighting, which is referred to by the terms for shooting; but *ha(ra)* is any kind of organized fighting either within or between districts. There is no special term for intradistrict fighting of a more or less haphazard kind, which is not seen as a matter of opposition between social units as such. Among the Gahuku-Gama (Read, 1954, pp. 34–42), the "tribe" is the largest group within which warfare is forbidden, distinguished by a common name and the exercise of force, and containing 300 to 1,000 members; it is divided into a number of "sub-tribes." I am not certain whether these would correspond to what I call a "district." The "tribe" is defined by political ties and oppositions, and is conterminous with the political unit. However, I prefer not to use the term "tribe" or "sub-tribe" for "district."

for specific purposes. In any encounter only segments of each district may be involved. Nevertheless, it is virtually always phrased as an issue between opposing districts and carried out in their names.

The social configuration, then, is one of contiguous districts linked by ties of relationship and opposition. A range of potential co-operation/antagonism extends outward from any one district, diminishing in intensity in accordance with sociogeographic distance. It remains relatively constant through time, despite variation in social perspective due to interdistrict movements. In each case it represents a core of closely knit districts surrounded by others with which relationships are more loosely conceived. Within this total field (of potential hostilities and friendships on an interdistrict basis) we can define at any given period for any given district a zone of social interaction which can be termed the ephemeral zone of political influence. All such zones overlap, signifying the crisscrossing of ties and opposition across the whole region we are considering, and even beyond it.

At another level, the interactory zone for each district may be reformulated for each individual within it, taking into account, for instance, the extension of cognatic kin ties. On the whole, however, the area of major strain includes districts connected by a network of interrelationships. Marriage and close relationship in this region are intimately correlated with warfare. The more closely districts are bound by kinship ties, the greater the likelihood of dissension and open hostility. The greater the distance between two districts, sociogeographically as well as genealogically speaking, the less the likelihood of warfare. Thus Kemiju (Jate), Moiife (Usurufa), Ofafina, and Asafina (Fore) are bitter enemies of Kogu, but they are also its main source of wives as well as its guests for certain festivals, ceremonies, and so on. They comprise the principal units in the zone of most intensive interaction centering on Kogu. Mainly for that very reason, because they are engaged jointly in so many transactions, because they come in contact with one another fairly regularly and are dependent on one another, and because their territories adjoin, there has been much more likelihood of dissension; it is also more convenient to exact punishment for a real or imagined injury and easier to retaliate in the event of a death by shooting or sorcery. Since so many Kogu men have and have had near-kin in these districts, we can understand better the conventional local warning, "Don't trust an affine." There is expectation of dissension, and this is reflected in real situations.

Each man always goes armed, carrying with him wherever he goes his bow and bundle of arrows; he wears his plumes and decorations and his plaited anklets. There is no need for him to be specially prepared because being prepared is part of ordinary living. It is partly for this reason that men sleep together in their communal houses away from women, so that they can be ready in the case of attack. Nevertheless, they seem often to have been caught unawares. Perhaps living under constant threat of raids blunts both expectation and excitement and leads to carelessness; but this is not the case when it comes to planning a raid or a fight. It is necessary to take into account the presence of women with brothers and other kin among the "enemy," or of men who may try to turn the situation to their personal advantage. Yet this alone is not always enough to restrain exuberance at such a time. Everyone knows when fighting preparations are going on without necessarily guessing the identity of the intended victims. Fighting magic may be carried out inside and in front of the men's house, large shields dragged out and tested and decorated with cassowary plumes, special leaves ritually given to the warriors, arrows anointed; and the warriors rub their bodies with grease and adorn themselves. Special songs and dances are performed around the men's house and in the village clearing.

Few interdistrict fights last longer than two or three days, but often raids and counter-raids will be made over an extended period. It is considered better to attack an enemy village when it is relatively unprepared,[5] sack it in the shortest possible time, and then disperse rapidly, reassembling on the track leading to the home village and entering it with triumphant singing. But in many cases the object of the attack may be prepared to fight back.

Peace ceremonies are held occasionally, when some sort of balance in the matter of killings and injuries can be said to exist between the participants or when at least one of them is exhausted.[6] But these pacts are not binding, especially over a long period, and they are sometimes designed only to lull an opponent into a false feeling of security.

The warrior leaders may begin negotiations by calling out to one another that it would be better to stop. This is a delicate procedure since, while still in the heat of the fight, it is necessary for them to trust one another. Assuming that two

[5] Fortune (1939, p. 35) remarks that the "use of surprise or of ambush, killing under cover of apparent peace before open battle is joined, is characteristic of New Guinea warfare."

[6] Seligmann (1910, pp. 544–45) mentions for the Wagawaga and Maivara that a formal peacemaking was customary "when it was felt that a respite was necessary from such severe inter-community feuds. . . . Probably such peace-makings did not often occur until the blood accounts between the two communities were tolerably even. . . ." See also F. E. Williams (1930, pp. 166–67).

groups are engaged, the peace ceremony will proceed in the following way. The warriors of each group assemble facing one another, holding their bows in readiness. Men from each side, usually the leaders, dance forward singing, waving before them a *tusefa* leaf, and plant it before the opposite side. ''We exchange the magical *tusefa* leaf, counteracting our enmity.'' Then the warriors dance before one another singing, with tightened bows threatening to shoot. Finally, the leaders step forward and break sugar cane, declaring that they will be friends, no longer fight, and now may eat together. The sugar cane rite symbolizes the dispersement of energy, the breaking of the fighting spirit. Crotons, too, are planted, and usually a feast follows. However, other peace ceremonies may take place after the fighting stops, when each side invites the other to a feast.

Retaliation

The pattern of interdistrict raiding and fighting, for these two features are inseparable here and constitute warfare as defined in this study, will emerge more clearly as our examples (such as the following) are presented.

Although bad feeling existed between Awanti Kasa [Jate] and Busarasa [Fore], Awanti called out inviting the others for a feast, ostensibly to negotiate a peace. A party of Busarasa men went down to Awanti. As they arrived Opavi [of Awanti] drew his bow and shot at them; they shot back. No one was injured, but the Busarasa men retired as quickly as they could, pursued by Awanti, who returned to their stronghold after a running skirmish. Next morning the Awanti men, complete with large shields, waited in ambush at Kagiapinti, near the Awanti-Busarasa boundary. As no Busarasa men appeared, some of them left their hiding place and came almost to Busarasa. There they surprised a number of warriors, and shot Riema [*inivi* lineage]. The Busarasa men pursued them, but when these Awanti men were joined by others, they withdrew to their villages with Riema's corpse. That day Busarasa mourned for the dead man; but next morning one of their villages, Kegati, was attacked at dawn by Keᶜjagana [Jate]. Leaving the corpse, they caught up their weapons and rushed to the defense of the village. In the course of this Ogia [Busarasa; *anumpa* lineage] was killed, and the Keᶜjegana men went away singing.[7] The Busarasa men carried Ogia back and placed him in the men's house at his village, where they mourned for him. Next morning they cut up the two corpses, made ovens, and feasted. On the following day Awanti again waited in ambush at Soinentapinti and were able to kill two Busarasa men who were caught unawares, although fully armed; these were Agosi [*inivi* lineage] and Igeᶜna [*anumpa* lineage].[8] Other Busarasa men were quickly on the scene and drove Awanti back with casualties. The Busarasa men then returned, carrying their dead. Next day the bodies were cut, ovens made, and the warriors feasted. The following morning, the women, heavily guarded by their menfolk, went to the gardens at Jabagamuti to dig sweet potatoes; but while so

---

[7] Riema and Ogia were *nanogai*. Kinship terms are given here in Jate; in most examples, however, they have been omitted in the interests of conciseness.

[8] These two men were *nenafu*. Agosi was a ''brother'' to Riema, *noka* to Ogia; Igeᶜna was ''father'' to Riema, ''son'' to Ogia.

engaged they were surrounded by Awanti, who shot among them and succeeded in killing Kokori [*inivi* lineage] and Agemu [*kasaru* lineage].[9] Again the attackers were beaten back by the Busarasa men, who gathered up their dead and returned to their villages. Next day the corpses were cooked and eaten.

Three or four days afterward Ke^cjagana again planned an attack and waited in ambush at Earaki [in Awanti, close to Busarasa]. From here they made a quick raid on an adjacent village but were repulsed by Busarasa, who ran after them and shot several men. In the fighting, however, Ibiru [*inivi* lineage] was shot and later carried back to Busarasa.[10] This man they buried at Kabumanti instead of eating, saying, "We cannot eat, because a big fight has come up." Then Awanti bribed Kasaru Moke with shells and pig meat to join in harrying Busarasa. Kasaru Moke men gathered together their weapons and shields and waited in ambush at Kakugori [Busarasa]. When Busarasa women, with armed warriors, came out to the gardens near this place, they were surrounded. Fighting followed, in which one woman, Ke^cja [originally from Ifusa, *tonerasa* lineage, wife of Erao, *inivi* lineage, Busarasa], was killed as well as her daughter, Aguja, the brother's child of Era^co.[11] Busarasa warriors managed to wound some of the Moke men and beat them back. They carried the two bodies back to their village, and on the following day the Busarasa women cooked and ate them, the men abstaining because of the severe fighting.

The Busarasa people were apparently becoming thoroughly frightened by now, after this series of reverses; they had reciprocated on each occasion but had not succeeded in showing superior strength. In fact, it was plain that they were considerably weakened; and their enemies, aware of this, continued to harry them. Next morning most men of the *anumpa* lineages collected their belongings and with their wives and children slipped away to Kasogana in the southeast. They were followed by men of the *kasaru* lineages, while the *inivi* and *kiki* lineages fled to Kasaiga, in Emasa. Some little time afterward Awanti men came surreptitiously to Emasa and to Ifusa and bribed them with pig meat and shells to shoot the Busarasa refugees, an offer which they accepted. Thus when Jaberukama [*kiki* lineage][12] was out in the bush, he was seized by men from Emasa and Ifusa and shot with arrows. He was later found by his friends, who carried his corpse first to Kasaiga and then, during the night, to Ibareranti at Busarasa. With those who remained there, they cooked and ate the body, taking some meat back to Kasaiga.

A few days afterward, Awanti, Moke, and Ke^cjagana warriors assembled and attacked the Busarasa people living at Kasaiga. After much skirmishing, the Busarasa people were driven back into the stockades they had erected; but this did not help them. The others broke through, razing their houses and palisades,

[9] These two men were *aku*. Kokori was "elder brother" to Riema, *aku* to Ogia, *nanogai* to Agosi, *nenafu* to Ige^cna; Agemu was *aku* to Riema, "son" to Ogia, "younger brother" to Agosi, *nanogai* to Ige^cna.

[10] This man was "brother" to Riema and Agosi, *noka* to Ogia, *nenafu* to Ige^cna, "elder brother" to Kokori, *aku* to Agemu.

[11] Aguja's father was Igierao, *inivi* lineage, Busarasa.

[12] This man was *nenafu* to Riema, Ogia, Agosi, and Ibiru, *nanogai* to Ige^cna, "elder brother" to Kokori, "younger brother" to Agemu.

killing a man, Jajabu [*anumpa* lineage],[13] and a woman, Osowanita [originally from Etazena, *pigaruri* lineage, but married to a Busarasa man, Moi, *inivi* lineage], and driving the others into the bush. When the enemy had departed, the Busarasa people returned, collected their dead, hastily buried them, and went to Amengkagori [Emasa]. Immediately they set to work erecting houses and surrounding them with a large stockade. Not long after they had finished, Ke︎ᶜjagana again attacked them. They remained within their stockade, while the Ke︎ᶜjagana men stayed exchanging shots for two days or so. By that time the Busarasa people had finished their food: "Where shall we find food? We only fight!" What was worse, they had no tobacco left. At first they dried *jari* gum leaves over a fire and smoked them, but later they began to feel hungry. In the night they sent a man to Moke with gifts of shells, asking them to cut a road through the bush so that they could escape to Kasogana. The Moke men did this, saying they would help them and would not shoot. Ke︎ᶜjagana, hearing of these plans, dispersed, and the *inivi* and *kiki* Busarasa went along the new road to Kasogana. On the road, however, they left Tabie, an *inivi* lineage man,[14] and his wife. Too tired to go further, these two said, "If they want to kill us, they can do so," and went on to Hagasiga [Emasa], where they slept. Next morning they moved into the taller pitpit cane, hiding there until they could slip away unnoticed. Finally they reached Aᶜmari [Moke]; there they remained for a while with others of their lineage and clan in houses originally built by Ora men.

By this time, however, some of the Moke people had had a change of heart. Waniᶜ, an *inivi* Ora man, a classificatory brother of Tabie, secretly approached him in the garden at Waipatati [Moke], telling him that they intended to fight. Waniᶜ also said he would help both him and his younger brother, Agavisa. In the meantime some Moke warriors had left for Amengkagori and finding it empty razed the village. Tabie, with his brothers Agavisa and Aguᶜnamu, his wife Mekuta [of *kasaru* lineage, Busarasa], his daughter Inamisuka, his son Abanumu, and *nanoferu* Mugaja, Agavisa's wife, with other women and young children, as well as Iniganda [*inivi* lineage],[15] guided initially by Waniᶜ, who soon left them, started off with their belongings for the bush where they were to hide until it was dark. The Moke warriors had returned. Hearing that Tabie and his companions intended to escape, they pressed on to Aᶜmari, where they found the Ora salt houses empty. Tabie, hearing their approach, sent Iniganda forward to guard the pathway along which his group was to travel, while he himself looked after the women and children; Aguᶜnamu and Agavisa served as the rearguard, stationed behind trees to block the Moke advance. As they were leaving, Mekuta was shot by a Moke man, Jonaᶜo, of the *keᶜafu* lineage. As she fell she called out a warning; her husband, turning, was also injured by an arrow. He called out to Agavisa, who turned and shot Jonaᶜo, killing him.

Shouting defiance to the approaching Moke men, Agavisa shot again at Jonaᶜo's corpse, crying out, "Tabie's brothers remain. We two, Agavisa and Aguᶜnamu! You surround us! And when the sun goes down you will shoot us, but until then

13 *Nenafu* to Jaberukama and Igeᶜna.
14 "Brother" to Riema, Agosi, and Ibiru, *noka* to Ogia, *aku* to Igeᶜna and Agemu, *nanogai* to Kokori, *nenafu* to Jaberukama and Jajabu.
15 Tabie was his *nanoferu*, having bled his nose and negotiated his betrothal.

we will fight!'' There was an exchange of arrows, but the Moke men got Jonaᶜo's body and some of them took it back to Moke. Desultory shooting continued until the Moke men were reinforced, and called out, ''We can kill you now.'' Agavisa and his brother continued shooting, being driven further away from Tabie, until they eventually made their escape into the thick bush. By this time Tabie had recovered. Cutting the strings tying several bundles of arrows, he filled his net bags with them and prepared for more fighting. He sent the women and children ahead to Iniganda and, leaving his dead wife, took his daughter Inamisuka on his shoulder. As he was making his way along, Moke men appeared and shot at him. Quickly he dropped his daughter at the base of a tree and drawing his bow ran along the track shooting at them. But some of them came through the bush and shot Inamisuka as she lay by the tree. Hearing his daughter's cry, Tabie became distracted. He rushed forward letting his arrows fly, killing a Moke man and one of their Oka allies, calling out, ''My name is Tabie! When the sun goes down, you can shoot me—but until then . . .!'' The fighting continued, Iniganda trying to protect the women and children; Mugaja and Abanumu, Tabie's son, were killed; others escaped to Kasogana. Finally Tabie disappeared into the tall pitpit cane, where he was joined afterward by Aguᶜnamu. They could hear the Moke men singing triumphantly, and presently made their escape to Emanti at Busarasa, which they found razed. They slept in the only remaining shelter there, a menstrual hut. Agavisa and Iniganda had fled to Inivi in Jate territory. Tabie and Aguᶜnamu went on to Ora, where they told Waniᶜ what had happened, and then in a roundabout way to Kasogana to tell the other members of their village and district. Some of them then fled to Inivi. Waniᶜ from Ora went out and buried the dead. For some time Tabie lived at Kasogana, but one day he killed an Oka man and returned to plant a croton over the grave of his son and daughter. He then went to Tukasinanti at Ora. Gradually people began drifting back to Busarasa to rebuild their villages, and Tabie did likewise.

This account has been given in some detail to show the rhythm of ''backing'' and ''counter-backing.'' It reveals, too, a number of other interesting points: for instance, the various methods of fighting adopted, the raid, the ambush, the open fight, as well as the sacking of villages, bribery, and the driving away of people from their home territory. Although the Busarasa men retaliated, inflicting some casualties, they were no match for their enemies. The Awanti wanted to make them suffer and enlisted the help of other districts for the purpose. Busarasa, by the way, is immediately adjacent to both Awanti Kasa and Moke, in much the same way as Kogu is to Moiife and Asafina.

Were it possible to analyze all of the available cases the result would resemble a huge checkerboard, each district being represented by a counter. Through time a continual movement will be observed, with the loss of relatively few counters. At another level of analysis, such examples provide illuminating evidence in terms of interpersonal relations. They offer a much more vivid commentary on social affairs than can be achieved by merely setting out the principles they seem to exemplify. We may know, in general terms, the form of a given society and how it functions; but it is the cultural content in relation to the persons who share it which provides significance and depth of meaning. It depends, of course, on what one is looking for in the matter of explanations. The multitude of details which appear in almost any action sequence, some of them seemingly irrelevant, help to provide answers to many important questions which concern us in this study.

When a grudge exists between two districts, one of which awaits an opportunity to retaliate and finally kills an unsuspecting visitor, here we have the basic ingredients of warfare. Viewed in isolation, it indicates a settlement. In wider perspective, it is further evidence of a breach between the two units. Almost anything is permissible in this context. There is no need, even, to declare war, because potential hostility from members of other districts is part of the normal process of living. Generally speaking, there is no "inter-national" law or (in Fortune's term) "inter-municipal" law, stipulating what should or should not be done. But because fighting usually takes place among districts within a certain range and involving persons more or less closely connected through affinal and other kinship ties, it is often suggested that there are, ideally, limits beyond which destruction should not go. Women and children, like the aged or the unarmed, are not ordinarily exempted, but if more than three or four people are killed in a single fight, there may be an outcry that the enemy "is shooting us like wild pigs." A great deal depends upon the attitude of the "strong" men in each village. "This is not fighting," they may say. "We are men, not pigs, not animals!" After killing or injuring someone on the opposite side, the victorious party usually stops shooting to dance and sing, and often retires at this stage while the others collect the body. The drawing of blood, or the killing of one victim, may be enough to stop the fight. This is not always so. There is a feeling that it should be like this, but no sanction or strong pressure of popular opinion is brought to bear to encourage it. It is considered, too, that a dead or wounded person should be left for his kin to recover, or at least his bones should be returned for final burial in his garden. More important, lineage and district loyalty is not seen as an all-or-none affair; neutrality in respect of certain relationships is taken for granted.[16] These

16 It is permissible even in the heat of fighting to refrain from shooting certain categories of kin, or to shout a warning. Indeed, such behavior is expected and is in no way condemned by either side or by its allies. What is condemned is the divulgence of plans, the warning before the event, or the acceptance of bribes for this purpose; even here the particular circumstances of each instance determine the attitude of the group.

are the main courtesies to be observed by opposing groups. Again, there are no sanctions to insure that they will be; but the zone of political interaction, emphasizing the interdependence of the component units, undoubtedly has some moderating influence.

Let us consider a few examples:

A young Tiroka boy, Gumage^c, said to have been caught and operated on by Amufi *sangguma* men, eventually died. His father, Patuja, carried the body to his lineage garden at Kasafiga and gave it to others to cook; he also killed a pig, which was cooked in a separate oven. In order to divine responsibility for the boy's death, a few bamboo containers of edible leaves were placed with the corpse. When cooked the meat was distributed, the father being given his son's head; the leaves were examined, and Amufi was named as the district responsible for the death. Nothing was done in the matter for some time. When the affair was almost forgotten, an Amufi visitor arrived at Tiroka. He was entertained in customary fashion and while the men were sitting around their communal house Patuja asked him whether he really came from Amufi. He replied that this was so. Patuja then went to his house, brought out his child's dried head, and placed it beside the stranger. The Amufi man began to tremble with fear; "Why do you do this?" But Patuja did not listen; he stood in front of him and drew his bow. The Amufi man cried out that he had not killed the child; but Patuja said he was lying and killed him. Later a party of Tiroka men carried the body to Amufi. The Amufi men accepted it with angry denials that they were to blame for the child's death: they accused Patuja of tricking them.

Apparently nothing further was done in the matter. Yet we are not to suppose that the event was entirely forgotten, merely that our evidence is not complete.

A party of Numparu warriors, out to avenge an injury, came to Gwegwepinaga [in Numparu], where they found an Agura man named Eteweri. They transfixed his body with many arrows, then piled kunai grass on it and set fire to it. When the fire had died down the corpse resembled a roasted animal. They then left the body as a decoy for the deceased's kin, who soon put in an appearance. As they were carrying it back to Agura the Numparu men shot at them until they were forced to abandon it. Finally, after a pitched fight in which no one was injured, the Agura people were able to get the body and hold a mortuary feast.

Jagana planned a surprise attack upon Tira^{c}e. A party of warriors set out for Kipanaga, near some Tira^{c}e gardens, and hid in the undergrowth. From this position they could observe men and women working in the gardens, making furrows, planting seed potatoes, and so on. One man, Aratizu, was standing on a raised mound keeping watch over his womenfolk, ready to warn the others of any suspicious movement in the surrounding bush. The Jagana men waited for his attention to wander. It so happened that an airplane passed overhead, and Aratizu looked up; the Jagana men seized their opportunity and shot him dead. In the confusion which followed they shot arrows indiscriminately among the Tira^{c}e men and women, none of whom was seriously injured, and after removing the arrow which had killed Aratizu the Jagana men hurriedly beat a retreat. Dancing and singing they entered Jagana victoriously, waving the arrow as well as *fetoba* (fern) and *kanu*[c] (edible leaves). The older men, children, and womenfolk gathered admiringly around them, examining the arrow and leaves, praising their prowess, exclaiming that their bellies were good because the death of Zezawajeti, previously shot by Tira[c]e, had now been avenged. Next morning they killed a pig, held a feast, and planted a croton over Zezawajeti's grave. Tira[c]e, to avenge Aratizu's death, bribed a Hopea man to perform sorcery on Dabulga, a Jagana man thought to be responsible for the shooting. The sorcery used was *naglisa*, but Dabulga recovered after treatment.

Arrows were often removed from a victim and exhibited, or tied to the outside of a stockade to serve as a reminder of what had taken place, or as a challenge to retaliation. The use of fern and edible leaves signifies that a death has occurred, for these are often cooked and eaten with a corpse.

Moiife men made a quick raid on some Kogu villages. In the fighting they killed Tomugu[c]o and retired singing. The Kogu men picked up the corpse and placed it in a hut. That same evening Kama [of Kogu], with a small party of men, set off for Moiife. Leaving the others to guard the road, he crept stealthily up to the stockade around one of the villages, climbed over, moved across the clearing to the women's houses, and waited. Presently a woman, Fuge[c] [originally from Numaga], emerged. Seeing him, she withdrew, asking, "Are you an enemy?" "I am a man of this place," he replied. [Both Kogu and Moiife are Usurufa-speaking districts, so he had no "alien" accent to alarm her.] She came out, and Kama shot her, quickly making his escape across the stockade to join the others. They returned singing to Kogu. Kama then went down to Ofafina with invitations to visit Kogu for the mortuary feast. Next morning a group of warriors came up with Kama. Tomugu[c]o's corpse was cut up and cooked with a pig, the meat distributed, and his bones finally buried in his garden. Kama, with the rest of his village, fled Kogu and went to live for a time at Ofafina, for they were afraid of Moiife. Soon afterward Moiife attacked other Kogu villages.

Interesting is the fact that Kama deliberately enlisted the help of Ofafina men by offering them a share of the feast and thus obtained their permission to use Ofafina as a refuge. What Ofafina hoped to get out of the bargain, besides the food, is not revealed. Also, apparently only Kama and his co-villagers made their escape, leaving the other Kogu villages to cope with Moiife. Other similar cases (for example, the dispersal of Busarasa) suggest that the district as the political unit was often split up, that it was not invariably a unit of interdependent segments, on the principle of one for all and all for one. A district faced, as Kogu was (and the above incident is only one of a long series of Kogu-Moiife fights, culminating in the temporary collapse of Kogu), and as Busarasa was, with a more powerful foe, and seeing no real opportunity for settlement (several offers from Kogu to Moiife had been treated with derision, their food trampled underfoot, and their shells taken), gradually began to "lose its nerve," to fear the inevitable outcome of remaining.

Some Agura men shot Ipevi, a younger brother of Kama, while he was at Moiife. Moiife called out to Kogu, and in particular to Kama, telling what had happened, and asking them to collect the body. They called back that they would fetch Ipevi later, and in the meantime would go in pursuit of the Agura men. Kama, with a party of warriors, arrived that evening at an Agura village, scaled the stockade, and surrounded the men's house before those inside were aware of their presence. They called for the others to come outside. When they refused, the Kogu men began to pull off the kunai roof and shot at the inmates as they emerged. Several Agura men were wounded, and one, Uriru, was killed by Kama. The fight continued until the Agura men were driven into the bush. Then Kama, pulling his arrow from the dead man, called to the others and without attacking the women's houses they returned singing to Kogu with the news. Then they went on to Moiife, where they placed the arrow taken from Uriru upright in the ground by Ipevi's legs, signifying that his death had been avenged. Next day the body was cooked and shared with Moiife, the bones finally being buried in Ipevi's garden and a croton planted over them.

Another incident in the feuding between Kogu and Moiife took place some little time after the first, when Kogu was again functioning as a united district and Kama and his lineage kin had returned to their own village. They were still on friendly terms with Ofafina. One evening a party of Kogu men raided Moiife and killed Kerifu, a Moiife woman. Next day Moiife raided a Kogu village, killing Kaju^ca and an Ofafina man, Pitiviva^co, who was present, and returned singing. Kogu held a mortuary feast and calling Ofafina carried the two corpses to the gardens and cut them up. They brought the meat back to the village, placed it in bamboo containers, and cooked it in an oven. The bones of the Kogu man were buried in his garden; but the Ofafina men pounded up all but a few of Pitiviva^co's bones, and removed the marrow and ate that in addition to the pounded fragments which were mixed with edible leaves. Kogu considered the death of Kaju^ca to have been balanced by their killing of Kerifu and planted a croton over his grave, but Ofafina soon afterward successfully raided Moiife.

No obvious reason, except hostility toward Moiife, is given for the death of Kerifu, and Kogu was ready to accept the killing of Kaju^ca in exchange. But how far can we rely on the planting of a croton over the grave of a person killed in this way as indicating that the affair is settled and not to be reopened? "A death for a death" is the conventional view-point. Yet it is obvious that this may be rationalized. Kogu's bad feeling toward Moiife was said to offer sufficient reason for the killing of Kerifu, yet to avoid further repercussions her death was held to balance that of Kaju^ca. But his death, even if the croton had been planted, might be held to warrant punitive action on the part of Kogu should the occasion arise. This is brought out in many examples; crotons are planted and vows are taken that the matter is settled, only to have it reopened later.

Crotons are planted not only when a death has been "backed" but also, among other reasons, to settle arguments. During my stay at Kogu we saw crotons planted for various reasons; some of the agreements were observed, some were not. It is the same with the planting of a croton over a grave. Further, should there be no croton over a grave an excuse may be found to plant one; an injury to an enemy, and not a killing, may then be enough. There is, however, some lack of agreement here. In some cases where a death has been successfully "backed" no croton is planted, and the grave is left unmarked.

A young woman from Ofafina, Jumu, went in marriage to a Jasuvi man. At the same time a party of Ofafina men raided Ora and shot an *anumpa* lineage woman named Inusa [a maternal grandparent of Jumu]. Fighting occurred between the two districts, but Ora failed to injure anyone. The affair was left in abeyance. It so happened that Jumu wanted to visit Ofafina to see her parents and brothers. Knowing that her path led through Ora and that the latter was at open enmity with Ofafina, the Jasuvi people advised her while passing through there to stay with Asiwa. "He is your classificatory father; stay with him. He will give you food and help you to reach Ofafina." [Asiwa, an *anumpa* man, was a brother's son of Inusa.] Jumu eventually arrived with her child at Ora and found Asiwa in his garden at Isagori. He was surprised to see her: "Your lineage kin came and killed an Ora woman. Why do you come before my eyes?" But he was sorry for her and gave her food. However, some other Ora men saw her and talking among themselves decided to kill her. A party of warriors hid in a clump of undergrowth near the track leading to Ofafina, waiting for her. Asiwa, who had heard their plans, told her: "They all want to kill you, but I will hide you. Don't come to the garden; but when it is dark and men sleep I will come and get you and take you some distance down the Ofafina road." He hid her and her child in a clump of pitpit cane in the middle of the garden and covered them with grass and returned to his village. Here the remaining men were sitting around an oven. Asiwa took some of the cooked food and returned to the garden, gave it to Jumu and the child, and covered up their hiding place again. His movements had been observed by Tawasa, an *anumpa* man who called him *nefaru* [age-mate]. Guessing what was taking place, he approached Asiwa, saying, "I can help you. We can take them. which way shall we go?" Asiwa, trusting his *nefaru*, replied that he would go in a roundabout way, bypassing the Ora men who were in ambush. Tawasa passed this information on to the others, who now ranged themselves along the proposed route. Tawasa then came back to Asiwa, who by this time had realized his mistake; but Tawasa stayed close to him, and there was little he could do. They went together to where Jumu was hidden, and Tawasa said, "Give her to me first, and I will copulate." Asiwa nodded approval, thinking that Tawasa might really help him now. Tawasa took hold of her. Jumu cried out to Asiwa, "My father! They all want to shoot me now; he too is doing it. You make this come about! Hold my head." Asiwa took her head on his lap and held it; her child sat alongside, and Tawasa proceeded to have coitus. Asiwa spoke to her, "My daughter, they are going to shoot you." When he had finished Tawasa got up and went away. Asiwa took hold of her arm and they left the garden for the Ofafina road. Just out of Ora they found shells piled on the track. Nearby Ora warriors were hidden, watching to see if Asiwa touched them. [The shells were to serve as a bribe: Asiwa could have them if he shot the woman.] Asiwa passed by them; but the Ora men emerged and said to him, "Ofafina shot us, and so now we want to kill this woman. If you do this you may have the shells." Asiwa replied, "I cannot take these shells; I am sorry for my daughter. If you shoot her, I can shoot you. You will have to shoot us both first." He turned away and leaving both the shells and the woman returned to his village. The Ora men then shot Jumu and her child and returned to where Asiwa was wailing, telling him that they had shot them and now he could bury them. Asiwa was angry. He said that he had wanted to protect them, but the others had tricked him, and that Ofafina would do likewise and come down and shoot them. He blamed Ora for bringing trouble on itself. He then went out, collected the two bodies, and buried them. Soon afterward Ofafina heard [ostensibly through Asiwa] what had happened. They came down to Ora and shot Namina [an *anumpa* woman, clan daughter of Asiwa] and Egina [also *anumpa*, clan daughter of Asiwa], and after general fighting returned singing and planted a croton. Asiwa called out to the Ora people, "I talked to you. Now you see what has happened. It is your own fault!" Ora buried the two women and planted crotons over their graves.

Several interesting points emerge here, and we pause to consider them. Asiwa was acting quite conventionally in befriending Jumu and expected help in this respect from his *nefaru*. Tawasa betrayed him. Asiwa did not blame him directly, any more than his own lineage and clan kin considered him to be behaving disloyally in hiding the woman from them. But Asiwa's actions were not beyond reproach, even according to local standards. Jumu might legitimately expect his protection; without it she would be exposed to any man's sexual attentions. Nevertheless, Asiwa, although allegedly helping her, was persuaded by his *nefaru* to let him copulate with her, thus, in effect, treating her as an unprotected person of no defined relationship. She herself recognized this and said that they meant to kill her; symbolizing this, Tawasa prepared to shoot her with his penis. Asiwa had "made this come about." The inference was that Asiwa was behaving contrary to expectation; he was creating a precedent for such action. Asiwa himself acknowledged this. Afterward he helped her only half-heartedly, knowing what would happen. He made no effort to avoid the danger or to send her back to Jasuvi or to another village or district; nor did he attempt to bribe his own kinsmen. He seems to have felt that the two should in fact be killed to "back" the previous death but continued to make a show of protection. The Ora men, mostly of his own lineage and clan (*anumpa*) tried to placate him, offering him shells to shoot Jumu and her child. They preferred that he should do it himself in order to avoid lineage and clan dissension. Asiwa rejected the offer and defied them. Although he did nothing to defend the victims, he warned the others that Ofafina would take revenge, and when this eventually happened taunted them. The resultant Ora deaths were, he said, due to their own acts. He talked so ''strongly'' that crotons were placed over the graves of the two Ora women to indicate ''backing'' when in reality no such revenge had taken place. Thus the killing of Jumu and her child served to balance the deaths of both the new victims as well as of Inusa. The fault was considered to lie with the Ora people themselves. This is almost an unprecedented situation where interdistrict troubles are concerned, for nearly always, irrespective of what may happen, the fault is ascribed to external agents. Further, this was not solely Asiwa's view but apparently was accepted by others or green crotons would not have been planted—or it was an attempt to avoid further conflict with Ofafina.

It was not unusual that Jumu should have come alone through enemy territory. Women do not always travel in the company of their husbands. Alone or in pairs, they move about fairly frequently within a certain range. They expect protection from certain male relatives—a *nenafu*, for instance, or ''father'' (like Asiwa); but they must be aware of the risks involved. There are many cases in which women traveling alone have been attacked, although as often they were not. In fact, it is said that desire for sexual adventure is often an underlying motive for traveling in this way. A husband rarely denies his wife the privilege of an occasional visit to her parents, and this may sometimes serve as an excuse. However, both men and women often visit relatives in other districts. They always run a risk in doing so, although they are not usually so foolhardy as to go to a hostile village or district as Jumu did. But this underlines what has been said before: fighting, revenge, and counter-revenge are so commonplace that people become accustomed to this state of affairs and are often careless about their own safety.

A Henagaru visitor, Tawari, was staying in the men's house at Tatagufa. During conversation one day he thoughtlessly discussed the killing of a Kemiju woman, Emuti^{c}mu, who had been holding a small child at the time of her death. Tawari boasted that he had been responsible, not suspecting that the child had now grown to manhood and was present in the house, for Emuti^{c}mu had been married to a Tatagufa man. Some other men present plucked at their skin to indicate that the child had become a man and would be ready to avenge his mother's death. But it was too late. The son, Etuifa [the local *tultul*], had heard and spoke: ''When I was small, you shot my mother. I have not forgotten''; and Warimpa, his lineage brother, added, "My mother, he shot her before; now we two would like to shoot him!" Tawari did not excuse himself. The other two men went out, and after sleeping Tawari left for Henagaru. Etuifa and Warimpa had gone to Fogo-finaga [near Tatagufa], where they lay in wait for Tawari and finally shot him. His wife, Jopelgebi [originally from Inivi], who was with him, embraced his dead body in grief. Then, picking up his bow and arrows, she threatened to shoot the two men. She shot several arrows, which missed their mark; but she was so possessed with fury that the others were afraid and did not attempt to shoot back. Eventually others arrived and disarmed her. Tewapi ["mouth-boy" of Kemiju and later *luluai*] carried the corpse back to Tatagufa, where Etuifa and Emuti^cmu's father, an old man named Enagiza, killed pigs and held a feast. They called out to Kemiju, who joined them. Both Tatagufa and Kemiju were "good belly," for the woman's death had been avenged. Tewapi buried Tawari's body, but Etuifa insisted that to make him "good belly" they should dig it up, cook, and eat it. Tewapi returned to the grave and proceeded to cut up the body, packing it into heaps for the Tatagufa and Kemiju women to take away and cook. [The widow did not share in this.] Henagaru did not avenge Tawari's death. His widow remained for a while at Kemiju but eventually went to Gwana, where she married.

There is no explanation for Henagaru's failure to "back" this killing, but it is assumed that they saw the Tatagufa-Kemiju combination as too strong for them and were content to leave the matter where it stood, one death offsetting the other. The widow did not return to her husband's district for fear of being considered to be in collusion with the killers and being killed in turn.

In the northern districts fighting has been officially suppressed by the Administration since 1947–48, yet the majority of examples we have collected cover approximately an eight to ten-year period up to 1953. For the southern area they are more recent, while those relating to Kogu, Moiife, Kemiju, and parts of Ofafina occurred before 1949. In both areas, however, the force of alien control is making itself felt, and fighting has become more and more spasmodic. This is true for the whole region, in varying degrees, as far north as Grufe and as far south as Busarasa and Moke, but not beyond these points. Even in the areas which are now relatively peaceful outbreaks do occur and would be much more frequent but for fear of the Government and Mission authorities, whose influence has been exerted largely at a distance. Informal local courts, like the Administration court at Kainantu, do not provide for the settlement of disputes in the way that fighting does. There is, for instance, no provision for "backing' a death diagnosed as the result of sorcery and ascribed to the action of a particular district. Only a very few sorcery cases have been tried by the Kainantu court, and these do not directly concern the region under discussion. To my knowledge, no cases of sorcery have been tried by the informal courts. Inevitably, there are now fewer deaths as a direct result of warfare.

In the northern districts spasmodic outbreaks have taken place.

A Tebinofi man named Agadjubu was living in Kogu.[17] He went one day with some companions to Jababi, where Epukano killed him with an ax, thinking he was alone and because Jababi had a death to avenge. His Kogu companions brought him home. They were followed by men from Jababi, Grufe, Tebinofi, and Tiroka [all Kamano], who came to look on the dead man. Kokote, the warrior leader of Kiave hamlet [in Kogu], rubbed himself with ashes and mud and harangued the onlookers: "All you Kamano men, we have listened to you when you spoke about alien ways.[18] Why did you do this thing? Now all the white men have come and told us to stop fighting. But you killed this man. You have tricked us." With this he drew his bow and shot at Gugativio, a Grufe man, wounding him. The gathering broke up in confusion, and the visitors scattered into the bush to take up positions. Kogu men rushed for their weapons, and a general fight followed. Finally the Kamano visitors retreated, to the accompaniment of showers of arrows. Kokote and his companions returned to carry the corpse to the gardens, where it was cooked and eaten, and a croton was planted over the bones.

In the southern region we find not so much outbreaks of fighting as efforts on the part of a representative of the Administration to suppress what is locally viewed as normal procedure:

Obebu, of the ke{^c}afu lineage in Moke, had a son, Afujaso [younger brother to Esoiba, the present Moke luluai]. It so happened that a section of the Hogateru district was driven away from its territory by Ke{^c}afu, Ke{^c}jagana, and Taramu and found refuge at Jegabamuti, not far away. While Obebu was planting cucumbers in his garden at Kabapati, Afujaso fell violently ill. He was carried home but on the following day became worse. Obebu and Esoiba were convinced that Hogateru had worked naglisa but had no proof of this. Esoiba therefore went to the Hogateru refugee village and obtained some urine and feces from the latrine. Returning, he mixed this with water and gave it to Afujaso to drink, the idea being that if he were under the influence of their sorcery he would respond violently and if not he would at least be unaffected by it. The sick boy's reaction was to become even worse. Obebu was doubly sure that the Hogateru people were to blame and sent Esoiba to them again. This time he obtained a small piece of kunai grass from the doorway of a Hogateru house, discolored by body grease and charcoal from people brushing past it. When this was shown to Afujaso he fell back in a coma. There was no doubt, then, that the Hogateru people were responsible. Obebu went up and spoke to them, "You have worked sorcery on

17 This man resembled in features and in physique a deceased Kogu man, and when Kogu visitors to Tebinofi saw him they said that the latter had "returned." They persuaded him to come and live with them, "taking up his old kinship ties."

18 Kokote is referring here to the Kamano as intermediaries between the Usurufa and the Europeans, since they were relatively close to Kainantu. See R. Berndt (1952–53, e.g., pp. 51, 53, 142).

my son. Throw the magic bundle into the water, counteract the sorcery so that he may recover. But the Hogateru men replied, "You come to our place and collect things [i.e., the feces and kunai] and you give them to your son. You come into our houses and collect ashes, you take our feces. We have given you these freely.[19] Now we are angry." Obebu answered, "Good, you have spoken," and went angrily away. Soon afterward Afujaso died. Just before the mortuary ceremony, Busarasa, Kasogana, and Ora made a combined attack on Moke, surrounding its various stockaded settlements. They were beaten back without loss of life, but Obebu was unable to find a pig to kill for the feast. The body of the dead boy was taken to the gardens where it was cooked and eaten by the women. The refugee Hogateru group left that same day for their own territory at Kivika [Hogateru] because they were afraid. As Moke was fully occupied in defending itself at the time, nothing was done immediately in the matter of "backing" Afujaso's death; Obebu, however, told his elder son, Esoiba, that he must attend to it later.

In about 1951, two Hogateru men returned to their old refugee village at Jegabamuti to collect sugar cane from the garden. As they were coming along a little frequented track Esoiba crept up and shot them, then arranged their bodies some distance apart. Several days afterward some Hogateru men came down to look for them and not far out from Kasa found the bodies already decomposing. The eyes of the two men had been eaten, so it is said, by Anitaratiza, a bush spirit inhabiting a patch of swampy ground nearby. They carried them home and buried them. A party of warriors then set out for Moke. They came up to a garden at Pomavinti where Takaba [a clan brother of Esoiba] was engaged in digging and shot at him. He escaped into the bush nearby and ran to the main village, warning the others, who instantly rushed out and found the Hogateru men at another garden, Jararinti. Here fighting took place, and a Moke man named Baneni [noka to Esoiba] was shot but not killed. The Hogateru men thought they had killed him and returned singing.

A little time afterward, before Moke could retaliate, two native police, Bagau and Tukam, arrived at Moke to establish an Administration base. A group of Hogateru men [sponsored by the classificatory father and younger brother of the two men] came to them and asked them to punish the Moke people by shooting them. The two native police "held court," summoning Esoiba as luluai with his kinsmen, in the presence of the Hogateru men. The case was discussed fully from both angles, and Esoiba told why he had killed the two Hogateru men. The Hogateru representatives denied their initial complicity. This was parried by Esoiba. There ensued a test of verbal strength which was won by the Hogateru men, repeating that they were not responsible for the original death, at the same time passing the hand across the nose, thus declaring the subject "taboo" and affirming the essential truth of their statement. Esoiba was forced to accept this and when questioned by the native police repeated, "They speak the truth.

---

[19] The Hogateru men apparently allowed Esoiba to collect these things openly. Thus they attempted to vindicate themselves, declaring their honesty and innocence; if they had worked the sorcery they would hardly have permitted this. By submitting to Esoiba's requests they hoped to show their good faith. They were angry now because Obebu accused them openly.

Another man must have killed my younger brother. I thought they had done it, and so I killed in return.'' The two police then asked Esoiba what he would do about it, and he replied that, in these circumstances, he would be willing to give compensation. The Hogateru men assented, and two pigs, paper, shells, waistbands, rope, and money were paid, the affair thus being settled.

In this example we see not only the settlement of what might have been a persisting feud but the beginning of a judicial procedure introduced by agents of external control, representing an extension of legal space in which the judgment is accepted by both parties. It might be suggested that this acceptance depended primarily on the authority of an alien arbitrator backed by the force of the Administration. Such, of course, is the case. Yet there seems to have been in the use of ''taboo gesture'' a sanction of some significance, with power to transcend interdistrict disagreement. Just what importance can be attached to it is uncertain, since beyond a few isolated examples there is little evidence that it is widely used in such circumstances. In essence it signifies that what has been said is true beyond dispute; the act, symbolizing the nose-bleeding rite (and thus expressing ''strength''), constrains the accuser to accept unconditionally by placing him in the wrong and making him liable to the payment of compensation. It is an act, moreover, of ''closing,'' or sealing, and has parallels in the endings of certain mythological stories, or in the planting of crotons in the peace ceremonies. The implication would seem to be that statements made by an accused person have a much wider acceptance when accompanied by an act of ''closing,'' in contrast to the usual rejection of an enemy's point of view. Because our evidence is slender in this direction, we are unable to postulate a wider legal influence. Were we to do so, its importance would be soon overshadowed by the evidence relating to interdistrict distrust and fighting. Too frequent use, for instance, would lead to its being discredited in the very situation in which it could serve as a mechanism of control.

Refugees

There is reason to believe that movements of displaced groups take place fairly frequently. Just how frequently we cannot be certain, for although our data are relatively full on the movements of such districts as Kogu, Moiife, Ke^cjagana, Kemiju, Tatagufa, Inivi, Busarasa, and Moke, this is not so for others. Thus we cannot be entirely sure that such movements are not due to numerical differences between districts, or unequal fighting strength. Where we do have detailed information it would seem that most districts, not all, are fairly equally matched, and at a given time can be said to have equal chances of success. Nevertheless, in many cases final collapse seems to have been swift.[20] It is rare for any one district to withstand a continuing, concerted attack.

The refugees so scattered cannot easily combine for fighting. This does not stop them from making occasional raids, but otherwise they prefer to wait until they are reunited. Once "on the run," as in the Busarasa case, they are likely to remain so until they are able to take up their own land again. A small exiled group, unable to return to its gardens and having lost its main items of wealth (pigs, for example), is very much dependent on the kindness of others; and this has to be paid for. But dispersal of this kind forces people into areas they would not normally visit. Consequently, it widens their interactory zone, bringing in new elements of common interest quite as much as of antagonism.

Kasa, Moke, and Henagaru combined to drive away Busarasa, sacking its stockaded settlements, until finally their inhabitants ran away to Waingamuti [in the vicinity of Emasa]. After some time had elapsed, Kasa and Moke sent word to the refugees that they were willing to settle the affair and be friends and suggesting that the Busarasa people should return. Then a party of warriors hid themselves in a patch of bush at Gusintamuti, on the road leading to Busarasa, stationing some old men on a nearby hill to keep watch. As the returning refugees approached, the old men began to sing. Tabie, a Busarasa warrior leader, at once suspected treachery and ordered the others to remain where they were while he and his younger brother, Kaperuti, went ahead: "If they don't shoot, follow us; otherwise return," they said. They went around to Jararinti, where they met a group of armed Kasa and Moke men who invited them to come forward and embrace. But their bows were tightened and Tabie spoke, "You are not to shoot us. You are not to tighten your bows. You deceive us!" and with this they turned to depart. The others tried to seize their shields, but Tabie and Kaperuti ran away under a shower of arrows. In the meantime the men at Gusintamuti emerged from the bushes and began to shoot at the assembled Busarasa people, who scattered, the men taking up positions from which to shoot. A Moke man held Tabie, but Kaperuti, turning, saw this and shot him dead. A number of Moke men ran forward shooting, but the two were able to parry the arrows with their shields. Kaperuti managed to get under cover in the bush at Tetieru, while Tabie remained on the road. But men went after Kaperuti and shot him dead, and returned singing to the others. Tabie, hearing this, called out in defiance, "Another man may come, and you can shoot him. But I am Tabie! You shoot my brother, you can't shoot me! Later you can surround me, and when the sun goes down you can shoot me—but not until then!" He went on shooting and then, escaping into the bush, came to Waipantata [Busarasa], where he hid. Seeing Karagiza, a Moke man, he shot him through the leg, calling out, "Later you can shoot me!" By

[20] We may say that panic develops as a result of fear and the feeling of possible entrapment. Cf. Quarantelli (1954, p. 275).

this time most of the Busarasa people had spread out into the bush and were making their way back to Waingamuti. The Kasa and Moke men returned to Kaperuti's body, and all shot at it; then they returned to their villages carrying their dead and wounded. Tabie came back to Waingamuti, where two Ora men, To^cwara and Wani^c [kasaru lineage men, classificatory fathers to him; this is not the Wani^c of the other Busarasa case], were visiting; he asked them to go to Tetieru to find and bring back his brother's body. They did so, and on their return Tabie began a mourning harangue, accusing his own people of desertion in the hour of need. "Here am I, a 'strong' man; but the others did not stand by us. And now Moke has shot my younger brother. . . ." With this he broke his bow and arrows and cut his ear. Next morning the usual mortuary ceremonies were held, a pig was killed, and the dead man's body rubbed with blood. Pig meat was given to the two Ora men, and the corpse was carried by four women [Asire from Ke^cjagana, a nogago, mother's brother's wife, of Tabie; Ampie of Busarasa, kiki lineage, a nogago; Wajaguta of Busarasa, inivi, a nogago; and Pegujema, Wajaguta's sister] to the garden of Kotuti, where it was cooked and brought back to the village.

A few days afterward a party of Busarasa men went down to their own district, where they found some Henagaru men and women digging in their garden at Gusami [Busarasa]. Aguja [inivi lineage, "brother" to Tabie] and Agavisa [an actual brother] drew their bows and shot one woman and returned singing to Waingamuti, where they planted a croton for Kaperuti. On the following day, Moke warriors ranged to attack Ora. Busarasa men, hearing what was happening, sent a message to Ora to drive the Moke men toward Tabieninggagori [at Busarasa], where they would be ready. A pitched fight took place between Ora and Moke, the latter being driven toward the Busarasa men, who attacked them from behind. In confusion the Moke men dispersed, with many injured and disappeared into the bush and tall kunai grass. Tabie managed to shoot one Moke man, Kamagu, calling out, "You have killed us, now we kill you. We back you!" Busarasa returned singing to their own district, where they planted another croton for Kaperuti, and Ora too returned home singing.

The "treachery" on the part of Moke and Kasa in sending a friendly message while intending to take advantage of the returning refugees and ambush them is a traditional part of warfare itself. It is not condemned as wrong behavior. Tabie accused them of deception, but this was not so much moral indignation as a statement of fact, calling attention to their superior strategy, their having, so to speak, put one over Busarasa.

Refugees are often ready to accept such an invitation to return. They may feel insecure at times on their own ground, but this feeling is intensified when away from it, especially if they have been dispersed. In this case, however, most of Busarasa was at Waingamuti and not scattered; and it was mainly on this account that it could combine with Ora to defeat Moke.

Occasionally there are cases of "mass killing" involving perhaps a dozen persons, rarely more. When this takes place the district affected is likely to split up and scatter.

Most of the Inivi men went to Tatagufa, leaving their womenfolk, children, and old people behind. During their absence Ke͏ͨjagana and Henagaru warriors sacked Inivi, killed a number of women and children [unspecified, but apparently something over two dozen], burned most of the houses, and after ravaging the gardens returned home. When the Inivi men heard the news they rushed back, collected their dead, and went to nearby Aisenaviga. Others, who had been hiding in the bush, joined them there. They erected stockades and built temporary houses. When the collective mortuary ceremony was over, they got together their surviving pigs and killed them, and took the meat and gave it to Ke͏ͨjagana and Henagaru. This was designed as a gift to insure that no further attack would be made upon them. The presents were accepted, but soon afterward messages reached the Inivi people at Aisenaviga that the others were making arrows. In fear, they scattered over the Jate territory, seeking refuge in several different districts.

This case shows that bribery was not really a satisfactory way of handling the situation. The Inivi men were thoroughly disturbed by the killing of so many of their women and children and the loss of their property. Fear more than anything else led them to offer propitiatory gifts to the enemy in an attempt to achieve temporary security. In doing this they exposed their weakness and their readiness to scatter at the least threat instead of fighting it out. It is interesting to note that some of them apparently went for refuge to Ke͏ͨjagana itself. It may be assumed that members of a segment which did retreat to an enemy were going to their *nenafu*, *aku*, and so on, confident of some active help from them in the face of other opposition. Also, perhaps, they hoped that once their district had scattered the others would lose interest and turn to fresh engagements.

The weakness here lay in the scattering of power and authority, each village or hamlet, even each lineage, having its leader who remained such until another "strong" man took his place. There was a more or less constant jockeying for position; and in such a process the system was flexible enough to allow of contrary views and clashes even within the village as well as within the district. The notion of a central authority is in one sense quite contrary to this way of thinking. Although component villages of a district rely to some extent on one another, they rely even more heavily on themselves and on their "strong" men. But these "strong" men are accustomed to asserting themselves, if necessary at the expense of others; and they are not interested in prolonged, concerted effort, as in the matter of defense. For this reason, too, a combined attack, with several reverses following quickly one after another, weakens morale to such an extent that a district readily breaks and scatters. Moreover, there is no ideal of wholehearted and absolute aggression in all conflict situations and in the face of all odds. If training points to the desirability of strength and aggressiveness, it also prepares people to yield to these qualities in others and to accept the domination of the strong, at least temporarily, when they cannot resist it.

Bribery

Bribery has already been discussed in relation to sorcery, but because it appears most frequently in interdistrict fighting a few words must be said here.

In our first example, bribery is used to bring about the death of a specified person:

Ifusa, Inivi, and Kimi^{c}agumu combined in a temporary alliance, each district contributing a party of warriors to fight Kemiju. A pitched battle ensued and part of Kemiju fled to Ofafina. Among the refugees were a man named Veganomu, his Inivi wife, Agenapisu, and his two children, Japega^{c}o and Foka^{c}ja. On the following day Veganomu started to return to Kemiju, leaving his wife and children behind, but was waylaid by Ifusa men who killed him and hid his body. It was found by Ofafina men who carried it back to the village where the corpse was cooked and eaten. Agenapisu returned to Kemiju with her children, but since she was an Inivi woman and feelings were running high against that district she went on to Inivi. There she remained with her parents. An Inivi man, Haisage^{c}a, who called her nenafu, looked after one of her children, Japega^{c}o, while Agenapisu retained the other. Eventually she married another nenafu, an Inivi man named Avagujamu.

Some time afterward several Kimi^{c}agumu men approached Haisage^{c}a and offered him a bribe: "You are looking after a Kemiju child. Leave him in the house and go hunting, and while you are away we will kill him." Haisage^{c}a, feeling bitter about Agenapisu's marriage to her other nenafu, and his hostility toward Kemiju being kindled in the face of an offer of shells, accepted and left the child unprotected. A party of Kimi^{c}agumu men entered the Inivi village of Uwipinaga while most of its people were away in the gardens, found the child, killed him, and continued to shoot arrows into his body. Hamina of Inivi, a classificatory father of the dead child, picked up his bow and arrows and began shooting at the Kimi^{c}agumu men. He was joined by his lineage son, Okizo, son of Haisage^{c}a; but they were no match for the others. Okizo received a leg wound, and the Kimi^{c}agumu men made their escape singing. In the disturbance which immediately followed, a half-hearted attempt was made to go after them, while Agenapisu hid her other child in the bush; but nothing was done in the matter because the Inivi men considered that it was not their business and Okizo's wounding was his own fault. A feast was held, Hamina killing a pig. The body of the child was cut up, cooked, and the meat distributed, the bones finally being buried in an Inivi garden at Asenaviga.

In another instance, bribes were offered to induce one district to engage in fighting with a second, or to kill a member of it, in an attempt to avoid an appearance of direct responsibility. This was not successful. The second district learned who had taken the initiative and retaliated, not against the district which had carried out the killing, but against the district which had given the bribe.

Kogu gave shells to Ofafina men, urging them to shoot some Anonana men; this arrangement was accepted by Ofafina. Anonana, hearing of it, prepared gifts to bribe Ofafina to shoot some Kogu men and sent an emissary, Iᶜaᶜgu, down to Ofafina with ropes of shells. He was greeted by an arrow in the chest. The Ofafina men heaped the shells on his chest and called out to Anonana that they had killed a man of that district. Enaᶜo of Kogu came with a couple of men and took the body and the shells to Anonana. A mortuary feast was held and the body buried. A little later a party of Anonana men went to Irafu men and offered them shells, with a request that they kill someone belonging to Ofafina. Irafu made a raid on Ofafina, killing a man, then brought a red croton to Anonana, where it was planted over the grave of Iᶜaᶜgu. A feast was held and pig meat given to Irafu. Ofafina held a mortuary feast for their dead man and afterward sent a war party to Anonana, raiding a village and killing several women. They returned singing to plant a croton over the grave of their dead man. This provoked an attack on Kogu by Anonana, and a series of raids involving these four districts continued for some months.

Bribery then tends to aggravate general hostility, drawing into its network more districts and leaving in its wake a number of deaths to be compensated. Not all of these are avenged, and there comes a time when either a peace ceremony is requested or one district has to flee. And then matters are left in abeyance.

Occasionally a member of a group receiving a bribe warns the third party of the impending attack.

Kogu held a bean feast, to which it invited Ifusa. Returning to their villages the Ifusa people were ambushed by a party of Kemiju men, who shot Ariruᶜna. Ifusa then approached Kogu and Moiife, offering shells if they would combine to fight Kemiju. They accepted and made ready to attack. In the meantime, Kama [from Kogu] went secretly to warn Kemiju, telling what had happened and suggesting that they keep watch. Moiife and Kogu, supported by some Anonana and Asafina men, and including Kama, set out for Kemiju, only to find its villages on the alert. There was an exchange of arrows until Kiwoinipa, of Kemiju, shot dead Ekuna of Asafina. The small party of Asafina men retired carrying his body and fighting came to a standstill. Kemiju then approached the Kogu men, offering them a pig to go down to Amufi and kill some people there. Kogu accepted it and returned home to hold a feast: Moiife and Anonana went home with nothing. Next day, a party of Kogu men set out for Amufi and waited in ambush at Timefinaga. Presently a large number of Amufi men on their way to fight Kemiju came in sight. As they passed the bush in which the Kogu men were hidden a number were picked off quite easily and the others scattered in confusion. The Kogu party returned by way of Kemiju, receiving more gifts. Soon afterward Amufi gave bribes to Ifusa, Kimiᶜagumu, Jafanagumu, Numparu, Anonana, Moiife, and Asafina. They made a combined raid with Amufi on Kemiju; a number of men on each side were injured, houses burned, and stockades broken down, and a Kemiju man, Nanimupana, killed. The various groups then retired to their separate districts, Amufi planting a croton.

Again this represents only part of a series of fights involving a number of districts brought into the fray for no other reason than that they are paid, or bribed, to do so. In such circumstances, those undertaking to avenge a death are not personally and emotionally involved. They may be compared to mercenary soldiers, paid to perform the task of another, and interested not so much in the deed as in the reward. Yet in most cases there is some personal involvement (for instance, consider the inter-actory zones involving these groups); and in accepting a bribe they are often taking the opportunity to benefit not only others but themselves. In many cases bribes are offered when it is understood that a grudge is held and needs only stimulus to find expression in action. Nevertheless, we have seen that the giver has no certainty that the agreement will be honored. Kogu did not kill any Kemiju men, and Kama (a prominent war leader) betrayed the plans to them. This was not, as it appears to be, treachery on the part of Kama, exposing his own district. It was a plan carefully worked out by the Kogu men, who pretended to Ifusa that they would fulfil their promise but engaged as allies two other districts, on one of which (Asafina) they wanted to take revenge; Moiife was brought in in order to allay suspicion. When the Asafina man had been killed by Kemiju men, and Kogu received a bribe from them instead of continuing to fight, the duplicity of the Kogu men was revealed to their allies. Their action was not condemned but viewed as part of the fortunes of war. Kogu was fortunate in extracting two bribes and achieving revenge on Asafina; Ifusa, Asafina, and Amufi, the main sufferers at Kogu's hands, obtained satisfaction at the expense of Kemiju.

Kemiju, Inivi, and Kimiᶜagumu combined to fight Amufi, and several raids took place without advantage to either party. Kemiju then approached Kogu and Anonana, offering a quantity of shells if they would fight Amufi. Agreeing to this, they joined Kemiju and Inivi and waited in ambush for the Amufi men, but the latter surprised and surrounded them and a general fight ensued. A number were injured on both sides. One Kemiju man, Eamena, severely wounded, was dragged from the field by a classificatory father, Nomaja from Anonana; but the Amufi men continued shooting, and Nomaja was in turn dragged away by his *nenafu*,

Ena^co of Kogu. The Amufi men then surrounded Eamena's body and shot arrow after arrow into it. Ena^co, who was *noka* to Eamena, hid behind some bushes and was able to shoot dead an Amufi man, Afu^cmupana. In a rage, the Amufi men plucked banana shoots, sugar cane, edible leaves, pitpit cane, yam runners, and so on and, removing the arrows from Eamena's body, planted these in their place in the many wounds, treating the body as a garden.[21] They then returned singing to Amufi. The others went back singing to their villages, as they too had achieved a kill. During the night, a party of Kemiju men recovered the body and taking it to a stream at Fajogopagir [close to Inivi] removed the leaves and plants, washing off the dirt and blood. They then carried it to Kemiju where a mortuary feast was held; a pig was given to Ena^co, as he had "backed" the killing of Eamena, and the pig was later divided among various Kogu and Anonana men. A croton was planted over Eamena's grave. Kogu and Anonana again joined with Kemiju and fought Amufi, and received more gifts.

Our final example (the occurrence is relatively rare) concerns the recovery of a bribe:

Kasaru and Busarasa warriors surrounded the stockade at one of the Moke villages and after bitter fighting managed to break through, causing general confusion and dispersal. Most of the Moke people went to Waregasiga, in Ifusa territory, where they built a settlement. By clearing some bush on Kemiju ground to make a garden, they incurred the anger of Kemiju, and arrow shots were exchanged. On another occasion two of the Moke men, Karama and Fi^cna [ke^cafu lineage, both *nefaru*], were occupied in a garden named Fajagogamofinaga, also located on Kemiju ground, when they were surrounded and shot by Kemiju men. Other Moke men rushed to their defense, and fighting took place, but Kemiju retired singing. The Moke men carried the bodies to Waregasiga, where a mortuary feast was held and the two men buried. The Moke people were extremely angry and approached two Ifusa warriors, Sinaju and Ago^cna, both *nefaru*, offering them a bribe of shells and bush beads, saying, "We are going back to our own ground. Later, you can kill a Kemiju man and bring the croton to us." The two men accepted this in the name of their district.

Next day the Moke people made preparations to leave, but a small group of Kemiju men under Nikinosavi came and hid near Waregasiga. They were seen by a small boy, Takaba; he quickly warned his classificatory father, Pejamu, who collected a number of warriors. These men quietly left the settlement unseen by their enemy and, circling, came up behind them. As the Kemiju men emerged from their hiding place and approached the stockade for the attack, Pejamu and his men surprised them and shot Nikinosavi. The others turned to flee, dragging their companion, but the Moke men continued to shoot, and they were forced to leave him behind. The Moke men then went to the gardens singing and planted a croton over the grave of Karama and Fi^cna. That evening they made an oven and early next day returned to Karawanti, in Moke, where they began to reconstruct

---

21 Rough treatment of a corpse is not unusual; the men are venting their rage because of the death of Afu^cmupana. This is not irresponsible behavior, but symbolic. The corpse is treated as if it were buried in a garden, as it or its bones usually are, and these various foods grow from it.

their houses and stockades. Obebu, a war leader, who had been responsible for offering the bribe to Ifusa, now desired to recover it. He sent an old Moke man, Antari, his classificatory father of a parallel lineage, to Ifusa, telling him, "Go and collect those shells from the two Ifusa men. They have killed no Kemiju men and have brought no croton to us." Antari went to them and demanded the return of the shells. At first they refused, explaining that they had worked sorcery on Nikinosavi and had thus made him vulnerable to Moke's arrow shots; for this reason they were entitled to receive the shells. But Antari was insistent, and at last they returned the shells with bad grace. On his return to Moke, Antari passed some Emasa villages, where he was accosted by a party of armed men who threatened to shoot him. In fear, he offered some of the shells he was carrying. These they accepted and in return gave him various foods and accompanied him to Kabumanti at Busarasa. Here he was met by another group of armed men who threatened to shoot him. He again offered some of his shells, which they accepted, giving him in return sugar cane and taro; he then went on to Moke with only a few shells remaining.

Next morning Obebu asked him where the shells were so that they could be redistributed among their original owners. But Antari replied, "Have you not heard my name, my reputation! I am a humbug [trickster] man. Emasa and Busarasa wanted to kill me, so I gave them away. So leave it, we will not talk about it again." Obebu answered, "You have made another fashion now," and went away in anger. He saw a pig belonging to Antari and, thinking of his lost shells, picked up a stick and killed it, calling out, "Your name is Antari; you remain! I am Obebu, a trickster man. Thus I remain!" Antari asked him why he had killed his pig, and Abebu replied, "Why did you lose our shells?" Antari began to wail over his dead pig, while Obebu called out to the others, "Antari has lost our shells, but I have killed his pig in compensation. We will now hold an oven and eat." So a feast was held.

Immediately following this incident Kasaru killed Tabasi, a Moke man, by *sangguma* sorcery. In return Moke men shot a Kasaru man named Manijema. They also raided Kemiju and killed a man to back the second death at Waregasiga.

The bribe would not have been returned unless Ifusa had been afraid of Moke. What is unusual is that Antari went alone through hostile districts to obtain it. It is not surprising that he was threatened by two districts and lost most of the shells. Obebu was well aware of these circumstances but expected Antari to defend the shells even with his life (although he himself probably would not have done so). An old man, in any case, is thought to be of relatively little importance. Antari was aware of Obebu's greed for the shells and admitted, when he referred to himself as a trickster, that he was in the wrong in having lost them. In admitting his fault, so to speak, he desired to leave it at that; no more need be said about it. But Obebu was angry and wanted compensation for the loss. He did not blame those who had taken the shells. Instead, he threw the blame on Antari and punished him in what he considered to be a satisfactory way.

Defense of Property

Immovable property such as houses, stockades, and entire gardens may be destroyed in the course of interdistrict fighting, and in such cases a number of people are likely to be involved. In contrast, pigs and garden produce are often stolen. A pig is a valuable commodity. It is not simply an item of food but a vital part of ritual and ceremonial life, especially necessary at mortuary feasts. The loss of a pig may be treated almost as seriously as the death of a near relative.

A few gardens are close to the village but most are some little distance away. The fences normally surrounding them are largely for protection against pigs and can be scaled without difficulty, so it is fairly easy to steal produce. It is not possible for garden owners to watch constantly. On most days one is likely to find groups of women or men in their gardens, but some gardens remain unvisited for several days, especially when seasonal cultivation is at an end. Many lie immediately beside patches of bush or near gardens belonging to neighboring districts; there is no great difficulty in taking produce from them without being observed. Two factors militate against interdistrict thefts of this sort—fear of discovery, with consequent fighting, and the low value (generally) placed on garden produce, in comparison with other commodities. There is no supernatural sanction against stealing. Although taboos may be placed on various food-producing plants or trees, these are usually in the nature of personal markings, indicating ownership; but certain crotons threatening sores or illness may be planted to discourage thieves.

A man does not shoot or steal a pig or take food from a garden because he is hungry or particularly wants it, although he may achieve some prestige from such a manifestation of "strength." The pig or garden produce is individually owned, but the act of aggression is directed ordinarily against the district unit rather than against an individual member of it. As in the matter of sorcery, retaliation occasionally may be left to the person who has suffered the loss. We cannot speak of punishment for theft in the same way as punishment for sorcery. The response which is provoked is one of defense of property, but it is normally a defensive action by the unit as a whole against the unit which is held responsible:

Three Kasa men, Umavia, Arao, and Pirinote [Umavia is *noka* to Arao and *nanogai* to Pirinote; Arao is *nanogai* to Pirinote], came to Moke in search of a *sangguma* victim. Unable to find one, they went instead to Esoiba's garden, cut three bunches of bananas, and returned to Kasa. Later, Esoiba came to his garden and found the bananas gone. He saw the tracks leading to Kasa and ran back to his village and told others. With three companions, Anggosu, a younger brother,

Oentuma, a younger brother's son, and Egasi, an elder brother's son, he set out for Kasa. They followed the tracks past Kabumanti and Etaviti [both in Busarasa] to Agari [a Kasa village]. From the adjacent bush they saw the three Kasa men preparing an oven for cooking the bananas. Esoiba said, "I would like to shoot them all. What shall I do? Shall I shoot?" Just then he heard a sound in the bush. Stealthily moving in the direction of the noise, they saw Igiwajubi of Kasa [nenafu to Umavia and Arao, nanogai to Pirinote] and his son Javita cutting wood. Here was the opportunity Esoiba wanted; he whispered to his companions that he would not shoot but would only frighten them. The Moke men surrounded Igiwajubi and Javita with drawn bows. "You have stolen our food," said Esoiba. "You always work sangguma against us. All this must stop!" The two Kasa men trembled with fear. Esoiba let fly an arrow just above Igiwajubi's head, and another into the tree beside him. Igiwajubi called out to the others at Agari, "Moke are shooting me!" Quickly Esoiba and his companions disappeared into the bush and ran back to Moke.

Almost straightaway, Iviropa and Govari of Kasa [Govari was a "younger brother" to Iviropa, Umavia a "father," Arao a nenafu, Pirinote a nanogai] got together a number of warriors. Passing through Kagiapingka [Kasa] and Kawapati [Busarasa] they came to Soenadapingka, a Moke garden, where they found a Moke woman named Aruaninta [wife of Takia, of Moke, who first called her "sister"; Esoiba called her "mother," and Takia "elder lineage brother." She called Esoiba's three companions younger brothers]. They shot at her, and she dodged some of the arrows but was wounded. They returned to Kasa singing. Esoiba, finding Aruaninta, carried her back to the village, where he and others removed the arrows. He was angry and said, "I did not kill any Kasa men, I only frightened them. Now they come and shoot you!" After about five days Aruaninta recovered.

In the meantime, Kasa men had collected at Kabiagiri for a ceremony. They sent a messenger to Moke asking whether the woman they had shot had died and if they had eaten or buried her. Moke sent no reply. Instead, a large number of warriors went by way of Soenadapingka to the Kasa villages. They surrounded the first, Kirunagasi, and stormed the stockade, forcing the inmates to escape to the next village, Kagiapingka, which they also surrounded and broke into, destroying houses and driving the inmates to Kabiagari [that is, Agari]. They stormed this village, too, and when it fell went on to Parianati. Here the defense was stronger and the fighting more bitter; a number of Kasa people were wounded. At last the defenses were broken down and a pitched fight ensued. One young Kasa man, Simi ["younger brother" to Umavia, Arao, Pirinote, and Govari; "son" to Iviropa], surrounded by Moke men ready to shoot him, was protected by Irasi [neimo to Esoiba, aku to Anggosu, toto to Oentuma and Egasi, brother to Aruaninta], a Moke man, who called out to the others, "This is my 'son.' You are not to shoot him. Shoot someone else." [He was married to Simi's father's sister, Geja.] But they pulled Simi away from Irasi and killed him. Most of the Kasa people were now dispersed, and a number of separate fights were taking place along the main road, in the bush, and in the gardens. In one of these a Miarasa man named Wainu was shot at, by mistake, by Esoiba. In another, Oentuma shot Kogia [nefaru to Umavia, nanogai to Arao and Govari, mother's brother to Pirinote, sister's son to Iviropa and "son" to Irasi], a Kasa man, in the knee, but he escaped into the bush, only to be wounded in the arm by Kuguni of Moke [*nefaru* to Esoiba, *nenafu* to Anggosu, "father" to Oentuma, Egasi, and Irasi, "brother" to Aruaninta]. Abandoning his weapons, he managed to get away. By this time most of the Kasa people had fled to surrounding districts or were hiding in the bush.

One man, E^cnagu [who called Iviropa "father," Umavia and Irasi "brother"; Arao *neimo*, Pirinote and Govari *noka*, and Kogia *nanogai*], an outstanding Kasa warrior, had left his bow and arrows near a tree in his flight. He returned to look for them and climbed a tree to see what was happening and whether the Moke men were still there. They had followed his movements but were afraid to tackle him. Esoiba found him in the tree and, standing at its base with bow taut, called out: "I, Esoiba, have come. You, E^cnagu! We will fight each other. You shoot at me, I'll shoot at you. We will see who dies." He then took aim. E^cnagu, who was unarmed, called out, "Oh, my brother, Esoiba! Before, we shot birds together; I looked after you. Now you are a big man. Do you mean to shoot me? Why do you want to do this? Think first before you shoot your arrow." [22] Esoiba loosened his arrow and began to cry, "Oh, brother, you speak the truth. I thought you were different; that is why I covered you with my arrow. Call out for your lineage kin, let them come and shoot the Moke men. Let them come and take you safely away." But E^cnagu replied, "Oh, brother, I am not afraid for my body. I am a no-good man. I am nothing. They can shoot me. Let them come and kill me." Esoiba then returned to his companions, who asked whether he had killed E^cnagu. When he replied that he had not, they were angry. "Why did you leave him?" they asked. Esoiba answered that he had fully intended to kill him but remembered that he was his brother; E^cnagu had spoken to him, and he had cried in shame and had therefore left him. "You go down and shoot him, if you want to."

Oentuma and Jagau [who called Esoiba *noka*, Anggosu and Egasi "brother," and Irasi *aku*] then went to the tree in which E^cnagu was sitting. They pulled their bows taut ready to shoot. E^cnagu called out, "You two men stay on the ground watching this tree. But I am a man. Only birds stay in trees; men stay at the base of the trees. We shoot birds in the trees, and they fall down and we eat them. It is not good to shoot a man as he sits in a tree. I will climb down and then you two can shoot me. I am not afraid of you." As he climbed down they shot him; he fell to the ground and they shot more arrows into his body. They called out to the other Moke men, who came and shot more arrows into the body. Then they returned to Moke singing.

The Kasa people returned to their villages and collected the dead bodies; Simi they ate, E^cnagu they buried. After about six days a party of Kasa men assembled and came through the bush near Pasapiti and Endavinti [Busarasa] to Kakasimuti in Moke territory. Here they surprised two Moke men, Aku [who

[22] E^cnagu was referring to a special relationship between himself and Esoiba, whom he called "elder brother." During their parents' time Kasa and Moke were on peaceful terms; E^cnagu's father and Esoiba's father had their noses bled at the same initiation rites and consequently called each other *nefaru*. They behaved to each other as *nefaru* usually do, calling to each other at times of feasting and so on. The sons of *nefaru* are brothers, or *nanogai*.

called Esoiba "father," Jagau nenafu, and Oentuma "brother"] and Kakaja [who called Esoiba aku, Aku nefaru, and Jagau and Oentuma, nenafu], carrying a pig to Eguniti in Moke. Among the Kasa men were Iviropa, Kogi, and Govari, who shot Aku many times; Kakaja escaped. They returned to Kasa singing and at Eberurati planted a croton over the grave of Simi.[23]

Moke people collected Aku's body. In the garden of Amugenagovinti they cooked and ate him and buried his bones. They then decided to plant a croton over his grave, as they had killed Simi before. Five days afterward a party of Moke men went down to Kasa and waited in ambush at Kabiagari. Here they managed to shoot Iviropa dead and, returning to Moke singing, planted another croton over Aku's grave. Kasa collected Iviropa's body, held a mortuary feast, and buried him at Paiagudi, planting a croton over his grave to indicate that compensation was still outstanding. Later several Kasa sangguma men came to Moke and found Tavanu, on whom they performed sorcery. When news of his death reached them they changed the red croton for a green one. After this a peace ceremony was arranged between them. [Tavanu called Esoiba "son," Jagau and Kakaja nenafu, Aku nefaru, and Oentuma "brother."] Tavanu's body was cut open preparatory to cooking but was found to be full of worms; he was therefore buried.

I have treated this case in some detail because it illustrates so well a series of repercussions following a simple case of stealing and because it brings out some interesting facets of interdistrict warfare—for instance, how far the course of fighting is influenced by the personal commitments of those taking part. Of course, only a few of the actual participants are mentioned here, but they are the main ones from the narrators' point of view. Irasi tries to save his wife's brother's son, and there is Esoiba's mistake in shooting at a Miarasa man. Especially, there is Esoiba's approach to E^cnagu. In conversation with him, Esoiba is reduced to tears and cries in shame; he is willing to sacrifice his own companions, offering to allow E^cnagu to escape. We cannot assess the sincerity of this offer (Esoiba himself assured me of his good faith, but this was some time afterward). E^cnagu apparently abased himself before his nanogai, offering to let the others shoot him, while Esoiba returned to his own companions telling them to shoot his nanogai if they wanted to. Examples of this sort give

[23] No croton was planted over E^cnagu's grave, since he was closely bound to Esoiba by the nanogai bond; they were of "one skin," although belonging to different districts. To plant a croton over his grave, indicating that compensation had been sought by killing a Moke man, would be against common practice. The expression used here, in pidgin English translation, is "no-good skin fasten, or join." Esoiba is here treated as E^cnagu's killer; i.e., as if it were an intralineage killing, when conventionally no compensation is sought and no croton planted over the grave. This is the convention should a man be killed by his nanogai. It must be added, however, that in practice revenge is normally sought. On the other hand, nanogai rarely kill each other. In the above case Esoiba, while he refused to take this action, was willing to let others do it for him.

us a vivid glimpse of personal attitudes and provide useful material concerning, for instance, conflicting ties of loyalty.

Finally, a case involving the theft of a pig:

Mage men shot a pig owned by an Ora man, Bunanu, took it home, and ate it. Bunanu with some companions followed the tracks leading to Mage. On the way, however, they were ambushed by a party of Mage warriors, one of whom, Apisagabara, shot Agosawanaga of Ora, his *nenafu* [Apisagabara called Bunanu classificatory father; Agosawanaga was lineage father to Bunanu]. The Ora men retired, but the Mage men followed them and were able to kill another Ora man, Eantenti [*nenafu* to Agosawanaga, *aku* to Bunanu, "brother" to Apisagabara]; they returned home singing. Ora responded by a raid on Mage without much result, and several days afterward, hearing that Mage was planning another attack, waited in ambush near the track leading into Wentagori. Here they were able to kill Jagogabara ["brother" to Apisagabara; classificatory brother to Eantenti and Agosawanaga; classificatory son to Bunanu]. Mage retired and held a mortuary feast, eating the dead man. On the next day they lay in wait near the road at Wentagori until a young Mage woman, Anta‑o, passed by on her way to the gardens. [She was "sister" to Jagogabara, classificatory sister to Agosawanaga, *ato* to Eantenti and Bunanu. Her husband was Tuiema of Ora, *noka* to Bunanu, Apisagabara, and Jagogabara, "brother" to Agosawanaga and Eantenti.] They shot at her, but the arrow killed her baby, and grazed her shoulder. They then retired as Ora men started shooting from their stockade. The child was eaten by the women. A little later Amegabara [*noka* to Bunanu, *nenafu* to Eantenti, "brother" to Agosawanaga and Tuiema, *ato* to Anta‑o] was digging a rat hole near the stockade door at Ke‑akasati. At first he was on his guard but became so absorbed in what he was doing that he did not notice the approach of some Mage warriors, who shot him dead. After some fighting the Mage men retired. Amegabara was then carried to the local men's house and eaten the following morning. There was an argument over mortuary payments. Asiwa [*neimo* to Bunanu and Eantenti, *noka* to Agosawanaga, "brother" to Tuiema] called the dead man "half brother," although Amegabara was the son of Asiwa's elder brother; he was therefore obliged to give goods to the deceased's elder brother, Nasumpi. [Although actually a brother's son to Asiwa, Nasumpi called him younger brother; he was also "brother" to Agosawanaga and Eantenti, *nenafu* to Bunanu, *nefaru* to Tuiema.] Asiwa held back in making his gifts and for this was sharply criticized by his lineage kin. With bad grace, therefore, he killed a pig and gave this with a new steel ax to Nasumpi. But as soon as he had given it, he regretted his action, became "hot belly," and took back the ax. Little else was done in the matter. Kasaru and Oka men were invited to the feast. As they were eating, Asiwa spoke to Nasumpi, endeavoring to justify his action: "Mage men do not live in rocky caves, nor in holes in the ground. I can shoot them. I can compensate for this death. They remain in their villages and are easy to kill. I shall do so instead of giving you this ax."

With a party of Ora men, Asiwa set out at night for Mage. When they neared the stockade, Asiwa went forward without the others and shot Kabuji [elder brother to Apisagabara, *noka* to Jagogabara, classificatory brother to Asiwa]. They returned to Ora singing and planted a croton over Amegabara's grave. Negotiations were then begun for a peace ceremony. Ora and Mage met, remaining some distance apart; and Ora said, "This fight must now stop. Our lands adjoin, they are almost one ground." Mage agreed and returned home, inviting Ora to come for the peace feast. In good faith, Ora men went to Mage, but were attacked there. In the fighting, Mage shot Ninikabara [nenafu to Bunanu, "brother" to Agosawanaga and Eantenti, nefaru to Tuiema and Amegabara, noka to Asiwa, "elder brother" to Nasumpi]. The Ora men carried the body back and cooked and ate it. Next day they returned to Mage but were again ambushed, and Iruea [nenafu to Bunanu and Eantenti, "brother" to Agosawanaga, Tuiema, and Amegabara, noka to Asiwa, "father" to Nasumpi, nefaru to Ninikabara] was killed; his body, too, was taken back to Ora and eaten.

On the following day Ora men surrounded the stockade of the Mage village of Umerajati. At last a youth, Akikikabara [son of Apisagabara, noka to Jagogabara], emerged, and they shot him. They returned home singing, while Mage held a mortuary feast and ate the body. In reprisal Mage came down to the gardens at Wentagori, where a woman was digging sweet potatoes. [She was Mempe, of Mage, "sister" to Apisagabara and Kabuji, "daughter" to Jagogabara, neimo to Bunanu, Eantenti, and Iruea; she called Agosawanaga and Asiwa "son" and Ninikabara classificatory brother. Her husband was Mantebuja.] They shot her and returned singing. The Ora people took her body into the village, where the women ate it. A small party of Ora men went to Mage and waited in ambush, eventually killing Jagu ["father" to Apisagabara, noka to Jagogabara, "brother" to Kabuji and Akikikabara; he called Mempe "mother"]. They came back singing and planted a croton over Mempe's grave. Almost immediately Mage warriors came to Ora, where they sacked Wentagori and wounded Asiwa's son. But Ora fought back and wounded Wario [who called Apisagabara, Kabuji, and Jagu "brother," Jagogabara noka, Akikikabara "son," and Mempe "mother"].

Up to this point, only the anumpa lineages of Ora had been involved in the fighting, but they now approached the kasaru lineages of Ora, asking them to join in the fight against Mage and giving them a pig. The kasaru Ora agreed, and after feasting a party of warriors from both clans went to Mage and surprised people in the gardens. General fighting took place; the Ora men killed one Mage woman and returned home singing. Mage held a mortuary feast and next day raided Ora, killing an Ora woman, Arawanta ["daughter" to Agosawanaga, Eantenti, Tuiema, Asiwa, Nasumpi, Ninikabara, and Iruea, "mother" to Bunanu], and a young girl, Kanuᶜmi ["sister" to Arawanta, but calling her mother]. After Mage left, singing, the Ora people carried their dead back to the village and ate them. On the following day, Mage again raided Ora and killed an unmarried girl, who was later eaten. Ora then raided Mage but lost Fegenu, son of Berebi [who called Bunanu noka, Agosawanaga, Eantenti, Tuiema, Asiwa, Ninikabara, and Nasumpi "brother," Iruea, Arawanta and Kanuᶜmi "son" and "daughter," Antaᶜo and Mempe ato], and Manabuta, a kasaru Ora man [who called Bunanu, Tuiema, Nasumpi, and Berebi "father," Agosawanaga, Asiwa, and Iruea "brother," Eantenti and Ninikabara nenafu, Antaᶜo and Mempe "mother," and Arawanta and Kanuᶜmi "sister"]. They injured a number of the enemy, killing some whose names are not known. They returned carrying the two dead men, who were eaten during the mortuary ceremonies. Then they went back to Mage and after some fighting shot Janarusa. [All the other Mage people mentioned here were of the *mage* lineages; Janarusa, however, was of the Mage *owabi*, or *ofafina*, lineages; he called Apisagabara and Akikikabara "son," Jagogabara "brother"]. They returned singing to plant a croton. Next morning they went again to Mage but found the villages deserted; during the night the inhabitants had fled to Ofafina. Disappointed, the Ora men returned home. Some weeks afterward they sent messages to the Mage people at Ofafina asking them to return: "Your ground, your bush, does not lie elsewhere; it remains here. Return to your own ground." Soon afterward Mage came back and a peace festival was held.

Such a case shows what can result from the killing of a pig belonging to someone in another district. In this particular series of raids, there were about eighteen deaths. Examples of this kind are not unusual. They tell us something about the general state of affairs before external influences were felt to any great extent, that is, between 1947–50, if we are to include the whole area as far south as Moke-Busarasa-Ora. Examination of the available cases for the whole region under discussion reveals an essential similarity in general content and orientation. There is variation as regards detail: less fighting in one area, more in another; some quarrels extending over a relatively long period (say several months), others finished in a single raid or fight; some involving several districts, others only the two immediately concerned. Interpersonal factors, the "pull" of some relationships at the expense of others, sometimes tend to modify existing hostile conditions, sometimes tend to intensify them.

In the present example, most of the fighting was between the *anumpa* lineages of Ora and the whole district of Mage. In this case Ora did not operate as a political unit. One noteworthy point is that the *anumpa* "paid" the other district segment, *kasaru*, to engage in combined action against Mage. Perhaps the most interesting features are the shooting of Agosawanaga by his *nenafu* Apisagabara; the killing by Mage warriors of Mempe, a Mage woman married to an Ora man; and the attempted killing of Anta°o, also a Mage woman married to an Ora man. This is a further demonstration of the gap between customary expectations and actuality: not all *nenafu* are closely linked in bonds of friendship; not all females receive help and protection from members of their own district, or even of their own clan. Where close relatives are concerned, they can reasonably expect this, but others may not be so scrupulous.

In this study I have no more than indicated some of the structural implications of the southern Fore alignments. Yet it should be remembered that the linked lineages of one name (i.e., the clan), although among the Fore they occupy different villages, regard themselves as comprising a social unit with common interests and aims. It is often the war-making unit. There is a tendency to rely on it rather than on the village or hamlet, insuring a greater numerical strength. Although only the larger districts seem to have these subpolitical formations fairly well developed, they are, on the whole, stronger than their neighbors, the Jate, Kamano, and Usurufa. More often than not, any given series of incidents here may spread over a longer period of time than in other linguistic units. But this arrangement does not decrease the likelihood of warfare.

Conclusions

Fighting was, and remains, the "breath of life" to these people, one of their main preoccupations. It has been sustained primarily in two ways. First, there has been the more or less consistent concentration on strength, on male dominance, and on the desirability of employing physical violence in a wide range of situations—pre-eminently, inter-district warfare. Second, there is pervasive distrust of neighbors, and even of others living in the same village or district. One outcome of this is the view that the best opponents are those who are weaker than oneself (or those, temporarily weaker, caught unaware or unarmed). There is no last-ditch standard here. Respect for strength involves a readiness to give way to it as well as to practice it. Coupled with this is the emphasis on self-assertion, with individual leaders basing their authority largely on force and likely to be supplanted at any time by rivals—leaders usually unable, or unwilling, to co-operate in any sustained defense in a time of crisis.

Warfare offers a key to the kind of political organization we find in this region. It isolates the political unit, the district, making it a more or less independent unit in opposition or potential opposition to all others. This structural isolation, however, is never absolute. Any district at a given time is the center of a zone of interaction in which districts within a certain range, regardless of linguistic affiliation, are temporarily associated for various purposes, including warfare. In warfare, the weaknesses of the political organization are most obvious. But in warfare, too, we find attempts to strengthen that organization by seeking temporary allies. The way in which these alliances are formed has a number of structural implications. The fact that they rest on the uncertain basis of bribery, where no agreement is necessarily binding, is significant in itself and partly accounts for their transitory nature. On the positive side, bribery helps to maintain the existing structural formation and to widen its scope.

Interdistrict warfare, resting on the principle of retaliation, can be seen

A warrior with drawn bow and shield takes part in a ceremony at Pintagori.

Typical stance of a warrior, with drawn bow, protected by large fighting shield tipped with cassowary plumes.

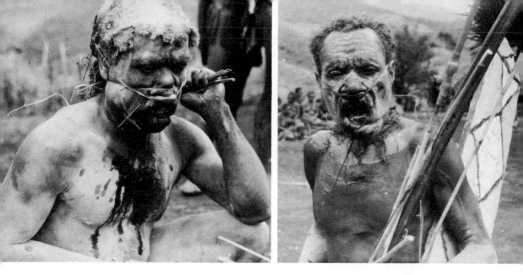

Actors in ceremonial farce in Kogu. Fiber has been used to flatten the nose and evert lips. Faces and chests are stained with blood to represent sufferers from yaws or leprosy.

Actor in ceremonial farce, his face distorted with fiber to simulate yaws or leprosy. Note variety of arrows.

in terms of "balancing." Any action designed to achieve this balance is likely to set in motion a series of similar actions, terminated only by a peace ceremony or by the forced withdrawal of one party. The solicitation of allies does not interfere with this basic patterning. This balancing consists of reverses and victories over a period of time, and at any one point in time will appear to be asymmetrical. However, this assumption demands further empirical analysis. From the few examples discussed here it would seem that a balancing is not always achieved, even over an entire sequence. One unit inflicting reverses on another may try to press home its advantage until its opponents withdraw, demoralized. On the other hand, peace negotiations may be sought only when both parties have suffered more or less equally or consider that they are fairly evenly matched. Ideally, then, in warfare a balancing of killings and "backings" is desired; but in reality this seems to be attained only over a period, regardless of divisions between fighting sequences, and in relation to total co-activity. This takes into consideration not only warfare but sorcery, for in any form of "balancing" (or "backing" and "counter-backing") sorcery is as important as more overt forms of aggressive action. A district dispersed by hostile action loses such political solidarity as it may have had. Its refugee segments are scattered over a relatively wide area and can no longer act in solidarity. Therefore, in the interactory sphere of any one group a unit may be "counted out," at any rate for the time being. The interactory sphere centering on it is also reformulated in relation to each new host district and its neighbors. And there is no evidence to suggest that the refugees remain in exile any longer than necessary—at least in the years before some of them were forced to remain in alien territory because of the suppression of warfare by the Administration.

Broadly speaking, then, the district (or, in some instances, a section of it acting independently) is the political and war-making unit, legitimizing the use of force in order to insure its own continuity. Social control is thus structurally manifested in the way warfare throws into relief the isolation of the district, at the same time underlining the dependence of each unit on other units, within a fluctuating zone of interaction. (Because of the absence of any central authority, even as an ideal, and the acknowledged political autonomy of the district, there is no advantage in speaking of interdistrict conflict as "civil war.") Warfare serves as a means of redressing a wrong by the mechanism known as "backing," operating almost solely on the interdistrict level (and, except for sorcery, was until recently the only means of proceeding against a member of another district). Such action normally is assumed to have the sanction of the political unit as a whole, even though all its male members may not participate. Warfare has the appearance of being regulative, since the retaliation on which it is based is designed to cause a return to a hypothetical status quo. The only way in which a harm, injury, or death can be wiped out is by achieving adequate compensation. In dealing with other districts, the use of force can bring satisfactory redress in much the same way as can judicial procedure. Although such is the primary aim of warfare in this region, it may rebound on the unit which initiated it in any given series, thus counteracting its regulative effects. Nevertheless, warfare as a regulative force is best seen as an "internal" means of maintaining social or political solidarity and of redressing wrongs outside the district.

In discussing cannibalism in this study, our primary concern is its association with violent behavior. We have seen that there are various cultural avenues through which aggression can be expressed legitimately. One of these is cannibalism, which is both a part of interdistrict warfare and a customary way of disposing of the dead.[1] (As Fortune put it, "Their bellies are their cemeteries.") We cannot pretend by any stretch of imagination that cannibalism is a form of social control, any more than eating or sexual activity may be. In concentrating on its more violent aspects, we can say, tentatively, that these indicate, rather, a *lack* of control. But even in the practice of cannibalism there are (as there must be) certain regulating influences. (These come into play, for instance, when there is disagreement in the treatment of a particular corpse.) It is this point which concerns us here.

Cannibalism and Violence

Today, in the northern areas of the eastern Highlands, the practice of cannibalism is carried out only surreptitiously, being forbidden by both the Administration and the Missions. In the south, at least during the time we lived in the region, it was a normal part of local behavior; but its more violent features are disappearing with the suppression of interdistrict

[1] See Landtman's description of burial cannibalism (1927, pp. 266–67), carried out only by men, among the Kiwai Papuans. They eat only their own dead, and not those of an enemy, because to do so would spoil the crops. Among the Kuni, however, enemies were eaten (Williamson, 1914, p. 180). The Bamu or Dibiri of the Fly River had no restrictions on the eating of the dead, according to Beaver (1920, p. 225). Among the Orokaiva, cannibalism did not occur within the tribe (Williams, 1930, pp. 160, 171). Seligmann (1910, p. 552) also speaks of restrictions. See also G. Róheim (1954, pp. 487–95). I shall not consider this subject in any detail—for instance, methods of preparing, cutting up, or cooking a corpse. Very occasionally, bodies are smoked and the heads of certain kin preserved in a special way.

I cannot agree with Honigmann (1954, pp. 379–82) that cannibalism is a manifestation of abnormality; while the material he presents (Eskimo, American Indian, and Marquesan) bears out this assumption, certain other forms of cannibalism are not treated. He mentions, however, that more investigation is needed.

warfare. It is not associated with head-hunting.[2] The bodies of both men and women are eaten; and enemies are eaten just as readily as kin or affines.[3] Such restrictions as there are (for instance, in respect of certain kin)[4] seem often to have been disregarded, especially by women. People do not normally eat victims of dysentery or of *guzigli*^c ("guria") sorcery; but otherwise the manner of death is of little consequence. On the other hand, not all the dead are eaten. From many examples it is clear that there are no fixed rules in operation, that in any given case the disposal of the corpse rests largely on personal preferences.

Dead human flesh, to these people, is food, or potential food.[5]

[2] See J. M. van der Kroef (1952, pp. 221–35); cannibalism and head-hunting do not necessarily go together.

[3] The person who has killed the victim may also eat, contrary to what is mentioned by Williams (1930, p. 174) for the Orokaiva, and by Seligmann (1910, p. 557) for the Wagawaga.

[4] It will be remembered that an *aku*, a mother's brother or sister's son, may be an actual wife's father. In that case he will not be eaten, since a man does not eat his parents-in-law, nor his male or female *nenafu*. Similarly a woman's parents will not eat her husband. A husband will not eat his deceased wife, although she will eat his body. Apart from this, men will eat the flesh of women just as often as that of men: there is no fear of absorbing the supposedly less aggressive qualities of the female.

A man will eat the flesh of his deceased grandparents, paternal and maternal, actual and classificatory, as well as those of his wife, in fact, all those whom he calls *negu* and *agu*: but not his sons' or daughters' children, nor his grandchildren through marriage. He will eat all those whom he calls "finger" in the third ascending, but not in the third descending, kinship grade. Women will rarely eat the flesh of a father, mother, brother, sister, father's sister, or *nenafu* (although such cases have been recorded), but restrictions relating to other classes of relatives do not seem to be strictly enforced.

Thus a man will eat the flesh of three classes of kin in his patrilineage, three on his father's maternal side, four on his maternal side, and three among his affines. The rest will normally be taboo to him, except for enemies to whom he bears no defined relationship. Within a man's own village are a number of females with whom he has either consanguineal (or quasi-consanguineal) or affinal ties, or sometimes both. He will not eat those whom he calls daughter, his own or brother's son's wife, mother or mother's sisters, son's son's wife, and so on; but this restriction does not apply to those married to second or third degree classificatory brothers or sons or sons' sons, and others genealogically related.

A man has a claim to part of the flesh of a deceased nephew or niece, an obligation which is reciprocal. A woman sends word to her own brother on the death of her child so that he may visit her husband's village, if it is not openly at enmity with his own. The brother-sister relationship implies this claim, which is extended in the classificatory sense.

[5] Beaver (1920, p. 249) says that the Purari Delta people viewed human meat as food, and highly appreciated it. Williams (1930, p. 170) says that the reason for cannibalism given by Orokaiva natives was the simple desire for good food. Seligmann (1910, pp. 548–64) speaks of cannibalism as the "solemn act of revenge which it was the duty of each community to take on behalf of its own members killed and eaten by other communities with whom it was at enmity." He is speaking generally. He admits that human flesh was sometimes eaten for pleasure. C. S. Belshaw (1954, p. 3) mentions that in Melanesia man himself was a resource: he was also the source of flesh.

It is said among the Fore that generations ago people never ate the dead. It so happened that an ancestor of the *moke* lineages of Moke, named Tawazi, was killed by *sangguma* sorcery. After his death the body was carried to Krawanti [in Moke], where it was cooked and portions of the meat distributed throughout the district. People tasting it expressed their approval. "This is sweet," they said. "What is the matter with us, are we mad? Here is good food and we have neglected to eat it. In future we shall always eat the dead, men, women, and children. Why should we throw away good meat? It is not right!" Since then people have always eaten the dead.

Among the Kamano, Usurufa, and Jate there are other stories to provide a precedent and to suggest, for instance, that the dead themselves approve of the practice. A point to be remembered here is that the diet of the region is apparently deficient in protein. Pigs are not really plentiful and, generally, are kept for ceremonial occasions. (Although there are special ways of cutting up a corpse, it is usually cooked in much the same way as a pig, and often eaten with one.) There is no evidence that people fight to obtain meat; but it is quite possible that this is one of the underlying motives in interdistrict warfare.

Although we cannot speak here of ritual cannibalism, the eating and disposal of a corpse are significant in terms of fertility.[6] Human flesh is not eaten to absorb the "power" or strength of the deceased,[7] nor do men consider that female flesh will have a weakening effect on them. Nor, generally speaking, does fear of the deceased's spirit provide an incentive —although a few people say that a malevolent ghost is likely to be more dangerous when its corpse is intact. Others say that the dead prefer to be eaten, and that this wish should be respected. In the ordinary course of events, when a man (or woman) dies in his own district, pigs are killed, a feast is held, and a mortuary distribution of goods takes place. The body is carried to one of the local gardens (ideally, one belonging to the dead person's lineage) and either buried or cut into portions there. If it is buried in the garden, this encourages the growth of crops by fertilizing the soil; the body is "given to the ground" in return for the food it will produce. (This is equivalent to giving up the body to Jugumishanta, who symbolizes the earth.) If it is cut up, the blood spilled is a libation both to the lineage ancestors and to Jugumishanta and has fertilizing properties as well. The actual eating of the body, as in the pig festivals, has the same

[6] Landtman (1927) notes that pieces of human flesh were placed in trees to increase crops and bones and tendons buried in gardens to promote growth. Cannibalism among the Kiwai was generally associated with garden fertility.

[7] As among, e.g., the Kuni (close to the Mafulu), where the flesh of a slain warrior gives strength to the eater (Williamson, 1914, p. 181). In the eastern Highlands there is no sense of contamination, such as noted by this writer.

significance. "Cut my body," a dying man or woman may say, "so that the crops may increase." "Eat my flesh so that the gardens may grow." Certain parts (penis, testes, vulva, hands, fingers, toes, hair, skull, or jaw) may be kept not only for sentimental reasons but also because they have a special efficacy. They may be hung around a child's neck to encourage his growth or rubbed on the back of a pig to make it fat. Pig fat may be kept in a skull, which enhances its power when used in anointing babies, children, and adults, or water may be drunk from a skull with the same purpose in mind. Human hair and human fat are believed to have curative properties. Ideally, the remaining bones are always placed in the deceased's lineage garden so that the crops will flourish. The same qualities are ascribed to the remains of enemy dead;[8] but in this case the body is not always cut up in a garden, and the bones should normally be bundled up and given to kin for burial.

People who die within their own village or district may be cut up soon afterward, or may be buried temporarily or exposed in some way so that the flesh decomposes.[9] There seems to be some preference for decomposed human meat, although other kinds of meat are generally eaten while fresh:

An old man named Kagusafinu of Ke^{c}jagana died. He was carried by his daughter's husband, Nusa^{c}e, to his lineage garden at Kepugufaga and buried there, with two ropes tied around his body and the ends left exposed above ground. After about two days Nusa^{c}e, with his wife and his mother and other women, returned to the grave where they exhumed the corpse, pulling it up by means of the ropes. In the meantime, heavy rain had seeped through the earth, and the moisture, so it is said, made the old man's body swell so that it resembled that of a young man. It was now ready to be eaten.

Often, apparently, a corpse is left buried for several days, then exhumed when decomposition is relatively well advanced:

Kiramaupa of Kemiju died of *krana* sorcery, allegedly administered by Kogu, and was buried at Vehomuga. On the afternoon of the sixth day following his death his corpse was exhumed. The maggots were scraped off and placed on banana leaves. The body was then cut up, the meat and bones being cooked in one oven, and the maggots, tied up in small leaf bundles, in another; these are regarded as a delicacy.

[8] Landtman (1927, pp. 151–52) mentions use of an enemy's penis or vulva as relics helpful in warfare among the Kiwai Papuans.

[9] Seligmann (1910, p. 550) says that, rarely, bodies were exhumed for eating soon after they had been buried. He quotes an example from Milne Bay (Sir Francis Winter, *Annual Report*, Papua, 1894–95), when the body was dug up a day after burial, and a case from Chalmers (1887) for South Cape, Bonarua group, and suggests (*ibid.*, p. 551) that it occurred over a wide area, particularly in the D'Entrecasteaux Group.

In other instances, special methods are employed to collect maggots:

Aniᶜo of Kogu died, allegedly killed by Kemiju with *naglisa* sorcery. After the mortuary feast his body was carried to his garden where it was placed under a tree and covered with small branches. Several days later members of his clan and their womenfolk returned to the spot bringing *gabiag* leaves [*omefahaida* leaves, usually eaten with pig meat]. Parting the top branches they found maggots in great abundance. They spread out the *gabiag* leaves and carefully shook the branches over them one by one so that the maggots fell on the leaves. Finally they rolled these up in bundles, with other edible leaves mixed with pig fat, and cooked them in bamboo containers. This was done several times until there were too many blowflies and the stench too great, when the remains were buried.

Decomposing flesh and maggots are relished, and fluids from the corpse are sometimes consumed:

Iasi, a Moiife man, fell by accident from a tree onto the protruding stump of a smaller tree and was impaled. Although seriously injured, he remained alive for several days. The wound began to fester. Pads of edible leaves were held to it, then cooked in bamboo containers and eaten.

In many cases, especially when the deceased was physically fit, the feces are not discarded. Thus in the case of Zejuᶜewa of Kemiju, who was shot by Jafanagumu, the feces were cut out with the belly and given to his wife, Doiiᶜgu, who cooked them in banana leaves mixed with *fezagupa* (edible fern leaves).

Some of the bones of the dead, but never all, may be crushed or pounded, sometimes chewed, and finally mixed with edible leaves, sprayed with salt, and cooked. Special parts of the body are occasionally given to specific persons, for instance, a man's penis to his wife, his head to his grandchild, and so on.[10] But there is no strict procedure in these matters.

When Opiᶜna of Moiife was shot by Kogu, his body was cut up and his penis given to a woman named Ketuᶜna, of no acknowledged relationship. She caused much amusement by holding this in her mouth and sliding it from side to side. Then she spat it out, and it was picked up by another woman who did the same with it, finally cutting it up into small pieces and eating them.

On another occasion a husband and wife, Hagina and Mugegli, of Keᶜjagana were killed, allegedly by *sangguma* sorcery performed by Keᶜafu. The bodies were carried to the garden of Itoka, at Keᶜjagana, and cut up beneath a clump of bamboos. The meat was cooked in two separate ovens and distributed among various men and women. Fenakizu, who called them "mother and father," cooked the woman's vulva separately and gave it to her son Nusaᶜe to eat. Nusaᶜe

10 Landtman (1927, p. 152) mentions the eating of a vulva, but with a specific purpose in view.

chewed away at the titbit, but the pubic hair caught in his teeth. He removed it, complaining that it was not properly cooked, but his mother pressed him to finish it, saying that it was only underarm hair. Jaju^{c}mi, Fenakisu's classficatory sister, had a pig's head which she gave Nusa^{c}e so that he could eat it with the vulva.

There is relatively little violence associated with eating the dead of one's own village or district, including women married into it. There may be quarrels, however, over the actual cutting up and distribution of the meat.[11] Also, as we shall see, some violence may be used in accelerating a person's death for the purpose of eating him. But cannibalism in association with interdistrict fighting offers scope for the expression of violent and aggressive behavior toward a victim. Although this aspect receives special attention here, it should be kept in mind that it is not invariably present. There are as many examples where enemy dead are untouched, or where the bodies are either taken back or cut up on the spot without such displays.

During a combined attack by Agura, Moiife, Kogu, Asafina, and Ofafina on Irafu, the village stockades were surrounded and finally broken down. A number of Irafu people of both sexes, and women of other districts, were killed, and the rest dispersed. Most of the bodies were left untouched, but Terebu of Agura found among the burning houses the corpse of an Agura woman named Augabara, whom he called *aku*. He was sorry for her and dragged the body out. Then he cut it up and made it into a couple of bundles, and called out for his wife, Jatu, to help him carry the meat home. The dead woman's mother, Itaso, showed her gratitude to Terebu by killing a pig and giving it to him.

In another combined raid by Kogu, Kemiju, Anonana, and Moiife on Asafina, a number of men and women, as well as children and aged of both sexes, were killed and their village demolished. A party of women belonging to the victorious groups were soon on the scene picking over the corpses, choosing those with the best meat. A Kemiju woman chose a young boy, a Kogu woman a child, an Anonana woman another young boy, and a Moiife woman took a man. The remainder were left for their kin.

Although near kin at times oppose the eating of a corpse, when this question comes up (that is, of eating as against burying) approval usually seems to be more or less unanimous. Often a dying man will say that he wishes to be eaten.

Mararita^{c}o of Asafina, for instance, was allegedly a victim of *sangguma* sorcery performed by Ora. Returning to his district he became ill and remained in his

---

[11] For instance, fighting may break out between those who want to bury the corpse and others who want to cut it up. On the other hand, it may be eaten surreptitiously by a small group of men or women, who exhume it secretly by night, cut it up, and take it to the men's house or (if women are responsible) to the menstrual hut.

house. Knowing that he was going to die he asked to be moved down to the creek. "Take me down to the water, and let me lie there. When I die, you must cut and eat me," he ordered.

Similarly, Waigigapa of Ofafina, a famous warrior as well as a large man physically, when suffering from the effects of *imusa* sorcery [allegedly carried out by Moiife], spoke to his kin: "I am dying from this poison. After I am dead let me lie for two days; on the third day cut and eat me."

When Kama's mother, Marei, was dying, she told him how her body should be cut after death and how it should be cooked. Water was to be poured into her eyes, leaves were to be placed on the oven stones on which her flesh was to cook and then given to his pigs so that they would grow large and their litters increase. Her bones, when buried in his garden, would increase the crops.[12] Kama did as he was ordered, at first doubting the efficacy of the leaves he fed to his pigs; but as the pigs grew fat and littered he knew she had spoken the truth.

Opposition to the eating of a near kinsman centers mainly, though not entirely, in the parent-child relationship and the mother's brother-sister's son (*aku*) relationship. Conventionally, parents should not eat their own children, and vice versa; and this rule is apparently observed more often than not. The opposition manifested in these two situations is of a rather different kind. In the parent-child case, and also in respect of *nenafu*, perhaps it may represent a more or less genuine reaction against seeing the body treated in this way, losing its individual identity so rapidly. (There is also the consideration that near kin of this sort are conventionally obliged to give a pig, or at least vegetables, to people living in the same district who eat the corpse. This is distinct from the ordinary distribution of goods at a mortuary feast.) In most recorded instances, such a response is soon overruled by majority opinion; but in the greater number of cases the bereaved parents, or son or daughter, do not try to prevent others from eating the corpse.

Ta'u, an old Kogu woman, died and the body was carried to the Negivi gardens where it was cut up. The flesh was then cooked and distributed. While people were eating, her son, Iso'so, began to run up and down the village asking why they had cut up his mother's body instead of burying it. Angrily he seized a firebrand and set alight the kunai roof of the house in which people were congregated for the feast. They rushed out, leaving parts of the corpse inside: the house soon burned down, charring the flesh and bones. Iso'so then killed a pig and gave it to the others as compensation.

[12] According to Landtman (1927, pp. 361, 366–67), the Kiwai mythical hero, Marunogere, prescribed that at his death his body should be divided among the people and kept for a garden medicine.

In another case, Efanu, a Moiife woman married to a Kogu man, Nariteja, died, allegedly as a result of *naglisa* sorcery inflicted by Asafina. Her son Nogona, with others, carried the body to his lineage garden where it was buried. On the following day, Nogona's wife, Tuwaᶜi, from Kemiju, dug up the corpse and began cutting it up. Her husband happened to see her doing this and in a rage drew his bow and shot her in the thigh. As she cried in pain, he said, "I buried her. Why did you remove her body and cut it?" Receiving no reply, he relented and told her that she could continue. She did so, cooking the meat, distributing some and eating some herself. In this case, it is not clear whether the wife was punished because she had cut up the corpse or because she had gone contrary to her husband—probably something of both.

In the *aku* relationship, opposition is not against the cutting of the corpse as such, and the practice itself is not in question. The *aku* objects to others usurping what he takes to be his privilege. This is one of the primary rights of the mother's brother-sister's son relationship, reflecting as it does the strong emotional alliance between siblings of opposite sex, and (when the parties involved are not at war) an *aku* may resist any infringement of his rights. Nevertheless, such situations are relatively rare; the dissension is usually focused on the distribution to which a person is entitled on the occasion of his *aku*'s death. At times the deceased's kin go to some trouble to hide the death from *aku* in order to evade payments.

Gugagava, a Keᶜjagana man, was shot by Busarasa during a raid on Toᶜjaforega. After the fighting the dead man's body was carried to his garden where men and women began to cut it up. Nusaᶜe of Kogu objected: "This is my *aku*. Whose *aku* are you cutting?" Smearing himself with ashes and mud, waving a stick above his head and wailing, he rushed among the women who were clustered around the corpse and drove them all away. Then he sat down before the corpse and taking hold of a leg began to cut it. Other men, mainly the deceased's lineage brothers, came up to him: "Our *aku*, why do you fight us like this? You have no shame!" Nusaᶜe then felt ashamed and let the women return to complete the cutting. To compensate for his action, he killed a pig and gave it to them; this was cooked in one oven and the human flesh in the other. Later, the dead man's lineage brothers reciprocated by killing a pig and giving it to Nusaᶜe.

In another case Nusaᶜe made a similar demonstration. Haniᶜigu, the small son of Ibuja, lineage sister to Nusaᶜe, married to Nagadjeᶜmi of Keᶜjagana, died from eating cucumber poisoned with *krana*. Nusaᶜe was away at the time, but the mortuary feast was held and a pig's head put aside for him. On his return, Nusaᶜe found people congregated around the corpse. His mother's brother's son and adopted brother, Meneke, offered him the pig's head, but Nusaᶜe pushed it aside, telling Meneke to eat it himself. He was angry because people were talking about cutting up the corpse without having asked him. He then smeared himself and his weapons with mud and ashes and came dancing across the village clearing, singing:

> nupagu noganeni
> hafaru noganeni
> uma^{c}a^{c}moka nunamiu
> ma^{c}moka   nunamiu . . .

"Numparu *aku*, Hafaru *aku*. That woman, you breast-feed him; this [another] woman, you breast-feed him." ["There are other *aku* from other districts, suckled by this woman and that. But this one was special to me, he was suckled by my 'sister'. "] Wailing, Nusa^{c}e rushed among the assembled people, shooting his arrows in all directions, shooting at pigs and setting alight houses. Everyone ran away into the bush; no one restrained him. At last, when he had calmed down, he came to his *aku*'s corpse, tied the hands and legs together with rope, and swinging it over his shoulders went to the gardens at Figamutaga above the village. Here he cut it up. The dead boy's father later gave gifts to Nusa^{c}e, in compensation.

In both cases, when opposition is shown by a son or an *aku*, some compensatory gifts pass between the parties concerned. A son compensates his lineage kin and others, although not when his wife is concerned; an *aku* either compensates or is compensated, depending on his rights in the case. When such cases do occur they are resolved with the minimum of internal dissension. It is recognized that a son, *nenafu*, or *aku* may cause some disturbance at such a time, and that usually the best thing to do is to let this run its course. For instance, no effort is made to restrain such a demonstration. The situation is resolved by appeasement or by inducing shame through public disapproval. Overwhelmingly, opinion is in favor of eating a corpse.

Occasionally, we are told, a "corpse" revives when the first cut is made:

Kawadji of Taramu died, supposedly from *naglisa* sorcery administered by Inivi. Members of his lineage treated him with special medicinal leaves and pig blood and fat, but to no effect; he apparently died. He was placed on a platform inside a house for two days while the mortuary feast was held and later carried to his garden. Here he was laid out for cutting and edible *fezagupa* fern leaves spread out ready for the meat. Various men and women held his body discussing which parts they wanted: one held his arm, another his head, and so on. As one began to cut his leg, he jumped up and cried out. The people clustered about him got such a fright that they ran away. When at last they returned Kawadji asked why they were cutting him, and they explained that he was supposed to be dead. Since he was still weak, they carried him back to the village; and as they did so he sang:

> managesamowoi afi^{c}ni negiwau
> haginamu agumu aigoni hagiu
> jaga tumafi haju haju. . . .

"This, my ear, [is] wild, foolish; knife cuts across thus: Animal, wild cat, it goes. . . ." [Kawadji becomes conscious of the knife, cutting him. "While my ears are deaf (i.e., while I am unaware of what's happening), you cut me as if you were cutting a wild animal."]

He changed his name to Fezagupa, after the edible leaves placed beside his body in readiness for the cutting. The scar of the cut on his leg is still visible.

Hastening a Death.

Although violence is not necessarily manifested in the practice of eating human meat, it may be present in the circumstances associated with it. For instance, steps may be taken to hasten the death of a person who is wounded or ill: [13]

An Ifusa man, Gagagiza, was wounded by Oka men in a raid. He was carried back to his village and placed in a house where he lay breathing heavily. Members of his lineage collected some sticks of sugar cane from the gardens and sitting beside him began to break it piece by piece. [This signifies the breaking of the man's bones, and supposedly induces him to die quickly. Pitpit cane or strong sticks may be used for the same purpose.] In this case the man soon died and was cut and eaten. [It is said that the dying man's spirit familiar (oni^c), a lizard, came and rested beside him; as he breathed heavily, so did the lizard; they both died at the same moment. Some mourned the man, others the lizard; it was later buried in his garden with his bones.]

A number of other examples show that this method is not uncommon, particularly where old people are concerned. Yet in some cases, apparently, people do not wait until a man is dead before they cut up his body.

An old Tevenofi man, Atavawanoja, was visiting his daughter at Kogu when he became ill. He was carried to a house where he lay in a semiconscious state for some days. Ena^co, his *aku*, considered that it was time he died and with the help of some women began to cut up his body while he was still alive; at first he struggled, but a few cuts of the bamboo knife stilled him. The flesh was eaten and the bones later buried in a garden at Amogronaga, his *aku*'s own garden, now occupied by Asafina. [14]

In another case, an old Ofafina woman, Ametu^c, became so weak that she remained indoors most of the time. Some Ofafina men decided that she would not live long and taking her out of the house carried her to the gardens. Here

[13] Landtman (1927, p. 267) mentions that the Kiwai killed and ate their own sick. "Oh, he got plenty fat," people are supposed to think on looking at a sick man; "more better you me [we] kill him, *kaikai* [eat]. No good wait [till] he die along sick [sickness], no more fat he stop."

[14] His bones were not returned to his own district, as they should have been. Often in such a case this is left to the discretion of the *aku*, who may return the bones only if compensated. No burial feast was held at Tevenofi for Atavawanoja, and hence there was no distribution of gifts to *aku*.

they began to cut her; she cried out, "I am alive; why do you cut me?" The others took no notice and continued cutting, first her legs and then her arms, while she cried and struggled. At last they slit her belly and she died. They filled their net bags with the meat and returned to the village where a feast was held; later the bones were buried beneath a clump of bamboo at Kazanagai.

In order to bring about the death of a person some subterfuge is normally used:

A young girl named Kokori of Numpagimi fell sick and spent most of her time sleeping in her hut. Certain men and women, without the knowledge of her lineage brothers, her father, and her husband, decided to kill her so they could eat her flesh: "She will die later: it is better for us to kill her while she lives. She is young and her flesh is good to eat now; later it may deteriorate as her sickness grows." So taking a rope they went to her house and strangled her, then carried out her body and hung it from a tree, making it appear that she had committed suicide. Then they pretended to find her and, wailing, called out to her kin and her husband. A mortuary feast was held and gifts offered by her husband; the body was cooked and eaten.

There is no way in which we can gauge how often the sick are killed. Generally the instigators are classificatory kin, *aku*, or women married into the district. Violence, here, is incidental; the aim is to have good meat before a protracted illness or increasing old age causes it to deteriorate. The sick or the aged person, it is assumed, will die soon anyway. Another factor is the virtual uselessness of anyone who is incapacitated and so unable to contribute actively to the life of the community. A long sickness may cause some inconvenience to the people immediately concerned; and while the healthy aged are of value in many ways, when they become ill they may be viewed as a nuisance. Nevertheless, much affection, patience, and care may be shown them; and near kin and spouse rarely take the initiative in hastening their death. There are exceptions; but with the Administration ban on cannibalism in the northern part of the region these features may gradually disappear.

Violence becomes correspondingly greater when enemies are concerned,[15] or when a stranger, for example, is caught with a man's wife:

A Hatia man named Auglimu and his wife Auguma fled from their district, near Taramu, to Emoatiga, in Ke'jagana. While they were there a visiting

[15] R. I. Skinner (K.5 of 1947/48, Patrol Report) observes that Moiife and Kogu people ate the bodies of fellow villagers killed in battle or by certain forms of sorcery. Enemies, he says, are not eaten. Special parts of the body, like testes, penis, brains, shoulders, and forehead, are eaten by the deceased's father or brothers. G. W. Toogood (No. 1 of 1949/50, Patrol Report) gives contrary information, to the effect that the flesh of kinsfolk is never eaten. G. Linsley (No. 8 of 1950/51, Patrol Report) states that these people consume their own dead kinsfolk, but enemies killed in battle are never eaten.

Friganu [Jate] man, Wajatorabio, made advances to Auguma. She received him several times in her house at night while her husband slept in the men's house. He became so persistent that she feared her husband would hear of it; hoping to evade trouble for herself, she went to Auglimu and told him that a man was worrying her. They decided that he would wait with his bow that night and she would hold the man when he came. When Wajatorabio visited her that night she lit a torch of paperbark and holding his arms called out to her husband. Auglimu came up and shot several arrows into his body. Then he dragged out the wounded man. A fire was built, and the husband began to cut off slices of flesh, while Wajatorabio cried out in pain. He then cut off both the man's arms, and left him to bleed to death. After the initial excitement, it is said, none of the other people took any further notice. Auguma and Auglimu took the arms of their victim into her house, where they roasted them over a fire, had a meal, and slept together. In the morning the villagers of Emoatiga cut up the corpse and called other Ke^cjagana people to the feast. Later the bones were collected and arranged round a tree near the village. A message was sent to Friganu, and the dead man's mother came down, collected the bones, and returned to her district; she killed a pig, and a mortuary feast was held.

The desire to punish and avenge an injury apparently was uppermost in the husband's mind. Cannibalism was only incidental, a way of achieving compensation. It should be noted that the killing occurred in a district not their own, while they themselves were refugees. It would have been a different matter had the victim belonged to Ke^cjagana.

In fighting involving Musa^cve and Irafu, among other districts, Musa^cve raided Irafu. After the fighting the Musa^cve people returned to their villages for the night. Before dawn next day Irafu, with Moiife as ally, raided Musa^cve. They stormed the stockades and, dispersing most of the inhabitants, managed to catch Kenegi^cwaio in the men's house. The Irafu and Moiife men pulled off some of the kunai roof and by shooting through the aperture managed to wound him. Then they set fire to the house and as Kenegi^cwaio emerged they again shot at him and he fell to the ground. Pulling the burning kunai from the roof, they threw it over him as he screamed, until finally he died. An Irafu man, Wajawaja, chewed off each ear of the corpse, singing at intervals. They then cut up the body and returned with it to Irafu, where they were joined by Moiife and Agura for the feast.

Such treatment of enemy victims apparently is not unusual in inter-district fighting. It provides an opportunity for venting one's anger and hostility, especially after the death of one of one's own lineage kin.

Kogu and Asafina made a combined attack on Moiife and were able to shoot Metaga, a Moiife man. The Moiife men beat back their enemies and chased them for some distance. Kogu and Asafina held their ground, returning the arrow shots, but eventually Moiife wounded an Asafina man named Kri^cme and forced the others back. The Moiife men then took their own dead warrior and Kri^cme as well. As they entered their district, they were greeted by all the women and children dancing and singing around them. They put Kri^{c}me in the center of the village clearing, where the people danced around him. It is said that he must have been in great pain, for the arrow with which he had been shot was still protruding. Nase^{c}ompa then came forward with a steel ax and began cutting at his knee; Kri^{c}me cried out, but Nase^{c}ompa severed the limb and threw it to one side. A woman danced forward singing, picked up the leg, and danced away. Still Kri^{c}me cried as Nase^{c}ompa cut off the other leg and threw it to a man who danced forward, singing, and carried it away. The same was done with one arm, then the other: still Kri^{c}me cried, until Nase^{c}ompa with a stroke of his ax severed the head, which was caught up by a dancing man and carried away. Then the trunk was cut up and various parts distributed. When the feast was finished the bones were tied up in croton leaves and fastened to the Moiife stockade.[16]

This illustrates the more formalized type of cannibalism associated with the eating of an enemy. The behavior is relatively well organized, except for the emotional effervescence expressed in the initial dancing and singing; but then it is customary to meet a victorious party in this way. Whether the cutting up of a victim while he is still alive is deliberate cruelty,[17] as in the case of the husband who killed his wife's lover, is difficult to say. There is little doubt, however, that the people who participated (and one must consider here that women of the Asafina lineages were present, including perhaps *nenafu* and other affines) appear to have enjoyed watching the man's suffering and hearing him cry as his limbs were hacked off. A number of men who took part in this particular feast, including Nase^{c}ompa himself, thought it great fun and laughed uproariously in discussing it, with no sign of embarrassment. Frankness in

[16] Asafina and Kogu were too much afraid to collect the bones from the stockade; they remained there until they fell and were scattered by pigs. Metaga was buried and a croton planted over his grave; Kogu also planted a croton for the death they had inflicted.

Another version of this incident, agreeing in the main points but emphasizing different details, was recorded by C. H. Berndt. The returning men called out to their womenfolk, and presumably especially to those from Asafina, "We are bringing one of your menfolk—don't cry, don't interfere. We are backing a death. . . ." The women are said to have answered, "No, it is good for you to kill him, he was killing us. . . ." Also, reference is made to Kri^{c}me's bravery. He said proudly, "You can kill me!" and at first did not cry out as the ax cut him.

[17] This is aggressive action: it is possibly cruelty, according to the usual definition of this term. But although there is undoubtedly a conscious or unconscious satisfaction derived, both in performing and in witnessing it, I am reluctant to regard it as sadism in view of the cultural stress on all forms of aggressive action. See, for example, Horney (1946, pp. 192–93, 200). Was there a desire to cause pain? Was the inflicting of suffering on others an intrinsic part? Certainly in many examples this appears to be so. Nevertheless, I do not think this can be regarded as deliberate torture. See Williams (1930, pp. 172–73). But compare with Seligmann (1910, p. 569), who mentions that prisoners taken in warfare were brought alive to the hamlet-cluster, where they would be tortured before being killed and eaten. Women, he says, were never tortured or assaulted.

these matters is the rule; this is an approved way of treating enemies. It follows the conventional method of cutting up a corpse, combining feasting with ceremony, and differs from cannibalism involving one's own kin or people living in the same village or district.

The Orgiastic Feast [18]

We may hesitate to classify the above example, involving the killing and cutting up of Kri^cme, as an orgiastic feast, since it was relatively well organized and controlled, and with no wild displays over, for instance, the division of the corpse.[19] But it seems that this is not always the case. Examples testify that at such a time, when victorious warriors return home, many men and women indulge in uncontrolled behavior, assaulting the corpse and fighting over the best portions of meat. This seems to have been so much a part of the situation as to arouse little comment. Women appear to have been the worst offenders.

In the course of fighting between Asafina and Ifusa, Asafina managed to kill an Ifusa warrior, who was abandoned by his retreating companions. The Asafina men collected his body and returned home with it, singing. They were met by a mob of their womenfolk and other men who had not accompanied the war party. As the corpse was being carried, they hacked at it, trying to cut off pieces of it. The men who were carrying it tried to prevent them, telling them to leave it until they had reached their own village, but they took no notice. A couple of older men began to beat off the crowd with sticks, thrashing them about the head and shoulders until blood flowed, but this did not stop them. "You can fight us," they said. "We will 'back' you by eating this man!" When the cutting was completed, they carried their joints of meat triumphantly home, where a feast was held.[20]

A large group of Tiroka men and women came to participate in the mortuary feast of a Kogu man, among them affines as well as *aku* and *nenafu* and so on. Agura and Moiife men and women were present for the same purpose. Feeling was running high against the Kamano, since this Kogu man had been shot by Numaga; Tiroka also belonged to the Kamano linguistic unit. The Agura and

[18] This does not conform completely to the accepted meaning. There is, for instance, no general and indiscriminate licentious revelry, as in the Greek sense. Nevertheless, it indicates fairly clearly the kind of situation with which we are concerned.

[19] See description by Seligmann (1910, pp. 553–59).

[20] A similar case occurred when an Asafina man died of sorcery away from his district. A Kogu man, Muga^ce, father of Kama, offered to carry the body back to Asafina for burial. With the aid of two companions he brought it to Kogu. Next morning Muga^ce, with a lineage brother, started off for Asafina with the corpse. They were leaving their village when a group of their own men and women surrounded them and began to hack at the body. Dropping it, the two men grabbed sticks and tried to beat them off, but the others took no notice and continued to hack at it. Eventually Muga^ce gave up and joined in with the others.

Moiife people felt that here was an excellent opportunity to obtain revenge, since they too had a score to settle with Numaga. Secretly they approached some Kogu men, who refused to aid them on the grounds that Tiroka were visitors come to mourn. Agura and Moiife were not deterred, however, and got together their weapons. Kogu warned the Tiroka men, who got up and began to depart. The Agura and Moiife men immediately followed them and began shooting; a running fight ensued, Tiroka returning the shots. Kogu remained watching and took no part. Agura and Moiife first shot Tabagana, then Kuguripana, then Futijana. Shooting continued until they reached Arufanu, near Agura, where several Tiroka men and a number of women were killed. The remaining Tiroka people disappeared into the bush and escaped home. Groups of Agura, Moiife, and Kogu men and women gathered around the corpses to cut them up. Most assembled at Arufanu, where more corpses were available for cutting. Here Unapi^{c}na of Kogu selected the corpse of a young woman named Pazu^{c}na; finding her attractive, he knelt between her legs and pulling them to his thighs began to copulate, cutting the body as he did so. A Kogu woman, Aria, came up, and said to him, "You are taking a long time. You are only pretending to cut. All the time you copulate." But having ejaculated he began again, at the same time slowly cutting off the woman's breasts. By this time Aria, a *nenafu* of his, became impatient and set to work on the corpse herself with her bamboo knife. She began to cut across the corpse's belly, but Unapi^{c}na was so intent on copulating that he did not notice how near her knife was. Aria, for her part, was careless. She cut further in and across, hacking away at the flesh; and since Unapi^{c}na's penis was in the woman's vagina, she cut most of it off. Unapi^{c}na fell back crying, blood flowing from the stump of his penis. Aria blamed him for what had happened. "You sit there copulating, not bothering to cut her up properly. This woman is dead, ready to be cut up for eating. I told you about it, but you continued copulating. Thus I cut off your penis!" Unapi^{c}na replied, "I looked at this Kamano woman; she was a good woman. I looked at her vulva, and I liked it; that is why I copulated. But now you have cut off my penis! What shall I do?" Aria removed the end of the penis she had cut off, popped it into her mouth, and ate it, and then continued with the cutting. Unapi^{c}na was helped back to his house, where he rested. Ovens were made and the meat cooked, amid dancing and singing. Unapi^{c}na was given the woman's vulva and surrounding flesh to eat.

In selecting this incident for discussion, I should mention that there are no other similar examples available. There are, however, many cases of men copulating with the dead, especially if the corpse is young and attractive.[21] In the above example, the bodies of other young women were available and are said to have been treated in much the same way. The men concerned acted quite openly; and their own women, far from resenting it, apparently enjoyed watching them. It is said that they themselves often squat over dead men, pretending to have coitus with them or playing with the penes of corpses. Both men and women smear themselves with blood and

---

[21] See Landtman (1917, p. 398), who mentions a Kiwai case told in a myth.

hang from their head and shoulders various parts of the body in much the same way as is done with the meat of pigs during the pig festival.

It is not, then, solely the warriors responsible for killing the victim or victims who enjoy these festivities, but other members and residents of the district, men, women, and children; and often, as in the case of other feasts, adjacent groups are invited to join in. Affinal kin rarely object, and should they do so their objection will be signified by refusal to participate. Just as often, however, dead victims are cut up without being subject to sexual abuse. The cooking of human meat in the village usually is carried out with no more disturbance than attends other cooking. Violent handling of the corpse is associated mainly with the actual dismember-ment, or with the period immediately after the killing, when warriors are aroused and their womenfolk share their excitement. There are a number of cases in which a small group of men or women, or even one person alone, may take an enemy corpse and retire with it and in private eat as much of it as they can. This is more usual where the dead of their own village or district are concerned. But it may be done also in the case of enemy dead abandoned after a fight.[22] Or they may exhume by night a newly buried corpse in an adjacent district[23] and eat it secretly.

Sexual Violence

The exhibition of sexual violence toward the dead is in keeping with what has already been said about other forms of sexual aggression and plural copulation. Where the living alone are concerned, this kind of activity is carried out either for enjoyment or to punish a woman branded as disobedient or promiscuous. In relation to the dead, however, the physical satisfaction involved is tinged with a desire to abuse the corpse. Coitus is viewed as an aggressive act, even when the partners are fond of each other. By copulating with a dead female, so we are led to believe, a

[22] Iguwa of Asafina, shot by Ifusa in the course of fighting, was left lying on the ground, his kin being afraid to return for him. Ibegeva of Kogu, son of Unapiᶜna of the severed penis, came out alone at night and brought the body back to his house, where he cut it up, storing some meat and disposing of the rest. He ate all of this himself, so we are told, cooking small pieces secretly over his fire. When he had finished the meat he was so bloated that people asked what he had been eating; he replied, nothing. Still his belly began to swell, and he was asked whether he had defecated lately. He answered, no. Some of his kin examined his rectum and found it blocked with human skin which had not been masticated. They removed it with a pair of wooden tweezers. Presently he became quite well again.

This is, of course, an unusual case, for most lone eaters of human flesh feel no ill effects. Usually, too, a person would share some of the meat with near-kin.

[23] Members of a hostile district are said to wait in ambush to shoot the corpse-robbers when they appear. Catherine Berndt has recorded several cases of this.

man not only derives personal pleasure but is also "attacking" the enemy; he is gaining an advantage not only over the dead woman but over her male kin.

Such violence occasionally overtakes women who throw themselves on the protection of men who are at war with their husbands or kin:

During fighting between Kogu and Moiife, Kogu sacked one of the Moiife villages, razing the houses and scattering the inhabitants. One young woman, Jawuriᶜna, originally from Agura but married to Japanu of Moiife, left her husband and went to Kogu. They asked her why she had come. She said that she was afraid and wanted to marry a Kogu man. They replied that they would not marry her but were ready to copulate with her. They put her in a house and visited her one by one for this purpose. This continued until the night of the third day after her arrival. Then they fastened the door of her house, surrounded it, and shot arrows through the walls. Finally they pulled off the kunai roof and shot her dead. Women took her body to the gardens and cut it up, the meat being placed in bamboo containers and cooked in an oven. Only the women ate. The men danced with drawn bows, refusing to join in because they were preparing to fight Moiife. "If we eat we won't shoot well." [24] Soon afterward they made another raid on Moiife.

In another example Kogu, Anonana, and Moiife combined to attack Asafina, demolishing a village and killing a number of people. Most of the remaining Asafina people fled; but one young woman remained hidden in the nearby bush for several days, afraid to come out or to go in search of her kin. She was found by four Kogu men, Goᶜari, Kumewiᶜna, Kavanempa, and Kama, who on seeing her made ready to shoot. But the girl called out, "Don't shoot me. Let me come with you to your village and marry one of you. Let me stay with you. There I will make you string net bags; there I will look after your pigs; there I will look after your gardens: I will plant food for you." Kumewiᶜna said he would marry her; he took hold of her, loosened her skirt, threw her to the ground, and copulated. When he had finished, the other three did the same in turn. When Kama had finished, he left his three companions and returned to his village, where he prepared an oven. In the meantime the others occupied themselves in copulating with the girl, but on Kama's return they shot her, cut up her body, divided the meat, and went back to the village where they cooked it. [25]

[24] There are no other cases where this is put forward as a reason for abstaining from human flesh, although this is implied in the Busarasa-Kasa fighting sequence mentioned in chap. 12. No further explanation was forthcoming. It was not because they had copulated with the woman, for this does not normally deter them. But before setting out to fight warriors rarely eat heavily, on the ground that this will make them drowsy and they will not be physically and mentally alert.

[25] The meat was shared mainly among the four men and their wives and children. The others asked where they had obtained the meat. They replied that they had found a "wild" or "bush" woman, had copulated with her, and then cut her up. This term is ordinarily used to refer to creatures which live in the bush, spirits for instance, or untamed pigs. It signifies contempt or abuse when used in reference to a human being.

A woman placing herself at the mercy of men of another district, when they bear no acknowledged relationship to her, can expect only this kind of treatment. We have seen that, even in peaceful times, a lone female, unprotected and having no strong kin in the district, is an easy victim for the men who enjoy her until they are bored. Yet there are numerous examples of women going alone to visit kin in another district and having to pass hostile villages on the way. Such women may be assaulted sexually; but the prospect of this does not usually deter them, and in fact the evidence suggests that it may sometimes have served as an incentive. The likelihood of being killed, however, would depend primarily on the relations existing between her husband's district or her own and that of her attackers. If there are deaths to be "backed" or grudges to be repaid, or if a state of hostility exists between them, she will be in danger of being killed. Almost invariably sexual intercourse will precede the shooting. She has a better chance of escaping this fate if she goes directly to a village where a large number of people are congregated and tries to claim their protection by reason of kin or quasi-kin ties. But this is likely to be of little use unless these ties are close and the men concerned are "strong" enough to assert themselves against her attackers.

The circumstances of sexual violence vary. For instance, the corpse of a dead female may be assaulted sexually before being returned to her husband or kin:

Kinamuju, originally from Agura but married to Goꞓari of Kogu, was sent to Moiife by her husband. Moiife had a grudge against Agura and therefore shot her. Two Kogu men, Wajanavi and Wozaꞓo, collected her body from Moiife and set off with it for Kogu. Before they had gone far they copulated with it in turn. They picked it up and carried it a little further, then copulated with it again. After resting they continued on their way. Coming to a stream, they put it down and copulated again. They spent some time there, finally wiping the dead woman's vulva and adjusting her skirt. Then they carried the body to her husband's village, calling out to Goꞓari and telling the circumstances of her death. She was placed on a platform in her house and a mortuary feast was held the following morning. Later the body was carried to the gardens and cut, cooked, and eaten. When the feasting was over, Goꞓari commended the two men who had brought her corpse from Moiife, and in gratitude, not knowing what they had done on the way, gave them a pig.

Here physical enjoyment was the sole concern of the two Kogu men. When this subject was discussed with them they insisted that if the woman in question were physically attractive, a "good woman" as the expression has it, this in itself provided sufficient reason. Men admitted that intercourse with a dead woman was less pleasurable than with a living one, yet they implied that there was more scope in such a case for rough treatment which could not be resisted.

Conclusion

In discussing cannibalism we have focused our attention primarily on violence. Cannibalism is associated with behavior which suggests aggressive self-assertion. Thus it sets a problem in relation to restraint; in other words, to the factors which restrict and regulate action, directing aggression into particular channels and discouraging it in others. There is, broadly speaking, a sharp difference between cannibalism involving near kin or members of the co-resident group and that involving an enemy. In the former, aggression is latent and fairly well controlled by common sentiment and emotion engendered by the death, reinforced in terms of relationship ties and obligation. A mortuary feast, for example, must be held, and this involves an outlay of wealth. Payments are made to the deceased's brothers, sisters, and *aku*, among others. Food must be assembled for a feast, in which most members of that district, as well as of certain others, normally participate. Afterward, there is frequently the matter of cutting up the corpse. Here opposition may appear and develop into open dissension. Awareness of such opposition (whether it be against the actual cutting up of a kinsman's corpse or merely against the infringement of the right to do so), even if it is only conventionally expressed, may serve to discourage violent action. But majority opinion, or what passes for this under pressure from the "stronger" or more determined, tends (or has tended, in the past) to override personal opinion and to support the practice of cannibalism on the basis of its general acceptability to the community as a whole. Associated with it, over and above the satisfaction derived from eating the flesh, is a series of "good" and beneficial qualities (relating to fertility, and to strengthening or healing or curing the living) to be gained thereby. Indirectly, and as an extension of this, aggressive action directed against the corpse is formally sanctioned; but the cutting up of the corpse is not ordinarily accompanied by violence, although quarreling and fighting may accompany the choice of various parts of the body. Violence becomes more apparent according to the distance (genealogically or in quasi-kin terms) between the deceased and the persons who take part in the cutting; but there are exceptions to this. It does not matter, in this respect, whether the corpse is cut up immediately or exhumed later for that purpose. When a corpse is exhumed, it is more often eaten by only a small group, who have obtained it secretly. There are no sanctions against this, although certain of the deceased's kin and the spouse may exact punishment if they object.

Conversely, in dealing with a person viewed as an enemy only the corpse and its disposal are of immediate consideration. Mortuary ceremonies for the deceased are of no concern to the participants, and the only specifically economic element involved is the possibility of gifts from the deceased's kin if the bones are returned. There are no accepted procedures to regulate the treatment of a dead or captured enemy. Again, moderating influences are discernible where kin ties are concerned; but these, in circumstances of hostility or in the heat of fighting, are restricted and can be overridden by adverse opinion. It is in such a setting, where relative freedom of individual action is permissible within the cultural context (which means only that it is allowable as long as it does not affect the ingroup or antagonize unduly those who acknowledge kin or affinal bonds with the deceased), that we find extreme violence in both dismembering and ill-treating the corpse. Such actions are canalized in what I have called orgiastic feasts which may be associated with such behavior. These range from the more or less formal ceremony (for example, when the corpse or living victim is cut up in the village clearing and distributed piece by piece to dancing and singing men and women) to the informal (for example, the cutting up and sexual abuse of corpses where they have fallen). They are, or were, conventional channels for the release of tensions which develop during a fight; they are, if one wants to view them in this way, the compensations or the rewards associated with it.

Two significant elements are so far apparent: first, the strong emphasis on personal choice in such matters; second, the discrepancy between ideal and actual in regard to the eating of the dead.

We can speak of the structural aspect of cannibalism insofar as it symbolizes "ingroup solidarity" as against "outgroup hostility," underlining the segmentary nature of the social units involved. On the organizational level, in terms of interrelation and interaction of individuals, the same principles already discussed are operative—for instance, in respect to the interactory zone of political influence, seen as an ephemeral unit of antagonism and co-operation. Since the co-resident group, the village (or district in its wider political setting), is the economic unit and its survival dependent on the successful co-operation of its male and female members (whatever their lineage affiliation), cannibalism may be viewed as an economic or perhaps supra-economic factor, immediately productive of food and, in long-range perspective, significant to group fertility.

Apart from such considerations, it is more fruitful to contrast the ideal with the actual, examining, for instance, who may or may not eat of a specific relative's flesh, or what should occur in relation to the disposal of a corpse, and so on. Men are rather more strict in this than their womenfolk. There is, generally speaking, closer conformity to the ideal in regard to near-kin (for example, the prohibition upon eating the flesh of a deceased parent, brother, sister, or *nenafu*). Variation takes place more frequently, for example, in the matter of a husband's eating the flesh of his dead spouse. It is accepted conventionally that a slain enemy should be left for his (or her) kin to collect after a fight, or, if killed else-where, that the body should be taken to the home village for disposal. This is one of the "ideal courtesies" of interdistrict warfare. Yet it seems that frequently the right is infringed and gives rise to the violence we have discussed. Even allowing for the fact that the body may be eaten by the victorious group, the bones, it is felt, should be returned. There are, however, a number of instances where this is neglected. Thus there is much closer correspondence between ideal and actual in regard to the dead of one's own group; but, as indicated, there may be opposition or dissension in regard to the actual disposal or cutting up of the corpse. Two different ideals or norms are here in conflict.

Within the sociocultural context the personal factor is of basic con-sideration, influencing the course of subsequent action, just as it is in other aspects of social and cultural belief and living. In our discussion this aspect has been most apparent. For instance, sometimes men may eat a corpse, sometimes women, or both sexes jointly, or some persons may abstain for no other reason than that they do not feel like it. It is evident, too, in the matter of violence done to a corpse, in the treatment of female victims, in choice of corpses on the field, in killing specific enemies, in deciding to exhume a body, and so on. Such considerations are directly relevant to any range of variation we may construct.

Throughout the region we are discussing, cannibalism is gradually giving way to disposal by burial under both Administration and Mission pressure. There is no specific argument against the practice of cannibalism beyond the fact that it is "something Europeans do not do." Increasing disfavor has made cannibalism more difficult to carry out in public. This is particularly the case in the northern area, while only beyond Mount Wanevinti does it continue in the way we have described. Instead, it is carried out surreptitiously in some districts and not at all in others. In the Kogu-Moiife-Kemiju area, corpses are no longer invariably buried in the gardens but are occasionally placed on platforms some little distance away, in the seclusion of the bush. The last public eating of the dead known to us in this area occurred late in 1951; surreptitiously, it is continuing. But through the enforced curtailment of interdistrict fighting, the chief source of dead enemies has been closed—and with it have ended the more aggressive elements associated with cannibalism. The curtailment has been abrupt on both these scores, prohibiting what were conventional channels for aggression and violence. Now the problem arises of how to divert such tendencies, which do not languish overnight, so to speak, merely because their traditional media of expression have been removed.

In any situation where districts are interacting with one another as separate units, the differences and cleavages within them are deprecated. The emphasis, then, is on common interests and unity of purpose; the forces which hold members of a district together, in contrast to all others, are assumed to be stronger than those which divide them. We have already seen that this conventional picture of intradistrict harmony does not faithfully reflect the actual situation, even though there is some measure of agreement between the two. When the focus shifts to intradistrict affairs, internal dissension becomes even more prominent.

The settlement of intradistrict breaches serves as a congenial basis for the emergence of a judicial procedure in changing social circumstances. Superficially this might not appear to be the case. One might be inclined to look for such a development in a wider social context; for example, interaction between districts, where breaches bring into play a system of retaliation which utilizes force and exacts compensation. If we follow Seagle here ("It is in the process of retaliation that custom is shaped into law."), certain forms of sorcery, warfare, and the like carried out between districts within an interactory zone are "legal." That is, they are legal expressions when action is taken on behalf of the social or political unit as such. Their "illegal" aspect may emerge when there is not even a nominal suggestion of majority approval.

When it comes to intradistrict offenses or disputes, the position is much less straightforward. They may be classified under three headings: (1) breaches within the lineage and clan; (2) breaches between members of different lineages belonging to one district; (3) breaches between lineage members of a district and other members of the co-resident group (predominantly women married into it). In all but the first, affinal kin may or may not be involved. The seriousness of offenses within the second category may depend on the degree of political independence of the district segments. Those in the third are treated in much the same way as interdistrict disputes, but with certain differences.

Under the first heading, then, come offenses involving members of the lineages occupying a village or hamlet-cluster. Traditionally there is no formal mechanism for dealing with homicide or other serious offenses within the clan. The killing or wounding of one lineage or clan member by another may provoke instant action—or none at all. In theory, a social unit cannot proceed against itself; and for ordinary purposes the lineage or the clan tries to present a solidary front to the outside world. In practice the offender himself, or a substitute, may be killed or wounded by someone who takes the initiative without united or majority backing from the unit involved; or he may be left entirely unpunished. The breach is best healed through non-action; here, it is the social group which is of primary consideration. The procedure adopted against an offender, although carried out by one or more persons and drawing in other kin, is not claimed to have majority support. It represents an attempt to regulate behavior, and right a wrong, by individual persons who have suffered from the breach. The procedure adopted is non-legal; it differs from action taken with social approval, by members or segments of a group, on an interdistrict basis.

Offenses within this category cover a fairly wide range, for example, homicide, infringement of sexual rights, infringement of land rights, theft. These are normally "wrong" when occurring in the confines of the district group. Group condemnation may be forthcoming in respect of them, but this is almost entirely at a verbal level. No joint force is exerted, and punishment is left in the hands of individual members. There is no central authority to maintain and enforce rules. The local "strong men," in any case, are interested primarily in maintaining their own position at the expense of others. Their authority does not derive from any popular mandate, or any formally expressed consensus, although they may have popular support for the very reason that they embody an ideal, or an approximation to it. Dissension between close brothers, or between members of different lineages within a district, may be aggravated by the emphasis on individual action as a means of achieving temporary ascendency. Further, opinion within the unit, even when concerned with fundamental moral wrongs (in local terms), is likely to be divided by conflicting personal interests. In respect of wrongs outside the political unit, it is usually (although not always) more uniform, more sharply crystallized, and more easily translated into action. The strong men, as self-appointed but publicly proclaimed leaders, can achieve something like a united front against an outsider and obtain support from their political unit (excluding "non-articulate" co-resident members, that is, women married into it).

In breaches between members of different lineages in one district, the response may take the form of individual action against a culprit; and again we can call it non-legal. Or it may lead to a consolidation of the respective lineages, underlining the opposition between them at the expense of the political unity of the district as a whole. Action taken between them, by way of "backing" and counter-backing, can then be described as having a legal quality (as in the case of interdistrict warfare). This is conventionally the case also in regard to breaches in our third category—those between lineage members of a district, and others who live in it but belong by birth or adoption to other units outside it. In such a situation, differences in affiliation are heavily underscored. However, an offense by a lineage member against a resident "alien" may provoke no retaliation from the unit to which the victim belongs. (This would usually apply, for instance, to action taken by a husband against his wife; but the nature of the relationship between them, and between their respective kin, makes this a special case.) Or retaliation may take place on a kin or lineage basis, without the support of the political unit or even of the village.

It can be said that the gravest crimes[1] in this region are those which take place within the political unit, becoming increasingly grave the more intimately they involve the lineage and clan. The more serious they are, the weaker the reaction on the part of the unit as such, perhaps on the basis that any concerted action may have undesirable repercussions on its solidarity. At least, this has been so in the past. Today, through the institution of the informal court, there has been a shift from an attitude of laissez faire to district responsibility in the handling of certain offenses within its boundaries.

Breaches coming within the scope of our first two categories may involve persons other than the two initially concerned, but they are usually settled fairly promptly. There may be payment of compensation, or an exchange of gifts, or the holding of a feast to indicate that friendly relations have been re-established. This is not always so when the issue is the killing of a lineage kinsman. However, generally speaking, we can observe here the principle of compensation for a wrong. There is no mechanism within the group to enforce the payment of indemnities; but this is the only way the breach can be healed.

In most of our examples in this section, response to an injury takes the form of retaliation; but it consists also of inflicting or threatening to inflict

---

[1] See Nadel (1947, pp. 501–3).

punishment, or forcing a settlement (variously defined: it may involve payment of compensation, or the retaliation may be sufficient). This is exactly the same procedure as that adopted by a judicial system, when the action used by it is legal, for it reacts against the infringement of laws. The intensification of popular opinion, crystallized into action, using a specific body (possessed of power to enforce penalty) as representative of that opinion, transforms custom into law. In our examples of intradistrict conflicts, separate individuals serve as agents of control, but they are not socially sponsored. What they act against may be regarded as a social wrong, but social awareness in the shape of concerted action is absent. Nevertheless, through the settlement of breaches within the political unit itself, non-legal procedure has set an example for legal and judicial procedure, concurrently with the growth of the embryonic court.

Breaches in the Lineage and Clan

A prominent source of conflict is rivalry between close brothers, but clashes may develop between other categories of kin as well. We shall not deal with quarrels between those who live in a district but do not belong to it by birth or adoption (e.g., co-wives). However, in many, perhaps most, arguments and fights they are directly involved.

Breaches between lineage and clan members may be precipitated by a variety of factors, the development of which is not always easy to trace. For instance, sibling rivalry may be of a conventional kind, intensified by two structural features which permeate their relationship. One is the principle of seniority (preference in certain matters, such as betrothal and land-inheritance, to an elder or senior brother). This is especially notice-able when the differences in status between them are most obvious, as in adolescence or early adulthood. The other is the junior levirate, the arrangement whereby a man's widow may pass to his younger brother. Actual friction appears when two kinsmen are in opposition, one striving to achieve ascendancy over the other in some situation. It implies a certain amount of jealousy tinged with resentment on the part of either or both. This may extend laterally to include patri-kin of the same generation, but it is less marked between "father" and "son" and rare between a "grand-father" and a "grandson." Restraints operate through a strong expression of sentiment or attachment to the lineage and the clan; and here the factor of self-interest is frankly stressed, pointing to mutual aid as neces-sary for both individual and group survival. The sexual dichotomy within the village throws the relations between men into sharper relief, obliging them to be in more constant and intimate contact with one another than with members of the opposite sex. In contrast to these conventionally strong ties between men of the same lineage and village, the equally conventional expectation of rivalry and friction may provide the spark which explodes a quarrel—the participants seizing on the slightest pretext to express latent aggressive feelings toward near kin. The close proximity in which they live, and the coincidence of common interests, provide a favorable setting for this.

Ajo^ce of Kogu was digging furrows in his father's garden when his lineage brother [father's brother's son], Gori^co, shot him dead. Gori^co held that Ajo^ce had trespassed on his garden; he was the elder and resented Ajo^ce's attempt to surpass him in strength and wealth. Ajo^ce's father, Muga^ce,[2] carried his son's body back to the village. In a rage he seized his bow and arrows and going to his elder brother, Kiepavi, the father of Gori^co, shot him dead and killed his domesticated cassowary, his dog, and his pig. Nothing was done in the matter, no sides were taken, and no compensation paid by either party. Kiepavi was eaten, together with his pig, dog, and cassowary, each being cooked in a separate oven. Ajo^ce was buried.

Nori of Kogu, elder brother to Kama, was working in his father's garden when his younger brother, Porare^cna, shot him dead. The reasons were the same as in the preceding case. Kama carried Nori back to his village and placed his body in state. He then got his bow and arrows [3] and wounded Arojabu, lineage son of Porare^cna. Various members of the lineage carried Arojabu back to the men's house, where his wound was treated; others chased Kama, shooting arrows at him but without effect. Kokote, a classificatory brother of Kama, helped him; and they shot Porare^cna's young daughter, Ario. Various members of the parallel lineages then turned their attention to Kokote and ran after him, too, shooting. The affair then settled down while Kama buried Nori, and a mortuary feast was held. Kemiju men who were *noka* and *aku* to Nori later exhumed his body and cut it up for a feast. Afterward hostility flared up once more. Supporters of Arojabu and Ario threatened Kama and shot at him, forcing him to leave Kogu as a refugee for Fomu. By similar pressure they forced Kokote to leave for Kemiju. It was primarily because of this that Kokote later split from his former lineage and set up his own, forming a new house-place. When Ario and Arojabu had completely recovered from their arrow wounds, Kama and Kokote returned to Anonana, adjoining Kogu, where they remained for some time at Watapi. A little later a pig festival was held at Kogu. Kama and Kokote gave gifts of pork to Arojabu and the girl, and the breach was healed.

Repercussions extended laterally and involved the taking of sides. Conflicting personal loyalties split normal clan and village solidarity. But even

[2] Ajo^ce was an elder brother of Kama. For slightly different versions of these two cases obtained from women, see Catherine Berndt (n.d.).

[3] In all cases of fighting, whether of the intra- or interdistrict variety, an arrow used to shoot a certain person is chosen from a bundle and its name remembered. There are several dozen varieties of arrows. In this case Kama selected a *katia*.

though Kama and Kokote were forced to flee the district for a time and seek refuge elsewhere, this cannot be said to have been due to pressure of group opinion and action. It was primarily on the personal level, and a commentary on their relative strength at that particular time. When aid is sought or given during intravillage dissension, those who stand together are not necessarily recognized as full or close kin. Kokote, for example, is a Kogu-affiliated man, a classificatory brother to Kama in a relationship not genealogically traceable, having genealogical ties with Anonana. On the other hand, in externally focused dissension brothers and patri-kin stand (generally speaking) as one. For general purposes, then, co-resident patri-kin may be caught up in quarrels among themselves; but once they are attacked from the outside, internal troubles are expected to disappear or be submerged in collective action.

But not all intravillage dissension leads directly to killing. A few blows, or arrows, or merely hard words may be exchanged between opposing persons or sides.

Five men were occupied in their gardens at Kogu—Nagajagani and Kiki^{c}o, who were full brothers, and their lineage brothers Kafajagi and Ta^{c}ona,[4] in addition to a lineage father, Hafoza. Their gardening land adjoined, and their separate plots were not clearly demarcated; but they all knew the approximate extent of each. Hafoza came down from the upper part of his plot and began to plant vegetables in the section belonging to Kiki^{c}o and his brother. Kiki^{c}o pointed out that Hafoza had overstepped his area, and he marked the dividing line by inserting an upright post. Hafoza pulled it out, threw it aside, and continued planting on Kiki^{c}o's side. Kiki^{c}o grew angry, and a heated argument ensued between them, each accusing the other of trespassing. Igena, full brother to Hafoza, then made his appearance and struck Kiki^{c}o, and a fight began, Hafoza joining in. Nagajagani began to hit Igena. Kafajagi took Kiki^{c}o's part; Ta^{c}ona threw himself at Kafajagi. By this time most of the villagers were on the scene, arguing at the tops of their voices the rights and wrongs of the case. Nusa^{c}e, a lineage brother of Kiki^{c}o, Nagajagani, Kafajagi, and Ta^{c}ona, and a lineage son of Hafoza and Igena, joined in the fight against Kiki^{c}o. Nagabara, who belonged to another village, classificatory brother to Nusa^{c}e but aku to the others, began to fight Nusa^{c}e, against whom he had a personal grudge. The whole village was now in an uproar. The wives of the men with their kin and friends were taking sides, and men were running from adjacent villages to join in the general scramble; others were rushing to their houses to get their weapons. The luluai of Kogu, Noka, intervened; gradually the fighting was brought to a standstill, and nothing else was done in the matter. Kiki^{c}o, who considered himself to be the wronged party, collected together his belongings and with his wife made an abortive attempt to leave Kogu for

4 Kiki^{c}o was elder brother to Nagajagani; Kafajagi younger lineage brother to Kiki^{c}o; Ta^{c}ona younger lineage brother to Kiki^{c}o and Kafajagi; Ta^{c}ona and Kafajagi elder lineage brothers to Nagajagani.

Kemiju. Sinotaba, *nefaru* to Nusa^c^e and lineage brother to Kiki^c^o, lineage son to Hafoza and Igena, and *aku* to Nagabara, persuaded him to remain.

The case is interesting because it shows how rapidly a quarrel can spread, drawing in people from other villages. Wives of male participants often take their cue from the men, and before long the original cause may be lost sight of and personal grudges come to the surface. The extent to which such petty quarreling and fighting become serious depends on factors of internal control. In the above example the *luluai*, as nominal representative of the Administration in Kogu, was thought to have power to enforce his order that the fighting should stop; his threat was upheld by remote alien authority. It succeeded because the people concerned knew that should they resist he would appeal to the Administration or its direct agents, the native police, and the ringleaders would be brought before an informal court and punished.

Breaches between District Lineages

Breaches between members of various lineages within the district are settled on a personal basis (i.e., by self-help), in much the same way as those occurring within the village. Social conscience in such matters becomes articulate only when affinal kin or members of other districts are implicated.

Jave of Kogu, wife of Kama of Kogu, was planting in her husband's garden a fringe of crotons, some taken from the nearby garden belonging to her husband's *noka* [sister's husband], Ena^c^o. Kama and Ena^c^o belonged to adjacent villages of Kogu, but their gardens adjoined. Ena^c^o angrily accused Jave both of trespassing and of stealing his plants; and taking up a stone ax he hit her about the head. Jave called to her husband, who came running. He and Ena^c^o began to quarrel, and fought together, using sticks. Next morning Ena^c^o approached Kama with overtures of friendship. They collected vegetable foods from their gardens and held a feast to settle the matter. None of the other men took sides in this dispute.

In some cases a killing within the district but outside the village is not followed by retaliation or by the planting of a croton to signify that revenge has been taken, although compensation of some sort is almost invariably given. In other cases it appears that retaliation does occur, as in interdistrict fighting; but the difference lies in the fact that the procedure is not clearly defined and rests on individual decision and action. Nevertheless, the scope for interpersonal and intervillage or interclan conflict is much greater than if only two or more co-villagers were concerned. There is more opportunity for units, as contrasted with persons, to be at odds with one another. Through the action of two or more of its members, one village may find itself opposed to another within the same district. This is rare, although examples have been recorded for some of the larger units, like Ke⁣ᶜjagana, Kemiju, Moke, and Ora. But however serious an intradistrict offense may be, a common tendency is to "play down" its importance for the sake of district unity, and if this is not possible to let the matter be handled by individuals who are directly and personally concerned.

When Kokote was a small child his father, Mota, was killed, allegedly by *naglisa* sorcery projected by a classificatory brother, Tamaja, living in an adjacent village. It was a question of jealousy over a woman. Mota died as he was cooking a small animal in the ashes of a fire in front of the men's house. Some years later, before Kokote had killed his first man, he happened to be practicing with his bow and arrows in front of the men's house. Unknowingly he placed a banana bud where his father's fire had been and using it as a mark began to shoot at it; his companions did the same. His lineage father, Noguᶜmu, watching nearby, remarked that this was the very spot where Kokote's father had been killed by sorcery, and the fact that Kokote was shooting arrows there indicated that he would avenge the death. Kokote then asked him who had been responsible for the sorcery. Angrily intent on revenge, he straightaway went in search of Tamaja's son, Tamiavena, and shot him dead. News of the killing soon spread, and men from both villages concerned gathered around Kokote asking why he had done it. Kokote told them. Nothing else was said in the matter; but Kokote and his lineage father and brothers collected together shells, ropes of bush beads, salt, arrows, waist bands, and skirts and gave them to the men of the village to which Tamiavena belonged. A croton was planted over Mota's grave.

Something has already been said about marital dissension. What happens in such cases when a man and wife belong to the same district? In a minor disagreement, kin of both the protagonists may be involved, as contrasted with what usually takes place when they come from different districts and most of the affines, if not all, are at a distance. Conventionally a husband has a considerable measure of authority over his wife, whether or not she comes from another district; but his lineage kin, especially those who have supplied some or all of the bridewealth, feel they have a right to interfere. A dispute between husband and wife remains largely a personal affair, a matter only for themselves and his kin, unless she appeals directly to her own kin; but if they live in the same district, in fairly close contact, she may not need to take the initiative. Quarrels of this sort on an intradistrict basis usually involve persons rather than units. They may lead to cleavages in local opinion, when this is formulated at all; when it is, this is normally on a local or kin basis, and does not involve the political unit as such. Where interdistrict marriage

Actors in ceremonial farces (discussed in Chapters 7 and 9).

Two participants in ceremonial drama, one dressed as a woman, at Maira (see Chapter 9).

Row of dancing men with bows and arrows, wearing cassowary plumes, during ceremony at Maira.

Two participants in ceremony at Pintagori. The man on the left wears a bird of paradise feather through his nasal septum; the man on the right, wearing a gourd mask, represents a spirit.

Two participants in a ceremony at Maira, wearing gourd masks and cassowary plumes, the eye and mouth apertures edged with corn. They represent bush spirits.

is concerned, public opinion is likely to be directed against the wife or husband, as the case may be, as representative of another and potentially hostile unit; and the resulting procedure may be termed legal. The behavior of the kin on either side, when they are able to have direct dealings with one another, does not differ radically whether they belong to the same district or not. The distinction rests on the relative crystallization of public opinion.

We shall consider two such cases. The first is an example of minor dissension between husband and wife, showing how other kin are drawn in:

Inaguja, a Kogu woman, was married to I'iva, also of Kogu. Although in a fairly advanced stage of pregnancy, she went to her garden to work. Her husband, with his *nenafu* Egina, also of Kogu [Egina called Inaguja "wife of my *nenafu*," or *nenafu*, and on I'iva's death would be eligible to marry her], decided to collect wild pandanus nuts growing near the garden at a small swamp in which lived a dangerous bush spirit. I'iva called out to his wife, telling her what they intended to do, and warned her to leave the garden and return to the village: "If you remain nearby in the garden this spirit, being disturbed by our cutting of the nuts, will emerge from the swamp and kill the spirit of the child within you. Later, when we have finished collecting them, you may return to the garden." Inaguja replied, "What is this you say? I can go on working!" Egina had gone on to the clump of pandanus and climbed one tree, while I'iva went over to remonstrate with his wife. But she was in a cantankerous mood and without saying anything further took up her digging stick and brought it down on his head. Blood flowed from his nostrils and mouth. I'iva's mother, Egasi, rushed up to her unconscious son and held his hand in great consternation. "What is the matter with you, Inaguja?" she asked. But Inaguja, without answering, lifted her digging stick and hit the old woman on the knee so that she too fell down beside her son. Egina, who had stopped to watch all this, saw that I'iva remained without moving. Thinking the matter serious, he called out to I'iva's younger brother, Ko'uja, who was in the village nearby: "Inaguja has felled your brother, who is lying here: and she has hit your mother, too." Ko'uja came rushing up with his bow and arrows and took aim ready to shoot. Inaguja, afraid, ran to the garden fence; as she was climbing over, Ko'uja shot her in the back, wounding her and she fell to the ground. In a rage Ko'uja continued shooting at the digging stick beside her, at the ground around her, and at sugar cane nearby. Having dissipated his anger he called out, "This woman fights my brother. I saw what was happening, and I became hot belly, and so I shot her. Come and carry her!" Inaguja's brother, Viagupa, now made his appearance and carried her into the village. Egina went over to I'iva and his mother and massaged them and, with Ko'uja, carried them back to the village where warmed leaves were applied to their wounds.

Another Kogu man, Ano'ja, elder clan brother to Egina and *nenafu* to both I'iva and Inaguja, approached old Juta', of Kogu, the father of I'iva and Ko'uja, saying, "Ko'uja has shot at your *nanoferu* [son's wife]." Catching up his bow and arrows and a stone ax, Juta' went to the house in which Ko'uja and I'iva were and called to them, "Come outside, you two. I have heard what has happened. Why did you shoot Inaguja? I worked hard to 'buy' this woman!" I^{c}iva, who had recovered, grabbed a stone ax and made as if to hit the old man, cutting him on the forehead. The old man collapsed crying and lay full length on his back. I^{c}iva placed the ax on his chest and ran away. Ko^{c}uja called after him, "Oh, I^{c}iva, I helped you over this woman, and I shot her. But why have you hit this old man, our father?" Drawing his bow he shot at I^{c}iva as he ran, wounding him in the thigh. I^{c}iva, who was not seriously injured, approached O^{c}zjura [his *nenafu*, elder full brother to Egina, who called Juta^c *aku*] for aid. Arrow shots were exchanged between I^{c}iva and O^{c}zjura, Ko^{c}uja and Ano^{c}ja. This continued until I^{c}iva called a halt and offered compensation. He killed a pig and gave it to his father, who had recovered, and another pig to Oz^{c}jura and Egina. The matter was considered settled. No payments were made to the wife, nor did her brother interfere.

Inaguja was not seriously wounded and soon recovered and returned to her husband. She later gave birth to a stillborn child. Her husband then said to her, "I told you so! That bush spirit killed its spirit when you disobeyed me."

Here the principle of "fair play" comes into operation. It hinges ultimately on the principle of reciprocity; but in this particular form it is a feature of intradistrict quarrels, not of those between districts— except from the interpersonal point of view, when the expression of hostility between certain persons depends on the relationship existing between them. Although the emotional content of any given relationship is just as strong in intradistrict affairs (Ko^{c}uja springs to help his brother; I^{c}iva claims aid from his *nenafu*), other considerations or other relationships may cut across it, according to circumstances or personal interests. For instance, Juta^c took the side of his daughter-in-law because she represented for him an outlay of bridewealth, involving personal energy on his part; he was intimately concerned in the matter, for serious injury to her would mean dissipation of these goods without hope of return. In addition, he thought she had been unfairly treated and was ready to take her part against his own son. Inaguja's own brother did not rush to protect her but considered she was to blame for what had happened. Ko^{c}uja made a choice between his father and his brother. This aspect of weighing a situation and taking sides (or abstaining from action altogether) is most noticeable in intradistrict disturbances, where the conventional expectations attaching to certain relationships are not the only factors to be considered. This is not to say that these can be discounted. It means simply that the element of what can be vaguely termed fair play in some situations, or self-interest in others, is of major importance.

The other case is more serious and involves the death of an erring wife. Extramarital activity is common enough and might almost be viewed as expected behavior, yet a husband, while knowing how general is this state of affairs, can view it with great concern when it affects him personally—as an act, moreover, designed by his wife to cause him direct harm by weakening him physically. What is more, within the district he can usually count on the active or passive support of his wife's male kin, including her brothers. Adultery on the part of a wife who belongs to the same district as her husband is likely to be judged more harshly on the whole than if she had come from outside it. As an "outsider," however, she may be potentially more dangerous to him. In that case, too, she can expect help from her male kin, who may be on hostile terms with her husband's district; and in fact this consideration may influence his behavior toward her. Within the district, her male kin would not have the same pressure of conventional antagonism to guide their response; and apart from them, in such a case, she may have no near kin to whom she may turn. (Even should she have *nenafu* or mother's brothers outside the district, she could rely only on their personal support and not on that of their agnatic kin—particularly if they knew that her own agnatic kin did not stand behind her.) On the other hand, the procedure may be taken out of the husband's hands altogether by his own or his wife's male kin.

During her husband's absence in another village, Awari of Ke^jagana, married to Ika^o of Ke^jagana, used to walk about at night, soliciting men.[5] Her husband's lineage kin knew about this, for some of them were personally involved. Mato^o, a clan brother of Ika^o and *tultul* of Henagaru, although really of Ke^jagana, approached her and complained that she was "making the men no good!" In response she asked for coitus. At this he became "hot belly." Seizing her by the arm, he took her to her father, Uau^c of Ke^jagana, and told him what was happening. They then took her to the gardens, where Uau^c held her while Mato^o shot her. Returning to the village, he called her brothers and told them where to find the body. With Uau^c, they carried her back to her house and laid her on a platform. The brothers got together their weapons and shields, and leaving the village waited in ambush near the road leading to the next village along which Mato^o was expected to come. Some friends warned him, and with Ika^o, who had returned, and his father, Fanofa, he too armed himself. Then Mato^o and Ika^o took the low road, while Fanofa came along the top road where the dead woman's brothers were waiting. On seeing him they emerged from their hiding place, but did not shoot Fanofa: "It is not good that we should shoot you. You have nothing to do with this." Then they went down to the other road, where shots were exchanged between them and Mato^o and Ika^o. When this had gone on for some time without anyone's being injured, the brothers asked that

---

[5] Unlike ordinary adultery or occasional extramarital intercourse, referred to by the usual terms for coitus, relatively blatant soliciting and consistent wandering around after men at night is termed *gumaja*, "stealing," or "theft." The inference is that the woman is stealing something (i.e., strength) which belongs not only to her husband but also to members of his lineage or village who have contributed to her bridewealth.

"pay" [compensation] be given them to settle the affair. This was agreed on, and they all returned to the village. Mato͡o and Ika͡o killed a pig and gave it with shells, waist bands, and so on to the dead woman's brothers, who returned to their village. Awari's body was buried but was exhumed by the women of Ika͡o's village, who cooked and ate it.

Awari's husband was not initially concerned and had no hand in her death. This was accomplished in conjunction with her own father, who sanctioned the shooting. Had he not done so, or had it been left for Ika͡o himself to take action, the affair might have gone differently. Her brothers reacted in the conventional way, ignoring the collaboration of Uau͡, but ready to accept terms and press for compensation rather than retaliate by killing (as they could have done quite easily when Fanofa came among them). Acceptance of compensation for the death of a sister, even when she is killed by her husband or his kin, is a preferred means of settlement in intradistrict disputes.

Intradistrict Theft

When property is stolen within the village or district, we find the same absence of organized measures for coping with the situation. Responsibility for defending personal property or punishing an offender is primarily an individual matter, although the punishment itself may have further consequences, bringing in other persons who consider themselves to be intimately concerned. Any action taken against a thief may provoke some sort of retaliation, while settlement in terms of compensation may also be sought, perhaps simultaneously. All procedure of this kind is on a personal basis and, as such, is non-legal. Cases of theft when members of other districts are concerned may provoke aggressive action far beyond what seems warranted by the relative value of the goods involved. The action against an offender may be fairly mild or it may comprise torture or death. It bears no consistent relationship to the type of commodity stolen or the kinship ties between the protagonists. Generally speaking, it depends on the offended person's inclinations and temper at the time, including consideration of past grudges, jealousy, or the attitude of the thief's kin toward him, and so on, influenced by the strong conventional condemnation of theft as an infringement of human rights. Because theft is regarded as an offense against the person in much the same sense as is a physical injury or a murder, it is likely to provoke similar consequences. It might seem possible, in view of the leniency shown to some offenders, to draw a distinction between offenses against property and offenses against the person. But leniency is no gauge. Thus in some intradistrict killings no steps may be taken, while others may bring severe penalties.

Anua of Kogu stole some tobacco leaves from the garden of his clan father, Apanofi, living in the same village. Apanofi noticed that some leaves were missing and following the tracks came to Anua. When asked, Anua denied any knowledge of the theft. Apanofi then drew his bow and shot at him, but without injuring him; arrow shots were exchanged harmlessly between them. Finally a halt was called, Anua killed a pig, the two ate together, and the affair was settled.

This is the simplest reaction to theft, except when for personal reasons the offended party does not proceed; he may, for instance, be "weak" in comparison with the thief. Only two parties are involved in this case. In others a number of persons may be drawn in on either side.

At Kogu a number of youths had been collecting pandanus nuts and were cooking and eating them. Old Igegu^{c}a, a lineage grandfather to them, had waited expectantly for some, but as they were not forthcoming complained, "Some people give me these!" The youths replied jeeringly, "Before, you ate! You have only decayed teeth, we have new teeth. We can eat!" Igegu^{c}a became angry and went to Negivi with his ax and some rope to collect pandanus nuts for himself. Having obtained a large quantity he was bundling them together when the youths came up to him and asked for some. He replied that as they had refused to give him any of theirs he would give them none of his. When they had gone he took the nuts to his garden, where he buried some. The rest he took home to the village, where he set about cooking and eating them. While he was so occupied another old man, Marepe^{c}na, a younger brother to him, came up and asked for a share. Igegu^{c}a refused on the grounds that among the youths who had withheld nuts from him were several sons of Marepe^{c}na: "Your sons cut pandanus nuts and ate them themselves without giving me any. I have hands, I have feet; thus I went myself and cut these nuts, cooking and eating them myself. I won't give you any." Marepe^{c}na was angry and turned away. Later he hid in the garden and watched Igegu^{c}a obtaining more nuts from the hiding place. That night, by moonlight, Marepe^{c}na went to the garden, found the hole, and dug up the nuts; he filled up his net bags and returned to Ta^{c}nefi, where he was living. Next morning he set to work cooking them, but was interrupted by his wife, Gubaja^{c}o of Kemiju, who asked how he had obtained them: "You didn't go into the bush. Where did you get them from? Perhaps some men stole them!" But he replied that he had been to the bush and cut them.

While Marepe^{c}na and his wife were talking, a young man, Timere^{c}gu, son of Igegu^{c}a, was passing on his way from the bush where he had been hunting birds. "Where were you in the bush?" he asked his father's brother. "Where did you cut these nuts?" "I was in the bush," insisted Marepe^{c}na. "There I cut them and now I am cooking them!" "Good," replied Timere^{c}gu. He gave Gubaja^{c}o one of the birds he had caught, and was given some sweet potatoes in return. Then he went to his father and told him, "Marepe^{c}na has stolen the nuts you hid in the garden. I saw him cooking them." Igegu^{c}a went to the garden and finding the nuts gone returned crying to the village. His son comforted him by saying, "Do not cry. Your son remains, he is not dead!" With this he picked up a net bag and went to Marepe^{c}na's house, where he found the nuts spread out. He quickly put most into his bag, leaving a few for Marepe^cna because he had gone to the trouble of cooking them. But at this moment Marepe^cna returned and seeing Timere^cgu taking the nuts he seized a piece of firewood and began hitting him about the head. Timere^cgu hit back, and called for his father. Igegu^ca came rushing up with a stone ax and finding his son lying on the ground hit Marepe^cna on the head. Egina of Kogu, whose sister was married to Igegu^ca, came up to help his *noka* and *aku*, lifting up Timere^cgu and hitting Marepe^cna. Another Kogu man, Ka^ceavu, *noka* to Marepe^cna, sprang to his help, fighting Igegu^ca. O^czjura, brother of Ka^ceavu, came to the help of Igegu^ca, whom he called lineage father, as he did Marepe^cna. By this time Marepe^cna's head was streaming with blood; a halt was called. He left Kogu and in this condition went to Moiife where lived several of his *nenafu*. When they saw the blood they were enraged and catching up their weapons returned with him. There they came upon Igegu^ca with Kokote, his adopted son, and arrow shots were exchanged between them. Kokote called out, "Why have you come you *nenafu*? What are you seeking?" And Igegu^ca offered compensation, which was agreed on. He then killed a pig and offered it to Marepe^cna, who also killed one and offered it to Igegu^ca; an oven was made, and all who had participated joined in the feasting; the two men embraced in friendship.

Marepe^cna, in appealing to his *nenafu* in another district (who were also *nenafu* to Igegu^ca), did so on an interpersonal basis with, so we are told, no intention of embroiling the whole of Moiife. It is conventional that *nenafu* should help *nenafu* in such matters, even taking sides with one against another. But as others outside this relationship are drawn into the argument there is more likelihood of an interdistrict rupture. The weakening effect which Marepe^cna's action had on his own village and district is obvious.

Theft may involve the supreme penalty, death:

A young unmarried Kogu girl, Ja^co, stole some salt from the house of her classificatory father, the same Marepe^cna. Finding the salt gone, he traced her to her house and began to beat her with a stick. She struggled and hit back. Two other men, Pinumaja and Krosi, lineage sons to Marepe^cna, grabbed their bows and arrows. They drew their bows and, dancing forward and backward, began to sing; coming near the girl they pretended to shoot but turned and danced away. Finally they danced forward and shot her. She cried out and fell back dead. Some Kogu women took her body to the gardens at Itojapa, cut it up, and cooked it; later they rubbed her bones with pig's grease and buried them there. No action was taken by the girl's near kin, no compensation was paid to anyone, and neither Marepe^cna nor his two lineage sons were censured for what they had done.

Although the girl was young and unmarried, her death deprived her kin of the bridewealth in which reasonably they could have expected to share in due course. Their apathy in the face of this may have been due in part to the emphasis on male dominance, which encourages men to show much less concern for the rights of a woman. Nevertheless, a woman can generally rely on her brothers. Here, we assume, they were influenced by the fact that relatively close patri-kin were involved; but had the victim been a man, this consideration would possibly not have restrained them. This is not to suggest that male dominance will of itself prevent men from helping a kinswoman or others from taking her part. But it is possible to say that punishment varies in severity according to the strength of the offender. It may, for instance, be harsher when a child or a woman is concerned—not because these are equated in status, but because taken into account will be men's conventional attitude toward women. Conversely, of course, the degree of severity may depend on the relative strength of the offended person. A woman, for instance, cannot normally retaliate, as a man can, by direct physical action against an adult male, although she may do so against a female offender or a child. Instead, conventionally, she resorts to sorcery; but there are exceptions to this.

Tagemusano, wife of Kikituwoifa of Numparu, went to the garden of her husband's elder brother Numatigiᶜa and broke some sugar cane.[6] She was observed in the act by Numatigiᶜa, who asked her, "You, woman, who gave you permission to break sugar here?" "I looked at my brother's garden and wanted this sugar, and so I broke it," she replied.[7] Numatigiᶜa, without saying anything further, took hold of Tagemusano and threw her to the ground. He took up a bamboo knife and proceeded to cut between each of her fingers, first on one hand and then on the other. She was too much afraid of him to cry or call out but defecated and urinated in fear.[8] He then chewed a wild ginger root and sprayed it on the open cuts to increase the pain. He did the same with the toes on each

[6] A wife has no right to take produce from the garden of her husband's brother. In some cases she may assume this right in regard to his younger brother, presuming on the expectation that the junior levirate may one day operate in her favor. The term used in the above case is *gumaja*, stealing.

[7] She was referring to the fact that as Numatigiᶜa was her husband's elder brother she called him *nepuᶜnimo* (my elder sibling-of-the-same-sex), and he reciprocated with the term *naganaᶜnimo* (my younger sibling-of-the-same-sex). Conventionally, the use of this term signifies that she views him as a sibling, not as an affine, and consequently expects help from him as she would from her own siblings. She has no right to help herself from his gardens; but in her reply she suggests that she equates him with her own brothers, into whose gardens she may go at any time to collect produce. Numatigiᶜa is not swayed by this suggestion.

[8] Numatigiᶜa, it should be mentioned, seems to have been generally much feared. He was a powerful warrior and strong man; according to comments, he was "a man no good," ready to quarrel with anyone, unwilling to participate in co-operative endeavors or fulfil his obligations. It was said, "All the men and women are frightened of him (i.e., he is unpredictable); no one will steal from his garden; no one will sleep in his house!" (Cf. Bateson's reference, 1936, pp. 161–63, to the two admired types of men among the Iatmul, the violent and the discreet: a man who lives up to the former ideal may be criticized for that very reason.)

foot. He left her lying unable to move and returned to the village, where, expecting trouble as a result of his action, he got together his bow and arrows and his ax and waited. It was not long before some Numparu men found Tagemusano, almost unconscious, lying in the garden, and called out to Kikituwoifa telling him what had presumably happened. Kikituwoifa, in a rage, asked his brother if this were true. Numatigi^{c}a, from the security of the house, explained. Tagemusano was then carried into the village and placed in her house. Her husband killed a pig and placed it before her. He got his bow and arrows and sat some little distance away from Numatigi^{c}a and spoke to him: "She stole from your garden, and you have punished her. Let us now embrace in friendship." [Kikituwoifa had no intention of doing this but was hoping to entice his brother outside.] Numatigi^{c}a replied that he would not come out. Kikituwoifa, becoming impatient, approached the house with drawn bow. Numatigi^{c}a came out, but just as his brother was about to release an arrow some of his male lineage kin took hold of him and prevented him. Eventually they persuaded him to leave Numatigi^{c}a. He returned to his wife's house. The pig was cut up and cooked, and he gave her some to eat. Next day, his anger had not cooled. He took up his position behind some bushes near the doorway of Numatigi^{c}a's house, waiting for him to emerge so that he could shoot him. Again his male lineage kin intervened and warned Numatigi^{c}a that his brother waited outside. This went on for several days; on each occasion the elder brother was warned and remained inside. By this time Tagemusano was feeling much better and was able to hobble about. Numatigi^{c}a then offered to compensate his younger brother, and this was accepted. He killed a pig and placed with it some skirts, rope, and paper; to reciprocate, Kikituwoifa also killed a pig. The meat was cooked and a feast held, and the affair was settled.

Punishment of this sort, involving "mild" torture of the culprit, has its appeal to the person performing it. The stated intention is to teach the offender a lesson. But although it is by no means rare, usually more direct punishment seems to be preferred. The fact that Numatigi^{c}a armed himself, awaiting events, indicates that he knew his behavior was not acceptable. Yet it would be unwise to press this point, for even the mildest punitive measure may provoke retaliation by the kin of the injured party.

Take the example of a Numparu youth, Fio^{c}eva, who developed sores. These became so severe that it was decided to segregate him, and a small house was built in the bush not far from the village. Each day his father, Afunopia, brought him food; but one day Fio^{c}eva stole some salt from Zonega^{c}au, his lineage father. Discovering who had taken it, Zonega^{c}au went to Afunopia, his lineage brother, requesting that a like amount be returned to him. Afunopia replied that this was bad, but later, when a pig was killed and he had salt available, he would give him some. Zonega^{c}au was apparently satisfied, but he continued to brood about the stolen salt. Going to Fio^{c}eva's house, he found him eating salt. In a rage he seized the youth, cut off part of one ear, and forced it into his mouth; then he cut off part of the other ear, and pushed that in, too. Fio^{c}eva was so frightened that he did not cry out. Zonega^{c}au then picked up the remainder of the salt and returned home, where he prepared his bow and arrows, expecting trouble from his lineage brother. Fio^c^eva ran to his father and showed him what had happened. Taking up his bow and arrows, Afunopia went in search of Zonega^c^au. After the two had exchanged a few arrows, a halt was called, and Zonega^c^au offered some salt to Fio^c^eva. Afunopia promised to give a pig to Zonega^c^au; and Fio^c^eva returned to his bush house.

Some few days after, when the salt was eaten, Fio^c^eva again stole some from Zonega^c^au. This time Zonega^c^au, holding him securely, cut between his fingers on each hand, rubbing salt into the wounds. He then rubbed a stick with salt and forced it up each nostril in turn [as in the nose-bleeding ritual]. Then he hit the boy about the head with a stick until blood flowed and left him lying unconscious. Afunopia, bringing his son's food, found him in this state. In a rage he picked up a stick, rushed to Zonega^c^au, and began to strike him. The two men fought until Afunopia dealt the other a severe blow on the head. Zonega^c^au called out to his son, Ikase^c^na, lineage brother to Fio^c^eva, to come to his aid; he did so, hitting Afunopia on the head. The fighting continued for some little time, until Afunopia offered compensation. He killed a dog and offered it to Zonega^c^au, who refused it and asked for a pig. Afunopia then killed a pig and gave it to him. Ikase^c^na also killed one and gave it to Fio^c^eva, who had now recovered and was being treated by his mother. Zonega^c^au killed one and gave it to his son. A feast was held, and they embraced one another in friendship.

Violent as was Zonega^c^au's treatment of Fio^c^eva, the resentment it engendered in his father was not so severe as to show unequivocal condemnation of it, and settlement was achieved in a relatively short time. The desire to cause suffering and humiliation to the culprit through violent action (apart from the ordinary procedure of beating with a stick or shooting with an arrow) will appear again in the setting of the informal courts.

Two Moiife men, Ifia^c^mu and Biwa, full brothers, stole an Irafu pig and brought it back to their village, where they left it under the protection of another Moiife man, Asai^c^, their *nenafu*. Kegu^c^, a Tira^c^e youth adopted by Waribu of Moiife [taking his kin relationship from his adoptive father] was a classificatory son to Ifia^c^mu and Biwa [Waribu being a father's brother's son to them] as well as to Asai^c^ [Waribu being his *nenafu*]. He stole the pig and ate it alone in the bush. Kau^c^o, elder brother to Asai^c^, *nenafu* to the other three men, and classificatory father to Kegu^c^, came on him finishing his feast. Such was his anger that he struck Kegu^c^; taking a rope he fastened it with a slip-knot about his neck and dragged him along the ground. Kegu^c^ cried out, "My father, let me go!" But Kau^c^o took no notice and struck him again, severely injuring him. Then he dug a fairly deep hole, threw the boy into it, and partially covered it up, placing a large log over it; all the time the boy kept crying. Kau^c^o returned to the village, where it was generally believed that Kegu^c^ had absconded with the pig to Tira^c^e. Next morning Kau^c^o came to the hole and could still hear Kegu^c^ crying faintly. He left him there and returned to the village. Next day he came again and still heard a faint whimper. On the following day he visited the grave and could hear no sound; he then filled in the hole with the rest of the earth.

Tiraᶜe after a time became suspicious of the disappearance of Keguᶜ, but it was not until Asaiᶜ's son succumbed to sorcery that the story came out. It was divined that Tiraᶜe had projected *naglisa*, and Kauᶜo indicated the probable reason for this, detailing what he had done. Waribu took no action because the boy had been an adopted son and feeling against Tiraᶜe was running high after Asaiᶜ's son's death.

This represents an extreme case, and such action taken against a culprit is relatively rare; yet it conforms to the general pattern of violent behavior, with a willingness to inflict pain on others if in a position to do so. This callousness is culturally determined and not indicative of a "psychopathological" state.

Conclusion

The conclusion of this chapter brings us to the end of Part 4, which has been concerned with coercive aspects of social control and with the various settings in which such control is exerted in greater or lesser degree. Suicide, sorcery, warfare, cannibalism, and the settlement of internal disputes have been explored in these terms. There may be disagreement as to the "rightness" of any particular action on the part of the person or persons against whom it is directed. But in all such cases the objection is framed as a specific matter. In a general sense, there is no question as to the acceptability of the means employed. Suicide, sorcery, and warfare are not "wrong" in themselves: they represent legitimate ways of coping with certain situations. What may be regarded as wrong, or unacceptable, is the choice of victims. People who complain about the consequences of sorcery, or warfare, are nonetheless ready to applaud the same procedures in different circumstances, when the outcome is to their advantage. And they are more than willing to make use of such procedures, or claim to do so, on their own account. Even though at any given point in time suicide, sorcery, or warfare may appear to have a disrupting effect on social relations, making for disorder and discontinuity in social affairs, in the long run they can be seen as means of regulating behavior and, in a more general sense, of maintaining order within the social system.

At this juncture, one may well ask, what *is* the social system? We have spoken of it as being co-extensive with the political unit, the district, but in the light of the last few chapters that assumption needs to be reviewed. A social system should be relatively self-contained, if not entirely so. It should include all those ingredients, both social and cultural, which its members consider essential to their existence. Is this the case with the district, the political unit? The fairly clear definition of principles underlying relations between districts, individual neutrality notwithstanding, contrasts with the absence of sanctions governing behavior toward members of other districts with whom no kin ties are acknowledged. (Treatment of enemy dead is a pertinent example.) But the same absence of formal sanctions marks intradistrict relations, in which, ideally, members should remain consistently on amicable terms. Controls operate to preserve the integrity of the district, not only in such matters as warfare and sorcery, but also as far as intradistrict breaches are concerned. Ostensibly, each district might appear to be an independent unit. It produces sufficient food to meet its own requirements. It can recruit members internally, as between its various segments, through marriage as well as through birth and adoption, with no need to draw upon outside sources. It has its own system of authority: its warrior leaders and religious leaders, its rules and practices relating to such matters as training its new members and reinforcing the appropriate attitudes and values of those who have reached adulthood.

But this independence is only nominal. There are other such units throughout the region, all viewed as socially equivalent despite the actual disparities between them—and all looking to others, outside themselves, as a necessary part of their social perspective. In other words, each is a subsystem, part of a whole, incomplete unless seen in relation to others. The real (functional) social system[9] is the wider interactory zone of opposition and co-operation or, to put it in a different way, the zone of political influence, of which any given district at any given time can be seen as the center. It influences the regulation of behavior within the district as well as between that district and all others within that zone. Broadly, it is thus possible to say that the controls we have been considering operate to maintain a form of balance between the units involved. This is demonstrated in the fluctuating range of friendship and hostility, opposition and co-operation, marriage and fighting, alliances and cleavages.[10] While in one sense such controls serve to sustain antagonism and

[9] See T. Parsons (1952, pp. 6, 19).

[10] For example, the zone of interaction centering on the Usurufa district of Kogu involves (in 1953), excluding alliances for fighting purposes, thirty-nine districts: all those in the Usurufa language unit, some Kamano, Jate, Fore and Koga. This is worked out on the basis of information from genealogies, which can be taken to cover a period of approximately fifty years. The reference here is in summary only. A fuller discussion of both procedure and content is still in manuscript form. The Kogu-centered interactory sphere, conceptualized from this point of view, is conveniently divided into four sections:

A = major sphere of intensive interaction (four districts are involved, plus Kogu).
B = supplementary major sphere, distinguished by the occurrence of more marriages and fewer killings (three districts are involved, plus Kogu).

enmity between districts, they also serve to stabilize the relations between them, in terms of intermittently co-operative endeavor, by pointing to the area of common understanding and common expectations within which such action takes place. It is in this way that social order is maintained: the balancing between conflict and co-operation, one cross-cutting the other, makes it clear that, whatever impression one might get from a single example at a single point in time, there is no question here of "normlessness" or anomie.

C=secondary sphere of intensive interaction (five districts are involved, plus Kogu).
D=spasmodic fighting and occasional marriages (remaining districts, twenty-seven, plus Kogu).

Some 66 per cent of the total Kogu male deaths by arrow are attributed to sphere A, as are 62 per cent of all the cases of sorcery and 41 per cent of the total marriages contracted by Kogu men; 61 per cent of Kogu women (that is, lineage members) are said to have been killed by members of districts within sphere A, while 41 per cent of their total marriages took place within this area. If we include sphere C as well, these two account for the greater number of killings and marriages involving Kogu. However, while most killings are confined to sphere A, the majority of marriages is shared between spheres A and B. Interaction is localized mainly within spheres A and B, but a residue is diffused over spheres C and D making the wider interactory zone functionally significant only at its center, and almost nonexistent peripherally.

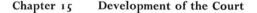

Part 5   Judicial Procedure

Chapter 15   Development of the Court

We have considered so far one type of response to intradistrict offenses, identifying it as non-legal. But should such a response be supported by majority opinion, or what passes for majority opinion, and action against an offender be delegated to a person (or persons) who may not otherwise be directly involved in the affair, it has an essentially legal quality. Typically, the core of the procedure is a meeting of representatives from segments of the unit concerned. The breach is talked over, and suggestions for settling it put forward. These may lead to combined action, or the matter may just be left in the hands of the individuals immediately affected.

The Embryonic Court

Traditionally, this procedure in regard to extradistrict disputes is relatively well-developed. Its focus is the men's house, which has a prominent position in every village. Men congregate there to discuss proposed raids or fights, rituals, and so on. In fact, most matters of vital importance to the district as a whole, or the segment in particular, are deliberated in the men's house before final decisions are made. Personal grievances, too, may be brought up and support requested for some likely course of action. This is especially the case where interdistrict questions are concerned. But these informal meetings are not courts. Nor do they involve any judicial procedure which, through inter- or intradistrict co-operation, could insure that accused persons are brought to trial. They serve mainly to crystallize opinion against an enemy in some specific situation. The opinions expressed are largely controlled or guided by the local "strong men," the warrior leaders. Here, just as much perhaps as in actual fighting, contests for power take place between these men. The ability to talk "strongly" is important to them. Forcefulness in speech is linked significantly with forcefulness in warfare. There is actually little opportunity for all male members at a lineage, village, or district meeting to express their views. Generally they are overridden by the more dominant men, who tend to serve as spokesmen for their respective units and to exercise a fair amount of authority. They do not necessarily act in concert, with uniform opinion.

In this region the concept of the strong man involves continual self-assertion within conventional and traditional confines, setting such a man in opposition to others who contest or are likely to contest his position either within or outside his own village. His strength, however, is relative and is apparent mainly in interdistrict disputes. Where internal breaches are concerned he is hampered considerably, since those immediately involved are personally affected to a greater degree than in the case of outside disputes and prefer to act for themselves. The authority of the village strong men is not enough in itself to influence popular opinion, if that were desired. Further, they do not necessarily represent that opinion as such, although they normally have popular support at times when district and village security is threatened from outside.

These gatherings in the men's house are a vital force in village life. Such meetings have to do mainly with interdistrict affairs on an "official" basis and show much less concern with internal matters. (Interpersonal associations between members of different districts continue more or less independently, except under hostile conditions.)

One problem here is that internal acts which may be considered morally wrong in local terms only give rise to weak sanctions on the basis of popular opinion. Further, the stress on individual strength, for instance, functions to counterbalance or reduce the effectiveness of popular support. But in some cases, for example when an adulterous wife is subjected to plural copulation, there is some social recognition of the punishment and some active support of it. The meeting in the men's house, then, serves as a basis for the emergence of the embryonic court.

Nevertheless, before embryonic courts could become articulated or functionally acceptable, the influence of alien pressure had to be experienced. They owe their existence to this. We can regard them as transition phenomena, a bridge between self-help and other forms of traditional procedure, and informal and administrative courts. They represent an adjustment and absorption of new ideas directly concerned with coercive controls, as manifested also in the informal court. Both may be simultaneously present in a single region. In some instances self-help, on the personal level, may be resorted to; in others, the embryonic court. Usually, however, the embryonic court gives place almost immediately to the informal court presided over by official, semi-official, or self-styled dignitaries.

When the Administration post was established at Kainantu, one of the first routine duties of the officials in charge was to hold courts, before which natives were brought for various offenses.[1] The patrol post became well known as a place of punishment. Although the new reasons for punishment did not always coincide with traditional ones, there was some broad correspondence. It was not long before the judicial system was appreciated[2] as a means of redressing personal wrongs, especially since the measures usually adopted by the natives themselves were frowned on

[1] W. E. H. Stanner (1953, pp. 25–27) discusses very briefly the judicial system in Papua-New Guinea. See also L. A. Mander (1954, pp. 255–57).

[2] By "appreciated" I mean that these people recognized authority substantiated by coercion, the essential ingredients of a judicial system and of other forms of alien control. This corresponded fundamentally with their own traditional concept of authority. See S. W. Reed (1945, p. 173). I do not mean, as Stanner has suggested (*ibid.*, p. 26), that "In spite of bewilderment, irritation and frequent disobedience, the natives developed respect for the incorruptible, implacable and, on the whole, very reasonable working of British law." This assumption has no basis in the situation we are discussing. British law as such, wrapped up as it is in *Native Administrative Ordinances*, is virtually unknown to them, as it is also, I would venture to say, to the native police. What they do know is the outward manifestation, which often bears little or no resemblance to conventional procedure. They fear and respect the Administration because of the power it possesses and the force it may at times use.

Nilles (1953, pp. 20–21) notes that Chimbu natives are heard to say, "That's the law

by the newcomers. The Administration, as it extended its control, banned forcibly most of the approved and traditional means of settling grievances, both within and between districts. All forms of armed combat such as warfare, raiding, and ordinary fighting were strictly forbidden, as well as all acts of homicide (which were punishable) and certain forms of sorcery. However, the Administration was not always able then (or, for that matter, in some cases today) to enforce such measures. The fact that some of these actions were forbidden was not universally understood, because the influence of the Administration has been much more widely experienced and acknowledged in the northern districts than in the south. Yet the official court was seen by these people as an alternative mode of settling differences, of righting wrongs, and of obtaining compensation for injury. When the traditional means of achieving such settlement were formally prohibited, although still not entirely removed, this "new" procedure was fairly rapidly assimilated and resulted in the embryonic court.

The embryonic courts spread thoughout the region in accordance with the extension and intensification of alien control. From the available evidence, it seems that the embryonic court would be already in operation some little time before an area or district was visited by a patrol—and before it was declared "under control." It functioned simultaneously with traditional control mechanisms, being accepted as a congenial innovation in this field. According to local sources, diffusion took place in much the following way:

> The administrative court, when it came to Kainantu, influenced all in its imme-
> diate vicinity. To settle disputes when armed combat was banned, people in
> districts near Kainantu imitated the court system by vesting greater authority in
> their leaders [or, rather, this authority was assumed by the strong men them-
> selves] and by focusing more attention on the meetings held in the men's houses.
> Settlement by armed combat was not precluded and in some cases involved them
> in direct conflict with the Administration. Their "court procedures," however,
> were imperfectly copied by men in adjacent districts who were drawn into them.
> Thus "Warena [Kamano-Agarabe] heard about them from Kainantu, Tevenu
> from Warena, Kanapa from Tevenu, Janabu from Kanapa, Onapina from Janabu,"

---

of the 'kiap' [Administration official] and we have to obey, and we do so because we do not want to go to jail." This would admirably sum up current attitudes toward European law in the eastern Highlands. But to say that the people themselves realize the benefits of the "new" law, that they acknowledge that "justice is done to everybody, to both strong and weak," is to speak in ideal terms, without paying sufficient attention to the empirical situation. To acknowledge that this could eventually be so is another matter altogether.

and so on; while "Waruna men went to Fomu to hear about them, Jurinavi men to Waruna, Fomu men to Jurinavi, Viteve men to Fomu, Irafu men to Viteve, Musa^cve men to Irafu, Kapifuna to Musa^cve, Sonofe to Hamaraga, Jababi to Numaga, Numaga men to Jababi, Taja and Forenofiga men to Numaga, Osena men to Taja, Irafu men to Osena, Moiife men to Irafu, Asafina men to Kogu, Kogu men to Asafina, Kemiju men to Kogu," and so on, southward through the region.

Conventional as this picture appears, with its suggestion of cross-fertilization, it gives some key to the spread of the notion of a court system. That this introduction of new procedure must have involved some alteration in values is true enough, but any reorientation which it occasioned could be attributed to the total effect of alien impact rather than to this aspect of it. On the whole, the spread was evidently less uniform than local accounts imply. Because the procedure was known in one district, that is not to say it was carried out there. Further, as native police came into these parts they held their own courts without reference to the Administration, meting out their own punishments and arranging settlements for their own personal gain. To some degree these molded the course the informal court was to take. In addition there was some interdistrict rivalry; one district instituted court proceedings, why shouldn't the next? This is what is said to have happened in the first embryonic court held at Kemiju, in about 1947.

A woman named Tiogliofa, married to a Moiife man named Pa^cu, deserted him and ran off to Kemiju, where she lived with Kibo^cnipati. Nothing was done immediately in the matter by Pa^cu or his kin. But Arojabu, a Kogu man, the woman's *nenafu* and a classificatory brother of Pa^cu, considered that the best way to settle the affair would be to hold a court. "Other people are making courts, why shouldn't I?" he asked. With this in mind he went to Kemiju and taking the woman by the arm brought her to the cleared place before the men's house. When all the men were assembled, including the strong men, as well as Kibo^cnipati and his male lineage kin, he set out the case, demanding compensation. "My brother 'bought' this woman; you must give me pay," he declared. The matter was discussed and Kibo^cnipati was instructed to give payment to him. Shells, ropes, waist bands, skirts, and so on were handed over. Arojabu returned with them to Kogu and later passed on some to Pa^cu. The affair was settled.

The payment was made by common consent after an amicable discussion by a body of men, led by strong men, who, by pressure of opinion exerted against Kibo^cnipati, obliged him to conform. But such a group did not constitute a judicial body, although it took the form of a rudimentary court. There is no certainty that opinions put forward at such a meeting can be enforced; and when members of other districts are present, as in this case, there is the likelihood of an interdistrict breach. The important point, however, is the substitution for coercion or threat of force, the usual means of settling differences between districts, of settlement by common discussion. This is, then, one function of the embryonic court. It does not do away with settlement by interdistrict fighting and sorcery but it does offer an alternative approach.

When an offense takes place, the offended person may call together a group of men, normally (almost inevitably) including warrior leaders; they hear, quite informally, the circumstances of the case and give approval for him to proceed in a way he, or they, may determine. There is thus likely to be some uniformity of opinion or some agreement here, and the group deciding on the action possibly considers itself representative of local opinion. Yet it has no real power either to enforce its judgments or to regulate the procedure which is carried out by the offended person. Nor is the offended person obliged to refer to this indeterminate representation of political authority.

The use of the embryonic court is more apparent, however, in matters where agreement is necessary or desirable so that any action involved will have majority support, or when help is sought from others, either within the village and district or outside it. This may be relevant in the case of a husband who wishes to proceed against his wife for desertion:

U^{c}ive, a Hafaru woman, went in marriage to Uni^{c}ma of Anonana. After some little time she left him and returned to her mother in Hafaru. While there she had intercourse with two of her *nenafu*, Wagunapavi and Mato^{c}o. This continued until her husband came to Hafaru to recover her; she ran away in fear. Uni^{c}ma eventually managed to find her and took her back to Anonana. He called out to Agura, "Tomorrow I will make a court. You all come." He sent the same message to Kogu. On the following day parties of men arrived from Agura and Kogu and assembled with Anonana men in the village cleared place. U^{c}ive was brought from her house by her husband and placed in the middle. She was then cross-questioned by various men, especially warrior leaders, but not by her husband. The circumstances of the case were already well known, as this had been generally discussed. The objects of the questioning were to establish her guilt by obtaining her admission; to discover who had had intercourse with her, and to dwell on this aspect for its entertainment value; to determine what form the punishment should take; and to administer it. The case in question, then, concerns a wife who has evaded the responsibilities of the marital union by deserting her husband and by adultery. A husband, traditionally, has a right to proceed against his wife on both counts. The questioning took much the following form: "Who copulated with you?" The woman replied, "Wagunapavi." "Who else?" "Mato^{c}o." "Who else?" She denied having had intercourse with others. But again and again the same question was repeated, with details relating to the sexual act. Waufaia of Anonana, elder brother to Uni^{c}ma, then took up a bamboo knife and cut off her skirts, leaving her naked. [The public stripping of a woman is designed to make her ashamed.] The questioning continued along the same lines, discussing her propensity for coitus and likening her desire to a desire for food. The men then took her out into the bush where they copulated with her in turn.

Later they brought her back to the village clearing for the second part of her punishment. Two pegs of wood were driven into the ground. She was placed full length on her back on the ground, her legs wide apart and each fastened with rope to a peg. An Anonana leader, chosen by the group, prepared a length of cane, warming it over a fire ready for the beating. He then began to beat her pubes; she cried out in pain. The men crowded around watching, with women and children on the outskirts. The beating continued until she lost sphincter control, to the amusement of the spectators who constituted the "court." Her husband, sitting among them, made no attempt to interfere; the proceedings were out of his hands. A length of rough-surfaced pandanus wood was then thrust into her vagina and moved up and down. The beating of her pubes continued until she was almost unconscious. Then the men dispersed. Various women of the Anonana villages, including her co-wife, released her and carried her back to her house. Here she was looked after, pig grease and warm water being poured into her vagina and warmed leaves applied to her swollen pubes. The treatment was continued for several days: it was several weeks, however, before she was sufficiently well to move freely. She did not return to her husband but went to Tiroka, where she married Oᶜupati.

The procedure set out here is not uncommon, although varying in severity, and represents an accepted type of punishment meted out to an adulterous wife. It is markedly similar to the proceedings and punishments undertaken by the informal court. It is not a new development, arising out of the superimposition of the embryonic court. This is, on the whole, a traditional way of exacting punishment. But the case demonstrates the main point: a body of men, comprising representatives from at least three districts, have been summoned together, have questioned the offending party, determined her guilt, passed opinion as to punishment, and administered it. The difference between this procedure and that of the informal court rests mainly in the delegation of authority and in the extension of its powers.

The gradual acceptance of such rudimentary courts by various districts has led to the development of the informal court itself. Even this has not meant the disappearance of procedures of self-help, or of the settlement of interdistrict disputes by armed aggressive action, although it has considerably modified and, in the northern areas, virtually replaced the latter. Self-help, without appeal to the court, continues for many minor as well as for a few major matters. Because it is often difficult to distinguish between procedure involving self-help and that involving the rudimentary court, I have called this transitional development embryonic, indicating it as the basis of the more clearly defined informal court. In the embryonic court, then, indigenous leaders of the political unit, or a segment of that unit, play a prominent part when a meeting is called in the event of an internal breach or to discuss settlement of an outstanding liability incurred by or due to a member of that unit (for example, compensation to be paid to an aggrieved husband or his representative). Statements are made on the procedure to be adopted and on the rights and wrongs of the case in question. But judgment rests on the consensus of expressed opinion—or on the most forcefully expressed opinion. It is "representative" of only one sex—and perhaps of only a certain number of members of that. The leaders are not always in a position to enforce the judgment. In most cases there is a struggle between traditional practice, in terms of personal self-help, and an undigested, alien procedure which has not gained sufficient hold, since political authority is relatively weak.

The Informal Court

The people in this area were given no time to adjust themselves to alien control. On the contrary, the change was thrust on them whether they wanted it or not. The more aggressive indigenous forms of control were declared illegal by the agents of external authority, who proceeded (aggressively) to suppress them. The superiority in strength and the apparently unlimited power of the newcomers provoked fear, and this fear was partly responsible for the development of the courts. The germ of the judicial procedure was no doubt alien-inspired, but the necessity to replace some of the coercive controls which had been banned was an important factor in its acceptance. For some little time there seems to have been an atmosphere of indecision, where the occasional use of traditional forms prevailed, as it continues to do in the far south. The change-over, however, was made fairly smoothly and without direct alien interference. There was no direct control of the emerging informal courts. Their very existence remained largely unknown to European officials, but not to the native police, who at times participate in them.[3]

[3] If the different conditions of their emergence are taken into account, a parallel can be found in the native courts which operated on Santa Ysabel during and after the occupation of this territory by the Japanese (see C. Belshaw, 1954, p. 113). These operated with varying success and with varying degrees of friction with the Administration.

Belshaw (op. cit., p. 159) mentions that in the Solomons courts became popular "because they provided a native-controlled justice at a time when European-controlled justice was disliked; but Councils were not so successful for a time since they were not given power and because the people turned them to uses which were incompatible with their existence in a framework of European-controlled administration."

The appearance of the informal court virtually coincides with the rise to power of officially appointed local dignitaries. During the infrequent visits of patrols to this region certain men were dubbed *luluai*, *tultul*, and "boss boy" (or "mouth-boy"). They became the official spokesmen of their respective districts and in some cases wore metal disks around their necks, peaked caps, and lava-lava cloths to indicate their position. Choice was often indiscriminate and rested primarily on the personal judgment of the European official, with minimum reference to the people generally. In some cases traditional war-leaders were chosen; in others, the new leaders did not even belong to the district to which they were allocated and did not correspond with the traditional warrior leaders; and then initial clashes between the "new" and the traditional authorities were almost inevitable. Some adjustment, however, took place, with the warrior leaders occasionally dictating the "policy" of the newly appointed *luluai*, *tultul*, and mouth-boy. The position was not incongruous, since, traditionally, the prestige of the warrior leader depended on individual achievement and strength and was not to any extent ascribed. (Slight evidence of hereditary headmanship is not significant in the context of this discussion.) The new leaders, too, relied on strength for the maintenance of their position. They rose to power through the strength of an alien body and, in turn, behaved aggressively in order to ratify their position. They were officially considered to be representatives as well as leaders of their people, authorized to act for them in all affairs affecting the Administration. They were placed in this position so that they could serve as intermediaries between Government representatives and the people of the district, and were obliged to translate and enforce the injunctions transmitted to them in that capacity.[4] These *luluai*, *tultul*, and mouth-boys were possessed of much more power than had ever been held by the cluster of warrior leaders within any one political unit. The immediate result was the establishment of a central authority for this unit, bringing its component segments more or less tightly together. But at the same time the indigenous context in which it would have been

---

[4] Possibly the *luluai* was entitled to hold meetings (or "courts") and to resolve minor offenses; but he was not given judicial powers by the Administration. As far as I can gather from conversation with Administration officials, these rights were officially denied him. Nilles (1953, p. 19), however, speaking for the Chimbu, mentions that "*luluais* are entitled to sit in court over all minor matters. In fact, all troubles and disputes except criminal cases have to be taken to the *luluai*. . . . Such court dealings are pressed to unreasonable excesses, especially by native officials who had no previous claims to leadership—merely in order to exercise the power bestowed upon them by the government. . . . The *luluai*, in making his decisions, is guided by native customary law."

functionally significant was done away with by the very emergence of such an authority.

Although most *luluai*, *tultul*, and mouth-boys were officially appointed, and this was the conventional picture, others, fulfilling the same functions, were self-appointed. The primary criteria were strength, aggressiveness, and dominance, and an official not possessing these necessary qualifications was soon superseded by another. In fact, strength and self-assertiveness were just those traits which were admired by the Administration, which in these newly opened areas believed in wielding power by the use of a strong arm. The local people, of course, were relatively well-adjusted to meet such an approach. The Administration, in delegating authority to its intermediaries, was speaking the language they best understood. The cultural impact, therefore, has not been so sharply defined in this area as it might have been in other circumstances. Although in many cases the *luluai*, *tultul*, and mouth-boy work in co-operation with one another, rivalry for supremacy is inevitable in a situation still permeated by traditional values.

In addition, a series of other men seeking power and influence have made their appearance. Although not contesting the positions described above, they have attempted to place themselves on a relatively equal footing with the three major authorities. These are mainly native evangelists, some officially sponsored by the Missions, others self-appointed, who conventionally profess to speak and act in unison with the Administration officials. At the top of this hierarchy, below the European missionaries, are native evangelists from other parts of New Guinea. The Lutherans, for instance, using the Kâte language from the northeast as a *lingua franca*, draw heavily on "native missionaries" and their families from the Kâte-speaking area. Next to them come the *babatara*, usually local men, but not all officially recognized; some have had no formal contact of any sort with European missionaries. In status they are sometimes said to be roughly equivalent to a *luluai*, but actually seem to approximate more closely to the *tultul* and the mouth-boy. The *babatara* is the "strong man" of the Mission. He is not afraid of threatening arrows or stockades, and but for the banning of warfare would possibly have been a local war-leader. Schoolboys may come into the same category as *babatara*; half a dozen or so under the *mozogi^cni* (teacher) at Kemiju are only youths, but others who have had some training (mainly instruction in biblical material, in reading and writing, and in the Kâte language) are scattered among the northern districts. Some clashes have occurred from time to time between the evangelists and others, but more usually their aims are seen as identical; and they, too, rely on "strength" as a basic criterion. Both parties are supported by alien control agents—the Administration, and the Missions. That is to say, although their status is primarily achieved, it is ratified by alien sanction and approval. It is thus more stable than that of the warrior leaders, who are forced to seek validation through alien support or relinquish any claim to authority. Under the circumstances, it has not been possible for them to form behind the scenes a conservative group upholding traditional standards, endeavoring to maintain the status quo, while influencing and surreptitiously directing the new authorities. There is no doubt that strong men continue to rise and to exert pressure on officially supported leaders; but the traditional emphasis on individual achievement, and the usually transitory position of the warrior leader, does not encourage either their opposition to or control of the new authorities. What results from alien appointments is not so much a clash of authority but rather a re-emphasis, such as could occur in a predominantly traditional situation—a changing-over or a re-ordering of personnel, dependent on the same basic criteria. Changes are taking place, however, on both organizational and structural levels. The crucial difference lies in the relative stability of authority, involving a shift from a diffusely oriented authoritarian power structure, dependent on individual exertion and rivalry, to one of narrowing choice and formalization within this sphere.

Particularly important in this situation are the native police. In the eyes of the people with whom they come in contact they have almost absolute authority and are apparently answerable for their actions to no one, although to some extent it is understood that they are subordinated to European officials. They have virtual control over all the officially appointed dignitaries in their region and can make or unmake them if they so desire. It is possibly true to say that they abuse their powers no more than do some of their directors, the European officials, and certainly no more than do the *luluai*, *tultul*, and mouth-boy, who behave in much the same way as the strong men of tradition. Abuse of power is a relative matter. If a strong man can get away with some action or other, and by so doing add to his prestige, well and good.

Informal courts are held mainly by native police, *luluai*, *tultul*, and mouth-boys, either separately or in conjunction, and occasionally by certain evangelists who have sufficient alien backing—or sufficient personal strength. Sometimes officials from several districts come together informally for this purpose, whether or not people from those particular districts are concerned. Native police in this region hold courts fairly frequently, but even more frequently they are held by other officials. Whoever presides, there is apparently no essential difference in procedure. The courts are designed primarily to settle grievances and offenses as they arise, without reference to the Administration court. Officially, from the Administration's point of view, this procedure is illegal: native police, for instance, are not supposed to hold their own courts. Occasionally a request for a court may be refused by a mouth-boy, and the complainant may then approach the *tultul*. Should he refuse or remain inactive, the other may then appeal to the *luluai* or a native police official. Rarely, is appeal made directly to a European official. There is no fixed approach in these matters, and choice of one rather than another is a matter of personal inclination. Once a court is set in motion, however, and judgment is passed, no appeal can normally be made to another court short of seeking European or police intervention.

A court is convened when a complainant approaches a local authority, who joins with other authorities and various male supporters to take the alleged offender into custody. Or the offender (or offenders) may be sought and brought before such an authority. In the majority of offenses a complaint must be lodged first. In some cases, however, a native police official may take action for personal reasons. On the occasion of interpersonal fights some local authority may intervene and then summon a court; but in most cases interdistrict fighting does not involve a court.

Persons so appealed to have, unofficially, the power to enforce punishment and to exact settlement, and the local people recognize their authority to act as arbitrators and to pass judgment. They acknowledge not only the leaders of their own district but those of others as well. In many reported cases, complainants have approached leaders of districts other than their own. This social recognition is important. On the whole, they appear to accept without question the alien-inspired authority structure which has been thrust on them. Their recognition rests on the assessment of their leaders' strength and aggressiveness. Without this it might not be so readily forthcoming. There is considerable reliance on these leaders and acknowledgment of their power to enforce their judgments. The injunctions as well as the judgments they put forward are accepted, because they are culturally congenial. The changing situation has produced a crystallization of popular opinion in relation to certain "wrongs"; and public support for the leaders who administer "justice" is apparently much more articulate than it has been in the past or than it is at present in those areas where the system has not yet been accepted.

Men who preside over an informal court have virtually absolute power, although generally their pronouncements are mostly in accordance with expressed local opinion. One might suggest that the holding of courts has become endemic in this region. The slightest injury or personal grievance may offer an excuse for a court. In fact, seeking pretexts to hold a court has become almost a pastime for some. In the interactory zone of Kogu, for instance, particularly during our second visit, rarely a day went by without at least one court being held. Again and again, for a variety of reasons, as the only European in the immediate area (apart from my wife), I was asked to hold courts, but always declined. People from as far distant as Mount Michael came to Kogu for this purpose while we were there.

The informal court is held in the village clearing, or in front of the men's house. Some interrogation, and perhaps some violence, may have taken place before the court convenes. The pattern varies according to circumstances. Normally, however, the presiding authority takes the central position, flanked by other dignitaries; the staff of office here is almost invariably the cane (used, in some cases, to administer justice). In front of them on one side sits the complainant, on the other the accused (or defendant); each may be supported by patri-kin, *nenafu*, *aku*, or others. The audience disposes itself as it pleases. It is all very informal; the complainant may be nursing a child, and children may play among the audience. Various witnesses are heard and sometimes cross-questioned. The complainant may give an impassioned speech or may leave the matter entirely in the hands of others (witnesses or kin). He may be interrupted at will by the court leaders, who will go over and over the matter. Repetition in discussion is the delight of such meetings, especially when the affair concerns sexual matters or when amounts for settlement are to be determined. Proceedings may continue for a couple of days or longer, usually depending on the entertainment value of the evidence. The accused is given an opportunity to speak, but when women are involved they may be bullied, and beatings may be administered to force admissions of guilt. Accuser and accused may come to blows, and the leaders intervene. Interrogation continues until punishment is determined and/or settlement takes place. The treatment of the accused depends very largely on his power to speak strongly, to insist on his point of view in defense; and his attitude of self-confidence may achieve an acquittal, with or without the obligation to pay indemnities. The authority is, officially, an impartial mediator, but this is rarely the case. There is little attempt to weigh various factors to achieve some degree of objectivity, and rarely does an acquittal takes place without some form of payment to accused or accuser.

When all the evidence, relevant and irrelevant (and in some cases the patience of the hearers), is exhausted, punishment, if this has been decided upon, takes place. Or it may take place during the proceedings, the discussion being adjourned till the following day. Or punishment may continue for several days until a final court is convened to "make the court [or talk] die [to settle the affair]." The guilty party may perhaps be placed in "calabus" (pidgin English term for jail or detention and similar to the American "calaboose," the Spanish "*calabozo*"). This is not a formal imprisonment. To "calabus" a person, as the term is used in the informal court, is to force him to undertake some special task. The native police official "calabuses" a man when he indents him for work on the roads,[5] for cultivating his gardens, and so on. This may extend over several weeks. There are cases of confinement in a pit or house by native police, who also, infrequently, use handcuffs or rope to tie a prisoner's legs and hands. A local official, such as a *luluai*, does not always "calabus" a guilty person. When he does, it is usually a woman who is forced to clean a village clearing, or weed a garden for several days, while a guard with drawn bow stands watch over her.

Decision as to punishment may be reached before the court is held, and the terms of punishment are not always discussed during the actual proceedings. It is arbitrary, dependent largely on personal factors—that is, as regards the active participants (the leaders themselves, the complainant, and the witnesses). Certain offenses, particularly those by a wife against a husband, nearly always involve some sort of relatively violent action. Offenses of a sexual nature usually provoke violent punishment, as other matters (involving, for instance, fighting between males or a decision on prestations) may not. The possibility of violent judgment is particularly satisfying to the complainant and the onlookers.

There is some reason to believe that if the punishment is not too severe it may also be suffered with some degree of excitement if not pleasure by the victim. The overt purpose of punishing is to discipline the guilty party, to impress on him the realization that he has committed an offense

[5] A native police official may force a whole village or district to engage in road work, i.e., "calabus" it. Several districts were treated in this way during our first period at Kogu because, one such official said, they had been holding too many ceremonies. In other cases, no explicit reasons were put forward. One Administration report mentioned that all the people of this region were co-operating extremely well in the making of roads.

of some magnitude, which is socially condemned. In addition, it appears
to serve a positive function in that it gives emotional satisfaction not only
to the person administering the punishment but also to the complainant
and the spectators. Many means of achieving excitement have been done
away with through the banning of warfare and cannibalism; but some of
the emotions expressed in these are diverted into the informal court, and
in this respect there is great similarity between them. Prior to alien contact, physical violence was recognized as a necessary part of ordinary social
life. Now, under the aegis of the informal court, it has been concentrated, as it were, and highlighted. This is of the utmost significance in
understanding punishment and violent behavior in such situations.

Coercive measures are left in the hands of the new leaders by those
whose own right to proceed against an offending party are curtailed. In
some cases, however, court procedure and punishment serve only as a
cloak for this, and personal satisfaction is achieved, but now with the
active approval of these authorities. It is as well to remember that such
men are appointed by aliens and that others have achieved their position
by self-assertiveness and indirect or inferred alien backing. While they are
officially representative of their people, it is often difficult to associate
this with positive social support. Such support as they have depends
largely on the element of fear. Although the local people may be afraid of
the *luluai* and *tultul*, this attitude is more apparent between all of them,
including these officials, and the native police. Fear of the police is
relatively constant, but fear of local officials depends on particular
circumstances and operates in specific contexts—when, for example,
one of these men exerts his authority during a court, or carries out orders
given to him by a native policeman or a European officer of the
Administration.

Generally speaking, although they may, if they can, seek to defend
themselves, women have no legal rights. Whether they are rightly or
wrongly accused is beside the point, and punishment is no criterion of
guilt. They can appeal to an authority so that a court is convened, but
once it is set in motion the verdict or the procedure adopted in reaching
it may turn against them. Only such women as are accused can normally
take an active part in court proceedings.

In the eastern Highlands there is no strict moral evaluation correlated
with a scale of severity, such as Nadel has noted. Variation in this matter,
as in other cultural and social contexts, is marked. It would be possible to
grade the various cases qualitatively, classifying offenses according to
native assessment; for instance, in descending order of seriousness, are

adultery, desertion of husband, assault, theft, and so on. This would also correspond with the relative frequency of such offenses. But frequency is no criterion of the gravity of the offenses, and crimes such as homicide are rarely brought before a court.

In a traditional assessment, offenses within the district provoke no social condemnation in terms of concerted action. Moral evaluation is not uniform through a given district; adultery may be condemned or condoned by different persons, depending on sex and circumstances. Not all cases are brought before a court, and although there seems to be some agreement in the matter of punishment for female offenders, and such punishment is usually more severe, it will vary according to the persons implicated in any given case. (A man may not be charged with adultery by his wife; but a charge may be brought against him by the husband of a woman with whom he has had sexual relations.)

The informal court, even though it is often (if we exclude the presence of native police) operative within a native setting, is primarily a mechanism of indirect alien control. It is concerned with the formal and coercive regulation of local behavior. Indirectly and subtly, therefore, it is actually a medium through which alien ideas are unofficially diffused. However divergent in attitude and action the alien and the local patterns of administering and enforcing the law may be, in general form they are not dissimilar. But the linkage here, between the local (as a merging of the traditional and the introduced) and the alien, is structurally significant. At the local level the court is concerned with the punishment of persons offending against more or less commonly accepted local standards, with the regulating of behavior in accordance with indigenous requirements, and with the maintenance and extension of alien control. It is thus concerned with conformity on two levels: on the one, with the standards and value acceptives set by the alien, on the other, with those traditionally derived. Whether and to what extent these coincide does not really alter the question or solve the problem.

The question, broadly, is one of accommodation, or reconciliation, between two very different ways of life; and, more specifically, between two peoples, one of which, formerly autonomous, is now politically subordinated to the other. The problem, from one point of view, is how the eastern Highlanders can be brought within the Australian-European framework of government with a minimum of friction and upset. In long-range perspective other issues emerge—whether, and in what context, they will regain their independence. In the present interim or transition period, the local people and the incoming aliens are both concerned with achieving some sort of rapprochement, although their reasons for wanting this are far from identical. The dual function of the court is significant here, as a "bridge" institution, mediating between the two systems of behavior and ideas. In the next chapter we shall look more closely at this assumption, focusing on the informal court in action.

The cases to be discussed here describe judicial procedure in the informal courts. They cover a period of approximately four to five years, from 1948–49 to 1953, and are drawn from most of the districts which came within the scope of our field work. The majority have to do with Kemiju-Kogu-Moiife and Busarasa-Moke-Ora. There is less evidence from the second area because informal courts there have been in operation only since about 1950, and very irregularly. Of the 107 cases which I have recorded in full,[1] most took place between 1951–53, and about 25 per cent of these I witnessed. Courts were held so frequently that it was impossible to keep track of them all, especially those outside the district in which we were then living.[2] Of the courts which could not be observed personally, I decided to concentrate on those for which relatively reliable first-hand information was available, that is, in which it was possible to contact personally not only the leaders involved but also the accused, the complainant, and the witnesses.

None of these 107 cases concern a homicide. When a murder took place, or there was an outbreak of interdistrict fighting, the tendency was to keep it hidden, as far as possible, from the European administration. A few instances were referred to officers of the Administration, who normally made use of native police to have the ringleaders brought to Kainantu or to Goroka. Such cases were not always recorded in the official court books. While we were in the area, then, killings were still treated in a traditional fashion, with relatively little outside interference. But homicides are infrequent now in the northern districts and in the south, as far as Mount Wanevinti (that is, up to March, 1953).

Of the 107 cases I recorded, only one concerns an accusation against an

[1] I have isolated these for discussion here because my information about them is relatively complete. They comprise the principal cases which came to my notice. It should be made quite clear that they do not represent a complete coverage of *all* the court cases in the area; e.g., they do not include a number of cases which my wife recorded after talking to women who had been observers or participants in them.

[2] A rather different situation is discussed by Honigmann (1949, e.g., p. 149) for Kaska society.

alleged sorcerer. The incidence of sorcery, or belief in it, has certainly not diminished, as far as I can gather. In fact, retaliation by this means, if information from genealogies (including the supposed cause of each death) is to be relied on, is possibly becoming more frequent, encouraged by the belief of the native police in various forms of sorcery, particularly of the *sangguma* type. Administrative officers find such cases as do come before them difficult to deal with, since punishment of supposed offenders reinforces local belief in the power of sorcery. It is taken to indicate that the Administration admits the reality of sorcery as an effective means of working harm against the person, and one to be treated like other offenses. Mission condemnation of sorcery, as a force operating against Christian influences, has the same implication.

Most of our 107 cases relate to adultery, assault, husband-desertion, and theft. "Adultery" (29 cases), since no men were tried for this offense, might be better described as extramarital relations on the part of a female. It is not always easy to distinguish adultery from promiscuity; the term *gumaja* ("steal") is normally used for the latter, but often in a rather arbitrary way. Under the heading of adultery come cases in which either one or more men approach a woman for sexual intercourse, or the woman herself takes the initiative. It includes cases of elopement and a woman's visit to her lover in another village or district. In one case, not listed here as adultery, two youths were accused of having sexual relations with another man's wife; but this charge was said to have been fabricated. Usually it is only when the affair is blatant, or when the couple are caught in the act by the husband or a third party, that the matter is brought to court. But, as we have seen, a husband conventionally regards infidelity on the part of his wife as directly harmful to himself; and his reaction to such news, especially when this is made public, is often violent. He wants to retaliate by publicly shaming her and inflicting physical pain; but he is anxious also to restore his damaged prestige. He may then either reinstate her as his wife or reject her.

In husband-desertion (16 cases), the common elements are a wife's dislike of her husband and her desire to find someone more congenial. She may go directly to her lover, or elope with him, or simply set off for another district in the hope of taking a lover there. Two additional cases concern dislike of a husband, two the rejection of a wife, three dissension between husband and wife, five attempted or actual abduction of a young woman, and three the abduction of a wife.

Under the general heading of assault (15 cases), three cases concern assault on a wife by a husband, together with accusations of promiscuity.

Thus 63 of the 107 cases, or almost 59 per cent of the total, relate either directly or indirectly to marital dissension. Dissension, in the majority of cases, takes the form of accusations of promiscuity and adulterous liaisons, sexual incompatibility, desire for sexual adventure, and so on. There is also one case of sexual assault (or rape) and five cases of co-wife dissension, rivalry for the affections and favors of a husband. That is, almost 65 per cent of the cases reported concern sexual matters.

Also included under the general heading of assault are three cases of fighting between individuals, three disputes over gardens, and one dispute over the position of a grave in a garden. Of slightly different type are two cases of interference in someone else's affairs and one involving a fight over land.

Another general category, which cuts across others, has to do with claims for compensation. These may or may not be made in cases of adultery but usually appear in those involving husband-desertion, seduction, and abduction. In addition, seven relate to the remarriage of widows, four to the evasion of bridewealth distribution, three to evasion of mortuary distribution, and one to the destruction of growing crops by a pig.

There are nine cases of theft, five of a general type and four referring to stolen pigs, etc. While intradistrict theft has been conventionally regarded as "wrong," on an interdistrict basis it was traditionally approved. Through the influence of the informal court, however, all theft, irrespective of district boundaries, has come to be acknowledged as a punishable offense.

In our present series only two new offenses have resulted from alien contact: one concerns "escape from a native evangelist's authority," the other "trouble over road work." A number of other offenses might be included in this category: for instance, failure to clean villages, dig latrines, build new houses, or restore or build official rest houses; disobedience; holding too many ceremonies; not offering tribute to native police; failure to report to a patrol taking census; and so on. For the most part, however, neglect of such obligations to the introduced regime is treated summarily and without a court. Generally speaking, in this part of the Highlands no men (as of March, 1953) are indentured for outside labor; census-taking, except in the northern districts, is only now becoming systematized; and there is no head tax. Officially, the Administration is committed to controlling and patrolling the region, and to supervising the building of roadways and the cleaning up of villages.

Our 107 cases may be taken as relatively representative, when considered in conjunction with examples of similar offenses as they were treated traditionally. But one group cannot be compared with the other in time, since there is a considerable overlap here. Further, there is no check on the number and the nature of the cases which have been brought before the courts in this region. Such an assessment, even for a single district, would be almost impossible to make. Despite these admitted deficiencies, the 107 cases give a fairly wide coverage and illustrate reasonably well the definition and treatment of offenses in this setting.[3]

Sexual Offenses

Case 1. *Wife taken in adultery:*

Circumstances: Zagia and her husband, Nikinosavi, both of Kemiju, were working in their garden, but Nikinosavi left her digging sweet potatoes while he returned to the village to make an oven. During his absence her *nenafu*, Hegofa^ca, also of Kemiju, came to the garden and invited her to come into the nearby bush. Nikinosavi, having prepared his oven, grew impatient and went to look for his wife. He found them copulating. Hegofa^ca got up and ran away, but Nikinosavi seized his wife.

Initial treatment of guilty woman: Nikinosavi immediately beat Zagia, asking her as he did so, "Am I a no-good man, that you should let another copulate with you? I am a good man! *Vo!* What is this vagina of yours?" He struck her vulva with his hand and kicked it.

Court proceedings: Nikinosavi then brought his wife back to the village, where he approached Tewapi, the local mouth-boy, telling what had happened and requesting a court. Tewapi immediately called a court. He and Ozaze^cna[4] sat in judgment, a small crowd gathered around them, and Nikinosavi repeated his complaint. Tewapi cross-examined Zagia. "How many men copulated with you?" "Only one," she replied. There followed a series of questions concerning the sexual act itself. Ozaze^cna then took Zagia aside and questioned her concerning the number of times she had had intercourse with Hegofa^ca. Zagia replied, "Six times he has copulated with me, and it tasted sweet!" On hearing this, Nikinosavi became angry and shouted that he was a good man: "Why does her vagina want another man's penis?"

Punishment: Tewapi and Ozaze^cna decided to leave the matter in the hands of the woman's husband, who took hold of one of Zagia's legs and dragged her about the village clearing, kicking her pubes. The matter was then considered to be settled. No action was taken against Hegofa^ca.

The informal nature of the native judicial system is quite obvious in this example. The husband receives social validation for his act of punishment

---

[3] I discuss the judicial procedure only briefly, reserving most of my data for a detailed study of both the informal court and the judicial system set up by the Administration.

[4] Ozaze^cna of Ke^cjagana, then living in Kemiju, had no official position, but in virtue of his association with Europeans (Administration and Mission) he assumed authority in such matters. He was also an assistant to Ijoki, a Lutheran Mission evangelist at Kemiju, and was called a "schoolboy."

through the authority of the men presiding over the court. The question
of whether these men represent majority opinion does not enter here. It
is sufficient that the judicial body should purport to represent it; it is
taken for granted that their actions meet with general approval.

Case 2. *Adulterous wife divorced but subsequently reinstated:*

Circumstances: Jowaja^ca, wife of Anaga of Tatagufa, committed adultery with a
young Tatagufa man, Aguvi, her *nenafu*, but was observed in the act by her husband [whom she was said not to like].

Court convened: Anaga immediately approached Ozaze^cna, who called together
a number of male friends. When they had assembled in the village clearing with a
fair-sized audience, Anaga described the circumstances in which he had found his
wife. Neither she nor Aguvi was present. Anaga asked Ozaze^cna, as judicial representative, to beat his wife in order to discipline her ["to make her understand"].
At this juncture Jowaja^ca was summoned and on arrival was cross-questioned by
Ozaze^cna in the following way: "A man copulated with you. Don't deny it, I
saw you! How many times have you copulated with him?" "Five times," she
replied. "Was his copulation sweet?" "Yes, it was sweet," she answered.[5] The
court was then adjourned.

Intermediate period: That evening Ozaze^cna visited Jowaja^ca in her house. To
test her out, he asked her to have coitus with him. But she replied that she was
his *ato* and could not. [Anaga is Ozaze^cna's younger lineage brother.] Ozaze^cna
then called out for Anaga, who was in the men's house, and when he arrived
indicated that he was going to lecture them both. He sent Anaga to collect wood
for a fire and to obtain a bamboo container of water. When he returned, Ozaze^cna
asked the woman, "Doesn't your husband copulate with you? Do you 'pull'
another man because you are not sexually satisfied? You must remain quietly with
him and copulate with him." He then turned to Anaga and asked whether he
copulated regularly with his wife. "If you don't copulate with her all the time
she will 'pull' another man." He then told them to remove their skirts. When
they had done so, Ozaze^cna told them to have coitus and watched while they did
so. Ozaze^cna then took up the bamboo container of water and poured water into
her vagina. When Anaga had rested, he was told to begin copulating again. This
continued throughout the night; the girl's vagina was washed after each act.
[This is said to be teaching the married couple one of the main activities of
marriage—i.e., copulation.]

Court resumed—punishment: The court was then resumed. Ozaze^cna took the
central position with a small crowd around him and Anaga and Jowaja^ca were
summoned. Discussion continued, going over the circumstances of the case. It
was then decided to punish the young woman. Her skirt was cut off and she was
told to sit down naked before the people. A large tin was obtained and filled with

---

[5] *Haga*, "sweet." The appetites for food and sex are generally regarded as comparable.
This kind of questioning is associated with sexual curiosity and pleasure on the part of the
court leaders and the audience, and with establishing her guilt (i.e., her active desire for
coitus with her lover).

stones and a special ceremonial emblem made.[6] She was made to stand up and a man's fringed skirt fastened around her, but not concealing her pubes. The wooden end of the emblem was then inserted into her vagina so that it protruded out and upward. Attached to the skirt behind her was a similar emblem. She was then told to place the tin of stones on her head and dance up and down. She began to dance to and fro across the village clearing, the emblems shaking as she did so. People crowded around to look at her, even coming from other villages and districts. They joked and laughed. Children rushed up and down with her, crying out and shouting obscenities.[7] When she stopped dancing or showed signs of exhaustion she was threatened with a bow and arrow and urged on. Throughout the day she continued to dance, holding the tin of stones on her head; sweat poured from her body, and her head was swollen from the weight she carried. During the late afternoon she could hardly move and showed extreme exhaustion. Her mother and father began to wail, and the latter called out, "Oh, my daughter what is this that you are doing? Give her back to us. Stop this punishment." But they did not intervene because they were afraid of Ozaze^cna.

Court continued: At sunset Ozaze^cna summoned Anaga and stopped Jowaja^ca's dancing. They again sat before him, surrounded by spectators. Ozaze^cna then asked the girl, "Is this," pointing to Anaga, "your first husband?" "Yes." Then Aguvi was called for the first time. "Is this your second husband?" "Yes." "Are you going to remain with your first husband?" "No, I want to go to my second husband, Aguvi." Ozaze^cna asked Aguvi, "Are you willing to marry her?" "Yes." Then Ozaze^cna asked Anaga, "Will Aguvi marry this woman and compensate you?" But Anaga became "hot belly" and refused to answer. Ozaze^cna then told Jowaja^ca to remain with Anaga, but she too refused to answer. Several times Ozaze^cna asked her but received no reply. Becoming angry he hit her, "to make her understand," then threw her to the ground and struck her pubes until they began to swell.

Intervening period: Women who called her "sister" came to her aid and carried her back to her house, where they treated her wounds and swellings with warmed leaves. Later her brother, Namania^ca, came and carried her to the adjacent village where her parents were living. They had been afraid to come for her.

Final court: On the following morning the court was resumed. Anaga and Aguvi were summoned and appeared before Ozaze^cna, who ordered Aguvi to give Anaga five items of wealth, since he had copulated five times with the woman. Aguvi then gave one ax, two strings of *gumugumu* shells, one rope of *girigiri* shells, and one of tambu shells. Anaga accepted the payment. Placing his index finger vertically on his nose, he signified his willingness to divorce Jowaja^ca, saying, "I do not like her; I will not remain married to her." She was then free to marry Aguvi if she wished. The court ended.

[6] I.e., a length of wood to which is attached with wax the jawbone of a pig, topped with a bunch of feathers. Such emblems, sometimes of beaten bark, are used generally during secular ceremonies.

[7] For the purpose of the dance she had been made into a man, wearing a male skirt and a symbolic penis "because she likes other men's penes." The object was to shame her publicly so that in future she would remain faithful to her husband.

Aftermath: Jowaja^ca did not marry Aguvi. She returned to her house in her husband's village and continued to cook food for him, sending it up to the men's house, but he always refused it, leaving it untouched. After she had recovered completely, he visited her at night and resumed sexual relations. When this had continued for some time Jowaja^ca called together all the men of the village; and when they had assembled, she said, "Other men continually copulate with their wives at night. Anaga always comes to me and copulates!" All the men laughed and talked among themselves: "He put his finger to his nose, yet he still copulates with her. You two continue copulating." Anaga was then considered to have remarried Jowaja^ca, and Aguvi had no further claims.

This case illustrates the wielding of authority by an unofficial administrator of justice, who has assumed his position because he is considered to have indirect alien backing and is also a "strong" man. His decisions are not referred to others, nor is there any agreement by, for instance, an informal body corresponding to a jury. The kind of punishment he selects, while not diverging fundamentally from the general pattern, varies according to his personal inclination. The emblem and the tin of stones are "personal touches," considered by Ozaze^cna himself and by others to be particularly choice and in keeping with the behavior of a "strong" man. (The notion is said to have been introduced by certain native police who were bribed by a group of Kamano districts in about 1946 to help them in an attack on others. After the fighting, a man who was visiting the defeated districts from the Jate area was punished in this way: but in this case an emblem is said to have been inserted into his anus as well as one in his penis.) The court is thus fulfilling the function not only of disciplining the culprit but also of giving pleasure to the local people as well as to the leaders themselves. Ozaze^cna enjoyed instructing Anaga and his wife in coitus, watching the dancing, and striking her. Although her parents objected when she appeared to be suffering, they were afraid to intervene in case they too would be brought into the court. An interesting point is the resumption of marital relations after formal divorce had been arranged. The attitude of the men when faced with Jowaja^ca's statement indicates how much such action depends on personal inclination and on the common agreement of those concerned. This in itself is enough to counteract the formal divorce measure and deny any rights to the interloper (irrespective of any payment he may have made; however, the payment in this case was made to compensate the infringement of the husband's rights).

Case 3. *Woman seduces youth in husband's absence and is caught in the act:*

Circumstances: Igidjub of Tatagufa had two wives, the first Anutavia, the second Uzegu. Igidjub spent most of his time with Uzegu, neglecting Anutavia and not accepting her food. She therefore committed adultery with a young Tatagufa man named Honiigo, who regularly visited her house at night. On one occasion, Honiigo's younger brother, Tuvuᶜvuo, visited Anutavia and remained talking with her. Tuvuᶜvuo was about sixteen years old and relatively inexperienced as far as older women were concerned. Anutavia told him that she was a Numparu woman and that it was the custom of Numparu women to sleep in the same house as the young men. Young men always slept in her house, she said. Tuvuᶜvuo believed her, having never been to Numparu. "It is our custom," she said, "to remove our skirts before sleeping." She took off her skirts and lay down by the fire to sleep, and Tuvuᶜvuo did the same. Anutavia, pretending to be asleep, opened her legs. Tuvuᶜvuo, who had been watching her, got up and began to copulate with her. But Igidjub's younger brother, Haᶜi, happened to be passing Anutavia's house and saw what was happening. He went at once to Inivi, where Igidjub was attending a local church service, and told him. Igidjub returned immediately and beat Tuvuᶜvuo about the head with a cane until blood flowed. By this time a crowd of Inivi men, under the leadership of three pseudo-evangelists, had reached Tatagufa and insisted that a court be held to discover the facts of the case. These three men, Haguefa, Epiri, and Magueva, gave instructions that all those concerned should come to Inivi for the court. Then they started back. On the way they met Tewapi, the Kemiju mouth-boy, and Ozazeᶜna, who were on their way to Tatagufa, and inquired what the others intended to do. The three men replied that all the women were copulating in the absence of their husbands and that they proposed to take the matter to court at Moiife, where they could approach Gunua, a native police official. However, they decided to return to Tatagufa and hold a court with Tewapi and Ozazeᶜna presiding.

Court convened: When Tewapi and Ozazeᶜna reached Tatagufa the Inivi people dispersed and a court was convened in the main village clearing. Igidjub and his wife, together with Haᶜi, Honiigo, and Tuvuᶜvuo, were summoned and took up positions in front of them; a crowd gathered around them. Statements were made by Igidjub and Haᶜi. Then the two leaders asked Anutavia whether she had "pulled" these two men [i.e., whether she had made the approaches]. Anutavia replied that the two men had "pulled" her and copulated. They then asked Honiigo how many times he had copulated with her, and he replied "five times" [i.e., "one hand," which when used vaguely may mean merely a number of times]. They then asked Tuvuᶜvuo what had happened, and he gave his version. "I was lying down, when I looked at her vulva; I liked it and planted my penis in the hole." [The expression "plant" is used here, as in gardening.] "Did his penis go inside your flesh [vagina]?" they asked Anutavia. "Yes, it tasted sweet." "Did his penis go inside your belly?" "Yes," she replied. The same questions were asked in reference to Honiigo and answered in the same way. After further discussion, including other details relating to intercourse, Tewapi and Ozazeᶜna decided that they would take the matter to Moiife and get the native police official there to hold a court.

Prisoners taken into custody; subsequent punishment: Honiigo and Tuvuᶜvuo had their hands fastened together with twine, while Igidjub held his wife, and all set off along the Kemiju road with Tewapi and Ozazeᶜna, and Haᶜi as witness. On the way, however, Tuvu^cvuo collapsed from the injuries he had received from the angry husband and was carried back to Tatagufa. Tewapi and Ozaze^cna then asked the woman if she had anything to say, but she did not reply. Ozaze^cna threw her to the ground and beat her on the buttocks with a cane and then, turning her over, beat her on the pubes. They afterward beat Honiigo and Tuvu^cvuo on the buttocks and body.

Public shaming: Later that afternoon the woman and the two youths were again summoned by Tewapi and Ozaze^cna and came to the village clearing where a crowd of people had assembled. Ozaze^cna then spoke to the culprits: "You surreptitiously copulate in her house at night, but now you must do it openly in the village clearing. Copulate here so that all may look at you." They took off the woman's skirts and made her lie down. Then they removed the fringed waist bands from Honiigo and Tuvu^cvuo and told them to mount the woman in turn, while the crowd pressed close to obtain a good view. But the two youths were ashamed and did not obey. Ozaze^cna then took Honiigo by the arm and dragged him over to Anutavia, forcing him to lie on her, but he would not copulate. Tewapi dragged him away, while Ozaze^cna led Tuvu^cvuo to Anutavia and forced him to lie on her. Men, women, and children were calling out to him, telling him to copulate so that they could watch. Tuvu^cvuo tightened his grasp on her and did as he was bid amid the laughter and acclamation of the onlookers. After ejaculation he jumped up and showed his penis, and was greeted with further shouts of acclamation.

Final court: Tewapi, Ozaze^cna, Igidjub, and the two youths sat down to consider the terms of compensation. After a certain amount of discussion it was decided that Honiigo and his younger brother should pay to the husband four sixpenny pieces,[8] two fowls, two varieties of shells, and some paper. When these were handed over, the affair was considered to be settled.

This case underlines the sexual flavor which attaches to the majority of cases of this type. There is obvious desire to take advantage of the situation, not only to express physical violence but also to achieve indirect sexual stimulation. Public shaming is said to be sufficient to deter a woman or a man from again committing adultery. But when the exhibition is greeted with excitement and pleasure by the onlookers it may not always have this effect. For example, Tuvu^cvuo's behavior is not strictly in accordance with an attitude of shame but displays rather a kind of bravado. But not all public copulation is greeted so enthusiastically by the crowd as a whole, depending partly on the presence of the woman's kin (her parents and her brothers). In other cases people may run away in "shame" when a public demonstration takes place; but those who do so are usually close kin and more often than not a number of spectators

---

[8] Money is filtering down into this region, although there is as yet little understanding of the relative values of the various coins. Silver but not copper coins are regarded as items of wealth, and used in the same way as shells, etc.

remain. There is a striking resemblance between this exhibition and those staged in the ceremonial farces.

Case 4. Adultery, raising the question of a child's legitimacy:

Circumstances: Kakau of Ifusa has a wife named Tinepia, or Ti͡cnepi, originally from Kogu. While returning from the gardens she met another Ifusa man, Oasi [*neimo* to her husband and herself], who held her arm and expressed a desire to copulate with her. She did not answer. He continued, "My vulva, you are there: my body cries to yours, but you do not hear!" She returned to the village, where she attended to the oven, and Oasi sat down near her. They looked at each other from time to time, and finally Oasi touched her hand and made a sign that she should go to the gardens. Later they met in the gardens, where she asked what he wanted. He repeated his previous statement, "I like your skin [body]; I eat your vulva." "Good," replied Tinepia. "Come and look at this thing." She lay on the ground, opening her skirt, and Oasi copulated with her. They then returned to the village by different roads. On the following day Tinepia went out to dig worms for fishing bait; Oasi followed, and they copulated again. But while they were thus engaged Oasi's *nenafu*, Agenamaso [a lineage brother of Kakau, and *ato* to the woman], saw them and asked, "What are you two doing?" They said nothing but sprang apart, the woman going to the gardens and Oasi returning to the village. Agenamaso went to find Kakau and told him what he had seen.

Court convened: Kakau immediately approached the local *tultul*, Kepiema [acknowledging no kin relationship to any of the parties concerned], who called a crowd of men together and sent others to seize Tinepia and Oasi. When they arrived they sat before him and he began cross-questioning. The woman blamed Oasi for "pulling" her, and Oasi admitted the truth of this. Details relating to the sexual act were then discussed in full. Kakau intervened to say that as a result of their coitus he was becoming ill. "All the time Oasi copulates with her. She cooks food for me which I eat unknowingly; thus she makes me ill." Kakau added, "Tinepia recently gave birth to a female child. But she is a promiscuous [*gumaja*] woman.[9] You, *kabawaja* ["boss" man], make this question come up!" Cross-questioning now centered on this topic, with Tinepia denying the accusation. The court was adjourned at dusk.

Intermediate period: That night and on the following day the guilty pair were not restrained. Waja͡cipi, the Numparu *luluai*, was summoned to Ifusa to join the Ifusa *tultul* in judging the case.

Court resumed: Waja͡cipi and Kepiema opened their court in the village clearing. Some men were sent to apprehend the guilty pair and the husband as well. When they arrived Waja͡cipi asked the woman, "Do you want to leave Kakau and go to Oasi?" She replied that she did not like Oasi and preferred to remain with her husband. Kakau, however, while wishing to retain his wife, questioned the legitimacy of her daughter. "I will keep my two sons that she bore," he said. "But as for the female child, Oasi can keep her and look after her, and later he

---

9 Kakau is here doubting the legitimacy of his daughter, whom he calls a *gumimofa͡cne* ("stolen child," child of a promiscuous union). He is in effect saying that the child is Oasi's and asks the *tultul* to discover the truth.

can provide her dowry." He continued in this strain, working himself into a rage; then, taking up an ax, he made a dash for Oasi but was restrained by the onlookers. While this was happening Tinepia sat placidly munching a cucumber. A lineage brother of Kakau, a youth named Aseu [who called the woman *ato*, but acknowledged no relationship to Oasi], hit Tinepia in the mouth. Kac︎i of Kogu, a clan brother to her [*noka* to Kakau and classificatory younger brother to Oasi], took her back to her house. The *luluai* and *tultul* then discussed the settlement. It was agreed that Oasi should give a fowl, shells, paper, and three shillings to Tinepia. The case was then closed. The goods were given to her, and she remained with her husband, who shared them. No punishment was carried out.

Here the very rare question of a child's legitimacy arises. Whether the husband was suspicious before his wife's infidelity was revealed we do not know; it is possible that he mentioned it simply to accentuate his grievance. The case was considered a tricky one, hence the Ifusa *tultul*'s request for help from the Numparu *luluai*. There is no fixed punishment for adultery. The question of whether an adulterous wife and her lover should be punished at all is often decided indirectly by the husband's own attitude and influence. In this case the court serves, it might almost be said, as a forum for discussion of a grievance, the authorities mediating. The fact that damages are here allocated to the wife is an admission that her lover is to blame and she is absolved. The position becomes explicable only when the presence of Kac︎i, her clan brother, is taken into account. He, as a "strong" man, had some indirect say in the matter. Her acquittal depended on that rather than on any impartial consideration by the court. It is true that a distinction is often, although not always, made between premeditated and desired extramarital liaisons and coitus under persuasion or duress—that is, between the woman who "pulls" a man and one who allows herself to be "pulled." Whether or not such a distinction is drawn is again dependent on the inclinations of those involved in the case.

Case 5. *Adultery, punished in accordance with the relationship existing between the guilty pair:*

Circumstances: Kiwiso, of Kogu, is the wife of Inafi, a self-styled *babatara* [Lutheran evangelist] of Anonana. While she was bathing one day Janini, a young Agura man, entered the water and held her vulva. She said nothing. He then waited for her on the bank; eventually, after filling her bamboo water container, she joined him. He held her arm and asked her for coitus. Still she did not reply, so he pushed her to the ground and copulated. She then returned to the village. Next day, when she went to the gardens, the same thing happened, and similarly on the following morning when she went into the bush. Janini then went away for several days and on returning found Kiwiso sick in her house. At night he entered and copulated with her. While he was doing so a Jagana man, Guc︎aifa, visiting the village, looked in through the doorway and saw them.[10] He asked what they were doing but received no reply. He then asked Kiwiso who was the man with her. She answered, "Janini." Gu^caifa seized her and dragged her from the house and tried to seize Janini, but he ran away. Gu^caifa took Kiwiso to her husband and told him what he had seen. Immediately the Kogu *luluai*, Noka, and the Numpari *luluai*, Waja^cipi, were summoned. Inafi threatened to beat Kiwiso but was restrained by the two officials, who said, "You are not to hit her yet, this talk has not died [i.e., has not been resolved by the court]."

Court convened: On the following morning the two *luluais* held a court in the village clearing. Kiwiso and her husband were summoned and a large crowd surrounded them. She was cross-questioned but would not admit that Janini had copulated with her. Accused of hiding information, she would admit nothing.[11] The court was adjourned.

Intermediate period: Kiwiso was taken to Noka's house in Kogu, where she remained in custody. On the following day she was forced to do manual work on the road between Kogu and Moiife; there her husband thrashed her, with the approval of the *luluais*. Late that afternoon Janini was apprehended, and he and Kiwiso were forced to carry large logs of wood from the bush to the village of Maira in heavy rain, in the custody of the husband and of Waja^cipi. That evening Kiwiso was put in her house with her husband and the two *luluais*. Inafi spoke angrily, "I am not another man [i.e., he asserts his status as her husband], I copulate with you; but you take another man's penis!" He accused her of spoiling his food [through adultery], making him sick. Then he took off her skirt and began pulling her *labia majora* again and again in a rage, punching her pubes, and finally kicking her.

Court resumed: On the following morning Noka took Kiwiso and held a court at Watapi, a nearby village in Anonana. Cross-questioning began, and she admitted that Janini had copulated four times with her. Noka became angry because she had refused to admit this before: "Why did you hide it? Don't you understand you must tell me the truth?" He hit her, and her husband joined in. The court was then adjourned.

Following events: Noka took Kiwiso and together with Inafi went along the road leading to Maira, in Kogu. On the way they met the Agura *tultul*, Anetu, who had Janini in custody; during the night Janini had tried to escape to Tira^ce. [Anetu called Janini "younger brother" and the woman classificatory sister; he was *noka* to Inafi.] They all returned to Watapi.

Court continued: The three officials cross-questioned the pair in front of the husband and a group of onlookers. The main concern was to see if Janini's information agreed with that supplied by Kiwiso. Inafi became angry and seizing his bow and arrows tried to attack Janini but was restrained by the officials. He

---

[10] During court evidence he said he had entered the house in order to obtain fire to light his pipe; before entering he had heard the noise they were making. He called Kiwiso classificatory mother and Inafi classificatory father but acknowledged no relationship to Janini.

[11] When questioned informally on being taken to her husband, she had admitted that she was lying naked by her fire asleep. Janini had copulated against her wishes, she said. Now, fearing punishment, she denied this.

also tried to hit Janini with an ax, but it was taken from him. The court was adjourned.

Intervening period: Kiwiso and Janini were taken back to Maira and kept in custody by the three officials. Inafi, who was dissatisfied with the court proceedings, especially in relation to the punishment of the offenders, approached Gunua, the native police official who was for a time stationed at Moiife. At first he said that they should all go to Kainantu to place the matter before the Administration court. There was conflict of opinion on this point, and it was decided to hold another court at Irafu.

Fourth court: All those concerned, including Inafi and the officials, went to Irafu.[12] In front of Gunua, in the village clearing, the whole matter was gone over again. When their guilt was established to Gunua's satisfaction, the court was adjourned.

Administration of punishment: The officials, Gunua, the husband, and the guilty pair, including a number of other men from Irafu, Agura, Numparu, and Kogu, assembled in a house to administer punishment. Gunua threw the woman to the ground and her skirt was removed. All the men examined her genitalia. She was then ordered to stand up with legs apart. Janini was forced to squat between them and told to put his mouth to her vulva. After he had done this for a time a sweet potato was put into Kiwiso's vagina and Janini was forced to nibble at this until he had completely eaten it. Finally, Janini was ordered to lie down on his back, while Kiwiso was made to squat over him, placing her vulva to his mouth. He was told to suck out the fluids, swallowing them. In the morning Inafi expressed his approval of this demonstration and declared that he was now "good belly." Gunua ordered Kiwiso and Janini to do manual work on the roads. The affair was settled,[13] no indemnity was paid, and Kiwiso remained with her husband.

This example demonstrates further the lack of order in these judicial proceedings, and the important part played by the aggrieved party (the husband), who can go contrary to local officials and bring the matter before the native police. Moreover, various local officials have the right to join in, whether or not the accused or the accuser belong to their districts. The particular form of punishment planned and carried out here symbolized the relationship existing between Kiwiso and Janini, who were classificatory siblings. A brother, even a classificatory one, may receive food from the hand of a sister; since this particular brother desires closer intimacy, so it is argued in this case, let him be forced to pay this penalty.

Case 6. *Adultery discovered by child, who wrongly accuses the local* luluai:

Circumstances: Negamopagli is married to a Numparu man, Wa^cuvefa. During a ceremony in Numparu, parties from Agura, Anonana, and Hafaru came together.

[12] The choice of this place was made by the Irafu *luluai*, Karimba, who was serving as "interpreter" for Gunua.

[13] There was an attempt to hold another court in Kogu so that I would pass judgment. The two were brought before me, but I refused to preside and the matter was dropped.

While the dancing and singing were in progress, Negamopagli remained in her house scraping potatoes for the communal oven. There she was visited by Govio, a Numparu man, her *nenafu* [classificatory brother to Wa^c^uvefa], who sat down to talk with her. After a while he seized her arm and they copulated. They arranged to meet again the following day in the nearby gardens of Sefenaga. Negamopagli told Govio that she liked his penis [she continued to contrast her lover's sexual proficiency with that of her husband]. On the following day they met and copulated at Sefenaga and arranged to meet that afternoon when Negamopagli went down to the stream for water. There they again had coitus and decided that next time he should visit her in her house. Next day Negamopagli gave her husband some seeds to plant; when he had left the village, Govio came to her house and copulated. During the night too he came to her and remained almost till dawn. Negamopagli tried to persuade him to go in case people should see them together. But Govio had grown careless and boasted that no others would come to her house. "This house belongs to me; they are not to interfere!" He began to copulate again; just then a small boy, Ijufa, who called Negamopagli mother,[14] entered the house and saw what they were doing. He spoke to Negamopagli, "Mother, why do you do that?" Govio quickly lay down on the ground, while she pulled a mat over him in an effort to hide him. She bundled the child out of the house, but he continued to ask her, "Mother, you make another custom [i.e., contrary to normal behavior]. I saw you! What were you doing?" Negamopagli told him she had been doing nothing. The boy, however, ran away to find her husband, Wa^c^uvefa, and reported what he had seen. The husband came to his wife's house and asked her the name of the man who had been with her. She replied, "What are you talking about? I have been asleep. I remained here by myself until this child came to my house." He searched the house, but Govio had made his escape. The boy then accused Waja^c^ipi, the Numparu *luluai*, of copulating with Negamopagli. Wa^c^uvefa angrily caught up his bow and arrows and called to members of his lineage and clan to support him. "My fathers, my brothers, come and help me. The *luluai* has copulated with my wife, and I will shoot him!"

Waja^c^ipi was occupied at his oven when Wa^c^uvefa came toward him with drawn bow. He asked what was the matter. Nopiglina, a lineage father of Wa^c^uvefa, with drawn bow, called out, "I can shoot him. You have copulated with my son's wife; that is why I am going to shoot you." But an elder brother of Waja^c^ipi, Kikituwoifa, came forward and spoke to Wa^c^uvefa's lineage kin: "Hear what he has to say first. Do not mark him thus with your arrows, as his spirit may escape." [I.e., as he breathes heavily in fear, his spirit may leave him.] The others put down their arrows, but Kikituwoifa rushed to his house and seizing his bow shot at Nopiglina, wounding him. Shots were then exchanged between the two parties until Waja^c^ipi brought it to a halt. "Hear what I have to say first; then you can decide whether you will mark me with your arrows."

Court convened: All those concerned went to the village clearing, where Wa^c^uvefa formally accused the Numparu *luluai* of having sexual relations with his wife. The *luluai*, although charged, presided; and the woman was brought before him. She was asked whether he had copulated with her and replied in the nega-

---

[14] Ijufa had been adopted by Wa^c^uvefa, his father's brother, since his parents were dead. He called Govio classificatory brother.

tive, naming Govio. Waja'ipi then became angry and, accusing her of trickery, threatened to shoot her. Turning to her husband he told him that, as they had threatened him and wrongly accused him, he himself would marry her. He turned to Negamopagli and told her she could consider herself his wife. He then upbraided the husband and his kin: "Why did you threaten me? Are you afraid of Govio?" He seized the woman; Wa'uvefa grabbed her other arm, and they began pulling. Finally Wa'uvefa apologized, saying that there had been a mistake, his son had deceived him; since the *luluai*'s house was near the woman's, he had jumped to the conclusion that Waja'ipi was with her: he had not seen the man's face. This apology was eventually accepted by Waja'ipi, who released the woman's arm and gave Wa'uvefa permission to beat her. Wa'uvefa did so, and afterward the court was resumed. It was established that Govio had slept with her, and the court was adjourned. Wa'uvefa approached the *luluai* for permission to shoot Govio, and permission was given.

Intermediate period: Wa'uvefa shot Govio in the arm. His lineage kin sprang to his aid and a general fight ensued, but no one was injured. A halt was called during the late afternoon, and the village settled down. Next day a feast was held to settle the affair. On the following night Govio again visited Negamopagli in her house; but Waja'ipi was on the lookout and surprised them copulating. Taking some rope he put it around their necks and pulled them out of the house, then called out to the rest of the village: "I have caught a *sangguma* man, I am holding him now!" He pushed the couple back into the house. All the people in the village rushed to the house, surrounding it, and pulled off the kunai grass roof. They then saw Waja'ipi with his two captives, who had their skirts removed.

Court resumed: The two culprits were taken to the village clearing, where the Numparu *tultul*, Aga'ufa [*nenafu* to the woman and her lover, *aku* to Waja'ipi, and clan brother to the husband], set on them. Waja'ipi ordered a large fire to be built. They dismantled the woman's house and piled kunai on it. He then told the onlookers to cluster around and watch. The pair were cross-questioned, and finally Waja'ipi spoke to them: "You two have hidden your copulation, but now you must do this before the eyes of all the people." He untied the rope around their necks. Govio said, "You now calabus me, I have no alternative," and with these words he took hold of Negamopagli and copulated. The onlookers pressed forward, while others heaped more kunai on to the fire to light the scene; they laughed and called out to them. When Govio had done he got up,[15] and he and the woman were led away to the *luluai*'s house where they were kept in custody.

Aftermath: Next morning Waja'ipi expressed a wish to take the couple to Kainantu in order to place the matter before the Administration court. Nopiglina, however, brought a pig and offered it to Waja'ipi, asking him to "make the court die" at Numparu and not take it to Kainantu. Waja'ipi agreed to this but refused the pig. He then called Govio and ordered him to compensate Negamopagli. Govio gave her a pig, as well as some money, and the affair was considered settled. Negamopagli remained with her husband.

---

[15] Expressing their delight at this entertainment, some men and women touched and caressed the sexual organs of the pair, drawing in their breath and making sucking sounds, remarking that they could eat them.

The events leading up to the convening of this court resemble traditional procedure. The case shows too that a *luluai* is not beyond accusation. However, his authority carries more weight than it would have under the traditional authority system, and his accusers have enough respect for the power he wields to listen to him and allow a court to be held. When this is convened he defends himself without trying to call in an impartial judge, proceeding essentially along the lines traditionally adopted by a "strong" man. Public copulation here (as in Case 3) provides an opportunity for entertainment. The laughter of the onlookers, partly perhaps in enjoyment of the others' discomfort, suggests some approval of the proceedings. This does not necessarily mean that individually they approve of adultery as such and would not themselves act as the aggrieved husband did; but the general attitude of those not intimately concerned in the case seems to encourage the practice of engaging more or less surreptitiously in extramarital relations.

The pair were not actually humiliated, however much the intention might have been to achieve this. They could be regarded, rather, as temporary celebrities. Certain of their near kin would not be present, however, nor would the woman's husband always remain to watch. Much depends on the personality of the pair. If they are able to carry it off with gusto as Govio and Negamopagli did, public opinion will acclaim them. But if they are constrained, like Honiigo and Anutavia (in Case 3), there is more likelihood of their humiliation. Public opinion may applaud the display but not, explicitly, the adultery. People may tolerate adultery in others but at the same time try to exact severe penalties when they themselves are affected; and often, nowadays at least, they do not hesitate to reveal a case if it comes to their notice.

The question is whether local officials taking action in such cases do so with wholehearted social approval. Adultery is an offense against a third party, the husband, not against society, although the conventional view may be that it is socially "bad." But the local official may see all individual injuries as his business, and his mediation here is not so much to punish offenders (although this may seem to be a primary object) as to limit and channelize coercive action by the aggrieved party; that is, to see that the breach is not widened and to heal it by gratifying or appeasing the husband. There is no expression of general public disapproval against adultery as such, nor are the couples caught in adultery ostracized in any way. Even if they are shamed publicly, this is only transitory; and I know of no cases of subsequent suicide by either party, as is occasionally the outcome of shame in other situations. In this example, too, the final judgment that compensation should be paid to the woman is tantamount to absolving her from all blame in the matter.

Case 7. Adultery with husband's parallel cousin, with subsequent offer to exchange husbands:

Circumstances: E꜀ejau꜀mi is married to Ekifa, a Numparu man. On the road leading to the gardens, her *nenafu*, Inoguepa [of Numparu; father's brother's son and *nefaru*, age-mate, to her husband], "pulled" her and they copulated. At night he visited her in her house. On the following morning, when E꜀ejau꜀mi was at the stream washing with other women, he threw a stick to attract her attention. She left the others and disappeared into the bush; but an Inivi woman, Ago꜀neniagli, wife of the Numparu *tultul*, Aga꜀ufa, saw her go and immediately went to tell her husband.[16] Returning together, they found the couple copulating. Aga꜀ufa asked what they were doing. Inoguepa answered that he had come down to wash but that the woman had "pulled" him and asked for coitus. He then asked the woman whether she had done so, and she replied that she had. The *tultul* then left them and returned to the village. There he reported the incident to Waja꜀ipi, the Numparu *luluai*, who asked why he had not brought them along as was his duty. However, he went to the garden where E꜀ejau꜀mi was digging sweet potatoes and asked whether the report was true. She replied, "I am a woman, I 'pulled' him. What of it? Five times we copulated!" He then seized her and took her to the village. In the meantime Inoguepa, too, had been caught and was brought before the *luluai*, who fastened their hands with rope and took them to his house.

Court convened: On the following morning the pair were taken to the village clearing. The *luluai* and *tultul* took up their positions, together with witnesses and the woman's husband and the usual crowd of onlookers. Cross-questioning began, and the two adhered to their previous statements. After details had been extracted, O꜀o꜀mia, wife of Inoguepa, spoke, asking her husband why he had gone down to the stream to wash. Obviously, she said, he had wanted E꜀ejau꜀mi. If this were the case, she said, "You, Inoguepa, can take her. We shall exchange husbands and I shall go to Ekifa." [Ekifa is her *nenafu*.] The officials agreed to this, and the *luluai* took hold of O꜀o꜀mia and led her over to Ekifa. But O꜀o꜀mia protested, saying that she did not mean this. She turned to Inoguepa and asked why he preferred the other woman to her. "You think she has a good thing, and mine is no good?" But he did not reply. "Good. This thing I have, you can leave it; you go and copulate with another woman!" The *luluai* then repeated that the women should exchange husbands.

At this juncture Kaina꜀au, father of Ekifa, appeared on the scene, closely followed by Igase꜀na, father of Inoguepa, both with axes. These men were full brothers. Each tried to hit the other's son. The *luluai* took away their axes, telling them that it was nothing to do with them; but after this outburst he withdrew his judgment and ordered Inoguepa to pay compensation to E꜀ejau꜀mi. O꜀o꜀mia helped her husband by paying the settlement costs herself; she gave a pig and five

---

[16] She bore no relationship to the other woman or her lover, but her husband called E꜀ejau꜀mi classificatory sister, her husband *nenafu*, and her lover classificatory brother.

shillings, handing this over to the *tultul*, who gave it to Eᶜejauᶜmi. The pig was killed and a feast held, the matter being settled.

Here the court's proceedings are left very much in the hands of witnesses, and the *luluai* in charge changes his views to conform to their wishes. The wife of the accused man, in paying the compensation he himself owes, is trying to regain his favor. It is most unusual for a woman, not herself accused, to appear before the court in this way. The errant wife again receives compensation, as in Case 6, but this time without action being taken against her. The husband, because his wife's lover is his *nefaru* as well as a parallel cousin (although this would not always deter him if he wished to proceed against him), takes no action.

Case 8. *Adulterous woman punished, then rescued and compensated:*

Circumstances: A Kemiju woman, Joᶜwaja, married to Arlgaᶜa of Tatagufa, committed adultery with Zuzu, also of Tatagufa. They were found by her husband, who took the matter to Walwalia, the local mouth-boy, and Drua, the *luluai*. These two officials seized the couple and brought them to the village clearing.

Court convened: The facts of the case were ascertained through cross-questioning. Zuzu was released and punishment for Joᶜwaja decided on.

Punishment: The two officials removed her skirt and handed her over to a number of young men to teach her to remain with her husband in future. These youths took her out into the bush to an old house which was used at night as a decoy for small animals. There they made a fire and each in turn copulated with her. When all had finished they wrapped some pandanus leaves in *faja* nettles and, heating the bundle in the fire, thrust it into her vagina. They then copulated in turn and replaced the pad of heated leaves, each man struggling to get at her. Tewapi, the Kemiju mouth-boy [her *nenafu*], came to the house and saw what was happening. When they saw him coming, some of them fled. He picked up a stick and began to beat the remaining youths, asking them, "What are you doing? She is no daughter of a pig! Why do you treat her so?" He then took Joᶜwaja back to her parents at Kemiju.

New court convened: When Joᶜwaja had recovered and her sores had healed, Tewapi took her to Tatagufa and called a court together. The two Tatagufa officials joined him. He insisted that all the youths who had copulated with her should come before the court, and after they had assembled he asked Joᶜwaja to pick out those who had been with her. When this was done, he ordered them each to compensate her. A heap of goods grew before her, fowl, money, paper, shells, matches, waistbands, salt, and so on. Tewapi then asked her whether she intended to remain with her husband without attempting adultery again. She replied that she would be good in future. The goods were then handed over to her, and she returned to her husband.

The punishment of plural copulation in order to discipline a wife is a traditional one; the court which preceded it was perfunctory and casual, classifiable as such only because the officials themselves heard the facts of the case and recommended appropriate measures. Of equal interest is the action of the Kemiju mouth-boy, who contravened the decision passed by the two Tatagufa officials. Tewapi is a "strong" man, with considerable influence, and believed to have support from the native police; the Tatagufa men were therefore ready to fall in with his ideas in the matter. In this case again the adulterous woman is compensated, although here she has undergone punishment. Zuzu, her lover, escaped without penalty.

Case 9. *Husband defends wife's adultery: case abandoned:*

Circumstances: Magumisu of Kemiju, married to Keno^cmo of Numparu, gave him their baby to mind, saying that she would go for wood and make a fire inside her house. Unsuspecting, he took the child and went to sit behind the row of women's houses. Taking up a container of water, she handed it to a young man named Amufiganu, also of Numparu, her *nenafu* [classificatory brother to Keno^cmo], scraping his hand as she did so to indicate that she wanted him. Then she obtained some fire wood and went into her house, where Amufiganu joined her and they began to copulate. Presently Keno^cmo called out to her that the baby was crying and asked her why she was such a long time. She called back that she was making a fire and would come when she had finished. The two continued to copulate. Her husband, growing impatient, came around to the house. Amufiganu got up and stood by the door and as Keno^cmo entered slipped outside. Keno^cmo, hearing the noise, asked his wife what had gone outside. She replied that it was only a pig; but Keno^cmo suspected that a man had been with her. Taking up a torch of kunai grass he looked around and found some semen on her sleeping mat. Turning, he asked her, "I remained outside; how did this semen get here?" When he repeated his question she became frightened and admitted that Amufiganu had been with her. News of the discovery soon spread. Amufiganu became afraid and during the night spoke to the Numparu *luluai*, Waja^cipi [his lineage brother, who called the woman *aku* and Keno^cmo classificatory younger brother], admitting what he had done. The *luluai* said that they would leave the matter till the morning. In the meantime, Amufiganu left Numparu and went to Kainantu.

Court convened: Next morning the *luluai* approached Keno^cmo and his wife and brought them to the village clearing to discuss the matter. The court was then adjourned. Magumisu left the village for Sosofenaga in the company of her brother Jaglio. Waja^cipi came after her and brought her to another village, Kagunaga. Here he called together a court and summoned the husband. After they had assembled, cross-questioning began; and when her guilt was established, Waja^cipi decided to take the court to the native police official. Keno^cmo interrupted and spoke against this. "You are not to take my wife. If she is taken there they will cut her vulva, they will damage her body!" He began to wail and, removing her skirt, showed the *luluai* her vulva. "Hers is a good vulva. If you take her there they will cut it with a razor." The *luluai* replied that he had thought he would take her to the other court in order to gratify the husband, but if this was his attitude he would leave it. The husband went on to explain, "Amufiganu copulated with her only once." The *luluai* then said, "All right, this is something belonging to yourself; we will not hold a court. You are strong, and I have nothing else to say; you have refused to hear me." The court was abandoned.

Aftermath: Waja͡ipi discussed the matter with the Kemiju mouth-boy, Tewapi, then *luluai*. Later Tewapi took it on himself to take the young woman into custody and put her to work on the road, thus contravening the decision of Waja͡ipi. The latter hearing of this went down to Kemiju and taking Magumisu from her road work returned her to Keno͡mo. "You are not to work on this road. Your husband threw away my words and the court was abandoned!" Nothing else was done in the matter.

This case illustrates the contention that procedure against the guilty party depends primarily on the attitude of the complainant. Here the husband made no direct accusation and the official investigated on the admission of the lover, who disappeared to the patrol base to escape punishment. The husband spoke against the decision that the court should proceed further, since he feared (with good reason, we may suppose) that his wife would be maltreated by the officials. He was anxious to justify her act of adultery, virtually to condone it by minimizing the sexual aspect. This was not, he suggested, repeated intercourse which could be said to infer alienation of marital affections; it was simply an isolated act of no account. (His attitude toward his wife's infidelity was not the customary one.) In opposing the *luluai*'s decision he was behaving as a "strong" man, and traditionally people are expected to give way before this kind of behavior. The *luluai* could have forced the issue and taken the woman to the police, but under pressure of the husband's words he reconsidered. Insistence might have led to internal friction; but, on the other hand, a deciding factor would possibly have been the *luluai*'s own relationship to Magumisu, as an *aku*. Tewapi's subsequent officious behavior was in keeping with his personality, which involved him at times in conflicts with officials of similar standing. But these, inevitable between "strong" men, are kept in check by "higher authority" (such as the native police, and the fear of European intervention) and rarely develop into a physical clash.

Case 10. Adultery not proven:

Circumstances: Agimu, married to Nagoteri of Kogu, was in the habit of giving food to Ka͡i, also of Kogu, since he called her *nanoferu*, son's wife, and her husband clan son. Nagoteri suspected that the two were indulging in sexual relations. Seeing her giving Ka͡i food one day, he became angry and accused her: "Whenever you go to the garden, he copulates with you." He took hold of her and threw her to the ground, then opening her legs looked at her vulva. "Yesterday

I did not have coitus with you, yet semen is there! Who has copulated with you?''
In a rage he broke off her skirt, leaving her naked, and taking up a stick beat her.
Agimu fought back and hit him in the groin, but he continued to beat her.
When they had finished fighting, Nagoteri dragged her naked to Kemiju and
placed the matter before Tewapi [see above].

Court convened: A number of men, with Tewapi presiding, assembled in the
village clearing, where the facts of the case were discussed. Ka^ci too was present.
Nagoteri demanded that his wife should compensate him since she had caused
him to become angry. Tewapi asked Agimu to show him her vulva. He then
called Nagoteri and Ka^ci and asked them to show him their penes; neither was
moist. Tewapi then closed the case, commenting that since no proof of the
woman's adultery was forthcoming he could not proceed. Nagoteri again demanded that Agimu should compensate him, but she refused on the grounds that
he had exposed her naked to the public eye and shamed her. The matter was
closed.

There are many cases of this type, when a husband suspects his wife of
committing adultery and seizes an opportunity to bring the matter to
court. Some represent merely an excuse for public airing of a grievance
and after this purpose has been served the court is abandoned for want of
decisive proof. Yet proof is not always necessary if the husband exerts
sufficient pressure on the presiding officials and insists on proceeding
further.

Case 11. *Adultery, with husband's subsequent punishment of wife:*

Circumstances: Ailotapi^cja, married to Waja of Asafina, committed adultery
with an Asafina youth, Agiru, her *nenafu*, a clan brother of Waja. Her husband
accused her: ''Here I 'bought' you and you became my wife, but you have become promiscuous [a *gumaja* woman]. You have made me ill; my belly pains.''
Taking up his bow and arrows, he seized her and dragged her into the bush,
where he sat down with her in a clearing. Then he asked her to tell him what the
women did in the menstrual hut and what they did at menstruation and at childbirth. As this is taboo between men and women,[17] Ailotapi^cja refused, saying,
''I do not understand these things.'' But Waja insisted. ''It is better that I should
not shoot you,'' he said. ''Tell me all about menstruation and childbirth.'' But
she replied that she did not know. He then told her to lie down so that he could
copulate with her and began to do so, then withdrew and stood before her,

[17] Men and women do not normally talk together about matters relating to menstruation and childbirth. These things are the concern of women, and men declare they know
nothing about them. That is not to say that men do not know about menstruation and
childbirth in relative detail. Discussing these matters with men I usually found that their
knowledge was fairly accurate. It is, however, an accepted convention that these are prohibited subjects between men and women. Waja's attitude here was that his wife had
caused a breach in their marital union, hence he was at liberty to break the existing convention between men and women. He was not seeking information on these topics but was
symbolically underlining the breach between himself and his wife.

taking up his bow and drawing it taut, leveling the arrow at her. "Come and drink my semen," he ordered her. She refused. "It is better that I should not shoot you; come and drink it!" he repeated. But Ailotapicja was afraid. Waja threw aside his bow and mounted her again, but just before ejaculation withdrew and placed his penis in her mouth. Then he left her and returned to the village. Ailotapicja was "hot belly." She went to the native police official, Gunua, at Moiife, and told him what had happened. Gunua accompanied her back to Asafina, where he apprehended Waja.

Court convened: Gunua held his court in the village clearing with a large group of onlookers. He asked Waja, "Are you a no-good man, that you make your wife drink semen?" Waja replied that his wife was promiscuous and that he did this to discipline her. Gunua then asked the young woman why she had complied. She explained that she had had no alternative, as her husband had threatened her with a bow. Gunua then hit her and kicked her and, turning to her husband, did the same to him. He then told them both that they must work on the road.

Aftermath: The husband and wife did manual work on the Moiife-Kemiju road for two weeks, during which time they resumed marital relations. When this period was completed Gunua released them, telling them not to do such a thing again. They returned to Asafina. A little later Gunua took Ailotapicja to Moiife and copulated with her; when he returned to the patrol base of Kainantu he took her with him, and she remained there.[18] Her husband was unable to proceed against Gunua.

This man, suspecting his wife of adultery, preferred to punish her himself rather than bring the matter before a court. There is a precedent for such behavior, as we have seen, in the excesses associated with plural copulation. Symbolically it is similar to the example in Case 5. Here Waja initially accused his wife of making him ill (he had eaten the food which she had cooked while indulging in an illicit liaison); therefore she must be forced to drink his seminal fluid. Traditionally, a wife would have no redress. The presence of officials, like the native police, provide her with a means of achieving redress; but such an approach, particularly when made directly to the police, is risky and would not have been attempted except on the spur of the moment and in extreme anger and fear of the husband.

Case 12. *Wife informs her husband of her adultery:*

Circumstances: Zebicsa is the wife of Anogacsa of Tatagufa. The pair went down to Hipuga [close to Kimicsagumu] to stay for a time. While Zebicsa was in the sugar cane garden, Kaneja, *tultul* of Hipuga, had intercourse with her. On the following

[18] Native police in this region commonly avail themselves of local women; they do not keep permanent mistresses but prefer variety. This takes place whether or not their own wives are present. The guardian or husband of the woman abducted by a native police officer rarely receives compensation, nor has he any redress; he is usually afraid to approach the Administration officials at Kainantu or elsewhere, because of the power of the native police. See Nilles (1953, p. 18) for the Chimbu district.

morning, when she went to the gardens, he did so again. Subsequently she went to the menstrual hut, but Kaneja visited her there. When she returned to the village, he had sexual relations with her on several occasions. Fearing discovery, she went to her husband and told him what was happening. He went to Moiife and reported the matter to the native police official, who ordered him to bring the *tultul* before him. Anoga^ca returned to Hipuga with Tewapi, the Kemiju mouth-boy, and others.

Court convened: On arrival at Hipuga, Tewapi held a court. After summoning all those concerned, he elicited the facts of the case. The court was then adjourned.

Intermediate period: Tewapi brought the woman to Kogu, where he set her to work removing grass from the village clearing at Maira while a man with drawn bow and arrow stood guard over her. Her husband and Kaneja also came to Kogu. During the night she was kept in an empty house, and Tewapi invited a number of Kogu men to visit her there. They made her lie down and pulling aside her skirt looked at her vulva and joked about it. Next morning Gunua, the native police official from Moiife, came to Kogu and apprehended Zebi^ca and the *tultul*. With Anoga^ca, Tewapi, and others, he started along the road to Moiife. On the way, however, he told Tewapi to break off her skirt. Naked, she was made to stand with legs apart, and Tewapi delegated to put earth into her vagina. When this was done two Kogu men, Ka^ci and Wajuba, who were unrelated to her, took her down to the nearby stream and washed her genitalia.

Court resumed: On arrival at Moiife, Gunua held a court and heard the evidence of the *tultul*. Zebi^ca was brought in but was not questioned. Gunua ordered the *tultul* to compensate the woman, the amount decided on being two pigs, two fowl, and two ropes of shells. One pig was handed over to him and the rest was given to Zebi^ca. The case was closed and the participants returned to their villages.

As in Case 6, a local official is not absolved because of his authority from appearance at a local court. An aggrieved husband can proceed against him as a rule only if, as in this case, he approaches the native police as direct representatives of alien authority; but, as we have seen in Case 11, he has no redress should one of the police have sexual relations with his wife. A police official, having an accused *tultul* or *luluai* before his court, will be more lenient than if the latter were a person of no consequence. He is apt to put other officials into a different category and permit them privileges which he would not allow in others; he contrasts them with the "bush *kanakas*," a term of abuse frequently used by his European superiors. Thus if a *tultul* or *luluai* is brought before his court and proven guilty he will not usually punish him physically but make him pay compensation.

Case 13. *Adultery attempted but not reported to husband:*

Circumstances: Ganizuja is the wife of Anaeva of Kogu. During her husband's absence, her *nenafu*, Ma^cju, of Kogu, opened the door of her house one night and attempted to hold her for intercourse. She could not see who it was and beat him off. He left her house but was seen by another man, who told Anaeva of this on his return. Anaeva waited for a while to see whether she would tell him of the incident, but she said nothing. He then approached Noka, the *luluai* of Kogu, asking him to investigate.

Court convened: Noka held a court outside the woman's house, in the presence of her husband and others. After a good deal of cross-questioning, Ganizuja admitted that a man had visited her house; she had been awakened by a noise, and a man grabbed hold of her. She had beaten him off. She was then asked why she had not told her husband about it and replied that she was afraid he might beat her. Noka suggested that the real reason for her reticence was a desire that the incident be repeated. "You were thinking about this man," he said. Maᶜju was then summoned and, when asked whether he was the man, admitted this. He then described what had taken place. Anaeva, on hearing his admission, became angry and hit Maᶜju on the mouth and nose again and again. He then turned to his wife and hit her. Presently Noka restrained him and ordered that the guilty pair be punished.

Punishment: The woman and Maᶜju were taken to the village clearing. Here her skirt was removed and she was beaten on the buttocks with a cane. Then Maᶜju's fringe was taken off and he too was beaten on the buttocks and on the penis. At this point Anaeva's brother, Nusaᶜe, objected to the court. "You make this court no good," he told Noka. [Nusaᶜe was protesting against the lightness of punishment inflicted on Maᶜju.] He and Noka then went to Gunua, the native police official at Moiife, and placed the matter before him. Gunua told them to bring all those concerned to Moiife so that he could settle the case.

Court reopened: When all assembled at Moiife, the evidence was gone over again. Gunua released the woman, but "calabused" Maᶜju. The court was dispersed. Maᶜju was put to work under guard in Gunua's garden. During the night he was handcuffed. He carried out this work for approximately a month.

The case shows that even if a wife does not commit adultery, and actually repulses a man's advances, she may be accused if she does not inform her husband of the incident at the earliest opportunity, an obligation made clear to her at her betrothal. It is argued that she has an ulterior motive in hiding the incident, and she is consequently judged guilty. A further point concerns dissatisfaction at an official's decision in the matter of punishment, here expressed by the husband's brother. Ordinarily no appeal is allowable at such a late stage, although appeal may be made to another authority if the one approached refuses to proceed. But circumstances vary; and this is a case of talking "strongly"; otherwise the dissenting person would not be heard. Here Nusaᶜe went over the head of the local *luluai* and appealed to a higher authority, the native police, to achieve his aim.

Case 14. *Woman seduced by husband's father:*

Circumstances: An Amufi woman, Afuveᶜmu, is married to Jokapa of Henagaru. She and her husband's father, Famia, were sleeping in a pig house where they were tending Jokapa's pigs.[19] During the night Famia got up to blow on the fire and observed his son's wife lying naked on the opposite side. As he looked at her desire grew and he mounted her and copulated. When he had finished Afuve^cmu got up and asked him why he had done that. He replied that he had done so only to mark her body. Afuve^cmu told him that he should not copulate with his son's wife and that she would go and tell her husband immediately. She left the pig house and went to the men's house in the village and told Jokapa what had happened. He went directly to the Henagaru *tultul*, Mato^co, his clan brother.

Court convened: Although it was nighttime, the *tultul* opened a court at the men's house and questioned Afuve^cmu concerning the incident. He then summoned Famia and asked him, "Why did you copulate with your son's wife?" He replied, "You are a no-good person talking about this. What I have done is finished. I have copulated with her and that is ended. Leave this talk. You go and eat [and forget about it]!" He then left the court and returned to the pig house. The court broke up and the *tultul* called after him, "You can't talk in this way. I will fight you."

Court resumed: The *tultul* then obtained rope and went to the pig house and tying Famia's hands together brought him to the men's house, where the court was resumed. He was again asked why he had copulated with his son's wife but gave the same reply. The *tultul* asked the onlookers what he should do, and a lineage brother of Famia, Have^ceva, spoke: "My son, Jokapa, he has copulated with your wife, a good woman. I will 'back' this and do the same to his wife!" But the *tultul* discarded this solution and closed the court.

Intervening period: Famia was kept in custody overnight and on the following morning the *tultul* took him and the young woman, in company with other men, down to Taramu, where he placed the matter before a native police official who was there at the time.

Court reopened: The police official, Boney, opened a court and heard the evidence of the young woman. He then asked Famia why he had copulated with her. Famia did not reply. Boney hit him and pulling off his pubic fringe drew back the prepuce of his penis, exposing the apex; taking up a firebrand, he burnt it. Famia was then thoroughly beaten and kept in custody, the police official intending to take him to Goroka to bring the matter before the Administration court. Afuve^cmu was also detained.

Aftermath: A party of Henagaru men went to Taramu and presented Boney with a pig, asking him to release Famia, since they were sorry for him. He consented to this, and the deputation returned to Henagaru with Famia and his daughter-in-law.

This shows the inadequacy of the local court in dealing with some cases. Much depends on the public support accorded the official presiding over it, and his relative strength. Here the *tultul* was at a loss when faced with

---

[19] A woman may sleep at night in a small hut, within or just outside the village, to watch over her own and her husband's pigs. It is not unusual for a woman to remain by herself even during periods of interdistrict fighting; but often she is accompanied by an older man or woman, or her parents-in-law.

Famia's stubbornness. He asked the onlookers to suggest a solution but discarded the suggestion offered by the accused man's lineage brother. Finally he placed the matter before the native police, absolving himself from all responsibility.

Case 15. *Alleged sexual relations:*

Circumstances: Two Keᶜjagana youths, Kugubeku and Avigo, clan brothers, were boasting of their sexual prowess. Kugubeku pretended that he had just copulated with a young girl, his *nenafu*. Avigo, believing him, remarked, "Is that true? Then I must find a girl with whom I may copulate. I can copulate with all the women!" "Good," replied Kugubeku. "We will do this and then talk about it afterward." During the night Avigo went to the house of Pugare [whom he called classificatory mother], wife of Kaᶜeavu, a Kogu man, *luluai* of Keᶜjagana. Opening the door, he looked at her; but he was so timid that he ran back to the men's house. Pugare, however, jumped up and running out of her house called out that Avigo had copulated with her. Two Keᶜjagana men, Kiaᶜnu and Tabaᶜo, clan brothers, who called the woman classificatory mother and Avigo clan brother, took hold of the youth and gave him a beating. They then called to Kaᶜeavu, telling him what had happened.

Court convened: On the following morning a court was held, presided over by the *luluai*, who was also the aggrieved husband. Avigo was brought before him and cross-questioned and revealed that he and Kugubeku had boasted together, Avigo saying he would look around for a girl with whom to have coitus. With this in mind he had gone to Pugare's house but had only looked in the door. The case was adjourned.

Intervening period: Kugubeku was apprehended and the two youths were kept in custody. The Keᶜjagana *luluai* approached the Henagaru *tultul*, his classificatory son, who called the two youths classificatory brothers, stating that Avigo had copulated with his wife and requesting aid in holding a court at which both youths could be tried.

Court resumed: The court was reopened on the village clearing. Avigo and Kugubeku were cross-questioned. Avigo was asked again and again whether he had had coitus with Pugare but denied the accusation and said that Pugare was lying. The two officials then turned their attention to Kugubeku and eventually obtained the name of his *nenafu*, Noᶜjugana [the one with whom he had allegedly copulated]. They asked whether he had had coitus with her. Kugubeku denied this, saying that he had only pretended to his friend. The Henagaru *tultul* then suggested that the two youths should be taken to the native police official at Moiife and the matter placed before him. They pleaded that the court should be made to "die" at Keᶜjagana under the direction of their own "boss men." "If we had copulated with these women," they held, "we could be sent to the native policeman, but as we didn't do this it is better that the matter should be settled on our own ground by our own leaders." This plea was accepted by the two officials, who decided on the punishment and the settlement of the case. The two youths were made to work on the road near Toᶜjaforega [in Keᶜjagana], carrying heavy stones from the nearby stream, for approximately two weeks.

When this was completed Avigo was ordered to give compensation [one pig and one fowl] to Pugare, and Kugubeku to do likewise [one fowl] to No꞉jugana, his *nenafu*. The affair was closed.

This case shows the reliance placed upon the word of Pugare, who made public Avigo's timid attempt not, we may assume, out of malice, but because if he were seen leaving her house at night only one possible construction would be placed on his visit. By making an outcry she was protecting herself. Yet in doing this she insisted that coitus had taken place, and here her motive becomes discernible. She was, as onlookers remarked, possibly concealing a lover—and it may have been his presence which prevented Avigo from pressing his attentions. Such undercurrents are not always revealed in court evidence: Avigo may have concealed Pugare's infidelity because she was his classificatory mother (although this did not prevent Ijufa from telling his father's brother of his "mother's" adultery in Case 6).

There is nothing untoward in the two youths discussing sexual matters and boasting of conquests. It is fairly common for a young man to meet and have coitus with a female *nenafu*, or with an older woman. It is only when this is brought to the attention of adults and the public guardians of morality, if we can so call the official leaders, that this is regarded with any degree of seriousness. At such a time the injunctions at initiation are recalled (when unmarried youths who have not completed the final stages are warned to avoid all association with females, not because coitus with them as such is frowned on but because such relations will have a weakening effect on a man).

During the court proceedings in this case no evidence was solicited from either of the two women named. Both youths were badgered, as is usual with those accused, to admit their guilt. Even when this guilt is in doubt, as it was here, for the women were not called to substantiate the accusation, they must still be punished and pay compensation. Yet their argument against being sent to the native police official for trial was considered and accepted.

Case 16. *Sexual assault on female child:*

Circumstances: A Numaga woman, Agumatu, left her two young children to play in the village while she went to the gardens. [Her son was called Waisa꞉tu; her daughter's name was not given.] A Numparu youth called Zana꞉i, the girl's *nenafu*, came over to where the children were playing and persuaded them to go into an empty house nearby. Here he got Waisa꞉tu to make his sister lie down; then he took out a razor from his bag and cut her vagina, making the entrance larger, and copulated with her. By this time the child was screaming, and Zana꞉i ran away. The girl's brother tried to quiet her; he then carried her into the village clearing, and called for their mother. When Agumatu came running, Waisa^ctu told what had happened. Wailing, she called to her husband, Pe^ceko, who seeing his daughter in this state became extremely angry. He rushed away to find Zana^ci and dragged him to the village clearing, where Ja^ciju [a "strong" man from Kogu and an unofficial deputy of the local *luluai*] took hold of him, opened his pubic fringe, and found blood on his penis. Both he and Pe^ceko gave him a thorough thrashing. They then took him to the Numaga *tultul*, Matanu, and reported the matter.

Court convened: A court was held in a village clearing in Numaga and the youth cross-questioned before a large group of onlookers. The official asked him why he had acted in that way; he replied that he did not know, that he had been mad at the time. No further evidence was heard, and the *tultul* struck him again and again until he was unconscious. Later he was carried to a house and revived; when he had recovered he returned to his home district, Numparu. No compensation was paid. The girl recovered.

Only two other cases of sexual assault on a small girl (excluding mythical instances) have been recorded for this region. Children, as we have observed, become aware of matters concerning sex at an early age and experiment accordingly. Although the girl mentioned in this case would be about six or seven years of age, and her brother about eight or nine, the shock would be due not so much to the act of coitus as to the pain and injury caused by the cutting. The youth who committed this offense tried to excuse himself by saying that he was temporarily mad. This is a common enough excuse, used to explain any action which receives condemnation and censure: "I was mad (*negi*)"; meaning that he was acting without a sense of responsibility, without considering the effects of his action.

Additional Aspects of Marital Dissension

Case 17. *Desertion, and attempted recovery of a wife:*

Circumstances: A young Moiife woman, Keara, was sent in marriage to Ka^conu of Tiroka. Ka^conu already had another wife, Etu^cu. After the birth of her first child Keara became ill, covered with sores, and her husband therefore refused to accept the food she cooked for him. She later went for medical attention to a native medical assistant [Administration "doctor boy"] stationed for a time at Moiife and subsequently recovered; but instead of returning to Ka^conu she went to live with a Moiife man named Kavari [a classificatory brother to Ka^conu, who called Keara *ato*; he had previously called her *nenafu*]. Ka^conu brought the matter to Gunua, the native police official then stationed at Moiife, requesting that action should be taken and his wife returned.

Court convened: Gunua called together a court. Keara and Kavari were summoned and cross-questioned, and the husband stated his case. Kavari explained that he had taken the woman after his classificatory brother had discarded her.

Keara substantiated this and added that her husband had not looked after her and had rejected the food she gave him. "I will not return to him," she said. "I will remain on my own ground." Ka^{c}i, a Kogu man, her *nenafu*, spoke in her favor, blaming the husband. The court was adjourned with the issue undecided.

Intervening period: Ka^{c}onu remained for a time at Moiife, awaiting events. In the meantime Keara began to give food to Ka^{c}i, who accepted it; both parties thus indicated their willingness to marry. When Ka^{c}onu saw this happening he became angry. He returned to Tiroka and obtained two fowl and five shillings and, bringing these back to Moiife, bribed Gudara of Moiife, Gunua's interpreter, to persuade Gunua to order his wife to return.

Court reopened: Gunua again called together all the parties concerned and ordered Keara to return to her husband. She refused. Ka^{c}onu then asked for his child, thinking that if he had the child the mother would also come. Gunua gave him custody of the child, and the case was closed.

Subsequent events: When Ka^{c}onu left Moiife for Tiroka with the child, Keara followed him and spent the night there; but on the following morning she took the child and fled to Kogu, where she remained with Ka^{c}i. Ka^{c}onu immediately approached Iojampana, the Tiroka *luluai*, and Joivu^{c}o, the local *babatara*, and explained the position. They came down to Kogu with him and apprehended Keara.

Further court: Assisted by the Kogu *luluai*, these two officials held a court. The husband, Ka^{c}i, and Keara were cross-questioned. Keara was told to return to her husband but refused. The Tiroka *luluai*, the *babatara*, and Ka^{c}onu then beat her with canes until blood flowed from her head.

Final settlement: Keara went to Gunua, at Moiife, and told him what had happened. He summoned Ka^{c}i and Ka^{c}onu to come before him, but the latter became frightened and returned to Tiroka. Ka^{c}i obtained a leg of pork and gave it to Gunua, asking that the matter be settled. Gunua told him to give compensation to Ka^{c}onu so that he, Ka^{c}i, could retain the woman. Ka^{c}onu was again summoned and appeared before Gunua. Ka^{c}i gave one pig, two fowl, some money, and a rope of shells. This was accepted by Ka^{c}onu, and the case was closed.

Here the wife's desertion of her husband was occasioned by his neglect and his refusal to accept food from her; this was not merely because she was sick but possibly because he was more interested in his first wife. Repeated refusal of a husband to eat the food his wife cooks for him is tantamount to rejecting her, and if she were young this in itself would force her to leave him. The husband does not always go so far as to divorce her by using a conventional sign (as in Case 2), because this invalidates [20]

---

[20] Of course, a husband having symbolically divorced his wife would not necessarily be deterred, in consequence, from attempting to recover her or achieve compensation. It would nullify his "right" to this, but even without that he could use force to achieve his end. I am not considering here divorce and remarriage in any detail. Before this could be done it would be necessary to discuss local terminology in relation to the "first," "second," and "third" husbands (and so on) with whom a woman may have casual or permanent associations.

his right to sue (by self-help or through the courts) for her recovery, or
for compensation from her next "husband." This case is important because it demonstrates the "strength" displayed by the woman. Her sustained refusal to return to her husband, even in the face of pressure from
the native police official who was bribed to decide in his favor, is a point
to which attention has already been drawn in emphasizing the traditional
value placed on a display of strength or purposefulness. Alien-sponsored
officials, like the native police, can also be influenced by it. Further, there
is the counteracting by the local authorities of the apathetic decision of
the police official, who did not take them to task because their co-operation was more useful to him than their antagonism, even if this could not
be expressed openly. And in any case he was in a position to give final
judgment.

Case 18. *Wife deserting husband to live with other men:*

Circumstances: Buruni of Tiroka was married to Ame^{c}ja of Agura. Her husband's pig, which she was tending, died, and allegedly for this reason she left
her husband and returned to Tiroka, where she lived with a Tiroka man,
Ave^{c}pavena. Her husband came crying to Tiroka and approached Ivegopa^{c}ve, a
local *luluai.*

Court convened: Ivegopa^{c}ve summoned Buruni to the village clearing and cross-
questioned her before her husband and a group of onlookers. He thrashed her
and returned her to Ame^{c}ja. The case was closed.

Aftermath: Returning to Agura, she remained with her husband for a time. Then
she left him for another Agura man and presently left him in his turn for yet
another Agura man.[21] Ame^{c}ja came crying to Noka, *luluai* of Kogu, and asked
him to deal with the matter.

Second court: Noka apprehended Buruni on the following day and held a court.
She was cross-questioned but offered no excuse for her behavior. "I go to marry
another man; we play together, and then my husband takes me back. It is like
this all the time. I am only playing!" Noka thrashed her, but her husband interfered, saying that if she were beaten "his belly would be no good." Noka continued to strike her with a cane, and when he had finished he handed her over to
Ame^{c}ja, with whom she remained.

The wife first left her husband for a relatively good reason, fearing his
anger at the death of his pig. It will be recalled that one of the duties of a
wife is to attend to her husband's pigs, feeding and watching over them
as if they were her own children; and neglect on her part can lead to
trouble. This, however, is not clear in the above case, and the real reason

[21] Her object was "amorous playing" (*janawa*) as contrasted with *gumaja*, promiscuous
relationships. The distinction is difficult to make, but the former seems to be regarded
more leniently.

emerges when she makes the statement that she wants to "play." It is this tendency in women, men say, which it is necessary to curb. In Case 7, when E꜀ejau꜀mi, accused of adultery, said, "I am a woman, I 'pulled' him. What of it?" the inference was that this in itself provided sufficient excuse. Some men go so far as to say that women's liking for coitus is insatiable; hence, notwithstanding the conventional attribution of aggressiveness to men, women are often described as the initiators of extramarital liaisons.

Case 19. *Desertion of husband, who is compensated but continues to press for wife's recovery.*

Circumstances: Mopi from Kabuje, south of Ja꜀agusa, came up to Busarasa [Kabumanti] with a group of refugees, having been driven away in the course of fighting. There she was given as wife to her *nenafu*, Haisa of Busarasa. The two, however, were always quarreling. Haisa beat her for no apparent reason and then copulated with her.[22] Mopi complained: "A human being gave birth to me! You fight me a little, and then you copulate with me a little. Later I will leave you and go to another man." On the following day her husband again beat her and copulated, and she repeated that she would soon leave him. Several days afterward she collected her belongings and went to Tajo꜀vima [also of Busarasa but acknowledging no genealogical relationship to herself or her husband]. She asked to live with him; he agreed and took her to Ifusa where he lived in his *aku*'s house. They spent four days together and then decided to return to Busarasa; Tajo꜀vima observed, "Why have we come to another place? I have a child of my own! If Haisa shoots me, my son can shoot him!" Back at Busarasa, Tajo꜀vima and Mopi lived together as man and wife. Presently, Haisa collected together some of his lineage brothers and approached Tajo꜀vima, who was prepared for him. Arrow shots were exchanged but neither was injured. When Haisa's anger had abated he told Tajo꜀vima that he wanted his wife back. Mopi protested, and clung to Tajo꜀vima's net bag. Jona꜀o, a warrior leader, clan son to Tajo꜀vima [acknowledging no relationship to Haisa], intervened and told Haisa that it was his own fault. "You always beat your wife. I told you about it before. Now she has left you for good to remain with Tajo꜀vima." Haisa asked for compensation, and the other man gave him a pig. However, Haisa was not yet satisfied and approached Takua, a native police official at Moke, asking that he insist on the return of his wife.

Court convened: Takua summoned Tajo꜀vima and Mopi to a court in front of his house. Haisa was present, together with some local authorities and a number of onlookers, and evidence was taken from the three persons concerned. Takua ordered Mopi to return to her husband, but she protested that she disliked him and that Tajo꜀vima had adequately recompensed him. Takua turned to Haisa and asked whether this was true. Haisa replied that he wanted both the woman and the compensation, the latter as payment for her desertion and infidelity.

At this juncture the court was adjourned for a short time. Jogo, son of

---

[22] This was possibly an accentuation of the aggressive aspect of coitus.

Tajoᶜvima, appeared on the scene with a pig which he presented to Takua. Takua asked, "Why do you give this to me?" Jogo replied, "I give it to you for nothing. I am sorry for my father, Tajoᶜvima." Takua accepted the gift [intended as a bribe].

Court resumed: Takua gave his decision. Speaking to Haisa, he said, "Tajoᶜvima has given you compensation. The matter is now closed. Mopi is to remain with Tajoᶜvima." Haisa left the court wailing, but the case was not reopened.

This case blends an attempt at traditional settlement with the authoritarian aspect of the informal court. The former, without the existence of the latter, would have been enough to settle the affair one way or another (that is, by fighting and/or by payment of compensation), but since an additional means of arbitration is now open to complainants it is used in an attempt to obtain satisfaction which the other has failed to give. The failure has taken place, actually, just because the alternative medium is now available. Entering into this is the question of bribery, as observed in Case 17. This is relatively common in courts convened by local authorities or native police. Bribes are offered whether or not the giver is considered to be in the wrong and are designed to influence the accepter and weight his decision. Bribery has the same function, now as in the past, in efforts to obtain allies in interdistrict fighting. It is primarily an attempt to form a transitory alliance to obtain a specific service, which when rendered automatically wipes out the debt. In practice, acceptance of it does not necessarily cause indebtedness, although there is a "moral obligation"; it is this which Jogo implied when he gave his pig. Further, and this is particularly noticeable in discussing the Administration judicial system, what I call "bribery" serves to explain fines paid into the court. These are not seen as an essential part of judicial procedure as such. A prisoner at Kainantu, faced with the alternatives of a fine or a jail sentence, will pay the fine, if he has the few necessary shillings, in the belief that he is bribing the Administration official to release him. Native police in outlying areas, like those we are discussing, usually encourage the practice of bribery (which is, after all, traditionally based), since no costs are rendered to a court but occasional bribes compensate the official for his trouble in hearing the cases brought before him.

Case 20. *Recovery of three runaway wives:*

Circumstances: The three wives of Namugu of Ivigoᶜi [close to Wanitavi, south of Moke] left him and went to live with other men in other districts. This whole region is "uncontrolled" by the Administration. During a patrol made by Bagau [or Bagaᶜau], a native police official at Moke, to obtain wild betel nut, Namugu approached him and requested the recovery of his wives.

Court convened: Bagau called together a court on a village clearing in Ivigoᶜi [the first ever held there]. Namugu, supported by male lineage kin, stated his case and presented Bagau with a pig. When asked why he had done this, Namugu replied, "Eat first, and then obtain my three wives and hand them over to me." Bagau agreed. The names of the three women were then obtained, together with those of the districts to which they had gone. After more discussion the court was adjourned.

Intervening period: The *luluai*s of Busarasa, Moke, and Wanitavi, with the mouth-boys of Ora and Moke, were present. Bagau sent the Busarasa and Moke *luluai*s to Wanikatɔ to apprehend one young woman, Kisema. The two mouth-boys were sent to Kamira to get Inuntu and the Wanitavi *luluai* to his district for Fomarenta. Inuntu and Fomarenta were found without trouble and brought immediately to Bagau. Kisema was frightened and ran away to the menstrual hut at Wanikato; but the two *luluai*s entered and dragged her out and, tying her to two poles, carried her back to Ivigoᶜi.

Court resumed: Bagau commended the local officials, telling them they were "strong" men. He reopened the court and heard the evidence again. He questioned the three women, but they were so frightened that they were unable to speak. Bagau then sent word to the three men with whom the women had been living, but they were afraid and would not come. As these districts were still hostile, Bagau did not press the point. As little else could be done apart from handing over the women to their husband, Bagau spoke to Namugu: "You killed a pig and gave it to me. You asked me to take action in this affair. I therefore sent men to get your wives and bring them back to you. All this has been hard work. These "boss men" [i.e., the *luluai*s and mouth-boys] want entertainment. You must spend the night copulating with your wives in front of us." The three women were brought into Bagau's house and told to remove their skirts. They lay down while Namugu copulated with each in turn, to the great amusement of the officials and others who had collected to watch. From time to time Namugu was threatened: "It is not good that Bagau should shoot you. Get on with your work!" On the following morning Bagau told Namugu that he could now take the women away.

Aftermath: Namugu was not willing to remain at Ivigoᶜi. "I cannot remain here after this public copulation. If I remain people may perform *sangguma* on me. I am afraid. I and my wives will return to Moke with you." They went back with Bagau and worked for some time in his garden. Later Bagau ordered them to return to their district, where they now live.

Namugu's unwillingness to remain at Ivigoᶜi was not simply because he had been forced to copulate with his wives in public but because the men with whom they had been living might retaliate when Bagau had gone. Nevertheless, there is an element of shame in a husband's having public coitus with his wives. For guilty lovers, as we have seen, this would be considered a suitable punishment; but the conditions are different when the claimant himself is placed in the position of a guilty party. By going to Moke with Bagau he evaded condemnation, since he was now considered to be "calabused" and could therefore expect sympathy on his return. Further, in this case the carrying out of public copulation was described as a form of entertainment for the officials and onlookers, while in other cases (although this element is obvious) it is explicitly designed as a disciplinary measure, with the entertainment factor secondary.

Case 21. *Rejection of wife:*

Circumstances: Taroᶜna of Anonana was married to two young women, Moru from Agura and Ozazona from Moiife. He much preferred Ozazona and told Moru that he did not like her and that she could leave him. Moru therefore went to Moiife, where she married Inafi, a *nenafu* of Taroᶜna. She left him, however, for Ovebu, also of Moiife and also a *nenafu* of Taroᶜna. In the meantime Ozazona died from dysentery, and Taroᶜna tried to recover Moru. Messages to her failed to persuade her to return.

Court convened: Taroᶜna collected his lineage brothers and approached Moru's male kin at Agura. They agreed to help him and, collecting further classificatory brothers and *nenafu* from Kogu, proceeded to Moiife, where they approached the local *luluai* and asked for his help. A court was held and Moru and Ovebu summoned. Taroᶜna gave evidence and requested the return of his wife, being supported in this by the woman's father and male lineage kin. Moru, however, rejected him. "I do not like him," she said. "I will stay with Ovebu." Taroᶜna then asked that compensation be paid to him by Ovebu. The *luluai* asked Ovebu whether he wished to keep Moru on these conditions. Ovebu agreed and gave a pig, leaf tobacco, various shells, salt, paper, a fowl, and bark skirts. This was accepted, and the case was closed.

This case underlines the point that a husband, after rejecting his wife, may reclaim her. He and or his lineage kin, although there are sometimes exceptions to this, have paid bridewealth, and the woman comes legally into their custody. Should he discard her, or allow her to remarry elsewhere, he can claim compensation. Her patri-kin normally may not make such a claim, although the husband may ask their aid. Payment of compensation by the man with whom she is living normally cancels the former husband's claim, although, as in Case 19, it may be pressed again. The position is not so clear on the remarriage of a widow, when either the deceased's patri-kin, in lieu of the junior levirate, or her own patri-kin may demand compensation. Should a woman be divorced, her husband may or may not relinquish all right to recovery or compensation; and this may or may not be taken up by her patri-kin. (In any case, the paternity of her subsequent offspring, if any, is not an issue here.) During inter-district warfare it is principally a matter of opportunity or expediency. Claims for compensation from a member of a hostile district can be put forward, so to speak, only at the point of an arrow. Occasionally, compensation will be paid if the districts concerned are friendly, but mediation in such matters is comparatively rare. Hence, whether a man proceeds against the man with whom his wife is living and demands her recovery or compensation, or whether her patri-kin, too, have claims, is still dependent on aggressive action.

With the appearance of the informal court, however, a certain crystallization has taken place. Traditionally, a man has rights over his wife. Even should she elope, or be rejected and go to another district, he may claim her recovery, or compensation for her loss. This right is backed by force and involves fighting; compensation may or may not be paid, and the woman may be killed, punished, or brought back. Today, a husband, providing he has not formally divorced his wife or publicly rejected her, can demand her return or, failing this, adequate compensation for her loss. If he wishes, he can proceed against her and the man with whom she is living and be more or less sure of achieving satisfaction. Thus, procedure against a wife is considerably facilitated under the court system. Further, whereas many second marriages (the first husband remaining alive) are made without compensatory payments to the first husband or to the woman's patri-kin, the informal court has made it almost obligatory for the second marriage to be validated by a payment if it is to be viewed as marriage.

Case 22. *Dislike of husband:*

Circumstances: Urolni, a Tiroka girl, expressed dislike for her husband, Ameja of Agura, and consistently refused to have sexual relations with him. He therefore took her to the men's house and explained the situation to the Agura *luluai,* Kopinefa [who called him lineage father and the girl "mother"].

Court convened: Urolni was taken into the men's house where a court was held with the *luluai* presiding and the inmates of the house as onlookers. Evidence was taken from Ameja and from Urolni, who reiterated that she disliked him. The *luluai* decided, with the approval of Ameja, that the only way to discipline her would be through plural copulation. Ameja, with several of his lineage brothers, then left the men's house, leaving Urolni with the others.

Disciplining: In the presence of the *luluai* several men had coitus with her. Then came the turn of Nomaja [*nenafu* to Ameja, lineage father to the *luluai,* but acknowledging no relationship to the woman]. Nomaja, a prominent performer in erotic farces and generally considered a great wit, squatted before Urolni and taking up her hands pretended to eat them. "Ah! This tastes good!" Then he pulled her labia majora and made as if to eat, remarking how good they were. The onlookers applauded. But at this juncture Urolni grabbed one of Nomaja's testes and pulled it. Nomaja let out a cry. She tugged at it again, and Nomaja pretended to eat her face, making sucking sounds. "How good this tastes. Oh my vulva! Loose me now—it pains!" But Urolni pulled it again, and Nomaja fell

Arojabu,
making a shell
headband.

A Fore man
wearing a hornbill
head decoration.

Jate women
at Taramu
(*left* and *below*).

Kogu woman.

Below: Jate woman
married in Kogu
(Nusaᶜe's mother,
Fenakizu).

over, pretending to die. "You have killed me now!" Urolni, becoming afraid, released his testicle. Nomaja jumped up and began to play with her vulva, passing remarks as the occasion demanded. Finally, he picked her up in his arms and carried her to a nearby stream. Here he threw her into the shallow water and began to copulate. But the stones of the creek bed hurt his knees, and he became angry. He picked her up again and carried her into the high pitpit cane. Here he took some creeper rope and fastened her legs apart, attaching each to a clump of pitpit. Squatting between them, he copulated and sucked at her face, pretending to eat it. On finishing he held her vulva and asked, "Oh, this thing! What has it eaten that it should have grown so big?" Urolni replied, "My mother gave me her vulva. You look at it! Don't talk about it any more; remain copulating with me!" Nomaja then copulated with her again. Afterward she said to him, "I have left my child behind. I will go and get it and come to you. I will leave my husband." Nomaja replied that he was unable to pay her husband compensation. However, they were not alone. Anetu, *tultul* of Agura [classificatory brother to the Agura *luluai*; he called Nomaja *neimo*, Ameja lineage brother, and the woman *ato*], had been watching them. When he heard their conversation he became angry and hit Urolni and dragged her back to her husband. She slept with him that night but on the following day went to Nomaja. The *luluai* and *tultul* thrashed her and returned her to Ameja, with whom she remained without further trouble.

There is no need to comment here beyond saying that this resembles closely the traditional way of disciplining a wife. The local officials played a minor part. Just how far it can be viewed as punishment varies according to the number of men participating and the kind of actions which accompany it. Of interest in this case is the attitude of the woman.

Case 23. *Assault by husband:*

Circumstances: Enujapizu, wife of Aguaguja of Kemiju, was sweeping the village clearing while holding her small child when an Imoga man named Weku came up to her and asked whether he could nurse it. Enujapizu, misunderstanding, thought he was asking her for coitus. Frightened, she threw the child to the ground and ran away. The child was unhurt, but her husband, who observed this, became very angry and struck her in the belly with a digging stick. The *luluai* of Kemiju apprehended both husband and wife, and brought them to a native police official who was then in that district.

Court convened: A court was held, presided over by the native police official in the company of the local *luluai*. Both husband and wife gave evidence. The wife was absolved of blame, and the police official declared that the husband should be punished for having assaulted his wife without adequate reason.

Punishment: Both husband and wife were taken to Moiife. Aguaguja was "calabused"—i.e., was ordered to dig a deep pit, into which he was put, with a guard placed over him. He remained there for several days, food being thrown down to him. His wife slept in a nearby house. Finally some of his lineage kin presented the police official with some fowl, and he was released.

Enujapizu acted here in accordance with what is traditionally and ideally required of a wife—that is, to repulse or refuse to listen to the words of any man other than her husband and certain recognized affinal and agnatic kin. The assumption is that a stranger, as Weku appeared to be, would ask her for only one thing. Had he approached her in private, her response might possibly have been different. But to engage her in conversation in public could have only one connotation to onlookers. The husband was angry because his child had been thrown to the ground, and in his view his action was entirely legitimate. The police official's decision to punish him must be considered interference with marital rights and responsibilities, and contrary to traditional procedure. That a husband can be punished for assault on a wife represents an extension of the common rights of the individual, although a curtailment of those of the husband over his wife. These common rights, in respect of women as of men, are usually couched in such terms as "I am a human being . . .!" but they become effective only when supported by personal manifestations of strength, or coercive action, designed to reaffirm them. They may be commonly acknowledged as an ideal, but they are individually oriented. The informal court, on the other hand, gives official support to such rights, recognizing that they exist and may be articulated through the judicial system. This recognition is basic to the formation of a legal system and to the crystallization of such rights into laws. It is just this process which may be observed in the functioning of the informal court.

Obtaining Compensation

Case 24. *Remarriage of widow and claim for compensation:*

Circumstances: Agemotoja of Tatagufa was the widow of Nanomi of Kemiju. Soon after the mourning period was over she returned to Tatagufa and lived with her *nenafu*, Kikinazi, classificatory brother to the dead man. The lineage brothers of Nanomi immediately requested Tewapi, the Kemiju mouth-boy, to approach Kikinazi for compensation.

Court convened: Arriving at Tatagufa, Tewapi summoned the woman and Kikinazi. Both were cross-questioned, and Tewapi ordered that she be returned or compensation be paid. Kikinazi was inclined to question this, but suddenly blood began to flow from Agemotoja's nose and she fainted.[23] Kikinazi, on seeing this, agreed at once. A pig, several ropes of different shells, bush beads, skirts, string, salt, a fowl, and arrows were collected and given to Tewapi, who took them back to Kemiju and distributed them among the male patri-kin of the deceased.

[23] This was taken as a sign that Kikinazi and the woman were indeed married. (Nose-bleeding was performed ritually before a betrothed wife was sent to her husband.)

The right to claim compensation in respect of a widow is vested primarily in the deceased's patrilineage which, should she remarry elsewhere, can proceed against the man with whom she is living. Its members have contributed to her bridewealth; if she marries into another lineage or clan, especially into another district, she becomes a loss, unless they are compensated with something approaching their original payment.

Case 25. Remarriage of widow and the payment of compensation:

Circumstances: Eogli, originally from Tiroka, was the widow of Tugana of Anonana. Lineage and clan brothers of the dead man waived their claims to her, and she went to a Kogu man, Api^cnuma, his classificatory younger brother, who paid no compensation to anyone. Manige^cmi, who called her sister, came down to Kogu and took her back to Tiroka, pretending that he wanted only to kill a pig there and give her some and then she could return. Instead, he gave her to another Tiroka man named Monigofave, her *nenafu*, who was already married to Ta^cija of Agura. Ta^cija then left Monigofave, went to Kogu, and married Wa^cjava, who paid no compensation. As a result of these marital moves, the lineage kin of Eogli's deceased husband, those of Api^cnuma, and those of Wa^cjava came to Tiroka, where they approached the local officials asking for a court and settlement of the affair.

Court convened: A discussion was held. The Anonana men withdrew their claim but insisted with Kogu that Eogli be returned to Api^cnuma. Monigofave, however, wanted to keep her. After a long drawn out discussion the Kogu men decided that, as they had gained one woman [i.e., Ta^cija], they would let Eogli go, provided compensation was paid by Monigofave to Api^cnuma. This was agreed upon. Monigofave handed over five ropes of shells and stated that he would claim nothing for the loss of Ta^cija; he formally placed his finger to his nose, divorcing her. Toward the conclusion of the court he made an attempt to obtain compensation for her, but the officials pronounced that he had already divorced her and could therefore make no claim. The court was closed.

The same theme as discussed in Cases 21, 24, and elsewhere appears here, where the rights of certain parties become more clearly delineated than under a purely traditional medium of settlement. The aspect of balancing by the "exchanging" of wives is an interesting point, since Ta^cija went to a Kogu man, although he was not the one who had been deprived of Eogli and was, moreover, only an adopted lineage member; and this was considered in the assessment of compensation. The small payment of five ropes of shells takes this aspect into account.

Case 26. Unequal distribution of bridewealth; repercussions arising from a claim
    for compensation:

Circumstances: A Kemiju man, Opieso, representing his lineage, contracted with Haga men that O^cagetu should marry his lineage son Tegeniazu. The marriage ceremony was held, the bridewealth handed over by the bridegroom's patri-kin, and Oᶜagetu came to her husband. During the distribution of bridewealth, which included a pig, the full brother of the girl, Maviatu, was ignored and given nothing. [He was apparently then in jail at Kainantu.] Some time afterward, he took his sister to Kopegeri, a native constable from Kainantu who was visiting Tatagufa for a few days, and asked him to intervene in the matter and obtain compensation for him. Kopegeri took the girl into custody and copulated with her. When he had done he passed her to two Sonofe men who had accompanied him, and they did the same. Next morning the constable summoned Tegeniazu to appear before him.

Court convened: Tegeniazu prepared himself for the ordeal by obtaining a small twig from a special tree and holding it in his cheek while being interrogated.[24] Kopegeri, his two unofficial Sonofe assistants, Maviatu, and his wife were assembled, with a large body of onlookers. The constable, as presiding dignitary, asked Tegeniazu why he had not given betrothal gifts to his wife's full brother. He replied that he had had no hand in the actual distribution; a pig had been given by his patri-kin, and for him the matter ended there; he could give nothing more, he said. Seeing the swelling in his cheek, Kopegeri told him to come closer so that he could look at it and asked whether it was a boil. Taking hold of Tegeniazu, he forced his mouth open and saw the magic twig and angrily asked what it was for. Receiving no answer, he punched Tegeniazu on the nose and struck him again and again until he managed to break loose and run away. After this Kopegeri dismissed the court and the complainant and returned the following day to Hamaraga, a native police post near Sonofe.

Aftermath: A few days later, Tatagufa men, to settle an outstanding debt, called out to Tegeniazu and gave him a pig. This he handed to his brother-in-law, who reciprocated by giving back Oᶜagetu; she returned with him to Kemiju. At this juncture Oᶜagetu's copulation with the three strangers was discussed. Tegeniazu, with some of his patri-kin, approached Kopegeri, requesting compensation from the two Sonofe men. This was refused, Kopegeri saying he would take the matter to the Administration court at Kainantu. [His object here apparently was to cast blame on the girl and accuse her of promiscuity.] He ordered that Oᶜagetu be apprehended and brought to him.

Capture of runaway wife: Hearing she was sought, Oᶜagetu ran away to Tatagufa. Kukuni, then Kemiju mouth-boy, unable to find her, approached Ozazeᶜna [see Case 1] at Tatagufa, asking him to search for her. Ozazeᶜna found her tracks leading into some dense kunai grass. Removing his lavalava,[25] he crawled into the undergrowth and eventually came upon the girl, who trembled and urinated in fright as he seized her. Although Ozazeᶜna was her *nenafu*, he apparently enjoyed the situation. He asked her whether she had looked at his penis.[26] She replied

---

[24] This is called "court magic," *kotijozai*; it is said to prevent the user from maltreatment and from punishment, and to insure that his case will be successful.

[25] A short cloth wraparound skirt worn in this region only by native officials, evangelists, and one or two others who have obtained cloth from the patrol base at Kainantu or the Mission at Raipinka.

[26] It will be remembered that Ozazeᶜna was naked. His question is said to have been designed to discover whether she was promiscuous.

that she had looked only at his face. He led her back to Tatagufa where she remained that night in his house. On the following morning he obtained rope and tied it around one of her arms, himself holding the other end. Oᶜagetu begged him to hide her. "If you hide me," she said, "you can copulate with me." But Ozazeᶜna replied that he was afraid of the police: if he hid her he would be put in jail. On the way to Kemiju she again asked him to release her: "Copulate with me, and let me run away." But Ozazeᶜna refused. Arriving at Kemiju, he handed the girl over to Kopegeri, telling him that she had tried to persuade him to copulate with her and release her. Kopegeri angrily asked Oᶜagetu why she had behaved in that way. Ozazeᶜna, he said, was doing what he had been requested to do. He then beat her and punched her on the nose until blood flowed.

Court held at Kainantu: The police official Kopegeri was now joined by another, Gawagli, and they started off for Kainantu with Oᶜagetu, the two previously mentioned Sonofe men, the girl's husband, the two Kemiju *tultuls*, Nabulga and Fenimu, three lineage brothers of the girl, Gogulmeroa, Mananiᶜo, and Tigie, and a *nenafu* of hers, Hegofa. All these reported to the European officer at Kainantu, who held a court. Kopegeri was charged, along with the two Sonofe men, with having sexual relations with the girl. But it is reported that Kopegeri denied this accusation, paid some money to the European official, and left the court.[27] The two Sonofe men were put in jail. All the others returned to their districts, Oᶜagetu going back to her husband.

The first part of this case shows the lengths to which a disgruntled brother-in-law may go if he has not received a share in his sister's bride-wealth distribution. Generally, he would proceed against those who had deprived him of it, but here is virtually an atypical case in which he endeavored to extort more from the bridegroom, who is not convention-ally responsible. (The arrangement, as we have seen, is made between his patri-kin and those of his wife.) The husband was in the right in refusing to pay more. However, his treatment (from which his magical twig did not protect him) in the court served to cast blame on him by making him appear guilty. His wife's brother held her as a hostage, so to speak, and released her only on receipt of compensation.

The remainder of the case arises from the action of the brother in placing his sister in the hands of the native police. The affair came to the notice of the Administration officer at Kainantu only through the appear-ance of another native policeman. In evidence at the Kainantu court the circumstances were revealed, and Kopegeri, instead of being put in jail for the offense, paid costs and so gained his release. (In local terms, he

[27] I.e., in denying this he is reported to have said, "I cannot go to calabus. I will throw away [i.e., pay an indemnity]. I will 'buy calabus' [i.e., pay costs for his release]." Kopegeri was later transferred to Goroka.

"bribed" an Administration official.)[28] The two Sonofe men were unable to do this. We saw in Case 11 that no local man would normally proceed against native police who had sexual relations with his wife or daughter (or, for that matter, assaulted her). The above case is an exception or, rather, an accident. The activities of native police are rarely reported in any detail, or in detrimental terms, to Administration officers, and there are only one or two cases on record for the whole region. One of the most outstanding recent (1952–53) cases concerned the shooting of a native at Ja^cagusa in the course of an attempt to take him into custody.

There is no need to comment on Ozaze^cna's behavior in capturing the girl: the sexual content is quite typical. Ideally she could expect aid from her *nenafu*, of whatever degree, but against this was Ozaze^cna's fear of the police and of the court. Ozaze^cna was specifically detailed to catch her and, presumably, would be punished if he failed. This does not explain why he reported her attempt to escape, knowing she would be punished for it; but Ozaze^cna's liking for this sort of violence is evident from the part he himself has played in the courts.

Assault

Case 27. *Quarrel over allocation of widow:*

Circumstances: Avaru of Inivi pressed his lineage father, Dunaga^ca, to obtain for him as wife a recently widowed Inivi woman, but Dunaga^ca protested that she was to go to another man. Avaru accused him of not having contracted a betrothal for him as was his duty, and demanded the widow. Both became angry and fought, and Dunaga^ca hit Avaru on the head with an ax. Avaru approached Ozaze^cna and asked for a court. Ozaze^cna set off for Margati, near Viteve, where the native constable, Kopegeri [see previous case], was then staying. On the following day Ozaze^cna accompanied Kopegeri and his two Sonofe adherents back to Inivi.

Court convened: Dunaga^ca and Avaru were apprehended and a court was held in the village clearing. The two men were cross-questioned. Dunaga^ca said he had hit Avaru in self defense, being first attacked with a stick and then with an ax, which Avaru had now hidden. Avaru denied this. After a number of accusations and counteraccusations, Dunaga^ca declared that he had hit Avaru with a stick and

---

[28] The case is reported in the Kainantu Register of District Courts, 127/49: 8-8-49. Constable Kumbagan (i.e., Kopegeri) was charged with adultery with O'areitu (i.e., O^cagetu); he was found guilty and fined the sum of £1, or alternatively sentenced to two months' imprisonment in Kainantu jail. The fine was paid. Some interesting points given in the evidence are not mentioned above. The constable, for instance, accused the woman's brother of sending her to him. The same Register notes (128/49: 8-8-49) that one Sonofe man was charged with adultery with the same woman and sentenced to two months' hard labor in Kainantu jail.

not with an ax. Avaru angrily asked the constable to take Dunagaᶜa to jail. "Let him say it was a stick! I know it was an ax." The constable ordered Dunagaᶜa to compensate Avaru by giving him a pig and also to give one to himself. "Would you like to go to the Kainantu jail, or would you like to pay these pigs?" Kopegeri asked. Dunagaᶜa then obtained the two pigs and handed them over. The constable also ordered that Avaru marry the widow. The court was closed, and the affair settled.

This case is straightforward, judgment being found against the offender, who was ordered to pay compensation to the injured party or be taken to Kainantu. Few would willingly choose the latter course. Procedure here, which concerns intravillage (or lineage) dissension, should be compared with that prevailing under the traditional system.

Case 28. *Quarrel over division of gardening land:*

Circumstances: Oguabipa of Kemiju was making a fence in his garden when Tegia, an elder lineage brother, accused him of trespassing, pointing out that he had ignored the croton barrier, and breaking down the fence. Oguabipa in a rage seized an ax and hit Tegia on the head. Kumuiko, Tegia's mother, hit Oguabipa with a stick. Oguabipa then sent to Gunua, the native police official at Moiife, and asked for a court.

Court convened: Gunua summoned Tegia to Moiife, and both men were cross-questioned. Both held that they were in the right. Gunua took away Oguabipa's ax and gave it to Tegia; but the Kemiju mouth-boy, Tewapi, intervened, pointing out that Oguabipa had a right to cultivate lineage land. The ax was then returned. Gunua ordered them both to embrace and forget their difference, and to supply him with vegetable food when their respective gardens were bearing. The case was closed.

Case 29. *Dissension between co-wives:*

Circumstances: Waiveku from Kogu and Agimu from Kemiju, married to Nagoteri of Kogu, were almost constantly quarreling. Finally Nagoteri approached Noka, the Kogu *luluai*, asking him to discipline them. Noka took them into custody while they were out collecting firewood and selected two very large logs of wood which he forced them to carry back to the village. As they walked along Noka struck at them with a cane until they defecated in pain and fear. Arriving at the village clearing they were met by Tuᶜavo, then *tultul* of Kogu, who asked Noka why he was doing this. Noka explained, adding that a court would be held.

Court convened: The two women were made to sit down in the middle of a circle of men and a court began. Noka and Tuᶜavo cross-questioned them but elicited no reasons for their constant quarreling. Presently they were made to lie down, and Tuᶜavo beat them with a cane; after this Noka told them not to quarrel in future but to live together amicably. Then he closed the court.

This is an example of discipline through force, traditionally the prerogative of a husband. Co-wives, ideally, should live together peace-ably, co-operating with each other and with their joint spouse. Men, however, accept the fact that co-wives commonly fight and quarrel and even, in a sense, expect it of them. It is viewed as being primarily the concern of the women themselves and conventionally outside the male sphere of action, unless their quarreling directly affects the husband. It is not the business of the husband's lineage and clan kin, as would be the adultery or promiscuity of a wife. Nevertheless, the informal court is now used generally for administering punishment and disciplining recalcitrant women, as well as men, superseding the husband's claim. It is not neces-sary for him to take the initiative in such a matter. Interpreting his duties widely, a local native official is likely to act of his own accord if co-wives disturb the peace by quarreling.

Theft

Case 30. *Woman steals pig from* luluai:

Circumstances: Ma^cju from Ke^cjagana, married to a Henagaru man, stole and killed a pig belonging to Janu^cna, the *luluai* of Henagaru. She took the carcass to her house, where she cut it up and cooked it in a wooden drum. Janu^cna, finding his pig gone, asked Ma^cju if she had seen it; she replied that she knew nothing about it. Soon after the *luluai*'s son entered her house and found blood sprinkled plentifully about. Assuming this to be from his father's pig, he reported the matter to him. Janu^cna went to her house and discovered that the drum con-tained meat; a bamboo container was full of fat; under her platform-bed he found the pig's head. While he was collecting this meat, Ma^cju, taking her child, ran away into the nearby bush and hid in a small house which had been erected adjacent to the gardens. Here Janu^cna found her, tied her hands together, and brought her back to the village where he placed her in his house. He then broke off her skirts so that she was naked. Her husband, Aguja of Henagaru, was in-formed of her offense but did not interfere. A number of people assembled at the house where Ma^cju was kept in custody.

Court convened: A court was summarily held. The *luluai* stated his case, but no evidence was heard from Ma^cju. The *luluai* expressed his intention of punishing her, and the court broke up. The *tultul* of Henagaru, Mato^co, tied a length of rope from her hands to his own and went to sleep.

Punishment: On the following morning the two men took the woman to a stream, near Vitegumatega, and chose a large tree stump which they forced her to carry on her head back to the village clearing. She was still naked. Before a fairly large crowd, two stakes were driven into the ground some distance apart. She was made to lie full length and her legs were attached to the pegs with rope; two more pegs were driven in, and her arms tied to these with a fifth for her head. The *luluai* and the *tultul* then took several canes and began to beat her pubes. They continued this intermittently throughout the day until almost sundown; several canes were broken and blood came from Ma^cju's vagina, ears, and mouth, her pubes being lacerated and swollen. They did not stop until she fainted. Women living in the village loosened the ropes and carried her back to her house, where they applied pads of warmed leaves to her wounds. Later that evening her husband came for her and carried her into the bush, where they remained in a small house "away from the eyes of men" [because they were both ashamed] until she had recovered.

The holding of the informal court was only perfunctory, for the *luluai* was both the complainant and the judge. There was no trial or hearing of evidence, nor any attempt at mediation. The *luluai* was acting broadly in accordance with the approved traditional practice of personal self-help. He paid lip service to the court in order to lend added authority to his decision, and in this he was aided by the *tultul*. But severity of punishment in the case of theft is normal and has not been modified by the establishment of the informal court. In some cases compensation is sought, but more frequently theft is regarded as a major offense (a personal injury), demanding an aggressive response. The culprit must be made to suffer. In this sense theft and promiscuity (the same term, *gumaja*, being used for both) are regarded in much the same light and considered to require similar punishment.

Here, too, enters the idea of shame (*agaze*). Shame often provokes resentment, with a desire to "hit back," to be avenged on the person who has caused it. But, generally speaking, when shame occurs before the informal court this reaction is blocked. The punished and shamed person cannot engage in physical retaliation against the "impersonal authority" of the court or the officials, although this does not necessarily mean that he feels no resentment toward the people directly responsible. A question here is how far we can call the court "impersonal" when it is controlled to such a large extent by personal factors, which determine judgment to a far greater degree than the administration of an impartial range of rules or laws would suggest. The point is, of course, that the latter are in a process of transition; and the personal factor is particularly significant, since a relatively wide range of alternatives is open to the authority applying the laws. It is not so much the impersonal authority of the court which prevents any direct aggressive reaction on the part of a shamed person but the alien power which supports the system of judicial procedure through the appointment of officials.[29]

[29] Although these courts are not directly sponsored by the Administration, support of the local officials and native police virtually amounts to this. These native authorities believe, or say they believe, that they are acting for the Administration; and it is this which is our immediate concern.

The shame which is denied aggressive outlet in one direction conceivably may be diverted into other channels—against other persons, or against the self. But this does not seem to have happened, perhaps because of the severity of the punishment (in many cases), and because of its social recognition. We might almost say that the informal court has brought about a change in the idea of shame, but this would not be entirely true, when suicide and other aspects are taken into account. One explanation possibly lies in the lack of suitable outlets, apart from sorcery. But it has already been suggested that there are degrees of shame. Nor does all punishment automatically produce this response in the person suffering it. There are instances where none is observable, although it may be present—for example, the bravado of the youth who copulates in public. But where an adulterous or promiscuous wife is discovered and brought before a court, the subsequent actions of the men controlling it are calculated to punish and discipline and, above all, to inculcate shame in the woman and her lover; to humiliate them before the onlookers, and, in a lesser degree, to humiliate their kin.

Case 31. *Theft of pig:*

Circumstances: Wanizara, mouth-boy of Kogu, gave his pig to Jaboroda, a young lineage brother, to tend. Jaboroda killed it and shared the meat with his clan sister, Ne͡ja, who put it in a net bag and hung it from a tree. Wanizara, finding his pig missing, questioned Jaboroda, who replied that it must have run away, or perhaps someone had stolen it; he had seen a man looking at it. Wanizara did not believe him, and later saw Jaboroda go to the net bag and take out a piece of meat. He hid by the tree and then took the bag back to the village.

Court convened: Wanizara called together a court, summoned Jaboroda, and before a group of men accused him of theft. For some time Jaboroda denied the accusation but eventually admitted that he had killed the pig. Wanizara then said he would punish him.

Punishment: Wanizara took his bow and arrows and shot one arrow after the other at Jaboroda, grazing his legs, causing a number of surface wounds. Ka͡ceavu, at that time *luluai* of Kogu, took a knife and cut between each of Jaboroda's fingers. The youth was carried to the men's house, where he eventually recovered. Immediately after the punishment Wanizara distributed the recovered pig meat among Kogu onlookers, refusing to eat any himself.

Here is a further example of one local authority, with the help of another, although himself the aggrieved party, passing judgment and administering punishment corresponding to what is thought to be the severity of the offense. It closely resembles the traditional procedure mentioned in Chapter 14.

Case 32. *Orphan punished for theft:*

Circumstances: Fuganaja^{c}mi and Togetu, the small son and daughter of a Numparu man, Tokenoja, were orphaned. Before dying, Tokenoja spoke to the girl, who was the elder, asking her to care for her brother. They continued to live with lineage kin and their womenfolk. Some time after the father's death, Fuganaja^{c}mi went to the garden of Oentuma, a clan father, and picked a number of cucumbers, damaging the plants and the furrows but eating only one. Oentuma, cutting sticks for his yam creepers, saw the boy. "Am I your father?" he asked. "You have eaten only one cucumber, yet you have picked many and destroyed the plants." Angrily he seized him and cut between the fingers of both his hands as well as the lobes of his ears. The boy ran crying to the village, where men and women, seeing the blood running freely, began to wail: "The child has no father, no mother!" They asked him what had happened; when he told them, many of them were indignant. His sister held Fuganaja^{c}mi's head and sang the following song, which she composed as she cried.

> aminejau agohe agohe agohe i i . . .
> agireana moruga hazafi
> ware^{c}fujamena gruheja
> kavineriana agohe agohe i i . . . .
> oa oa o o o vio wi ae . . .

"Look at this boy, look! [From] Agireana, a red banana leaf, leaf [red], from loosened vine he shows you. Look!" That is, "All you people, look at this boy from Agireana [Numparu]. He is like a red banana leaf [i.e., stained with blood]. This red leaf [blood] falls from the severed vines [veins; sinews of his hands and ear lobes]. He is showing you. Look!"

The boy was taken to his sister's house. She went to Waja^{c}ipi, the *luluai* of Numparu, and told him what had happened.

Court convened: Waja^{c}ipi returned to the village with Togetu and summoned Oentuma and his wife, who had been present in the garden during the cutting of Fuganaja^{c}mi. Before a group of people he cross-questioned them and condemned Oentuma's action, declaring that he would punish them both.

Punishment: He fastened husband and wife together, tying their hands and legs, and took them to an empty house. Here a large fire was made and the couple placed close to it. Wood was piled upon it until they sweated and were scorched and blisters appeared on their bodies. They were then taken outside and their ropes cut.

Compensation: Waja^{c}ipi told them to choose between being taken to jail and paying compensation to Fuganaja^{c}mi. He told them how angry he was at their cutting the boy's fingers and ears, especially since he was an orphan [*meguza mofa^{c}ni*]. Oentuma got a pig and two fowl and gave them to Fuganaja^{c}mi in the presence of the *luluai*, who made the pronouncement that orphaned children could take food from the gardens of lineage and clan kin without being accused of stealing. Fuganaja^{c}mi, however, gave Oentuma two fowl in return, and the matter was settled. After a few weeks the boy recovered.

This case shows the traditional type of punishment carried out by an aggrieved person on a child who damages and steals from his garden. It is similar to that already discussed; the difference rests mainly in the fact that public opinion is roused in the child's favor, as he is an orphan who has no parent to provide him with regular meals (although orphans are generally treated with kindness by members of their patri-kin and their wives) or to stand by him in trouble. The extent of public opinion in this respect is seen in their wailing and in the sister's song. Yet, incensed as they were, they did not themselves act against the perpetrator of the punishment; and it was the sister who approached the *luluai* and requested his intervention. The *luluai* condemned the behavior of Oentuma and apprehended him and his wife, who by her presence had allegedly condoned the offense. Further, Oentuma in acting by himself was contravening the authority of the *luluai*, who alone had the power to punish transgressors. This was a further reason for his prompt action and indignation, although it is not explicitly mentioned. However, even if Oentuma's act was condemned and the orphan sympathized with, the boy's offense was acknowledged in the giving of two fowl to Oentuma.

Case 33. *Theft and attempted seduction:*

Circumstances: A youth named Tuvuvuᶜo of Tatagufa stole a dog belonging to a Jafanagumu man, killed and cooked it, and shared it among some Tatagufa men and youths. A piece was given to Aguja, who kept it aside and, awaiting an opportunity, offered it to a young woman, Nezitavena, his *nenafu*, the wife of another Tatagufa man, Janu. Giving it to her, he said, "My vulva! I offer you this dog meat. Eat first, and later I will come and copulate with you." She accepted the meat but did not eat it. Instead she reported his request to her husband, who became angry. Getting his bow and arrows he went in search of Aguja, who escaped to Moiife. Giving up the pursuit, Janu went to the Kemiju mouth-boy, Tewapi, and asked that a court be held.

Court convened: A number of Kemiju men accompanied Tewapi to Moiife, where they held a court, summoning Aguja. Evidence was heard from Janu, but Aguja protested at being tried without the presence of the woman. "Get Nezitavena and hear what she has to say. I did not copulate with her." The court was adjourned.

Aftermath: Aguja, in the company of Tewapi, the Kemiju *luluai* [Etuifa], the *tultul* [Fenimu], and Janu, started off for Tatagufa. On the road to Kemiju the officials began to beat Aguja with sticks. He protested that the court was adjourned and that they had not heard him yet, but they continued to beat him. By the time he reached Kemiju his head, arms legs, and body were lacerated and swollen. There in a village clearing they threw him to the ground and gave him another beating. He protested that they had tricked him and were punishing him without a hearing, but they took no notice. By the time they had finished with him at Kemiju he was unconscious, his face and body swollen and bleeding. They then carried him down to Tatagufa and put him in the village clearing. Ozazeᶜna spoke angrily to the local officials, asking why they had not heard Aguja's case before punishing him, but they made no reply. Ozazeᶜna took Aguja to his house, where he applied warmed leaves and rubbed him with hot water until he revived. Nothing else was done in the matter. The case was not reopened, Nezitavena was not questioned, nor was the case of theft between Tatagufa and Jafanagumu considered.

In this case the situation in relation to the informal court and its organization is presented, so to speak, in a nutshell. A culprit, whether he is or not judged guilty, once charged before a native authority comes under his immediate power and jurisdiction. He may measure his strength against the presiding official and the court, and in so doing, in some instances, can achieve some degree of consideration; but primarily his is a situation of subordination, and he cannot, either conventionally or in practice, react against his judges. Nor is he assured of "justice" (in the European sense),[30] or of an adequate hearing, although this may be allowed him on occasions. The organization of the informal court rests on the conflict of individual opinion, and the personal element overshadows any attempt at impartiality. The informal court is not a court of equity. The judge or "mediator" is not primarily concerned with weighing evidence presented to him by both complainant and accused and by specific witnesses, or in hearing different points of view. An accusation is not explored for accuracy, nor are the peculiar circumstances of a case taken into account when delivering judgment. Judgment or decision is made at the personal level and (generally speaking, although more than one authority may be present during court proceedings) not in collaboration with a group roughly equivalent to a jury. The official is intent on punishing an offender, and only a small percentage of cases is concerned solely with the matter of settlement by compensation.

Conclusion

The adaptation of the informal court to traditional modes of action, settling differences and disciplining those who go contrary to indigenous standards, is perhaps one of its most striking features. The similarity, or continuity, is located primarily in the content itself, especially in relation to procedure against the transgressor and the punishment meted out to him. Comparing this with corresponding behavior discussed in other chapters, it does not seem that alien contact has brought about any marked changes in basic values. But there has been some organizational change through the superimposition and growth of the judicial system

[30] See G. Gurvitch (1947, pp. 42–44).

itself. The courts were not forced on these people, nor do they represent
an attempt by an alien governing body to exert control through its own
judicial system. They are, nevertheless, of alien inspiration. Their development within the traditional framework is, as it were, a reaction to
contact; but it is a reaction which has taken place very largely in local
terms, having been adapted rather flexibly to local conditions and standards. It has hastened the changes in indigenous mechanisms of control.
And at the same time it is indirectly assisting the imposition of Administration control.

Our examples show that the changes which have taken place are structurally important. They have resulted from a reorganization in the
authority system, with the virtual disappearance of the warrior leaders as
such in consequence of more direct methods of alien control, notably the
banning of interdistrict warfare. The outlawing of this traditional form of
activity has made the informal court possible. It has led, as we have seen,
to a redefinition of the interactory zone, with a weakening of the political
unit as a body capable of acting more or less independently. The district,
fairly "strong" in the past (as it remains in many cases) in spite of its
inherent weaknesses, has become less effective since its boundaries have
been broken down through the extension of legal space.

Conventionally, all dissension, disputes, or offenses against person or
property, in fact all violence involving injury to another person, all types of
physical aggression, should now come under the jurisdiction of the court,
which alone (i.e., apart from Europeans and police) has the right to
arbitrate and to employ physical punishment in respect of adults. That
right has passed from the person and from the political unit to the judicial
body, supported by the restructuring of power and authority. This change
alone is important because it appears to run counter to much of what is
taught during the processes of socialization and enculturation. How is this
dilemma resolved?

Aggressive action is now, or is in the process of being, curtailed, and is
in the hands of local authorities. Here we find the main emphasis on
physical punishment and on violence, which provides if not active physical
satisfaction at least vicarious satisfaction for both men and women in
being party to, or witnessing, or demanding it. In view of the preceding
material, this seems to offer one explanation we seek when we ask why
the informal court has been so well assimilated and is serving so much as a
pseudotraditional mechanism, when it has been set up in contradiction to
others which have been forcibly suppressed. Much of the violence, the
physical punishment, the emphasis on sexuality, and so on, represents

merely a diversion, a re-direction of traditional modes of action. The excitement of the cannibal feast, the violence of warfare, the personal satisfaction of settling differences and of retaliating for an injury, have been, or are, giving way before the impact of alien control and the operation of the informal court; but they reappear in the punishment administered by that court, in the violence inflicted on a guilty person, in the floggings, in the stripping and sexual abuse of women, in public copulation, and so on. These features are culturally congenial and show a striking resemblance to those carried out under the traditional system. In this respect, then, the apparent contradiction or inconsistency has been resolved. People may still achieve satisfaction through violence and aggression, although not in the same fashion as before, since that right is now restricted to the authorities controlling the court. Their identification as "strong" men is not incompatible with traditional standards, since their power rests on similar criteria. The major difference is that they have become stronger "strong" men and are sponsored by an alien government so that their tenure of office is more stable. But this is still dependent on strength of action, which is appreciated both by themselves and by the alien.

The offenses treated by the informal courts are, with some minor differences, essentially the same as before—mainly marital dissension, adultery, or promiscuity. This is reflective of the traditional situation, and it is neither by accident nor design that in the cases considered here these themes predominate. There is a comparatively high incidence of adultery and promiscuity, which has been linked with the emphasis on aggressive behavior. The ambivalent attitude toward this has been noted as well as the conventional condemnation of it by males in relation to females. Here, as elsewhere, there is a conflict in values. Whereas the court has proved itself capable of coping with most of these offenses—adultery and other sexual offenses, evasion of legitimate settlement and compensation, theft and assault, and so on—it has not attempted to interfere with the more subtle or indirect forms of aggression, such as sorcery.

The most prominent offenses treated in the courts are those relating to sexual offenses and theft. In each case the punishment meted out is similar to traditional forms. Women accused of adultery or promiscuity are almost always condemned and punished. In the past there was more opportunity to evade this, but with the widening of legal space offenders can more easily be apprehended. And the same is true of those accused of theft. Although punishable within the political unit, it often escaped notice when carried out between districts—or served as an impetus to warfare. Whereas it was formerly considered legitimate to steal from one's enemies, the establishment of interdistrict (or supradistrict) authority and order has made this an offense. The position in relation to sexual offenses is more difficult to discuss without reiterating what has already been said about its traditional context. Reference should be made to this, for under the court system it has not radically changed, except in legal crystallization, in the "hardening" of public opinion against offenders, and in the procedure adopted by an aggrieved person. Cases of sexual offense excite the greatest interest and are particularly absorbing to the authorities investigating and passing judgment, as well as to the onlookers. This "hardening" is a matter of formality; it is a "hardening" of procedure rather than of attitudes.

With the blocking of many avenues for aggressively violent action as a result of alien control, the sexual aspect has been accentuated, particularly in relation to female subjects. This has a certain entertainment value, as has been emphasized. In this sense the court is performing a dual function. This accounts for its obvious popularity. These people do not seem to tire of holding courts, and a variety of trivial reasons provides an opportunity to appeal to local authority. When a court is held, the authority is not only presented with an opportunity to parade his importance and increase his "strength," he also obtains entertainment and satisfaction in fulfilling his duties, especially in inflicting punishment. The complainant, being more handicapped than previously, nevertheless achieves satisfaction through the discomfort of the accused and, occasionally, the material advantage of compensation. The onlookers and witnesses are entertained as they would be with a particularly well-acted farce, only here the circumstances are much more "real" and topical.

The accused, and in a lesser degree his or her immediate circle, is the only person seriously upset by the proceedings, perhaps suffering acute pain and injury and being shamed before co-villagers and kin. But however severe the punishment, it is possible that shame and pain are balanced against the satisfaction obtained through notoriety. This is possibly one reason why shame, when allegedly experienced, is not followed by an aggressive reaction against the person who has caused it or against the self. Shame is balanced by the exhaustion which is an outcome of punishment and by the satisfaction derived from awareness of the enjoyment of onlookers—the sensual pleasure of being stripped naked and paraded before others, of being forced to public copulation or subjected to plural copulation, and so on. These are compensatory factors, when considered in their cultural context. Both men and women are culturally conditioned to accept more or less severe physical treatment in the course of every day. Further, adultery and promiscuity on the part of women are now, under the courts, punished less severely than in the past (although women now have fewer opportunities to escape the consequences of such action).

Under the traditional system a relatively wide range of action was open to the aggrieved husband; and this in some cases included the shooting of both the woman and her lover, or a duel between the men concerned and a severe beating of the woman. It could involve interdistrict warfare. Under the informal court, however, there is no death penalty. Woman's "legal" position is considerably bettered, since she can persuade a court that she will not return to her husband, and, instead, her lover can pay compensation to him. What is more, she herself may receive compensation in the event of an alleged or an attempted seduction, and so on. She may be punished, whether or not she is guilty, yet receive compensation, which is calculated to balance the punishment.

All decision in the court rests with the local authority controlling it. For that matter, the procedure is dependent not on a specific formalized pattern but on the local authority's idea of how a court should be conducted, broadly based on a general understanding as to the course it should follow. An appeal is made, the official convenes the court, evidence is heard, judgment is given, and the decision is put into operation. This procedure varies according to circumstances. The power of the authority is, conventionally speaking, absolute; and there is, ordinarily, no appeal. This again is in marked contrast to traditional procedure. The official's decisions are made on the basis of his own experience (with some reference to the expressed opinion of the complainant). In this respect he is open to bribery, offered in order to weight an accusation or to insure that punishment will result. There is, as I have said, no impartial consideration of all the facts involved, no formal attempt to defend the accused in order to balance the charges of the complainant. The official or officials in charge may or may not consult others within or outside that district; and sometimes the court may be under the direction of a man who is not an officially designated authority. His (or their) decisions take into account what is considered by the group to be "right" and "wrong" behavior, and the application of the law is flexible enough, since it is neither formalized nor codified, to meet the demands of those appealing for satisfaction. The fact that an accusation has been made is often sufficient to convict a person, even before the court hearing. This comes out in cases when the accused is punished or abused before court is convened.

While people may recognize more or less clearly what sorts of activity are "wrong" (*haviza*, bad thing) and what are "good" (*kanari*, or *so^c e*) on the basis of ideal criteria, assessment does not normally take place until accusation is made. *Havi(za)* activity is not labeled as "wrong" until action, verbal or otherwise, is taken against it. Adultery condoned by a husband is not actually *havi(za)*, although ideally all female adultery and infidelity is so; it will be condemned as such only when the husband expresses active disapproval and appeals to the court, or himself punishes his wife. Relative strength can also override condemnation of *havi(za)*. On the whole, the judicial system fulfils a useful function in maintaining law and order within the community; but it does so on essentially the same basis as has been traditionally prescribed and its operation depends very much on the personal qualities of the local authority.

Through the process of the informal court, traditional rules are being transformed into laws. This, as we have seen, stems primarily from the fact that the judicial system is invested not only with social support but also with power to enforce its jurisdiction. It has assumed the "personal" responsibility previously operative in the settlement of intradistrict (or intrapolitical unit) disputes. And it has taken over the power of the political unit to proceed against others. This pseudocrystallization of law, however, does not refer to the political unit alone. It extends regardless of district or linguistic boundaries.[31]

But the judicial system depends for its existence not so much on the collective wish or affirmation of the people, who do not envisage it as an institution upholding their "rights," but on the individual authorities who must administer the emergent laws and impose penalties when laws are broken. These authorities have been appointed by aliens (or have, directly or indirectly, alien-derived prestige) to "keep order" in the area in which they are stationed. For this purpose they are invested with power, deriving from their recognition by and the support of the Administration. They are, in the first place, agents through which alien control is exerted, and most noticeably so when a breach of the peace takes place. To achieve this they have imposed new coercive controls, but only through the invalidation and outlawing of traditional media. They have made use of indigenous measures as far as possible, and the court system has developed as a medium through which these coercive mechanisms of control can operate. The court appears as a traditionally oriented institution supported by the social system in which it functions.

---

[31] See Wolff (1950, p. 102). Simmel associates the scale of a community, and the greater freedom, mobility, and individualization of its members, with the crystallization of customs into law.

The purpose of the Administration's Department of District Services and Native Affairs is the establishment of law and order in an attempt to bring the Highlanders within the scope of the Australian judicial system, to make the region settled and "safe," and to incorporate it within the existing political system of the Trust Territory of New Guinea. To accomplish this it must rely primarily on force. No other avenues are at present open to it. Formal education in this area is, so far, largely in the hands of the Missions and, in practice, of a rather narrow and specialized kind. As yet it has achieved only pacification, in varying degrees, and the reassembling of control mechanisms through the establishment of "new" institutions. But the local people have done more than accept this attempt at control. Given the inescapable fact of alien dominance, they have contributed actively to it. In one sense, and superficially, it has almost the appearance of self-government; but not entirely so, since most of the men in whom the power primarily rests are dependent on the Administration. Although under the native police in the new hierarchy, they have assumed much of the executive responsibility usually shouldered in such circumstances by the alien government during initial years of contact and pacification. But they are still under the surveillance of both native police and European officials. The native police may delegate some of their duties to local authorities and content themselves simply with inspection and with the occasional taking of prisoners to the patrol base at (e.g.) Kainantu. Such inspection includes the putting down of interdistrict fighting and the supervision of the cleaning of villages, the making of roads, latrines, rest-houses and so on. Their presence and their routine actions, apart from anything else, are helping directly to change local conditions. European officers also patrol the region, with duties fundamentally similar in type to those of the native police, but more far-reaching, including the taking of the census and the rounding up of patients for medical treatment.

In addition, the Missions are active. Although European missionaries do not often visit these parts, apart from the trips made by the missionary in

charge of the Taramu outstation, an increasing number of native evangelists is sent out after inadequate training at the main bases. Not only do
they reinforce and underline the injunctions of the native police and
Administration officers, but they are committed, at least nominally, to
the superimposition, more or less completely, of a new system which
they themselves understand only imperfectly. This means the undermining of existing values over a wide area of social living, even to the
extent of condemning almost all traditional belief and activity as uncongenial to Christianity, or to their version of Christianity, which is not
necessarily the same as that of the European missionaries of their particular church. In their teaching they encourage haircutting and the wearing of cotton lavalavas and dresses, and they discourage or prohibit the use
of pig fat for oiling the hair or body or anointing new-born babies, the
seclusion of women during menstruation, separate sleeping and eating
quarters for husband and wife, sacred ritual and ceremony and the objects
associated with it, sorcery, cannibalism, garden burial, and so on. Their
views are illustrated from time to time in short morality plays, on much
the same lines as traditional dramas and farces.

In spite of this, the local people lose sight of the fact that these changes
are, directly and indirectly, sponsored by aliens and designed to have far-
reaching effects. It is perhaps partly on this account that, on the whole,
the pacification of this region has taken such a smooth, uninterrupted
course. A working assumption, highly relevant here, is that when either
an innovation or an alien importation first makes its appearance it does not
do so in a vacuum. Certain of its features predispose those to whom it is
introduced either to accept or reject it.[1] The situation was congenial for
the introduction of the embryonic and informal courts, for the forms of
coercive control which they employ, and for the new allocation of power
through the appointment of *luluais* and *tultuls*. The process was one of
reassembling.[2] Even in the traditional situation we might expect something of this sort to take place; but the inspiration, or impetus, in this
case comes from alien sources.

Further, little friction has resulted between the indigenous and alien
agents of control since, up to a point, their aims unintentionally coincide.
This unexpected, apparent acceptance is due, we may suggest, to corre-

---

[1] H. G. Barnett (1953, p. 313), speaking here of "determinants among the range of
potential acceptors."

[2] R. Firth (1951, p. 82); S. F. Nadel (1951, p. 101). In R. Berndt (1954a, pp. 273–
74), I spoke of this in reference to certain reaction movements in this region, pointing
out that they were dependent on traditional background, experience, and ideology.

spondence in the matter of certain basic values. Even where these do not coincide, a *rapprochement* has taken place at a superficial level, since the Administration regulations relating to Native Affairs are formulated mainly to deal with native conditions and, except for a few outstanding features, do not attempt to enforce Australian-European law. By introducing control mechanisms similar to those already present in traditional life, the Administration is going part of the way toward meeting native ideas. Alien legal concepts need not prove difficult to assimilate in such a situation, provided they are sufficiently broad to incorporate or accommodate existing rules, even if these are modified in the process. They can become effective more readily if indigenous features are utilized indirectly, as they are here.

In adopting the informal court, the eastern Highlanders are accepting nothing which is not "usable" within their own organization and structure. In adapting it to their own use they do not seriously envisage it as serving the interests of the Administration.[3] Likewise the Administration is not aware of the institutional significance of that court or of the main purposes it serves. From its point of view the informal courts are illegal, whether they are controlled by local native officials or by native police.[4]

---

[3] This is not to say that these people are unaware of forces of external control. They were made conscious of the presence of Europeans and of their power (strength) to exert their point of view during the initial phases of contact, and since. Further, they have been able to adjust to this situation fairly adequately by means of rationalization (see R. Berndt, 1952–53, 1954a). But it is clear that they are ignorant of the extent of this control and do not understand that the alien Administration is there to stay—that they will be more or less permanently under its jurisdiction and that their own traditional life is faced with such far-reaching changes. They appear to believe that those changes which are made now are only superficial or tentative and that the present position will not last. Some of them point out that the Administration, like the Missions, withdrew during the war years, when the people around Kainantu and Goroka themselves reverted to warfare, fighting, and self-help. (The Highlanders throughout most of the region with which we are concerned were not affected, since at that time they were "uncontrolled"; yet they were broadly aware of what was taking place further north.) This, they say, could happen again; and in any case they apparently cannot envisage their complete subjugation to an alien power, however strong it might appear to be at the moment. They have had temporary setbacks before in the course of interdistrict fighting.

[4] J. Nilles (1953, p. 17) says that Administration officers for the Chimbu region (Central Highlands) are advised to observe as far as possible in lesser offenses (not stipulated) the native customs of retaliation. He adds that, in spite of settlement of a case by the Administration officer, the complainant will settle it later according to native practice if not satisfied; also (*ibid.*, p. 18), that the native police "are not supposed to exercise any judiciary power in local courts presided over by the *luluai*, but the latter would hardly ever make a decision without the approval of the policeboy present." We have seen already that in the Chimbu region (*ibid.*, p. 19) courts under a *luluai* are permitted, and his powers extend to mediating in minor disputes that are brought to him.

In principle there can be no compromise here, under the current view that the Administration itself, although it may delegate its authority in certain contexts, constitutes the only political system; and court decisions must be made within this framework. From the alien point of view, the establishment of local village councils with defined legal rights perhaps would offer a solution. Yet there is little likelihood that these would be successful in the immediate future, since the informal court rests primarily on authoritarian control; and in the final reckoning traditional ideology and values in this sphere would be uncongenial to the Administration.[5]

Thus while superficially there appears to be acceptance of alien control, it is acceptance mainly in native terms. Resistance to external pressures is potentially all the stronger on that account and likely to continue in varying degrees, although it may not be openly manifested, as long as this position remains.[6] Because the eastern Highlanders have been left so much to their own devices, and because their traditional values have not been radically changed but merely rechannelized, they have responded eagerly to the Administration's demands; and this has appeared to be merely passive submission to alien control. Such is the position as we find it today. But as alien influence is intensified, from both the Administration and the Missions, indigenous or semi-indigenous mechanisms of control will come more strongly under attack; and so, simultaneously, will the underlying value orientation.[7]

The Administration Court

Almost as soon as it came into this part of the Highlands, the Administration tried to introduce its own judicial system. This was designed mainly to control local activities considered to run counter to its own interests and those of the people themselves. The imposition and maintenance of "law and order" are viewed as basic to the spread of the new political system.[8] In the immediate vicinity of Administration centers the

[5] See R. Berndt (1957a, pp. 39–55).

[6] For instance, in the vicinity of Kainantu and Goroka, conditions are such, and alien influence so intensive, that the informal court (like other "independent" coercive controls) cannot function. Here the Administration court has become one of the main positive agents of social change, "by punitive measures rather than by adjustment of interests" (Stanner, 1953, p. 27).

[7] C. Belshaw (1954, pp. 83, 84) expresses a contrary view, speaking generally for Melanesia (on the basis of data relating to New Caledonia, the New Hebrides, and the British Solomon Islands).

[8] See Stanner (1953, pp. 18–31) and compare with J. Nilles (1953, p. 17), where he discusses briefly how government law was brought and applied to the Chimbu people.

people are under relatively firm judicial control. In the southern districts, away from Kainantu and Goroka, they are aware of the mechanism known as "calabus," but in its official form this has remained largely a background threat and not a matter of immediate concern. Nevertheless, as alien control is extended and tightened in this region, the "new" judicial system must come to play a greater part in their lives. Even now, more people are being drawn into it. Prisoners may be brought back by patrols, or occasionally by native police, particularly when an incident is considered serious. Also, more frequently, people go so far as to appeal to any European officer, asking him to "hold a court" on the spot, under the impression that more severe punishment will be inflicted on an accused person and that the accused will be more fearful of the consequences. Perhaps the strongest threat of all in these southern districts is that the matter will be taken to the official court at Kainantu, a threat often employed by local officials and native police to discourage opposition.[9]

The official courts held by the Administration have jurisdiction over relatively minor offenses. For serious cases, and here the personal opinion of the Administration officer is often a deciding factor, there is the "superior court"; that is, the district court. The same officials may preside over either, and for practical purposes no distinction need be drawn, except insofar as court registers are concerned.[10]

What interests us here is the nature of the offenses which come before the official court, in the light of what we have seen of the informal court. In Chapter 16 it was pointed out that of the 107 cases available most could be labeled "sexual offenses," being concerned either directly or indirectly with marital dissension, which is usually sexually based, adultery, promiscuity, sexual incompatibility, and so on.

In considering offenses brought before the Kainantu Court of Native

[9] Many aspects of the Administration judicial system are not locally understood. I have mentioned this already in connection with the payment of fines, regarded as bribery. Questions may arise which are not specifically covered by Administration Regulations, and conflict may take place between indigenous "custom" and the new code based on European law. At present this is mainly confined to some instances of physical assault, murder, fighting, and sorcery. But as alien control is intensified, more indigenous types of offense are bound to be brought before the Administration courts. As Belshaw (1954, p. 107) has commented, ". . . when there is a conflict between Melanesian custom and European law, it is not always clear to the Melanesian whether the official will uphold custom or regard it as 'repugnant' and over-ride it."

[10] I am not dealing here with the composition and procedure of the Administration courts. Nilles (1955, p. 20) notes the distinction between the Court of Native Affairs and the High Court. Many aspects relating to such courts should be considered, however, in a more detailed study; for instance, the position of interpreters. Nilles (*ibid.*, p. 17) mentions bribery in this connection, in relation to native police at the Chimbu station.

Affairs, I am relying primarily on the Register in which all cases are recorded from July 12, 1948; no earlier records are available. My information covers cases from that date until February 29, 1952. The offenses
recorded here relate to the whole subdistrict of Kainantu and only incidentally to the region under discussion. (At least twelve, and possibly
more, refer to the southern Kamano, Usurufa, Jate, and Fore areas.)

Over a period of three years and seven months, 263 cases are recorded,
at a time when the population under the immediate jurisdiction of the
Kainantu court (comprising only a part of the subdistrict) was several
thousand. Of these 263 cases, 151 (seven from our southern region), or
more than 57 per cent, relate to "sexual offenses." This total is made up
as follows: 139 are adultery cases, the complainant being usually the
aggrieved husband, but occasionally the wife. Where a man is accused, the
record reads "male has an adulterous relation with a female"; where a
woman is accused (i.e., is considered to have taken the initiative), the
record reads "female has an adulterous relation with a male." The circumstances of the case determine the penalty, which ranges from six
weeks' to six months' hard labor for a male, or the same period of light
labor for a female. The usual term of imprisonment is two to four months.
Seven cases (one from the southern region) concern adultery with native
police. Under the same general heading come two cases of a woman
attempting to entice another female away from her husband for immoral
purposes, two of a woman forced to have sexual intercourse with a man
other than her husband, and one of a man who behaved "in an indecent
manner" before a female.

Within the category generally referred to as "assault," 62 cases are
recorded (three from the southern region): that is, a little under 24 per
cent of the total. Of these, twenty refer to men assaulting females (in a
number, several men are charged with physical assault on a female),
especially husbands beating or injuring their wives. The penalty is usually
two weeks' to four months' hard labor, depending on the circumstances.
Here too are classified eight cases of a man "unlawfully laying hold of a
female." This is possibly a sexual offense, for it implies that sexual intercourse is desired. For example:

The complainant was Iane'me, an Anona woman, the defendant a *tultul*,
Bi'bowa, of the same district. (124/49: 25-7-1949). The woman was outside her
house when the defendant came up and placed his hand over her breasts. He tried
to persuade her to go inside, saying he wanted to speak to her. She refused and
walked away. The *tultul* came behind and caught hold of her wrists; she threw
him off. He was sentenced to one month's hard labor.

There are twenty-four cases of assault on males by males; three on females by females; two on males by native police; one on a male by a medical *tultul*; two on males by females.

In two cases there is a parallel with what we have seen in the informal courts:

One (7/48–49: 23–7–1948) concerns Iaiungo, a female of Tebinofi, and Komobe, a *tultul* of Onki. The charge was "having used his authority wrongfully to injure the complainant" [sentenced to fourteen days' hard labor in the Kainantu jail, or ten shillings fine]. The evidence mentions that this *tultul* had a stone placed upon the complainant's head and then forced her to walk around with this as a punishment. The stone weighed ten pounds. The *tultul* in defense said that when he had previously visited Kainantu he had heard a government officer insist on an improvement of village morals; there had, apparently, been a great number of cases of adultery. With this in mind, said the *tultul*, he had punished the woman, since she was promiscuous.

In the second case (46/50: 3–6–1950) the complainant was a female, Irewantanano of Ozana [Oijana], the defendant Iaroka, the *luluai* of Sainapa, who "did unlawfully strike the complainant" [sentenced to two months' hard labor]. In the evidence we are told that the *luluai* came to Ozana to make inquiries about "some trouble between the woman and a man named Auetna." It is then assumed, although this is not specifically stated, that an informal court was held. The *luluai* instructed a man named Saramoka to remove the woman's skirt; she was then forced to lie face downward across a log and was beaten on the buttocks with a cane. The *luluai*'s defense was that he had punished her for having had sexual intercourse with Auetna.

In the next category there is the general heading "behaving in a riotous manner." This includes outbreaks of fighting between either persons or groups. In seventeen cases (one relating to the southern region) several men are involved, in one case several females, and in one a man and a woman. Classified separately are two cases of "threatening language or action against another male," three cases of sorcery against males (one relating to the southern region), and eight cases of theft (involving the killing of a pig, the stealing of sweet potatoes, a blanket, clothing, a shovel, and a small sum of money).

Eighteen additional cases represent new offenses created by the Administration. For instance, two concern "setting fire to grass land not their own"; one, "refusal to maintain roads"; six, escape from custody or prison (males); two, native police assisting in the escape of prisoners; three, absconding from the Kainantu hospital; two, neglect to apply for medical attention; and two, disobeying the orders of a medical *tultul*.

The cases available from the Register of district courts (twenty-six altogether) cover a period of two years and nine months (from April 20,

1949, to January 31, 1952, no earlier records being obtainable), and the whole Kainantu subdistrict, with only two examples from the southern region. Seven are murder cases, six (including the two southern cases) involving males, and one a woman who killed another woman.

In this case (23/49: 4–8–1949) Kaupa, a Barabuna woman, killed Uera, of the same district. The defendant said she had put salt in her house but on going to get it found it hidden elsewhere. Uera was the only other person who had entered the house. Kaupa was angry; she went to the gardens where Uera was working and taking up a spade struck her on the head with the iron blade, killing her.

In the next major category, "grievous bodily harm" (that is, deliberate wounding and injury), nine cases are given: five concern injury to females by males; two, injury to females by females; two, injury to males by males.

Two of these (3/50 and 4/50: 6–9–1950) concern Bora, *luluai* of Kamanakera, who "did unlawfully wound with intent to disfigure" Naiko and Meru, both females of the same district. In her evidence Naiko said that she had gone to Aiyura with a female friend, Meru, to see her husband, Obara, who was working at the government agricultural station. Some time afterward two men, Peta and Naria, came from Kamanakera and told them that the *luluai* had ordered them to return. They did so and on their arrival the *luluai* took them both into custody. He built a fire over which he heated a length of wire, and when it was red hot forced them to lie face downward on the ground and beat them with it across their backs. The *luluai* then instructed another man, Ora'o, to sit on Naiko's back while he cut off her right ear with a bamboo knife. The same was then done to Meru. Naiko ran to her husband, who took her to the Administration officer at Kainantu. Peta, in giving evidence, confirmed the above statement, adding that the *luluai* had told him that Naiko and Meru had refused to obey him: "I want to straighten out this trouble of their not listening to what I say and walking about away from the village." On arrival at Kamanakera, Peta said, the *luluai* told them, "You won't obey my orders, and you continue to walk about and go where you like. I must teach you to hear what I say." The *luluai*, in defense, excused himself on the same grounds as in the above case (i.e., 7/48–49): "When I was appointed *luluai* the government officer told me that I was to look after my people and to see that everything was in order at my place. These two women would not listen to what I said and kept walking about to various places for immoral purposes. I then cut off the right ear of each to teach them to hear what I say in future." [The sentence is not recorded.]

There are four cases of carnal knowledge: one concerns intercourse with a woman without her consent; two, "unlawfully and indecently dealing with a girl under the age of twelve years"; and one, "unlawful carnal knowledge of a girl under seventeen years." Four cases of theft (of bananas, a newspaper, a shovel, and scissors) are recorded, and two classified as "damages to" (a pig and other property).[11]

This brief glance at the number and variety of offenses and "crimes" treated by the native and district courts at Kainantu offers some interesting points of comparison with those treated by the informal courts further south. The distinction between offense and crime, according to relative seriousness, is not made in the same way in the informal courts. However, if we wish to draw some such distinction, we can call "minor offenses" those which are usually settled by payment of compensation (e.g., in relation to the remarriage of a widow, evasion of bridewealth or mortuary distribution, and so on) and "crimes" those involving adultery, promiscuity, and theft and assault, when punishment is more likely to take some physical form. So Administration law would grade these, although there is a tendency to accord an equal weighting to adultery and promiscuity, guided perhaps by native opinion. Others, like "riotous behavior" (fighting), murder, some forms of physical assault, and sorcery, are now introduced as "offenses" and "crimes" by the Administration, where in a traditional situation they would be resolved in ways already indicated. The informal court, it will be recalled, does not ordinarily handle these cases. Should the informal court continue to exist (although this is unlikely, as alien control is intensified and responsibility taken increasingly out of the hands of local authorities) grading of crimes will probably become more severe.

The Administration court allows a wife to bring charges (e.g., of

---

[11] Compare with those given by Stanner (1953, p. 27), who lists convictions of natives in the New Guinea courts during the period 1930–41. The significant trends of which he speaks are meaningless unless population figures are supplied and the peculiar conditions of various districts taken into account. It is noticeable, however, that a number of offenses (for instance, absent from quarters, gambling, intoxicating liquor, unauthorized ceremonies, neglect of road maintenance, neglect to clean villages, disobedience of lawful orders, spreading false reports, and failure to report for census) refer to superimposed alien conditions or those peculiar to contact situations. It is true that, as Reed (1943, p. 173) points out, on the whole the enforcement of law is becoming more strict and the number of punishable offenses is growing. But the position is more difficult to gauge where indigenous or general categories of offense like adultery, promiscuity, assault, fighting, theft, and so on are concerned, for offenses may be said to increase with tighter Administration control merely because it is taking over indigenous responsibility. There is nothing to suggest that there is an actual increase of offenses in these spheres, since the indigenous position is not known. Where the indigenous population is not "in control" of its own circumstances and does not assume responsibility for maintaining law and order, since this has passed to the Administration, then, with the keeping of records, significant trends can be gauged if figures are available over a period of years.

adultery) against her husband; the informal court does not.[12] In such cases she is more likely to accuse the "other woman," who is often sentenced to imprisonment with light labor, while the husband is released, being considered the seduced party. (A woman so accused and sentenced may be regarded in the south as *gumaja*, "promiscuous," and here a parallel can be drawn with traditional criteria.)

The Administration courts treat a great number of sexual offenses, mostly adultery and promiscuity, comparable to those treated in the informal courts. They seem to stem mainly from current local trends and not necessarily from the special circumstances of alien impact. This point is borne out when we consider what we can call the traditional situation. There is the same aim behind such accusations, the desire to punish the offender, not a wish to divorce the husband or wife in question; adultery, in itself, rarely leads to the severing of marital ties. Explanations must be sought on the indigenous level, and these have already been indicated. If adultery were punishable in western European society, one might suggest that the courts could not cope with the situation.[13] This problem is one which the New Guinea Administration would do well to delegate to local authorities or leave to the persons concerned.

The other striking feature concerns those cases (7/48–49, 46/50, 3/50, and 4/50) which refer to what is actually informal court procedure and Administration attitudes toward it. The Administration considers that in such circumstances the local officials have overstepped their authority, which they hold not in their own right but in virtue of their appointment. When charged, such *luluais* and *tultuls* try to justify their actions by saying that they have been told to keep order in their particular districts. Here is expressed the basis of conflict between the European representatives of the Administration and the local authorities they have appointed. The official may act as a "strong" man only within certain limits. When he exceeds these, he is likely to be reminded of his subordinate place in the new hierarchy. This is not simply a conflict between individual persons and the Administration but a question of contrasting interests, aims, and ideologies. The *luluais* and *tultuls* can "control" their districts only through the application of coercive sanctions, which are traditionally

---

[12] Cf. Nilles (1953, p. 19): "Almost every person [in the Chimbu region], including women, may bring complaints to court" [i.e., the *luluai*'s informal court].

[13] Normally, as Belshaw points out (1954, p. 84), the Administration machine is not dependent on "Melanesian" approval before the exactment of a law. "The only partial exceptions to this are the adultery laws of the Solomon Islands and New Hebrides, which specifically make adultery a criminal as well as a civil offence in order to support what is believed to be Melanesian custom."

congenial. When these in turn (as in the above cases) are declared illegal, the main prop of their authority is removed, and they are reduced to the unsatisfying role of intermediaries or agents (deprived of full executive powers) of the Administration, relying on threat rather than on action. This change has not yet taken place further south, where local authorities are executives in the traditionally accepted manner, simply making use, as they consider, for their own purpose of the power possessed by the Administration; but, when it does come, it must involve a reorientation of existing values.

Part 6   Conclusions

Chapter 18   Social Order

Talking about social control means, in general terms, talking about social order, or, in any specific instance, the way in which a given social system maintains itself through time. It brings up a number of questions concerning the nature of that system, in both ideal and actual terms, and the patterning of social relationships within it. How is conformity conceived and what measures are taken to achieve it? Conversely, what is meant by nonconformity and how or to what extent and in what circumstances is it discouraged?

In this study the processes of socialization have been seen as fundamentally part of social control, not to be isolated from it. At the same time, for convenience in discussion, a line has been drawn between these processes and coercion and the social order. In exploring these fields just as much attention has been paid to "content" as to "form." What is

393

taught, what kinds of action are approved or disapproved, is taken as no less important than the methods of teaching and the ways of expressing approval or disapproval. In presentation of the material I have depended to a great extent on actual cases recorded from participants or my own observation, using these as a basis for discussion instead of attempting to extract and tabulate relevant items. Inevitably, some selection and interpretation has already taken place. They no longer represent the "raw material" of action; nevertheless, they offer some guide to the variations and crosscurrents which are inseparable from it.

We are concerned, then, with relations between persons, and with the choices and decisions which confront them in that field; we are equally concerned with the wider system of which these are only a part, and with relations between the units or subsystems which comprise it.

Social Relations, in Summary

In the region of the eastern Highlands, one major dichotomy affecting interpersonal relations is that between kin and non-kin. The second of these has more than negative significance, although its negative qualities become more apparent with sociogeographic distance. Certainly it points to the assumption that the rules governing behavior between kin of various kinds do not apply; but it suggests also that in such circumstances a person is free to adopt, without misgivings, the kind of behavior typically displayed between enemies, or potential enemies. Limiting factors are not absent, but they are at a minimum. Affines who were not previously kin, which in itself implies that they belong to different districts, represent in practice an intermediate or "bridge" category. Formally they may be classed as kin, distinguished by special terms and special sets of obligations and privileges, but because the basis of this type of relationship is a marriage link and not a link of descent they are likely to be treated in certain circumstances in the same way as non-kin. This is, to some extent, a matter of membership in different and, at times, opposed social units. However, quasiconsanguineal kinship also cuts across district boundaries and even across the demands ordinarily associated with such membership. Affinal bonds are much more vulnerable to fluctuations in interdistrict relations and subject to intradistrict pressures. They are expected to reflect interdistrict as well as interpersonal conflicts and antagonisms as certain other kin relations are not, and they are not qualified by any convention of neutrality in war.

Kin ties of any sort outside the district are viewed as primarily individual ties, without formal significance for interdistrict relations, and not

Upper left:
Dancers in ceremony in Kogu.

Upper right:
Konu smoking his bamboo
pipe (Kogu).

Kokote outside house
at Maira.

Men after a ceremony in
Kogu, wearing feathered
headbands. One has casso-
wary plumes; others carry
weapons. The man on the
right carries a drum, recently
introduced into this area.

After a ceremony in Kogu. The man wears a feathered headband. On the left is part of an emblem and cassowary plume.

A participant after a ceremony in Kogu. The man wears cassowary feathers and a bird of paradise plume. Feather down has been stuck to his body.

representing or leading to alliances on an interdistrict basis. But because the existing authority system in the district can be described as person-centered rather than office-centered, the importance of these ties may be maximized or minimized according to circumstances. The same is the case with interdistrict marriages, setting up as they do affinal bonds between persons who may or may not have acknowledged one another as kin. They provide additional grounds for conflict as well as for co-operation; but they also give these a personal relevance, offsetting the tendency to conceive of the interplay between districts in relatively impersonal terms. The personal ties which are thus created, or accorded an extra dimension, may serve as a basis for a closer relationship which competes with intradistrict loyalties—for example, in time of war giving warning, help, or shelter to members of other districts. A "strong" man is better able to do this openly and has a greater chance of influencing local opinion. In his case, such ties can be extended to take on, at least temporarily, more than individual or person-to-person significance.

The kin/non-kin dichotomy, then, does not coincide with the distinction which is made between those who are members of any given district and those who are not. Nevertheless, there is a strong tendency to identify the two in principle. Nor are all types of kin regarded as being, generally and consistently, of equal importance. The main social units outside the elementary family recruit their members on the basis of agnatic kinship, actual or assumed. Corporate action is associated pre-eminently with this sort of kinship, which serves to select the human material comprising these units although it does not determine their shape. This appears most clearly in the lineage, or rather in the ideal concept of the lineage (see Chapter 3), with the assumption of continuity through time and the restriction on lateral spread inferred in the use of the term "finger" (or "fingernail").

Viewed internally, the lineage represents, at one level, a way of ordering kin, drawing together one set of agnates rather than another, and providing a base line for personal identification. Viewed from outside, it represents a unit interacting with other "like" units, which actually are not uniform either in size or in span. Co-resident members of a lineage and of a village, respectively, act jointly for certain purposes and take part in certain common tasks such as those associated with gardening or with various rituals. This is the case also with the district, which convention-ally subsumes its component lineages and villages in any transactions with other districts. We have seen that this is not always a straightforward matter, particularly in respect of the larger districts, where unity may be nominal at best. But ordinarily the district is, or was, the major political as well as the major ritual unit. Its corporateness hinges not so much on the exigencies of day-to-day social living as on collective action in war and in other enterprises where its members act in its name with or against members of other districts.

For practical purposes, the lineage (and to a lesser degree the linked lineages acknowledging common descent) can be described as the unit of greatest solidarity. The relationships within it, between its co-resident members, are marked by the absence of formal restrictions ón the use of personal names, on speech, or on movement; that is, minor restraints are lacking. But there is one major restraint which is seen as overriding or superseding all person-to-person relationships within or outside it. Its members are expected to refrain from attempting to injure one another by direct violence or by sorcery and from encroaching on one another's property (gardening land or produce; and, in one sense, wives). On the contrary, they are expected to further one another's interests and actively to co-operate for what is assumed to be the common good. But this expectation alone is not enough to insure conformity.

Although, generally, there is no intense pressure to obtain either land or the food it provides, to cite two sources of possible conflict, this does not obviate clashes in which either is put forward as a central issue. Differentiation of authority and privileges within the unit, on the basis of ascribed status, provides ample room for such disagreements. These are played down to some extent. For instance, rivalry between brothers for women is formally countered by restraints between a man and his brother's wife, by the junior levirate, and by the arrangement whereby a married man and his wife may adopt his younger brother, thus reorientating their social relationship, including their formal generation alignment. In the same way the bond between brother and sister, emphasizing a woman's links with her patri-kin even at the expense of those with her husband, is part of the ideal of lineage unity. But status is not simply a matter of ascription. It rests also on achievement. This is particularly relevant here, where self-assertion is so highly valued. "Training for aggression," as one may call the process of socialization, takes place within a framework of assumptions about the use of that aggression. For example, it is to be directed only against other districts, or at least other lineages, or sets of linked lineages. In practice it is not so easily limited and is likely at times to have intradistrict and even intralineage or intra-village repercussions. The presence of women from other districts—wives, mothers, son's wives, and so on—may deflect hostility from its own members; but these women also represent sources of friction both between the members of the district and between districts.

Conformity—Nonconformity

Any relationship between two persons embodies a set of rules, involving expectations about such matters as their rights and obligations in respect of each other. At one level, there is the ideal behavior associated with that relationship; however, as the examples indicate, people do not ordinarily act in complete accordance with the ideal but approximate it in varying degrees. Their own awareness of "what actually happens" also serves as a guide to action. The ideal, then, is not necessarily a rule which people strive to follow. Often it is a symbol of the unattainable, of what might be under different conditions, rather than a standard or norm directly relevant to actual behavior in any particular case. (Because of the interdependence between ideal and norm, the one influencing the other through time, the "ideal" can never be irrelevant, but on any given occasion it may appear to be so, since its influence is likely to be reflected primarily in the norm, or the "rules," and only secondarily or indirectly in everyday behavior itself.) Because no such relationship exists in isolation, either conceptually or in reality, in any situation it is crosscut by other relationships, bringing in different and perhaps conflicting commitments, and qualified on the part of the actors by considerations deriving from past experience and anticipations about the future. Almost invariably the situation is flexible enough to allow for choice among alternatives, which may fall inside or outside the range of conformity.

Nadel (1951), like Parsons and Shils (1952), has drawn attention to the "normal range" of variability within which socialization and enculturation take place. This corresponds to the ordinary range of variation which can be formulated for any given item of social or personal behavior, although some lend themselves more readily than others to handling in quantitative terms. At some point along this range, in any given case, is the boundary which marks off tolerated or acceptable behavior from that considered to be dangerous or undesirable to the person or unit concerned. This is subject to corrective measures, varying in intensity and severity, designed to resolve the situation in which such an offense occurs and to induce or coerce the actor responsible to redirect his behavior so that it falls within the accepted range. In my terms, however, this is not "deviation" unless the actor consistently refuses to conform, rejects the prevailing norms within his social unit, and fails to respond to the controlling influences exerted against him.[1] Even then, this is to some extent a relative matter. It raises the question of subsystems or subcultures within a society, subscribing to more or less differing moral values, and the "legitimacy" of minority standards in a system where in principle majority decisions are regarded as paramount.

In the region under discussion this particular issue of minority versus majority is hardly relevant. Differences or conflicts in values do not take this form and certainly are not conceptualized in these terms; and in the current contact situation the Administration, like the Missions, does not acknowledge the legitimacy of majority opinions unless they are acceptable to itself. Nevertheless, it is important to remember that most offenses which have occurred here in the "traditional" context, excluding those which have been introduced recently and for which there are said to be no local precedents, are part of the cultural configuration. They represent alternative modes of action which at any given time may or may not be condemned in relation to specific categories of persons. For instance, there is the "double standard," in the light of which certain conduct is legitimate only for men. Thus, having more than one spouse concurrently and openly indulging in extramarital affairs are generally tolerated where a man is concerned, but not so for a woman. As moral standards change for various reasons, particularly with the impact of alien values and alien pressures, alternatives once condemned may be condoned, or those within the range of tolerated variation may be condemned. To put it simply, offenses are offenses only because they are declared to be so, and opinion in relation to them can change according to changes in moral values.

In regard to some aspects of behavior, the range of tolerated behavior may be so wide that the issue of nonconformity seems to have no practical relevance. In regard to others, a significant factor, as we have seen, is the emphasis which is placed on individual achievement, even, in extreme cases, at the expense of close patri-kin. It is by asserting himself against others, making them do what he wants or doing what he wants with them, that a man shows himself to be "strong." In choosing action to bring about the consequences he desires, he may go contrary to socially accepted rules; he may be able to ignore or override them, virtually invalidating them so that corrective or punitive measures do not operate

---

[1] For a rather different view, taking the "criminal" to be a "deviant" who is confirmed in his special role by the sanctions applied to him after his refusal to conform, see T. Parsons (1952, e.g., pp. 310–11). For further discussion see T. Parsons (1956, e.g., p. 310).

against him—or operate only in a weak and ineffective way. That is, by making a show of strength he need not be confined within the range of generally tolerated behavior.[2]. He is not a deviant if, through his strength, he widens the range of such behavior, the range of conformity, to suit his own actions; whereas, in other cases, for weaker or more submissive persons, the range does not expand in this way. The employment of relevant control mechanisms is dependent on the expression of "strength." It is not simply a matter of differences between ideal and actual behavior but rests more fundamentally on the contrasts or conflicts which are part of the system of values itself.

Ordinarily, however, setting aside this point for the moment, one of the strongest influences which keeps decisions and associated behavior within the range of conformity is the expected reaction of others. The "most significant others," in this context, are those on whom a person depends for present or future support in matters which he considers to be important. Consistent day-to-day interaction takes place with a relatively small circle of persons and as a matter of direct personal contact. Generally speaking, for an adult male, the nucleus of this circle, apart from his own wife or wives, consists of agnatic kin and their wives plus various other kin who may be, but usually are not, co-resident. For an adult female the perspective is obviously different, since apart from her own children most of the people with whom she is in more or less continuous contact are related to her only affinally; and in many cases the district in which she is living is not the one which, conventionally, has first claim on her loyalty. But for both men and women, irrespective of the total population of the linguistic unit or of the district, controls have been mediated in the past largely through face-to-face relations; and the position remains much the same today, when authority has taken on a more impersonal aspect. (On the local scene, however, the machinery of administration still operates to a considerable extent within this personal framework. Native officials do not assume that their formal position is independent of their own commitments and interests, including those of kinship.) This is a point which LaPiere, for instance, has emphasized in his study of social control, although to him it is the "desire for social status," derived through such interpersonal associations, which "induces conformity to the norms or standards of the group."[3]

I do not want to intrude a discussion of "membership" and "reference

---

[2] Cf. G. Bateson's comments (1936, p. 31) on Iatmul "respect" for a "law-breaker" with "sufficient force of personality."

[3] R. T. LaPiere (1954, e.g., p. vi *et passim*).

groups." Nor do I want to imply that pressure from kin as such is the main factor, even though the issue of kinship is not entirely separable here from other facets of social relations. But there are areas of behavior in which forceful coercive action is not employed or threatened and yet some measure of conformity seems to be achieved. We have seen that stealing within the district is likely to meet with a fairly severe response. Assault or killing may lead to sharp retaliatory action of a "self-help" kind, but is too serious to provoke organized sanctions. Instead, once the first reaction is over, efforts are directed principally toward healing the breach, re-establishing friendly relations between the parties concerned, rather than in efforts to balance the offense or punish the offender. In contrast to both these categories of "wrong," but in this case perhaps because they are not considered of a serious nature, there is no institutionalized means of enforcing conformity to the rules which govern behavior between sets of persons (pre-eminently, between kin). Physical coercion may be used on an individual basis, in an attempt to remedy a grievance and bring a relationship back to normal. Otherwise it is not seen as a means of regulating such conduct, whether or not the protagonists belong to the same district. No deliberate majority pressures are exercised to make a son dutiful toward a father, or a mother's brother toward a nephew, or a brother affectionate toward a sister, to restrain two male *nenafu* from fighting each other, and so on. The principal sanctions here are informal and diffuse, hinging on the relative interdependence of such persons in the field of social affairs.

One notable exception concerns the relations between husband and wife, and between contracting parties in a marriage. In certain circumstances a man may proceed against his wife in a way which can be called "legal," but until recently she had no "legal" right to proceed against him. For example, if a wife's adultery is brought openly to her husband's attention the consequences are likely to involve other persons besides themselves, whether these take the form of violent revenge or of demands for compensation from the wife's lover. Now, with the informal court, a judicial mechanism has been brought into operation, providing punishment for offenses and at the same time a warning against them, often combining the two in a dramatic public spectacle. The court, in the northern part of the region, also serves as a medium of punishment and/or settlement in disputes relating to bridewealth.

In what can be called broadly the traditional environment, the pattern of these relationships, the kinds of expectation associated with them, was closely bound up with the nature and patterning of alignments within the wider social system. The focusing of agnatic ties in local clusters calling for various degrees of allegiance contrasts with the scatter of all other close relatives except maternal patri-kin. Loyalty to one's agnatic kin was phrased as a matter of survival, a *desiderandum* which carried its own justification. But just because of this, underlining as it did the bond between brother and sister and extending it to their offspring as well, and because most women marry outside their own districts, maternal filiation was perceived as offering an inherent threat to lineage and district solidarity. The suggestion was that members who had close ties of this sort in another district might be subverted by bribery or affection or both to favor that district in preference to their own, while hiding their treachery by continuing to reside in their own. At the same time, possible deserters were made aware of the risk to themselves inherent in such a step by the insistence that personal security depended on identification with male patri-kin, ideally associated with a specific locality. This was highlighted as the unit of maximum loyalty and consistent support. Collaborating with others against it, while remaining ostensibly part of it, was tantamount to cutting oneself off from it in varying degrees without obtaining equivalent support from any other unit. Change of residence would make such a person even more vulnerable, because the same principle of agnatic loyalties would be invoked against him in times of crisis by his new neighbors. His allegiance would be suspect to all parties concerned. The circularity of this approach is obvious, with the socialization of boys in particular both reflecting and reinforcing the assumptions on which its rests. Although it is basic to the situation, we have seen that, as one would expect, it merely influences and does not determine the course of events, not least because of the conflicting emphasis on individual achievement. But it is this rather than the exercise of organized sanctions which is invoked as a major threat in discouraging nonconformity over a fairly wide area of behavior.

A boy is taught that it is in his own interest to conform, to act on the advice which his elders put forward. He is allowed what appears to be a relatively free choice. The decision is ostensibly left with him, with an opportunity to reject that advice. The range of tolerated variation, here, seems wide enough to include even behavior which is conventionally unacceptable. Both during and after the initiation rituals, in regard to nose-bleeding, cane-swallowing, wariness of women, and participation in warfare, there is always an apparent margin of choice. This means, of course, that pressures are not immediately obvious.

Responsibility for punishing those who do not conform is not shifted from one category of individual kin to another, for example from a father to a mother's brother; nor, in any marked degree, from human to super-natural beings, although the supernatural enters into the sphere of ritual and also into the sphere of certain taboos and omens, for example those relating to various local sites; nevertheless, a distinction is drawn be-tween senior kin who teach, encourage, advise, and care for their juniors and the sources of possible injury or deprivation. We Who Guide And Help are demarcated from Those Who Punish Or Hurt. During initia-tion rituals, when some of the actions to which young men are subjected appear to be severe, they are told that only by these means will they be able to avoid, or resist, or divert to other targets experiences of a much more painful and unpleasant kind. The promise of "strength through suffering," according to the prescribed formula, offers a straightforward way of living up to the physical and emotional demands of the local environment. It would be misleading to draw a parallel with adults who inflict pain on children, "for their own good," as a disciplinary measure, because the ritual is not viewed as punishment and does not have the same moral connotation. From the material at hand, although quantitative data on this aspect are lacking, it seems that these people do not willingly punish their children by force, except in moments of rage; and rage excuses a great deal, whether the victims are children or adults. But, particularly as a child learns his way in the world outside his immediate family, it is made clear to him that the sources of harm and danger are normally "others," not his own circle of male kin and associates.

Contrasting Male-Female Qualities

One source of danger is said to be in female qualities which are inimical and weakening to men. The intentions of individual women are a second-ary consideration, although men claim that women can make deliberate use of these powers to suit their own purposes. At first glance it might seem that this is a matter of exaggerating differences, mainly physiological differences, and insisting that they are incompatible. The ritual imitation of certain female characteristics may appear to support this, but it can also be viewed as a conflict on the basis of likeness. Women, too, are taught as they grow to adulthood that it is good to fight, to be strong, and to assert themselves. Their training lacks the specific focus of that given the men, with its sharpening of attitudes and techniques. Nevertheless, they are assumed to share the same broad aim of self-development—although not the same means of achieving it. For both sexes there are acknowledged to be certain limits within which, in the ordinary course of events, hostility may not or should not be openly expressed. But, in addition, women are subjected to a further restriction which is more consistently enforced: they are not to use either physical violence or sorcery against men. There are only two exceptions. First, of a minor sort, are ritual attacks when young male initiates are brought back to the men's house; second, and probably more important, is the kind of "fighting" which is identified with sexual intercourse and with some of the preliminaries associated with it. (For example, it is said that a widow who violently resists or fights a suitor thereby shows her interest in him and her readiness to accept him.) And it is in this area of sexual intimacy that men are most vulnerable.

Apart from these, the separation of permissible conflict areas for both sexes means that direct clashes between them are less likely or more easily resolved when they do happen—because men have control of the major weapons. Women's antagonisms and grievances conventionally find outlet against other women, not against men. (Typically, jealous co-wives turn on each other rather than on their joint husband.) Their standards of achievement in this respect seem to be focused on men as a yardstick for conduct. Often this is a matter of inference; but in some cases it is made explicit, for instance when a woman who has acted bravely or shown more than ordinary initiative responds with evident pride to the statement (from men) that she is "not a woman now but a man." And this in spite of the fact that in their mythology Jugumishanta usually receives far more attention than her male counterpart. Formally, in all male-female relationships, especially on occasions when physical force comes into the picture, men are dominant, women submissive. In one sense women provide a background against which men can highlight their own achievements, a foil for their display of "strength." The contrast itself appears to stimulate men and enhance their sense of self-esteem, even though the injunctions and precautions relating to women show that their submission is regarded as by no means complete. Men must work to develop their strength, because the measuring rod here is the relative strength not only of other men but, at least potentially, of women.

In spite of the fact that some fights between women have been reported to end in death for one of the participants and injury to others, women are not normally afraid of what other women may do to them, especially since the same weapons are available to them all. This is not the case between women and men. Whereas men may express fear of women's "natural" powers, women quite realistically express fear of what men, armed with axes and bows and arrows, may see fit to do to them. On the whole, in spite of individual exceptions, men are better able to control women in a crisis than women are men. Up to a point, a woman can get her own way in a variety of matters. She may force her husband to give up a new wife or refuse to marry a man she does not like. But she must be careful not to be caught in a position of weakness; and women are more vulnerable in this respect than are men.

In the past, the assumption that women are to blame for various ills and misfortunes which afflict men served as a partial check against open adultery on the part of wives. It is hard to say just how effective cane-swallowing was thought to be in such cases. Taking a wife to court for adultery is not an equivalent remedy insofar as the husband's own "health" is concerned. Among the Usurufa, for instance, court action and cane-swallowing are recognized as serving different purposes. When cane-swallowing is no longer consistently practiced, as in the northern part of the region, we need not expect on that account more adultery cases to appear in the courts.

Inculcation of Fear and Aggression

Men, then, shift responsibility for certain kinds of trouble to women, ostensibly because this is a latent attribute of the sex, even while they acknowledge that in any given instance the trouble may be precipitated by other factors. But for both men and women there is another source of possible danger which is just as important, and that is the hostile intentions of "other districts." Children start to learn this quite early in life, first in a casual way as they listen to the talk of their elders, and later through deliberate inculcation. The potential hostility of other districts provides a reason for intradistrict co-operation. Sometimes this is merely inferred; but often men draw on it explicitly in urging others to accept some particular course of action. The menace of "other districts" is held up as a threat, with both direct and indirect bearing on internal affairs. In the dramatic performances staged in the men's house at initiation periods, boys are shown what is likely to happen if they disobey the rules. Thus a man who commits adultery with the wife of a fellow member of the village or district is likely to be attacked by the angry husband and suffer personal injury, perhaps death. But the further implications of his action may be pointed out to him: fighting within the unit weakens that unit, and a unit needs to be strong to resist attack from outside if its members and the unit itself are to survive.

It is in this context that we are to understand the statement made to the young initiates, "Some boys hear what we say; others do not." Direct orders or prohibitions are employed only sparingly, and the instructors or guardians themselves need not appear as the agents of punishment or disciplinary force. The two categories, "women" and "other districts," are made to serve in this capacity, either separately or in combination. The preferred line of approach is, "If you do [or fail to do] this, such and such may [or will] happen." Apparent freedom of choice masks strong indirect compulsion. There is no "ultimate sanction," and the matter is framed in fairly simple terms, with empirical evidence to show that the threatened disasters are present and "real"; but this way of putting it, without obviously forcing decisions, accords very well with the emphasis on individual responsibility.

Essentially the appeal is to fear, whatever subsidiary factors may intervene. Both fear and aggression are deliberately fostered, the one reinforcing and accounting for the other. The linkage between them is most apparent in the sphere of interdistrict relations. During initiation training, for instance, they are often referred to in virtually the same breath. Neither is put forward in isolation. In both formal and informal teaching they are presented as part of a complex of assumptions, in which one necessarily implies the other: that members of other districts (apart from a few of one's own kin) are likely to attack, as they have done in the past, using either sorcery or direct violence; that one must be able to defend oneself in the face of this threat; and that, where possible and expedient, attack is the best form of defense. It is clear that we cannot understand this position in terms of individual anxiety, maladjustment, or paranoia. Where the social situation is so defined by all the members of all districts concerned, it has a "reality" independent of the personal characteristics of any one of them. There is no information available as to the course of its development in the past; it confronts us as "given," the origin of which we cannot explore. It may be useful to see it as an example of a "self-fulfilling prophecy,"[4] a self-generating and closed system, one which carries its own momentum, so to speak, and from which it is difficult to break away. Even the Administration, forcibly intervening and taking steps to alter this state of affairs (that is, to halt the warmaking, sorcery-accusation cycle), in one sense itself has been incorporated into the system, as representing a new and more powerful unit, which achieves its ends merely through superior strength. Obviously it is not enough to suppress open warfare, thus removing the threat of armed attack from other local units, as long as the basic values continue to be perpetuated, because warfare comprises only one expression of these values, even though

---

[4] R. Merton (1949/57, pp. 128–29, 421–36); see also K. R. Popper (1957, p. 13).

it provides "visible evidence" of the state of affairs which is assumed to exist.

The kind of situation in which physical violence seems to be most satisfying, insofar as we can judge this, is one in which the victim is unable to retaliate or at least temporarily is lacking in supporters who can take up the challenge. Interdistrict affairs offer the best scope for this, as a sphere in which such violence is not only legitimate but highly approved, and the treatment of enemy corpses, for instance, with the opportunities it affords for exciting activity, is part of this picture.

Personal Choice

To speak in these general terms is not to lose sight of variations in individual behavior, where physical aggression against other persons is concerned. Mechanisms of control locate the context within which this may or should take place; and, as sometimes in suicide, it may even be turned against the self as the best means of injuring or punishing others. But most people do not commit suicide, most people are not outstanding in "strength," and even in situations where physical violence is an acceptable form of behavior not everyone has recourse to it. The examples set out in this study illustrate the interplay of various factors in any particular case, with considerations of personal interest or pressure of interpersonal relationships helping to shape the choices that are made. Neither the accounts put forward nor the construct statements about "what happens" (as contrasted with "what should happen") ignore this factor of differences in individual response, conventionalized (as it often is) in the distinction between "strong" and weak.

Traditionally, the rights and rules upheld and sanctioned by public opinion and sentiment, variously expressed, could be contravened on occasion according to the "strength" of the persons concerned. With the introduction of the informal court these rights and rules have become more tightly defined and more strictly enforced. There is not the same scope for personal violation without accompanying condemnation or censure. Controls, up to a point, show signs of operating more equitably. Nevertheless, the traditional theme of strength-through-aggression has not been seriously curtailed but only diverted into new channels, and it still exerts considerable influence. Whether certain actions lead to the holding of a court (and determine its subsequent outcome) is still very much a matter of personal attitude and decision. It does seem, however, that personal choice is more restricted when the informal court is operative. The forces of coercion are much more clearly defined than they were, mainly because they are supported by agents of external control.

In the courts, the use of force is a one-way affair. The victim, however much he is shamed and humiliated, cannot respond in the same coin, although sorcery still offers one possible means of retaliation. The desire to retaliate is blocked by the powers assumed to reside in the persons controlling the courts, with their aura of Administration support. It may be displaced, diverted into other channels, but it does not take the form of direct physical aggression against the offenders or (when suicide is seen as revenge) against the self. It may possibly be dissipated in the course of everyday living—for example, in sexual associations, in the excitement of watching similar demonstrations in which others are punished and humiliated; and the suggestion has been made that the punishment itself, focusing dramatically on the victim in a public display, may afford him some pleasure or satisfaction. In any case, there are well-established precedents for such failure to answer force with force—when a woman is subjected to plural copulation, when a strong man overrides a weaker, and so on. The probability of submission is latent in any relationship where power or authority are unequally distributed; for example, between a strong man, or local authority, and others; between elder and younger (or senior and junior) brothers; between men and women; between a husband's parents and his wife; or, initially and perhaps most consistently, between parent and child. On a larger scale it appears in the relatively swift collapse of social units under attack, their readiness to scatter without making a co-ordinated stand.

Here, of course, the factor of long-range choices comes in. Because in the past there has been no fixed hierarchy of adult status other than that of males versus females, "strength" and "weakness" are perceived as relative qualities subject to change through time. Children become adults, growing stronger as their parents grow weaker. With adulthood, disparity in age between brothers loses much of its significance. "Strong" men cannot hold their positions indefinitely in the face of competition from others (or this was assumed to be the case until just recently); and those who are powerless today may achieve power tomorrow. The succession of victories and defeats for any one district, or any one person, is conceived as an attempt to achieve a balance through time, although the score at any given moment may reveal a debit rather than a credit.

An important feature of this long-range view of the relations between persons and between social units, extending to the non-human world as well, is the principle that all injuries must be reciprocated, not necessarily in kind. In practice, as the examples indicate, for reasons of expediency, lack of incentive, or conflicting pressures, steps are not always taken to implement it; but such exceptions are usually deprecated or glossed over to provide a show of conformity, without affecting the validity of the code itself. At one level, fear of possible attack is given as a reason for the use of aggressive measures such as physical force and sorcery. At another level, these measures are deliberately employed as a means of retaliation in order to balance the account between districts, to compensate for a real or imagined injury or wrong, although from the viewpoint of the victim and his unit these measures, in themselves, represent an injury or wrong. Both tend to form part of a repetitive sequence. At the same time they serve as mechanisms of control, which may be countered by similar mechanisms operating from a different source. Sorcery is usually confined to this sphere, but occasionally it enters into intradistrict relations. Two factors which are used locally to explain this departure from the norm also play some part in interdistrict affairs. One is a serious rift in the district, or village, or lineage, which may lead to a redefinition of the units concerned. The other is bribery as a customary means of instigating or sustaining short-term alliances.

Warfare and sorcery, traditionally legitimate ways of proceeding against other districts, are now condemned by the ruling Administration. Warfare has been declared illegal, a punishable offense, because the Administration reserves to itself the right to control the use of force between adults. Sorcery is in a rather different category. It is the belief in it rather than the alleged performance of it which is under attack, since the Administration is reluctant to accord it the same empirical status as overt physical aggression. Even fighting between individual persons, where local reaction formerly depended on the context in which it took place (for example, it was discouraged between kin and between co-wives if their joint husband was inconvenienced by it; encouraged between non-kin with different district allegiances), or on their relative strength, is now coming to be regarded consistently as an offense. There is continuity here in that the new "strong" men, the native officials and their adherents, in practice still rely on physical violence and the threat of violence to assert their authority and punish offenders and (subject only to the European officials) regard it as being their prerogative.

Mechanisms of control such as these obviously do not always operate to reduce or restrain conflict. They may resolve it temporarily in one situation while, in a broader perspective, serving to reinforce it. This is due in part to conflicting or incompatible features within the value system itself. Probably the most outstanding of these is the pervasive emphasis on direct and indirect aggression as a means not only of defense-through-attack but also of self-expression in a wide range of situations. Taken in conjunction with the ideal of individual self-assertion, it operates against the ideal of unity and co-operation within the various agnatically based units, the lineage, village, clan, and district. In terms of the crude dichotomy of in-group versus out-group (which is relevant here, particularly at the interdistrict level), it undermines the foundations of in-group loyalty and cohesion, encouraging the very weakness which it is allegedly designed to prevent.

There is some local awareness of this position—but only in its implications for action. The solution is seen ideally in compartmentalization: consistent co-operation, mutual aid, within a certain range of persons; conflict, or spasmodic co-operation, outside it. The major examples of role-conflict are shaped by this framework. Take, for example, the case of an interdistrict marriage and the roles of wife and mother, sister and daughter. There is an incipient clash here, determined by the system of social alignments, with personality factors playing only a subsidiary part.

In contrast, the *nenafu* role is, as it were, ideally held constant outside the field of lineage or district loyalties, insulated from them by the convention of personal neutrality. For the most part, it is not seen as incompatible with other roles. When it coincides with some other role (for example, that of *nefaru* "age-mate" or of spouse), its strongly co-operative tone has the effect of reinforcing this quality and reducing the likelihood of conflict. Spouses who were originally *nenafu* are expected to be more affectionate and less vulnerable to interdistrict tensions than those who were not. The *nenafu* role, then, is, ideally, unhampered by the latent conflicts which mark even the relationship between close brothers. Even though a marriage between two *nenafu* alters the content of the relationship between their respective siblings, this is indicated clearly enough by changes in terminology (see Chapter 3), that is, by the dropping of the term *nenafu*. Where the term continues to be used, the behavior conventionally associated with it is straightforward and consistent, not expected to change course suddenly under the pressure of outside events. The main dilemma facing a *nenafu* has to do with the fact that this is not a simple dyadic relationship, and that genealogical closeness outside the immediate range of actual or adopted cross-cousins is not the only criterion influencing the choice of one line of action as against another. In situations where a person has, say, two close *nenafu* who are at odds with each other and both call on him for help, he must choose between remaining passive, and so failing to fulfil his *nenafu* role, or deciding in favor of one of them, and so evading his responsibility to the other and, in fact, by opposing or even attacking him, going contrary to the behavior that a *nenafu* has every right to expect of him. Rarely, he may attempt to mediate between them. This, however, has to do with choice between a number of "alters" toward whom the *nenafu* type of behavior is viewed as appropriate and not with contradictions within the role itself, or, necessarily, between it and others. The same consideration enters into all relationships between persons or social units—that is, the choice, in any given situation, of one course of action rather than another, on the basis of long-range or short-range interests. Where such interests are perceived as conflicting, the result may be a cleavage between the persons or units concerned. Where they are perceived as congruent, a view sometimes stimulated by bribery, the result may be an alliance, if only on a temporary basis. This is, of course, putting the matter too simply. For one thing, it implies a deliberate calculation of advantages versus disadvantages which need not be present. The decision to act may be taken suddenly, in accordance with a person's mood at the time, or merely because he seizes on it as the "right thing" for him to do. For another, it suggests too sharp a distinction between conflict and co-operation.

Institutionalization of Conflict

Conflict of principles, of roles, of interests, and, consequently, of persons is to be found in one form or another in all social systems. But one of the most interesting features of this particular region is the way in which conflict has been institutionalized. In considering this, let me recapitulate briefly.

The social context within which people interact is a shifting one, contracting and expanding in accordance with the perspective of the actors. In certain circumstances they are engrossed in kin or quasi-kin roles on an individual basis. In others, they appear as members of various social units. In any action sequence, one of these roles is likely to predominate. The whole process of socialization, from the viewpoint of the person subjected to it, consists of learning how to adjust his behavior and expectations in accordance with these shifting frames of reference; how to apply his knowledge, his "home-made model," in actual situations. His experience in those situations, and the formal and informal discussions which insure that, up to a point and for most practical purposes, most local "models" agree—all this is reflected in his own working model, at the same time an abstract of "reality" and a guide to it.

One such frame of reference, affecting a wide range of behavior, hinges on membership in one district instead of another. The district, the political unit, is not structurally independent. Although the local label for it (the "big name") is noncommital, neither denying nor underlining its territorial significance, in social terms it maintains its identity as a unit only as it is contrasted with other structurally similar units. This is true, too, for the lineage and the clan but less obviously and consistently so. There is no specific word, in any of the four languages we studied, for the interactory zone which can be delineated at any one time in relation to any one district. These people do not formulate their position in this way. Nevertheless, their comments, both general and particular (for example, "explaining" some incident), suggest that if they turned their attention to a systematic consideration of this question some such picture would emerge, at least in rough outline.

Usually they emphasize the need for reciprocity in interdistrict as in all other affairs, particularly where grudges or injuries are concerned. Adult male members of each district keep a rough tally of the gains and losses of that district in relation to others, continuously trying to adjust the balance in their own favor. To put it more accurately, they keep a series of tallies, because not all the items involved are of the same order, and the various accounts are kept more or less separate. Deaths, illnesses, or injuries due to open violence or attributed to sorcery, are not in the same category as the holding of ceremonies or feasts. The content of the delayed "exchange" differs in each case, even though there is some overlapping when payment of compensation is substituted for retaliation in kind. Interdistrict marriages, however, are not weighed on the same scales. For the persons immediately concerned the debit-credit assessment looms large; but for the districts, as units, the point is rather that these represent informal links which should be taken into account in their formal dealings with each other.

The assumption is often made, sometimes explicitly and sometimes not, that the districts most often and most bitterly at enmity with one's own are those with which its members have contracted the greatest number of marriages and in which they thus have, among them, the greatest number of affines. This assumption does not always hold good, but it approximates what seems to be the actual position.[5] Certainly it points quite plainly to

[5] Cf. Radcliffe-Brown's interpretation (1951, p. 20) of a somewhat similar statement from the Gusii of East Africa ("Those whom we marry are those whom we fight"). As he explains this, it signifies that "The taking of a woman in marriage is represented as in some sense an act of hostility against her kin." This interpretation, which is put forward as a general statement, does not adequately account for the situation as we find it here.

See also, e.g., M. Gluckman (1956, p. 69).

the kind of interaction which is expected between such units—neither wholly co-operative nor wholly conflicting, but incorporating both aspects as a legitimate and necessary part of the relations between them. There is no question of differentiating, as some societies do, between the people one fights and the people from whom one obtains a spouse. Here, in general terms, the two categories coincide because both are activities characterizing a close social relationship as contrasted with the relationship existing between strangers.[6] Within this interactory sphere are found the bitterest and most hostile as well as the most affectionate ties.[7] At one level these are of a personal kind, indicating the spread of kinship and affinal bonds; at another level they find expression in the fluctuating alignments between districts, alternating between friendship and hostility.

Thus the formal picture of districts interacting as units is not identical with the interaction of their individual members. Some of these, for instance, might remain neutral in respect of certain individual members of the enemy, or even render them active assistance. Kogu might be fighting Kemiju, but this state of affairs would not be binding on various persons in either of those units in respect of one another. This undertone of personal kin commitments is seen as primarily an individual affair,

[6] The ordinary unilinear scale for measuring social distance will not serve the kind of situation we have here. The criteria usually employed in assessing and measuring social distance are those of perceived closeness of interest or identification, in terms of friendly versus inimical attitudes. (See, e.g., T. Newcomb, 1952, p. 573; Kimball Young, 1948, p. 261; B. F. Green, 1954, p. 353.) This means that strangers who are perceived as neutral or indifferent if not friendly are "closer" than enemies with whom there is a well-established relationship of hostility. The scale, then, indicates gradations along a friendly-hostile continuum largely on the basis of subjective reporting within a relatively standardized framework. It selects from and simplifies the "real" situation, in which the two cannot always be distinguished so sharply. Of course the problem of definition is critical here—what do we mean by "social distance"? It seems to me that assessing subjective feelings of friendship and hostility, viewing these as antithetical, is not the same thing as assessing social distance, although it goes part of the way toward it. Choice indicating the "social acceptability" of another person is not identical with choice indicating a "desire to interact with" that person. Objective analysis of the degree of interaction between the subjects concerned would provide another clue, at least as important, insofar as interpersonal relations are concerned; but in part the problem is one of conceptualization, of agreement as to just what is being measured. It would be out of place to pursue this question here, but for discussion of it, see, e.g., G. Lindzey and E. F. Borgatta (1954, pp. 411, 423); also C. H. Proctor and C. P. Loomis (1951, pp. 561–85, especially p. 583, "communication data").

[7] J. French (in Cartwright and Zander, eds., 1953, p. 128) sees a necessary correlation between interdependence and potential conflict in social relations. J. Whiting (1953, p. 286) makes the same point in regard to people living in intimate contact; they are at once the main source of both frustration and gratification. This is another way of saying, as Weber did (1949, p. 26), that "Conflict cannot be excluded from social life." See also R. M. MacIver and C. G. Page (1950, p. 65); G. Simmel (1955, pp. 44–47).

inseparable from the movements of various districts toward and against one another but at the same time not to be confused with them. Nevertheless, the very fact that neutrality on this personal basis is conventionally upheld, and not merely a matter of individual sentiment, indicates that "total war" is neither expected nor desired. Individual neutrality helps to keep the lines of communication and co-operation open even during periods of intense fighting when the combatants seem to regard one another as devoid of every human right. Like the assumption that there should be a limit to the number of deaths in any one encounter, it points to the broader setting of common agreement within which such cleavages take place.

In considering the question of social order the broader setting is of critical importance. Because no district is self-contained but relies on others like itself to make up its social world, we can speak of the district as a subsystem, the social system being the zone of interaction centered on any one district. Naturally, this will be an abstraction, which can be made at any point in time; but such an abstraction will reveal the nature of social order, throwing into relief both structural alignments and the cultural content on which they depend. Thus linguistic affiliations cut across the interactory zone and are viewed in one sense as contrasting with it, in another as complementary to it.

Intradistrict pressures, designed to insure solidarity against "outsiders," help to maintain a position of opposition and conflict in relation to all other districts as such. Conversely, the expectation and actuality of conflict serve to underline the separate identity of any one district as against others, perpetuating social (if not always territorial) boundaries. It is in this context that we can see most plainly the attempt to achieve balance, or order, in social affairs.[8] Obviously, a complete balancing is never attained on either an interdistrict or an interpersonal level. Nevertheless, the principle of reciprocity, as conceived here, has this controlling or "equilibrating" quality. We could say that it has to do with restoring the status quo, provided we understand by this the state of relations between social units, or between persons, with content or environment a secondary matter. Allowance is made for variation in detail. It is the balancing of the relationship itself that counts, although conventionally accepted means are advocated in order to arrive at this balance.

But in one field in particular it is probably true to say that the means are taken to be just as important as the ends. Where warfare is concerned, aggressive actions are treated as both pleasurable and "good" in

[8] Cf. R. Firth (1951, p. 82).

themselves, apart from the stated objective in any series of encounters. Warfare in this sense appears as an "antagonistic game," as Simmel put it,[9] in which the "opposing teams" enjoy the encounter and at the same time compete to score a greater number of goals and so claim a victory. Up to a point this could be termed competition; but the "play" aspect of warfare, its excitement and thrill, are inseparable from the risk and danger associated with it. If warfare is a game, it is a deadly one. The immediate goals are the killing, or at least (though this represents only a temporary triumph) the wounding, of other human beings, active participants or not. The system allows for and encourages a certain expenditure of human material. Provided the "rules" are observed (the neutrality of various kin, the acknowledgment that killing should have its limits), this human material may be disposed of in any way the combatants see fit; and even after death it can still be used as a challenge to one's opponents or as tangible evidence of their defeat. But there are no sanctions to enforce the "rules" except the principle of reciprocity itself: the understanding that retaliation is likely to follow, that grievances can be long-lasting, and that the greater the number of killings the more outstanding the debt to be finally settled. In any case, in this scheme of things, wholesale destruction is not desired. The sole intent is that a district keep slightly ahead of its enemies, insofar as it can manage this. Opponents are not there to be annihilated; they are there to be fought. Even if this means driving them away for a time, they are still "in the game"; and, with interdistrict alignments so flexible, they may be needed later on as allies and friends.

Warfare here is not a consequence of hunger for food or, as a general rule, for land. The capture of women, pigs, or even children is incidental. The struggle, basically, is for power and for the prestige that goes with it. Just as rivalry within the district is a feature of relations between adult male peers, particularly in terms of their relative strength, so the relations between districts are marked by the same desire to show the superior strength of one against another. This can be achieved in a small way by destroying gardens, burning houses, stealing pigs, and other provocative acts, or, on a larger scale, by driving away whole villages or districts. But the real test is to show that one has the power of life or death over members of another district—to kill without being killed in return, and to taunt the bereaved district with its defeat. "We [are strong enough to] kill you; but you can't kill us!" In the local view this is the supreme con-

[9] G. Simmel (1955, pp. 34–35). See also R. Merton (1957, p. 157), pointing to the significance for the maintenance of social relationships of "satisfactions deriving from competition itself," as against "almost exclusive concern with the outcome."

trol one human being can exercise over another as an individual or as representative of a social unit. In warfare, victories and defeats are ultimately calculated in these terms; and districts are bound to one another just as much by their defeats, by the debts and obligations which these involve, as by the commitments entailed in their more peaceful transactions. This is the case with sorcery as well, although here the imputation of responsibility in any particular case may appear to have an "unrealistic"[10] quality as contrasted with the more straightforward evidence provided by direct physical injury. But as a means of expressing interdistrict suspicion and hostility sorcery has been a substitute for open warfare; and today in the controlled areas it is a strongly favored alternative, although it lacks the display and swagger of warfare and the exhilaration of co-ordinated physical action.

Warfare and sorcery, in threat and actuality, thus bring into play the oft-cited principle of unity through opposition, the drawing together of the "in-group" in the face of a common enemy. But over and above this, opposition between districts within the zone of interaction (and, conceptually, within the zone of potential interaction) is seen as being, itself, a unifying force. It is not so much that conflict unites; the point is that between one district and another conflict is one of the accepted ways of behaving, just as it is between persons, with varying provisos and restraints in each case. The opposition between districts finds expression in a number of different ways, but it crystallizes most sharply, and in local terms most satisfyingly, in the open clashes of warfare.

The local conception of social order, then, does not minimize the importance of conflict but, if anything, overvalues it. To say that conflict here is a form of co-operation may obscure the significant distinctions which can be drawn between them; but the same point has often been made, from Simmel's[11] "conflict as a form of sociation" to Radcliffe-Brown's[12] "relationship of opposition, which is not at all the same thing as strife or enmity, but is a combination of agreement and disagreement, of solidarity and difference," and Jessie Bernard's[13] reminder that the "opposite of co-operation is not conflict but *anomie*." The positive and negative effects of conflict have received varying emphasis from social

[10] Cf., e.g., R. M. Williams, Jr. (1947, p. 40); L. Coser (1956, pp. 48–59).

[11] Cf. G. Simmel (1955, p. 13). See also J. Bernard (1957, p. 44) and W. G. Sumner's references to "antagonistic co-operation" (1906/40, pp. 16–18, 49, 346).

[12] A. R. Radcliffe-Brown (1951, p. 22). His reference here is to Aboriginal Australia, distinguishing this mixed type of "relationship between persons or groups" from enmity and strife, and from "simple solidarity."

[13] J. Bernard (1957, p. 78); see also J. Bernard (1950, pp. 11–16).

scientists in the past and have been differently assessed and evaluated. To Coser its positive effects have not received the consideration they deserve.[14] Merton[15] suggests that sociologists have been concerned more with stability and "with the 'maintenance' of social systems" than with the "potentialities for change" in them, a point to which the study of conflict is especially relevant. But to Ogburn and Nimkoff, sociologists are "competition conscious" and have devoted more attention to "competition, rivalry, and conflict" than they have to such issues as co-operation, accommodation, and adjustment.[16]

I do not want to engage in a general discussion on this topic, since my principal concern here has been the regulation of social behavior and the problem of social order in one particular region. At the same time, this situation does not exist in isolation. It is of interest not just for its own sake, although something of this sort may very well be concerned too, but because it provides us with one more example of the ways in which human beings live together in society; and it is through such examples that we increase our knowledge of social process and social structure in a range of different contexts.

In some respects this case is a specialized one, or at least represents a minority position. At an individual level, apart from the male-female dichotomy, there is no fixed status hierarchy. The tremendous stress on achieved status goes hand in hand with the notion that all adult males are potentially equal, as adult females are in their own sphere, and that any who try hard enough can be a "strong" man with control over others. Because hereditary leadership is so weak as to be almost negligible, and authority is highly personalized, over a period the power to enforce decisions is diffused among a number of "strong" men, who exercise it largely on their own initiative. The emphasis on individualism serves as a check on co-ordinated action and reduces the ability of any social unit to withstand attacks from outside. At the district level there is the same assumption of rivalry among equals, even though not all districts are comparable in population or in size. There are no fixed alliances and no attempt by any one district to dominate another over a long period. Nor is there any attempt to "line up" into two mutually opposing camps, with a consequent hardening of relations between them. Just as the cross-cutting of individual ties helps to prevent rigidity in interdistrict affairs,

14 L. Coser (1956, p. 16). I shall not deal with other aspects which Coser raises in this study and in a subsequent briefer statement (1957, pp. 197–207).

15 R. Merton (1957, p. 122).

16 W. F. Ogburn and M. F. Nimkoff (1946, pp. 345–46).

so the mixed friendly-hostile relations existing over a series of districts,[17] including the prevalence of bribery based on mutual distrust and the desire to seize an advantage, discourages the formation of solidary groups or blocs. And because each district's zone of interaction varies in certain respects from those of its neighbors, not incorporating quite the same range of units, this in turn helps to keep fluid the relations between them. The notion of reciprocity, the assumption of potential equality, and the demand that through time a "balance" be achieved in social affairs (except only in the male-female relationship; and this finds its own balance in ritual)—all this, on the whole, insures that, in spite of obvious inequalities, every district, like every adult, has a sporting chance in the struggle which, in one form or another, is an essential part of social living.

In this system conflict can be seen[18] "as a mode of integrating groups," "a form of social balance," because, essentially, it takes place within a framework of consensus.[19] The local acknowledgment that conflict and co-operation should both be accorded more or less equal weighting over a period can be seen, for example, in the conception of warfare as a "see-sawing" or "tug of war"[20] arrangement. The training for aggression which is a feature of the socialization of boys, stimulated by the warnings that "other districts" offer threats to their personal survival and to that of their district, is not taken to its logical conclusion; but it carries with it its own checks, equally bound up with the notion of self-interest as well as, less obviously, with that of the "common good." As far as we can tell, there are no protests against the system as such. The basic assumptions on which human life depends (in the narrowly conceived local sense) are not seriously questioned. Disagreements and conflicts of interest take place within this system of beliefs and behavior, just as social cleavages and re-formations (breakaways resulting in new lineages, shifting district alliances, the movement and resettlement of refugees) are viewed as an inevitable part of the existing social order.

Today this picture is changing rapidly, although the people concerned are not fully aware of it. The authority system within the district has become formalized, with fewer opportunities for rivalry between

[17] Cf. E. Colson (1953, p. 211); M. Gluckman (1956, p. 74); L. Coser (1956, pp. 75–77).

[18] M. Gluckman (1949, p. 10); G. Simmel (1955, p. 16 n); D. J. Hager (1956, p. 7).

[19] See, e.g., M. Gluckman (1955, p. 23); G. Simmel (1955, pp. 15, 20, 25–26); L. Coser (1956, pp. 73, 74); R. Faris (1948, p. 517 n).

[20] This is the kind of situation S. F. Nadel (1957, p. 131) speaks of in reference to "conflict relationships" and "balanced opposition." See also E. E. Evans-Pritchard (1940/50, p. 134); R. Aron (1957, p. 181).

"strong" men insofar as this particular hierarchy is concerned. The social system has been thrown off balance by the intrusion of a factor which, by tacit agreement, appears to have been consistently avoided in the traditional relations between districts; that is, an overwhelming and far-reaching defeat, through superior force, by a social unit which is not prepared to bow to the "rules." The fact that this social unit has entered the situation from outside, and in size and complexity has no parallel in the region, does not alter the position. The "game" is being broken up by a player who acknowledges different "rules" and disallows the traditionally recognized goals.

This is not a comparative study. It has focused on one empirical situation, in an attempt to indicate some of its main features. Of necessity it has been selective as regards both topics and details; but by considering events and persons within the broad framework of social control we come nearer to viewing the social system and its cultural content in a holistic fashion.

Concentrating on one particular region represents, of course, only one step, although an essential one, in the process of understanding what goes on within it. Another way of approaching it, once ethnographic material is available, is to consider it in relation to other societies and cultures which impinge on it or are pertinent in some other way to our examination. Enough material has already been published on Papua and New Guinea to indicate many points of similarity to the situation we have been discussing. There is a fruitful field here for comparative examination in the "controlled" sense.[21] Outside this range is the issue of its more general relevance in the study of human behavior and ideas both in relation to other situations with which it has a number of close parallels and in relation to more broadly based propositions concerning diversities and uniformities in social living generally.

The actors in this study are gardening and hunting people, non-literate, non-industrialized, with a relatively poor technology and few durable material possessions. Their scheme of living is a fairly simple one, confined to a world which even today, although expanding, is small and circumscribed. We could speak here of relative homogeneity, provided we do not imply that there are no conflicting ideals or standards, no choices, or that one member can be readily substituted for another of the same age and sex. There is virtually no occupational or craft specialization, no institutionalization of "experts" in any given field. Economic transactions

[21] Cf. F. Eggan (1954, pp. 755–59); I. Schapera (1953, pp. 359–61).

are on a small scale, with no conceptual distinction between producer and consumer. Face to face relations are of primary importance and largely framed in kinship terms. There is no social stratification of a hereditary kind; ascribed status does not involve grading in a prestige hierarchy. Apart from distinctions on the basis of sex and age, or seniority, all members are exposed to the same broad processes of socialization; and, conventionally, all have equal opportunity of access to the rewards, tangible and otherwise, which these societies have to offer. In other words, there is no formal differentiation between them as far as achievement is concerned. The same goals, and the same means of attaining them, are open to everyone. Between adults of the same sex, just as between social units, there is the assumption of interaction between equals or potential equals, whether this takes the form of competition or cleavages, exchange of goods or services, or collaboration in some joint enterprise.

In comparison with the wider span of known human behavior, the range of variation within this region is limited. In spite of local differences, it would not be hard to map out common social and cultural features for the eastern Highlands, for the Highlands as a whole, and even for all Papua and New Guinea, following these into the islands of Melanesia on the east and parts of Indonesia on the west. This suggests that before the coming of Europeans the impact of the outside world, in the larger sense, was mediated through people who were in many ways very much like themselves, and apparently it was not such as to interfere drastically with their basic assumptions about living. The crosscurrents of different ideas which reached them seem to have been accommodated without a major upheaval in the system itself.

Because they do not make use of artificial aids (such as bamboo-pipe irrigation) like some of their neighbors on the southeast, they are more directly dependent on seasonal rainfall for the growth of crops. The wet season, from approximately November to April, is the gardening period, providing a surplus of food which is a feature of ceremonial displays and distribution. The dry season or "sun time," when gardening is at a minimum, is the period of hunting and food collecting.

"Mythological time" may be represented as a continuing dialectic between the present and the past, identifying them for certain purposes and separating them for others, while holding up the past as a source of values and rules for the present. In contrast, gardening time, as a narrower version of "seasonal time," is based on a regularly recurring sequence of events: clearing and burning, preparing the soil, planting seeds, tending the growing crops, harvesting the produce, and storing the seeds in preparation for the next planting season. In spite of occasional upsets, the cyclical conception of "gardening time" seems to conform very closely to the actual course of events. To a large extent, the organization of ritual follows the same pattern, especially the pig festivals, dependent as they are on the fattening and maturing of pigs. This notion of cyclical repetition is clearly reflected in the principles underlying interaction between districts, particularly in regard to warfare and sorcery. In that case, however, what actually happens is much less orderly than the statements of principle would imply. In the same way the lineage paradigm is neatly and regularly cyclical, as contrasted with the on-the-ground units into which it is translated in everyday experience.

This kind of society has been spoken of as "repetitive" or, in a rather different conceptual sense, "tradition-oriented." It is sometimes held to represent a special case, on the grounds that orientation toward change and evaluation of change are crucial factors in any society and that generalizations deriving from "backward-looking" societies can have no relevance to the study of "forward-looking" societies. This is a matter of degree and emphasis rather than of sharply defined contrast, since all societies pay some attention to seasonal time, whether or not they make use of other conceptions such as chronological time; all acknowledge some sort of continuity with the past and anticipate or plan for future events; and none is rigidly opposed to the idea of change in regard to some spheres of living, however conservative it may seem in regard to others. Nevertheless, it would certainly be true to say that here, more than in many other societies, there is a strongly articulated conception of "balance" and order, simply framed in terms of reciprocity, or "backing," and in terms of recurrent sequences. In both cases there is the assumption of a return to some hypothetical status quo or, as one may put it, a "strain toward equilibrium."

Traditionally, force is not institutionalized in coping with breaches within the political unit. Instead, reliance is placed on the practical implications of interdependence and on the results of early training in order to enmesh its members in such a way that physical coercion can be kept to a minimum. The term "self-regulating" is sometimes used for this kind of system, where on the whole most people appear to conform to the "rules" even though there are few organized pressures to compel them to do so. At the same time, the "rules" themselves are flexible enough to allow for a certain amount of variation.

Social controls operate on the basis of what is considered to be "good" or "bad," the "right" or "wrong" way of behaving in any given situation. They hinge, that is to say, on social standards or values operating in a particular society. Difficulties often arise in attempting to identify these values, especially since they may vary in priority, and at any point where choice is involved they may be in conflict. Moreover, choices themselves are limited not only by regulative pressures but by the boundaries of traditional knowledge and experience.

In the eastern Highlands (or in any other society, for that matter), it is not enough to consider the dimension of social structure—how it is conceptualized locally, how the anthropologist formulates it, what is its counterpart in actuality. It is as important to know the values and basic assumptions of the people concerned,[22] from inferences based on such sources as myth and ritual and observation of behavior, and from individual accounts both in construct terms and in respect of personal attitudes in specific contexts. Knowing what is being taught in the process of socialization, and how and by whom, helps us to understand what keeps the system going. It provides us with a generalized picture which can be used both in construct to balance against what actually happens in adult life and, specifically, in focusing on the career of any particular person. In the present study it was not possible to follow a set of persons through time, from childhood through initiation and subsequent adult experiences. Instead, both training and adult activity were explored more or less simultaneously, so that what we have is an assumption of close relationship between the two, supported by statements on this score from adults on the basis of their own upbringing. In the course of more or less formal training (and outside it), we have seen that there are often discrepancies between what people say should be done ideally in certain circumstances, what they actually say should be done in particular circumstances, and what, in fact, they do. The case material set out in this study points up this kind of variation, among others (for example, between persons or categories of persons).

Inconsistencies and potentially conflicting features, however, do not appear solely at the level of action. They are an intrinsic part of a system of belief and action, not least as expressed in mythology and ritual in either direct or symbolic form. In this sense, they can be seen as validated or sanctioned. Similarly, mechanisms of social control support the elements of tension and conflict just as they support the more conservative elements of co-operation and consistency. They may uphold violent behavior or be directed against it. The legal response to an offense may be identical with the offense itself; killing, for instance, may be either a

22 Cf. S. N. Eisenstadt (1959, pp. 216, 217).

crime or a means of punishment. Here the difference lies not so much in the content of the action as in the definition of the circumstances in which it may take place. Individual "self-help" is demarcated from action authorized by or on behalf of the social unit concerned. In the region we have been discussing the distinction between them is becoming more sharply crystallized with the development of the informal court and the consolidation of Administration control; but in regard to warfare and sorcery the position is traditionally clear enough to allow us to speak of them as "legal institutions" similar to the judicial system, although less formalized and regularized. The majority of offenses in this region are culturally patterned and represent conventional, if not always tolerated, alternatives. It is difficult in this context to speak of deviant behavior, since the definition of an offense is, in most cases if not all, relative to the person, the unit, and the circumstances of the case in question.

Is this to be viewed as "looseness," in the sense of a lack of co-ordination? Or should we identify it as flexibility, which implies a capacity to adjust and be receptive?[23] From the evidence put forward it would seem that the second alternative is the more appropriate, when we consider the apparent ease with which these people have responded to alien demands and adopted and adapted new forms of control. Not all the changes now under way have been forced on them. Many of them have been accepted enthusiastically, even to the extent of anticipating the wishes of the Administration and the Missions.

When, in regard to a particular system, we talk about the maintenance of social order, it is obvious that we are dealing with a construct, an abstraction from the real situation; we are defining the system in a way which allows for changes and adjustments through time. How far we conceptualize it as the same system rather than a different one depends very largely on how much variation we see as being tolerated, as against how much continuity. For example we could speak, here, of patterned relations between social and political units, which provide a setting for the patterning of relations between persons, in a system which is framed loosely enough to accommodate a fairly wide divergence between the ideal construct, or constructs, as an abstraction from reality, and local recognition of what does in fact happen. What might appear to be irregularities in the actual situation, such as the splitting up or dispersal of units under pressure from others, or the uneven breaking away of groups of persons to form new lineages, do not disturb that construct,

[23] Cf. B. F. Ryan and M. A. Straus (1954, pp. 198–205, 223), although their concept of "loose structure" is applicable only in part to this situation.

and may even help to reinforce it. It seems that only a small proportion of the population would be uprooted in this way at any one time, and then only within certain limits—not enough to upset local views about what is going on or to lead to reassessment of the principles which are thought to be involved. Such movements take place within a framework of assumptions about "what ought to be" as well as what is happening.

With Administration control, however, it is clear that insofar as the traditional system is directly reflected in actual events, not separated from them, it is now no longer "the same" as before. Warfare has been forbidden, refugees "frozen" in positions away from their home areas, rituals and ceremonies seriously curtailed. This means that the main avenues for interaction between districts, as districts, are no longer open. In addition, the informal courts now cut across district boundaries; and, although the Administration court takes these units into account, they are irrelevant to its functioning. Loss of political autonomy, the centralization of authority under external control, the declining importance of district membership (including the dispersal of persons on an individual rather than a district basis, as in recruiting for outside employment), the formalization of leadership: this combination of factors, operating more or less simultaneously, must indicate a new social system, at least in a number of important respects.

Values and basic beliefs are under fire from both Missions and Administration. A few assumptions have been reinforced: gardening is "good," "strength" is an important quality in social relations, and (in Mission teaching) the creation of the earth and of human and other forms of life came about through the actions of a supernatural Being described in anthropomorphic terms. Nevertheless, a whole series of critical assumptions has been challenged: that fighting is good; that bloodletting of a ritual kind is necessary to healthy living; that men and women should not consistently eat and sleep together; that burying the dead in gardens increases the fertility of the soil; that human flesh is a legitimate as well as a desirable food. The range of potential interaction has widened enormously, but the range within which direct physical violence is unacceptable has also increased. Aggressive action against all persons outside a certain nucleus, variously defined according to circumstances, was condemned by the victim or his associates but not as a general principle. Now, however, it is no longer justifiable in such terms but increasingly in others —in terms of punishment for an alleged offense.

Obvious changes of this sort are more easily delineated and more readily detected. It is more difficult to deal with changes in the traditional sphere, before European contact, because of the lack of adequate data. But it does seem that there we could speak of changes as taking place within the framework of a system, and allowed for within it, even though modifying it in the process. The conception of change as cyclical, or repetitive ("History repeats itself."), may be contrasted with the view that change is linear or progressive.[24] The distinction in any given context may or may not correspond with locally held ideas about change. Cumulative, nonreversible changes may be taking place in a system which is not locally conceptualized in that way. One question here is how much time-depth we need for our analysis before we can speak of rate or degree or direction of change or the maintenance of order in a system. The longer the time span, the greater the confidence with which such an assessment can be made.

When we look at a situation at one point in time, we may be inclined to overemphasize its asymmetrical aspects. In this region the movement of refugees, the bitterness of sorcery accusations, the apparent disorder of fighting, the violence often associated with cannibalism, could very well overshadow less spectacular but equally significant features. To a stranger, the "exotic" looms large. Because life in the eastern Highlands of New Guinea is based on rather different premises, it is not easy at first to see what principles may underlie the multitude of details which confronts him. Event jostles event, statement jostles statement, in bewildering variety. The cutting up of experience into items of case material comes later, as part of the process of examining "what happened." So, in the eastern Highlands, the excitement and romance at first obscures its more mundane qualities. The range of tolerated behavior seems so wide, and so loosely structured, the apparent contradictions so numerous, that it is tempting to see this as a society well on the way to anomie. It is only in trying to consider it in some sort of time perspective, however inadequate, and in relation to the principles which the people themselves ascribe to it, that its regularities and consistencies become clear.

I have been concerned in this study with social control and social order, in both its narrower and its wider aspects, applying certain propositions to the empirical situation as we find it in the eastern Highlands. But it seemed to me that my primary concern had to be the exploration of that situation; and it was with this in mind that I considered the sociocultural

[24] For conceptions of time as "reversible" or "nonreversible," see, e.g., C. Lévi-Strauss (1953, p. 530). See also Leach's treatment of *gumsa-gumlao*, representing fluctuations within a range rather than a series of progressive, nonreversible "differences" (E. R. Leach, 1954).

system, or systems, represented here. Only by viewing these more or less as a whole can we understand, for instance, the operation of regulative factors and the importance and significance of basic values and cultural emphases in all co-activity and structural alignments. Moreover, it is within this framework that we may discover answers to some of the questions raised from time to time throughout this study, in which my aim has been to explain, to some extent at least, the nature and process of belief and action in the eastern Central Highlands of New Guinea.

Bibliography
(Works cited and consulted)

ADLER, A.
1945   The Practice and Theory of Individual Psychology (trans. P. Radin). London: Kegan Paul, Trench & Trubner.
ALBRECHT, M. C.
1954   "The Relationship of Literature and Society," American Journal of Sociology, LIX, 5.
ALLEN, C. K.
1951   Law in the Making. (5th edition.) Oxford: Clarendon Press.
ALLPORT, G. W., BRUNER, J. S., and JANDORF, E. M.
1950   "Personality Under Social Catastrophe," in C. Kluckhohn and H. Murray (eds.), Personality in Nature, Society, and Culture. New York: Knopf.
ARON, R.
1957   "Conflict and War from the Viewpoint of Historical Sociology," in The Nature of Conflict. ("UNESCO Tensions and Technology Series.") New York: International Sociological Association.
AUFENANGER, H.
1941   "Vom Leben und Denken eines Papua-Stämmes im Bismarck-gebirge, Anthropos, XXXVI.
AUFENANGER, H., and HÖLTKER, G.
1940   Die Gende in Zentral-neuguinea: Ergänzungsbände zur Ethnographie Neu-guineas. Wien-Mödling: Missionsdruckerei St. Gabriel.
BARNETT, H. G.
1953   Innovation: The Basis of Cultural Change. New York: McGraw-Hill.
BARTLETT, F. C. (ed.)
1946   The Study of Society, Methods and Problems. London: Kegan Paul, Trench & Trubner.
BARTON, R. F.
1919   "Ifugao Law." ("University of California Publications in American Archaeology and Ethnology," Vol. 15, No. 1.)
1949   The Kalingas: Their Institutions and Custom Law. Chicago: University of Chicago Press.
BATESON, G.
1934   "Field Work in Social Psychology in New Guinea." ("Proceedings of the First International Congress of Anthropological and Ethno-logical Sciences.") London.

1936   *Naven: A Survey of the Problems Suggested by a Composite Picture of the Culture of a New Guinea Tribe Drawn from Three Points of View.* Cambridge: Cambridge University Press. (Stanford: Stanford University Press, 1958.)

BEAVER, W. N.

1920   *Unexplored New Guinea.* London: Seeley, Service.

BELSHAW, C. S.

1954   *Changing Melanesia: Social Economics of Culture Contact.* Melbourne: Oxford University Press.

1957   *The Great Village.* London: Routledge & Kegan Paul.

BERNARD, J.

1950   "Where is the Modern Sociology of Conflict?" *American Journal of Sociology*, LVI, 1.

1957   "The Sociological Study of Conflict," in *The Nature of Conflict.* ("UNESCO Tensions and Technology Series.") New York: International Sociological Association.

BERNARD, L. L.

1939   *Social Control in Its Sociological Aspects.* New York: Holt.

1944   *War and Its Causes.* New York: Holt.

BERNATZIK, H. A.

1935   *Südsee.* London: Constable.

BERNDT, C. H.

1953   "Socio-Cultural Change in the Eastern Central Highlands of New Guinea," *Southwestern Journal of Anthropology*, IX, 1.

1954   "Translation Problems in Three New Guinea Highland Languages," *Oceania*, XXIV, 4.

n.d.   "Myth in Action" (elsewhere titled "Myth in Conflict: A Study of Myth in the Eastern Central Highlands of New Guinea"). Ph.D. thesis, 1955, London School of Economics, University of London.

1960   "The Concept of Primitive," *Sociologus*, X, 1.

1957   "Social and Cultural Change in New Guinea: Communication, and Views About 'Other People'," *Sociologus*, VII, 1.

1959   "The Ascription of Meaning in a Ceremonial Context, in the Eastern Central Highlands of New Guinea," in J. D. Freeman and W. R. Geddes (eds.), *Anthropology in the South Seas.* New Plymouth (New Zealand): Avery Press.

BERNDT, R. M.

1951   *Kunapipi: A Study of an Australian Aboriginal Religious Cult.* Melbourne: Cheshire. (New York: International Universities Press.)

1952   *Djanggawul: An Aboriginal Religious Cult of North-Eastern Arnhem Land.* London: Routledge & Kegan Paul. (Melbourne: Cheshire. New York: Philosophical Library.)

1952–53 "A Cargo Movement in the Eastern Central Highlands of New Guinea," *Oceania*, XXIII, 1, 2, and 3.

1954*a* "Reaction to Contact in the Eastern Highlands of New Guinea," *Oceania*, XXIV, 3 and 4.

1954*b* "Kamano, Jate, Usurufa and Fore Kinship of the Eastern Highlands of New Guinea," *Oceania*, XXV, 1, 2, and 3 (1954–55).

1954*c* "Contemporary Significance of Pre-Historical Stone Objects in the Eastern Central Highlands of New Guinea," *Anthropos*, XLIX.

1955*a* "Murngin (Wulamba) Social Organization," *American Anthropologist*, LVII, 1.

1955*b* "Cannibalism," *World Science Review*, December.

1955*c* "Interdependence and Conflict in the Eastern Central Highlands of New Guinea," *Man*, LV, 116.

1956 "Anthropology and Education," *Educand*, II, 2.

1957*a* "The Changing World in New Guinea," *Australian Quarterly*, XXIX, 1 (or *South Pacific*, IX, 6).

1957*b* "An Anthropologist looks at Literature," *Meanjin*, XVI, 2.

1958 "A 'Devastating Disease Syndrome': Kuru Sorcery in the Eastern Central Highlands of New Guinea," *Sociologus*, VIII, 1.

1960 Review article: *The Kuma*, by M. Reay, *Journal of the Polynesian Society*, LXIX, 3.

n.d. "Political Structure of the Eastern Central Highlands of New Guinea," in forthcoming volume (K. E. Read, ed.).

n.d. "Religion in the Eastern Highlands of New Guinea," in forthcoming volume (M. Meggitt, P. Lawrence, R. Glasse, eds.).

BERNDT, R. and C.

1942–45 "A Preliminary Report of Field Work in the Ooldea Region, Western South Australia," (*Oceania* Reprint). Sydney: Australian National Research Council.

1951 *Sexual Behaviour in Western Arnhem Land.* ("Viking Fund Publications in Anthropology," No. 16.) New York.

1954 *Arnhem Land, Its History and Its People.* Melbourne: Cheshire.

BETTELHEIM, B.

1952 "Individual and Mass Behaviour in Extreme Situations," in G. E. Swanson, T. M. Newcomb, E. L. Hartley (eds.), *Readings in Social Psychology*. New York: Holt.

BETTELHEIM, B., and JANOWITZ, M.

1952 "Ethnic Tolerance: A Function of Social and Personal Control," in Swanson, Newcomb, Hartley (eds.), *Readings in Social Psychology*. New York: Holt.

BIDNEY, D.

1953*a* "The Concept of Value in Modern Anthropology," in A. L. Kroeber (ed.), *Anthropology Today: An Encyclopedic Inventory*. Chicago: University of Chicago Press.

1953*b* *Theoretical Anthropology*. New York: Columbia University Press.

BLACK, R. H.
   1956   "The Epidemiology of Malaria in the South West Pacific: Changes
           Associated with Increasing European Contact," *Oceania*, XXVII, 2.

BLOCH, H. A.
   1952   *Disorganization: Personal and Social*. New York: Knopf.

BOAS, F.
   1938   *The Mind of Primitive Man*. (Revised edition.) New York:
           Macmillan.

BOHANNAN, P.
   1957   *Justice and Judgment among the Tiv*. London: Oxford University Press.

BROWN, P.
   1952   "Changes in Ojibwa Social Control," *American Anthropologist*, LIV, 1.
   1960   "Chimbu Tribes . . . ," *Southwestern Journal of Anthropology*, XVI, 1.

BURRIDGE, K. O. L.
   1953   "Social Control in Tangu." Ph.D. thesis, Australian National
           University.

CAMERON, W. B., and McCORMICK, T. C.
   1954   "Concepts of Security and Insecurity," *American Journal of Sociology*,
           LIX, 6.

CANNON, W. B.
   1942   "Voodoo Death," *American Anthropologist*, XLIV.

CAPELL, A.
   1948–49   "Distribution of Languages in the Central Highlands, New
             Guinea," *Oceania*, XIX, 2, 3, and 4.
   1950   *Survey of Linguistic Research*. (South Pacific Commission, Project S.5,
           Report No. 1, Vol. 1.)

CASSIRER, E.
   1946   *The Myth of the State*. New Haven: Yale University Press.

CAVAN, R. S.
   1928   *Suicide*. Chicago: University of Chicago Press.

CHINNERY, E. W. P.
   1934   "Mountain Tribes of the Mandated Territory of New Guinea from
           Mt. Chapman to Mt. Hagen," *Man*, XXXIV, 140.

CHINNERY, E. W. P., and BEAVER, W. N.
   1915   "Notes on the Initiation Ceremonies of the Koko, Papua," *Journal of
           the Royal Anthropological Institute*, XLV.

COHEN, M. R., and NAGEL, E.
   1949   *An Introduction to Logic and Scientific Method*. London: Routledge &
           Kegan Paul.

COLSON, E.
   1953   "Social Control and Vengeance in Plateau Tonga Society," *Africa*,
           XXIII, 3.

COOLEY, C. H.
  1918   *Social Process*. New York: Scribner.
  1929   *Social Organization*. (Revised edition.) New York: Scribner.
CORY, H.
  1953   *Sukuma Law and Custom*. (International African Institute.) London: Oxford University Press.
COSER, L.
  1956   *The Functions of Social Conflict*. London: Routledge & Kegan Paul.
  1957   "Social Conflict and the Theory of Social Change," *British Journal of Sociology*, VII, 3.
CROTTY, J.
  1951   "First Dictionary of Tchaga Language, Central Highlands, New Guinea," *Anthropos*, XLVI.
DAVIE, M. R.
  1929   *The Evolution of War*. New Haven: Yale University Press.
DAVIS, A.
  1952   "Socialization and Adolescent Personality," in Swanson, Newcomb, Hartley (eds.), *Readings in Social Psychology*. New York: Holt.
DAVIS, K.
  1956   *Human Society*. (Revised edition.) New York: Macmillan.
DETZNER, H.
  1920   *Vier Jahre unter Kannibalen*. Berlin: August Scherl.
DIAMOND, A. S.
  1935   *Primitive Law*. London: Watts.
  1951   *The Evolution of Law and Order*. London: Watts.
DOLLARD, J., DOOB, L. W., MILLER, N. E., MOWRER, O. H., and SEARS, R.
  1939   *Frustration and Aggression*. New Haven: Yale University Press.
DONOGHUE, J. D.
  1957   "An Eta Community in Japan: The Social Persistence of Outcaste Groups," *American Anthropologist*, LIX, 6.
DOOB, L. W., and SEARS, R.
  1939   "Factors Determining Substitute Behaviour and the Overt Expression of Aggression," *Journal of Abnormal (Social) Psychology*, XXXIV.
DUBOIS, C.
  1944   *People of Alor: A Social-Psychological Study of an East Indian Island*. Minneapolis: University of Minnesota Press.
DURKHEIM, E.
  1899–1900   "Deux lois de l'évolution pénale," *L'année sociologique*, 4.
  1947   *The Division of Labor in Society* (trans. G. Simpson). Glencoe, Ill.: Free Press.
  1950   *The Rules of Sociological Method* (ed. G. E. G. Catlin). Glencoe, Ill.: Free Press.

1951   *Suicide* (trans. J. A. Spaulding and G. Simpson). Glencoe, Ill.: Free
        Press.

1954   *The Elementary Forms of the Religious Life* (trans. J. W. Swain). (Revised
        edition.) London: Allen & Unwin.

EDEL, A.

1953   "Some Relations of Philosophy and Anthropology," *American
        Anthropologist*, LV, 5.

EGGAN, D.

1950   "The General Problem of Hopi Adjustment," in Kluckhohn and
        Murray (eds.), *Personality in Nature, Society, and Culture*. New York:
        Knopf.

EISENSTADT, S. N.

1959   "Primitive Political Systems," *American Anthropologist*, 61.

EGGAN, F.

1954   "Social Anthropology and the Method of Controlled Comparison,"
        American Anthropologist, LVI, 5.

ELKIN, A. P.

1953a   *Social Anthropology in Melanesia*. (South Pacific Commission.) Mel-
        bourne: Oxford University Press.

1953b   "Delayed Exchange in Wabag Subdistrict, Central Highlands of New
        Guinea, with Notes on the Social Organization," *Oceania*, XXIII, 3.

EVANS-PRITCHARD, E. E.

1931   "Sorcery and Native Opinion," *Africa*, IV, 1.

1937   *Witchcraft, Oracles and Magic among the Azande*. Oxford: Clarendon
        Press.

1950   *The Nuer*. (Revised edition.) Oxford: Clarendon Press.

1951a   *Social Anthropology*. London: Cohen & West.

1951b   *Kinship and Marriage Among the Nuer*. Oxford: Clarendon Press.

FARIS, R.

1955   *Social Disorganization*. (Revised edition.) New York: Ronald Press.

FENTON, W. N.

1941   "Iroquois Suicide: A Study in the Stability of a Culture Pattern."
        (Smithsonian Institution, Bureau of American Ethnology Bulletin No.
        128; "Anthropological Papers," No. 14.) Washington, D.C.

FIRTH, R.

1940   *The Work of the Gods in Tikopia*. ("London School of Economics
        Monographs on Social Anthropology"; 2 vols.) London.

1949   "Authority and Public Opinion in Tikopia," in M. Fortes (ed.),
        Social Structure: Studies Presented to A. R. Radcliffe-Brown. Oxford:
        Clarendon Press.

1951   *Elements of Social Organization*. London: Watts.

1953   "The Study of Values by Social Anthropologists" (The Marett
        Lecture), *Man*, CCXXXI.

1957a   *We, The Tikopia: A Sociological Study of Kinship in Primitive Polynesia.* (Revised edition.) London: Allen & Unwin.

1957b   (ed.), *Man and Culture.* London: Routledge & Kegan Paul.

FISCHER, A., and FISCHER, J. L.

1961   "Culture and Epidemiology: A Theoretical Investigation of Kuru," *Journal of Health and Human Behaviour,* II.

FORD, C. S., and BEACH, F. A.

1951   *Patterns of Sexual Behaviour.* New York: Harper.

FORDE, DARYLL (ed.)

1954   *African Worlds: Studies in the Cosmological Ideas and Social Values of African Peoples.* (International African Institute.) London: Oxford University Press.

FORTES, M.

1944   "The Significance of Descent in Tale Social Structure," *Africa,* XIV, 7.

1945   *The Dynamics of Clanship Among the Tallensi.* (International African Institute.) London: Oxford University Press.

1949   *The Web of Kinship Among the Tallensi.* (International African Institute.) London: Oxford University Press.

1953   "The Structure of Unilineal Descent Groups," *American Anthropologist,* LV, 1.

FORTES, M., and EVANS-PRITCHARD, E. E. (eds.)

1950   *African Political Systems.* (International African Institute; revised edition.) London: Oxford University Press.

FORTUNE, R.

1932   *Sorcerers of Dobu: The Social Anthropology of the Dobu Islanders of the Western Pacific.* London: Routledge.

1935   *Manus Religion: An Ethnological Study of the Manus Natives of the Admiralty Islands.* (The American Philosophical Society.) Philadelphia.

1939   "Arapesh Warfare," *American Anthropologist,* XL.

1947a   "The Rules of Relationship Behaviour in One Variety of Primitive Warfare," *Man,* XLVII, 115.

1947b   "Law and Force in Papuan Societies," *American Anthropologist,* XLIX, 2.

FRENCH, J.

1944   "Organized and Unorganized Groups under Fear and Frustration," in K. Lewin, C. E. Meyers, J. Kalhorn, M. L. Farber, and J. R. P. French, *Authority and Frustration Studies in Topological and Vector Psychology, III.* ("University of Iowa Studies in Child Welfare," Vol. XX.) Iowa City: University of Iowa Press.

1953   "The Disruption and Cohesion of Groups," in D. Cartwright and A. Zander (eds.), *Group Dynamics: Research and Theory.* New York: Row Peterson.

GAJDUSEK, D. C., and ZIGAS, V.

1957   'Degenerative Diseases of the Central Nervous System in New Guinea: The Endemic Occurrence of 'Kuru' in the Native Population," *New England Journal of Medicine*, CCLVII.

1958   "Untersuchungen über die Pathogenese von Kuru," *Klinische Wochenschrift*, XXXVI, 10.

1959   "Pathological and Epidemiological Study of an Acute Progressive Degenerative Disease of the Central Nervous System among Natives of the Eastern Highlands of New Guinea," *National Institute of Neurological Diseases . . . and Public Health Department, Territory of Papua and New Guinea*, March.

GAJDUSEK, D. C., ZIGAS, V., and BAKER, J.

1961   "Studies on Kuru: III, Patterns of Kuru Incidence: Demographic and Geographic Epidemiological Analysis," *American Journal of Tropical Medicine and Hygiene*, X, 4.

GAJDUSEK, D. C., and REID, L. H.

1961   "Studies on Kuru: IV, The Kuru Pattern in Moke, a Representative Fore Village," *American Journal of Tropical Medicine and Hygiene*, X, 4.

GIBBS, J. P., and MARTIN, W. T.

1958   "Status Integration and Suicide," *American Sociological Review*, XXIII, 2.

GINSBERG, M.

1946   "The Problems and Methods of Sociology," in F. C. Bartlett (ed.), *The Study of Society, Methods and Problems*. London: Kegan Paul, Trench & Trubner.

1947   *Reason and Unreason in Society: Essays in Sociology and Social Philosophy.* (London School of Economics.) London: Longmans, Green.

1953   "On the Diversity of Morals" (The Huxley Memorial Lecture), *Journal of the Royal Anthropological Institute*.

GITLOW, A. L.

1947   "Economics of the Mount Hagen Tribes, New Guinea." ("American Ethnological Society Monographs," No. 12.)

GLADWIN, T., and SARASON, S. B.

1953   *Truk: Man in Paradise.* ("Viking Fund Publications in Anthropology," No. 20.) New York.

GLASSE, R. M.

1961   "A Kuru Bibliography," *Oceania*, XXXI, 4.

GLUCKMAN, M.

1949   *Malinowski's Sociological Theories.* ("Rhodes-Livingstone Papers," No. 16.) Cape Town: Oxford University Press.

1954   *Rituals of Rebellion in South-East Africa.* (The Frazer Lecture, 1952.) Manchester University Press.

1955a   *The Judicial Process Among the Barotse of Northern Rhodesia.* Manchester: Manchester University Press.

1955b   *Custom and Conflict in Africa.* Oxford: Blackwell.

1956   "Political Institutions," in E. E. Evans-Pritchard *et al.*, *The Institutions of Primitive Society.* Oxford: Blackwell.

GOLD, M.

1958   "Suicide, Homicide, and the Socialization of Aggression," *American Journal of Sociology*, LXIII, 6.

GOODENOUGH, W. H.

1952   "Ethnological Reconnaissance in New Guinea." ("University Museum Bulletin," No. 17.) Philadelphia.

1953   "Ethnographic Notes on the Mae People of New Guinea's Western Highlands," *Southwestern Journal of Anthropology*, IX, 1.

GREEN, B. F.

1954   "Attitude Measurement," in G. Lindzey (ed.), *Handbook of Social Psychology*, Vol. I. Cambridge, Mass.: Addison-Wesley.

GURVITCH, G.

1945   "Social Control," in G. Gurvitch and W. Moore (eds.), *Twentieth Century Sociology.* New York: Philosophical Library.

1947   *Sociology of Law.* London: Kegan Paul.

HADDON, A. C.

1924   *The Races of Man and Their Distribution.* Cambridge: Cambridge University Press.

HADLOCK, W. S.

1947   "War Among the Northeastern Woodland Indians," *American Anthropologist*, XLIX.

HAGER, D. J.

1956   "Introduction: Religious Conflict," in D. J. Hager *et al.* (eds.), "Religious Conflict in the U.S.," *Journal of Social Issues*, XII, 3.

HALBWACHS, M.

1930   *Les Causes du Suicide.* Paris: Libraire Felix Alcan.

HALLOWELL, A. I.

1946   "Some Psychological Characteristics of the Northeastern Indians," in F. Johnson (ed.), *Man in Northeastern North America.* ("Papers of the Robert S. Peabody Foundation for Archaeology," Vol. 3.) Andover, Mass.: Phillips Academy.

1949   "The Social Function of Anxiety in a Primitive Society," in D. G. Haring (ed.), *Personal Character and Cultural Milieu.* (Revised edition.) Syracuse: Syracuse University Press.

1950   "Aggression in Saulteaux Society," in Kluckhohn and Murray (eds.), *Personality in Nature, Society, and Culture.* New York: Knopf.

1953   "Culture, Personality, and Society," in A. L. Kroeber (ed.), *Anthropology Today: An Encyclopedic Inventory.* Chicago: University of Chicago Press.

HARING, D. G. (ed.)

1949   *Personal Character and Cultural Milieu.* (Revised edition.) Syracuse: Syracuse University Press.

HELD, G. J.

1957   *The Papuas of Waropen.* The Hague: Martinus Nijhoff.

HENRY, A. F., and SHORT, JR., J. F.

1954   *Suicide and Homicide.* Glencoe, Ill.: Free Press.

HENRY, J.

1940   "Some Cultural Determinants of Hostility in Pilagá Indian Children," *American Journal of Orthopsychiatry*, X.

HERSKOVITS, M. J.

1949   *Man and His Works: The Science of Cultural Anthropology.* New York: Knopf.

HERZOG, G.

1949   "Linguistic Approaches to Culture and Personality," in S. S. Sargent and M. W. Smith, *Culture and Personality.* ("Proceedings of an Interdisciplinary Conference Held under the Auspices of the Viking Fund," 1947.) New York: Viking Fund.

HIDES, J. G.

1935   *Through Wildest Papua.* London: Blackie.

HOEBEL, E. A.

1940   "The Political Organization and Law Ways of the Comanche Indians." (American Anthropological Association Memoir No. 54.)

1946   "Law and Anthropology," *Virginia Law Review*, XXXII.

1954   *The Law of Primitive Man: A Study in Comparative Legal Dynamics.* Cambridge, Mass.: Harvard University Press.

1958   *Man in the Primitive World.* (Revised edition.) New York: McGraw-Hill.

HOERNLÉ, A. W.

1937   in I. Schapera (ed.), *The Bantu-Speaking Tribes of South Africa.* (International African Institute.) London: Oxford University Press.

HOGBIN, H. I.

1934   *Law and Order in Polynesia: A Study of Primitive Legal Institutions.* London: Christophers.

1938a   "Social Advancement in Guadalcanal," *Oceania*, VIII, 3.

1938b   "Social Reaction to Crime," *Journal of the Royal Anthropological Institute*, LXVIII.

1939   *Experiments in Civilization: The Effects of European Culture on a Native Community of the Solomon Islands.* London: Routledge.

1944   "Native Councils and Courts in the Solomon Islands," *Oceania*, XIV, 4.

1945   "Notes to Native Local Administrations in the British Solomon Islands," *Oceania*, XVI, 1.

1947   "Shame: Social Conformity in a New Guinea Village," *Oceania*, XVII, 4.

1948   in M. Fortes (ed.), *Social Structure: Studies Presented to A. R. Radcliffe-Brown*. Oxford: Clarendon Press.

1951   *Transformation Scene: The Changing Culture of a New Guinea Village*. London: Routledge & Kegan Paul.

1958   *Social Change*. London: Watts.

HOGBIN, H. I., and WEDGWOOD, C. H.

1953   "Local Grouping in Melanesia," *Oceania*, XXIII, 4; XXIV, 1.

HOLLINGSHEAD, A. B.

1941   "The Concept of Social Control," *American Sociological Review*, VI, 2.

HOMANS, G. C.

1951   *The Human Group*. London: Routledge & Kegan Paul.

HONIGMANN, J. J.

1949   *Culture and Ethos of Kaska Society*. ("Yale University Publications in Anthropology," No. 40.) New Haven.

1954   *Culture and Personality*. New York: Harper.

1959   *The World of Man*. New York: Harper.

HORNEY, K.

1946   *Our Inner Conflicts: A Constructive Theory of Neurosis*. London: Kegan Paul.

HU HSIEN-CHIN

1944   "The Chinese Concepts of 'Face'," *American Anthropologist*, XLVI (reprinted in D. G. Haring [ed.], *Personal Character and Cultural Milieu*. Revised edition; Syracuse: Syracuse University Press, 1949).

JACQUART, C. J.

1908   *Le Suicide*. Brussels (cited by P. Sorokin, *Contemporary Sociological Theories*. New York and London: Harper, 1928).

JEFFREYS, M. D.

1952   "Samsonic Suicide, or Suicide of Revenge Among Africans," *African Studies*, II (cited by E. Goffman, "On Face-Work: An Analysis of Ritual Elements in Social Interaction," *Psychiatry*, XVIII [1955], 221–22).

JOHNSON, E. S.

1956   *Theory and Practice of the Social Studies*. New York: Macmillan.

KABERRY, P. M.

1941–42   "Law and Political Organization in the Abelam Tribe, New Guinea," *Oceania*, XII, 4.

KAUFMANN, F.

1944   *Methodology of the Social Sciences*. New York: Oxford University Press.

KEESING, F.

1952   "Research Opportunities in New Guinea," *Southwestern Journal of Anthropology*, VIII, 2.

KLEIN, V.

1946   *The Feminine Character: History of an Ideology*. London: Routledge & Kegan Paul.

KLUCKHOHN, C.

1944   "Navaho Witchcraft." ("Papers of the Peabody Museum," Vol. 22, No. 2.) Cambridge, Mass.

1953   "Universal Categories of Culture," in A. L. Kroeber (ed.), *Anthropology Today: An Encyclopedic Inventory*. Chicago: University of Chicago Press.

KLUCKHOHN, C., and MURRAY, H. (eds.)

1950   *Personality in Nature, Society, and Culture*. New York: Knopf.

KLUCKHOHN, F.

1957   "Value Orientations," in R. R. Grinker, *Toward A Unified Theory of Human Behavior*. New York: Basic Books Inc.

KROEBER, A. L. (ed.)

1953   *Anthropology Today: An Encyclopedic Inventory*. Chicago: University of Chicago Press.

KROEF, VAN DER, J. M.

1952   "Some Head-Hunting Traditions of Southern New Guinea," *American Anthropologist*, LIV, 2.

LANDIS, P. H.

1939   *Social Control, Social Organization and Disorganization in Process*. Chicago: Lippincott.

LANDTMAN, G.

1917   *The Folk-Tales of the Kiwai Papuans*. (Acta Societatis Scientiarum Fennicae, Vol. 47.) Helsingfors.

1927   *The Kiwai Papuans of British New Guinea*. London: Macmillan.

LAPIERE, R. T.

1954   *A Theory of Social Control*. London: McGraw-Hill.

LASSWELL, H. D., and KAPLAN, A.

1952   *Power and Society: A Framework for Political Enquiry*. London: Routledge & Kegan Paul.

LAWRENCE, P.

1952   "Sorcery Among the Garia," *South Pacific*, VI, 3.

1956   "Lutheran Mission Influence on Madang Societies," *Oceania*, XXVII, 2.

LEACH, E. R.

1954   *Political Systems of Highland Burma: A Study of Kachin Social Structure*. (London School of Economics.) London: Bell.

LEAHY, M., and CRAIN, M.

1937   *The Land That Time Forgot: Adventures and Discoveries in New Guinea*. London: Hurst and Blackett.

LÉVI-STRAUSS, C.

1945   "L'Analyse structurale en linguistique et en anthropologie," *Word*, I, 1.

1949   *Les Structures élémentaires de la parenté*. Paris: Presses universitaires de France.

1953   "Social Structure," in A. L. Kroeber (ed.), *Anthropology Today: An Encyclopedic Inventory*. Chicago: University of Chicago Press.

LINTON, R.

1945   *The Cultural Background of Personality*. New York: Appleton-Century.

1952   in Swanson, Newcomb, Hartley (eds.), *Readings in Social Psychology*. New York: Holt.

1954   "The Problem of Universal Values," in R. F. Spencer (ed.), *Method and Perspective in Anthropology*. Minneapolis: University of Minnesota Press.

LINDZEY, G., and BORGATTA, E. F.

1954   "Sociometric Measurement," in G. Lindzey (ed.), *Handbook of Social Psychology*, Vol. I. Cambridge, Mass.: Addison-Wesley.

LLEWELLYN, K. N., and HOEBEL, E. A.

1941   *The Cheyenne Way*. Norman: University of Oklahoma Press.

LOWIE, R. H.

1927   *Primitive Society*. (Revised edition.) New York: Liveright.

1950   *Social Organization*. London: Kegan Paul.

LUMLEY, F. E.

1926   *Means of Social Control*. New York (cited by P. Sorokin, *Contemporary Sociological Theories*. New York and London: Harper, 1928).

1928   *Principles of Sociology*. New York (cited by P. Sorokin, *Contemporary Sociological Theories*. New York and London: Harper, 1928).

LUNDBERG, G. A.

1939   *Foundations of Sociology*. New York: Macmillan.

LUZBETAK, L. J.

1956   "Worship of the Dead in the Middle Wahgi (New Guinea)," *Anthropos*, LI.

1958   "The Middle Wahgi Culture: A Study of First Contacts and Initial Selectivity," *Anthropos*, LIII.

MACIVER, R. M., and PAGE, C. H.

1950   *Society*. London: Macmillan.

MAINE, H.

1939   *Ancient Law*. (Revised edition.) London: John Murray.

MAIR, L. P.

1948   *Australia in New Guinea*. London: Christophers.

1953   in A. Phillips (ed.), *Survey of African Marriage and Family Life*. (International African Institute.) London: Oxford University Press.

MALINOWSKI, B.

1915   "Natives of Mailu," *Transactions of the Royal Society of South Australia*, XXXIX. Adelaide.

1920   "War and Weapons Among the Natives of the Trobriand Islands," *Man*, V.

1922   *Argonauts of the Western Pacific*. London: Routledge.

1934   Introduction to H. I. Hogbin's *Law and Order in Polynesia*. London: Christophers.

1941   "An Anthropological Analysis of War," *American Journal of Sociology*, XLVI.

1944   *A Scientific Theory of Culture and Other Essays*. Chapel Hill: University of North Carolina Press.

1949   *Crime and Custom in Savage Society*. (Revised edition.) London: Routledge & Kegan Paul.

1952   *Sexual Life of Savages*. (Revised edition.) London: Routledge.

MANDER, L. A.

1954   *Some Dependent Peoples of the South Pacific*. Leiden: Brill.

MANNHEIM, K.

1949   *Man and Society in an Age of Reconstruction: Studies in Modern Social Structure*. London: Routledge & Kegan Paul.

MEAD, M.

1928   *Coming of Age in Samoa*. New York: Morrow.

1930a   "Social Organization of Manua." (Bernice P. Bishop Museum Bulletin No. 76.) Honolulu.

1930b   *Growing Up in New Guinea*. New York: Morrow.

1934   "Kinship in the Admiralty Islands." ("American Museum of Natural History, Anthropological Papers," Vol. 34, Part 2.) New York.

1935   *Sex and Temperament in Three Primitive Societies*. London: Routledge.

1940   "The Mountain Arapesh. II. Supernaturalism." ("American Museum of Natural History, Anthropological Papers," Vol. 37, Part 3.) New York.

1949   "The Mountain Arapesh. V. The Record of Unabelin . . . ." ("American Museum of Natural History, Anthropological Papers," Vol. 41, Part 3.) New York.

1950   *Male and Female*. London: Gollancz.

1956   *New Lives for Old*. London: Gollancz.

MEEK, C. K.

1950   *Law and Authority in a Nigerian Tribe*. London: Oxford University Press.

MEGGITT, M. J.

1956   "The Valleys of the Upper Wage and Lai Rivers, Western Highlands, New Guinea," *Oceania*, XXVII, 2.

1957   "The Ipili of the Porgera Valley, Western Highlands District, Territory of New Guinea," *Oceania*, XXVIII, 1.

1958   "The Enga of the New Guinea Highlands: Some Preliminary Observations," *Oceania*, XXVIII, 4.

MEISER, L.

1937   "Das Haus im Mt. Hagen Gebirge," *Anthropos*, XXXII.

Bibliography   441

MERTON, R. K.
  1957   *Social Theory and Social Structure.* (Revised edition.) Glencoe, Ill.:
          Free Press.
MILLER, N. E., and DOLLARD, J.
  1945   *Social Learning and Imitation.* London: Kegan Paul.
MILLER, N. E., SEARS, R., MOWRER, H., DOOB, L. W., and DOLLARD, J.
  1941   "The Frustration-Aggression Hypothesis," *Psychological Review*,
          XLVIII.
MISHKIN, B.
  1940   "Rank and Warfare Among the Plains Indians." ("Monographs of the
          American Ethnological Society," No. 3.) Augustin, New York.
MORSELLI
  1879   *Il Suicido*, Milan (cited by P. Sorokin, *Contemporary Sociological Theories*.
          New York and London: Harper, 1928).
MURDOCK, G. P.
  1949   *Social Structure.* New York: Macmillan.
MURPHY, R. F.
  1957   "Intergroup Hostility and Social Cohesion," *American Anthropologist*,
          LIX, 6.
MURRAY, H. A.
  1949   "Research Planning: A Few Proposals," in Sargent & Smith (eds.),
          Culture and Personality. ("Proceedings of an Interdisciplinary Confer-
          ence Held under the Auspices of the Viking Fund," 1947.) New
          York: Viking Fund.
NADEL, S. F.
  1942   *A Black Byzantium.* (International African Institute.) London: Oxford
          University Press.
  1946   "The Interview Technique in Social Anthropology," in F. C. Bartlett
          (ed.), *The Study of Society, Methods and Problems.* London: Kegan Paul,
          Trench & Trubner.
  1947   *The Nuba: An Anthropological Study of the Hill Tribes in Kordofan.* Lon-
          don: Oxford University Press.
  1951   *The Foundations of Social Anthropology.* London: Cohen & West.
  1953a   in "Problems of Process: Methods," *An Appraisal of Anthropology
          Today* (Sol Tax, ed.). Chicago: University of Chicago Press.
  1953b   "Social Control and Self-Regulation," *Social Forces*, XXXI, 3.
  1954   *Nupe Religion.* London: Routledge & Kegan Paul.
  1957   *The Theory of Social Structure.* Melbourne: Melbourne University Press.
NEWCOMB, T. M.
  1952   *Social Psychology.* London: Tavistock.
NEWCOMB, W. W., JR.
  1950   "A Re-examination of the Causes of Plains Warfare," *American
          Anthropologist*, LII, 3.

NILLES, J.

1943–44 "Natives of the Bismarck Mountains, New Guinea," *Oceania*, XIV, 2; XV, 1.

1950 "The Kuman of the Chimbu Region, Central Highlands, New Guinea," *Oceania*, XXI, 1.

1953 "The Kuman People: A Study of Cultural Change in a Primitive Society in the Central Highlands of New Guinea," *Oceania*, XXIV, 1 and 2.

NOON, J. A.

1949 *Law and Government of the Grand River Iroquois.* ("Viking Fund Publications in Anthropology," No. 12.) New York: Viking Fund.

NORTHROP, F. S. C.

1949 in *Ideological Differences and World Order.* New Haven: Yale University Press.

1953 "Cultural Values," in A. L. Kroeber (ed.), *Anthropology Today: An Encyclopedic Inventory.* Chicago: University of Chicago Press.

OGBURN, W. F., and NIMKOFF, M. F.

1946 *Sociology.* Boston: Houghton Mifflin.

OLIVER, D. L.

1955 *A Solomon Island Society: Kinship and Leadership Among the Siuai of Bougainville.* Cambridge, Mass.: Harvard University Press.

PARK, R. E., and BURGESS, E. W.

1917 "Social Control," Proceedings of the American Sociological Society, XII.

1921–22 *Introduction to the Science of Sociology.* Chicago: University of Chicago Press.

PARKINSON, R.

1907 *Dreissig Jahre in die Südsee.* Stuttgart: Strecken u- Schröder.

PARSONS, T.

1949a *Essays in Sociological Theory Pure and Applied.* Glencoe, Ill.: Free Press.

1949b *The Structure of Social Action: A Study in Social Theory with Special Reference to a Group of Recent European Writers.* Glencoe, Ill.: Free Press.

1952 *The Social System.* London: Tavistock.

PARSONS, T., and BALES, R. F.

1955 *Family, Socialization and Interaction Process.* Glencoe, Ill.: Free Press.

PARSONS, T., BALES, R. F., SHILS, E. A.

1953 *Working Papers in the Theory of Action.* Glencoe, Ill.: Free Press.

PARSONS, T., and SHILS, E. A. (eds.)

1952 *Toward a General Theory of Action.* Cambridge, Mass.: Harvard University Press.

PAUL, B. D.

1953 "Interview Techniques and Field Relationships," in A. L. Kroeber (ed.), *Anthropology Today: An Encyclopedic Inventory.* Chicago: University of Chicago Press.

PERISTIANY, J. G.

1956 "Law," in E. E. Evans-Pritchard *et al.*, *The Institutions of Primitive Society*. Oxford: Blackwell.

PHILLIPS, A. (ed.)

1953 *Survey of African Marriage and Family Life*. London: Oxford University Press.

PIERS, G., and SINGER, M. B.

1953 *Shame and Guilt: A Psychoanalytic and a Cultural Study*. Springfield, Ill.: C. C. Thomas.

POPPER, K. R.

1957 *The Poverty of Historicism*. London: Routledge & Kegan Paul.

POSPISIL, L.

1958 "Kapauku Papuans and their Law" ("Yale University Publications in Anthropology, No. 54"). New Haven.

PROCTOR, C. H., and LOOMIS, C. P.

1951 "Analysis of Sociometric Data," in M. Jahoda *et al.* (eds.), *Research Methods in Social Relations* . . ., Part 2. New York: Dryden.

QUARANTELLI, E. L.

1954 "The Nature and Conditions of Panic," *American Journal of Sociology*, LX, 3.

RADCLIFFE-BROWN, A. R.

1913 "Three Tribes of Western Australia," *Journal of the Royal Anthropological Institute*, XLIII.

1922 *The Andaman Islanders*, Cambridge (Glencoe, Ill.: Free Press, 1948).

1950a Introduction to *African Systems of Kinship and Marriage* (A. R. Radcliffe-Brown & Daryll Forde, eds.; International African Institute.) London: Oxford University Press.

1950b Preface to *African Political Systems*. (International African Institute.) London: Oxford University Press.

1951–52 "The Comparative Method in Social Anthropology," *Journal of the Royal Anthropological Institute*, LXXXI, 1 and 2.

1952 *Structure and Function in Primitive Society*. London: Cohen & West.

READ, K. E.

1947 "Effects of the Pacific War in the Markham Valley, New Guinea," *Oceania*, XVIII, 2.

1949 "Notes on Some Problems of Political Confederation," *South Pacific*, III, 12; IV, 1.

1950 "The Political System of the Ngarawapum," *Oceania*, XX, 3.

1951 "The Gahuku-Gama of the Central Highlands," *South Pacific*, V, 8.

1952a "Missionary Activities and Social Change in the Central Highlands of Papua and New Guinea," *South Pacific*, V, 11.

1952b "*Nama* Cult of the Central Highlands, New Guinea," *Oceania*, XXIII, 1.

1952c "Land in the Central Highlands," *South Pacific*, VI, 7.

1954a   "Cultures of the Central Highlands, New Guinea," *Southwestern Journal of Anthropology*. (A section of this essay appears in *South Pacific*, VII, 9.)

1954b   "Marriage Among the Gahuku-Gama of the Eastern Central Highlands of New Guinea," *South Pacific*, VII, 10.

1955   "Morality and the Concept of the Person Among the Gahuku-Gama," *Oceania*, XXV, 4.

REAY, M.

1953   "Social Control Amongst the Orokaiva," *Oceania*, XXIV, 2.

1959   *The Kuma, Freedom and Conformity in the New Guinea Highlands*. Melbourne: Melbourne University Press.

REED, S. W.

1943   *The Making of Modern New Guinea*. Philadelphia: American Philosophical Society.

RHYS, L.

1942   *High Lights and Flights in New Guinea*. London: Hodder & Stoughton.

RICHARDS, A. I.

1946   "Field Work Methods in Social Anthropology," in F. C. Bartlett (ed.), *The Study of Society, Methods and Problems*. London: Kegan Paul, Trench & Trubner.

1956   *Chisungu*. London: Faber.

RIESMAN, D.

1950   *The Lonely Crowd*. New Haven: Yale University Press.

1954   *Individualism Reconsidered, and Other Essays*. Glencoe, Ill.: Free Press.

RÓHEIM, G.

1954   "Cannibalism in Duau, Normanby Island, D'Entrecasteaux Group, Territory of Papua," *Mankind*, IV, 12.

ROSS, E. A.

1929   *Social Control: A Survey of the Foundation of Order*. (Revised edition.) New York: Macmillan.

ROSS, W.

1936   "Ethnological Notes on the Mount Hagen Tribes of New Guinea," *Anthropos*, XXXI.

ROUCEK, J. S., *et al*.

1956   *Social Control*. (Revised edition.) Princeton, N. J.: Van Nostrand.

RYAN, B. F., and STRAUS, M. A.

1954   "The Integration of Sinhalese Society." (*Research Studies of Washington State College*, Vol. XXII, No. 4.) Pullman.

RYAN, D'A. J.

1955   "Clan Organization in the Mendi Valley, Southern Highlands of Papua–New Guinea," *Oceania*, XXVI, 2.

SALISBURY, R. F.

1956a   "Asymmetrical Marriage Systems," *American Anthropologist*, LVIII, 4.

1956b   "Unilineal Descent Groups in the New Guinea Highlands," *Man*, LVI.

SARGENT, S. S., and SMITH, M. W.
1949   *Culture and Personality*. ("Proceedings of an Interdisciplinary Conference Held under the Auspices of the Viking Fund," 1947.) New
York: Viking Fund.

SCHAPERA, I.
1937 (ed.) *The Bantu-Speaking Tribes of South Africa*. (International African
Institute.) London: Oxford University Press.
1940   *Married Life in an African Tribe*. London: Faber & Faber.
1953   "Some Comments on Comparative Method in Social Anthropology,"
(Wenner-Gren Foundation Supper Conference), *American Anthropologist*, LV, 3.
1955   *A Handbook of Tswana Law and Custom*. (Revised edition.) London:
Oxford University Press.
1957   "Malinowski's Theories of Law," in R. Firth (ed.), *Man and Culture*.
London: Routledge & Kegan Paul.

SCHILDER, P.
1951   *Psychotherapy*. New York: Norton (cited by J. M. A. Weiss, "The
Gamble with Death in an Attempted Suicide," *Psychiatry*, XX, 1).

SCHINDLER, A. J.
1952   "Land Use by Natives of Aiyura Village, Central Highlands, New
Guinea," *South Pacific*, VI, 2.

SEAGLE, W.
1937   "Primitive Law and Professor Malinowski," *American Anthropologist*,
XXXIX.
1941   *The Quest for Law*. New York: Knopf.

SEGERSTEDT, T. T.
1948   "Social Control as Sociological Concept." (*Uppsala Universitets
Årsskrift*.) Leipzig.

SELIGMANN, C. G.
1910   *The Melanesians of British New Guinea*. Cambridge: Cambridge University Press.

SELVIN, H. C.
1958   "Durkheim's *Suicide* and Problems of Empirical Research," *American
Journal of Sociology*, LXIII, 6.

SHILS, E. A., and FINCH, H. A. (eds. and trans.)
1949   *Max Weber on the Methodology of the Social Sciences*. Glencoe, Ill.: Free
Press.

SIMMEL, G.
1955   *Conflict* (trans. K. H. Wolff). Glencoe, Ill.: Free Press.

SIMMONS, R. T., GRAYDON, J. J., ZIGAS, V., BAKER, L. L., and GAJDUSEK, D. C.
1961   "Studies on Kuru: V, A Blood Group Genetical Survey of the Kuru
Region and other parts of Papua–New Guinea," *American Journal of
Tropical Medicine and Hygiene*, X, 4.

SMALL, A. A., and VINCENT, G. E.
   1894   *An Introduction to the Study of Society*. New York: American Book Company.

SMITH, W. M.
   1938   "The War Complex of the Plains Indians." (*Proceedings of the American Philosophical Society*, Vol. LXXVIII.)

SMITH, W. R.
   1894   *Lectures on the Religion of the Semites*. Edinburgh: Black.

SOROKIN, P.
   1928   *Contemporary Sociological Theories*. New York and London: Harper.
   1937   *Social and Cultural Dynamics*. New York: American Book Co.
   1949   *Society, Culture, and Personality*. New York: Harper.

SPEIER, H.
   1941   "The Social Types of War," *American Journal of Sociology*, XLVI.

SPENCER, R. F. (ed.)
   1954   *Method and Perspective in Anthropology*. Minneapolis: University of Minnesota Press.

SPOEHR, A.
   1950   "Observations on the Study of Kinship," *American Anthropologist*, LII, 1.

STANNER, W. E. H.
   1953   *The South Seas in Transition*. Sydney: Australasian Publishing Co.

STEINMETZ, S. R.
   1907   *Die Philosophie des Krieges*, Leipzig (cited by P. Sorokin, *Contemporary Sociological Theories*. New York and London: Harper, 1928).

SULLIVAN, H. S.
   1949   "Multidisciplined Co-ordination of Interpersonal Data," in Sargent and Smith (eds.), *Culture and Personality*. ("Proceedings of an Inter-disciplinary Conference Held under the Auspices of the Viking Fund," 1947.) New York: Viking Fund.

SUMNER, W. G.
   1940   *Folkways*. (Revised edition.) New York and Boston: Ginn.

SWANSON, G. E., NEWCOMB, T. M., HARTLEY, E. L. (eds.)
   1952   *Readings in Social Psychology*. New York: Holt.

THURNWALD, H.
   1937   *Menschen der Südsee, Charaktere und Schicksale*. Stuttgart: F. Enke.

THURNWALD, R.
   1931–34   *Die menschliche Gesellschaft, V: Werden, Wandel, und Gestaltung des Rechts*. Berlin: W. de Gruyter.

TIMASHEFF, N. S.
   1939   *An Introduction to the Sociology of Law*. Cambridge, Mass.: Harvard University Press.

TURNER, V. W.

1957   *Schism and Continuity in an African Society.* Manchester: Manchester University Press.

TURNEY-HIGH, H. H.

1942   "The Practice of Primitive Warfare." ("University of Montana Publications in Social Science," No. 2.) Missoula.

1949   *Primitive War: Its Practice and Concepts.* Columbia: University of South Carolina Press.

VIAL, L. G.

1940   "Stone Axes of Mt. Hagen, New Guinea," *Oceania,* XI, 2.

VICEDOM, G. F., and TISCHNER, H.

1943   *Die Mbowamb, Die Kultur der Hagenberg-stämme im Östlichen Zentral-Neuguinea.* (Monographien zur Völkerkunde Herausgegeben vom Hamburgischen Museum für Völkerkunde; 3 vols.) Hamburg.

VOGT, E. Z.

1955   *Modern Homesteaders.* Cambridge: The Belknap Press of Harvard University Press.

WALLIS, W. D.

1947   "The Canadian Dakota." ("American Museum of Natural History, Anthropological Papers," Vol. 47, Part 1.) New York.

WARNER, W. L.

1958   *A Black Civilization.* (Revised edition.) New York: Harper.

WATSON, J. B.

1960   "A New Guinea 'Opening Man'," in J. B. Casagrande (ed.), *In the Company of Man.* New York: Harper.

WEDGWOOD, C. H.

1930   "Some Aspects of Warfare in Melanesia," *Oceania,* I, 1.

WEISS, J. M. A.

1957   "The Gamble with Death in an Attempted Suicide," *Psychiatry,* XX, 1.

WHITING, B.

1950   *Paiute Sorcery.* New York: Viking Fund Publications in Anthropology, No. 15.

WHITING, J. W. M.

1941   *Becoming a Kwoma: Teaching and Learning in a New Guinea Tribe.* New Haven: Yale University Press.

WHITING, J. W. M., and CHILD, I. L.

1953   *Child Training and Personality: A Cross-Cultural Study.* New Haven: Yale University Press.

WILLIAMS, F. E.

1930   *Orokaiva Society.* London: Oxford University Press.

1940   *Drama of Orokolo: The Social and Ceremonial Life of the Elema.* Oxford: Clarendon Press.

1941   "Group Sentiment and Public Justice," *American Anthropologist,* XLIII.

WILLIAMS, R. M., JR.

1947   "Reduction of Intergroup Tensions." ("Social Science Research Council Bulletin," No. 57.) New York.

WILLIAMSON, R. W.

1914   *The Ways of the South Sea Savage.* London: Seeley, Service.

WILSON, A. T. M., TRIST, E. L., and CURLE, A.

1952   "Transitional Communities and Social Reconnection: A Study of the Civil Resettlement of British Prisoners of War," in Swanson, Newcomb, Hartley (eds.), *Readings in Social Psychology.* New York: Holt.

WILSON, M.

1954   "Nyakyusa Ritual and Symbolism," *American Anthropologist,* LVI, 2.

WOLFF, K. H.

1950   *The Sociology of Georg Simmel.* Glencoe, Ill.: Free Press.

WRIGHT, Q.

1951   *A Study of War.* (Revised edition; 2 vols.) Chicago: University of Chicago Press.

YOUNG, K.

1948   *Handbook of Social Psychology.* London: Routledge & Kegan Paul.

ZIGAS, V., and GAJDUSEK, D. C.

1957   "Kuru: Clinical Study of a New Syndrome Resembling Paralysis Agitans in Natives of the Eastern Highlands of Australian New Guinea," *Medical Journal of Australia,* II, 21.

Index of Local (Personal) Names